The UCAS Guide to getting into
JOURNALISM, BROADCASTING, MEDIA PRODUCTION AND PERFORMING ARTS

For entry to university and college in 2013

378·41

Published by: UCAS Rosehill New Barn Lane Cheltenham GL52 3LZ

Produced in conjunction with GTI MEDIA LTD

© UCAS 2012

UCAS, a company limited by guarantee, is registered in England and Wales number: 2839815
Registered charity number: 1024741 (England and Wales) and SC038598 (Scotland)

UCAS reference number: PU038013
Publication reference: 12_045
ISBN: 978-1-908077-21-9
Price £15.99

We have made all reasonable efforts to ensure that the information in this publication was correct at time of publication. We will not, however, accept any liability for errors, omissions or changes to information since publication. Wherever possible any changes will be updated on the UCAS website (www.ucas.com).

UCAS and its trading subsidiary, UCAS Media Limited, accept advertising for publications that promote products and services relating to higher education and career progression. Revenue generated by advertising is invested by UCAS in order to enhance our applications services and to keep the cost to applicants as low as possible. Neither UCAS nor UCAS Media Limited endorse the products and services of other organisations that appear in this publication.

Further copies available from UCAS (p&p charges apply):

Contact Publication Services PO Box 130 Cheltenham GL52 3ZF

email: publicationservices@ucas.ac.uk or fax: 01242 544806

For further information about the UCAS application process go to www.ucas.com.
further information about the CUKAS application process is available at www.cukas.ac.uk.

If you need to contact us, details can be found at www.ucas.com/about_us/contact_us or at CUKAS www.cukas.ac.uk/aboutus/contactus

UCAS QUALITY AWARDS

CONTENTS

Foreword

THINKING ABOUT JOURNALISM, MEDIA AND
PERFORMING ARTS?

Finding the higher education course that's right for you
at the right university or college can take time and it's
important that you use all the resources and guides
available to you in making this key decision. We at
UCAS have teamed up with TARGETjobs.co.uk to
provide you with *The UCAS Guide to getting into
Journalism, Broadcasting, Media Production and
Performing Arts* to show you how you can progress
from being a student to careers in journalism, media
and performing arts. You will find key information on
what the subject includes, entry routes and real-life
case studies on how it worked out for others.

Once you know which subject area you might be
interested in, you can use the listings of all the full-time
higher education courses in art and design to see
where you can study your subject. The course entry
requirements are listed so you can check if getting in
would be achievable for you. There's also advice on
applying through UCAS, telling you what you need to
know at each stage of the application process in just six
easy steps to starting university or college.

We hope you find this publication helps you to choose
and make your application to a course and university or
college that is right for you.

On behalf of UCAS and TARGETjobs.co.uk I wish you
every success in your research.

Mary Curnock Cook, Chief Executive, UCAS

At TARGETjobs we champion paid work experience for UK university students. Find internships and placements across all sectors, plus take part in the TARGETjobs Undergraduate of the Year awards.

TARGETjobs.co.uk

the best possible start to your career

Introducing journalism, media and performing arts

It could be you...

... presenting a popular arts programme   – television presenter

... writing a monthly column for a top women's magazine   – features editor

... performing *La Traviata* around the world   – opera singer

... becoming the new JK Rowling   – writer

... performing with the Royal Ballet Company   – dancer

... receiving an Oscar in Hollywood   – film director

... and lots more besides. Could a career in journalism, media and performing arts be for you? The aim of this guide is to help you decide. For the purposes of this book 'journalism, media and performing arts' includes broadcasting and media production.

A CAREER IN JOURNALISM, MEDIA AND PERFORMING ARTS?

- Your experience counts more than your degree subject – see **Which area?** starting on page 19
- Admissions tutors look for creativity, self-confidence and an ability to entertain – see **The career for you?** starting on page 51
- Despite the low pay, graduates love their work – see **Case studies** starting on page 61

JOURNALISM, MEDIA AND PERFORMING ARTS
IN CONTEXT

Say the words 'journalism, media and performing arts' to people outside the sector, and they'll invariably start talking about TV shows, films and tabloid journalists. But those on the inside know it's a much more diverse field than this, with a myriad of roles, sectors and sub-sectors.

Under the previous government, much money was invested in the arts, to great effect; under the current government funding was cut to many arts organisations as part of its general policy to reduce the deficit. However, the cuts announced by Arts Council England in 2011 were less dramatic than feared, although inevitably cuts from other organisations as well as government funding cuts are having an impact on career prospects in the sector for the time being.

However, this should not put you off pursuing your dream of working in journalism, media or arts. In spite of continuing economic difficulties, the arts continue to make a considerable contribution to our economy. This is recognised by the Department for Culture, Media and Sport, which reported in December 2011 that 1.5 million people were employed in the creative industries or in creative roles in other industries; that the creative industries contributed nearly 3% of the UK's Gross Value Added in 2009; and that in 2011, 5.1% of all companies came under the category of creative industries.

If you're interested in a possible career in journalism, media and performing arts, then this guide can help you. Read on to discover:

- the main roles on offer
- the skills admissions tutors look for
- how to get in and the routes to qualification
- advice from journalism, media and performing arts graduates in different sectors.

Why journalism, media and performing arts?

Choose a career that is...

CREATIVE

Few careers can claim to be as creative as journalism, media and performing arts. You will be paid to think creatively at all times. There is also an unrivalled sense of satisfaction and achievement in seeing your ideas come to life in the finished product.

VARIED

Your journalism, media and performing arts background will enable you to work in a huge variety of careers sectors, from magazine journalism to web-based writing and from theatrical production to broadcast journalism. Read **Which area?** beginning on page 19 to find out more about the full range of journalism, media and performing arts careers.

FUN

Read the case studies of the journalism, media and performing arts graduates in this book and you'll find that they all really love their work. Being 'creative' and 'artistic' is something they have developed a special interest in during their studies, pursued as a hobby, or have always enjoyed doing as they grew up. And now they're getting paid to do it! As well as being a fun career, journalism, media and performing arts also make things fun for other people – whether it's making authors such as Jane Austen accessible or popularising history from the Romans to the Tudors.

A STRONG INFLUENCE ON OUR DAY-TO-DAY LIVES

Journalism, media and performing arts have a crucial influence on what we wear, read, sit on, look at, enjoy, and almost everything we buy. We read about the latest

health and beauty trends in magazines like
Cosmopolitan or *FHM* and find out about current affairs
through the television or radio. As a new student in
higher education, you'll probably enjoy going to the
cinema or theatre with your friends.

ADDING 'VALUE'

This may seem a little obscure at first, but the
journalism, media and performing arts sector is also
'valued' by people. For example, an uplifting theatrical
or television production can enthral viewers or

encourage people to start reading pieces of literature
that they never dreamed they would like. Newspaper or
magazine articles and reports help keep us informed
about what is happening on a local, national and
international scale, often prompting us to take action,
for example in helping to save the environment. Finally,
we have an innate appreciation of journalism, media
and performing arts; a song or a film can give pleasure
and uplift the senses.

WHAT IS SO GOOD ABOUT A CAREER IN JOURNALISM, MEDIA AND PERFORMING ARTS?

'I feel at home and the most myself when I am performing.'
Jason Andrew Guest, professional dancer, page 70

'I love seeing my finished videos on the website. It is rewarding to have an end product that you have researched,
scripted, filmed and edited. My long-term aim is to be a TV presenter.'
Amie Parker-Williams, video producer and presenter, page 68

'I love the variety of the job. As a session musician I get to play many different styles and meet lots of exciting
people. Setting up my own business I have had to learn new skills and I have grown in confidence socially.'
Rex Pearson, professional session guitarist, page 64

'I enjoy getting ideas across and telling stories using images and sounds: I find this a more natural process than
using words. It is really satisfying to have an end product and I enjoy being creative.'
Phillipa Beasley, post-production runner, page 66

'I have done a placement with The Big Issue, where I wrote short news items and undertook research for longer
stories. As this coincided with the Edinburgh Festival I was able to interview comedians, do vox pops out on the
street and gain experience of feature writing.'
Catherine Ritchie, final year journalism student, page 62

Focus your career with the TARGETjobs Careers Report. Using biographical data, information about your interests and insightful psychometric testing, the Careers Report gives you a clear picture of jobs that match your skills and personality.

TARGETjobs.co.uk

the best possible start to your career

A career in
journalism, media
and performing arts

A career in journalism, media and performing arts

Thousands of students are accepted onto journalism, media and performing arts degrees in the UK each year. On graduating, many immediately start employment within the UK, though interestingly only some 24% of journalism graduates, 23% of performing arts graduates and 15% of media studies graduates work in a field directly relevant to their degree six months after graduation. Many can be found in what may be considered more temporary jobs such as clerical, catering and retail. This reflects the fact that there are more applicants than there are places and that many aspiring performers and writers must do casual work while looking for their big break. Since working in the media or performing arts is more a vocation – a 'calling' if you like – than a career, these individuals are happy to do this to try to reach their goal.

WHERE THEY WORK

Freelance/self-employed

This is the most common employment option in journalism, media and performing arts and in many ways is one of the hardest paths to follow early on in your career. It relies on the reputation you build for yourself to ensure a continuous stream of work, and when you're fairly new to a profession, gaining valuable contacts can take a while. Freelancing is a common route among writers, producers, editors, photographers, actors and musicians, all of whom rely on the strength of their portfolio to secure new work and need to maintain a good relationship with current and past clients.

Large national companies

Major TV, radio, newspaper and magazine companies are recruiters of graduates, and a few offer training schemes to recruit new blood each year. Competition for places is extremely fierce so you will need excellent experience, heaps of motivation and plenty of ideas to be considered.

Smaller organisations and voluntary groups

On a more regional level, some people find work in local theatres, radio stations and newspapers. You may find yourself mucking in and doing all sorts of odd jobs while waiting for your big break, and salaries can vary from being on the minimum wage to being non-existent! Supplementing your monthly pay cheque with proceeds from another job is a fairly common experience among graduates trying to make it on their own.

WHICH AREA?

There are so many career paths to choose from in this sector that in some ways journalism, media and performing arts students are spoilt for choice.

Many of the skills required for some of the key roles are also highly transferable; for example, an actor could decide to use his or her years of experience to start directing plays or films. That said, the skills required for each particular profession are in many ways becoming more precise, which means that, in many media and performing arts sectors, the further down one route you go, the harder it could be to transfer across to other fields. It is rare for a fine art photographer to work as a newspaper photographer in a war zone, for instance. You would therefore be wise to take time at this stage to find out the key differences in each of the main journalism, media and performing arts sectors before embarking on your course. Have a look at the **Which area?** section, starting on page 19, to read outlines of some of the main fields in which you can specialise.

JOURNALISM, MEDIA AND PERFORMING ARTS STATISTICS

Typical media studies graduate destinations

Retail, catering, waiting and bar staff	28%
Other occupations	15%
Clerical and secretarial occupations	11%
Arts, design, culture and sports professionals	18%
Commercial, industrial and public sector managers	9%

Typical performing arts graduate destinations

Arts, design, culture and sports professionals	24%
Retail, catering, waiting and bar staff	23%
Education professionals	12%
Clerical and secretarial occupations	9%
Commercial, industrial and public sector managers	6%

Reproduced with kind permission of HECSU/AGCAS, What do graduates do? 2011
All data comes from the HESA Destination of Leavers of Higher Education Survey 2009/10

Trends

Different parts of the journalism, media and performing arts sector are subject to different trends and pressures.

ECONOMIC

Like most areas of work, journalism, media and performing arts are dependent on the state of the economy to flourish or flounder. In an economic downturn, people will still buy newspapers and magazines, watch the television and listen to the radio, and go to the cinema or theatre, although perhaps not so much. However, most of the organisations that produce these media depend for much or some of their income on advertisers, who may decrease or cut their advertising spend. This means that newspapers, magazines, TV companies and so on have to find the money from elsewhere and potentially make cutbacks.

In the current economic climate, the arts are also being severely affected by funding cuts by the government, local authorities, the Arts Council and other arts organisations. Inevitably this will affect opportunities in the sector for everyone, new graduates included. However, artists are creative, innovative types, so if you're really determined to succeed in this sector, don't let the current situation put you off pursuing your ambitions.

TECHNOLOGY

Technology plays a huge role these days in the ways films are made, television and radio programmes are broadcast and compiled, and music is produced. Photographers have largely changed from film to digital software, while film editors are increasingly using digital techniques rather than splicing. Anyone hoping for a career in this sector must be prepared to learn about the relevant and rapidly changing technology.

TASTE

Of all the things that affect journalism, media and performing arts, trends in popular and critical taste are of vital importance. Think about musicals, for example. These experienced something of a slump until a couple of recent BBC reality TV shows sparked the nation's interest by searching for the next Maria and Joseph. Films too are subject to audience preferences: consider the trend for adapting children's classic books into films that rely on fantastic computer-generated animation such as *The Lord of the Rings*, *The Chronicles of Narnia* and *The Golden Compass*.

PAY

Salaries vary greatly in this diverse employment sector. At the bottom end, it is common for those starting out to work voluntarily (for free) or just for expenses on internships or work placements in order to get a foot in the door, to build their portfolio and make good contacts. Many people in this sector are also self-employed or work on a freelance basis, charging hourly, daily, or on a contract basis. Rates depend on the sector, location and experience of the person; for example, an actor in a West End theatre may be paid a minimum weekly wage ranging from £472.56 to £577.58 (depending on the size of the theatre), or in independent theatre, £400 (2011-12 rates). Regional newspaper journalists can often start off on a very low rate, at £12,000 for example, although their salary will increase with experience.

WORKING CONDITIONS

Your work will vary greatly according to the sector and nature of the job you do. And just because you're self-employed or freelance doesn't mean that you can set your own hours; writers often can do so but theatre directors, actors, dancers, musicians and producers, for example, will need to work the hours a project dictates. In most fields, the working hours are long, erratic and unsocial with frequent late-night, early-morning, weekend and holiday working. Travelling and working away from home is a common occurrence and flexibility over where you work is essential.

www.ucas.com
www.cukas.ac.uk

at the heart of connecting people to higher education

Which area?

Actor

WHAT DO THEY DO?

Actors portray a writer's character through their words, body language and movements, normally according to the instructions of a director, although some work is based on improvisation. Their work is incredibly varied, from performing each night on a stage to television and radio serials or film acting. Typical activities include:

- attending auditions and rehearsals
- researching to prepare themselves for their role
- working with other cast members and the director to interpret a script
- performing either for an audience or in front of a camera
- doing 'voice-overs' for commercials or recording talking books
- helping out behind the scenes.

It's easy to romanticise the working life of an actor but the reality is that nearly 80% of an actor's time is spent between acting jobs. Therefore they will need other sources of income to pay the rent, such as taking on casual jobs (waiting on tables or temporary admin roles, for example), which give them the freedom to stop at short notice if a role comes their way.

WHERE DO THEY WORK?

Many actors work in theatres or in television or film studios, but sometimes outdoor scenes are necessary, which can be in any weather and at any temperature. Working hours tend to be long and unsocial, rehearsing during the day and performing at night in theatres, while on film or TV sets actors typically start early and finish late. Actors typically work all over the UK, sometimes touring abroad. Auditions are often held at very short notice so you will need to be prepared to travel without much warning. Spending time away from home is common and a normal social life is impossible during projects.

WHAT SKILLS DO THEY NEED?

Apart from the ability to act, the following skills are also essential:

- good communication skills
- empathy
- flexibility
- a proactive approach
- punctuality and reliability
- teamwork skills
- a thick skin to take criticism from directors, critics and the audience
- self-confidence
- stamina and self-motivation.

Other skills and talents may be developed on the job, such as singing, dancing or playing a musical instrument, and these can help boost employment prospects.

ROUTES TO QUALIFICATION

Experience, talent, hard work and – if we're being totally honest here – *luck* are as important as qualifications in this field. Work experience in theatres or television production companies can help you gain a better understanding of the industry as a whole and could provide good contacts for the future. Or why not consider working as an entertainer in a holiday camp or resort to gain some much-needed experience?
A performing arts degree may help your chances although many top actors have done well without one.

Participation in a drama society at school or university is essential, while work experience as an 'extra' can give you an insight into what the profession is like, although people who make a living as an extra rarely go on to become fully fledged actors.

PROSPECTS

It is difficult to define a standard career route for actors. Some will spend their entire career moving from one job to the next without further responsibility or pay, whereas others will gain fame and fortune and will be at the top of their profession.

FURTHER INFORMATION

- Equity **www.equity.org.uk**
- The London Academy of Music and Dramatic Art (LAMDA) **www.lamda.org.uk**
- National Council for Drama Training **www.ncdt.co.uk**

Broadcast journalist

WHAT DO THEY DO?

Broadcast journalists investigate and report on current affairs for news programmes on the television and radio, taking a neutral and unbiased stance in order to reflect the news as honestly as possible to a wide audience. They are involved in various media roles, such as editing, reporting and presenting. Typical duties can include the following:

- coming up with ideas for stories and features
- following up leads from many different sources
- researching and writing their stories
- gathering evidence
- advising their crews on what to film or record
- pitching their ideas to editors
- presenting their stories 'on air'
- interviewing experts and the general public.

WHERE DO THEY WORK?

News happens at all times of the day and night, and of course at weekends, so you'll have to be prepared to work long and unsocial hours, usually in shifts. These can start in the early morning or late evening, on weekdays, weekends and during public holidays.

This industry is unpredictable, with most people employed on short-term contracts or as freelancers, which means you may have to travel to find work. Opportunities are available throughout the UK, although if you want to work for one of the major networks you must be prepared to work in London or large regional cities.

WHAT SKILLS DO THEY NEED?

You will need great physical and emotional stamina to cope with work that is unpredictable, stressful and subject to tight deadlines. You will also need to have the following skills and attributes:

- an interest in the news (obviously!)
- good general knowledge
- excellent written and oral communication skills
- self-confidence
- resilience under pressure
- analytical skills to sort through different sources of information
- an ability to present often complex information in a comprehensible way
- an understanding of technical equipment
- sensitivity, empathy and tact
- creativity and originality.

A great way to get a foot in the door is through (often unpaid) work experience. Both the BBC and Independent Television (ITV) offer small journalism traineeship schemes but competition is fierce for places. You may want to contact editors and producers directly to ask for a work experience placement or the chance to shadow them for a short period of time. The local press is also a good place to start – try your newspaper or your local hospital radio – and don't forget to get involved with any student media opportunities.

Routes to qualification

There are three different ways to get into broadcast journalism:

- a traineeship directly after graduating
- moving from print journalism after a few years' experience
- by completing a postgraduate qualification in journalism, with the National Council for the Training of Journalists (NCTJ) or the Broadcast Journalism Training Council (BJTC). This is the most common route.

PROSPECTS

In TV you will normally start as a newsroom assistant or researcher and then progress into a reporting role, specialising in a particular field once you've gained more experience or even moving into a presenting role. Another possible option is to go into investigative or documentary journalism, or if you'd prefer to stay behind the camera you can work as a programme editor or sub-editor.

In radio, trainees receive greater responsibility earlier on, and may even be solely responsible for a newsroom from the very beginning. The most natural career progression would be to join a large commercial or network station, or to go into TV work.

FURTHER INFORMATION

- Broadcast Journalism Training Council **www.bjtc.org.uk**
- The National Council for the Training of Journalists (NCTJ) **www.nctj.com**
- Skillset (The Sector Skills Council for Creative Media) **www.skillset.org**

Commissioning editor

WHAT DO THEY DO?

Commissioning editors in the book publishing industry identify potential authors and support them from the commissioning stage right through to publication. Thus they play an important role in creating and constantly adding to a publishing house's booklists and, subsequently, helping their profits. To do this effectively, commissioning editors must know their field inside-out. They do this by attending book fairs, looking at catalogues and lists, and even by conducting surveys to see what sort of books are currently in demand.

Magazine commissioning editors ask writers to produce articles and features according to the remit of their magazine. They must ensure that the work they commission is of interest to their readers and is completed on time.

In both book and magazine publishing, this is not an entry-level job: you will need proven experience and ability in order to do it well. Commissioning editors normally start off in a junior position and work their way up within the company or by switching employers.

WHERE DO THEY WORK?

Commissioning editors normally work in an office environment, with occasional trips out to meetings or fairs, both in the UK and abroad. Working hours can often be long when leading up to a deadline, particularly in magazine publishing where such deadlines can occur once a week or month. The publishing world is mainly centred around the South East, with London, Oxford and Cambridge being hotspots.

WHAT SKILLS DO THEY NEED?

Commissioning editors need the following skills:

- a great knowledge of, and enthusiasm for, the field in which they work
- an eye for spotting talent
- business sense
- great interpersonal skills
- self-motivation
- the ability to plan and work to deadlines
- IT ability
- organisational skills
- an eye for detail.

While you may have gained such skills in other settings, work experience and entry-level experience are essential to get a job as a commissioning editor. Many publishing houses and magazines offer work experience schemes or placements, which can be a great source of contacts – essential in this very competitive field.

ROUTES TO QUALIFICATION

Any graduates can work in publishing, but scientific and academic publishers often stipulate that candidates have a degree in the relevant field. Publishing degrees and masters can help you get your foot in the door, as they are evidence of your commitment to working in a very competitive sector and will give you skills to set you apart from other applicants. Check out and apply for postgraduate courses at www.ukpass.ac.uk.

An entry-level post in a publishing house will normally be that of an editorial assistant, where you will carry out everyday tasks such as copy-editing, proofreading and writing text for book jackets. You may then move on to work as a desk editor or associate editor before finally becoming a commissioning editor.

In the magazine world, a degree in publishing is not essential. A postgraduate qualification in journalism might help improve your chances but nothing is as important as contacts, so make this a priority. Normally you would start off as a junior writer on a magazine, before perhaps taking a post as deputy features editor before becoming a features or commissioning editor.

PROSPECTS

Successful commissioning editors in publishing houses can work up the career ladder to become publishers. Commissioning editors working on magazines, meanwhile, can eventually become editors, responsible for the overall look and content of their product.

FURTHER INFORMATION

- Society for Editors and Proofreaders **www.sfep.org.uk**
- National Council for the Training of Journalists (NCTJ) **www.nctj.com**

Copy-editor and proofreader

WHAT DO THEY DO?

Publishing copy-editors and proofreaders check that books, newspapers and other texts are suitable for publication by ensuring the accuracy and accessibility of their information, language and grammar. This may involve correcting typos, checking that facts are correct, ensuring that the publication's house style and tone are adhered to, and rewriting anything that isn't quite right or doesn't meet the appropriate standards. It can also involve preparing documents for the design stage by flagging up codes for the designers and suggesting images and photographs. This role can be done in-house, especially in smaller publishing houses, but increasingly work is being farmed out to specialist freelancers.

WHERE DO THEY WORK?

If you work as an in-house copy-editor or proofreader, you will normally be based in an office environment, while freelancers work from home. The latter situation gives you much more flexibility as to when you actually work, as long as you meet deadlines. Freelancers can work in most parts of the country but most in-house opportunities are found in London and the South East. Working hours can be long when a deadline is approaching. Those employed on a freelance basis might find that projects have extremely tight deadlines – publishers often tend to contact you at the very last minute and expect a quick turnaround!

If you decide to go down the freelance route, it's worth bearing in mind that it can be difficult to gain sufficient work to earn a living. Publishing houses often have a list of preferred copy-editors and proofreaders, often with staff who have gone from working in-house to working at home, so perseverance is essential to get started in this field. Additionally, working on your own can be quite lonely and you may miss the buzz and camaraderie of an office.

WHAT SKILLS DO THEY NEED?

Successful copy-editors and proofreaders have the following skills and attributes:

- an excellent knowledge of English
- a methodical approach
- great attention to detail: you're employed to pick up other people's mistakes, but there's no one to correct yours
- accuracy and concentration
- the ability to multitask as you may be working on several projects at once
- a tactful manner to suggest corrections to authors
- self-motivation, especially for freelancers, to get the work done
- IT and computer skills (much editing and proofreading these days is done on-screen)
- business and numerical skills (for example, to deal with tax returns, National Insurance contributions and negotiating pay rates).

ROUTES TO QUALIFICATION

Any graduate can work in this field, although some scientific or academic publishers require a degree in a relevant field. A degree or postgraduate qualification in either publishing or the media may improve your chances.

Experience is extremely important, so try to get involved with university magazines or find some work experience at bookshops, libraries and publishers. Some graduates will start in a junior role in a publishing house – for example, as an editorial assistant – and then work their way up, often going freelance once their careers are more firmly established.

PROSPECTS

The salary you receive will depend on what type of work you do and for which company. Understandably, larger publishers tend to pay better rates although this is not always the case.

If you become quite experienced in your field and build up a good rapport with your company or clients, you may be offered project management roles. This would involve seeing a publication through from concept to finish and can command higher fees because of the increased responsibility.

FURTHER INFORMATION

- The Society for Editors and Proofreaders **www.sfep.org.uk**

Dancer

WHAT DO THEY DO?

Dancers are like actors in that they portray characters, but they do so primarily through movement, often to music, with the guidance of a choreographer or through improvisation. There are a huge variety of dance genres, from ballet and tap to contemporary and jazz dance. As well as performing, dancers often become involved with education and therapy.

This job is extremely competitive and physical and tends to have a short shelf-life – dancers rarely go on performing professionally beyond their forties. As with all performing arts careers, dancers must promote themselves in order to get work, at least until they are an established name. It is also a career marked by periods of unemployment in which dancers will need to take on other jobs to bring home money. Performance itself makes up a fairly small part of a dancer's life. Instead, they will usually combine dancing with fields such as teaching, arts promotion and administration, normally to fit around their dancing commitments.

WHERE DO THEY WORK?

Dancers work in a variety of settings, from gyms and dance halls, where they practise nearly every day, to theatres and other performance centres, when they are part of a production. Working hours are very antisocial, with performances typically taking place in the evenings and at weekends, six or even seven days a week. Contract work is common and offered on a short-term basis so you can expect periods of intensive work followed by quieter times when you will need to look for further contracts.

Travel is almost an essential part of a dancer's career, with opportunities both in the UK and abroad. Most work is available in large cities rather than smaller communities.

WHAT SKILLS DO THEY NEED?

Dancers need the following skills to succeed:

- a thorough training in dance
- physical stamina to cope with daily rehearsals and performances
- perseverance to find work and maintain contacts
- the ability to work both as part of a team and on an individual basis.

ROUTES TO QUALIFICATION

Most dancers start training at a very young age; this is usually not a profession that you can enter later in life and it's unlikely that you will be able to start a career after graduating if you have not followed a dancing path. Dance degrees are normally offered at specialist colleges or universities and focus on the theoretical side of dance, although performance forms a part of the course.

PROSPECTS

After a dancing career, a popular choice is teaching, either on a private basis or for public-sector organisations. Other possible areas include choreography and dance administration, or working in a community to run workshops for groups of people such as young people or those with disabilities.

FURTHER INFORMATION

- British Theatre Dance Association **www.btda.org.uk**
- National Dance Teachers' Association **www.ndta.org.uk**
- young-dancers **www.young-dancers.org**

Film and video editor

WHAT DO THEY DO?

Film or video editors take a variety of raw camera footage, dialogue, sound effects and graphics, select which ones they want and put them together to make a final 'cut', which is the version you will see on television or at the cinema. Much of the editing is done with computer or digital technology within a special suite, often beside a director to ensure the final product meets their vision. However, some production companies still use the more traditional method of cutting film and then arranging shots into the desired order.

WHERE DO THEY WORK?

Editors in these fields often work on a freelance basis, on short-term contracts for post-production studios and TV companies. They will work either alone or as part of a small team, often in very small, enclosed surroundings. Freelance editors can work from home in their own editing suites.

Working hours can vary. If you work in-house then you can expect a steadier stream of work and normal nine-to-five hours, but long hours and weekend work are common when a deadline approaches. Freelancers tend to work in shorter, more intense bursts, with shorter deadlines. However, they can also experience periods of unemployment until the next project comes in.

WHAT SKILLS DO THEY NEED?

Film and video editors must be able to use editing software packages competently. Without this, you can forget a career in this area, so look out for courses on the AVID, Lightworks or Final Cut Pro packages. While these can be expensive, they will provide you with the specific skills required for the industry. You will also need the following skills:

- a keen eye for detail
- a creative approach
- good listening skills
- teamwork
- self-motivation
- organisational and self-management skills
- oral and written communication skills.

ROUTES TO QUALIFICATION

Graduates from all degrees can in theory pursue a career in this field but taking a course in media and communication, photography, television, film, fine art or information technology could increase your chances. Experience is vital, as you will need to show that you have had experience of working in a film/video environment, either in production or post-production. Most film or video editors do not step straight into this role either – they tend to start out as runners and work their way up.

PROSPECTS

Gaining experience before trying to get a job is advisable, for example by joining a student film-making society (or starting one!) or undertaking voluntary placements with relevant employers. As a graduate your first job may be as a runner or trainee, so you need to be positive about working your way up from the bottom, learning new skills quickly and networking. The next stage could be to secure an assistant editor post, before becoming an editor. Structured career paths exist in some of the larger organisations, although there is huge competition for a relatively small number of jobs.

Freelance film or video editors tend to work on smaller projects to begin with. With increasing experience they will be able to find work on larger, more complex productions. In general, success in this career depends to a large extent on your practical experience, evidence of your achievements and personal contacts.

FURTHER INFORMATION

- British Film Institute **www.bfi.org.uk**
- Skillset (The Sector Skills Council for Creative Media) **www.skillset.org**

Features editor

WHAT DO THEY DO?

Features editors work for magazines, newspapers and websites, and are responsible for coming up with ideas for features on a weekly or monthly basis. Magazines and websites can vary in size from specialist publications on particular topics to glossy women's magazines and gossip 'mags'. Larger consumer magazines include features on fashion, beauty and lifestyle, as well as celebrity interviews, while specialist publications look at news and developments in their particular field.

Typically, features editors will do some or all of the following tasks:

- attend regular features meetings to come up with ideas for future editions
- plan each issue's features
- manage and commission both in-house and freelance writers
- draw up and send out briefs for features to writers
- edit features and ensure that they are accurate and that they meet house style
- write features
- liaise with the design department on layouts and illustrations
- proofread their pages before going to press.

WHERE DO THEY WORK?

Features editors work mainly in an office environment, although they sometimes will attend photoshoots and meetings. If writing is involved as part of their job, they may also take trips to research a topic or to interview relevant people.

Working hours tend to be fairly regular, particularly on magazines, with an average day lasting from 9am until 6pm. However, be prepared to work longer hours in the days running up to print, especially in newspapers and weekly magazines. While newspapers and magazines are based throughout the UK, the majority are in London so you may have to consider living in the capital.

WHAT SKILLS DO THEY NEED?

Since all media professions are popular, potential candidates have to prove their worth to get the job over hundreds of others. Typical skills include:

- top-notch organisation skills; often you'll be planning future issues while finishing current ones
- determination to get the job done on time and to an excellent standard
- the ability to take criticism... and often to give it
- strong interpersonal skills and a sociable nature
- creativity and an eye for an idea
- natural curiosity and an interest in people
- self-confidence and a professional approach.

Getting a foot on the career ladder can be tough. Make the most of any school or university vacations to seek work experience in the local and national press, as well as in any student-led magazines and newspapers. While much of this will be unpaid, you will be gaining invaluable contacts and an insight into the industry.

ROUTES TO QUALIFICATION

Most features editors are graduates who have worked their way up in journalism to get to this senior post: most have at least five years' experience in a writing capacity or as a deputy features editor before they move into this role. Degree discipline is usually not important, unless you are working on highly specialist magazines; recruiters view experience as more valuable than qualifications. However, a postgraduate qualification in journalism is often valued highly.

PROSPECTS

You'll probably start your career as a junior writer, working up to senior writer and then possibly deputy editor before becoming a features editor. This career route can take at least three to five years and you might have to move from one publication to another as positions arise. A features editor can then aim for the highest job as editor but this can take a long time to achieve as there are relatively few positions at the top.

FURTHER INFORMATION

- National Council for the Training of Journalists (NCTJ) **www.nctj.com**
- Periodical Publishers Association (PPA) **www.ppa.co.uk**

Magazine journalist

WHAT DO THEY DO?

Magazine journalists research and write both news articles and features for local, national and sometimes international magazines. There are thousands of magazines in the UK, ranging from women's lifestyle glossies to specialist titles on areas such as fly-fishing, so the articles that magazine journalists write must reflect the interests of their readers.

Magazine journalists may specialise in writing either news or features, and are normally also involved in sub-editing, in which they take another person's article and make amendments. While the work is still predominantly focused on paper-based products, web writing is becoming increasingly popular. In whatever medium they work, magazine journalists will typically research a subject or story and talk to the appropriate people, and then write an article based on their findings.

WHERE DO THEY WORK?

Magazine journalists work in a variety of places. Those employed directly by magazines or websites are based in an office environment, while those who work as freelancers (around 80% of features are written by freelancers) are home-based. All journalists will frequently go out to meetings to interview people or carry out research relevant to their feature.

Regular working hours are not common in this industry, with tight deadlines meaning that you are unlikely to enjoy a nine-to-five existence. Long and unsocial hours are common. While most major magazines are based in London and the South East, the availability of freelance work means that you can work from all over the UK.

WHAT SKILLS DO THEY NEED?

Successful magazine journalists need to be:

- highly literate
- curious
- good with technology (eg computers)
- up-to-date with current affairs
- good at working with other people
- interested in whatever magazine(s) they write for.

The best way to get noticed by employers is to find relevant work experience. Try writing for your student newspaper or magazine and, during the holidays, try to organise work experience placements on local, regional and national newspapers and magazines.

If you are considering a career as a freelancer, you may have to do some unpaid work first in order to build up a portfolio that you can then show to potential commissioning editors. Alternatively you could start as a staff writer and then go freelance.

ROUTES TO QUALIFICATION

Most features writers are graduates so a degree really is a prerequisite. If you want to write for a specialist field, you will often need to have a degree in that area in order to be considered. Postgraduate diplomas in journalism are not essential but they can be helpful in giving you an awareness of the industry and some skills that are required.

PROSPECTS

Career progression depends on a variety of factors. If you are working for an employer, you could start off as a staff writer, progressing to sub-editor. With a few years' experience under your belt, you may be able to land a job as chief editor. Thanks to the writing skills and commercial nous you'll develop, you could also move into related areas of work such as PR or marketing. Freelancers have more flexibility but must be highly proactive networkers, keep up with technological developments and produce good work to deadline to keep bringing the work in.

FURTHER INFORMATION

- National Council for the Training of Journalists (NCTJ) **www.nctj.com**
- Periodical Publishers Association (PPA) **www.ppa.co.uk**

Musician

WHAT DO THEY DO?

Musicians can work in several different fields within the music industry – as an instrumental performer, as a composer and as a singer. Normally they will specialise in a particular type of music such as pop, classical, jazz, etc. Some musicians are employed as part of a regular group (for example, in orchestras), while others will freelance and play whenever demand dictates. This often involves performing live or in a recording studio, either in a group or on their own. Practising on a daily basis is as important as performance to ensure that their skills and talents are always at the top of their field.

WHERE DO THEY WORK?

Musicians commonly work on a self-employed basis, although some are employed in orchestras and other groups of musicians. Freelance musicians will testify to the unreliability of their work – taking on a part-time job to pay the bills is often part and parcel of a music career. Musicians tend to practise at home and then perform in theatres or recording studios, at any time of the day and night. Unsociable working hours are common as performances tend to be in the evenings and at weekends. Working in holiday seasons is also unavoidable.

If your main passion is to play in an orchestra or perhaps as part of a backing group for a pop star, you will normally need to be based in London or another big city, where opportunities are most prevalent. Travel is common, as musicians often go on tour both in the UK and abroad.

WHAT SKILLS DO THEY NEED?

To get ahead in the music industry you need to know how to network. This involves making contacts and keeping in touch with them so they think of you when they are planning their next musical project. Experience is essential to attract the attention of musical directors. Other desirable skills include:

- **teamwork**: to get on in large and small groups of musicians
- **accuracy**: to play a piece of music well
- **confidence**: to perform in front of large audiences
- **stamina**: to cope with the amount of rehearsals and performances
- **language skills**: to be able to sing in other languages (if opera's your thing) and communicate with international musicians.

To build up your portfolio of experience, make the most of opportunities at school and university to perform with amateur orchestras and groups. Talk to musicians currently working in your preferred field to see what they have to say about getting your career off the ground, and ask if they can introduce you to anyone of influence.

ROUTES TO QUALIFICATION

Many musicians and composers have a degree in music but this is not always essential – talent and ability in your chosen instrument is of greater importance. However, music degrees do give you the opportunity to develop performance skills as well as concentrating heavily on the theory side of music.

If you want to play in an orchestra or sing in an opera house you will normally need to attend an audition and then work for them for a trial period. Unfortunately contracts aren't always offered at the end, even if you have played well, and trials can last from a few sessions to a few years.

PROSPECTS

There are so many different kinds of music, and hence of musicians, that it is impossible to describe a typical career path. Many musicians, whatever genre they specialise in, will be self-employed, and may need to make ends meet by taking on regular part-time work, which could be related to music – for example, teaching music or working in arts administration. Self-employment is not the only option: there are permanent positions, for example in orchestras, in teaching (whether private tuition, in schools or in further or higher education), and in arts administration or management. People don't tend to go into music for the pay – only a few famous soloists (instrumental or singers) can command considerable pay packets.

FURTHER INFORMATION

- Musicians' Union **www.musiciansunion.org.uk**
- Association of British Orchestras **www.abo.org.uk**
- Incorporated Society of Musicians (ISM) **www.ism.org**

Newspaper journalist

WHAT DO THEY DO?

Newspaper journalists carry out a similar role to magazine journalists except that they work for newspapers. They can be found working in the local, regional, national and sometimes international press. Journalists normally start off as a junior reporter and are given work from the news desk as stories roll in. The juicier topics tend to be snapped up by the more senior reporters but it is the journalist's task to make even the most dull, everyday story interesting. Topics covered include news, culture, sport and science, local and national events, and entertainment. Contacts in such areas as the police and emergency services are essential as they provide a much-needed stream of ideas.

WHERE DO THEY WORK?

Newspaper journalists will work from a central office but will often be out and about researching stories and talking to sources. There are opportunities with regional and local papers throughout the UK but if you want to work for one of the nationals, you'll probably have to move to London. Generally you will need to be flexible about where you're based in this career, particularly when you're starting out.

Hours can be very long and unsocial, as you will have to be ready to investigate a story when it happens, often at the drop of a hat. Early on in your career, particularly, you will often work on a shift basis – early and late shifts are common.

WHAT SKILLS DO THEY NEED?

It's often said that journalists need a thick skin and a dogged sense of determination to get ahead in this field. This is true, of course! You will also need the following skills and attributes:

- excellent written and oral communication skills
- an eye for a good story and the ability to write it up in an interesting manner
- the ability to keep to strict deadlines
- stamina to cope with long hours and often stressful conditions
- self-motivation.

Some national and regional newspaper groups offer a small number of traineeships but competition for these is extremely fierce, so prior experience is essential even to be considered. Try working for student publications and use your holidays to arrange work experience placements or work-shadowing possibilities. These can be in other forms of media such as radio and television.

ROUTES TO QUALIFICATION

Gone are the days when you could become a hack by starting off as a tea boy and working your way to the top. Most newspaper journalists now have degrees and many also take a postgraduate qualification in journalism. Some newspapers offer places on graduate training schemes, in which you will spend two years learning on the job.

PROSPECTS

The most common career route is to start as a general reporter on a local or regional newspaper and then move your way up the career ladder to specialise in a certain area. Other journalists may leave the regional press and start in a more junior job with the nationals. Another alternative would be to join a news desk or to work in production.

FURTHER INFORMATION

- National Council for the Training of Journalists (NCTJ) **www.nctj.com**

Photographer

WHAT DO THEY DO?

Photographers take pictures of people, objects and places in order to capture their essence or to convey a particular message through the image. The work varies from portraits of individuals and groups, to capturing the horror of war or photographing an aesthetically pleasing plate of food. However, it is rare for a photographer to be a jack of all trades – he or she will almost always specialise in a particular area such as fine art, fashion or advertising.

Many photographers are self-employed, although some work for such different employers as media companies, publishers and in education. Typical tasks include:

- liaising with clients about what they want from the photos
- researching sites for photoshoots in advance
- using a wide variety of technical equipment, such as lenses, cameras and computers
- advising human subjects on how to pose
- arranging still-life objects according to a brief.

Many graduates start out as a photographer's assistant, which tends to involve doing much of the photographer's admin work.

WHERE DO THEY WORK?

Photographers work in many different settings – from an office in a workplace or at home to attending shoots in studios or even outside... and in all weathers! Hours can be very long on projects and you may experience the opposite states of being too busy one moment and twiddling your thumbs the next. During quiet periods, it is essential to keep motivated to look for work and network with any contacts you have made. Working conditions themselves can be uncomfortable (a photoshoot in the snow, for instance) and even downright dangerous (for example, taking photos in a war zone). Most work can be found in London but there are opportunities throughout the UK, depending on your specialism.

WHAT SKILLS DO THEY NEED?

To be a top photographer, you need to be able to work as part of a team, as well as on your own. You will also need to be:

- **personable** – to get on with a wide range of people
- **dedicated** – to keep looking for jobs
- **technically minded** – the digital world has reached photography thoroughly and image manipulation is popular.

To stand a chance of getting regular, well-paid work you will need a portfolio to show potential employers and clients. Websites are a popular marketing tool these days too. To gain experience and build your portfolio, join any photographic societies and take your own pictures as often as possible. Read relevant magazines and check out the displays at local and national galleries. Work experience with a photographer can be both an insight into the industry and a way to get a foot in the door.

ROUTES TO QUALIFICATION

Graduates of any degree discipline can work in photography if they have the talent. However, art and design, digital imaging, graphics, media studies and photography can all help. Postgraduate courses are not essential but in specialist fields such as fashion and advertising it can be advantageous to do a further qualification in a relevant area of photography.

PROSPECTS

Some will decide to start their photographic career by building valuable experience working as a photographic assistant or in a photographic picture library. There is a relatively small number of opportunities for photographers to work for an employer, including as a staff photographer on a newspaper or in highly specialised capacities such as a museum or medical photographer.

Most photographers are self-employed. The decision then is whether to specialise and build up your reputation in a particular niche – for example, portraits, fashion or reportage – or whether to be more flexible and generalist. Keeping up-to-date with the latest equipment and technology is vital.

FURTHER INFORMATION

- British Institute of Professional Photography (BIPP) **www.bipp.com**
- The Association of Photographers (AOP) **www.the-aop.org**
- The British Press Photographers' Association (BPPA) **www.thebppa.com**

Presenter – radio and television

WHAT DO THEY DO?

Presenters of radio and television are the voices and faces of news, current affairs and popular culture. Radio presenters will host their own shows, which may have a theme (Eddie Mair's news programme on BBC Radio 4, for example), or will play music according to what their listeners will like, such as Radio 1's breakfast show with Chris Moyles. Television presenters normally work on shorter programmes and will specialise in a very particular field. Areas include news programmes, chat shows, children's entertainment, game shows and consumer programmes.

Presenters don't just start work when the cameras roll, or the microphone is turned on, however. A good deal of preparation goes on behind the scenes for several hours before the programme begins, with presenters rehearsing what they are going to say and often writing a script to follow. After their programme there may be meetings to plan for the next show, too.

WHERE DO THEY WORK?

Radio presenters work in studios within radio stations, although occasionally they may do outside broadcasts from live events. The same applies to television presenters, who will work in television studios, sometimes in front of a live studio audience.

Hours can be long and unsocial, particularly if you are doing early morning or late night shows. Both the radio and television operate throughout the night and during weekends and holidays, so chances are you will be working at some periods when your friends and family are at home.

WHAT SKILLS DO THEY NEED?

Presenting is often viewed as a glamorous career and therefore competition for places can be hard. Normally the following skills and attributes are required:

- a smart appearance (for television)
- a pleasant speaking voice (for both TV and radio)
- good interpersonal skills to deal with audience members and interviewees
- determination to get this far in the first place
- an unflappable nature – television and radio are often live and mistakes or problems happen. You need to be able to deal with issues as and when they arise and cope with the director shouting into your earpiece.

To stand a chance of a career in this area, get as much experience as possible while you're studying. Write to major broadcasters and local radio stations and ask for work experience or work-shadowing opportunities. Try to build up a good network of contacts to whom you can turn when you start your job search. A stint working on local or hospital radio can be invaluable and will give you the opportunity of recording your show to play to potential employers. Drama experience is helpful for teaching you how to present, so join a student theatre company or go on a short course if you can.

ROUTES TO QUALIFICATION

While there is no definitive route to becoming a presenter, most do have degrees. Subject matter is normally not important but those with a media or performing arts degree may enjoy a small advantage. What's more important is enthusiasm for the area plus relevant experience and good contacts.

Most presenters start out as journalists or researchers, while some have had previous experience in another field of the arts such as acting or music. Some may be experts in the area in which they present, such as sports, politics or the arts.

PROSPECTS

There is no structured career path for radio and TV presenters. Looking for voluntary opportunities can be a useful way of building up experience and showing your commitment (for example, working for a hospital or local community radio station). New presenters often start on the least popular slots – the early morning or late evening ones. Career development may then be a case of working their way to prime time slots once they establish a reputation. However, it is a very competitive industry that is under pressure due to the current economic climate, so achieving success will require a great deal of determination, the ability to spot opportunities and a gift for networking.

FURTHER INFORMATION

- Broadcasting Entertainment Cinematograph and Theatre Union (BECTU) **www.bectu.org.uk**
- Broadcast Journalism Training Council **www.bjtc.org.uk**
- National Council for the Training of Journalists (NCTJ) **www.nctj.com**
- Skillset (The Sector Skills Council for Creative Media) **www.skillset.org**

Producer – radio

WHAT DO THEY DO?

Radio producers are the people behind the scenes who provide the ideas and content for the broadcasts that presenters give on the radio and internet. They also manage the audience response to these programmes and work with presenters, DJs and sound engineers. Sometimes they may find themselves covering other roles in presenting and reporting.

WHERE DO THEY WORK?

Broadcasting roughly falls into three main areas: public radio, commercial radio and voluntary radio, and opportunities for producers exist in each. Studio-based work is the norm but producers often go out on location to interview people, research a programme and cover live events. Hours can be long, unsocial and unpredictable and travel away from home is not uncommon.

Half of the people working in radio are based in London but that also means that half the opportunities are in other areas. Local, regional and voluntary radio exists in cities throughout the UK although you may have to relocate to a larger place to get the bigger jobs.

WHAT SKILLS DO THEY NEED?

Radio producers need many skills, which include the following:

- self-confidence
- strong written and spoken communication skills
- organisation
- the ability to cope under pressure and work to tight deadlines
- curiosity and an eye for a good feature
- teamwork and the ability to work independently
- a talkative and lively nature, but also good at listening
- a willingness to use different forms of technology.

ROUTES TO QUALIFICATION

Any graduate can have a career in this area but broadcast journalism and journalism graduates may have a slight edge. You could always opt for a postgraduate diploma or MA in radio production but don't forget that experience and excellent skills matter more than a piece of paper. Training takes place on the job in all aspects of radio production, from technical aspects to presenting and editing.

PROSPECTS

Progression is possible in this field but it must be driven by you. Since many producers work on a freelance basis, they will often move from one job to another and undertake short-term projects, although long-term opportunities are available. To find out about these you will need to set up a good network of contacts as jobs are rarely advertised. You will probably also end up specialising in a particular field such as news, culture or sport.

FURTHER INFORMATION

- Skillset (The Sector Skills Council for Creative Media) **www.skillset.org**
- Broadcast Journalism Training Council **www.bjtc.org.uk**

Producer – television and film

WHAT DO THEY DO?

Producers are the head honchos in television, film and video. They will often come up with the idea for a project and they will see it through from conception until distribution. This will involve working with directors, other production staff and sometimes actors to get the job done, and it is becoming more and more common for producers to offer directing skills too. Fundraising to finance a project is also an important task, as is ensuring that a film doesn't stray too much from its proposed budget.

The difference between a producer and a director is mainly that producers deal with the practical aspects of a project, while a director is more focused on the artistic and interpretative side.

WHERE DO THEY WORK?

Working environments are incredibly varied, with producers being based in offices, studios and on location – often all in the same day! Hours are irregular and long and will involve weekend, evening and early morning work. Most of the jobs are in London but there are large production companies based in regional cities such as Birmingham, Manchester, Cardiff, Edinburgh and Glasgow. Working away from home is common. There are good opportunities for those who want to work on a freelance or self-employed basis but this does entail low job security.

WHAT SKILLS DO THEY NEED?

This is not an entry-level job: it requires a good deal of experience within the relevant industry, perhaps as an assistant producer, a researcher or a scriptwriter. Knowledge of programme- or film-making techniques is essential, as are directing and editing skills. The following are also vital:

- self-confidence
- excellent communication skills
- management skills
- creativity
- time-management skills
- leadership ability
- networking skills – jobs are rarely advertised and mostly gained from word of mouth
- stamina to cope with often long spells of stressful and intense working.

Be prepared for fierce competition and don't underestimate the importance of building up your own network of contacts. Try to gain much-valued experience by contacting production companies and asking to spend some time observing what goes on. Keep track of what's happening in the industry and look out for jobs as a runner in the first instance. Join any student film or theatre societies and if possible make a reel of the work you have contributed to as evidence of your capabilities.

ROUTES TO QUALIFICATION

Careers in this field are not subject-dependent but subjects focusing on media studies, photography, film, IT, multimedia and broadcasting can confer a certain advantage because they normally teach practical skills in production. If you opt for a degree in a non-related field, consider a postgraduate qualification to boost your chances and improve your skills. However, most of the training is on the job.

PROSPECTS

Most programme-makers and producers in television, film and video are self-employed and work on short-term contracts, whose length will depend on the project at hand. It is possible to move between film, video and television as the skills are often transferable. Some producers will start their own production company once they have built a good reputation and made enough contacts.

FURTHER INFORMATION

- Skillset (The Sector Skills Council for Creative Media) **www.skillset.org**

Theatre director

WHAT DO THEY DO?

Theatre directors interpret scripts for plays or musical scores in order to bring them to life on the stage. They do this by working closely with their creative and production teams and, to a certain extent, are dictated to by their budget. Most work on a freelance basis or on fixed-term contracts, although some are employed as 'resident' directors in some repertory companies.

Large theatre companies decide in advance which plays they wish to put on and then consider which directors they would like to use to do this. In smaller companies, the theatre director will do this in addition to his or her creative job. It is normal to start out as an assistant director or as an actor, writer, designer, stage manager or producer.

WHERE DO THEY WORK?

Directors work in theatres, predominantly, unless they are putting on performances in other places such as outdoor theatres or other theatrical settings. Working hours are unsocial by nature as performances occur when people are not at work or school and able to attend. It is not unusual for directors to put in more hours than they have been contracted to do, from rehearsals right through to the first performance. Typical contracts can last from one to three years. You need to be flexible about where you're willing to work as travel is common, both within the UK and abroad.

WHAT SKILLS DO THEY NEED?

Directors need the following skills to succeed:

- creativity
- artistic vision, to bring a play from page to stage
- teamwork
- time-management skills
- tact and diplomacy (many actors have fragile egos)
- an understanding of the technical aspects of stage performance
- research skills
- interpersonal skills
- practical acting and stage management experience.

Experience is vital so take any opportunity to become involved in the theatre, from amateur dramatic groups to student societies. Try to gain some work experience at your local theatre, or why not aim for a visit to one of the nationals? See as many productions as possible and make notes about aspects of the performances that you enjoyed or ways you could do things differently. By working behind the scenes at a theatre you will be in a good position to understand how a theatre runs and the many different aspects a director needs to take into account.

ROUTES TO QUALIFICATION

Any graduate can work within this field but the following degrees might help your prospects:

- drama/theatre studies
- music
- creative/performing arts
- English
- languages.

You don't need to have a postgraduate qualification under your belt if you have a relevant degree or practical experience. If you do decide to go for a postgraduate qualification, make sure that the course you choose places an emphasis on practical skills.

PROSPECTS

It is not uncommon for directors to start their careers by setting up their own small theatre company, or by directing a production for a touring company. To apply for senior roles with established theatre companies a director would need several years' experience. A good head for business is also essential, as it's often necessary to negotiate funding as well as make sure productions bring in enough money to assure the future of the organisation one is working for. An experienced director could start a new company or work as a director in an already established company, overseeing the annual cycle of productions. With enough experience, another option would be to move into directing in television or film.

FURTHER INFORMATION

- The Independent Theatre Council **www.itc-arts.org**
- Theatrical Management Association (TMA) **www.tmauk.org**

www.ucas.com
www.cukas.ac.uk

at the heart of connecting people to higher education

The career for you?

Is journalism, media and performing arts for you?

Building a successful career in journalism, media and performing arts requires more than the ability to act, sing, dance, write or produce. It also requires certain skills and personal qualities or 'attributes'. To help you decide if a career in journalism, media and performing arts is for you, we suggest you think about the following three areas:

- what **you** want from your future work
- what a journalism, media and performing arts course typically involves
- which skills and qualities admissions tutors in this field typically seek in new recruits.

WHAT DO YOU WANT IN YOUR FUTURE WORK?

You may not have an instant answer for this, but your current studies, work experience and even your hobbies can help give you clues about the kind of work you enjoy and the skills you have already started to develop. Start with a blank sheet of paper and note down the answers to the questions opposite to help get you thinking. Be as brutally honest with yourself as you can – don't write what you think will impress your teachers or parents. Write what really matters to you, and you'll start to see a pattern emerge.

- When you think of your future, in what kind of environment do you see yourself working? For example in an office, outdoors, nine-to-five, relaxed or high-pressured?
- What are your favourite hobbies outside school?
- What is it about them you enjoy? For example working with people, figuring out how things work?
- What are your favourite subjects in school and what is it about them that you enjoy most? For example being able to create something new, or working with people?
- What do you dislike about the other subjects you're studying? ('The teacher' doesn't count!)
- Which aspects of your work experience have you most enjoyed?

WHAT DO JOURNALISM, MEDIA AND PERFORMING ARTS COURSES INVOLVE?

Not surprisingly, the skills you'll require for a successful career in journalism, performing arts or media will also be required at various stages of your studies. Therefore, it is important to know what journalism, media and performing arts courses entail before you apply so that you're sure it's the kind of work you will enjoy. For example, one common misconception about media and performing arts courses is that they are purely practice based. While it's true that most courses include some practical tasks and assessments, you'll have to study the theoretical and historical side of media and performing arts – precisely how much will depend on the individual course syllabus.

WHAT SKILLS WILL YOU NEED?

Despite the many differences in journalism, media and performing arts sectors, the underpinning skillset they all require is broadly the same: talent, which employers will mostly discern from your portfolio and other experience. Beyond this, the following are the other key skills required of any potential journalism, media and performing arts student.

- **Creativity** – not just the artistic skill, but the capacity to use it to produce new perspectives or new productions.
- **Capacity for sustained effort** – working in this sector involves not just creating, but the patience and perseverance to rework and change your work, not once, but often many times, until you or your client are happy with the finished product.
- **A thick skin and a self-critical attitude** – in this field, your work – your *self* – will be on display, not just to your peers and tutors but also to the wider public and eventually the wider community. Therefore it is important from the outset that you learn to turn even the sharpest of criticisms into constructive feedback that you can use to improve your work.

- **Perseverance** – many, if not most, of the people working in this sector do so on a freelance basis. That means a lot of people repeatedly compete for the same job, the same contract, the same writing slot. As any writer, editor, actor, dancer or musician will tell you, rejection is far too common for their liking! However, rather than sitting and brooding on it, you need to keep trying to find work and not lose your self-belief or become downhearted or dejected.

In addition to these general skills shared and sought by all fields in journalism, media and performing arts, admissions tutors will also look for sector-specific skills related to their field. For example:

- would-be **musicians** will need to have excellent performance skills and be able to sight-read
- if you're planning on making a career as a **dancer**, you must have a high level of personal fitness and plenty of years' experience behind you – most dancers have been studying since they were tiny tots
- **writers** must be brimming with ideas and have excellent literary knowledge
- potential **directors** must also be keen actors and have bold creative visions that they are not scared of sharing with an audience.

Alternative careers

If you're looking for something a little less mainstream, a journalism, media and performing arts qualification can open the door to some alternative career paths.

MUSIC THERAPIST

Music therapists are allied health professionals who typically work as part of a therapeutic team headed by a psychiatrist. They are usually employed in health authorities, hospitals, schools, prisons and mental health centres. Their aim is to help in treatment by encouraging self-expression through music. To qualify, you typically need to take a postgraduate diploma. In addition to the formal qualifications, you'll also need great emotional sensitivity for this work, which is conducted on a one-to-one or small group basis over long periods of time.

Further information
British Society for Music Therapy **www.bsmt.org**
The UCAS Guide to getting into Nursing, Healthcare and Social Work
(see page 143)

TEACHER

As a teacher, you can influence future generations of actors, musicians, writers, and so on. It is usually preferable to have some experience of your own to draw upon, and many teachers in this area combine teaching with performance or writing. As a teacher, you will work with students to interpret plays, novels and music, as well as helping them to come up with their own creations, stage their own performances or find outlets for their writings. All state sector schools require a postgraduate qualification in teaching, which can be done either as a one-year, full-time course or as on-the-job training. Private schools do not ask for this qualification although increasingly they prefer candidates who offer it. University lecturers will normally have a relevant postgraduate qualification plus experience in their field.

Further information
Training and Development Agency for Schools
www.tda.gov.uk
The UCAS Guide to getting into Teaching and Education
(see page 143)

Professional bodies

Professional bodies are responsible for overseeing a particular profession or career area, ensuring that people who work in the area are fully trained and meet ethical guidelines. Professional bodies may be known as institutions, societies or associations. They generally have regulatory roles: they make sure that members of the profession are able to work successfully in their jobs without endangering lives or abusing their position.

Professional bodies are often involved in training and career development, so courses and workplace training may have to follow the body's guidelines. In order to be fully qualified and licensed to work in your profession of choice, you will have to follow the professional training route. In many areas of work, completion of the professional training results in gaining chartered status – and the addition of some extra letters after your name. Other institutions may award other types of certification once certain criteria have been met. Chartered or certified members will usually need to take further courses and training to ensure their skills are kept up-to-date.

WHAT PROFESSIONAL BODIES ARE THERE?

Not all career areas have professional bodies. Those jobs that require extensive learning and training are likely to have bodies with a regulatory focus. This includes careers such as engineering, law, construction, health and finance. If you want to work in one of these areas, it's important to make sure your degree course is accredited by the professional body – otherwise you may have to undertake further study or training later on.

Other bodies may play more of a supportive role, looking after the interests of people who work in the sector. This includes journalism, management and arts-based careers. Professional bodies may also be learned bodies, providing opportunities for further learning and promoting the development of knowledge in the field.

CAN I JOIN AS A STUDENT?

Many professional bodies offer student membership – sometimes free or for reduced fees. Membership can be extremely valuable as a source of advice, information and resources. You'll have the opportunity to meet other students in the field, as well as experienced professionals. It will also look good on your CV, when you come to apply for jobs.

See below for a list of professional bodies and other useful organisations in the fields of journalism, media and performing arts.

ALL SECTORS

Arts Council England
www.artscouncil.org.uk

Arts Council of Northern Ireland
www.artscouncil-ni.org

Arts Council of Wales
www.artswales.org.uk

Creative Scotland
www.creativescotland.com

Skillset (The Sector Skills Council for Creative Media)
www.skillset.org

PUBLISHING

National Council for the Training of Journalists (NCTJ)
www.nctj.com

Periodical Publishers Association (PPA)
www.ppa.co.uk

Society for Editors and Proofreaders (SfEP)
www.sfep.org.uk

Society of Young Publishers
www.thesyp.org.uk

JOURNALISM

Chartered Institute of Journalists
http://cioj.co.uk

Broadcast Journalism Training Council (BJTC)
www.bjtc.org.uk

National Council for the Training of Journalists (NCTJ)
www.nctj.com

National Union of Journalists (NUJ)
www.nuj.org.uk

CREATIVE WRITING

The Society of Authors
www.societyofauthors.org

The Writers' Guild of Great Britain
www.writersguild.org.uk

BROADCASTING, FILM AND VIDEO

Broadcasting Entertainment Cinematographic and Theatre Union (BECTU)
www.bectu.org.uk

Directors Guild of Great Britain
www.dggb.org

Stage Management Association
www.stagemanagementassociation.co.uk

Student Radio Association
www.studentradio.org.uk

THEATRE

Broadcasting Entertainment Cinematographic and Theatre Union (BECTU)
www.bectu.org.uk

Directors Guild of Great Britain
www.dggb.org

Equity - The British Actors Union
www.equity.org.uk

National Council for Drama Training
www.ncdt.co.uk

The Society of British Theatre Designers
www.theatredesign.org.uk

PERFORMANCE

Arts & Humanities Research Council (AHRC)
www.ahrc.ac.uk

Associated Board of the Royal Schools of Music (ABRSM)
www.abrsm.org

Association of British Choral Directors
www.abcd.org.uk

Association of British Orchestras
www.abo.org.uk

The British Association of Teachers of Dancing
www.batd.co.uk

British Dance Council
www.british-dance-council.org

Council for Dance Education & Training (CDET)
www.cdet.org.uk

Dance UK
www.danceuk.org

Equity - The British Actors Union
www.equity.org.uk

Incorporated Society of Musicians
www.ism.org

Musicians' Union
www.musiciansunion.org.uk

National Association of Youth Theatres (NAYT)
www.nayt.org.uk

National Council for Drama Training
www.ncdt.co.uk

National Dance Teachers' Association
www.ndta.org.uk

Graduate destinations

Journalism, media and performing arts
HESA Destination of Leavers of Higher Education Survey

Each year, comprehensive statistics are collected on what graduates are doing six months after they complete their course. The survey is co-ordinated by the Higher Education Statistics Agency (HESA) and provides information about how many graduates move into employment (and what type of career) or further study and how many are believed to be unemployed.

The full results across all subject areas are published by the Higher Education Careers Service Unit (HECSU) and the Association of Graduate Careers Advisory Services (AGCAS) in *What Do Graduates Do?*, which is available from **www.ucasbooks.com**.

	Journalism, media & performing arts
In UK employment	63.7%
In overseas employment	1.7%
Working and studying	5.0%
Studying in the UK for a higher degree	5.4%
Studying in the UK for a teaching qualification	2.3%
Undertaking other further study or training in the UK	2.3%
Studying overseas	0.2%
Not available for employment, study or training	3.1%
Assumed to be unemployed	10.6%
Other	5.7%

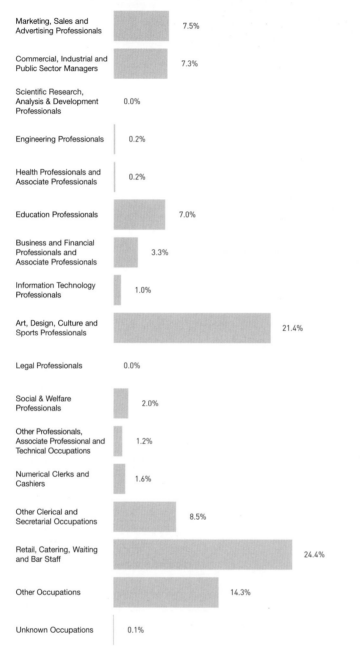

Marketing, Sales and Advertising Professionals	7.5%
Commercial, Industrial and Public Sector Managers	7.3%
Scientific Research, Analysis & Development Professionals	0.0%
Engineering Professionals	0.2%
Health Professionals and Associate Professionals	0.2%
Education Professionals	7.0%
Business and Financial Professionals and Associate Professionals	3.3%
Information Technology Professionals	1.0%
Art, Design, Culture and Sports Professionals	21.4%
Legal Professionals	0.0%
Social & Welfare Professionals	2.0%
Other Professionals, Associate Professional and Technical Occupations	1.2%
Numerical Clerks and Cashiers	1.6%
Other Clerical and Secretarial Occupations	8.5%
Retail, Catering, Waiting and Bar Staff	24.4%
Other Occupations	14.3%
Unknown Occupations	0.1%

Reproduced with the kind permission of HECSU/AGCAS, *What Do Graduates Do? 2011*.
Data from the HESA Destinations of Leavers from Higher Education Survey 09/10

Case studies

Just what can you do with a journalism, media and performing arts degree? The following graduate profiles show you the wealth of exciting careers awaiting you!

Final year journalism student

Glasgow Caledonian University

CATHERINE RITCHIE

Route into journalism:

Highers – English, maths, history, geography, chemistry, biology, Advanced Higher English (2008); BA journalism, Glasgow Caledonian University (graduating 2012)

WHY JOURNALISM?

English and writing were my strongest subjects at school alongside an interest in current affairs. I was keen to study a vocational degree with good employment prospects where I could use my skills. In the sixth form my school helped me find work placements at both Orkney Today, where I had the chance to write local news articles, and BBC Radio Orkney. This experience confirmed my interest in studying journalism.

TELL US ABOUT YOUR DEGREE

I am in the final year of a four-year journalism degree. The course is accredited by the National Council for the Training of Journalists (NCTJ) and the Broadcast Journalism Training Council (BJTC), and sitting NCTJ preliminary exams is an important part of the course. There is a focus on the practical skills needed for journalism as well as essential background knowledge, such as media law.

In the first two years my course included modules on shorthand, news and feature writing, and how to structure a news story. We spent time in the university radio studio and learnt how to produce news stories using video.

The third year included a module called 'News Days'. The university set up a working newsroom where, assisted by guest journalists, we worked in small teams on TV, radio and print projects. This year topics will include media ethics, editorial management and a dissertation. Throughout the degree there have been opportunities for work placements.

WHAT DID YOUR WORK PLACEMENTS INVOLVE?

I responded to an offer from one of our guest journalists to spend a week at Clyde and Forth Media on a news-writing placement for one of their papers. Here I had the chance to write articles from press releases and events reported to the paper and interview people over the phone.

Following this I did a sub-editing placement one day a week for four months for the same news group. I learnt about the processes for collating stories and pictures, writing headlines and captions and using computer software templates to transfer text and images on to the page. For both placements I was office based, working normal office hours.

I have also done a placement with The Big Issue, where I wrote short news items and undertook research for longer stories. As this coincided with the Edinburgh Festival I was able to interview comedians, do vox pops out on the street and gain experience of feature writing.

WHAT HAS BEEN YOUR BIGGEST CHALLENGE?

Having the confidence on placements to do tasks without assistance. It is very different during university simulations, where tutors can step in and help you. When you are working for a real company and anxious to make a good impression you don't want to make mistakes!

AND THE BEST BITS?

I really enjoyed the sub-editing placement. It is not a side of journalism I had previously considered but I have found I have an aptitude for it and there is a lot more to how stories and images are presented on the page than meets the eye. Clyde and Forth Media invited me back and I now work for them as a page layout editor, fitting shifts around my university timetable.

CATHERINE'S TOP TIPS

Be proactive and never be afraid to ask around for work experience; even a short placement can lead to employment or a contact to help you find further experience.

Professional session guitarist

REX PEARSON

Route into music:

A levels – media studies, biology, psychology, physics (2003); BA music practice, University of Central Lancashire (2006); MA PGCE in secondary music, Goldsmiths, University of London (2009)

WHY MUSIC?

Mine was not a traditional route! I was originally interested in a career in forensics but didn't get the grades at A level to get to the universities of my choice. At the time I was teaching myself guitar and practising for long hours each day. I was passionate about wanting to be able to play well and began to wonder if I could also make a living from performing. Encouraged by a careers adviser I applied for a music practice degree through Clearing and by performing well at an audition I was successful in getting a place.

HOW DID YOU GET WHERE YOU ARE TODAY?

At university being around other musicians and being introduced to different artists and styles really propelled my playing. The lecturers were also very supportive and open to creative ways of thinking and playing rather than just following traditional routes. My performance skills improved as we regularly played for student events and to the public.

After graduating I decided to move to London, one of the main centres for session musicians and where many music artists are based. I spent a year focusing on my playing and trying to make contacts. This was demanding but I was successful in playing at the African Music Awards supporting a couple of artists including Tinchy Stryder. It is difficult to break into the right circles; you are competing against a lot of other guitarists and it is hard to make enough money to live on session playing alone.

I decided I needed another avenue for my music career, so I began to offer private guitar lessons. I then took this further by doing a postgraduate certificate in education (PGCE) in secondary music which led to employment in a school sixth form. I now work here three days a week running their A level Music Technology course and providing individual guitar tuition.

WHAT DOES YOUR JOB INVOLVE?

The job is very varied. I balance teaching with continuing to play as a session musician and sixth months ago I launched my own business, Rex Pearson.com. This is a website that features my own unique teaching method, based on how I taught myself, and provides free online lessons. Currently I am busy writing a beginner guitar book to accompany the website and visiting universities to see if they would be interested in promoting my teaching method to their students.

WHAT HAS BEEN YOUR BIGGEST CHALLENGE?

Networking, without a doubt! Success is often not about how good your playing is but about the contacts you pick up, and in the music business this means getting into the right crowd.

AND THE BEST BIT?

My dream is to get my guitar teaching method into schools, colleges and universities across the UK. It also goes without saying I also want to be a top session player!

REX'S TOP TIPS

Networking is the key to success. Treat everyone you meet with respect – you never know who they might turn out to be and how making contact with them might benefit you in the future. Be organised – and always find time to practise.

Post-production runner

Editworks

PHILLIPPA BEASLEY

Route into media production:
A levels – media studies, fine art, 3D design, English language (2007); art and design foundation diploma, Reading College (2008); BSc television and broadcasting, University of Portsmouth (2011)

WHY MEDIA PRODUCTION?

Originally interested in art and design, I started a degree in fine art at the University of Portsmouth. During this time I enjoyed volunteering at the university TV studios and decided that I wanted to transfer to a skills-based course with employment prospects. I changed direction to the BSc television and broadcasting degree and have never looked back!

HOW DID YOU GET WHERE YOU ARE TODAY?

The course gave an introduction to all areas of TV broadcasting and was heavily practical. Projects mirrored working in the television industry; we made live TV shows each week and had a chance to film the university graduation ceremony.

I became particularly interested in editing as I enjoy getting ideas across and telling stories using images and sounds: I find this a more natural process than using words. It is really satisfying to have an end product and I enjoy being creative. I learnt to use Avid, industry-level editing software specific to the television industry.

After graduation I worked for a small production company, filming corporate promotional videos. This was a good experience but my heart was set on working in television editing. I sent my CV and showreel (portfolio of video clips) in response to a vacancy on Mandy.com, a good source of film and TV production vacancies. It was a very competitive process, but I was successful in gaining work as a post-production runner.

WHAT DOES YOUR JOB INVOLVE?

I work for Editworks, a small (it has 12 edit suites, large companies can have up to 200!) but very busy post-production house just outside Soho. The company edits television programmes such as The Graham Norton Show, Russell Howard's Good News and Take Me Out.

I am a runner which, as the name suggests, involves running errands to deliver and collect tapes, as well as other duties such as organising breakfasts, lunches and tea rounds. Although basic, the job is important as tapes of edited material have to be delivered to tight deadlines. The hours can be very long with early starts and late nights.

The pay is not much more than the minimum wage but this is the traditional route into media production; most people start off as a runner.

The role includes training to move up the career ladder. I have been learning the technical skills and processes needed to work as a junior technician and have just been promoted to junior edit assistant.

WHAT HAS BEEN YOUR BIGGEST CHALLENGE?

With such tight deadlines the atmosphere can be very intense and frenetic, and sometimes stressful when you are asked to help sort out a problem.

AND THE BEST BITS?

Gaining more experience of using industry software like Avid, and receiving training to move upwards in the company are the plus sides to my role. I have been able to watch editors at work, see footage prior to broadcast and when the programme is aired have an understanding of how it was assembled. In the future I'd like to edit documentaries or work as an audio editor, working on dubs and voice-overs.

PHILLIPPA'S TOP TIPS

Get as much work experience as you can at university. Make sure you have experience that will make your CV stand out and set you apart from other graduates. Have a positive attitude to being a runner – it is a basic but essential role. If you do it well you can open up opportunities for yourself to move up the career ladder.

Video producer and presenter

CNET UK

AMIE PARKER-WILLIAMS

Route into media:
A levels – media studies, film studies, English literature (2008); BA multimedia journalism, Canterbury Christchurch University (2011)

WHY MEDIA?

My A level in media studies involved making a music video. I loved filming, editing and being in front of the camera; this helped me decide to study for a media degree. I also have a particular interest in sport and my ultimate aim is to be a TV sports presenter.

HOW DID YOU GET WHERE YOU ARE TODAY?

I decided to keep my options open by taking a multimedia journalism degree, knowing that most TV presenters start off as journalists. My course was very practical and included skills such as learning to use Final Cut Pro editing software, which I use in my current job. A module in web design was also very useful, which included how to write for websites.

During my course I was proactive in finding work placements to gain experience in a variety of media settings. I worked as a runner (helping out with basic tasks) for The Gadget Show and BBC Radio Kent. I also wrote articles for Sky News online and as this is broadcast live I found out about the pressures of working to tight deadlines!

Before the end of my course I began to send my showreel (a CD with clips of the best bits of the videos I had made at university) to various employers. This demonstrated my experience of making videos, my editing skills in putting a showreel together, and featured myself presenting. I was successful in securing a full-time job as a video producer and presenter.

WHAT DOES YOUR JOB INVOLVE?

I work for CNET UK, a consumer technology website that features news about gadgets and new products. Each month I produce a number of consumer technology video reviews for the site. I am also responsible for putting together a weekly report on mobile phones and one on the latest apps. The role involves writing a script for myself to present to camera, and then in a studio, setting up the camera, auto-cue and lighting and filming and then editing the video.

Not all videos are shot in the studio; sometimes we choose an outside location to present a product more aptly. I also go out to technology shows either to film a colleague presenting or to be in front of the camera myself, or to interview other people. I then return to the studio to edit the footage so it can go online as quickly as possible, especially if we have information on a product not yet launched.

WHAT HAS BEEN YOUR BIGGEST CHALLENGE?

Writing scripts to present to camera is time consuming and challenging. Thorough research is needed to ensure I include all the key features of a product, and there is pressure to produce a video quickly so it can go online to deadline.

AND THE BEST BITS?

I love seeing my finished videos on the website. It is rewarding to have an end product that you have researched, scripted, filmed and edited. My long-term aim is to be a TV presenter: I would love to be a children's presenter on Blue Peter and ultimately a sports presenter.

AMIE'S TOP TIPS

Get as much work experience as you can while you are still at university. Don't wait for vacancies; research and find suitable companies yourself and target your application so it is specific to the company. Take the trouble to find out the appropriate person to send this to.

Professional dancer

JASON ANDREW GUEST

Route into performing arts:
A levels – performance studies, music, media studies (2008); BA dance, Liverpool Institute of Performing Arts
(2011)

WHY PERFORMING ARTS?

When I was eleven I started acting classes to boost my self-confidence (I had been bullied at school) and in a short time I knew performing was what I wanted to do as a career.

HOW DID YOU GET WHERE YOU ARE TODAY?

As well as secondary school I also attended a performing arts school at weekends, where I learnt to act, dance and sing. This involved taking exams and performing in a show at the end of each year. It was

hard work but gave me plenty of experience to apply for performing arts degrees.

I studied for a degree in dance at the Liverpool Institute of Performing Arts (LIPA). Here I received thorough training in dance and related performance skills. Dancing (and acting and singing) is both physically and mentally challenging and the course gave me the necessary support and confidence to attend auditions and cope with rejection.

LIPA also run courses in theatre management, stage design and sound. Performing arts, technical theatre and theatre management students are able to work side-by-side on productions. This really helped me understand what goes into putting on a professional show.

During the course I was selected, along with five others, to dance on a Mel C music video by a choreographer/visiting lecturer. In the final year casting directors and agents came to see us perform. An agent invited me to sign on with them and offered me a two-month tour with Hair, the musical.

WHAT DOES YOUR JOB INVOLVE?

I have toured twice with *Hair* in the Netherlands, Germany and Austria. Every role in this production is an ensemble part, involving dancing, singing and some acting, so I had to learn my own lines, singing part and choreographed dance routines. The tour started with a three-day rehearsal period followed by a premiere night. After this I had free time up until 3pm each day and then warmed up for an evening performance, finishing work around 11pm. We were given hotel accommodation right next to the theatre, so we could be available to do extra rehearsals at short notice. Being a performer involves working in a close team and I have made some great friends.

My next job is performing with *Starlight Express* in Germany. The show runs for 15 months in one theatre and each week will involve doing eight performances (with one day off) for the entire run.

When I am not performing I run workshops and lead rehearsals at my old performing arts school and for a Liverpool theatre group.

WHAT HAS BEEN YOUR BIGGEST CHALLENGE?

The audition process is tough. It can involve a first audition, followed by two recalls and then a final round. It can be disheartening to get a long way through the process and still not get the part. You have to be tough to cope with rejection and keep trying. As each contract is only for a short period you are continually searching for the next job.

AND THE BEST BITS?

The adrenaline rush when I am on stage. I feel at home and the most myself when I am performing.

JASON'S TOP TIPS

Don't be put off by the audition process: although it is hard to cope with rejection it makes you more determined as a person. Don't go into performing arts unless you are really passionate about it – it is more a way of life than a job.

Entry routes

Entry routes

UNDERGRADUATE COURSES

Unlike in many other professions, there is no single route that all students must follow to be successful in these career sectors – most degrees are acceptable, although relevant journalism, arts and media degrees can sometimes give an advantage. Some graduates will have done a degree in a relevant area, some will have done something entirely different while pursuing their artistic interests in their spare time, and others will have stopped studying altogether to try to join the workforce. That said, very few people go straight from school into journalism, media and performing arts careers nowadays, as most employers look for individuals who have gained nationally recognised qualifications alongside any relevant experience. Take a look at the 'Routes to qualification' information in each area of work (pages 19–49) to read about any specific subject requirements.

Don't let the vast range of courses on offer confuse you. Most courses on the same subject will follow a similar syllabus but institutions may vary in how they allocate time to each particular topic. On some courses, for example, students study subjects one after another, while others prefer to teach numerous aspects of the course simultaneously through projects that last several weeks. Most courses last for three years, full-time, with some institutions offering a four-year course if you combine journalism, media or performing arts with a language.

POSTGRADUATE COURSES

Most students will leave their studies after completing their undergraduate degree (or HND) to get their foot on the first rung of the journalism, media and performing arts career ladder. However, most of those who stay on to complete postgraduate studies do so for one of three main reasons.

- **To specialise in a particular field** – for example, an actor or director wishing to specialise in performance practice.
- **To stand out from the crowd** – a postgraduate qualification is one way to give yourself an edge over other applicants in particularly competitive fields, such as journalism.
- **To gain a teaching qualification** – for example, a Professional/Postgraduate Certificate in Education (PGCE) in drama, media, performing arts or related fields.

If you are considering a postgraduate degree, you can research and apply for a range of postgraduate courses at different higher education institutions at **www.ukpass.ac.uk**.

However, the possible advantage a postgraduate qualification may give you should be weighed against not only the additional cost, but also the delay before you join the job market.

Connect with us...

 www.facebook.com/ucasonline

 www.twitter.com/ucas_online

 www.youtube.com/ucasonline

What others say...

What others say…

These are extracts from case studies in previous editions of this book. They give some insights into the experiences and thoughts of people who were once in the same position as you.

HOLLIE CLEMENCE – REPORTER

I have always loved writing and talking to people so a job where I get to do both every day is perfect for me. As an undergraduate I wrote for the university newspaper and did work experience at local newspapers. The more experience I had, the more I was certain the journalism was the career for me.

Learning shorthand was pretty tough – like learning a new language. It got a bit easier once I figured out that transcribing my favourite television programmes was good practice!

The best feeling of each week is just after the magazine goes to press, when you finally appreciate the excitement of getting all your news in and the rush of the deadline.

EMMA HAWES - PRODUCTION EDITOR

In my second year, encouraged by my tutor, I took a module in publishing production. I began to apply for work experience at publishing companies and secured three weeks' unpaid work experience at a large local press. I really enjoyed my time and this spurred me on to apply for production roles. Two months before the end of the degree I started job hunting. It was a lot of additional work, during what was already a stressful time. But it definitely paid off, as I started in my current job one week after graduation.

MARK WRIGHT – FINAL YEAR MEDIA PRODUCTION STUDIES STUDENT

Be enthusiastic and assertive – production environments can be very busy places and you can easily get lost in the crowd. Use your colleagues' knowledge to your advantage: don't be afraid to ask those more experienced than you how to perform tasks correctly. Be organised – you then stand a better chance of coping with the pressure of time constraints. Lastly, understand the importance of teamwork individuality will only get you so far in the media industry!

ABBIE CUNLIFFE – COMMERCIAL RADIO PROGRAMMER

My degree involved community work projects, using theatre and TV, and from these I became interested in how media affects people. I took an active part in the university radio station, including becoming a DJ.

I am a commercial programmer – a middleman between commercial output and programming output. My role is to ensure the client's message is conveyed to the audience and the commercial content is engaging for the listener. I manage campaigns that involve competitions, giveaways and promotional events.

The hours can be long, especially just before we launch a campaign, and there is occasional weekend and evening work.

You've got to be motivated to find a job in radio; I was sending out 15 to 20 applications a day at one stage.

Get work experience, even in unpaid, at your local radio station as this may lead to paid work. And most importantly, stay positive: it goes a long way!

MARTIN SCOTT POWELL – FREELANCE PHOTOGRAPHER

I left school at 17 and trained and worked as a jewellery designer and goldsmith, before leaving to embark on my world trip. A year later, and full of enthusiasm for photography, I got a place on a BA course in photography, film and imaging.

When I graduated I worked as a photographer's assistant for six months and then moved to New York. I am a freelance fashion, portrait and fine art photographer. I try to keep regular hours if I'm working on portfolios or editing, but shoot days usually start much earlier. That said, I feel as though I'm working all the time; I always think about work! That's the bug of being self-employed.

ANTJE HILDEBRANDT – FREELANCE DANCE PRACTITIONER

I find it a challenge to stay motivated, to always look and apply for opportunities in the dance arena specifically, and the arts generally, and to keep up my dance practice now that I don't have the regular framework of a course. To overcome this challenge you have to really love and believe in what you are doing and show endurance and the ability to motivate yourself. I have to say that staying in touch with my tutors after graduating has been of great help to me as they can assist with applications, references and personal and professional support.

But what makes it so great is that I am earning enough money to support myself and at the same time having enough time to keep up my dance practice. I am also having a lot of contact with people on a daily basis and I am doing work that is varied and interesting; working in a creative place I am able to see a lot of films and performances.

DANIEL HALFORD – SELF-EMPLOYED RECORDING ENGINEER

To successfully enter this area of work, the ground has to be prepared long before graduation. Most of the industry works on a personal contact and referral basis, which requires networking and building up relationships with people who might be in a position to offer you work. This can start at any time – the earlier the better.

You need to get some experience under your belt; if you attend a concert or recording session, speak to the engineer to find out not just what they have done but why they've done it. Lack of underlying basics can spoil your chances – you need to be able to read music enough to follow a score and to learn the correct way to set up and take down equipment.

JEAN JOLLANDS – FEATURES EDITOR

My top tips are – always have loads of ideas ready, dress to impress, always meet a deadline and don't believe that anyone is better than you!

LISA HOGAN – PR AND MARKETING ADVISER

My degree required me to do placement module in two PR settings and I hated the agency placement I did in my second year. I started to wonder if PR was right for me, but decided to try an in-house role as soon as I could, and secured a two week unpaid summer placement in the university PR office. On finishing the placement I was offered a full-time paid job for the whole of that summer, so I did my third year placement there, and worked as a paid member of staff every Wednesday as well.

My work for the university press office involved drafting press releases, compiling press cuttings and helping to launch an internal communications magazine and website called Fuse, aimed at university students and staff.

When I graduated I applied for a job that one of our lecturers emailed around. I was invited for interview, and was rung the next day to say I hadn't got it but that I had come a close second. The reason I had done so well was because of my experience working on the university magazine. Then I had a lucky break – someone left a job similar to the one I'd applied for and I was offered her position.

Applicant
journey

SIX EASY STEPS TO A UNIVERSITY, COLLEGE OR CONSERVATOIRE

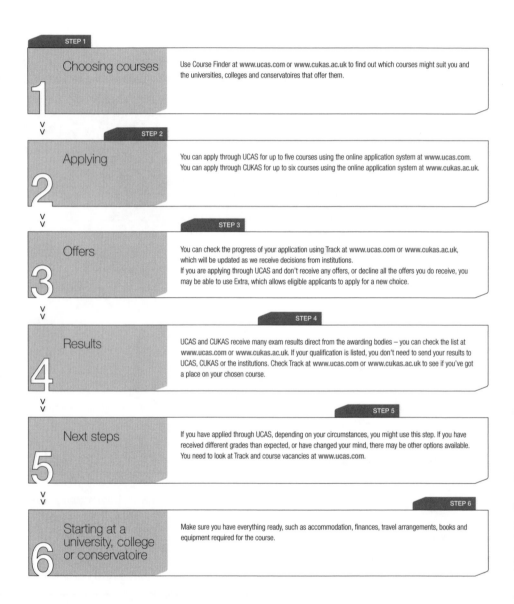

STEP 1

1 Choosing courses

Use Course Finder at www.ucas.com or www.cukas.ac.uk to find out which courses might suit you and the universities, colleges and conservatoires that offer them.

STEP 2

2 Applying

You can apply through UCAS for up to five courses using the online application system at www.ucas.com. You can apply through CUKAS for up to six courses using the online application system at www.cukas.ac.uk.

STEP 3

3 Offers

You can check the progress of your application using Track at www.ucas.com or www.cukas.ac.uk, which will be updated as we receive decisions from institutions.
If you are applying through UCAS and don't receive any offers, or decline all the offers you do receive, you may be able to use Extra, which allows eligible applicants to apply for a new choice.

STEP 4

4 Results

UCAS and CUKAS receive many exam results direct from the awarding bodies – you can check the list at www.ucas.com or www.cukas.ac.uk. If your qualification is listed, you don't need to send your results to UCAS, CUKAS or the institutions. Check Track at www.ucas.com or www.cukas.ac.uk to see if you've got a place on your chosen course.

STEP 5

5 Next steps

If you have applied through UCAS, depending on your circumstances, you might use this step. If you have received different grades than expected, or have changed your mind, there may be other options available. You need to look at Track and course vacancies at www.ucas.com.

STEP 6

6 Starting at a university, college or conservatoire

Make sure you have everything ready, such as accommodation, finances, travel arrangements, books and equipment required for the course.

Choosing courses

1

Step 1 – Planning your application

Planning your application is the start of your journey to finding a place at a university, college or conservatoire.

This section will help you decide what course to study and how to choose a university, college or conservatoire where you'll enjoy living and studying. Find out about qualifications, degree options, how they'll assess you, and coping with the costs of higher education.

ENTRY REQUIREMENTS

This section covers routes into journalism, media and performing arts from qualifications such as A levels and Scottish Highers.

Which subjects?

The good news for would-be performers and media professionals is that the range and number of subjects you need to take at sixth form level is quite flexible. However, you will usually need to offer a minimum of two – and preferably three – A levels, and at least one of these should be in an arts subject. Many drama, theatre studies and performing arts courses require an A level in one of these areas. Other useful A level subjects include English literature and languages, while science subjects can be helpful for people interested in scientific writing or programme making. However, we strongly advise that you check with the admissions tutors at your shortlisted institutions on their preferred subjects and grades.

Save with UCAS Card

If you're in Year 12, S5 or equivalent and thinking about higher education, sign up for the **FREE** UCAS Card to receive all these benefits:

- information about courses and unis
- expert advice from UCAS
- exclusive discounts for card holders

Which grades?

The sort of grades you will need for a degree in a media studies or performing arts-related area varies from one institution to the next. Some institutions require a minimum of two A levels but three is the norm. Offers can be made either using the Tariff (see page 124 for further details) or through specified grades. Since competition for places on courses is very competitive, good grades will boost your chances of being offered a place, though you won't be expected to achieve as highly as candidates for areas such as law and medicine.

UCAS CARD

At its simplest, the UCAS Card scheme is the start of your UCAS journey. It can save you a packet on the high street with exclusive offers to UCAS Card holders, as well as providing you with hints and tips about finding the best course at the right university or college. If that's not enough you'll also receive these benefits:

- frequent expert help from UCAS, with all the essential information you need on the application process
- free monthly newsletters providing advice, hints, tips and exclusive discounts
- tailored information on the universities and courses you're interested in
- and much more

If you're in Year 12, S5 or equivalent and thinking about higher education for autumn 2013, sign up for your FREE UCAS Card today to receive all these benefits at **www.ucas.com/ucascard**.

Choosing courses

1

Choosing courses

USE COURSE FINDER AT WWW.UCAS.COM AND WWW.CUKAS.AC.UK TO FIND OUT WHICH COURSES MIGHT SUIT YOU, AND THE UNIVERSITIES, COLLEGES AND CONSERVATOIRES THAT OFFER THEM.

Start thinking about what you want to study and where you want to go. This section will help you, and see what courses are available where in the listings (starting on page 149). Check that the entry requirements required for each course meet your academic expectations.

Use the UCAS and CUKAS websites – www.ucas.com and www.cukas.ac.uk have lots of advice on how to find a course. CUKAS (the Conservatoires UK Admissions Service) processes applications for practice-based music courses, and some drama and dance courses, at UK conservatoires. Go to the students' section of the websites for the best advice or go straight to Course Finder to see all the courses available through UCAS or Course Search for CUKAS. Our maps of the UK at www.ucas.com/students/choosingcourses/choosinguni/map/ and www.cukas.ac.uk/students/choosingcourses/choosingaconsandcourse/map show you where all the universities, colleges and conservatoires are located.

Watch UCAStv – at www.ucas.tv there are videos for UCAS applicants on *How to choose your course* and *Attending events* as well as case studies from students talking about their experiences of finding a course at university or college.

Attend UCAS conventions – UCAS conventions are held throughout the country. Universities and colleges have exhibition stands where their staff offer information about their courses and institutions. Details of when the conventions are happening are shown at www.ucas.com/conventions. The Compose your future event provides a fantastic opportunity for those interested in performing arts, music, dance, drama, broadcasting and multimedia production - see page 88 for details.

Look at websites and prospectuses – universities, colleges and conservatoires have prospectuses and course-specific leaflets on their courses. Your school or college library may have copies or go to the university's or conservatoire's website to download a copy, or ask them to send one to you.

Go to university, college and conservatoire open days – most institutions offer open days to anyone who wants to attend. See the list of universities, colleges and conservatoires on www.ucas.com and www.cukas.ac.uk and the UCAS *Open Days* publications (see the Essential reading chapter) for information on when they are taking place. Aim to visit all of the universities, colleges or conservatoires you are interested in before you apply. It will help with your expectations of studying there and make sure the course is the right one for you.

League tables – these can be helpful but bear in mind that they attempt to rank institutions in an overall order reflecting the views of those that produce them. They may not reflect your views and needs. Examples can be found at www.thecompleteuniversityguide.co.uk, www.guardian.co.uk/education/universityguide, www.thetimes.co.uk (subscription service) and www.thesundaytimes.co.uk (subscription service). See page 92 for more information about league tables.

Do your research – speak and refer to as many trusted sources as you can find. Talk to someone already doing the job you have in mind. The section on 'Which area?' on page 19 will help you identify the different areas of journalism, media and performing arts you might want to enter.

DECIDING ON YOUR COURSE CHOICES

Through UCAS you can initially apply for up to five courses. Remember you don't have to make five course choices. Only apply for a course if you're completely happy with both the course and the university or college and you would definitely be prepared to accept a place.

Through CUKAS you can apply for a maximum of six courses. You only need to apply to the highest level of course in which you are interested through CUKAS. If you are not sure which level of course you should apply for, please contact the conservatoire direct to discuss.

How do you find out more information to make an informed decision and narrow down your course choices? First of all, look up course details in this book or online on **www.ucas.com** or **www.cukas.ac.uk**.

This will give you an idea of the full range of courses and topics on offer. You may want to study a specific area of journalism, media or performing arts by itself, but there are also many courses which also include additional options, such as a modern language (check out the degree subjects studied by our case studies). You'll quickly be able to eliminate institutions that don't offer the right course, or you can choose a 'hit list' of institutions first, and then see what they have to offer.

Once you've made a short(er) list look at university, college and conservatoire websites, and generally find out as much as you can about the course, department and institution. Don't be afraid to contact them to ask for more information, request their prospectus or arrange an open day visit.

YOUR CHANCE TO CHECK OUT THE COURSES

If you don't fancy reading through a pile of prospectuses, why not visit the 'Compose your future' exhibition offered at the Manchester Central Convention Complex on 8 October 2012.

This event offers you a fantastic opportunity to chat to course leaders and those involved in performing arts, music, dance, drama, broadcast and multimedia production courses. You can also watch live performances given by current undergraduates within further and higher education or attend interactive workshops. This is an unrivalled opportunity for you to meet representatives from major providers of media and performing arts in the UK, and to collect as much information as possible.

For further details, please visit the Compose your future website, **www.ucasevents.com/compose** or contact UCAS Media Events tel: 01242 544 979, email: events@ucas.ac.uk.

√

UCAS

Confused about courses?

Indecisive about institutions?

Stressed about student life?

Unsure about UCAS?

Frowning over finance?

Help is available at
www.ucasbooks.com

1 Choosing courses

Choosing your institution

Different people look for different things from their university, college or conservatoire course, but the checklist on the next page sets out the kinds of factors all prospective students should consider when choosing their institution. Keep this list in mind on open days, when talking to friends about their experiences, or while reading prospectuses and websites.

TOP TIP

Don't be afraid to pick up the phone – admissions officers welcome enquiries directly from students, rather than careers officers phoning on your behalf. It shows you're genuinely interested and committed to your own career early on.

WHAT TO CONSIDER WHEN CHOOSING YOUR MEDIA AND PERFORMING ARTS COURSE	
Location	Do you want to stay close to home? Would you prefer to study at a city or campus university, at a college or a conservatoire?
Grades required	Use the Course Finder/Course Search facilities on the UCAS and CUKAS websites, www.ucas.com and www.cukas.ac.uk; to view entry requirements for courses you are interested in. Also, check out the institution's website or call up the admissions office. Some institutions specify grades required, eg AAB, while others specify points required, eg 340. If they ask for points, it means they're using the UCAS Tariff system, which awards points to different types and levels of qualification. For example, an A grade at A level = 120 points; a B grade at A level = 100 points. The full Tariff tables are available on pages 124-133 and at www.ucas.com.
Employer links	Ask the course tutor or department about links with employers, such as theatres, publishing houses, magazines etc. Find out if the course involves visiting lecturers from the professional side of the industry, and where they typically come from.
Graduate prospects	Ask the careers office for their list of graduate destinations.
Cost	Ask the admissions office about variable tuition fees and financial assistance. Also find out what fees are charged for studio time and/or equipment.
Degree type	Do you want to study music, drama or media etc on its own (single honours degree) or 50/50 with another subject (joint degree) or as one of a few subjects (combined degree)?
Coursework	How is the course taught? Ask about the number of lectures and tutorials per week, the amount of one-to-one work, and how you will build a portfolio of achievement or be involved in project work. Also ask about the split between practical and contextual work.
Course assessment	What proportion of the assessment is based on your project work and how much is based on written assignments? Do you have to do a performance as part of your final assessment?
Facilities for media and performing arts	Check out their musical and theatrical facilities; unlike most subjects, where most time is spent in lecture theatres and seminars etc, media and performing arts courses involve a lot of hands-on work in workshops. Also, find out if there is a university or college careers adviser dedicated to media and performing arts.
'Fit'	Even if all the above criteria stack up, this one relies on gut feel – go and visit the department if you can, and see if it's 'you'. For example, check out any end-of-year performances or recitals to give you a good idea of the type and level of work the course produces. Also ask about lecturers' own particular interests; many will have personal web pages somewhere on the departmental website.

Choosing courses

League tables

The information that follows has been provided by Dr Bernard Kingston of The Complete University Guide.

League tables are worth consulting early in your research and perhaps for confirmation later on. But never rely on them in isolation – always use them alongside other information sources available to you. Universities typically report that over a third of prospective students view league tables as important or very important in making their university choices. They give an insight into quality and are mainly based on data from the universities themselves. Somewhat confusingly, tables published in, say, 2012 are referred to as the 2013 tables because they are aimed at applicants going to university in that following year. The well known ones - *The Complete University Guide*, *The Guardian*, *The Times*, and *The Sunday Times* - rank the institutions and the subjects they teach using input measures (eg entry standards), throughput measures (eg student : staff ratios) and output measures (eg graduate prospects). Some tables are free to access

whilst others are behind pay walls. All are interactive and enable users to create their own tables based on the measures important to them.

The universities are provided with their raw data for checking and are regularly consulted on methodology. But ultimately it is the compilers who decide what measures to use and what weights to put on them. They are competitors and rarely consult amongst themselves. So, for example, *The Times* tables differ significantly from *The Sunday Times* ones even though both newspapers belong to the same media proprietor.

Whilst the main university rankings tend to get the headlines, we would stress that the individual subject tables are as least as important, if not more so, when deciding where to study. All universities, regardless of their overall ranking, have some academic departments that rank highly in their subjects. Beware also giving much weight to an institution being a few places higher or lower in the tables – this is likely to be of little significance. This is particularly true in the lower half of the main table where overall scores show considerable bunching.

Most of the measures used to define quality come from hard factual data provided by the Higher Education Statistics Agency (HESA) but some, like student satisfaction and peer assessment, are derived from surveys of subjective impressions where you might wish to query sample size. We give a brief overview of the common measures here but please go to the individual websites for full details.

- **Student satisfaction** is derived from the annual National Student Survey (NSS) and is heavily used by The Guardian and The Sunday Times.
- **Research assessment** comes from a 2008 exercise (RAE) aimed at defining the quality of a university's research (excluded by The Guardian).
- **Entry standards** are based on the full UCAS Tariff scores obtained by new students.
- **Student : staff ratio** gives the number of students per member of academic staff.
- **Expenditure figures** show the costs of academic and student services.
- **Good honours** lists the proportion of graduates gaining a first or upper second honours degree.
- **Completion** indicates the proportion of students who successfully complete their studies.

- **Graduate prospects** usually reports the proportion of graduates who obtain a graduate job – not any job – or continue studying within six months of leaving.
- **Peer assessment** is used only by The Sunday Times which asks academics to rate other universities in their subjects.
- **Value added** is used only by The Guardian and compares entry standards with good honours.

All four main publishers of UK league tables (see Table 1) also publish university subject tables. The Complete University Guide and The Times are based on four measures: student satisfaction, research quality, entry standards and graduate destinations. The Sunday Times uses student satisfaction, entry standards, graduate destinations, graduate unemployment, good degrees and drop-out rate, while The Guardian uses student satisfaction (as three separate measures), entry standards, graduate destinations, student-staff ratio, spend per student and value added. This use of different measures is one reason why the different tables can yield different results (sometimes very different, especially in the case of The Guardian which has least in common with the other tables).

League tables compiled by The Complete University Guide (**www.thecompleteuniversityguide.co.uk**) and The Guardian (**www.guardian.co.uk**) are available in spring, those by The Times (**www.thetimes.co.uk**) and The Sunday Times (**www.thesundaytimes.co.uk**) in the summer.

Table 1 – measures used by the main publishers of UK league tables

	Universities	Measures	Subjects	Measures
The Complete University Guide	116	9	62	4
The Guardian	119	8	46	8
The Sunday Times	122	8	39	6
The Times	116	8	62	4

THINGS TO WATCH OUT FOR WHEN READING SUBJECT LEAGUE TABLES

- Journalism will usually be in a more general table with other media studies and sometimes communication studies as well.
- Music and drama may be included in broader tables of the performing arts.

WHO PUBLISHES JOURNALISM, BROADCASTING, MEDIA PRODUCTION AND PERFORMING ARTS LEAGUE TABLES?

The Complete University Guide	Communication and media studies Drama, dance and cinematics Music
The Guardian	Drama and dance Media Studies, communications and librarianship Music
The Sunday Times	Communication and information studies Media studies
The Times	Communication and media studies Drama, dance and cinematics Music

www.ucas.com

www.cukas.ac.uk

at the heart of connecting people to higher education

Choosing courses

1

How will
they choose you?

Universities, colleges and conservatoires receive thousands of applications each year for only a limited number of places. So how can you make your UCAS or CUKAS application stand out from the others?

ACADEMIC ABILITY

Degrees can be intellectually demanding. Not only will you possibly be learning about the basics of your chosen discipline(s) for the very first time but you will also be expected to work on them in greater analytical depth than you have been used to before at GCSE and A level (or equivalent). Therefore, in order for admissions tutors to be certain that you have what it takes to cope with the course, you will have to show you have the academic ability to take on new ideas.

SELF-MOTIVATION AND SELF-DISCIPLINE

Studying at a university, college or conservatoire is very different from school and sixth form. In the latter settings, you will have followed a set course, normally following a study pattern suggested by your teachers. Homework set each night will have ensured that you completed your study regularly and on time.

In higher education, tutors and lecturers do not have the time to keep tabs on their students in the same way. Whereas your A level teachers will have helped motivate you to finish your work on time, university tutors will hand out reading lists and essay titles in advance and will expect you to complete them on time without constant reminders.

This can, understandably, be daunting for some people. Certainly, time management and self-motivation are skills you hone in higher education but it also helps if your referee can write about any instances where you have shown an ability to work well on your own, as this is how you will be studying throughout your undergraduate course.

DEVOTION TO YOUR CHOSEN SUBJECT

Make no mistake about it, people who choose to work in either the media or performing arts do so because they love what they do. Financial rewards can be low not just at the start but for years to come. You also may have to face the reality that, while you love acting or dancing or writing, you might never be a George Clooney or JK Rowling. Acknowledgement of this and a proven love of your subject (through writing for student newspapers, undertaking unpaid work experience or working at your local theatre) will help convince admissions tutors that you are devoted to their subject.

The tutors who select students on to their courses also want to see evidence that you have carefully considered what a degree in performing arts and the media will involve and why it appeals to you so much. After all, you don't necessarily need a degree in these areas to get a job in them, so why have you chosen to specialise in media even earlier than some of your peers? Only you will know the reasons why you're fascinated by these subject areas and it's your job to convey this enthusiasm in your UCAS or CUKAS application.

DO SOME READING

This is related to the previous point. A good way to prove to potential admissions tutors that you have an interest in their field is to find out their specialist academic areas and do some reading into these, potentially from books or academic papers that they have written. Additionally, contact the relevant department and ask for their first-year reading list, if this is not available online. You do not need to read everything on it but if you choose two or three books that most appeal to you and read them in some depth it will show a commitment to both the subject and the relevant institution's course.

Be warned, though: don't think that merely mentioning a few key books will automatically get you through. Admissions tutors will know if you're lying, so unless you can make a few valid points about why you enjoyed their books, don't bother: it could do more harm than good.

WORK EXPERIENCE

While relevant work experience is not essential to gain a place in media and the performing arts, if you have had any, do include details of it in your personal statement (see below). A job working as an usher at a theatre, or perhaps work shadowing a journalist, can give you valuable insight into these sorts of careers, as well as real inspiration to study what it is that drives them – and show admissions tutors you are really committed to your chosen field. Make sure you give details of anything you learned during the time and explain how it has led you to make the decisions you are taking today. Please see page 117 for more information about work experience.

YOUR PERSONAL STATEMENT

Your personal statement can really enhance your application. It is here that you can show evidence of all the above issues – academic attainment, self-discipline, work experience, a desire for your chosen subject. Most institutions place much importance on personal statements as this is where your own voice comes through, so make the most of it and use it to your advantage. Be honest but not over-friendly and give well-reasoned statements. And above all make sure it's free from mistakes and easy to read. There's nothing more offputting for an admissions tutor than an application and personal statement that have glaring grammatical and spelling mistakes.

As this is such an important part of your application, it's worth drafting it a few times. Ask your family or friends and teacher to check it, not only for mistakes but also to see if you're leaving anything out that should be in... or equally if there's anything that should come out.

Please see page 115 for more advice about your personal statement.

AUDITION

CUKAS applicants will normally need to attend auditions before the conservatoires can make their decisions. This usually involves giving a live audition at the conservatoire, but in some cases applicants are allowed to send in recordings or videos. Some conservatoires have audition centres in other countries to cater for international applicants.

The audition process will vary between conservatoires. When conservatoires invite applicants to audition they will provide advice on what the audition will include and what kinds of pieces should be prepared.

For further information to help you perpare for auditions, download the Conservatoires UK advice leaflet *Making the Most of Your Audition* from **www.cukas.ac.uk**.

wondering how much higher education costs?

need information about student finance?

Visit www.ucas.com/students/studentfinance and find sources for all the information on student money matters you need.

With access to up-to-date information on bursaries, scholarships and variable fees, plus our online budget calculator. Visit us today and get the full picture.

www.ucas.com/students/studentfinance

1

Choosing courses

The cost of higher education

The information in this section was up-to-date when this book was published. You should visit the websites mentioned in this section for the very latest information.

The cost of studying in the UK

As a student, you will usually have to pay for two things: tuition fees for your course, which for most students do not need to be paid for up front, and living costs such as rent, food, books, transport and entertainment. Fees charged vary between courses, between universities and colleges and also according to your normal country of residence, so it's important to check these before you apply. Course fee information is supplied to UCAS by the universities and is displayed in Course Finder at **www.ucas.com** and on conservatoire websites accessible through **www.cukas.ac.uk**.

Student loans

The purpose of student loans from the Government is to help cover the costs of your tuition fees and basic living costs (rent, bills, food and so on). Two types are available: a tuition fee loan to cover the tuition charges and a maintenance loan to help with accommodation and other living costs. Both types of student loan are available to all students who meet the basic eligibility requirements. Interest will be charged at inflation plus a fixed percentage while you are studying. In addition, many other commercial loans are available to students studying at university or college but the interest rate can vary considerably. Loans to help with living costs will be available for all eligible students, irrespective of family income.

Find out more information from the relevant sites below:

England: Student Finance England –
www.direct.gov.uk/studentfinance
Northern Ireland: Student Finance Northern Ireland –
www.studentfinanceni.co.uk
Scotland: Student Awards Agency for Scotland –
www.saas.gov.uk
Wales: Student Finance Wales –
www.studentfinancewales.co.uk or
www.cyllidmyfyrwyrcymru.co.uk

Bursaries and scholarships

- The National Scholarships Programme gives financial help to students studying in England. The scheme is designed to help students whose families have lower incomes.
- Students from families with lower incomes will be entitled to a non-repayable maintenance grant to help with living costs.
- Many universities and colleges also offer non-repayable scholarships and bursaries to help students cover tuition and living costs whilst studying.
- All eligible part-time undergraduates who study for at least 25% of their time will be able to apply for a loan to cover the costs of their tuition, which means they no longer have to pay up front.

There will be extra support for disabled students and students with child or adult dependants. For more information, visit the country-specific websites listed above.

1 Choosing courses

International students

APPLYING TO STUDY IN THE UK

Deciding to study in the UK is very exciting. You need to think about what course to do, where to study, and how much it will cost. The decisions you make can have a huge effect on your future but UCAS and CUKAS are here to help.

How to apply

Whatever your age or qualifications, if you want to apply for any of the over 35,000 courses listed at 300 universities and colleges on the UCAS website, you must apply through UCAS at www.ucas.com. If you are unsure, your school, college, adviser, or local British Council office will be able to help. Further advice and a video guide for international students can be found on the non-UK students' section of the website www.ucas.com/international/.

UCAS applicants may apply on their own or through their school, college, adviser, or local British Council if they are registered to use Apply. If you choose to use an education agent's services, check with the British Council to see if they hold a list of certificated or registered agents in your country. Check also on any charges you may need to pay. UCAS charges only the application fee (see below) but agents may charge for additional services.

What is CUKAS?

The Conservatoires UK Admissions Service (CUKAS) is an admissions service operated by UCAS. CUKAS provides a central application service for practice-based music courses, and some drama and dance courses, at seven conservatoires in the UK. CUKAS processes applications for the following types of full-time and part-time courses in music, dance and drama:

- undergraduate degree level courses
- postgraduate degree level courses
- postgraduate certificate and diploma courses
- courses with no award.

Applicants must apply through CUKAS for any courses listed on Course Search on the CUKAS website www.cukas.ac.uk. Further advice for international students can be found on the non-UK section of the website at www.cukas.ac.uk/students/wheretostart/nonukstudents.

The Guildhall School of Music and Drama and the Royal Academy of Music do not recruit through CUKAS. Please contact these conservatoires for advice on how to apply.

When you apply through CUKAS you can apply for up to six choices. All CUKAS applications are made online, and students apply on their own rather than through a centre.

How much will my application cost?
UCAS – If you choose to apply to more than one course, university or college you need to pay £23 when you apply. If you only apply to one course at one university or college, you pay £12.

CUKAS – All applicants have to pay an application fee of £16 to CUKAS to cover the processing of their applications. This fee applies to single and multiple choices. CUKAS applicants also have to pay audition fees – the fees vary between conservatoires. All the conservatoires in the CUKAS application system, except Leeds College of Music, require you to pay your audition fees at the time of application. Leeds College of Music requires you to pay once you have been invited to audition. Please see page 112 'How to apply through CUKAS' for more information.

What level of English?
UCAS provides a list of English language qualifications and grades that are acceptable to most UK universities and colleges, however you are advised to contact the institutions directly as each have their own entry requirement in English. For more information go to www.ucas.com/students/wheretostart/nonukstudents/englangprof.

Links to information on conservatoires' websites about English language requirements can be found at www.cukas.ac.uk/students/wheretostart/nonukstudents/englishlang.

INTERNATIONAL STUDENT FEES

If you study in the UK, your fee status (whether you pay full-cost fees or a subsidised fee rate) will be decided by the UK institution you plan to attend. Before you decide which university, college or conservatoire to attend, you need to be absolutely certain that you can pay the full cost of:

- your tuition fees (the amount is set by institutions, so contact them for more information - visit their websites where many list their fees. Fee details will also be included on Course Finder at www.ucas.com and www.cukas.ac.uk from mid-July)
- the everyday living expenses for you (and your family) for the whole time that you are in the UK, including accommodation, food, gas and electricity bills, clothes, travel and leisure activities
- books and equipment for your course
- travel to and from your country.

You must include everything when you work out how much it will cost. You can get information to help you do this accurately from the international offices at universities, colleges and conservatoires, UKCISA (UK Council for International Student Affairs) and the British

Council. There is a useful website tool to help you manage your money - **www.studentcalculator.org.uk**.

Scholarships and bursaries are offered at some institutions and you should contact them for more information. In addition, you should check with your local British Council for additional scholarships available to students from your country who want to study in the UK.

LEGAL DOCUMENTS YOU WILL NEED

As you prepare to study in the UK, it is very important to think about the legal documents you will need to enter the country.

Everyone who comes to study in the UK needs a valid passport. If you do not have one, you should apply for one as soon as possible. People from certain countries also need visas before they come into the UK. They are known as 'visa nationals'. You can check if you require a visa to travel to the UK by visiting the UK Border Agency website and selecting 'Studying in the UK?' so, please check the UK Border Agency website at **www.ukba.homeoffice.gov.uk** for the most up-to-date guidance and information about the United Kingdom's visa requirements.

When you apply for your visa you need to make sure you have the following documents:

- A confirmation of acceptance for studies (CAS) number from the university, college or conservatoire where you are going to study. The institution must be on the UKBA Register of Sponsors in order to accept international students.
- A valid passport.
- Evidence that you have enough money to pay for your course and living costs.

- Certificates for all qualifications you have that are relevant to the course you have been accepted for and for any English language qualifications.

You will also have to give your biometric data.

Do check for further information from your local British Embassy or High Commission. Guidance information for international students is also available from UKCISA and from UKBA.

ADDITIONAL RESOURCES

There are a number of organisations that can provide further guidance and information to you as you prepare to study in the UK:

- British Council
  www.britishcouncil.org
- Education UK (British Council website dealing with educational matters)
  www.educationuk.org
- English UK (British Council accredited website listing English language courses in the UK)
  www.englishuk.com
- UK Border Agency (provides information on visa requirements and applications)
  www.ukvisas.gov.uk
- UKCISA (UK Council for International Student Affairs)
  www.ukcisa.org.uk
- Directgov (the official UK government website)
  www.direct.gov.uk
- Prepare for Success
  www.prepareforsuccess.org.uk

Applying

2

Step 2 – Applying through UCAS

You apply through UCAS using the online application system, called Apply, at **www.ucas.com**. You can apply for a maximum of five choices, but you don't have to use them all if you don't want to. If you apply for fewer than five choices, you can add more at a later date if you want to. But be aware of the course application deadlines (you can find these in Course Finder at **www.ucas.com**).

IMPORTANT DATES FOR 2013 ENTRY	
Early June 2012	UCAS Apply opens for 2013 entry registration.
Mid-September 2012	Applications can be sent to UCAS.
15 October 2012	Application deadline for the receipt at UCAS of applications for all medicine, dentistry, veterinary medicine and veterinary science courses and for all courses at the universities of Oxford and Cambridge.
15 January 2013	Application deadline for the receipt at UCAS of applications for all courses except those listed above with a 15 October deadline, and some art and design courses with a 24 March deadline.
25 February 2013	Extra starts (see page 122 for more information about Extra).
24 March 2013	Application deadline for the receipt at UCAS of applications for art and design courses except those listed on Course Finder at www.ucas.com with a 15 January deadline.
31 March 2013	If you apply by 15 January, the universities and colleges should aim to have sent their decisions by this date (but they can take longer).
9 May 2013	If you apply by 15 January, universities and colleges need to send their decisions by this date. If they don't, UCAS will make any outstanding choices unsuccessful on their behalf.
30 June 2013	If you send your application to us by this date, we will send it to your chosen universities and colleges. Applications received after this date are entered into Clearing (see page 136 for more information about Clearing).
3 July 2013	Last date to apply through Extra.
August 2013 (date to be confirmed)	Scottish Qualifications Authority (SQA) results are published.
15 August 2013	GCE and Advanced Diploma results are published (often known as 'A level results day'). Adjustment opens for registration (see page 137 for more information about Adjustment).

DON'T FORGET...

Universities and colleges guarantee to consider your application only if we receive it by the appropriate deadline. Check application deadlines for your courses on Course Finder at www.ucas.com.

If you send it to UCAS after the deadline but before 30 June 2013, universities and colleges will consider your application only if they still have places available.

See page 113 for when to apply through CUKAS.

Applying

2

How to apply through UCAS

You apply online at www.ucas.com through Apply – a secure, web-based application service that is designed for all our applicants, whether they are applying through a UCAS-registered centre or as an individual, anywhere in the world. Apply is:

- easy to access – all you need is an internet connection
- easy to use – you don't have to complete your application all in one go: you can save the sections as you complete them and come back to it later
- easy to monitor – once you've applied, you can use Track to check the progress of your application, including any decisions from universities or colleges. You can also reply to your offers using Track.

Watch the UCAStv guide to applying through UCAS at www.ucas.tv.

APPLICATION FEE

For 2013 entry the fee for applying through UCAS is £23 for two or more choices and £12 for one choice.

DEFERRED ENTRY

If you want to apply for deferred entry in 2014, perhaps because you want to take a year out between school or college and higher education, you should check that the university or college will accept a deferred entry application. Occasionally, tutors are not happy to accept students who take a gap year, because it interrupts the flow of their learning. If you apply for deferred entry, you must meet the conditions of any offers by 31 August 2013 unless otherwise agreed by the university or college. If you accept a place for 2014 entry and then change your mind, you cannot reapply through us in the 2014 entry cycle unless you withdraw your original application.

1 GET SCHOOL OR COLLEGE 'BUZZWORD'

Ask your UCAS application coordinator (may be your sixth form tutor) for your school or college UCAS 'buzzword'. This is a password for the school or college.

2 REGISTER

Go to **www.ucas.com/students/apply** and click on **Register/Log in to use Apply** and then **register**. After you have entered your registration details, the online system will automatically generate a username for you, but you'll have to come up with a password and answers to security questions.

3 COMPLETE SEVEN SECTIONS

Complete all the sections of the application. To access any section, click on the section name at the left of the screen and follow the instructions. The sections are:

Personal details – contact details, residential status, disability status

Additional information – only UK applicants need to complete this section

Student finance – UK students can share some of their application details with their student finance company. Finance information is provided for other EU and international applicants

Choices – which courses you'd like to apply for

Education – your education and qualifications

Employment – eg work experience, holiday jobs

Statement – see page 115 for personal statement advice.

Before you can send your application you need to go to the **View all details** screen and tick the **section completed** box.

4 PASS TO REFEREE

Once you've completed all the sections, send your application electronically to your referee (normally your form tutor). They'll check it, approve it and add their reference to it, and will then send it to UCAS on your behalf.

- Important details like date of birth and course codes will be checked by Apply. It will alert you if they are not valid.
- We strongly recommend that the personal statement and reference are written in a word processing package and pasted in to Apply.
- If you want to, you can enter European characters into certain areas of Apply.
- You can change your application at any time before it is completed and sent to UCAS.
- You can print and preview your application at any time. Before you send it you need to go to the **View all details** screen and tick the **section completed** box.
- Your school, college or centre can choose different payment methods. For example, they may want us to bill them, or you may be able to pay online by debit or credit card.

NOT APPLYING THROUGH A SCHOOL OR COLLEGE

If you're not currently studying, you'll probably be applying as an independent applicant rather than through a school, college or other UCAS-registered centre. In this case you won't be able to provide a 'buzzword', but we'll ask you a few extra questions to check you are eligible to apply.

If you're not applying through a UCAS-registered centre, the procedure you use for obtaining a reference will depend on whether or not you want your reference to be provided through a registered centre. For information on the procedures for providing references, visit www.ucas.com/students/applying/howtoapply/reference.

INVISIBILITY OF CHOICES

Universities and colleges cannot see details of the other choices on your application until you reply to any offers or you are unsuccessful at all your choices.

You can submit only one UCAS application in each year's application cycle. You may apply through both UCAS and CUKAS (see page 112) in the same application cycle, but if you hold a confirmed place in both systems, you will have to withdraw from one of these places.

APPLICATION CHECKLIST

We want this to run smoothly for you and we also want to process your application as quickly as possible. You can help us to do this by remembering to do the following:

- ✓ check the closing dates for applications – see pages 107 and 113
- ✓ check the student finance information at www.ucas.com/students/studentfinance/ and course fees information in Course Finder at www.ucas.com
- ✓ start early and allow plenty of time for completing your application – including enough time for your referee to complete the reference section
- ✓ read the online instructions carefully before you start
- ✓ consider what each question is actually asking for – use the 'help'
- ✓ pay special attention to your personal statement (see page 115) and start drafting it early
- ✓ ask a teacher, parent, friend or careers adviser to review your draft application – particularly the personal statement
- ✓ if you get stuck, watch our videos on YouTube, where we answer your frequently asked questions on completing a UCAS application at www.youtube.com/ucasonline
- ✓ if you have extra information that will not fit on your application, send it direct to your chosen universities or colleges after we have sent you your Welcome letter with your Personal ID – don't send it it to us
- ✓ print a copy of the final version of your application, in case you are asked questions on it at an interview.

compose
your future

Find out about performing arts, music, dance, drama, broadcast, multimedia production courses and much more

Would you like the chance to talk to representatives from a wide range of colleges and universities, to pick up prospectuses and see live performances by undergraduates?

UCAS Compose your future exhibition is an annual event that offers the opportunity to find out more about higher education courses in performing arts, music, dance, drama, broadcast, multi-media production and related subjects, and the chance to meet organisations of a particular interest to prospective students.

The event will also feature:

- Workshops:
  Interactive sessions
  e.g. performance masterclasses
  Presentation sessions e.g. how to apply

- Live performances from current and past students from exhibiting institutions

TO FIND OUT MORE OR TO BOOK, PLEASE VISIT THE WEBSITE WWW.UCASEVENTS.COM/COMPOSE, OR CALL 01242 544645

UCAS

Applying

2

How to apply through CUKAS

WHAT IS CUKAS?

The Conservatoires UK Admissions Service (CUKAS) is an admissions service operated by UCAS. CUKAS provides a central application service for practice-based music courses, and some drama and dance courses, at seven conservatoires in the UK:

Birmingham Conservatoire
Leeds College of Music
Royal College of Music
Royal Northern College of Music
Royal Conservatoire of Scotland
Royal Welsh College of Music and Drama
Trinity Laben Conservatoire of Music and Dance.

The Guildhall School of Music and Drama and the Royal Academy of Music are members of Conservatoires UK (CUK) but do not recruit through CUKAS. Applicants should apply directly to these conservatoires.

CUKAS processes applications for the following types of full-time and part-time courses in music, dance and drama:

- undergraduate degree level courses
- postgraduate degree level courses
- postgraduate certificate and diploma courses
- courses with no award.

Applicants must apply through CUKAS for any courses listed on Course Search on the CUKAS website **www.cukas.ac.uk.**

WHEN TO APPLY

You can apply online through the CUKAS website **www.cukas.ac.uk** from early July, for courses that mostly start in September or October the following year. The online application system provides detailed help text to guide you through the application process.

The closing date for 2013 entry on-time applications is 1 October 2012. Conservatoires must give equal consideration to all applications received by this date.

We will process all applications received from 2 October 2012 to 31 August 2013, but these are classed as late and will only be considered by the conservatoires if they still have vacancies after considering all the on-time applications. If you are applying after 1 February 2013, you should contact the conservatoires to check if they still have vacancies before making an application.

APPLICATION AND AUDITION FEES

You can apply for a maximum of six choices; the application fee is £16 for 2013 entry regardless of how many choices you make.

All the conservatoires in the CUKAS application system, except Leeds College of Music, require you to pay your audition fees at the time of application. Leeds College of Music requires you to pay once you have been invited to audition.

The amount of the audition fee varies depending on the type of course and whether:

- the audition is a live performance or a recording
- separate auditions are required for two study areas, for example, different instruments, acting or drama production
- the audition is held in the UK or abroad
- the application is 'on-time' or 'late' (received at CUKAS by 1 October 2012 or after 1 October 2012 respectively for music courses; please see conservatoire websites for application deadlines for dance and drama courses).

Some conservatoires will waive audition fees for applicants who are unable to pay if they are able to provide evidence of hardship.

REFERENCES

You must provide details of two referees - one to comment on your academic ability; and the other to comment on your practical ability.

WHAT HAPPENS NEXT?

Once we have received your completed application, we then:

1. process your application
2. send it to your chosen conservatoire(s)
3. send you a Welcome letter confirming your personal details and choices.

After this stage, invitations for auditions are sent by conservatoires.

THE AUDITION

The audition process will vary between conservatoires. If you are invited for audition, the conservatoire will provide advice on what the audition will include and what kind of pieces you should prepare. Further information to help you prepare for auditions is available in the Conservatoires UK (CUK) leaflet *Making the Most of Your Audition*, which you can download from the CUKAS website at **www.cukas.ac.uk**.

TRACK

After you have submitted your application to CUKAS, you can use the Track service to:

- follow the progress of your application to see details of auditions, decisions and any offers
- change your postal address, email address and/or telephone number

- make additional choices (if you have not already made six)
- reply to your offers.

Please note, CUKAS does not operate an Extra or Clearing service.

APPLYING THROUGH CUKAS AND UCAS

You may apply through both CUKAS and UCAS (see page 108) in the same application cycle, but if you hold a confirmed place in both systems, you will have to withdraw from one of these places.

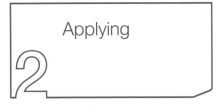

Applying

The personal statement

Next to choosing your courses, this section of your application will be the most time-consuming. It is of immense importance as many institutions rely solely on the information in the application, rather than interviews and admissions tests, when selecting students. The personal statement can be the deciding factor in whether or not they offer you a place. If it is an institution that interviews, it could be the deciding factor in whether you get called for interview.

Keep a copy of your personal statement – if you are called for interview, you will almost certainly be asked questions based on it.

Tutors will look carefully at your exam results, actual and predicted, your reference and your own personal statement. Remember, they are looking for reasons to offer you a place – try to give them every opportunity to do so!

A SALES DOCUMENT

The personal statement is your opportunity to sell yourself, so do so. The university, college or conservatoire admissions tutor who reads your personal statement wants to get a rounded picture of you to decide whether you will make an interesting member of the institution, both academically and socially. They want to know more about you than the subjects you are studying at school.

HOW TO START

At **www.ucas.com** you'll find several tools to help you write a good personal statement.

- Personal statement timeline, to help you do all your research and plan your statement over several drafts and checks.
- Personal statement mind map, which gives you reminders and hints on preparation, content and presentation, with extra hints for mature and international applicants.
- Personal statement worksheet, which gets you to start writing by asking relevant questions so that you include everything you need. You can also check your work against a list dos and don'ts.

Include things like hobbies and work experience (see pages 97 and 117), and try to link the skills you have gained to the type of course you are applying for. Describe your career plans and goals. Have you belonged to theatre groups, dance groups or orchestras, or held positions of responsibility in the community? If you're applying for journalism, have you visited a news organisation? Try to give evidence of your ability to undertake higher level study successfully by showing your commitment and maturity. If you left full-time education a while ago, talk about the work you have done and the skills you have gathered or how you have juggled bringing up a family with other activities – that is solid evidence of time management skills. Whoever you are, make sure you explain what appeals to you about the course you are applying for.

Visit **www.ucas.tv** to view the video to help guide you through the process, and address the most common fears and concerns about writing a personal statement.

WHAT ADMISSIONS TUTORS LOOK FOR	WHAT TO TELL THEM
<ul><li>Your reasons for wanting to take this subject in general and this particular course.</li><li>Your communication skills – not only what you say but how you say it. Your grammar and spelling must be perfect.</li><li>Relevant experience – practical things you've done that are related to your choice of course.</li><li>Evidence of your teamworking ability, leadership capability, independence.</li><li>Evidence of your skills, for example: IT skills, empathy and people skills, debating and public speaking, research and analysis.</li><li>Other activities that show your dedication and ability to apply yourself and maintain your motivation.</li></ul>	<ul><li>Why you want to do this subject - how you know it is the subject for you.</li><li>What experience you already have in this field – for example work experience, school projects, hobbies, voluntary work.</li><li>The skills and qualities you have as a person that would make you a good student, for example anything that shows your dedication, communication ability, academic achievement, initiative.</li><li>Examples that show you can knuckle down and apply yourself, for example running a marathon or your Extended Project.</li><li>If you're taking a gap year, why you've chosen this and (if possible) what you're going to do during it.</li><li>About your other interests and activities away from studying – to show you're a rounded person. (But remember that it is mainly your suitability for the particular course that they're looking to judge.)</li></ul>

CUKAS applicants

You should make your personal statement truly convey your aspirations, personality, feelings about music and experience. Showing understanding of today's music profession, which is competitive and requires versatility, is helpful and indicates a suitable temperament. It is up to you how you write your statement, but we suggest you include some or all of the following points.

- Your reasons for choosing the courses you have listed. Remember that each conservatoire will be able to see which other conservatoires you have applied to.
- What interests you about your chosen study area (whether playing an instrument, singing, conducting or composing).
- Your experience of playing your chosen instrument(s), or in singing, conducting or composing, or in any other activity related to the course(s) to which you have applied.
- Membership of national and/or international orchestras, choirs or chamber groups, for example NYO, NYC, EUYO.

WORK EXPERIENCE

The value of work experience is the skillset it gives you, which in turn helps you produce better work, both practical and academic. Describing the work experience you've had, what you learned from it and the skills you gained, will also help your personal statement to stand out from the crowd.

What work experience can I get?

Although there are no formalised work experience schemes offered by employers in the media and performing arts fields, some do offer work placements or ad hoc 'shadowing schemes', where you shadow a professional for a week or a few days: for these you'll have to apply direct to the company. There is also the possibility of 'taster days' offered by careers organizations in conjunction with employers, and increasingly the chance of work experience placements through your school.

However, you will need to use all your initiative to get experience in the field of performing arts and media that interests you. Remember that voluntary experience counts too, as does any involvement in relevant activities at school.

Here are a few examples of work experience that could help you gain that place (and be sure you're heading in the right direction for you!):

- Helping organise school music concerts
- Getting involved in plays or dance shows (backstage, lighting, costumes, production, acting etc)
- Contributing to the school magazine (writing, taking photographs, editing, helping with layout)
- Writing your own blog, reviewing plays, books or computer games
- Making your own films, putting on an exhibition of photography (yours or someone else's)
- Any kind of experience, however humble, in a company that works in the area that interests you. Be proactive: write to or telephone companies (local newspapers and radio/TV companies, theatre companies, photography studios), explain what you are hoping to study and where, and ask if you could come in for a few days to help or shadow an employee.

Even work experience that is not related to performing arts or media can work in your favour. The trick is to identify and describe the professional and personal skills you developed that are relevant to the work or skills required in media and performing arts: there are many of these, including teamworking, learning new skills quickly, solving problems, practical hands-on work, working with the public and communication skills.

Offers

3

Step 3 – Offers

Once we have sent your UCAS application to your chosen universities and colleges, they will all consider it independently and tell us whether or not they can offer you a place. Some universities and colleges will take longer to make decisions than others. You may be asked to attend an interview, sit an additional test or provide a piece of work such as an essay or art portfolio before a decision can be made.

INTERVIEWS

Many universities (particularly the more popular ones, running competitive courses) use interviews as part of their selection process. Universities will want to find out why you want to study your chosen course at their institution, and they want to judge whether the course is suitable for you and your future career plans. Interviews also give you an opportunity to visit the university and ask any questions you may have about the course or their institution.

If you are called for interview, the key areas they are likely to cover will be:

- evidence of your academic/communications/artistic/musical ability
- your capacity to study hard
- your commitment to a career in journalism, media and performing arts, best shown by work experience
- your awareness of current issues that may have an impact on your chosen field of study
- your creativity, and its interaction with attention to detail
- your interpersonal skills.

CUKAS applicants will normally need to have auditions before the conservatoires can make their decisions. Please see page 113 for more information.

A lot of the interview will be based on information supplied on your application – especially your **personal statement** - see page 115 for tips about the personal statement.

Whenever a university, college or conservatoire makes a decision about your application, we record it and let you know. You can check the progress of your application using Track at **www.ucas.com** or **www.cukas.ac.uk**. These are secure online services which give you access to your application using the same username and password you used when you applied. You use it to find out if you have been invited for audition or interview, or need to provide an additional piece of work, as well as check to see if you have received any offers. Whenever there is any change in your application status, we email you to advise you to check Track.

Types of offer - UCAS

Universities can make two types of offer: conditional or unconditional.

Conditional offer

A conditional offer means the university or college will offer you a place if you meet certain conditions – usually based on exam results. The conditions may be based on Tariff points (for example, 300 points from three A levels), or specify certain grades in named subjects (for example, A in drama, B in English, C in French).

Unconditional offer

If you've met all the academic requirements for the course and the university or college wants to accept you, they will make you an unconditional offer. If you accept this you'll have a definite place. However, there might be other requirements, such as medical or financial conditions, that you need to meet before you can start your course.

Types of offer - CUKAS

Guaranteed unconditional - the conservatoire is satisfied, from the information you have given, that you have already met the conditions for entry.

Guaranteed conditional - the conservatoire has made the offer subject to you meeting certain conditions, usually examination results.

Reserve unconditional - the conservatoire is satisfied, from the information you have given, that you have already met the conditions for entry and have offered a place on their reserve list.

Reserve conditional - the conservatoire has offered a place on its reserve list subject to your meeting certain conditions, usually examination results.

For any type of offer, through UCAS or CUKAS, there may be some non-academic requirements:

- For courses that involve contact with children and vulnerable adults you may need to have criminal record checks before you can start the course.
- For students who are not resident in either the UK or the EU, there may be some financial conditions to meet.

When you have received decisions for all your choices, you must decide what you want to accept and you do this by using Track. You will be given a deadline by which to decide what to accept.

Replying to offers - UCAS

When you have received decisions for all your choices, you must decide which offers you want to accept. You will be given a deadline in Track by which you have to make your replies. Before replying, get advice from family, friends or advisers, but remember that you're the one taking the course so it's your decision.

Firm acceptance

- Your firm acceptance is your first choice - this is your preferred choice out of all the offers you have received. You can have only one firm acceptance.
- If you accept an unconditional offer, you are entering a contract that you will attend the course, so you must decline any other offers.
- If you accept a conditional offer, you are agreeing that you will attend the course at that university or college if you meet the conditions of the offer. You can accept another offer as an insurance choice.

Insurance acceptance

- If your firm acceptance is a conditional offer, you can accept another offer as an insurance choice. Your insurance choice can be conditional or unconditional and acts as a back-up, so if you don't meet the conditions for your firm choice but meet the conditions for your insurance, you will be committed to the insurance choice. You can only have one insurance choice.
- The conditions for your insurance choice would usually be lower than your firm choice.
- You don't have to accept an insurance choice if you don't want one; but if you do you need to be certain that it is an offer you would accept.

For more information watch our video guides *How to use Track*, *Making sense of your offers*, and *How to reply to your offers* at **www.ucas.tv**.

Replying to offers - CUKAS

You may only be able to accept one offer as your first choice, or you may be able to accept two offers and state your first and second choices. The number of offers you can accept will depend on the type of offers.

- If you accept a guaranteed unconditional offer you

will be expected to take up this place. You cannot accept any other offer as a second choice.
- If you accept a guaranteed conditional offer as your first choice, you will also be expected to take up this place provided you meet the conditions. You cannot accept any other offer as a second choice.
- If you accept a reserve unconditional or a reserve conditional offer as your first choice, you may accept any type of offer as your second choice.

What if you have no offers?

If you have used all five choices on your UCAS application and either received no offers, or decided to turn down any offers you have received, you may be eligible to apply for another choice through Extra. Find out more about Extra on page 122.

If you are not eligible for Extra, in the summer you can contact universities and colleges with vacancies in Clearing. See page 136 for more information.

If you have applied through CUKAS and do not receive any offers, you can reapply in the next application cycle. CUKAS does not operate an Extra or Clearing service.

design
your future

Find out about art, design, media and other creative courses

The UCAS Design your future event is an excellent opportunity for students from Years 10,11,12 and foundation level to talk to representatives from a wide range of art colleges and universities, pick up prospectuses, and attend art and design study related workshops.

Some subjects covered include: Art; Design; Media; Architecture; Web Design; Fashion; Ceramics and many more…

Events are taking place in both London and Manchester and will include around one hundred exhibitors, from Universities and Colleges, to organisations of particular interest to prospective students.

TO FIND OUT MORE OR TO BOOK, PLEASE VISIT THE WEBSITE WWW.UCASEVENTS.COM/DESIGN OR CALL 01242 544645

Offers

3

Extra

Extra allows you to make additional choices through UCAS, one at a time, without having to wait for Clearing in July. It is completely optional and free, and is designed to encourage you to continue researching and choosing courses if you are holding no offers. The courses available through Extra will be highlighted on Course Finder, at **www.ucas.com**.

From 25 February – early July
The Extra service is available to eligible UCAS applicants through Track at **www.ucas.com**.

CUKAS does not operate an Extra service.

Who is eligible?
You will be eligible for Extra if you have already made five choices and:

- you have had unsuccessful or withdrawal decisions from all five of your choices, or

- you have cancelled your outstanding choices and hold no offers, or
- you have received decisions from all five choices and have declined all offers made to you.

How does it work?
We contact you and explain what to do if you are eligible for Extra. If you are eligible a special Extra button will be available on your Track screen. If you want to use Extra you should:

- tick the 'Available in Extra' box in the Study Options section when looking for courses on Course Finder
- choose a course that you would like to apply for and enter the details on your Track screen.

When you have chosen a course, the university or college will be able to view your application and consider you for a place.

What happens next?

We give universities and colleges a maximum of 21 days to consider your Extra application. During this time, you cannot be considered by another university or college. If you have not heard after 21 days you can apply to a different university or college if you wish, but it is a good idea to ring the one currently considering you before doing so. If you are made an offer, you can choose whether or not to accept it.

If you accept an offer, conditional or unconditional, you will not be able to take any further part in Extra.

If you are currently studying for examinations, any offer that you receive is likely to be an offer conditional on exam grades. If you already have your examination results, it is possible that a university or college may make an unconditional offer. If you accept an unconditional offer, you will be placed. If you decide to decline the offer, or the university or college decides they cannot make you an offer, you will be given another opportunity to use Extra, time permitting. Your Extra button on Track will be reactivated.

Once you have accepted an offer in Extra, you are committed to it in the same way as you would be with an offer through the main UCAS system. Conditional offers made through Extra will be treated in the same way as other conditional offers, when your examination results become available.

If your results do not meet the conditions and the university or college decides that they cannot confirm your Extra offer, you will automatically become eligible for Clearing if it is too late for you to be considered by another university or college in Extra.

If you are unsuccessful, decline an offer, or do not receive an offer, or 21 days has elapsed since choosing a course through Extra, you can use Extra to apply for another course, time permitting.

Advice

Do the same careful research and seek guidance on your Extra choice of university or college and course as you did for your initial choices. If you applied to high-demand courses and institutions in your original application and were unsuccessful, you could consider related or alternative subjects or perhaps apply for the subject you want in combination with another. Your teachers or careers advisers, or the universities and colleges themselves can provide useful guidance. Course Finder at www.ucas.com is another important source of information. Be flexible, that is the key to success. But you are the only one who knows how flexible you are prepared to be.

Visit www.ucas.tv to watch the video guide on how to use Extra.

Offers

3

The Tariff

Finding out what qualifications are needed for different higher education courses can be very confusing.

The UCAS Tariff is the system for allocating points to qualifications used for entry to higher education. Universities and colleges can use the UCAS Tariff to make comparisons between applicants with different qualifications. Tariff points are often used in entry requirements, although other factors are often taken into account. Information on Course Finder at **www.ucas.com** provides a fuller picture of what admissions tutors are seeking.

The tables on the following pages show the qualifications covered by the UCAS Tariff. There may have been changes to these tables since this book was printed. You should visit **www.ucas.com** to view the most up-to-date tables.

FURTHER INFORMATION?

Although Tariff points can be accumulated in a variety of ways, not all of these will necessarily be acceptable for entry to a particular higher education course. The achievement of a points score therefore does not give an automatic entitlement to entry, and many other factors are taken into account in the admissions process.

The Course Finder facility at **www.ucas.com** is the best source of reference to find out what qualifications are acceptable for entry to specific courses. Updates to the Tariff, including details on how new qualifications are added, can be found at **www.ucas.com/students/ucas_tariff/**.

HOW DOES THE TARIFF WORK?

- Students can collect Tariff points from a range of different qualifications, eg GCE A level with BTEC Nationals.
- There is no ceiling to the number of points that can be accumulated.
- There is no double counting. Certain qualifications within the Tariff build on qualifications in the same subject. In these cases only the qualification with the higher Tariff score will be counted. This principle applies to:
    - GCE Advanced Subsidiary level and GCE Advanced level
    - Scottish Highers and Advanced Highers
    - Speech, drama and music awards at grades 6, 7 and 8.
- Tariff points for the Advanced Diploma come from the Progression Diploma score plus the relevant Additional and Specialist Learning (ASL) Tariff points. Please see the appropriate qualification in the Tariff tables to calculate the ASL score.
- The Extended Project Tariff points are included within the Tariff points for Progression and Advanced Diplomas. Extended Project points represented in the Tariff only count when the qualification is taken outside of these Diplomas.
- Where the Tariff tables refer to specific awarding organisations, only qualifications from these awarding organisations attract Tariff points. Qualifications with a similar title, but from a different qualification awarding organisation do not attract Tariff points.

HOW DO UNIVERSITIES AND COLLEGES USE THE TARIFF?

The Tariff provides a facility to help universities and colleges when expressing entrance requirements and when making conditional offers. Entry requirements and conditional offers expressed as Tariff points will often require a minimum level of achievement in a specified subject (for example, '300 points to include grade A at A level chemistry', or '260 points including SQA Higher grade B in mathematics').

Use of the Tariff may also vary from department to department at any one institution, and may in some cases be dependent on the programme being offered.

In July 2010, UCAS announced plans to review the qualifications information provided to universities and colleges. You can read more about the review at **www.ucas.com/qireview**.

WHAT QUALIFICATIONS ARE INCLUDED IN THE TARIFF?

The following qualifications are included in the UCAS Tariff. See the number on the qualification title to find the relevant section of the Tariff table.

1 AAT NVQ Level 3 in Accounting
2 AAT Level 3 Diploma in Accounting (QCF)
3 Advanced Diploma
4 Advanced Extension Awards
5 Advanced Placement Programme (US and Canada)
6 Arts Award (Gold)
7 ASDAN Community Volunteering qualification
8 Asset Languages Advanced Stage
9 British Horse Society (Stage 3 Horse Knowledge & Care, Stage 3 Riding and Preliminary Teacher's Certificate)
10 BTEC Awards (NQF)
11 BTEC Certificates and Extended Certificates (NQF)
12 BTEC Diplomas (NQF)
13 BTEC National in Early Years (NQF)
14 BTEC Nationals (NQF)
15 BTEC QCF Qualifications (Suite known as Nationals)
16 BTEC Specialist Qualifications (QCF)
17 CACHE Award, Certificate and Diploma in Child Care and Education
18 CACHE Level 3 Extended Diploma for the Children and Young People's Workforce (QCF)
19 Cambridge ESOL Examinations
20 Cambridge Pre-U
21 Certificate of Personal Effectiveness (COPE)
22 CISI Introduction to Securities and Investment
23 City & Guilds Land Based Services Level 3 Qualifications
24 Graded Dance and Vocational Graded Dance
25 Diploma in Fashion Retail
26 Diploma in Foundation Studies (Art & Design; Art, Design & Media)
27 EDI Level 3 Certificate in Accounting, Certificate in Accounting (IAS)
28 Essential Skills (Northern Ireland)
29 Essential Skills Wales
30 Extended Project (stand alone)
31 Free-standing Mathematics
32 Functional skills
33 GCE (AS, AS Double Award, A level, A level Double Award and A level (with additional AS))
34 Hong Kong Diploma of Secondary Education (from 2012 entry onwards)
35 ifs School of Finance (Certificate and Diploma in Financial Studies)
36 iMedia (OCR level Certificate/Diploma for iMedia Professionals)
37 International Baccalaureate (IB) Diploma
38 International Baccalaureate (IB) Certificate
39 Irish Leaving Certificate (Higher and Ordinary levels)
40 IT Professionals (iPRO) (Certificate and Diploma)
41 Key Skills (Levels 2, 3 and 4)
42 Music examinations (grades 6, 7 and 8)
43 OCR Level 3 Certificate in Mathematics for Engineering
44 OCR Level 3 Certificate for Young Enterprise
45 OCR Nationals (National Certificate, National Diploma and National Extended Diploma)
46 Principal Learning Wales
47 Progression Diploma
48 Rockschool Music Practitioners Qualifications
49 Scottish Qualifications
50 Speech and Drama examinations (grades 6, 7 and 8 and Performance Studies)
51 Sports Leaders UK
52 Welsh Baccalaureate Advanced Diploma (Core)

Updates on the Tariff, including details on the incorporation of any new qualifications, are posted on www.ucas.com.

UCAS TARIFF TABLES

1

AAT NVQ LEVEL 3 IN ACCOUNTING	
GRADE	TARIFF POINTS
PASS	160

2

AAT LEVEL 3 DIPLOMA IN ACCOUNTING	
GRADE	TARIFF POINTS
PASS	160

3

ADVANCED DIPLOMA

Advanced Diploma = Progression Diploma plus Additional & Specialist Learning (ASL). Please see the appropriate qualification to calculate the ASL score. Please see the Progression Diploma (Table 47) for Tariff scores

4

ADVANCED EXTENSION AWARDS	
GRADE	TARIFF POINTS
DISTINCTION	40
MERIT	20

Points for Advanced Extension Awards are over and above those gained from the A level grade

5

ADVANCED PLACEMENT PROGRAMME (US & CANADA)	
GRADE	TARIFF POINTS
Group A	
5	120
4	90
3	60
Group B	
5	50
4	35
3	20

Details of the subjects covered by each group can be found at www.ucas.com/students/ucas_tariff/tarifftables

6

ARTS AWARD (GOLD)	
GRADE	TARIFF POINTS
PASS	35

7

ASDAN COMMUNITY VOLUNTEERING QUALIFICATION	
GRADE	TARIFF POINTS
CERTIFICATE	50
AWARD	30

8

ASSET LANGUAGES ADVANCED STAGE			
GRADE	TARIFF POINTS	GRADE	TARIFF POINTS
Speaking		Listening	
GRADE 12	28	GRADE 12	25
GRADE 11	20	GRADE 11	18
GRADE 10	12	GRADE 10	11
Reading		Writing	
GRADE 12	25	GRADE 12	25
GRADE 11	18	GRADE 11	18
GRADE 10	11	GRADE 10	11

9

BRITISH HORSE SOCIETY	
GRADE	TARIFF POINTS
Stage 3 Horse Knowledge & Care	
PASS	35
Stage 3 Riding	
PASS	35
Preliminary Teacher's Certificate	
PASS	35

Awarded by Equestrian Qualifications (GB) Ltd (EQL)

10

BTEC AWARDS (NQF) (EXCLUDING BTEC NATIONAL QUALIFICATIONS)			
GRADE	TARIFF POINTS		
	Group A	Group B	Group C
DISTINCTION	20	30	40
MERIT	13	20	26
PASS	7	10	13

Details of the subjects covered by each group can be found at www.ucas.com/students/ucas_tariff/tarifftables

11

BTEC CERTIFICATES AND EXTENDED CERTIFICATES (NQF) (EXCLUDING BTEC NATIONAL QUALIFICATIONS)					
GRADE	TARIFF POINTS				
	Group A	Group B	Group C	Group D	Extended Certificates
DISTINCTION	40	60	80	100	60
MERIT	26	40	52	65	40
PASS	13	20	26	35	20

Details of the subjects covered by each group can be found at www.ucas.com/students/ucas_tariff/tarifftables

12

BTEC DIPLOMAS (NQF) (EXCLUDING BTEC NATIONAL QUALIFICATIONS)			
GRADE	TARIFF POINTS		
	Group A	Group B	Group C
DISTINCTION	80	100	120
MERIT	52	65	80
PASS	26	35	40

Details of the subjects covered by each group can be found at www.ucas.com/students/ucas_tariff/tarifftables

13

BTEC NATIONAL IN EARLY YEARS (NQF)					
GRADE	TARIFF POINTS	GRADE	TARIFF POINTS	GRADE	TARIFF POINTS
Theory				Practical	
Diploma		Certificate		D	120
DDD	320	DD	200	M	80
DDM	280	DM	160	P	40
DMM	240	MM	120		
MMM	220	MP	80		
MMP	160	PP	40		
MPP	120				
PPP	80				

Points apply to the following qualifications only: BTEC National Diploma in Early Years (100/1279/5); BTEC National Certificate in Early Years (100/1280/1)

14

BTEC NATIONALS (NQF)					
GRADE	TARIFF POINTS	GRADE	TARIFF POINTS	GRADE	TARIFF POINTS
Diploma		Certificate		Award	
DDD	360	DD	240	D	120
DDM	320	DM	200	M	80
DMM	280	MM	160	P	40
MMM	240	MP	120		
MMP	200	PP	80		
MPP	160				
PPP	120				

15

BTEC QUALIFICATIONS (QCF) (SUITE OF QUALIFICATIONS KNOWN AS NATIONALS)					
EXTENDED DIPLOMA	DIPLOMA	90 CREDIT DIPLOMA	SUBSIDIARY DIPLOMA	CERTIFICATE	TARIFF POINTS
D*D*D*					420
D*D*D					400
D*DD					380
DDD					360
DDM					320
DMM	D*D*				280
	D*D				260
MMM	DD				240
		D*D*			210
MMP	DM	D*D			200
		DD			180
MPP	MM	DM			160
			D*		140
PPP	MP	MM	D		120
		MP			100
	PP		M		80
				D*	70
		PP		D	60
			P	M	40
				P	20

16

BTEC SPECIALIST (QCF)			
GRADE	TARIFF POINTS		
	Diploma	Certificate	Award
DISTINCTION	120	60	20
MERIT	80	40	13
PASS	40	20	7

UCAS TARIFF TABLES

17

CACHE LEVEL 3 AWARD, CERTIFICATE AND DIPLOMA IN CHILD CARE & EDUCATION

AWARD		CERTIFICATE		DIPLOMA	
GRADE	TARIFF POINTS	GRADE	TARIFF POINTS	GRADE	TARIFF POINTS
A	30	A	110	A	360
B	25	B	90	B	300
C	20	C	70	C	240
D	15	D	55	D	180
E	10	E	35	E	120

18

CACHE LEVEL 3 EXTENDED DIPLOMA FOR THE CHILDREN AND YOUNG PEOPLE'S WORKFORCE (QCF)

GRADE	TARIFF POINTS
A*	420
A	340
B	290
C	240
D	140
E	80

19

CAMBRIDGE ESOL EXAMINATIONS

GRADE	TARIFF POINTS
Certificate of Proficiency in English	
A	140
B	110
C	70
Certificate in Advanced English	
A	70

20

CAMBRIDGE PRE-U

GRADE	TARIFF POINTS	GRADE	TARIFF POINTS	GRADE	TARIFF POINTS
Principal Subject		Global Perspectives and Research		Short Course	
D1	TBC	D1	TBC	D1	TBC
D2	145	D2	140	D2	TBC
D3	130	D3	126	D3	60
M1	115	M1	112	M1	53
M2	101	M2	98	M2	46
M3	87	M3	84	M3	39
P1	73	P1	70	P1	32
P2	59	P2	56	P2	26
P3	46	P3	42	P3	20

21

CERTIFICATE OF PERSONAL EFFECTIVENESS (COPE)

GRADE	TARIFF POINTS
PASS	70

Points are awarded for the Certificate of Personal Effectiveness (CoPE) awarded by ASDAN and CCEA

22

CISI INTRODUCTION TO SECURITIES AND INVESTMENT

GRADE	TARIFF POINTS
PASS WITH DISTINCTION	60
PASS WITH MERIT	40
PASS	20

23

CITY AND GUILDS LAND BASED SERVICES LEVEL 3 QUALIFICATIONS

GRADE	TARIFF POINTS			
	EXTENDED DIPLOMA	DIPLOMA	SUBSIDIARY DIPLOMA	CERTIFICATE
DISTINCTION*	420	280	140	70
DISTINCTION	360	240	120	60
MERIT	240	160	80	40
PASS	120	80	40	20

24

GRADED DANCE AND VOCATIONAL GRADED DANCE

GRADE	TARIFF POINTS	GRADE	TARIFF POINTS	GRADE	TARIFF POINTS
Graded Dance					
Grade 8		Grade 7		Grade 6	
DISTINCTION	65	DISTINCTION	55	DISTINCTION	40
MERIT	55	MERIT	45	MERIT	35
PASS	45	PASS	35	PASS	30
Vocational Graded Dance					
Advanced Foundation		Intermediate			
DISTINCTION	70	DISTINCTION	65		
MERIT	55	MERIT	50		
PASS	45	PASS	40		

25

DIPLOMA IN FASHION RETAIL

GRADE	TARIFF POINTS
DISTINCTION	160
MERIT	120
PASS	80

Applies to the NQF and QCF versions of the qualifications awarded by ABC Awards

26

DIPLOMA IN FOUNDATION STUDIES (ART & DESIGN AND ART, DESIGN & MEDIA)	
GRADE	TARIFF POINTS
DISTINCTION	285
MERIT	225
PASS	165

Awarded by ABC, Edexcel, UAL and WJEC

27

EDI LEVEL 3 CERTIFICATE IN ACCOUNTING, CERTIFICATE IN ACCOUNTING (IAS)	
GRADE	TARIFF POINTS
DISTINCTION	120
MERIT	90
PASS	70

28

ESSENTIAL SKILLS (NORTHERN IRELAND)	
GRADE	TARIFF POINTS
LEVEL 2	10

Only allocated at level 2 if studied as part of a wider composite qualification such as 14-19 Diploma or Welsh Baccalaureate

29

ESSENTIAL SKILLS WALES	
GRADE	TARIFF POINTS
LEVEL 4	30
LEVEL 3	20
LEVEL 2	10

Only allocated at level 2 if studied as part of a wider composite qualification such as 14-19 Diploma or Welsh Baccalaureate

30

EXTENDED PROJECT (STAND ALONE)	
GRADE	TARIFF POINTS
A*	70
A	60
B	50
C	40
D	30
E	20

Points for the Extended Project cannot be counted if taken as part of Progression/Advanced Diploma

31

FREE-STANDING MATHEMATICS	
GRADE	TARIFF POINTS
A	20
B	17
C	13
D	10
E	7

Covers free-standing Mathematics - Additional Maths, Using and Applying Statistics, Working with Algebraic and Graphical Techniques, Modelling with Calculus

32

FUNCTIONAL SKILLS	
GRADE	TARIFF POINTS
LEVEL 2	10

Only allocated if studied as part of a wider composite qualification such as 14-19 Diploma or Welsh Baccalaureate

33

GCE AND VCE									
GRADE	TARIFF POINTS	GRADE	TARIFF POINTS	GRADE	TARIFF POINTS	GRADE	TARIFF POINTS	GRADE	TARIFF POINTS
GCE & AVCE Double Award		GCE A level with additional AS (9 units)		GCE A level & AVCE		GCE AS Double Award		GCE AS & AS VCE	
A*A*	280	A*A	200	A*	140	AA	120	A	60
A*A	260	AA	180	A	120	AB	110	B	50
AA	240	AB	170	B	100	BB	100	C	40
AB	220	BB	150	C	80	BC	90	D	30
BB	200	BC	140	D	60	CC	80	E	20
BC	180	CC	120	E	40	CD	70		
CC	160	CD	110			DD	60		
CD	140	DD	90			DE	50		
DD	120	DE	80			EE	40		
DE	100	EE	60						
EE	80								

34

HONG KONG DIPLOMA OF SECONDARY EDUCATION					
GRADE	TARIFF POINTS	GRADE	TARIFF POINTS	GRADE	TARIFF POINTS
All subjects except mathematics		Mathematics compulsory component		Mathematics optional components	
5**	No value	5**	No value	5**	No value
5*	130	5*	60	5*	70
5	120	5	45	5	60
4	80	4	35	4	50
3	40	3	25	3	40

No value for 5** pending receipt of candidate evidence (post 2012)

UCAS TARIFF TABLES

35

IFS SCHOOL OF FINANCE (NQF & QCF)			
GRADE	TARIFF POINTS	GRADE	TARIFF POINTS
Certificate in Financial Studies (CeFS)		Diploma in Financial Studies (DipFS)	
A	60	A	120
B	50	B	100
C	40	C	80
D	30	D	60
E	20	E	40

Applicants with the ifs Diploma cannot also count points allocated to the ifs Certificate. Completion of both qualifications will result in a maximum of 120 UCAS Tariff points

36

LEVEL 3 CERTIFICATE / DIPLOMA FOR iMEDIA USERS (iMEDIA)	
GRADE	TARIFF POINTS
DIPLOMA	66
CERTIFICATE	40

Awarded by OCR

37

INTERNATIONAL BACCALAUREATE (IB) DIPLOMA			
GRADE	TARIFF POINTS	GRADE	TARIFF POINTS
45	720	34	479
44	698	33	457
43	676	32	435
42	654	31	413
41	632	30	392
40	611	29	370
39	589	28	348
38	567	27	326
37	545	26	304
36	523	25	282
35	501	24	260

38

INTERNATIONAL BACCALAUREATE (IB) CERTIFICATE					
GRADE	TARIFF POINTS	GRADE	TARIFF POINTS	GRADE	TARIFF POINTS
Higher Level		Standard Level		Core	
7	130	7	70	3	120
6	110	6	59	2	80
5	80	5	43	1	40
4	50	4	27	0	10
3	20	3	11		

39

IRISH LEAVING CERTIFICATE			
GRADE	TARIFF POINTS	GRADE	TARIFF POINTS
Higher		Ordinary	
A1	90	A1	39
A2	77	A2	26
B1	71	B1	20
B2	64	B2	14
B3	58	B3	7
C1	52		
C2	45		
C3	39		
D1	33		
D2	26		
D3	20		

40

IT PROFESSIONALS (iPRO)	
GRADE	TARIFF POINTS
DIPLOMA	100
CERTIFICATE	80

Awarded by OCR

41

KEY SKILLS	
GRADE	TARIFF POINTS
LEVEL 4	30
LEVEL 3	20
LEVEL 2	10

Only allocated at level 2 if studied as part of a wider composite qualification such as 14-19 Diploma or Welsh Baccalaureate

UCAS TARIFF TABLES

42

MUSIC EXAMINATIONS					
GRADE	TARIFF POINTS	GRADE	TARIFF POINTS	GRADE	TARIFF POINTS
Practical					
Grade 8		Grade 7		Grade 6	
DISTINCTION	75	DISTINCTION	60	DISTINCTION	45
MERIT	70	MERIT	55	MERIT	40
PASS	55	PASS	40	PASS	25
Theory					
Grade 8		Grade 7		Grade 6	
DISTINCTION	30	DISTINCTION	20	DISTINCTION	15
MERIT	25	MERIT	15	MERIT	10
PASS	20	PASS	10	PASS	5

Points shown are for the ABRSM, LCMM/University of West London, Rockschool and Trinity Guildhall/Trinity College London Advanced Level music examinations

43

OCR LEVEL 3 CERTIFICATE IN MATHEMATICS FOR ENGINEERING	
GRADE	TARIFF POINTS
A*	TBC
A	90
B	75
C	60
D	45
E	30

44

OCR LEVEL 3 CERTIFICATE FOR YOUNG ENTERPRISE	
GRADE	TARIFF POINTS
DISTINCTION	40
MERIT	30
PASS	20

45

OCR NATIONALS					
GRADE	TARIFF POINTS	GRADE	TARIFF POINTS	GRADE	TARIFF POINTS
National Extended Diploma		National Diploma		National Certificate	
D1	360	D	240	D	120
D2/M1	320	M1	200	M	80
M2	280	M2/P1	160	P	40
M3	240	P2	120		
P1	200	P3	80		
P2	160				
P3	120				

46

PRINCIPAL LEARNING WALES	
GRADE	TARIFF POINTS
A*	210
A	180
B	150
C	120
D	90
E	60

47

PROGRESSION DIPLOMA	
GRADE	TARIFF POINTS
A*	350
A	300
B	250
C	200
D	150
E	100

Advanced Diploma = Progression Diploma plus Additional & Specialist Learning (ASL). Please see the appropriate qualification to calculate the ASL score

UCAS TARIFF TABLES

48

ROCKSCHOOL MUSIC PRACTITIONERS QUALIFICATIONS					
GRADE	TARIFF POINTS				
	Extended Diploma	Diploma	Subsidiary Diploma	Extended Certificate	Certificate
DISTINCTION	240	180	120	60	30
MERIT	160	120	80	40	20
PASS	80	60	40	20	10

49

SCOTTISH QUALIFICATIONS							
GRADE	TARIFF POINTS	GRADE	TARIFF POINTS	GRADE	TARIFF POINTS	GROUP	TARIFF POINTS
Advanced Higher		Higher		Scottish Interdisciplinary Project		Scottish National Certificates	
A	130	A	80	A	65	C	125
B	110	B	65	B	55	B	100
C	90	C	50	C	45	A	75
D	72	D	36				
Ungraded Higher		NPA PC Passport					
PASS	45	PASS	45				
		Core Skills					
		HIGHER	20				

Details of the subjects covered by each Scottish National Certificate can be found at www.ucas.com/students/ucas_tariff/tarifftables

50

SPEECH AND DRAMA EXAMINATIONS							
GRADE	TARIFF POINTS	GRADE	TARIFF POINTS	GRADE	TARIFF POINTS	GRADE	TARIFF POINTS
PCertLAM		Grade 8		Grade 7		Grade 6	
DISTINCTION	90	DISTINCTION	65	DISTINCTION	55	DISTINCTION	40
MERIT	80	MERIT	60	MERIT	50	MERIT	35
PASS	60	PASS	45	PASS	35	PASS	20

Details of the Speech and Drama Qualifications covered by the Tariff can be found at www.ucas.com/students/ucas_tariff/tarifftables

51

SPORTS LEADERS UK	
GRADE	TARIFF POINTS
PASS	30

These points are awarded to Higher Sports Leader Award and Level 3 Certificate in Higher Sports Leadership (QCF)

52

WELSH BACCALAUREATE ADVANCED DIPLOMA (CORE)	
GRADE	TARIFF POINTS
PASS	120

These points are awarded only when a candidate achieves the Welsh Baccalaureate Advanced Diploma

Results

4

Step 4 – Results

You should arrange your holidays so that you are at home when your exam results are published because, if there are any issues to discuss, admissions tutors will need to speak to you in person. We receive many UK exam results direct from the exam boards – check the list at www.ucas.com or www.cukas.ac.uk.

If your qualification is listed, we send your results to the universities, colleges or conservatoires that you have accepted as your firm and insurance choices through UCAS, or first and second choices if you applied through CUKAS. If your qualification is not listed, you must send your exam results to the universities, colleges or conservatoires where you are holding offers.

After you have received your exam results check Track to find out if you have a place on your chosen course.

If you have met all the conditions for your firm or first choice, the university, college or conservatoire will confirm that you have a place. Occasionally, they may still confirm you have a place even if you have not quite met all the offer conditions; or they may offer you a place on a similar course.

If you have not met the conditions of your firm or first choice and the university, college or conservatoire has not confirmed your place, but you have met all the conditions of your insurance or second offer, your insurance university, college or conservatoire will confirm that you have a place.

When a university, college or conservatoire tells us that you have a place, we send you confirmation by letter.

RE-MARKED EXAMS

If you ask for any of your exams to be re-marked, you must tell the universities, colleges or conservatoires where you're holding offers. If a university, college or conservatoire cannot confirm your place based on the initial results, you should ask them if they would be able to reconsider their decision after the re-mark. They are under no obligation to reconsider their position even if your re-mark results in higher grades. Don't forget that re-marks may also result in lower grades.

The exam boards tell us about any re-marks that result in grade changes. We then send the revised grades to the universities, colleges or conservatoires where you're holding offers. As soon as you know about any grade changes, you should also tell them.

'CASHING IN' A LEVEL RESULTS

If you have taken A levels, your school or college must certificate or 'cash in' all your unit scores before the exam board can award final grades. If when you collect your A level results you have to add up your unit scores to find out your final grades, this means your school or college has not 'cashed in' your results.

We receive only cashed in results from the exam boards, so if your school or college has not cashed in your results, you must ask them to send a 'cash in' request to the exam board. You also need to tell the universities, colleges or conservatoires where you're holding offers that there'll be a delay in receiving your results and call our Customer Service Unit to find out when your results have been received.

When we receive your 'cashed in' results from the exam board we send them straight away to the universities, colleges or conservatoires where you're holding offers.

WHAT IF YOU DON'T HAVE A PLACE?

UCAS only - If you have not met the conditions of either your firm or insurance choice, and your chosen universities or colleges have not confirmed your place, you are eligible for Clearing. In Clearing you can apply for any courses that still have vacancies (but remember that admissions tutors will still be reading your original statement). Clearing operates from mid-July to late September 2013 (page136).

BETTER RESULTS THAN EXPECTED?

UCAS only - If you obtain exam results that meet and exceed the conditions of the offer for your firm choice, you can for a short period use a process called Adjustment to look for an alternative place, whilst still keeping your original firm choice. See page 137 for information about Adjustment.

Next steps

Step 5 – Next steps

You might find yourself with different exam results than you were expecting, or you may change your mind about what you want to do. If so, there may be other options open to you.

CLEARING

Clearing is a service that helps people without a place find suitable course vacancies. It runs from mid-July until the end of September, but most people use it after the exam results are published in August.

You could consider related or alternative subjects or perhaps combining your original choice of subject with another. Your teachers or careers adviser, or the universities and colleges themselves, can provide useful guidance.

Course vacancies are listed at **www.ucas.com** and in the national media following the publication of exam results in August. **Once you have your exam results,**

if you're in Clearing you need to look at the vacancy listings and then contact any university or college you are interested in.

Talk to the institutions; don't be afraid to call them. Make sure you have your Personal ID and Clearing Number ready and prepare notes on what you will say to them about:

- why you want to study the course
- why you want to study at their university or college
- any relevant employment or activities you have done that relate to the course
- your grades.

Accepting an offer - you can contact as many universities and colleges as you like through Clearing, and you may informally be offered more than one place. If this happens, you will need to decide which offer you want to accept. If you're offered a place you want to be formally considered for, you enter the course details in

Track, and the university or college will then let you know if they're accepting you.

ADJUSTMENT

If you receive better results than expected, and meet and exceed the conditions of your conditional firm choice, you have the opportunity to reconsider what and where you want to study. This process is called Adjustment.

Adjustment runs from A level results day on 15 August 2013 until the end of August. Your individual Adjustment period starts on A level results day or when your conditional firm choice changes to unconditional firm, whichever is the later. You then have a maximum of five calendar days to register and secure an alternative course, if you decide you want to do this. If you want to try to find an alternative course you must register in Track to use Adjustment, so universities and colleges can view your application.

There are no vacancy listings for Adjustment, so you'll need to talk to the institutions. When you contact a university or college make it clear that you are applying through Adjustment, not Clearing. If they want to consider you they will ask for your Personal ID, so they can view your application.

If you don't find an alternative place then you remain accepted at your original firm choice.

Adjustment is entirely optional; remember that nothing really beats the careful research you carried out to find the right courses before you made your UCAS application. Talk to a careers adviser at your school, college or local careers office, as they can help you decide if registering to use Adjustment is right for you.

More information about Adjustment and Clearing is available at www.ucas.com. You can also view UCAStv video guides on how to use Adjustment and Clearing at www.ucas.tv.

CUKAS does not operate a Clearing or Adjustment service.

IF YOU ARE STILL WITHOUT A PLACE TO STUDY:

If you haven't found a suitable place, or changed your mind about what you want to do, there are lots of other options. Ask for advice from your school, college or careers office. Here are some suggestions you might want to consider:

- studying a part-time course (there's a part-time course search at www.ucas.com from July until September)
- studying a foundation degree
- re-sit your exams
- getting some work experience
- studying in another country
- reapplying next year to university or college through UCAS
- taking a gap year
- doing an apprenticeship (you'll find a vacancy search on the National Apprenticeship Service (NAS) website at **www.apprenticeships.org.uk**)
- finding a job
- starting a business.

More advice and links to other organisations can be found on the UCAS website at **www.ucas.com/students/nextsteps/advice**.

Starting at a
university, college
or conservatoire

Step 6 – Starting at a university, college or conservatoire

Congratulations! Now that you have confirmed your place at university, college or a conservatoire you will need to finalise your plans on how to get there, where to live and how to finance it. Make lists of things to do with deadlines and start contacting people whose help you can call on. Will you travel independently or call on your parents or relatives to help with transport? If you are keeping a car, have you checked out parking facilities and told your insurance company?

Make sure you have everything organised, including travel arrangements, essential documents and paperwork, books and equipment required for the course. The university or conservatoire will send you joining information – contact the Admissions Office or the Students' Union if you have questions about anything to do with starting your course.

Freshers week will help you settle in and make friends, but don't forget you are there to study. You may find the teaching methods rather alien at first, but remember there are plenty of sources of help, including your tutors, other students or student mentors, and the Students' Union.

Where to live - unless you are planning to live at home, your university, college or conservatoire will usually be able to provide you with guidance on finding somewhere to live. The earlier you contact them the better your chance of finding a suitable range of options, from hall to private landlords. Find out what facilities are available at the different types of accommodation and check whether it fits within your budget. Check what you need to bring with you and what is supplied. Don't leave it all to the last minute – especially things like arranging a bank account, checking what proof of identity you might need, gathering together a few essentials like supplies of a mug and coffee, insurance cover, TV licence etc.

Student finance - you will need to budget for living costs, accommodation, travel and books (and tuition fees if you are paying them up front). Learn about budgeting by visiting **www.ucas.com** or **www.cukas.ac.uk**, where you will find further links to useful resources to help you manage your money. Remember that if you do get into financial difficulties the welfare office at the institution can help you change tack and manage better in future, but it is always better to live within your means from the outset and if you need help, find it before the situation gets stressful.

Useful contacts

CONNECTING WITH UCAS

You can follow UCAS on Twitter at
www.twitter.com/ucas_online, and ask a question or
see what others are asking on Facebook at
www.facebook.com/ucasonline. You can also watch
videos of UCAS advisers answering frequently asked
questions on YouTube at
www.youtube.com/ucasonline.

There are many UCAStv video guides to help with your
journey into higher education, such as *How to choose
your courses, Attending events, Open days,* and
How to apply. These can all be viewed at
www.ucas.tv or in the relevant section of
www.ucas.com.

If you need to speak to UCAS, please contact the
Customer Service Unit on 0871 468 0 468 or 0044
871 468 0 468 from outside the UK. Calls from BT
landlines within the UK will cost no more than 9p per
minute. The cost of calls from mobiles and other
networks may vary.

If you have hearing difficulties, you can call the Text
Relay service on 18001 0871 468 0 468 (outside the
UK 0044 151 494 1260). Calls are charged at normal
rates.

CONTACTING CUKAS

If you need help or advice on your individual application, you can contact the CUKAS Customer Service Unit on 0871 468 0 470 (or 0044 871 468 0 470 from outside the UK). UK BT landline calls will cost no more than 9p per minute. Calls from mobiles and other networks may vary.

If you have hearing difficulties, call the Text Relay service on 18 001 0871 468 0 470 (0044 151 494 1260 outside the UK).

CAREERS ADVICE

The Directgov Careers Helpline for Young People is for you if you live in England, are aged 13 to 19 and want advice on getting to where you want to be in life.

Careers advisers can give you information, advice and practical help with all sorts of things, like choosing subjects at school or mapping out your future career options. They can help you with anything that might be affecting you at school, college, work or in your personal or family life.

Contact a careers adviser at
www.direct.gov.uk/en/youngpeople/index.htm.

Skills Development Scotland provides a starting point for anyone looking for careers information, advice or guidance.
www.myworldofwork.co.uk.

Careers Wales – Wales' national all-age careers guidance service.
www.careerswales.com
or **www.gyrfacymru.com**.

Northern Ireland Careers Service website for the new, all-age careers guidance service in Northern Ireland.
www.nidirect.gov.uk/careers.

If you're not sure what job you want or you need help to decide which course to do, give learndirect a call on 0800 101 901 or visit
www.learndirect.co.uk.

GENERAL HIGHER EDUCATION ADVICE

National Union of Students (NUS) is the national voice of students, helping them to campaign, get cheap student discounts and provide advice on living student life to the full - **www.nus.org.uk**.

STUDENTS WITH DISABILITIES

If you have a disability or specific learning difficulty, you are strongly encouraged to make early direct contact with individual institutions before submitting your application. Most universities and colleges have disability coordinators or advisers. You can find their contact details and further advice on the Disability Rights UK website - **www.disabilityalliance.org**.

There is financial help for students with disabilities, known as Disabled Students' Allowances (DSAs). More information is available on the Directgov website at
www.direct.gov.uk/disabledstudents.

YEAR OUT

For useful information on taking a year out, see
www.gap-year.com.

The Year Out Group website is packed with information and guidance for young people and their parents and advisers. **www.yearoutgroup.org**.

Essential reading

UCAS has brought together the best books and resources you need to make the important decisions regarding entry to higher education. With guidance on choosing courses, finding the right institution, information about student finance, admissions tests, gap years and lots more, you can find the most trusted guides at **www.ucasbooks.com**.

The publications listed on the following pages and many others are available through **www.ucasbooks.com** or from UCAS Publication Services unless otherwise stated.

UCAS PUBLICATION SERVICES
UCAS Publication Services
PO Box 130, Cheltenham, Gloucestershire GL52 3ZF

f: 01242 544 806
e: publicationservices@ucas.ac.uk
// www.ucasbooks.com

ENTIRE RESEARCH AND APPLICATION PROCESS EXPLAINED

The UCAS Guide to getting into University and College
This guide contains advice and up-to-date information about the entire research and application process, and brings together the expertise of UCAS staff, along with insights and tips from well known universities including Oxford and Cambridge, and students who are involved with or have experienced the process first-hand.

The book clearly sets out the information you need in an easy-to-read format, with myth busters, tips from students, checklists and much more; this book will be a companion for applicants throughout their entire journey into higher education.
Published by UCAS
Price £11.99
Publication date January 2011

NEED HELP COMPLETING YOUR APPLICATION?

How to Complete your UCAS Application 2013
A must for anyone applying through UCAS. Contains advice on the preparation needed, a step-by-step guide to filling out the UCAS application, information on the UCAS process and useful tips for completing the personal statement.
Published by Trotman
Price £12.99
Publication date May 2012

Insider's Guide to Applying to University
Full of honest insights, this is a thorough guide to the application process. It reveals advice from careers advisers and current students, guidance on making sense of university information and choosing courses. Also includes tips for the personal statement, interviews, admissions tests, UCAS Extra and Clearing.
Published by Trotman
Price £12.99
Publication date June 2011

How to Write a Winning UCAS Personal Statement
The personal statement is your chance to stand out from the crowd. Based on information from admissions tutors, this book will help you sell yourself. It includes specific guidance for over 30 popular subjects, common mistakes to avoid, information on what admissions tutors look for, and much more.
Published by Trotman
Price £12.99
Publication date March 2010

CHOOSING COURSES

Progression Series 2013 entry
The 'UCAS guide to getting into…' titles are designed to help you access good quality, useful information on some of the most competitive subject areas. The books cover advice on applying through UCAS, routes to qualifications, course details, job prospects, case studies and career advice.

New for 2013: information on the pros and cons of league tables and how to read them.

The UCAS Guide to getting into…
Art and Design
Economics, Finance and Accountancy
Engineering and Mathematics
Journalism, Broadcasting, Media Production and
  Performing Arts
Law
Medicine, Dentistry and Optometry
Nursing, Healthcare and Social Work
Psychology
Sports Science and Physiotherapy
Teaching and Education
Published by UCAS
Price £15.99 each
Publication date: June 2012

UCAS Parent Guide
Free of charge.
Order online at **www.ucas.com/parents**.
Publication date February 2012

Open Days 2012

Attending open days, taster courses and higher education conventions is an important part of the application process. This publication makes planning attendance at these events quick and easy.
Published annually by UCAS.
Price £3.50
Publication date January 2012

Heap 2013: University Degree Course Offers

An independent, reliable guide to selecting university degree courses in the UK.

The guide lists degree courses available at universities and colleges throughout the UK and the grades, UCAS points or equivalent that you need to achieve to get on to each course listed.

Published by Trotman
Price £32.99
Publication date May 2012

ESSENTIAL READING

Choosing Your Degree Course & University

With so many universities and courses to choose from, it is not an easy decision for students embarking on their journey to higher education. This guide will offer expert guidance on the questions students need to ask when considering the opportunities available.
Published by Trotman
Price £24.99
Publication date April 2012

Degree Course Descriptions

Providing details of the nature of degree courses, the descriptions in this book are written by heads of departments and senior lecturers at major universities. Each description contains an overview of the course area, details of course structures, career opportunities and more.
Published by COA
Price £12.99
Publication date September 2011

CHOOSING WHERE TO STUDY

The Virgin Guide to British Universities

An insider's guide to choosing a university or college. Written by students and using independent statistics, this guide evaluates what you get from a higher education institution.
Published by Virgin
Price £15.99
Publication date May 2011

Times Good University Guide 2013

How do you find the best university for the subject you wish to study? You need a guide that evaluates the quality of what is available, giving facts, figures and comparative assessments of universities. The rankings provide hard data, analysed, interpreted and presented by a team of experts.
Published by Harper Collins
Price £16.99
Publication date June 2012

A Parent's Guide to Graduate Jobs

A must-have guide for any parent who is worried about their child's job prospects when they graduate.

In this guide, the graduate careers guru, Paul Redmond, advises parents how to help their son or daughter:

- increase their employability
- boost their earning potential
- acquire essential work skills
- use their own contacts to get them ahead
- gain the right work experience.

Published by Trotman
Price £12.99
Publication date January 2012

Which Uni?

One person's perfect uni might be hell for someone else. Picking the right one will give you the best chance of future happiness, academic success and brighter job prospects. This guide is packed with tables from a variety of sources, rating universities on everything from the quality of teaching to the make-up of the student population and much more.
Published by Trotman
Price £14.99
Publication date September 2011

Getting into the UK's Best Universities and Courses

This book is for those who set their goals high and dream of studying on a highly regarded course at a good university. It provides information on selecting the best courses for a subject, the application and personal statement, interviews, results day, timescales for applications and much more.
Published by Trotman
Price £12.99
Publication date June 2011

FINANCIAL INFORMATION

Student Finance - e-book

All students need to know about tuition fees, loans, grants, bursaries and much more. Covering all forms of income and expenditure, this comprehensive guide is produced in association with UCAS and offers great value for money.
Published by Constable Robinson
Price £4.99
Publication date May 2012

CAREERS PLANNING

A-Z of Careers and Jobs

It is vital to be well informed about career decisions and this guide will help you make the right choice. It provides full details of the wide range of opportunities on the market, the personal qualities and skills needed for each job, entry qualifications and training, realistic salary expectations and useful contact details.
Published by Kogan Page
Price £16.99
Publication date March 2012

The Careers Directory

An indispensable resource for anyone seeking careers information, covering over 350 careers. It presents up-to-date information in an innovative double-page format. Ideal for students in years 10 to 13 who are considering their futures and for other careers professionals.
Published by COA
Price £14.99
Publication date September 2011

Careers with a Science Degree

Over 100 jobs and areas of work for graduates of biological, chemical and physical sciences are described in this guide.

Whether you have yet to choose your degree subject and want to know where the various choices could lead, or are struggling for ideas about what to do with your science degree, this book will guide and inspire you. The title includes: nature of the work and potential employers, qualifications required for entry, including personal qualities and skills; training routes and opportunities for career development and postgraduate study options.
Published by Lifetime Publishing
Price £12.99
Publication date September 2010

Careers with an Arts and Humanities Degree

Covers careers and graduate opportunities related to these degrees.

The book describes over 100 jobs and areas of work suitable for graduates from a range of disciplines including: English and modern languages, history and geography, music and the fine arts. The guide highlights: graduate opportunities, training routes, postgraduate study options and entry requirements.
Published by Lifetime Publishing
Price £12.99
Publication date September 2010

'Getting into...' guides

Clear and concise guides to help applicants secure places. They include qualifications required, advice on applying, tests, interviews and case studies. The guides give an honest view and discuss current issues and careers.

Getting into Oxford and Cambridge
Publication date April 2011
Getting into Veterinary School
Publication date February 2011
Published by Trotman
Price £12.99 each

DEFERRING ENTRY

Gap Years: The Essential Guide

The essential book for all young people planning a gap year before continuing with their education. This up-to-date guide provides essential information on specialist gap year programmes, as well as the vast range of jobs and voluntary opportunities available to young people around the world.
Published by Crimson Publishing
Price £9.99
Publication date April 2012

Gap Year Guidebook 2012

This thorough and easy-to-use guide contains everything you need to know before taking a gap year. It includes real-life traveller tips, hundreds of contact details, realistic advice on everything from preparing, learning and working abroad, coping with coming home and much more.
Published by John Catt Education
Price £14.99
Publication date November 2011

Summer Jobs Worldwide 2012
This unique and specialist guide contains over
40,000 jobs for all ages. No other book includes
such a variety and wealth of summer work
opportunities in Britain and aboard. Anything from
horse trainer in Iceland, to a guide for nature walks
in Peru, to a yoga centre helper in Greece, to an
animal keeper for London Zoo, can be found.
Published by Crimson Publishing
Price £14.99
Publication date November 2011

Please note all publications incur a postage and packing
charge. All information was correct at the time of
printing.

For a full list of publications, please visit
www.ucasbooks.com.

Courses

Courses

Keen to get started on your career in journalism, media or performing arts career? This section contains details of the various degree courses available at UK institutions.

EXPLAINING THE LIST OF COURSES

The list of courses has been divided into subject categories (see page 152).

We list the universities and colleges by their UCAS institution codes. Within each institution, courses are listed first by award type (such as BA, BSc, FdA, HND, MA and many others), then alphabetically by course title.

All practice-based music, drama, and dance courses offered through CUKAS can be found between pages 297 – 305.

You might find some courses showing an award type '(Mod)', which indicates a combined degree that might be modular in design. A small number of courses have award type '(FYr)'. This indicates a 12-month foundation course, after which students can choose to apply for a degree course. In either case, you should contact the university or college for further details.

Generally speaking, when a course comprises two or more subjects, the word used to connect the subjects indicates the make-up of the award: 'Subject A and Subject B' is a joint award, where both subjects carry equal weight; 'Subject A with Subject B' is a major/minor award, where Subject A accounts for at least 60% of your study. If the title shows 'Subject A/ Subject B', it may indicate that students can decide on the weighting of the subjects at the end of the first year. You should check with the university or college for full details.

Each entry shows the course code and the duration of the course. Where known, the entry contains details of the minimum qualification requirements for the course, as supplied to by the universities, colleges or conservatoires. Bear in mind that possessing the minimum qualifications does not guarantee acceptance to the course: there may be far more applicants than places. You may be asked to attend an interview or audition, present a portfolio or sit an admissions test.

Courses with entry requirements that require applicants to disclose information about spent and unspent convictions and may require a Criminal Records Bureau check, are marked '**CRB Check:** Required'.

Before applying for any course, you are advised to contact the institution to check any changes in entry requirements and to see if any new courses have come on stream since the lists were approved for publication. To make this easy, each institution's entry starts with their address, email, phone and fax details, as well as their website address. You will also find it useful to check the entry requirements section of Course Finder at **www.ucas.com** or **www.cukas.ac.uk**.

LIST OF SUBJECT CATEGORIES

The list of courses in this section has been divided into the following subject categories

PUBLICITY STUDIES

B22 UNIVERSITY OF BEDFORDSHIRE
PARK SQUARE
LUTON
BEDS LU1 3JU
t: 0844 8482234 f: 01582 489323
e: admissions@beds.ac.uk
// www.beds.ac.uk

PP25 BA Journalism and Public Relations
Duration: 3FT Hon
Entry Requirements: *Foundation:* Pass. *GCE:* 200. *SQAH:* BCC.
SQAAH: BCC. *IB:* 24. *OCR ND:* M1 *OCR NED:* P1 Interview
required.

P3P2 BA Media Practices with Public Relations
Duration: 3FT Hon
Entry Requirements: *Foundation:* Pass. *GCE:* 200. *SQAH:* BCC.
SQAAH: BCC. *IB:* 24. *OCR ND:* M1 *OCR NED:* P1

P210 BA Public Relations
Duration: 3FT Hon
Entry Requirements: *Foundation:* Pass. *GCE:* 200. *SQAH:* BCC.
SQAAH: BCC. *IB:* 24. *OCR ND:* M1 *OCR NED:* P1

P211 BA Public Relations
Duration: 4SW Hon
Entry Requirements: *Foundation:* Pass. *GCE:* 200. *SQAH:* BCC.
SQAAH: BCC. *IB:* 24. *OCR ND:* M1 *OCR NED:* P1

B25 BIRMINGHAM CITY UNIVERSITY
PERRY BARR
BIRMINGHAM B42 2SU
t: 0121 331 5595 f: 0121 331 7994
// www.bcu.ac.uk

P9P2 BA Media and Communication (Public Relations)
Duration: 3FT Hon
Entry Requirements: *Foundation:* Pass. *GCE:* BBC. *SQAH:* ABBB.
SQAAH: BBC. *IB:* 30.

B50 BOURNEMOUTH UNIVERSITY
TALBOT CAMPUS
FERN BARROW
POOLE
DORSET BH12 5BB
t: 01202 524111
// www.bournemouth.ac.uk

P210 BA Public Relations
Duration: 4SW Hon
Entry Requirements: *GCE:* 320. *IB:* 32. *BTEC SubDip:* M. *BTEC Dip:* DM. *BTEC ExtDip:* DDM.

B80 UNIVERSITY OF THE WEST OF ENGLAND, BRISTOL
FRENCHAY CAMPUS
COLDHARBOUR LANE
BRISTOL BS16 1QY
t: +44 (0)117 32 83333 f: +44 (0)117 32 82810
e: admissions@uwe.ac.uk
// www.uwe.ac.uk

PP52 BA (Hons) Journalism and Public Relations
Duration: 3FT Hon
Entry Requirements: Contact the institution for details.

B94 BUCKINGHAMSHIRE NEW UNIVERSITY
QUEEN ALEXANDRA ROAD
HIGH WYCOMBE
BUCKINGHAMSHIRE HP11 2JZ
t: 0800 0565 660 f: 01494 605 023
e: admissions@bucks.ac.uk
// bucks.ac.uk

PN25 BA Public Relations and Marketing Communications
Duration: 3FT Hon
Entry Requirements: *GCE:* 200-240. *IB:* 24. *OCR ND:* M1 *OCR NED:* M3

C10 CANTERBURY CHRIST CHURCH UNIVERSITY
NORTH HOLMES ROAD
CANTERBURY
KENT CT1 1QU
t: 01227 782900 f: 01227 782888
e: admissions@canterbury.ac.uk
// www.canterbury.ac.uk

N1PJ BA Entrepreneurship with Film, Radio & Television Studies
Duration: 3FT Hon
Entry Requirements: *GCE:* 240. *IB:* 24.

PP23 BA Public Relations, Media and Marketing
Duration: 3FT Hon
Entry Requirements: *GCE:* 240. *IB:* 24.

C30 UNIVERSITY OF CENTRAL LANCASHIRE
PRESTON
LANCS PR1 2HE
t: 01772 201201 f: 01772 894954
e: uadmissions@uclan.ac.uk
// www.uclan.ac.uk

NPF2 BA Management and Public Relations
Duration: 3FT Hon
Entry Requirements: *GCE:* 240-280. *SQAH:* AABB-BBBC. *IB:* 28. *OCR ND:* D

NP52 BA Marketing and Public Relations
Duration: 3FT Hon
Entry Requirements: *GCE:* 240-280. *SQAH:* AABB-BBBC. *IB:* 28.
OCR ND: D

P211 BA Public Relations
Duration: 3FT Hon
Entry Requirements: *GCE:* 260-300. *SQAH:* AABB-BBBC. *IB:* 28.
OCR ND: D

P213 BA Public Relations (Business Communication)
Duration: 4SW Deg
Entry Requirements: *GCE:* 260-300. *SQAH:* AABB-BBBC. *IB:* 28.
OCR ND: D

P218 BA Public Relations (Business Communication)
Duration: 3FT Hon
Entry Requirements: *GCE:* 260-300. *SQAH:* AABB-BBBC. *IB:* 28.
OCR ND: D

P2L2 BA Public Relations (Business Communication) with International Study
Duration: 4SW Hon
Entry Requirements: *GCE:* 260-300. *SQAH:* AABB-BBBC. *IB:* 28.
OCR ND: D

P215 BA Public Relations (Entertainment)
Duration: 4SW Hon
Entry Requirements: *GCE:* 260-300. *SQAH:* AABB-BBBC. *IB:* 28.
OCR ND: D

P222 BA Public Relations (Entertainment)
Duration: 3FT Hon
Entry Requirements: *GCE:* 260-300. *SQAH:* AABB-BBBC. *IB:* 28.
OCR ND: D

L2P2 BA Public Relations (Entertainment) with International Study
Duration: 4SW Hon
Entry Requirements: *GCE:* 260-300. *SQAH:* AABB-BBBC. *IB:* 28.
OCR ND: D

P214 BA Public Relations (Political Communication)
Duration: 3FT Hon
Entry Requirements: *GCE:* 260-300. *SQAH:* AABB-BBBC. *IB:* 28.
OCR ND: D

P219 BA Public Relations (Political Communication)
Duration: 4SW Hon
Entry Requirements: *GCE:* 260-300. *SQAH:* AABB-BBBC. *IB:* 28.
OCR ND: D

P2LF BA Public Relations (Political Communication) with International Study
Duration: 4SW Hon
Entry Requirements: *GCE:* 260-300. *SQAH:* AABB-BBBC. *IB:* 28.
OCR ND: D

P210 BA Public Relations (Sandwich)
Duration: 4SW Hon
Entry Requirements: *GCE:* 260-300. *SQAH:* AABB-BBBC. *IB:* 28.
OCR ND: D

P216 BA Public Relations (Sports)
Duration: 4SW Hon
Entry Requirements: *GCE:* 260-300. *SQAH:* AABB-BBBC. *IB:* 28.
OCR ND: D

P221 BA Public Relations (Sports)
Duration: 3FT Hon
Entry Requirements: *GCE:* 260-300. *SQAH:* AABB-BBBC. *IB:* 28.
OCR ND: D

L2PG BA Public Relations (Sports) with International Study
Duration: 4SW Hon
Entry Requirements: *GCE:* 260-300. *SQAH:* AABB-BBBC. *IB:* 28.
OCR ND: D

NP22 BA Public Relations and Management
Duration: 3FT Hon
Entry Requirements: *GCE:* 240-280. *SQAH:* AABB-BBBC. *IB:* 28.
OCR ND: D

NPM2 BA Public Relations and Marketing
Duration: 3FT Hon
Entry Requirements: *GCE:* 240-280. *SQAH:* AABB-BBBC. *IB:* 28.
OCR ND: D

P220 BA Public Relations with International Study
Duration: 4SW Hon
Entry Requirements: *GCE:* 260-300. *SQAH:* AABB-BBBC. *IB:* 28.
OCR ND: D

C55 UNIVERSITY OF CHESTER
PARKGATE ROAD
CHESTER CH1 4BJ
t: 01244 511000 f: 01244 511300
e: enquiries@chester.ac.uk
// www.chester.ac.uk

NP22 BA Business Management and Marketing & Public Relations
Duration: 3FT Hon
Entry Requirements: Contact the institution for details.

PNF5 BA Marketing & Public Relations and Advertising
Duration: 3FT Hon
Entry Requirements: *GCE:* 240-280. *SQAH:* BBBB. *IB:* 26.

PW23 BA Marketing & Public Relations and Commercial Music Production
Duration: 3FT Hon
Entry Requirements: *Foundation:* Pass. *GCE:* 260-300. *SQAH:* BBBB. *IB:* 28.

PW26 BA Marketing & Public Relations and Digital Photography
Duration: 3FT Hon
Entry Requirements: *GCE:* 240-280. *SQAH:* BBBB. *IB:* 26.

NP52 BA Marketing & Public Relations and Events Management
Duration: 3FT Hon
Entry Requirements: *GCE:* 240-280. *SQAH:* BBBB. *IB:* 26.

PPFH BA Marketing & Public Relations and Film Studies
Duration: 3FT Hon
Entry Requirements: *GCE:* 240-280. *SQAH:* BBBB. *IB:* 26.

PPF5 BA Marketing & Public Relations and Journalism
Duration: 3FT Hon
Entry Requirements: *GCE:* 240-280. *SQAH:* BBBB. *IB:* 26.

PPFJ BA Marketing & Public Relations and Media Studies
Duration: 3FT Hon
Entry Requirements: *GCE:* 240-280. *SQAH:* BBBB. *IB:* 26.

PN21 BA Marketing & Public Relations and Radio Production
Duration: 3FT Hon
Entry Requirements: *Foundation:* Pass. *GCE:* 260-300. *SQAH:* BBBB. *IB:* 28.

PC2P BA Marketing & Public Relations and Sport Development
Duration: 3FT Hon
Entry Requirements: *GCE:* 240-280. *SQAH:* BBBB. *IB:* 26.

PP2I BA Marketing & Public Relations and Television Production
Duration: 3FT Hon
Entry Requirements: *Foundation:* Pass. *GCE:* 260-300. *SQAH:* BBBB. *IB:* 28.

E42 EDGE HILL UNIVERSITY
ORMSKIRK
LANCASHIRE L39 4QP
t: 01695 657000 f: 01695 584355
e: study@edgehill.ac.uk
// www.edgehill.ac.uk

P210 BA Public Relations
Duration: 3FT Hon
Entry Requirements: *GCE:* 280. *IB:* 26. *OCR ND:* D *OCR NED:* M2

NP52 BSc Marketing with Public Relations
Duration: 3FT Hon
Entry Requirements: *GCE:* 280. *IB:* 26. *OCR ND:* D *OCR NED:* M2

E59 EDINBURGH NAPIER UNIVERSITY
CRAIGLOCKHART CAMPUS
EDINBURGH EH14 1DJ
t: +44 (0)8452 60 60 40 f: 0131 455 6464
e: info@napier.ac.uk
// www.napier.ac.uk

PN35 BA Communication, Advertising and Public Relations
Duration: 3FT/4FT Ord/Hon
Entry Requirements: Contact the institution for details.

G14 UNIVERSITY OF GLAMORGAN, CARDIFF AND PONTYPRIDD
ENQUIRIES AND ADMISSIONS UNIT
PONTYPRIDD CF37 1DL
t: 08456 434030 f: 01443 654050
e: enquiries@glam.ac.uk
// www.glam.ac.uk

JP92 BSc Live Event Technology
Duration: 3FT Hon
Entry Requirements: *GCE:* BBC. *IB:* 25. *BTEC SubDip:* M. *BTEC Dip:* D*D. *BTEC ExtDip:* DMM. Interview required.

G70 UNIVERSITY OF GREENWICH
GREENWICH CAMPUS
OLD ROYAL NAVAL COLLEGE
PARK ROW
LONDON SE10 9LS
t: 020 8331 9000 f: 020 8331 8145
e: courseinfo@gre.ac.uk
// www.gre.ac.uk

P210 BA Public Relations and Communications
Duration: 3FT Hon
Entry Requirements: *GCE:* 280. *IB:* 24.

H60 THE UNIVERSITY OF HUDDERSFIELD
QUEENSGATE
HUDDERSFIELD HD1 3DH
t: 01484 473969 f: 01484 472765
e: admissionsandrecords@hud.ac.uk
// www.hud.ac.uk

WP22 BA Fashion, Communication and Promotion
Duration: 3FT/4SW Hon
Entry Requirements: *GCE:* 300. *SQAH:* BBBB. *IB:* 28. Interview required. Portfolio required.

N5P2 BA Marketing with Public Relations
Duration: 4SW/3FT Hon
Entry Requirements: *GCE:* 300. Interview required.

WP3F BA Music and Promotion
Duration: 3FT Hon
Entry Requirements: *GCE:* 240. *BTEC ExtDip:* MMM. Interview required.

L23 UNIVERSITY OF LEEDS
THE UNIVERSITY OF LEEDS
WOODHOUSE LANE
LEEDS LS2 9JT
t: 0113 343 3999
e: admissions@leeds.ac.uk
// www.leeds.ac.uk

P900 BA Communications and Media
Duration: 3FT Hon
Entry Requirements: *GCE:* ABB. *SQAH:* AAABB. *SQAAH:* ABB. *IB:* 34.

P390 BA New Media
Duration: 3FT Hon
Entry Requirements: *GCE:* BBB. *SQAH:* AAABB-AABBB. *SQAAH:* BBB. *IB:* 32.

L27 LEEDS METROPOLITAN UNIVERSITY
COURSE ENQUIRIES OFFICE
CITY CAMPUS
LEEDS LS1 3HE
t: 0113 81 23113 f: 0113 81 23129
// www.leedsmet.ac.uk

P210 BA Public Relations
Duration: 3FT/4SW Hon
Entry Requirements: *GCE:* 260. *IB:* 26.

P2N5 BA Public Relations with Marketing
Duration: 3FT/4SW Hon
Entry Requirements: *GCE:* 260. *IB:* 26.

RP42 BA Spanish and Public Relations
Duration: 3FT/4SW Hon
Entry Requirements: *GCE:* 220. *IB:* 26.

L39 UNIVERSITY OF LINCOLN
ADMISSIONS
BRAYFORD POOL
LINCOLN LN6 7TS
t: 01522 886097 f: 01522 886146
e: admissions@lincoln.ac.uk
// www.lincoln.ac.uk

PN25 BA Advertising and Marketing
Duration: 3FT Hon
Entry Requirements: *GCE:* 260.

PP52 BA Journalism and Public Relations
Duration: 3FT Hon
Entry Requirements: *GCE:* 280.

L51 LIVERPOOL JOHN MOORES UNIVERSITY
KINGSWAY HOUSE
HATTON GARDEN
LIVERPOOL L3 2AJ
t: 0151 231 5090 f: 0151 904 6368
e: courses@ljmu.ac.uk
// www.ljmu.ac.uk

NP12 BA Business and Public Relations
Duration: 3FT/4SW Hon
Entry Requirements: *GCE:* 260. *IB:* 28.

L68 LONDON METROPOLITAN UNIVERSITY
166-220 HOLLOWAY ROAD
LONDON N7 8DB
t: 020 7133 4200
e: admissions@londonmet.ac.uk
// www.londonmet.ac.uk

NPM2 BA Advertising, Marketing Communication and Public Relations
Duration: 3FT Hon
Entry Requirements: *GCE:* 240. *IB:* 28.

NP82 BA Events Management and Public Relations
Duration: 3FT Hon
Entry Requirements: *GCE:* 240. *IB:* 28.

P210 BA Public Relations
Duration: 3FT Hon
Entry Requirements: *GCE:* 240. *IB:* 28.

M40 THE MANCHESTER METROPOLITAN UNIVERSITY
ADMISSIONS OFFICE
ALL SAINTS (GMS)
ALL SAINTS
MANCHESTER M15 6BH
t: 0161 247 2000
// www.mmu.ac.uk

NP52 BA Public Relations and Digital Communications Management
Duration: 3FT Hon
Entry Requirements: *IB:* 29.

PP21 BA Public Relations and Digital Communications Management (Exchange)
Duration: 4FT Hon
Entry Requirements: *IB:* 29.

NP5F BA Public Relations and Digital Communications Management (Sandwich)
Duration: 4SW Hon
Entry Requirements: *IB:* 29.

N77 NORTHUMBRIA UNIVERSITY
TRINITY BUILDING
NORTHUMBERLAND ROAD
NEWCASTLE UPON TYNE NE1 8ST
t: 0191 243 7420 f: 0191 227 4561
e: er.admissions@northumbria.ac.uk
// www.northumbria.ac.uk

P3P2 BA Hons Mass Communications with Public Relations
Duration: 3FT Hon
Entry Requirements: Contact the institution for details.

PP92 BSc Communication and Public Relations
Duration: 3FT Hon
Entry Requirements: *GCE:* 280. *SQAH:* BBCCC. *SQAAH:* BCC. *IB:* 25. *BTEC Dip:* D*D*. *BTEC ExtDip:* DMM. *OCR NED:* M2

Q25 QUEEN MARGARET UNIVERSITY, EDINBURGH
QUEEN MARGARET UNIVERSITY DRIVE
EDINBURGH EH21 6UU
t: 0131474 0000 f: 0131 474 0001
e: admissions@qmu.ac.uk
// www.qmu.ac.uk

PN25 BA Public Relations and Marketing
Duration: 4FT Hon
Entry Requirements: *GCE:* 260. *IB:* 28.

PP23 BA Public Relations and Media
Duration: 4FT Hon
Entry Requirements: *GCE:* 260. *IB:* 28.

R36 ROBERT GORDON UNIVERSITY
ROBERT GORDON UNIVERSITY
SCHOOLHILL
ABERDEEN
SCOTLAND AB10 1FR
t: 01224 26 27 28 f: 01224 26 21 47
e: UGOffice@rgu.ac.uk
// www.rgu.ac.uk

P9P2 BA Communication with Public Relations
Duration: 4FT Hon
Entry Requirements: *GCE:* CCC. *SQAH:* BBCC. *IB:* 26.

P210 BA (Hons) Public Relations
Duration: 4FT Hon
Entry Requirements: Contact the institution for details.

S21 SHEFFIELD HALLAM UNIVERSITY
CITY CAMPUS
HOWARD STREET
SHEFFIELD S1 1WB
t: 0114 225 5555 f: 0114 225 2167
e: admissions@shu.ac.uk
// www.shu.ac.uk

P210 BA Public Relations
Duration: 3FT Hon
Entry Requirements: *GCE:* 260.

PP23 BA Public Relations and Media
Duration: 3FT Hon
Entry Requirements: *GCE:* 260.

S28 SOMERSET COLLEGE OF ARTS AND TECHNOLOGY
WELLINGTON ROAD
TAUNTON
SOMERSET TA1 5AX
t: 01823 366331 f: 01823 366418
e: enquiries@somerset.ac.uk
// www.somerset.ac.uk/student-area/considering-a-degree.html

P240 BA Design: Advertising (Top-Up)
Duration: 1FT Hon
Entry Requirements: HND required.

S30 SOUTHAMPTON SOLENT UNIVERSITY
EAST PARK TERRACE
SOUTHAMPTON
HAMPSHIRE SO14 0RT
t: +44 (0) 23 8031 9039 f: + 44 (0)23 8022 2259
e: admissions@solent.ac.uk
// www.solent.ac.uk/

PN25 BA Advertising and Public Relations (Top-Up)
Duration: 1FT Hon
Entry Requirements: Interview required. HND required.

QP32 BA English and Public Relations
Duration: 3FT Hon
Entry Requirements: *Foundation:* Distinction. *GCE:* 240. *SQAAH:* AA-CCD. *IB:* 24. *BTEC ExtDip:* MMM. *OCR ND:* D *OCR NED:* M3

QP3F BA English and Public Relations
Duration: 4SW Hon
Entry Requirements: *Foundation:* Distinction. *GCE:* 240. *SQAAH:* AA-CCD. *IB:* 24. *BTEC ExtDip:* MMM. *OCR ND:* D *OCR NED:* M3

W2P2 BA Fashion with Public Relations
Duration: 3FT Hon
Entry Requirements: *Foundation:* Distinction. *GCE:* 240. *SQAAH:* AA-CCD. *IB:* 24. *BTEC ExtDip:* MMM. *OCR ND:* D *OCR NED:* M3
Portfolio required.

PH26 BA Public Relations and Communication
Duration: 3FT Hon
Entry Requirements: *Foundation:* Distinction. *GCE:* 240. *SQAAH:* AA-CCD. *IB:* 24. *BTEC ExtDip:* MMM. *OCR ND:* D *OCR NED:* M3

P2Q3 BA Public Relations and Communications with International Foundation Year
Duration: 4FT Hon
Entry Requirements: *GCE:* 240.

S72 STAFFORDSHIRE UNIVERSITY
COLLEGE ROAD
STOKE ON TRENT ST4 2DE
t: 01782 292753 f: 01782 292740
e: admissions@staffs.ac.uk
// www.staffs.ac.uk

PP25 BA Sports PR and Journalism
Duration: 3FT Hon
Entry Requirements: *GCE:* 260.

S84 UNIVERSITY OF SUNDERLAND
STUDENT HELPLINE
THE STUDENT GATEWAY
CHESTER ROAD
SUNDERLAND SR1 3SD
t: 0191 515 3000 f: 0191 515 3805
e: student.helpline@sunderland.ac.uk
// www.sunderland.ac.uk

NP12 BA Business Management and Public Relations
Duration: 3FT Hon
Entry Requirements: *GCE:* 260-360. *OCR ND:* D *OCR NED:* M3

N1P2 BA Business Management with Public Relations
Duration: 3FT Hon
Entry Requirements: *GCE:* 260-360. *OCR ND:* D *OCR NED:* M3

XPH2 BA Childhood Studies and Public Relations
Duration: 3FT Hon
Entry Requirements: *GCE:* 260-360.

X3P2 BA Childhood Studies with Public Relations
Duration: 3FT Hon
Entry Requirements: Contact the institution for details.

MP92 BA Criminology and Public Relations
Duration: 3FT Hon
Entry Requirements: *GCE:* 260-360. *OCR ND:* D *OCR NED:* M3

M9P2 BA Criminology with Public Relations
Duration: 3FT Hon
Entry Requirements: *GCE:* 260-360. *OCR ND:* D *OCR NED:* M3

PW25 BA Dance and Public Relations
Duration: 3FT Hon
Entry Requirements: *GCE:* 260-360. *IB:* 31. *OCR ND:* D *OCR NED:* M3

W5P2 BA Dance with Public Relations
Duration: 3FT Hon
Entry Requirements: *GCE:* 260-360. *IB:* 31. *OCR ND:* D *OCR NED:* M3

W4P2 BA Drama with Public Relations
Duration: 3FT Hon
Entry Requirements: *GCE:* 260-360. *OCR ND:* D *OCR NED:* M3

Q1P2 BA English Language & Linguistics with Public Relations
Duration: 3FT Hon
Entry Requirements: *GCE:* 260-360. *OCR ND:* D *OCR NED:* M3

Q3P2 BA English with Public Relations
Duration: 3FT Hon
Entry Requirements: *GCE:* 260-360. *OCR ND:* D *OCR NED:* M3

LP52 BA Health & Social Care and Public Relations
Duration: 3FT Hon
Entry Requirements: *GCE:* 260-360.

L5P2 BA Health & Social Care with Public Relations
Duration: 3FT Hon
Entry Requirements: Contact the institution for details.

MP12 BA Law and Public Relations
Duration: 3FT Hon
Entry Requirements: *GCE:* 260-360. *OCR ND:* D *OCR NED:* M3

RP12 BA Modern Foreign Languages (French) and Public Relations
Duration: 3FT Hon
Entry Requirements: *GCE:* 260-360. *IB:* 31. *OCR ND:* D *OCR NED:* M3

PR22 BA Modern Foreign Languages (German) and Public Relations
Duration: 3FT Hon
Entry Requirements: *GCE:* 260-360. *IB:* 31. *OCR ND:* D *OCR NED:* M3

PR24 BA Modern Foreign Languages (Spanish) and Public Relations
Duration: 3FT Hon
Entry Requirements: *GCE:* 260-360. *IB:* 31. *OCR ND:* D *OCR NED:* M3

L2P2 BA Politics with Public Relations
Duration: 3FT Hon
Entry Requirements: *GCE:* 260-360. *OCR ND:* D *OCR NED:* M3

P210 BA Public Relations
Duration: 3FT Hon
Entry Requirements: *GCE:* 260-360. *IB:* 30.

PN21 BA Public Relations and Business Management
Duration: 3FT Hon
Entry Requirements: *GCE:* 260-360. *OCR ND:* D *OCR NED:* M3

PM29 BA Public Relations and Criminology
Duration: 3FT Hon
Entry Requirements: *GCE:* 260-360. *OCR ND:* D *OCR NED:* M3

PW24 BA Public Relations and Drama
Duration: 3FT Hon
Entry Requirements: *GCE:* 260-360. *OCR ND:* D *OCR NED:* M3

PX23 BA Public Relations and Education
Duration: 3FT Hon
Entry Requirements: *GCE:* 260-360. *OCR ND:* D *OCR NED:* M3

PQ23 BA Public Relations and English
Duration: 3FT Hon
Entry Requirements: *GCE:* 260-360. *IB:* 31. *OCR ND:* D *OCR NED:* M3

PQ21 BA Public Relations and English Language/Linguistics
Duration: 3FT Hon
Entry Requirements: *GCE:* 260-360. *OCR ND:* D *OCR NED:* M3

PV21 BA Public Relations and History
Duration: 3FT Hon
Entry Requirements: *GCE:* 260-360. *OCR ND:* D *OCR NED:* M3

PP25 BA Public Relations and Journalism
Duration: 3FT Hon
Entry Requirements: *GCE:* 260-360. *OCR ND:* D *OCR NED:* M3

PW26 BA Public Relations and Photography
Duration: 3FT Hon
Entry Requirements: *GCE:* 260-360. *OCR ND:* D *OCR NED:* M3

PL22 BA Public Relations and Politics
Duration: 3FT Hon
Entry Requirements: *GCE:* 260-360. *OCR ND:* D *OCR NED:* M3

PC28 BA Public Relations and Psychology
Duration: 3FT Hon
Entry Requirements: *GCE:* 260-360. *IB:* 31. *OCR ND:* D *OCR NED:* M3

PL23 BA Public Relations and Sociology
Duration: 3FT Hon
Entry Requirements: *GCE:* 260-360. *OCR ND:* D *OCR NED:* M3

PX21 BA Public Relations and TESOL
Duration: 3FT Hon
Entry Requirements: *GCE:* 260-360. *OCR ND:* D *OCR NED:* M3

P2N1 BA Public Relations with Business Management
Duration: 3FT Hon
Entry Requirements: *GCE:* 260-360. *OCR ND:* D *OCR NED:* M3

P2XH BA Public Relations with Childhood Studies
Duration: 3FT Hon
Entry Requirements: *GCE:* 260-360.

P2M9 BA Public Relations with Criminology
Duration: 3FT Hon
Entry Requirements: *GCE:* 260-360. *OCR ND:* D *OCR NED:* M3

P2W5 BA Public Relations with Dance
Duration: 3FT Hon
Entry Requirements: *GCE:* 260-360. *IB:* 31. *OCR ND:* D *OCR NED:* M3

P2W4 BA Public Relations with Drama
Duration: 3FT Hon
Entry Requirements: *GCE:* 260-360. *OCR ND:* D *OCR NED:* M3

P2X3 BA Public Relations with Education
Duration: 3FT Hon
Entry Requirements: *GCE:* 260-360. *OCR ND:* D *OCR NED:* M3

P2Q3 BA Public Relations with English
Duration: 3FT Hon
Entry Requirements: *GCE:* 260-360. *OCR ND:* D *OCR NED:* M3

P2Q1 BA Public Relations with English Language/Linguistics
Duration: 3FT Hon
Entry Requirements: *GCE:* 260-360. *OCR ND:* D *OCR NED:* M3

P2L5 BA Public Relations with Health & Social Care
Duration: 3FT Hon
Entry Requirements: *GCE:* 260-360.

P2V1 BA Public Relations with History
Duration: 3FT Hon
Entry Requirements: *GCE:* 260-360. *OCR ND:* D *OCR NED:* M3

P2P5 BA Public Relations with Journalism
Duration: 3FT Hon
Entry Requirements: *GCE:* 260-360. *OCR ND:* D *OCR NED:* M3

P2R1 BA Public Relations with Modern Foreign Languages (French)
Duration: 3FT Hon
Entry Requirements: *GCE:* 260-360. *OCR ND:* D *OCR NED:* M3

P2R2 BA Public Relations with Modern Foreign Languages (German)
Duration: 3FT Hon
Entry Requirements: *GCE:* 260-360. *OCR ND:* D *OCR NED:* M3

P2W6 BA Public Relations with Photography
Duration: 3FT Hon
Entry Requirements: *GCE:* 260-360. *OCR ND:* D *OCR NED:* M3

P2L2 BA Public Relations with Politics
Duration: 3FT Hon
Entry Requirements: *GCE:* 220-360. *OCR ND:* D *OCR NED:* M3

P2L3 BA Public Relations with Sociology
Duration: 3FT Hon
Entry Requirements: *GCE:* 260-360. *OCR ND:* D *OCR NED:* M3

P2C6 BA Public Relations with Sport
Duration: 3FT Hon
Entry Requirements: *GCE:* 260-360. *OCR ND:* D *OCR NED:* M3

P2X1 BA Public Relations with TESOL
Duration: 3FT Hon
Entry Requirements: *GCE:* 260-360. *OCR ND:* D *OCR NED:* M3

X1P2 BA TESOL with Public Relations
Duration: 3FT Hon
Entry Requirements: *GCE:* 260-360. *OCR ND:* D *OCR NED:* M3

NP82 BA Tourism and Public Relations
Duration: 3FT Hon
Entry Requirements: *GCE:* 260-360. *IB:* 31. *OCR ND:* D *OCR NED:* M3

N8P2 BA Tourism with Public Relations
Duration: 3FT Hon
Entry Requirements: *GCE:* 220-360. *IB:* 31. *OCR ND:* D *OCR NED:* M3

P2C8 BA/BSc Public Relations with Psychology
Duration: 3FT Hon
Entry Requirements: *GCE:* 260-360. *OCR ND:* D *OCR NED:* M3

CP62 BA/BSc Sport and Public Relations
Duration: 3FT Hon
Entry Requirements: *GCE:* 260-360. *OCR ND:* D *OCR NED:* M3

C6P2 BSc Sport with Public Relations
Duration: 3FT Hon
Entry Requirements: *GCE:* 260-360. *OCR ND:* D *OCR NED:* M3

U20 UNIVERSITY OF ULSTER
COLERAINE
CO. LONDONDERRY
NORTHERN IRELAND BT52 1SA
t: 028 7012 4221 f: 028 7012 4908
e: online@ulster.ac.uk
// www.ulster.ac.uk

P9P2 BSc Communication with Public Relations
Duration: 3FT Hon
Entry Requirements: *GCE:* 260-280. *IB:* 24.

P2N5 BSc Communication, Advertising and Marketing
Duration: 4SW Hon
Entry Requirements: *GCE:* AAA. *SQAH:* AAAAA. *SQAAH:* AAA. *IB:* 39.

Q9P2 BSc Language & Linguistics with Public Relations
Duration: 3FT Hon
Entry Requirements: *GCE:* 260-280. *IB:* 24.

P210 BSc Public Relations (DPP)
Duration: 4SW Hon
Entry Requirements: *GCE:* 320-340.

U65 UNIVERSITY OF THE ARTS LONDON
272 HIGH HOLBORN
LONDON WC1V 7EY
t: 020 7514 6000x6197 f: 020 7514 6198
e: c.anderson@arts.ac.uk
// www.arts.ac.uk

WP22 BA Fashion Public Relations
Duration: 3FT Hon
Entry Requirements: *IB:* 28. Interview required.

P210 BA Public Relations
Duration: 3FT Hon
Entry Requirements: *IB:* 28. Foundation Course required. Interview required. Portfolio required.

W05 THE UNIVERSITY OF WEST LONDON
ST MARY'S ROAD
EALING
LONDON W5 5RF
t: 0800 036 8888 f: 020 8566 1353
e: learning.advice@uwl.ac.uk
// www.uwl.ac.uk

P210 BA Public Relations
Duration: 3FT Hon
Entry Requirements: *GCE:* 240. Interview required.

W50 UNIVERSITY OF WESTMINSTER
2ND FLOOR, CAVENDISH HOUSE
101 NEW CAVENDISH STREET,
LONDON W1W 6XH
t: 020 7915 5511
e: course-enquiries@westminster.ac.uk
// www.westminster.ac.uk

P210 BA Public Relations
Duration: 3FT Hon
Entry Requirements: *GCE:* BBB. *SQAH:* AAAAA-BBBBB. *SQAAH:* AAA-BBB. *IB:* 30. *OCR ND:* D *OCR NED:* D2 Interview required.

W80 UNIVERSITY OF WORCESTER
HENWICK GROVE
WORCESTER WR2 6AJ
t: 01905 855111 f: 01905 855377
e: admissions@worc.ac.uk
// www.worcester.ac.uk

NP52 BA Business, Advertising & Public Relations
Duration: 3FT/4SW Hon
Entry Requirements: *GCE:* 280. *IB:* 25. *OCR ND:* D *OCR NED:* M3

NP21 BA Business, Entrepreneurship & Public Relations
Duration: 3FT/4SW Hon
Entry Requirements: *GCE:* 280. *IB:* 25. *OCR ND:* D *OCR NED:* M3

NP62 BA Business, Human Resource Management & Public Relations
Duration: 3FT/4SW Hon
Entry Requirements: *GCE:* 280. *IB:* 25. *OCR ND:* D *OCR NED:* M3

NP22 BA Business, Management & Public Relations
Duration: 3FT/4SW Hon
Entry Requirements: *GCE:* 280. *IB:* 25. *OCR ND:* D *OCR NED:* M3

NP5F BA Marketing, Advertising & Public Relations
Duration: 3FT/4SW Hon
Entry Requirements: *GCE:* 280. *IB:* 25. *OCR ND:* D *OCR NED:* M3

MEDIA STUDIES

A40 ABERYSTWYTH UNIVERSITY
ABERYSTWYTH UNIVERSITY, WELCOME CENTRE
PENGLAIS CAMPUS
ABERYSTWYTH
CEREDIGION SY23 3FB
t: 01970 622021 f: 01970 627410
e: ug-admissions@aber.ac.uk
// www.aber.ac.uk

VP1H BA Hanes a'r Cyfryngau
Duration: 3FT Hon
Entry Requirements: *GCE:* 300. *IB:* 29.

VP13 BA History and Media
Duration: 3FT Hon
Entry Requirements: *GCE:* 300. *IB:* 30.

QP5H BA Irish Language & Literature/Film & Television Studies
Duration: 4SW Hon
Entry Requirements: *GCE:* 300-320. *IB:* 32.

P300 BA Media and Communication Studies
Duration: 3FT Hon
Entry Requirements: *GCE:* 300-320.

A44 ACCRINGTON & ROSSENDALE COLLEGE
BROAD OAK ROAD,
ACCRINGTON,
LANCASHIRE, BB5 2AW.
t: 01254 389933 f: 01254 354001
e: info@accross.ac.uk
// www.accrosshighereducation.co.uk/

PP39 BA Broadcasting, Film and Communication
Duration: 3FT Hon
Entry Requirements: *GCE:* 160. Interview required.

PP3P FdA Film and Digital Media
Duration: 2FT Fdg
Entry Requirements: Contact the institution for details.

A60 ANGLIA RUSKIN UNIVERSITY
BISHOP HALL LANE
CHELMSFORD
ESSEX CM1 1SQ
t: 0845 271 3333 f: 01245 251789
e: answers@anglia.ac.uk
// www.anglia.ac.uk

P391 BA Film Studies and Media Studies
Duration: 3FT Hon
Entry Requirements: *GCE:* 220-260. *SQAH:* BCCC. *SQAAH:* CC.
IB: 24.

P300 BA Media Studies
Duration: 3FT Hon
Entry Requirements: *GCE:* 220-260. *SQAH:* BBCC. *SQAAH:* BC.
IB: 24.

P310 BSc Media and Internet Technology
Duration: 3FT Hon
Entry Requirements: *GCE:* 150. *SQAH:* BBCC. *SQAAH:* BC. *IB:* 24.

B06 BANGOR UNIVERSITY
BANGOR UNIVERSITY
BANGOR
GWYNEDD LL57 2DG
t: 01248 388484 f: 01248 370451
e: admissions@bangor.ac.uk
// www.bangor.ac.uk

PH00 BA Astudiaethau'r Cyfryngau
Duration: 3FT Hon
Entry Requirements: Contact the institution for details.

W3P3 BA Astudiaethau'r Cyfryngau a Cherddoriaeth
Duration: 3FT Hon
Entry Requirements: *GCE:* 260-300. *IB:* 28.

WPQ0 BA Creative Studies
Duration: 3FT Hon
Entry Requirements: *GCE:* 240-260. *IB:* 28.

WQ93 BA Creative Studies and English Language
Duration: 3FT Hon
Entry Requirements: *GCE:* 240-260. *IB:* 28.

WR91 BA Creative Studies and French
Duration: 4FT Hon
Entry Requirements: *GCE:* 240-260. *IB:* 28.

WR92 BA Creative Studies and German
Duration: 4FT Hon
Entry Requirements: *GCE:* 240-260. *IB:* 28.

WR93 BA Creative Studies and Italian
Duration: 4FT Hon
Entry Requirements: *GCE:* 240-260. *IB:* 28.

WW93 BA Creative Studies and Music
Duration: 3FT Hon
Entry Requirements: *GCE:* 260-300. *IB:* 28.

WR94 BA Creative Studies and Spanish
Duration: 4FT Hon
Entry Requirements: *GCE:* 240-260. *IB:* 28.

WP83 BA Creative Writing and Media Studies
Duration: 3FT Hon
Entry Requirements: Contact the institution for details.

PWQ1 BA Diwydiannau Creadigol
Duration: 3FT Hon
Entry Requirements: Contact the institution for details.

Q3P3 BA English Language with Media Studies
Duration: 3FT Hon
Entry Requirements: *GCE:* 240-300. *IB:* 28.

R1P3 BA French with Media Studies
Duration: 3FT Hon
Entry Requirements: *GCE:* 240-260. *IB:* 28.

R2P3 BA German with Media Studies
Duration: 4FT Hon
Entry Requirements: *GCE:* 240-260. *IB:* 28.

PP53 BA Journalism and Media Studies
Duration: 3FT Hon
Entry Requirements: *GCE:* 260-300. *IB:* 28.

P306 BA Media Studies
Duration: 3FT Hon
Entry Requirements: *GCE:* 260-300. *IB:* 28.

PQ3H BA Media Studies and English
Duration: 3FT Hon
Entry Requirements: *GCE:* 260-300. *IB:* 28.

PW33 BA Media Studies and Music
Duration: 3FT Hon
Entry Requirements: *GCE:* 260-300. *IB:* 28.

LP33 BA Media Studies and Sociology
Duration: 3FT Hon
Entry Requirements: *GCE:* 260-300. *IB:* 28.

P3R1 BA Media Studies with French
Duration: 3FT Hon
Entry Requirements: *GCE:* 260-300. *IB:* 28.

P3R2 BA Media Studies with German
Duration: 3FT Hon
Entry Requirements: *GCE:* 260-300. *IB:* 28.

P3R3 BA Media Studies with Italian
Duration: 3FT Hon
Entry Requirements: *GCE:* 260-300. *IB:* 28.

P3R4 BA Media Studies with Spanish
Duration: 3FT Hon
Entry Requirements: *GCE:* 260-300. *IB:* 28.

P3WK BA Media Studies with Theatre
Duration: 3FT Hon
Entry Requirements: *GCE:* 260-300. *IB:* 28.

R4P3 BA Spanish with Media Studies
Duration: 4FT Hon
Entry Requirements: *GCE:* 240-260. *IB:* 28.

B20 BATH SPA UNIVERSITY
NEWTON PARK
NEWTON ST LOE
BATH BA2 9BN
t: 01225 875875 f: 01225 875444
e: enquiries@bathspa.ac.uk
// www.bathspa.ac.uk/clearing

NP19 BA Business & Management/Media Communications
Duration: 3FT Hon
Entry Requirements: *GCE:* 220-280. *IB:* 24.

WP99 BA Creative Writing/Media Communications
Duration: 3FT Hon
Entry Requirements: *GCE:* 220-280. *IB:* 24.

WP49 BA Dance/Media Communication
Duration: 3FT Hon
Entry Requirements: *GCE:* 220-280. *IB:* 24. Interview required.

WP4H BA Drama Studies/Media Communications
Duration: 3FT Hon
Entry Requirements: *GCE:* 220-280. *IB:* 24.

XP13 BA Education/Media Communications
Duration: 3FT Hon CRB Check: Required
Entry Requirements: *GCE:* 220-280. *IB:* 24.

XP39 BA Education/Media Communications
Duration: 3FT Hon CRB Check: Required
Entry Requirements: *GCE:* 220-280. *IB:* 24.

QP39 BA English Literature/Media Communications
Duration: 3FT Hon
Entry Requirements: *GCE:* 220-280. *IB:* 24.

VP93 BA Heritage/Media Communications
Duration: 3FT Hon
Entry Requirements: *GCE:* 220-280.

VP19 BA History/Media Communications
Duration: 3FT Hon
Entry Requirements: *GCE:* 220-280. *IB:* 24.

P390 BA Media Communications
Duration: 3FT Hon
Entry Requirements: *GCE:* 220-280. *IB:* 24.

PW93 BA Media Communications/Music
Duration: 3FT Hon
Entry Requirements: *GCE:* 220-280. *IB:* 24. Interview required.

PP34 BA Media Communications/Publishing
Duration: 3FT Hon
Entry Requirements: Contact the institution for details.

WPQ3 BA Photography and Digital Media
Duration: 3FT Hon
Entry Requirements: *GCE:* 220-280. *IB:* 24. Interview required.
Portfolio required.

WP6H BA/BSc Film & Screen Studies/Media Communications
Duration: 3FT Hon
Entry Requirements: *GCE:* 220-280. *IB:* 24.

DP69 BA/BSc Food & Nutrition/Media Communications
Duration: 3FT Hon
Entry Requirements: *GCE:* 220-280. *IB:* 24.

PV3M BA/BSc Media Communications/Philosophy & Ethics
Duration: 3FT Hon
Entry Requirements: *GCE:* 220-280. *IB:* 24.

PC98 BA/BSc Media Communications/Psychology
Duration: 3FT Hon
Entry Requirements: *GCE:* 220-280. *IB:* 24.

PL93 BA/BSc Media Communications/Sociology
Duration: 3FT Hon
Entry Requirements: *GCE:* 220-280. *IB:* 24.

WPP3 DipHE Film & Screen Studies/Media Communications
Duration: 2FT Dip
Entry Requirements: *GCE:* 220-280. *IB:* 24.

B22 UNIVERSITY OF BEDFORDSHIRE
PARK SQUARE
LUTON
BEDS LU1 3JU
t: 0844 8482234 f: 01582 489323
e: admissions@beds.ac.uk
// www.beds.ac.uk

P300 BA Media Practices (Mass Communications)
Duration: 3FT Hon
Entry Requirements: *Foundation:* Pass. *GCE:* 200. *SQAH:* BCC. *SQAAH:* BCC. *IB:* 24. *OCR ND:* M1 *OCR NED:* P1

B24 BIRKBECK, UNIVERSITY OF LONDON
MALET STREET
LONDON WC1E 7HX
t: 020 7631 6316
e: webform: www.bbk.ac.uk/ask
// www.bbk.ac.uk/ask

PP53 BA Journalism and Media
Duration: 3FT Hon
Entry Requirements: *GCE:* ABC. *SQAH:* AAAA-AABB. *IB:* 30. Interview required.

B25 BIRMINGHAM CITY UNIVERSITY
PERRY BARR
BIRMINGHAM B42 2SU
t: 0121 331 5595 f: 0121 331 7994
// www.bcu.ac.uk

QP33 BA English and Media
Duration: 3FT Hon
Entry Requirements: *GCE:* 300. *IB:* 26.

003P HND Media and Communication
Duration: 2FT HND
Entry Requirements: *GCE:* 120.

B32 THE UNIVERSITY OF BIRMINGHAM
EDGBASTON
BIRMINGHAM B15 2TT
t: 0121 415 8900 f: 0121 414 7159
e: admissions@bham.ac.uk
// www.birmingham.ac.uk

RP83 BA Modern Languages and Film Studies
Duration: 4FT Hon
Entry Requirements: *GCE:* ABB. *SQAH:* ABBBB. *SQAAH:* AB. *IB:* 32.

B41 BLACKPOOL AND THE FYLDE COLLEGE AN ASSOCIATE COLLEGE OF LANCASTER UNIVERSITY
ASHFIELD ROAD
BISPHAM
BLACKPOOL
LANCS FY2 0HB
t: 01253 504346 f: 01253 504198
e: admissions@blackpool.ac.uk
// www.blackpool.ac.uk

P300 BA Contemporary Media Practice
Duration: 3FT Hon
Entry Requirements: *Foundation:* Merit. *GCE:* 220. *IB:* 24. Interview required. Portfolio required.

B50 BOURNEMOUTH UNIVERSITY
TALBOT CAMPUS
FERN BARROW
POOLE
DORSET BH12 5BB
t: 01202 524111
// www.bournemouth.ac.uk

P392 BA Digital Media Design
Duration: 3FT Hon
Entry Requirements: *GCE:* 300. *IB:* 31. *BTEC SubDip:* M. *BTEC Dip:* DM. *BTEC ExtDip:* DDM.

LP23 BA Politics and Media
Duration: 3FT Hon
Entry Requirements: *GCE:* 300. *IB:* 31. *BTEC SubDip:* M. *BTEC Dip:* DM. *BTEC ExtDip:* DDM.

P300 FdA Media Practice
Duration: 2FT Fdg
Entry Requirements: Contact the institution for details.

B56 THE UNIVERSITY OF BRADFORD
RICHMOND ROAD
BRADFORD
WEST YORKSHIRE BD7 1DP
t: 0800 073 1225 f: 01274 235585
e: course-enquiries@bradford.ac.uk
// www.bradford.ac.uk

GP43 BA Computing and Media with Foundation Year (International stream)
Duration: 4FT Hon
Entry Requirements: *GCE:* 120.

P300 BA Media Studies
Duration: 3FT Hon
Entry Requirements: *GCE:* 240. *IB:* 24.

P3W6 BA Media Studies with Cinematics
Duration: 3FT Hon
Entry Requirements: *GCE:* 240. *IB:* 24.

WP63 BA Photography for Digital Media
Duration: 3FT Hon
Entry Requirements: *GCE:* 240. *IB:* 24. Interview required.

HP63 BSc Media Technology and Production
Duration: 3FT Hon
Entry Requirements: *GCE:* 260. *IB:* 24. Interview required.

B72 UNIVERSITY OF BRIGHTON
MITHRAS HOUSE 211
LEWES ROAD
BRIGHTON BN2 4AT
t: 01273 644644 f: 01273 642607
e: admissions@brighton.ac.uk
// www.brighton.ac.uk

QP33 BA English Language and Media
Duration: 3SW Hon
Entry Requirements: *GCE:* BBB. *IB:* 28.

QP3H BA English Literature and Media Studies
Duration: 3FT Hon
Entry Requirements: *GCE:* ABB. *IB:* 34.

DP43 BA Environment and Media Studies
Duration: 3FT/4SW Hon
Entry Requirements: *GCE:* BBB. *IB:* 30.

P300 BA Media Studies
Duration: 3FT Hon
Entry Requirements: *GCE:* BBB. *IB:* 30.

PX33 BA Media Studies and Education
Duration: 3FT Hon
Entry Requirements: *GCE:* BBB. *IB:* 32.

PL33 BA Media Studies and Sociology
Duration: 3FT Hon
Entry Requirements: *GCE:* BBB. *IB:* 28.

PQ33 BA Media and English Literature
Duration: 3SW Hon
Entry Requirements: *GCE:* BBB. *IB:* 30.

B80 UNIVERSITY OF THE WEST OF ENGLAND, BRISTOL
FRENCHAY CAMPUS
COLDHARBOUR LANE
BRISTOL BS16 1QY
t: +44 (0)117 32 83333 f: +44 (0)117 32 82810
e: admissions@uwe.ac.uk
// www.uwe.ac.uk

PL36 BA Media Culture and Practice
Duration: 3FT Hon
Entry Requirements: *GCE:* 320.

P251 BA Media and Journalism
Duration: 3FT Hon
Entry Requirements: Contact the institution for details.

B84 BRUNEL UNIVERSITY
UXBRIDGE
MIDDLESEX UB8 3PH
t: 01895 265265 f: 01895 269790
e: admissions@brunel.ac.uk
// www.brunel.ac.uk

PP93 BSc Communication and Media Studies
Duration: 3FT Hon
Entry Requirements: *GCE:* BBB. *SQAAH:* BBB. *IB:* 32. *BTEC ExtDip:* DDD.

LP33 BSc Sociology and Media Studies
Duration: 3FT Hon
Entry Requirements: *GCE:* BBB. *SQAAH:* BBB. *IB:* 32. *BTEC ExtDip:* DDD.

LP39 BSc Sociology and Media Studies (4 year Thin SW)
Duration: 4SW Hon
Entry Requirements: *GCE:* BBB. *SQAAH:* BBB. *IB:* 32. *BTEC ExtDip:* DDD.

B90 THE UNIVERSITY OF BUCKINGHAM
YEOMANRY HOUSE
HUNTER STREET
BUCKINGHAM MK18 1EG
t: 01280 820313 f: 01280 822245
e: info@buckingham.ac.uk
// www.buckingham.ac.uk

Q3P0 BA Communication (EFL) and Media Studies
Duration: 2FT Hon
Entry Requirements: *GCE:* CCC. *SQAH:* BBCC. *SQAAH:* CCC. *IB:* 30.

Q3P3 BA English Studies with Media Communications
Duration: 2FT Hon
Entry Requirements: *GCE:* BBC-BCC. *SQAH:* BBBB-BBBC. *SQAAH:* BBC-BCC. *IB:* 33.

N5P3 BSc Marketing with Media Communications
Duration: 2FT Hon
Entry Requirements: *GCE:* BBB-BBC. *SQAH:* ABBB-BBBB. *SQAAH:* BBB-BBC. *IB:* 34.

C8P3 BSc Psychology with Media Communications
Duration: 2FT Hon
Entry Requirements: *GCE:* BBB. *SQAH:* ABBB. *SQAAH:* BBB. *IB:* 34.

B92 BROOKSBY MELTON COLLEGE
MELTON CAMPUS
ASFORDBY ROAD
MELTON MOWBRAY
LEICESTERSHIRE LE13 0HJ
t: 01664 850850 f: 01664 855355
e: heenquiries@brooksbymelton.ac.uk
// www.brooksbymelton.ac.uk

016W HND Media (Moving Image)
Duration: 2FT HND
Entry Requirements: *GCE:* 160. Interview required. Portfolio required.

B94 BUCKINGHAMSHIRE NEW UNIVERSITY
QUEEN ALEXANDRA ROAD
HIGH WYCOMBE
BUCKINGHAMSHIRE HP11 2JZ
t: 0800 0565 660 f: 01494 605 023
e: admissions@bucks.ac.uk
// bucks.ac.uk

NP53 BA Advertising Management and Digital Communications
Duration: 3FT Hon
Entry Requirements: *GCE:* 200-240. *IB:* 24. *OCR ND:* M1 *OCR NED:* M3

NP13 BA Business and Digital Media Communications
Duration: 3FT Hon
Entry Requirements: *GCE:* 200-240. *IB:* 24. *OCR ND:* M1 *OCR NED:* M3

CP63 BA Football Business and Media
Duration: 3FT Hon
Entry Requirements: *GCE:* 200-240. *IB:* 24. *OCR ND:* M1 *OCR NED:* M3

C10 CANTERBURY CHRIST CHURCH UNIVERSITY
NORTH HOLMES ROAD
CANTERBURY
KENT CT1 1QU
t: 01227 782900 f: 01227 782888
e: admissions@canterbury.ac.uk
// www.canterbury.ac.uk

MP9H BA Applied Criminology and Film, Radio & Television Studies
Duration: 3FT Hon
Entry Requirements: *GCE:* 240. *IB:* 24.

M9PH BA Applied Criminology with Film, Radio & Television Studies
Duration: 3FT Hon
Entry Requirements: *GCE:* 240. *IB:* 24.

GP5H BA Business Computing and Film, Radio & Television
Duration: 3FT Hon
Entry Requirements: *GCE:* 240. *IB:* 24.

G5PH BA Business Computing with Film, Radio & Television
Duration: 3FT Hon
Entry Requirements: *GCE:* 240. *IB:* 24.

P3G5 BA Film, Radio & Television Studies with Business Computing
Duration: 3FT Hon
Entry Requirements: *GCE:* 240. *IB:* 24.

LP23 BA Global Politics and Media and Communications
Duration: 3FT Hon
Entry Requirements: *GCE:* 240. *IB:* 24.

L2PA BA Global Politics with Media and Communications
Duration: 3FT Hon
Entry Requirements: *GCE:* 240. *IB:* 24.

L2P3 BA International Relations with Media and Communications
Duration: 3FT Hon
Entry Requirements: *GCE:* 240. *IB:* 24.

P9LG BA Media & Communications with Politics & Governance
Duration: 3FT Hon
Entry Requirements: *GCE:* 240. *IB:* 24.

P300 BA Media and Communications
Duration: 3FT Hon
Entry Requirements: *GCE:* 240. *IB:* 24.

PL36 BA Media and Communications 'International Only'
Duration: 4FT Hon
Entry Requirements: Interview required.

P3L2 BA Media and Communications with Global Politics
Duration: 3FT Hon
Entry Requirements: *GCE:* 240. *IB:* 24.

P3B9 BA Media and Communications with Health Studies
Duration: 3FT Hon
Entry Requirements: *GCE:* 240. *IB:* 24.

P3LG BA Media and Communications with International Relations
Duration: 3FT Hon
Entry Requirements: *GCE:* 240. *IB:* 24.

LP2H BA Politics & Governance and Media & Communications
Duration: 3FT Hon
Entry Requirements: *GCE:* 240. *IB:* 24.

L2PJ BA Politics & Governance with Media and Communications (International Only)
Duration: 4FT Hon
Entry Requirements: Interview required.

L9P3 BA Politics and Governance with Media and Communications
Duration: 3FT Hon
Entry Requirements: *GCE:* 240. *IB:* 24.

TP73 BA/BSc American Studies and Media and Communications
Duration: 3FT Hon
Entry Requirements: *GCE:* 240. *IB:* 24.

TPR3 BA/BSc American Studies and Media and Communications (With a Year in USA)
Duration: 4FT Hon
Entry Requirements: Contact the institution for details.

TTP3 BA/BSc American Studies with Film, Radio & Television Studies (With a Year in USA)
Duration: 4FT Hon
Entry Requirements: Contact the institution for details.

T7P3 BA/BSc American Studies with Media and Communications
Duration: 3FT Hon
Entry Requirements: *GCE:* 240. *IB:* 24.

TRP3 BA/BSc American Studies with Media and Communications (With a Year in USA)
Duration: 4FT Hon
Entry Requirements: Contact the institution for details.

PN31 BA/BSc Business Studies and Media and Communications
Duration: 3FT Hon
Entry Requirements: *GCE:* 240. *IB:* 24.

GPK3 BA/BSc Computing and Film, Radio & Television
Duration: 3FT Hon
Entry Requirements: *GCE:* 240. *IB:* 24.

G4PH BA/BSc Computing with Film, Radio & Television Studies
Duration: 3FT Hon
Entry Requirements: *GCE:* 240. *IB:* 24.

X3P3 BA/BSc Education Studies with Media and Communications
Duration: 3FT Hon   CRB Check: Required
Entry Requirements: *GCE:* 240. *IB:* 24.

PQ33 BA/BSc English Literature and Media and Communications
Duration: 3FT Hon
Entry Requirements: *GCE:* 240. *IB:* 24.

Q3P3 BA/BSc English Literature with Media and Communications
Duration: 3FT Hon
Entry Requirements: *GCE:* 240. *IB:* 24.

W6P3 BA/BSc Film, Radio & Television Studies and Media and Communications
Duration: 3FT Hon
Entry Requirements: *GCE:* 240. *IB:* 24.

P3MX BA/BSc Film, Radio & Television Studies with Applied Criminology
Duration: 3FT Hon
Entry Requirements: *GCE:* 240. *IB:* 24.

PR31 BA/BSc French and Media and Communications
Duration: 3FT Hon
Entry Requirements: *GCE:* 240. *IB:* 24.

R1PH BA/BSc French with Media and Communications
Duration: 3FT Hon
Entry Requirements: Contact the institution for details.

LP73 BA/BSc Geography and Media and Communications
Duration: 3FT Hon
Entry Requirements: *GCE:* 240. *IB:* 24.

BP93 BA/BSc Health Studies and Media and Communications
Duration: 3FT Hon
Entry Requirements: *GCE:* 240. *IB:* 24.

MP23 BA/BSc Legal Studies and Media and Communications
Duration: 3FT Hon
Entry Requirements: *GCE:* 240. *IB:* 24.

M2PH BA/BSc Legal Studies with Media and Communications
Duration: 3FT Hon
Entry Requirements: *GCE:* 240. *IB:* 24.

NP53 BA/BSc Marketing and Media and Communications
Duration: 3FT Hon
Entry Requirements: *GCE:* 240. *IB:* 24.

PW36 BA/BSc Media and Communications and Film, Radio and Television Studies
Duration: 3FT Hon
Entry Requirements: *GCE:* 240. *IB:* 24.

PW33 BA/BSc Media and Communications and Music
Duration: 3FT Hon
Entry Requirements: *GCE:* 240. *IB:* 24.

CP83 BA/BSc Media and Communications and Psychology
Duration: 3FT Hon
Entry Requirements: *GCE:* 260. *IB:* 24.

LP33 BA/BSc Media and Communications and Sociology and Social Science
Duration: 3FT Hon
Entry Requirements: *GCE:* 240. *IB:* 24.

P3T7 BA/BSc Media and Communications with American Studies
Duration: 3FT Hon
Entry Requirements: *GCE:* 240. *IB:* 24.

PHT7 BA/BSc Media and Communications with American Studies (With a Year in USA)
Duration: 4FT Hon
Entry Requirements: Contact the institution for details.

P3N1 BA/BSc Media and Communications with Business Studies
Duration: 3FT Hon
Entry Requirements: *GCE:* 240. *IB:* 24.

P3GK BA/BSc Media and Communications with Digital Media
Duration: 3FT Hon
Entry Requirements: *GCE:* 240. *IB:* 24.

P3X3 BA/BSc Media and Communications with Education Studies
Duration: 3FT Hon   CRB Check: Required
Entry Requirements: *GCE:* 240. *IB:* 24.

PHQ3 BA/BSc Media and Communications with English Literature
Duration: 3FT Hon
Entry Requirements: Contact the institution for details.

P3W6 BA/BSc Media and Communications with Film, Radio and Television Studies
Duration: 3FT Hon
Entry Requirements: *GCE:* 240. *IB:* 24.

P3R1 BA/BSc Media and Communications with French
Duration: 3FT Hon
Entry Requirements: *GCE:* 240. *IB:* 24.

P3L7 BA/BSc Media and Communications with Geography
Duration: 3FT Hon
Entry Requirements: *GCE:* 240. *IB:* 24.

P3NM BA/BSc Media and Communications with Marketing
Duration: 3FT Hon
Entry Requirements: *GCE:* 240. *IB:* 24.

P3W3 BA/BSc Media and Communications with Music
Duration: 3FT Hon
Entry Requirements: *GCE:* 240. *IB:* 24.

P3C8 BA/BSc Media and Communications with Psychology
Duration: 3FT Hon
Entry Requirements: *GCE:* 260. *IB:* 24.

P3L3 BA/BSc Media and Communications with Sociology and Social Science
Duration: 3FT Hon
Entry Requirements: *GCE:* 240. *IB:* 24.

P3VP BA/BSc Media and Communications with Theology
Duration: 3FT Hon
Entry Requirements: Contact the institution for details.

W3P3 BA/BSc Music with Media and Communications
Duration: 3FT Hon
Entry Requirements: *GCE:* 240. *IB:* 24.

C8P3 BA/BSc Psychology with Media and Communications
Duration: 3FT Hon
Entry Requirements: *GCE:* 260. *IB:* 24.

L3P3 BA/BSc Sociology & Social Science with Media & Communications
Duration: 3FT Hon
Entry Requirements: *GCE:* 240. *IB:* 24.

VP63 BA/BSc Theology and Media and Communications
Duration: 3FT Hon
Entry Requirements: *GCE:* 240. *IB:* 24.

V6PH BA/BSc Theology with Media and Communications
Duration: 3FT Hon
Entry Requirements: *GCE:* 240. *IB:* 24.

N1P3 BSc Business Studies with Media and Communications
Duration: 3FT Hon
Entry Requirements: *GCE:* 240. *IB:* 24.

N5P3 BSc Marketing with Media and Communications
Duration: 3FT Hon
Entry Requirements: *GCE:* 240. *IB:* 24.

GP43 BSc/BA Digital Media and Media and Communications
Duration: 3FT Hon
Entry Requirements: *GCE:* 240. *IB:* 24.

G4P3 BSc/BA Digital Media with Media and Communications
Duration: 3FT Hon
Entry Requirements: *GCE:* 240. *IB:* 24.

L7P3 BSc/BA Geography with Media and Communications
Duration: 3FT Hon
Entry Requirements: *GCE:* 240. *IB:* 24.

GP4J FdA Broadcast and Interactive TV
Duration: 2FT Fdg
Entry Requirements: *GCE:* 120. *IB:* 24.

003P HNC Interactive Media
Duration: 1FT HNC
Entry Requirements: Contact the institution for details.

C15 CARDIFF UNIVERSITY
PO BOX 927
30-36 NEWPORT ROAD
CARDIFF CF24 0DE
t: 029 2087 9999 f: 029 2087 6138
e: admissions@cardiff.ac.uk
// www.cardiff.ac.uk

PP53 BA Journalism, Media and Cultural Studies
Duration: 3FT Hon
Entry Requirements: *GCE:* AAB. *SQAAH:* AAB. *IB:* 35. Admissions Test required.

PQ53 BA Journalism, Media and English Literature
Duration: 3FT Hon
Entry Requirements: *GCE:* AAB. *SQAAH:* AAB. *IB:* 35. Interview required. Portfolio required.

C20 CARDIFF METROPOLITAN UNIVERSITY (UWIC)
ADMISSIONS UNIT
LLANDAFF CAMPUS
WESTERN AVENUE
CARDIFF CF5 2YB
t: 029 2041 6070 f: 029 2041 6286
e: admissions@cardiffmet.ac.uk
// www.cardiffmet.ac.uk

QP33 BA English and Contemporary Media
Duration: 3FT Hon
Entry Requirements: *GCE:* 260. *IB:* 24. *BTEC ExtDip:* DMM. Interview required.

C30 UNIVERSITY OF CENTRAL LANCASHIRE
PRESTON
LANCS PR1 2HE
t: 01772 201201 f: 01772 894954
e: uadmissions@uclan.ac.uk
// www.uclan.ac.uk

P3P0 BA Communication and Film & Media
Duration: 3FT Hon
Entry Requirements: *GCE:* 260-300. *IB:* 28. *BTEC Dip:* D*D*. *BTEC ExtDip:* DMM. *OCR ND:* D *OCR NED:* M2

QP33 BA English for International Communication (Top-up)
Duration: 1FT Hon
Entry Requirements: Contact the institution for details.

PW36 BA Film and Media Studies
Duration: 3FT Hon
Entry Requirements: *GCE:* 240-260. *IB:* 28. *OCR ND:* D *OCR NED:* M3

N5P3 BA Marketing Management with Digital Media
Duration: 4SW Hon
Entry Requirements: *GCE:* 260-300. *SQAH:* AABB-BBBC. *IB:* 28. *OCR ND:* D

WP6H BA Photography
Duration: 3FT Hon
Entry Requirements: *GCE:* 240-260. *IB:* 28. *OCR ND:* D *OCR NED:* M3

WP23 BSc Film and Television Graphics Production
Duration: 3FT Hon
Entry Requirements: *GCE:* 300. *SQAH:* AAAB. *IB:* 30. *OCR ND:* D *OCR NED:* D2

HP63 BSc Media Production & Technology
Duration: 3FT Hon
Entry Requirements: *GCE:* 300. *SQAH:* AAAB. *IB:* 30. *OCR ND:* D *OCR NED:* D2

C55 UNIVERSITY OF CHESTER
PARKGATE ROAD
CHESTER CH1 4BJ
t: 01244 511000 f: 01244 511300
e: enquiries@chester.ac.uk
// www.chester.ac.uk

PN35 BA Advertising and Media Studies
Duration: 3FT Hon
Entry Requirements: *GCE:* 240-280. *SQAH:* BBBB. *IB:* 26.

NPDJ BA Business Management and Media Studies
Duration: 3FT Hon
Entry Requirements: *GCE:* 240-280. *SQAH:* BBBB. *IB:* 26.

P399 BA Commercial Music Production and Media Studies
Duration: 3FT Hon
Entry Requirements: *Foundation:* Pass. *GCE:* 260-300. *SQAH:* BBBB. *IB:* 28.

WP6H BA Digital Photography and Media Studies
Duration: 3FT Hon
Entry Requirements: *GCE:* 240-280. *SQAH:* BBBB. *IB:* 26.

NP8J BA Events Management and Media Studies
Duration: 3FT Hon
Entry Requirements: *GCE:* 240-280. *SQAH:* BBBB. *IB:* 26.

P398 BA Film Studies and Media Studies
Duration: 3FT Hon
Entry Requirements: *GCE:* 240-280. *SQAH:* BBBB. *IB:* 24.

PP35 BA Journalism and Media Studies
Duration: 3FT Hon
Entry Requirements: *GCE:* 240-280. *SQAH:* BBBB. *IB:* 26.

P901 BA Radio Production and Media Studies
Duration: 3FT Hon
Entry Requirements: Contact the institution for details.

CPP3 BA Sport Development and Commercial Music Production
Duration: 3FT Hon
Entry Requirements: *Foundation:* Pass. *GCE:* 260-300. *SQAH:* BBBB. *IB:* 28.

CPPH BA Sport Development and Media Studies
Duration: 3FT Hon
Entry Requirements: *GCE:* 240-280. *SQAH:* BBBB. *IB:* 26.

CPQ3 BA Sport Development and Radio Production
Duration: 3FT Hon
Entry Requirements: *Foundation:* Pass. *GCE:* 260-300. *SQAH:* BBBB. *IB:* 28.

CP6J BA Sport Development and TV Production
Duration: 3FT Hon
Entry Requirements: *Foundation:* Pass. *GCE:* 260-300. *SQAH:* BBBB. *IB:* 28.

C58 UNIVERSITY OF CHICHESTER
BISHOP OTTER CAMPUS
COLLEGE LANE
CHICHESTER
WEST SUSSEX PO19 6PE
t: 01243 816002 f: 01243 816161
e: admissions@chi.ac.uk
// www.chiuni.ac.uk

WP83 BA English & Creative Writing and Media Studies
Duration: 3FT Hon
Entry Requirements: *GCE:* BCC. *SQAH:* BBBB-BBBC. *SQAAH:* BCC. *IB:* 28. *BTEC ExtDip:* DMM.

PQ33 BA English and Media Studies
Duration: 3FT Hon
Entry Requirements: *GCE:* BCC. *SQAH:* BBBB-BBBC. *SQAAH:* BCC. *IB:* 30. *BTEC ExtDip:* DMM.

QP33 BA International English Studies and Media Studies
Duration: 3FT Hon
Entry Requirements: *GCE:* BCC. *SQAAH:* BCC. *IB:* 28.

P390 BA Media Production
Duration: 3FT Hon
Entry Requirements: *GCE:* BCC. *SQAAH:* BCC. *IB:* 28.

P300 BA Media Studies
Duration: 3FT Hon
Entry Requirements: *GCE:* BCC. *SQAAH:* BCC. *IB:* 28. *BTEC ExtDip:* DMM.

C60 CITY UNIVERSITY
NORTHAMPTON SQUARE
LONDON EC1V 0HB
t: 020 7040 5060 f: 020 7040 8995
e: ugadmissions@city.ac.uk
// www.city.ac.uk

PL33 BSc Media Studies and Sociology
Duration: 3FT Hon
Entry Requirements: *GCE:* AAB. *SQAH:* BBBBC. *IB:* 32.

C78 CORNWALL COLLEGE
POOL
REDRUTH
CORNWALL TR15 3RD
t: 01209 616161 f: 01209 611612
e: he.admissions@cornwall.ac.uk
// www.cornwall.ac.uk

XP33 FdSc Wildlife Education & Media
Duration: 2FT Fdg
Entry Requirements: *GCE:* 120. Interview required.

C85 COVENTRY UNIVERSITY
THE STUDENT CENTRE
COVENTRY UNIVERSITY
1 GULSON RD
COVENTRY CV1 2JH
t: 024 7615 2222 f: 024 7615 2223
e: studentenquiries@coventry.ac.uk
// www.coventry.ac.uk

PP53 BA Journalism and Media
Duration: 3FT/4SW Hon
Entry Requirements: *GCE:* BCC. *SQAH:* BCCCC. *IB:* 28. *BTEC ExtDip:* DMM. *OCR NED:* M2 Interview required. Portfolio required.

P300 BA Multimedia Computing
Duration: 3FT/4SW Hon
Entry Requirements: *GCE:* BCC. *SQAH:* BCCCC. *IB:* 28. *BTEC ExtDip:* DMM. *OCR NED:* M2

C93 UNIVERSITY FOR THE CREATIVE ARTS
FALKNER ROAD
FARNHAM
SURREY GU9 7DS
t: 01252 892960
e: admissions@ucreative.ac.uk
// www.ucreative.ac.uk

WP13 BA Arts & Media
Duration: 3FT Hon
Entry Requirements: *GCE:* 220. *IB:* 24. *BTEC ExtDip:* PPP. Interview required. Portfolio required.

C99 UNIVERSITY OF CUMBRIA
FUSEHILL STREET
CARLISLE
CUMBRIA CA1 2HH
t: 01228 616234 f: 01228 616235
// www.cumbria.ac.uk

NP83 BA Adventure and Media
Duration: 3FT Hon
Entry Requirements: *GCE:* 220. *SQAH:* BBBB. Interview required.

D26 DE MONTFORT UNIVERSITY
THE GATEWAY
LEICESTER LE1 9BH
t: 0116 255 1551 f: 0116 250 6204
e: enquiries@dmu.ac.uk
// www.dmu.ac.uk

NP13 BA Business and Media & Communication
Duration: 3FT/4SW Hon
Entry Requirements: *GCE:* 280. *IB:* 28. *BTEC Dip:* D*D*. *BTEC ExtDip:* DMM. *OCR NED:* M2 Interview required.

PWH4 BA Drama Studies and Media & Communication
Duration: 3FT Hon
Entry Requirements: *GCE:* 260. *IB:* 28. *BTEC Dip:* D*D*. *BTEC ExtDip:* DMM.

QP33 BA English Language and Media & Communication
Duration: 3FT Hon
Entry Requirements: *GCE:* 260. *IB:* 28. *BTEC Dip:* D*D*. *BTEC ExtDip:* DMM.

PQ33 BA English and Media & Communication
Duration: 3FT Hon
Entry Requirements: *GCE:* 260. *IB:* 28. *BTEC Dip:* D*D*. *BTEC ExtDip:* DMM.

P390 BA Film Studies and Media & Communication
Duration: 3FT Hon
Entry Requirements: *GCE:* 260. *IB:* 28. *BTEC Dip:* D*D*. *BTEC ExtDip:* DMM.

PPH5 BA Journalism and Media & Communication
Duration: 3FT Hon
Entry Requirements: *GCE:* 260. *IB:* 28. *BTEC Dip:* D*D*. *BTEC ExtDip:* DMM.

NP53 BA Marketing and Media & Communication
Duration: 3FT/4SW Hon
Entry Requirements: *GCE:* 280. *IB:* 28. *BTEC Dip:* D*D*. *BTEC ExtDip:* DMM. *OCR NED:* M2 Interview required.

P300 BA Media and Communication (with pathways)
Duration: 3FT Hon
Entry Requirements: *GCE:* 260. *IB:* 28. *BTEC Dip:* D*D*. *BTEC ExtDip:* DMM.

HP63 BSc Media Technology
Duration: 3FT/4SW Hon
Entry Requirements: *GCE:* 300. *IB:* 28. *BTEC ExtDip:* DDM. Interview required.

D39 UNIVERSITY OF DERBY
KEDLESTON ROAD
DERBY DE22 1GB
t: 01332 591167 f: 01332 597724
e: askadmissions@derby.ac.uk
// www.derby.ac.uk

PT37 BA American Studies and Film & Television Studies
Duration: 3FT Hon
Entry Requirements: *Foundation:* Distinction. *GCE:* 260-300. *IB:* 28. *BTEC Dip:* D*D*. *BTEC ExtDip:* DMM. *OCR NED:* M2

NP23 BA Business Management and Film & Television Studies
Duration: 3FT Hon
Entry Requirements: *Foundation:* Distinction. *GCE:* 260-300. *IB:* 28. *BTEC Dip:* D*D*. *BTEC ExtDip:* DMM. *OCR NED:* M2

PW38 BA Creative Writing and Film & Television Studies
Duration: 3FT Hon
Entry Requirements: *Foundation:* Distinction. *GCE:* 260-300. *IB:* 28. *BTEC Dip:* D*D*. *BTEC ExtDip:* DMM. *OCR NED:* M2

PW35 BA Dance & Movement Studies and Film & Television Studies
Duration: 3FT Hon
Entry Requirements: *Foundation:* Distinction. *GCE:* 260-300. *IB:* 28. *BTEC Dip:* D*D*. *BTEC ExtDip:* DMM. *OCR NED:* M2

PQ33 BA English and Film & Television Studies
Duration: 3FT Hon
Entry Requirements: *Foundation:* Distinction. *GCE:* 260-300. *IB:* 28. *BTEC Dip:* D*D*. *BTEC ExtDip:* DMM. *OCR NED:* M2

MP13 BA Film & Television Studies and Law
Duration: 3FT Hon
Entry Requirements: *Foundation:* Distinction. *GCE:* 260-300. *IB:* 28. *BTEC Dip:* D*D*. *BTEC ExtDip:* DMM. *OCR NED:* M2

PW33 BA Film & Television Studies and Popular Music (Production)
Duration: 3FT Hon
Entry Requirements: *Foundation:* Distinction. *GCE:* 260-300. *IB:* 28. *BTEC Dip:* D*D*. *BTEC ExtDip:* DMM. *OCR NED:* M2

LP33 BA Film & Television Studies and Sociology
Duration: 3FT Hon
Entry Requirements: *Foundation:* Distinction. *GCE:* 260-300. *IB:* 28. *BTEC Dip:* D*D*. *BTEC ExtDip:* DMM. *OCR NED:* M2

PW3K BA Film & Television Studies and Theatre Studies
Duration: 3FT Hon
Entry Requirements: *Foundation:* Distinction. *GCE:* 260-300. *IB:* 28. *BTEC Dip:* D*D*. *BTEC ExtDip:* DMM. *OCR NED:* M2

P300 BA Media Studies
Duration: 3FT Hon
Entry Requirements: *Foundation:* Distinction. *GCE:* 260. *IB:* 28. *BTEC Dip:* D*D*. *BTEC ExtDip:* DMM. *OCR NED:* M2

PQHJ BA Media Studies and English
Duration: 3FT Hon
Entry Requirements: *Foundation:* Distinction. *GCE:* 260-300. *IB:* 28. *BTEC Dip:* D*D*. *BTEC ExtDip:* DMM. *OCR NED:* M2

PVH1 BA Media Studies and History
Duration: 3FT Hon
Entry Requirements: *Foundation:* Distinction. *GCE:* 260-300. *IB:* 28. *BTEC Dip:* D*D*. *BTEC ExtDip:* DMM. *OCR NED:* M2

PMH1 BA Media Studies and Law
Duration: 3FT Hon
Entry Requirements: *Foundation:* Distinction. *GCE:* 260-300. *IB:* 28. *BTEC Dip:* D*D*. *BTEC ExtDip:* DMM. *OCR NED:* M2

PWJ3 BA Media Studies and Popular Music Production
Duration: 3FT Hon
Entry Requirements: *Foundation:* Distinction. *GCE:* 260-300. *IB:* 28. *BTEC Dip:* D*D*. *BTEC ExtDip:* DMM. *OCR NED:* M2

PLH3 BA Media Studies and Sociology
Duration: 3FT Hon
Entry Requirements: *Foundation:* Distinction. *GCE:* 260-300. *IB:* 28. *BTEC Dip:* D*D*. *BTEC ExtDip:* DMM. *OCR NED:* M2

PCJ6 BA Media Studies and Sport & Exercise Studies
Duration: 3FT Hon
Entry Requirements: *Foundation:* Distinction. *GCE:* 260-300. *IB:* 28. *BTEC Dip:* D*D*. *BTEC ExtDip:* DMM. *OCR NED:* M2

PWJ4 BA Media Studies and Theatre Studies
Duration: 3FT Hon
Entry Requirements: *Foundation:* Distinction. *GCE:* 260-300. *IB:* 28. *BTEC Dip:* D*D*. *BTEC ExtDip:* DMM. *OCR NED:* M2

PT3R BA Professional Writing and American Studies
Duration: 3FT Hon
Entry Requirements: *Foundation:* Distinction. *GCE:* 260-300. *IB:* 28. *BTEC Dip:* D*D*. *BTEC ExtDip:* DMM. *OCR NED:* M2

PM39 BA Professional Writing and Applied Criminology
Duration: 3FT Hon
Entry Requirements: *Foundation:* Distinction. *GCE:* 260-300. *IB:* 28. *BTEC Dip:* D*D*. *BTEC ExtDip:* DMM. *OCR NED:* M2

PNJF BA Professional Writing and Business Management
Duration: 3FT Hon
Entry Requirements: *Foundation:* Distinction. *GCE:* 260-300. *IB:* 28. *BTEC Dip:* D*D*. *BTEC ExtDip:* DMM. *OCR NED:* M2

PW3N BA Professional Writing and Dance & Movement Studies
Duration: 3FT Hon
Entry Requirements: *Foundation:* Distinction. *GCE:* 260-300. *IB:* 28. *BTEC Dip:* D*D*. *BTEC ExtDip:* DMM. *OCR NED:* M2

PL3F BA/BSc Media Studies and International Relations & Global Development
Duration: 3FT Hon
Entry Requirements: *Foundation:* Distinction. *GCE:* 260-300. *IB:* 28. *BTEC Dip:* D*D*. *BTEC ExtDip:* DMM. *OCR NED:* M2

PC33 BA/BSc Professional Writing and Zoology
Duration: 3FT Hon
Entry Requirements: *Foundation:* Distinction. *GCE:* 260-300. *IB:* 28. *BTEC Dip:* D*D*. *BTEC ExtDip:* DMM. *OCR NED:* M2

KP13 BSc Architectural Design and Film & Television Studies
Duration: 3FT Hon
Entry Requirements: *Foundation:* Distinction. *GCE:* 260-300. *IB:* 28. *BTEC Dip:* D*D*. *BTEC ExtDip:* DMM. *OCR NED:* M2

E14 UNIVERSITY OF EAST ANGLIA
NORWICH NR4 7TJ
t: 01603 591515 f: 01603 591523
e: admissions@uea.ac.uk
// www.uea.ac.uk

P300 BA Media Studies
Duration: 3FT Hon   CRB Check: Required
Entry Requirements: *GCE:* AAB. *SQAAH:* AAB. *IB:* 33. *BTEC ExtDip:* DDD. Interview required.

PL32 BA Media and Politics
Duration: 3FT Hon   CRB Check: Required
Entry Requirements: *GCE:* ABB. *SQAAH:* ABB. *IB:* 32. *BTEC ExtDip:* DDM.

LP33 BA Society, Culture and Media
Duration: 3FT Hon   CRB Check: Required
Entry Requirements: *GCE:* ABB. *SQAAH:* ABB. *IB:* 32. *BTEC ExtDip:* DDM. Interview required.

QP93 BA Translation, Media and Honours Language
Duration: 3FT Hon   CRB Check: Required
Entry Requirements: *GCE:* AAB. *SQAAH:* AAB. *IB:* 33. *BTEC ExtDip:* DDD. Interview required.

QP9H BA Translation, Media and Honours Language(s)
Duration: 4FT Hon   CRB Check: Required
Entry Requirements: *GCE:* ABB. *SQAAH:* ABB. *IB:* 32. *BTEC ExtDip:* DDM. Interview required.

E28 UNIVERSITY OF EAST LONDON
DOCKLANDS CAMPUS
UNIVERSITY WAY
LONDON E16 2RD
t: 020 8223 3333 f: 020 8223 2978
e: study@uel.ac.uk
// www.uel.ac.uk

PL31 BA Business Economics/Media Studies
Duration: 3FT Hon
Entry Requirements: *GCE:* 240. *IB:* 24.

NP23 BA Business Management/Media Studies
Duration: 3FT Hon
Entry Requirements: *GCE:* 240. *IB:* 24.

M9P3 BA Criminology with Media Studies
Duration: 3FT Hon
Entry Requirements: *GCE:* 240. *IB:* 24.

LP63 BA Cultural Studies/Media Studies
Duration: 3FT Hon
Entry Requirements: *GCE:* 240. *IB:* 24.

XP33 BA Early Childhood Studies/Media Studies
Duration: 3FT Hon
Entry Requirements: *GCE:* 240. *IB:* 24.

PQ33 BA English Literature/Media Studies
Duration: 3FT Hon
Entry Requirements: *GCE:* 240. *IB:* 24.

N8P3 BA Events Management with Media Studies
Duration: 3FT Hon
Entry Requirements: *GCE:* 240. *IB:* 24.

P390 BA Film Studies with Media Studies
Duration: 3FT Hon
Entry Requirements: *GCE:* 240. *IB:* 24.

W2PJ BA Graphic Design with Media Studies
Duration: 3FT Hon
Entry Requirements: *GCE:* 240. *IB:* 24.

PV31 BA History/Media Studies
Duration: 3FT Hon
Entry Requirements: *GCE:* 240. *IB:* 24.

NP63 BA Human Resource Management/Media Studies
Duration: 3FT Hon
Entry Requirements: *GCE:* 240. *IB:* 24.

P5P3 BA Journalism Studies with Media Studies
Duration: 3FT Hon
Entry Requirements: *GCE:* 240. *IB:* 24.

PP53 BA Journalism Studies/Media Studies
Duration: 3FT Hon
Entry Requirements: *GCE:* 240. *IB:* 24.

NP53 BA Marketing/Media Studies
Duration: 3FT Hon
Entry Requirements: *GCE:* 240. *IB:* 24.

V000 BA Media & Creative Industries option - Media Studies
Duration: 3FT Hon
Entry Requirements: *GCE:* 240. *IB:* 24.

P300 BA Media Studies
Duration: 3FT Hon
Entry Requirements: *GCE:* 240. *IB:* 24.

P3W6 BA Media Studies with Animation
Duration: 3FT Hon
Entry Requirements: *GCE:* 240. *IB:* 24.

P3N2 BA Media Studies with Business Management
Duration: 3FT Hon
Entry Requirements: *GCE:* 240. *IB:* 24.

P3QJ BA Media Studies with English Literature
Duration: 3FT Hon
Entry Requirements: *GCE:* 240. *IB:* 24.

P391 BA Media Studies with Film Studies
Duration: 3FT Hon
Entry Requirements: *GCE:* 240. *IB:* 24.

P3P5 BA Media Studies with Journalism Studies
Duration: 3FT Hon
Entry Requirements: *GCE:* 240. *IB:* 24.

P3WF BA Media Studies with Multimedia Design Technology
Duration: 3FT Hon
Entry Requirements: *GCE:* 240. *IB:* 24.

P3WH BA Media Studies with Music Culture
Duration: 3FT Hon
Entry Requirements: *GCE:* 240. *IB:* 24.

P3WA BA Media Studies with Theatre Studies
Duration: 3FT Hon
Entry Requirements: *GCE:* 240. *IB:* 24.

W2PH BA Multimedia Design Technology with Media Studies
Duration: 3FT Hon
Entry Requirements: *GCE:* 240.

WP33 BA Music Culture/Film Studies
Duration: 3FT Hon
Entry Requirements: *GCE:* 240. *IB:* 24.

W6P3 BA Photography with Media Studies
Duration: 3FT Hon
Entry Requirements: *GCE:* 240. *IB:* 24. Portfolio required.

PLH9 BA Third World Development/Media Studies
Duration: 3FT Hon
Entry Requirements: *GCE:* 240. *IB:* 24.

L5P3 BA Youth & Community Work with Media Studies
Duration: 3FT Hon
Entry Requirements: *GCE:* 240. *IB:* 24.

GP5J BA/BSc Business Information Systems/Media Studies
Duration: 3FT Hon
Entry Requirements: *GCE:* 240. *IB:* 24.

IP13 BA/BSc Computing and Media Studies
Duration: 3FT Hon
Entry Requirements: *GCE:* 240. *IB:* 24.

B1P3 BA/BSc Human Biology/Media Studies
Duration: 3FT Hon
Entry Requirements: *GCE:* 240. *IB:* 24.

G6P3 BSc Software Engineering with Media Studies
Duration: 3FT Hon
Entry Requirements: *GCE:* 240. *IB:* 24.

E29 EAST RIDING COLLEGE
LONGCROFT HALL
GALLOWS LANE
BEVERLEY
EAST YORKSHIRE HU17 7DT
t: 0845 120 0037
e: info@eastridingcollege.ac.uk
// www.eastridingcollege.ac.uk/

P304 FdA Applied Digital Media
Duration: 2FT Fdg
Entry Requirements: *GCE:* 120.

E42 EDGE HILL UNIVERSITY
ORMSKIRK
LANCASHIRE L39 4QP
t: 01695 657000 f: 01695 584355
e: study@edgehill.ac.uk
// www.edgehill.ac.uk

PW38 BA Creative Writing and Media
Duration: 3FT Hon
Entry Requirements: *GCE:* 280. *IB:* 26. *OCR ND:* D *OCR NED:* M2

PW34 BA Drama and Media
Duration: 3FT Hon
Entry Requirements: *GCE:* 300. *IB:* 26. *OCR ND:* D *OCR NED:* M1
Interview required.

PQ33 BA English and Media
Duration: 3FT Hon
Entry Requirements: *GCE:* 280. *IB:* 26. *OCR ND:* D *OCR NED:* M2

P3W6 BA Film Studies with Film Production
Duration: 3FT Hon
Entry Requirements: *GCE:* 280. *IB:* 26. *OCR ND:* D *OCR NED:* M2

P3V1 BA Film Studies with History
Duration: 3FT Hon
Entry Requirements: *GCE:* 280. *IB:* 26. *OCR ND:* D *OCR NED:* M2

P307 BA Media (Film and Television)
Duration: 3FT Hon
Entry Requirements: *GCE:* 280. *IB:* 26. *OCR ND:* D *OCR NED:* M2
Interview required.

PW33 BA Media, Music and Sound
Duration: 3FT Hon
Entry Requirements: *GCE:* 280. *IB:* 26. *OCR ND:* D *OCR NED:* M2

E59 EDINBURGH NAPIER UNIVERSITY
CRAIGLOCKHART CAMPUS
EDINBURGH EH14 1DJ
t: +44 (0)8452 60 60 40 f: 0131 455 6464
e: info@napier.ac.uk
// www.napier.ac.uk

N5P3 BA Marketing with Digital Media
Duration: 3FT/4FT Ord/Hon
Entry Requirements: *GCE:* 230.

E70 THE UNIVERSITY OF ESSEX
WIVENHOE PARK
COLCHESTER
ESSEX CO4 3SQ
t: 01206 873666 f: 01206 874477
e: admit@essex.ac.uk
// www.essex.ac.uk

MP93 BA Criminology and the Media
Duration: 3FT Hon
Entry Requirements: *GCE:* ABB-BBB. *SQAH:* AAAB-AABB.

LP33 BA Media, Culture and Society
Duration: 3FT Hon
Entry Requirements: *GCE:* ABB-BBB. *SQAH:* AAAB-AABB.

PL33 BA Media, Culture and Society (Including Year Abroad)
Duration: 4FT Hon
Entry Requirements: *GCE:* ABB-BBB. *SQAH:* AAAB-AABB.

P300 BA Media, Culture and Society (including foundation year)
Duration: 4FT Hon
Entry Requirements: Contact the institution for details.

E78 EUROPEAN SCHOOL OF ECONOMICS
8/9 GROSVENOR PLACE
BELGRAVIA
LONDON SW1X 7SH
t: 020 7245 6148 f: 020 7245 6164
e: admissions@eselondon.ac.uk
// www.eselondon.ac.uk

P9P3 BA Organisational Communication with Media Management
Duration: 3FT Hon
Entry Requirements: *GCE:* A-C. Interview required.

E81 EXETER COLLEGE
HELE ROAD
EXETER
DEVON EX4 4JS
t: 0845 111 6000
e: info@exe-coll.ac.uk
// www.exe-coll.ac.uk/he

WP23 FdA Graphic Communication
Duration: 2FT Fdg
Entry Requirements: *GCE:* 160.

PP35 FdA Journalism and Practical Media
Duration: 2FT Fdg
Entry Requirements: *GCE:* 160.

F66 FARNBOROUGH COLLEGE OF TECHNOLOGY
BOUNDARY ROAD
FARNBOROUGH
HAMPSHIRE GU14 6SB
t: 01252 407028 f: 01252 407041
e: admissions@farn-ct.ac.uk
// www.farn-ct.ac.uk

P394 BSc Media Production (New Media)
Duration: 3FT Hon
Entry Requirements: *GCE:* 180-200. *OCR ND:* M2 *OCR NED:* M3
Admissions Test required.

G14 UNIVERSITY OF GLAMORGAN, CARDIFF AND PONTYPRIDD
ENQUIRIES AND ADMISSIONS UNIT
PONTYPRIDD CF37 1DL
t: 08456 434030 f: 01443 654050
e: enquiries@glam.ac.uk
// www.glam.ac.uk

P300 BA Film and Video
Duration: 3FT Hon
Entry Requirements: *GCE:* ABB. *IB:* 27. *BTEC SubDip:* M. *BTEC Dip:* DD. *BTEC ExtDip:* DDM. *OCR NED:* M1 Interview required.

PP35 BA (Hons) Media, Culture and Journalism
Duration: 3FT Hon
Entry Requirements: *GCE:* BCC. *IB:* 24. *BTEC SubDip:* M. *BTEC Dip:* D*D. *BTEC ExtDip:* DMM. *OCR NED:* M2 Interview required.

G28 UNIVERSITY OF GLASGOW

71 SOUTHPARK AVENUE
UNIVERSITY OF GLASGOW
GLASGOW G12 8QQ
t: 0141 330 6062 f: 0141 330 2961
e: student.recruitment@glasgow.ac.uk
// www.glasgow.ac.uk

PQ32 MA Comparative Literature/Film and Television Studies

Duration: 4FT Hon
Entry Requirements: *GCE:* ABB. *SQAH:* AAAB-ABBB. *IB:* 34.

G42 GLASGOW CALEDONIAN UNIVERSITY

STUDENT RECRUITMENT & ADMISSIONS SERVICE
CITY CAMPUS
COWCADDENS ROAD
GLASGOW G4 0BA
t: 0141 331 3000 f: 0141 331 8676
e: undergraduate@gcu.ac.uk
// www.gcu.ac.uk

PP93 BA Media and Communication

Duration: 4FT Hon
Entry Requirements: *GCE:* BBC. *SQAH:* ABBB-BBBB. *IB:* 24.

G50 THE UNIVERSITY OF GLOUCESTERSHIRE

PARK CAMPUS
THE PARK
CHELTENHAM GL50 2RH
t: 01242 714501 f: 01242 714869
e: admissions@glos.ac.uk
// www.glos.ac.uk

P300 BA Creative Media

Duration: 3FT Hon
Entry Requirements: Contact the institution for details.

G56 GOLDSMITHS, UNIVERSITY OF LONDON

GOLDSMITHS, UNIVERSITY OF LONDON
NEW CROSS
LONDON SE14 6NW
t: 020 7048 5300 f: 020 7919 7509
e: admissions@gold.ac.uk
// www.gold.ac.uk

LP63 BA Anthropology and Media

Duration: 3FT Hon
Entry Requirements: *GCE:* ABB. *SQAH:* BBBBB. *SQAAH:* BBB.

PP39 BA Media and Communication with Foundation Year (Integrated Degree)

Duration: 4FT Hon
Entry Requirements: Interview required.

P300 BA Media and Communications

Duration: 3FT Hon
Entry Requirements: *GCE:* AAB. *SQAH:* AAABB. *SQAAH:* AAB.
Interview required.

PQ33 BA Media and Modern Literature

Duration: 3FT Hon
Entry Requirements: *GCE:* AAB. *SQAH:* ABBBB. *SQAAH:* ABB. *IB:* 34. Interview required.

LP33 BA Media and Sociology

Duration: 3FT Hon
Entry Requirements: *GCE:* ABB. *SQAH:* BBBBB. *SQAAH:* BBB.
Interview required.

H36 UNIVERSITY OF HERTFORDSHIRE

UNIVERSITY ADMISSIONS SERVICE
COLLEGE LANE
HATFIELD
HERTS AL10 9AB
t: 01707 284800
// www.herts.ac.uk

Q1PH BA English Language & Communication with Film

Duration: 3FT Hon
Entry Requirements: *GCE:* 300.

Q1P3 BA English Language & Communication with Media Cultures

Duration: 3FT Hon
Entry Requirements: *GCE:* 300.

Q3PH BA English Literature with Film

Duration: 3FT Hon
Entry Requirements: *GCE:* 300.

Q3P3 BA English Literature with Media Cultures

Duration: 3FT Hon
Entry Requirements: *GCE:* 300.

V1PH BA History with Film

Duration: 3FT Hon
Entry Requirements: *GCE:* 300.

V1P3 BA History with Media Cultures

Duration: 3FT Hon
Entry Requirements: *GCE:* 300.

P300 BA Mass Communications

Duration: 3FT Hon
Entry Requirements: *GCE:* 300.

V5PH BA Philosophy with Film

Duration: 3FT Hon
Entry Requirements: *GCE:* 300.

V5P3 BA Philosophy with Media Cultures

Duration: 3FT Hon
Entry Requirements: *GCE:* 300.

P304 BSc Multimedia Technology (Extended)

Duration: 4FT/5SW Hon
Entry Requirements: Contact the institution for details.

H49 UNIVERSITY OF THE HIGHLANDS AND ISLANDS
UHI EXECUTIVE OFFICE
NESS WALK
INVERNESS
SCOTLAND IV3 5SQ
t: 01463 279000 f: 01463 279001
e: info@uhi.ac.uk
// www.uhi.ac.uk

QP53 BA Gaelic and Media Studies
Duration: 4FT Hon
Entry Requirements: *GCE:* C. *SQAH:* CCC. Interview required.

H60 THE UNIVERSITY OF HUDDERSFIELD
QUEENSGATE
HUDDERSFIELD HD1 3DH
t: 01484 473969 f: 01484 472765
e: admissionsandrecords@hud.ac.uk
// www.hud.ac.uk

G4P3 BA Interactive Multimedia
Duration: 3FT/4SW Hon
Entry Requirements: *GCE:* 280.

P300 BA Media and Popular Culture
Duration: 3FT Hon
Entry Requirements: *GCE:* 280. Interview required.

H72 THE UNIVERSITY OF HULL
THE UNIVERSITY OF HULL
COTTINGHAM ROAD
HULL HU6 7RX
t: 01482 466100 f: 01482 442290
e: admissions@hull.ac.uk
// www.hull.ac.uk

TP73 BA American Studies and Film Studies
Duration: 3FT Hon
Entry Requirements: *GCE:* 280-320. *IB:* 28. *BTEC ExtDip:* DMM.

WP83 BA Creative Writing and Media, Culture and Society
Duration: 3FT Hon
Entry Requirements: *GCE:* 280-320. *IB:* 28. *BTEC ExtDip:* DMM.

QP33 BA English and Film Studies
Duration: 3FT Hon
Entry Requirements: *GCE:* 280-320. *IB:* 30. *BTEC ExtDip:* DDM.

RP13 BA French and Film Studies
Duration: 4FT Hon
Entry Requirements: *GCE:* 280-320. *IB:* 28. *BTEC ExtDip:* DMM.

RP23 BA German and Film Studies
Duration: 4FT Hon
Entry Requirements: *GCE:* 280-320. *IB:* 28. *BTEC ExtDip:* DMM.

RP33 BA Italian and Film Studies
Duration: 4FT Hon
Entry Requirements: *GCE:* 280-320. *IB:* 28. *BTEC ExtDip:* DMM.

VP53 BA Philosophy and Film Studies
Duration: 3FT Hon
Entry Requirements: *GCE:* 280-320. *IB:* 28. *BTEC ExtDip:* DMM.

LP3H BA Sociology and Media Studies
Duration: 3FT Hon
Entry Requirements: *GCE:* 280-320. *IB:* 28. *BTEC ExtDip:* DMM.

RP43 BA Spanish and Film Studies
Duration: 4FT Hon
Entry Requirements: *GCE:* 280-320. *IB:* 28. *BTEC ExtDip:* DMM.

K12 KEELE UNIVERSITY
KEELE UNIVERSITY
STAFFORDSHIRE ST5 5BG
t: 01782 734005 f: 01782 632343
e: undergraduate@keele.ac.uk
// www.keele.ac.uk

PN31 BA Business Management and Media, Communications and Culture
Duration: 3FT Hon
Entry Requirements: *GCE:* ABB.

PM39 BA Criminology and Media, Communications & Culture
Duration: 3FT Hon
Entry Requirements: *GCE:* BBC.

PQ33 BA English and Media, Communications & Culture
Duration: 3FT Hon
Entry Requirements: *GCE:* BBB.

PN33 BA Finance and Media, Communications & Culture
Duration: 3FT Hon
Entry Requirements: *GCE:* ABB.

PF38 BA Geography and Media, Communications & Culture
Duration: 3FT Hon
Entry Requirements: *GCE:* BBC.

PV31 BA History and Media, Communications & Culture
Duration: 3FT Hon
Entry Requirements: *GCE:* BBB.

PL37 BA Human Geography and Media, Communications & Culture
Duration: 3FT Hon
Entry Requirements: *GCE:* BBC.

PN36 BA Human Resource Management and Media, Communications & Culture
Duration: 3FT Hon
Entry Requirements: *GCE:* ABB.

PLH2 BA International Relations and Media, Communications & Culture
Duration: 3FT Hon
Entry Requirements: *GCE:* BBB.

PM31 BA Law and Media, Communications & Culture
Duration: 3FT Hon
Entry Requirements: *GCE:* ABB.

PN35 BA Marketing and Media, Communications & Culture
Duration: 3FT Hon
Entry Requirements: *GCE:* ABB.

PW33 BA Media, Communications & Culture and Music
Duration: 3FT Hon
Entry Requirements: *GCE:* BBC.

PJ39 BA Media, Communications & Culture and Music Technology
Duration: 3FT Hon
Entry Requirements: *GCE:* BBC.

PV35 BA Media, Communications & Culture and Philosophy
Duration: 3FT Hon
Entry Requirements: *GCE:* BBB.

PL32 BA Media, Communications & Culture and Politics
Duration: 3FT Hon
Entry Requirements: *GCE:* BBB.

PL33 BA Media, Communications & Culture and Sociology
Duration: 3FT Hon
Entry Requirements: *GCE:* BBC.

P9V0 BA Media, Communications and Culture with Humanities Foundation Year
Duration: 4FT Hon
Entry Requirements: *GCE:* CC. Interview required.

CP83 BSc Applied Psychology and Media, Communications and Culture
Duration: 4FT Deg
Entry Requirements: *GCE:* BBC.

PF35 BSc Astrophysics and Media, Communications & Culture
Duration: 3FT Hon
Entry Requirements: *GCE:* BBC.

PC37 BSc Biochemistry and Media, Communications & Culture
Duration: 3FT Hon
Entry Requirements: *GCE:* BBC.

PC31 BSc Biology and Media, Communications & Culture
Duration: 3FT Hon
Entry Requirements: *GCE:* BBC.

FP43 BSc Forensic Science and Media, Communications & Culture
Duration: 3FT Hon
Entry Requirements: *GCE:* BBC.

PG31 BSc Mathematics and Media, Communications & Culture
Duration: 3FT Hon
Entry Requirements: *GCE:* BBC.

PFH8 BSc Media, Communications & Culture and Physical Geography
Duration: 3FT Hon
Entry Requirements: *GCE:* BBC.

PF33 BSc Media, Communications & Culture and Physics
Duration: 3FT Hon
Entry Requirements: *GCE:* BBC.

PC38 BSc Media, Communications & Culture and Psychology
Duration: 3FT Hon
Entry Requirements: *GCE:* BBC.

K60 KING'S COLLEGE LONDON (UNIVERSITY OF LONDON)
STRAND
LONDON WC2R 2LS
t: 020 7836 5454 f: 020 7848 7171
e: prospective@kcl.ac.uk
// www.kcl.ac.uk/prospectus

Q3P3 BA English with Film
Duration: 3FT Hon
Entry Requirements: *GCE:* AAAb. *SQAH:* AAB. *SQAAH:* AA. *IB:* 38.

R1P3 BA French with Film (4 years)
Duration: 4FT Hon
Entry Requirements: *GCE:* ABBc. *SQAH:* AABBB. *IB:* 34.

R2P3 BA German with Film (4 years)
Duration: 4FT Hon
Entry Requirements: *GCE:* ABB-BBBc. *SQAH:* AABBB-ABBBB. *IB:* 32.

R4P3 BA Hispanic Studies with Film (4 years)
Duration: 4FT Hon
Entry Requirements: *GCE:* ABBc. *SQAH:* AABBB. *IB:* 34.

K84 KINGSTON UNIVERSITY
STUDENT INFORMATION & ADVICE CENTRE
COOPER HOUSE
40-46 SURBITON ROAD
KINGSTON UPON THAMES KT1 2HX
t: 0844 8552177 f: 020 8547 7080
e: aps@kingston.ac.uk
// www.kingston.ac.uk

NP13 BA Business and Media & Cultural Studies
Duration: 3FT Hon
Entry Requirements: *GCE:* 280. *IB:* 30.

WPV3 BA Creative Writing and Media & Cultural Studies
Duration: 3FT Hon
Entry Requirements: *GCE:* 260-360. *IB:* 30.

LPH3 BA Criminology and Media & Cultural Studies
Duration: 3FT Hon
Entry Requirements: *GCE:* 260-360. *SQAH:* BBCCC. *SQAAH:* BBC.

WP5H BA Dance and Media & Cultural Studies
Duration: 3FT Hon
Entry Requirements: *GCE:* 300-360. Interview required.

WPK3 BA Drama and Media & Cultural Studies
Duration: 3FT Hon
Entry Requirements: *GCE:* 300-360. *SQAH:* BBCCC. *SQAAH:* BBC.

LP13 BA Economics (Applied) and Media & Cultural Studies
Duration: 3FT Hon
Entry Requirements: *GCE:* 260-360. *IB:* 24.

QP3H BA English Literature and Media & Cultural Studies
Duration: 3FT Hon
Entry Requirements: *GCE:* 260-360.

PH90 BA Film Studies and Media & Cultural Studies
Duration: 3FT Hon
Entry Requirements: *GCE:* 260-360. *IB:* 30.

VPH3 BA History of Art, Des & Film and TV & New Broadcasting Media
Duration: 3FT Hon
Entry Requirements: *GCE:* 240.

VP33 BA History of Art, Design & Film and Media & Cultural Studies
Duration: 3FT Hon
Entry Requirements: *GCE:* 260-360.

LPF3 BA Human Rights and Media & Cultural Studies
Duration: 3FT Hon
Entry Requirements: *GCE:* 260-360.

LP2H BA International Relations and Media & Cultural Studies
Duration: 3FT Hon
Entry Requirements: *GCE:* 260-360.

PP53 BA Journalism and Media & Cultural Studies
Duration: 3FT Hon
Entry Requirements: *GCE:* 260-360. *SQAH:* BBCCC. *SQAAH:* BBC. *IB:* 25.

P300 BA Media & Cultural Studies
Duration: 3FT Hon
Entry Requirements: *GCE:* 280. *IB:* 30.

PLH2 BA Media & Cultural Studies and Politics
Duration: 3FT Hon
Entry Requirements: *GCE:* 260-360.

PC38 BA Media & Cultural Studies and Psychology
Duration: 3FT Hon
Entry Requirements: *GCE:* 260-360.

PLH3 BA Media & Cultural Studies and Sociology
Duration: 3FT Hon
Entry Requirements: *GCE:* 260-360. *IB:* 30.

PJ90 BA Media & Cultural Studies and Television & New Broadcasting Media
Duration: 3FT Hon
Entry Requirements: *GCE:* 260-360.

P3R1 BA Media & Cultural Studies with French
Duration: 3FT Hon
Entry Requirements: *GCE:* 260-360.

P3C8 BA Media & Cultural Studies with Psychology
Duration: 3FT Hon
Entry Requirements: *GCE:* 260-360.

P3R4 BA Media & Cultural Studies with Spanish
Duration: 3FT Hon
Entry Requirements: *GCE:* 260-360.

C8P3 BA Psychology with Media & Cultural Studies
Duration: 3FT Hon
Entry Requirements: *GCE:* 260-360.

P302 BA (Hons) Media Skills (Top-Up)
Duration: 1FT Hon
Entry Requirements: Contact the institution for details.

PN31 BSc Media Technology with Business
Duration: 3FT Hon
Entry Requirements: *GCE:* 240-280. Interview required.

PN3C BSc Media Technology with Business
Duration: 4SW Hon
Entry Requirements: *GCE:* 240-280. Interview required.

L14 LANCASTER UNIVERSITY
THE UNIVERSITY
LANCASTER
LANCASHIRE LA1 4YW
t: 01524 592029 f: 01524 846243
e: ugadmissions@lancaster.ac.uk
// www.lancs.ac.uk

QP33 BA English Language in the Media
Duration: 3FT Hon
Entry Requirements: *GCE:* AAB. *SQAH:* ABBBB. *SQAAH:* AAB. *IB:*
35.

**QP3H BA English Language in the Media
(Study Abroad)**
Duration: 3FT Hon
Entry Requirements: *GCE:* AAA. *SQAH:* AAABB. *SQAAH:* AAA. *IB:*
36.

PV35 BA Film Studies and Philosophy
Duration: 3FT Hon
Entry Requirements: *GCE:* AAB. *SQAH:* ABBBB. *SQAAH:* AAB. *IB:*
35.

PL33 BA Film Studies and Sociology
Duration: 3FT Hon
Entry Requirements: *GCE:* AAB. *SQAH:* ABBBB. *SQAAH:* AAB. *IB:*
35.

LP63 BA Media and Cultural Studies
Duration: 3FT Hon
Entry Requirements: *GCE:* ABB. *SQAH:* BBBBB. *SQAAH:* BBB. *IB:*
32.

L24 LEEDS TRINITY UNIVERSITY COLLEGE
BROWNBERRIE LANE
HORSFORTH
LEEDS LS18 5HD
t: 0113 283 7150 f: 0113 283 7222
e: enquiries@leedstrinity.ac.uk
// www.leedstrinity.ac.uk

QP33 BA English and Media
Duration: 3FT Hon
Entry Requirements: *GCE:* 240. *IB:* 24.

P300 BA Media
Duration: 3FT Hon
Entry Requirements: *GCE:* 280. *IB:* 25. *OCR NED:* M2

PN35 BA Media and Marketing
Duration: 3FT Hon
Entry Requirements: *GCE:* 280. *IB:* 25. *OCR NED:* M2

L27 LEEDS METROPOLITAN UNIVERSITY
COURSE ENQUIRIES OFFICE
CITY CAMPUS
LEEDS LS1 3HE
t: 0113 81 23113 f: 0113 81 23129
// www.leedsmet.ac.uk

P302 BA Media, Communication, Cultures
Duration: 3FT Hon
Entry Requirements: *GCE:* 260. *IB:* 24.

L34 UNIVERSITY OF LEICESTER
UNIVERSITY ROAD
LEICESTER LE1 7RH
t: 0116 252 5281 f: 0116 252 2447
e: admissions@le.ac.uk
// www.le.ac.uk

PV33 BA Film Studies and the Visual Arts
Duration: 3FT Hon
Entry Requirements: *GCE:* BBB. *SQAH:* BBBBB. *SQAAH:* BBB. *IB:*
30.

P900 BA Film and Media Studies
Duration: 3FT Hon
Entry Requirements: *GCE:* BBB. *SQAH:* BBBBB. *SQAAH:* BBB. *IB:*
30.

PL33 BA Media and Sociology
Duration: 3FT Hon
Entry Requirements: *GCE:* BBB. *SQAH:* BBBBB. *SQAAH:* BBB. *IB:*
30.

L46 LIVERPOOL HOPE UNIVERSITY
HOPE PARK
LIVERPOOL L16 9JD
t: 0151 291 3331 f: 0151 291 3434
e: administration@hope.ac.uk
// www.hope.ac.uk

**NP43 BA Accounting and Media &
Communication**
Duration: 3FT Hon
Entry Requirements: *GCE:* 300-320. *IB:* 25. Interview required.

**VP33 BA Art & Design History and Media &
Communication**
Duration: 3FT Hon
Entry Requirements: *GCE:* 300-320. *IB:* 25.

**VP63 BA Biblical Studies and Media &
Communication**
Duration: 3FT Hon
Entry Requirements: *GCE:* 300-320. *IB:* 25.

**NP23 BA Business Management and Media &
Communication**
Duration: 3FT Hon
Entry Requirements: *GCE:* 300-320. *IB:* 25.

VP6H BA Christian Theology and Media & Communication
Duration: 3FT Hon
Entry Requirements: *GCE:* 300-320. *IB:* 25.

GPKH BA Computing and Media & Communication
Duration: 3FT Hon
Entry Requirements: *GCE:* 300-320.

LP3H BA Criminology and Media & Communication
Duration: 3FT Hon
Entry Requirements: *GCE:* 300-320. *IB:* 25.

WP53 BA Dance and Media & Communication
Duration: 3FT Hon
Entry Requirements: *GCE:* 300-320. *IB:* 25. Interview required.

XP33 BA Education and Media & Communication
Duration: 3FT Hon   CRB Check: Required
Entry Requirements: *GCE:* 300-320. *IB:* 25.

QP3H BA English Language and Media & Communication
Duration: 3FT Hon
Entry Requirements: *GCE:* 300-320. *IB:* 25.

QP33 BA English Literature and Media & Communication
Duration: 3FT Hon
Entry Requirements: *GCE:* 300-320. *IB:* 25.

WP1H BA Fine Art and Media & Communication
Duration: 3FT Hon
Entry Requirements: *GCE:* 300-320. *IB:* 25. Interview required. Portfolio required.

VPD3 BA History and Media & Communication
Duration: 3FT Hon
Entry Requirements: *GCE:* 300-320. *IB:* 25.

LP23 BA International Relations and Media & Communication
Duration: 3FT Hon
Entry Requirements: *GCE:* 300-320. *IB:* 25.

MP13 BA Law and Media & Communication
Duration: 3FT Hon
Entry Requirements: *GCE:* 300-320. *IB:* 25.

NP53 BA Marketing and Media & Communication
Duration: 3FT Hon
Entry Requirements: *GCE:* 300-320. *IB:* 25.

P300 BA Media & Communication
Duration: 3FT Hon
Entry Requirements: *GCE:* 300-320. *IB:* 25.

PW33 BA Media & Communication and Music
Duration: 3FT Hon
Entry Requirements: *GCE:* 300-320. *IB:* 25.

PN38 BA Media & Communication and Tourism
Duration: 3FT Hon
Entry Requirements: *GCE:* 300-320. *IB:* 25.

PV63 BA Media & Communication and World Religions
Duration: 3FT Hon
Entry Requirements: *GCE:* 300-320. *IB:* 25.

L51 LIVERPOOL JOHN MOORES UNIVERSITY
KINGSWAY HOUSE
HATTON GARDEN
LIVERPOOL L3 2AJ
t: 0151 231 5090 f: 0151 904 6368
e: courses@ljmu.ac.uk
// www.ljmu.ac.uk

PQ33 BA English and Media & Cultural Studies
Duration: 3FT Hon
Entry Requirements: *GCE:* 260. *IB:* 28.

P300 BA Media Professional Studies
Duration: 3FT Hon
Entry Requirements: *GCE:* 280. *IB:* 29.

LP63 BA Media, Culture, Communication
Duration: 3FT Hon
Entry Requirements: *GCE:* 260. *IB:* 28.

HP63 BSc Broadcast and Media Production
Duration: 3FT/4SW Hon
Entry Requirements: *GCE:* 280. *OCR ND:* M2 *OCR NED:* M2 Interview required.

L62 THE LONDON COLLEGE, UCK
VICTORIA GARDENS
NOTTING HILL GATE
LONDON W11 3PE
t: 020 7243 4000 f: 020 7243 1484
e: admissions@lcuck.ac.uk
// www.lcuck.ac.uk

103P Dip Media and Humanities
Duration: 1FT Oth
Entry Requirements: Contact the institution for details.

L68 LONDON METROPOLITAN UNIVERSITY
166-220 HOLLOWAY ROAD
LONDON N7 8DB
t: 020 7133 4200
e: admissions@londonmet.ac.uk
// www.londonmet.ac.uk

W000 BA Art, Media, Design Extended Degree
Duration: 4FT Hon
Entry Requirements: *GCE:* 80. *IB:* 28. Interview required. Portfolio required.

P301 BA Media Practice
Duration: 3FT Hon
Entry Requirements: Contact the institution for details.

NP83 BA Music Industry and Events Management
Duration: 3FT Hon
Entry Requirements: *GCE:* 240. *IB:* 28.

PPH9 BSc Media and Communications
Duration: 3FT Hon
Entry Requirements: Contact the institution for details.

PP35 BSc Media, Communications and Journalism
Duration: 3FT Hon
Entry Requirements: Contact the institution for details.

P3J9 BSc Music Technology (Audio Systems)
Duration: 3FT Hon
Entry Requirements: Contact the institution for details.

L75 LONDON SOUTH BANK UNIVERSITY
ADMISSIONS AND RECRUITMENT CENTRE
90 LONDON ROAD
LONDON SE1 6LN
t: 0800 923 8888 f: 020 7815 8273
e: course.enquiry@lsbu.ac.uk
// www.lsbu.ac.uk

QP33 BA English and Media Studies
Duration: 3FT Hon
Entry Requirements: *GCE:* 240. *IB:* 24.

PQH3 BA (Hons) Film and English Studies
Duration: 3FT Hon
Entry Requirements: *GCE:* 240. *IB:* 24.

PP39 BA (Hons) Film and Media Studies
Duration: 3FT Hon
Entry Requirements: *GCE:* 240. *IB:* 24.

PL33 BSc Media and Cultural Studies
Duration: 3FT Hon
Entry Requirements: *GCE:* 240. *IB:* 24.

M10 THE MANCHESTER COLLEGE
OPENSHAW CAMPUS
ASHTON OLD ROAD
OPENSHAW
MANCHESTER M11 2WH
t: 0800 068 8585 f: 0161 920 4103
e: enquiries@themanchestercollege.ac.uk
// www.themanchestercollege.ac.uk

PN31 BSc Media and Creative Business
Duration: 1FT Hon
Entry Requirements: Portfolio required. HND required.

M40 THE MANCHESTER METROPOLITAN UNIVERSITY
ADMISSIONS OFFICE
ALL SAINTS (GMS)
ALL SAINTS
MANCHESTER M15 6BH
t: 0161 247 2000
// www.mmu.ac.uk

P306 BA Film, TV and Cultural Studies
Duration: 3FT Hon
Entry Requirements: *GCE:* 280. *IB:* 28. *BTEC Dip:* D*D*. *BTEC ExtDip:* DMM.

P307 BA Film, TV and Cultural Studies (Foundation)
Duration: 4FT Hon
Entry Requirements: *GCE:* 160.

P304 BSc Digital Media and Communications
Duration: 3FT Hon
Entry Requirements: *GCE:* 240.

HP63 BSc Media Technology
Duration: 3FT/4SW Hon
Entry Requirements: *GCE:* 280. *IB:* 28.

HPP3 BSc Media Technology (Foundation)
Duration: 4FT/5SW Hon
Entry Requirements: *GCE:* 160. *IB:* 24. *BTEC Dip:* MM. *BTEC ExtDip:* MPP.

M80 MIDDLESEX UNIVERSITY
MIDDLESEX UNIVERSITY
THE BURROUGHS
LONDON NW4 4BT
t: 020 8411 5555 f: 020 8411 5649
e: enquiries@mdx.ac.uk
// www.mdx.ac.uk

NP53 BA Advertising, Public Relations and Media
Duration: 3FT Hon
Entry Requirements: *GCE:* 200-300. *IB:* 28.

WP83 BA Creative and Media Writing
Duration: 3FT Hon
Entry Requirements: *GCE:* 200-300. *IB:* 28.

P5PJ BA Journalism with Media & Cultural Studies
Duration: 3FT Hon
Entry Requirements: *GCE:* 200-300. *IB:* 28.

LP63 BA Media and Cultural Studies
Duration: 3FT Hon
Entry Requirements: *GCE:* 200-300. *IB:* 28.

PP43 BA Publishing, Media and Cultural Studies
Duration: 3FT Hon
Entry Requirements: *GCE:* 200-300. *IB:* 28.

N21 NEWCASTLE UNIVERSITY
KING'S GATE
NEWCASTLE UPON TYNE NE1 7RU
t: 01912083333
// www.ncl.ac.uk

PQL0 BA Media, Communication and Cultural Studies
Duration: 3FT Hon
Entry Requirements: *GCE:* AAB. *SQAH:* AAABB. *IB:* 35. *BTEC ExtDip:* DDD.

N23 NEWCASTLE COLLEGE
STUDENT SERVICES
RYE HILL CAMPUS
SCOTSWOOD ROAD
NEWCASTLE UPON TYNE NE4 7SA
t: 0191 200 4110 f: 0191 200 4349
e: enquiries@ncl-coll.ac.uk
// www.newcastlecollege.co.uk

W6P3 FdA Television and Media Practice
Duration: 2FT Fdg   **CRB Check:** Required
Entry Requirements: *GCE:* 120-160. *OCR ND:* P2 *OCR NED:* P3
Interview required.

N36 NEWMAN UNIVERSITY COLLEGE, BIRMINGHAM
GENNERS LANE
BARTLEY GREEN
BIRMINGHAM B32 3NT
t: 0121 476 1181 f: 0121 476 1196
e: Admissions@newman.ac.uk
// www.newman.ac.uk

BP93 BA Counselling Studies and Media & Communication
Duration: 3FT Hon
Entry Requirements: *Foundation:* Distinction. *GCE:* 260. *IB:* 24.
BTEC ExtDip: DMM. *OCR ND:* M2 *OCR NED:* M2

W4P3 BA Drama with Media & Communication
Duration: 3FT Hon
Entry Requirements: *Foundation:* Distinction. *GCE:* 260. *IB:* 24.
BTEC ExtDip: DMM. *OCR ND:* M2 *OCR NED:* M2

XP33 BA Education Studies and Media & Communication
Duration: 3FT Hon
Entry Requirements: *Foundation:* Distinction. *GCE:* 260. *IB:* 24.
BTEC ExtDip: DMM. *OCR ND:* M2 *OCR NED:* M2

X3P3 BA Education Studies with Media & Communication
Duration: 3FT Hon
Entry Requirements: *Foundation:* Distinction. *GCE:* 260. *IB:* 24.
BTEC ExtDip: DMM. *OCR ND:* M2 *OCR NED:* M2

GP53 BA IT and Media & Communication
Duration: 3FT Hon
Entry Requirements: *Foundation:* Distinction. *GCE:* 260. *IB:* 24.
BTEC ExtDip: DMM. *OCR ND:* M2 *OCR NED:* M2

G5P3 BA IT with Media & Communication
Duration: 3FT Hon
Entry Requirements: *Foundation:* Distinction. *GCE:* 260. *IB:* 24.
BTEC ExtDip: DMM. *OCR ND:* M2 *OCR NED:* M2

NP23 BA Management & Business and Media & Communication
Duration: 3FT Hon
Entry Requirements: *Foundation:* Distinction. *GCE:* 260. *IB:* 24.
BTEC ExtDip: DMM. *OCR ND:* M2 *OCR NED:* M2

N2PH BA Management & Business with Media & Communication
Duration: 3FT Hon
Entry Requirements: *Foundation:* Distinction. *GCE:* 260. *IB:* 24.
BTEC ExtDip: DMM. *OCR ND:* M2 *OCR NED:* M2

PC38 BA Media & Communication and Applied Psychology
Duration: 3FT Hon
Entry Requirements: *Foundation:* Distinction. *GCE:* 260. *IB:* 24.
BTEC ExtDip: DMM. *OCR ND:* M2 *OCR NED:* M2

PW31 BA Media & Communication and Art & Design
Duration: 3FT Hon
Entry Requirements: *Foundation:* Distinction. *GCE:* 260. *IB:* 24.
BTEC ExtDip: DMM. *OCR ND:* M2 *OCR NED:* M2

PW34 BA Media & Communication and Drama
Duration: 3FT Hon
Entry Requirements: *Foundation:* Distinction. *GCE:* 260. *IB:* 24.
BTEC ExtDip: DMM. *OCR ND:* M2 *OCR NED:* M2

PQ33 BA Media & Communication and English
Duration: 3FT Hon
Entry Requirements: *Foundation:* Distinction. *GCE:* 260. *IB:* 24.
BTEC ExtDip: DMM. *OCR ND:* M2 *OCR NED:* M2

PV35 BA Media & Communication and Philosophy, Religion & Ethics
Duration: 3FT Hon
Entry Requirements: *Foundation:* Distinction. *GCE:* 260. *IB:* 24.
BTEC ExtDip: DMM. *OCR ND:* M2 *OCR NED:* M2

PV36 BA Media & Communication and Theology
Duration: 3FT Hon
Entry Requirements: *Foundation:* Distinction. *GCE:* 260. *IB:* 24.
BTEC ExtDip: DMM. *OCR ND:* M2 *OCR NED:* M2

PL35 BA Media & Communication and Working with Children, Young People & Families
Duration: 3FT Hon
Entry Requirements: *Foundation:* Distinction. *GCE:* 260. *IB:* 24.
BTEC ExtDip: DMM. *OCR ND:* M2 *OCR NED:* M2

C8P3 BA Psychology with Media & Communication
Duration: 3FT Hon
Entry Requirements: *Foundation:* Distinction. *GCE:* 280. *IB:* 25.
BTEC ExtDip: DMM. *OCR ND:* M2 *OCR NED:* M2

V6P3 BA Theology with Media & Communication
Duration: 3FT Hon
Entry Requirements: *Foundation:* Distinction. *GCE:* 260. *IB:* 24.
BTEC ExtDip: DMM. *OCR ND:* M2 *OCR NED:* M2

LMP3 BA Working with Children Young People and Families with Media and Communication
Duration: 3FT Hon
Entry Requirements: *Foundation:* Distinction. *GCE:* 260. *IB:* 24.
BTEC ExtDip: DMM. *OCR ND:* M2 *OCR NED:* M2

N38 UNIVERSITY OF NORTHAMPTON
PARK CAMPUS
BOUGHTON GREEN ROAD
NORTHAMPTON NN2 7AL
t: 0800 358 2232 f: 01604 722083
e: admissions@northampton.ac.uk
// www.northampton.ac.uk

G4PH BSc Web Design/Media Production
Duration: 3FT Hon
Entry Requirements: *GCE:* 260-280. *SQAH:* AAA-BBBB. *IB:* 24.
BTEC Dip: DD. *BTEC ExtDip:* DMM. *OCR ND:* D *OCR NED:* M2

N77 NORTHUMBRIA UNIVERSITY
TRINITY BUILDING
NORTHUMBERLAND ROAD
NEWCASTLE UPON TYNE NE1 8ST
t: 0191 243 7420 f: 0191 227 4561
e: er.admissions@northumbria.ac.uk
// www.northumbria.ac.uk

NP53 BA Advertising and Media
Duration: 3FT Hon
Entry Requirements: *GCE:* 300. *SQAH:* BBBBC. *SQAAH:* BBC. *IB:* 26.

PP35 BA Media and Journalism
Duration: 3FT Hon
Entry Requirements: *GCE:* 300. *SQAH:* BBBBC. *SQAAH:* BBC. *IB:* 26.

LP33 BA Media, Culture and Society
Duration: 3FT Hon
Entry Requirements: *GCE:* 300. *SQAH:* BBBBC. *SQAAH:* BBC. *IB:* 26.

P301 BA Hons Mass Communications
Duration: 3FT Hon
Entry Requirements: Contact the institution for details.

P3N5 BA Hons Mass Communications with Advertising
Duration: 3FT Hon
Entry Requirements: Contact the institution for details.

P3N1 BA Hons Mass Communications with Business
Duration: 3FT Hon
Entry Requirements: Contact the institution for details.

N91 NOTTINGHAM TRENT UNIVERSITY
DRYDEN BUILDING
BURTON STREET
NOTTINGHAM NG1 4BU
t: +44 (0) 115 848 4200 f: +44 (0) 115 848 8869
e: applications@ntu.ac.uk
// www.ntu.ac.uk

PQ33 BA English and Media
Duration: 3FT Hon
Entry Requirements: *GCE:* 260. *BTEC ExtDip:* DMM. *OCR NED:* M2

PR32 BA Film & TV and German
Duration: 3FT Hon
Entry Requirements: *GCE:* 260. *BTEC ExtDip:* DMM. *OCR NED:* M2

RP13 BA French and Film & TV
Duration: 3FT Hon
Entry Requirements: *GCE:* 260.

RP23 BA German and Media
Duration: 4FT Hon
Entry Requirements: *GCE:* 260. *BTEC ExtDip:* DMM. *OCR NED:* M2

LP93 BA Global Studies and Media
Duration: 3FT Hon
Entry Requirements: *GCE:* 260. *BTEC ExtDip:* DMM. *OCR NED:* M2

RP33 BA Italian and Media
Duration: 4FT Hon
Entry Requirements: *GCE:* 260. *BTEC ExtDip:* DMM. *OCR NED:* M2

PQ31 BA Linguistics and Media
Duration: 3FT Hon
Entry Requirements: *GCE:* 260. *BTEC ExtDip:* DMM. *OCR NED:*
M2

P300 BA Media (with specialist pathways)
Duration: 3FT Hon
Entry Requirements: *GCE:* 280. *BTEC ExtDip:* DMM. *OCR NED:*
D2

LP33 BA Media and Communication & Society
Duration: 3FT Hon
Entry Requirements: *GCE:* 260. *BTEC ExtDip:* DMM. *OCR NED:*
M2

PR39 BA Media and European Studies
Duration: 3FT Hon
Entry Requirements: *GCE:* 260. *BTEC ExtDip:* DMM. *OCR NED:*
M2

PV31 BA Media and History
Duration: 3FT Hon
Entry Requirements: *GCE:* 260. *BTEC ExtDip:* DMM. *OCR NED:*
M2

LP23 BA Media and International Relations
Duration: 3FT Hon
Entry Requirements: *GCE:* 260. *BTEC ExtDip:* DMM. *OCR NED:*
M2

VP53 BA Philosophy and Media
Duration: 3FT Hon
Entry Requirements: *GCE:* 260. *BTEC ExtDip:* DMM. *OCR NED:*
M2

RP43 BA Spanish and Media
Duration: 4FT Hon
Entry Requirements: *GCE:* 260. *BTEC ExtDip:* DMM. *OCR NED:*
M2

O66 OXFORD BROOKES UNIVERSITY
ADMISSIONS OFFICE
HEADINGTON CAMPUS
GIPSY LANE
OXFORD OX3 0BP
t: 01865 483040 f: 01865 483983
e: admissions@brookes.ac.uk
// www.brookes.ac.uk

QP93 BA English Language and Communication/Communication,Media and Culture
Duration: 3FT Hon
Entry Requirements: Contact the institution for details.

PP43 BA Publishing Media/Film Studies
Duration: 3FT Hon
Entry Requirements: *GCE:* BBC.

PL32 BA/BSc Communications, Media and Culture/International Relations
Duration: 3FT Hon
Entry Requirements: *GCE:* BBC.

PR31 BA/BSc Film Studies/French Studies
Duration: 4SW Hon
Entry Requirements: *GCE:* BBC. *IB:* 31.

P304 BSc Media Technology
Duration: 3FT Hon
Entry Requirements: *GCE:* BBC. *IB:* 30. Interview required.

P56 UNIVERSITY CENTRE PETERBOROUGH
PARK CRESCENT
PETERBOROUGH PE1 4DZ
t: 0845 1965750 f: 01733 767986
e: UCPenquiries@anglia.ac.uk
// www.anglia.ac.uk/ucp

P300 BA Media
Duration: 3FT Hon
Entry Requirements: *GCE:* 120. Interview required.

P60 PLYMOUTH UNIVERSITY
DRAKE CIRCUS
PLYMOUTH PL4 8AA
t: 01752 585858 f: 01752 588055
e: admissions@plymouth.ac.uk
// www.plymouth.ac.uk

C1P3 BSc Science and the Media
Duration: 1FT Hon
Entry Requirements: Contact the institution for details.

P80 UNIVERSITY OF PORTSMOUTH
ACADEMIC REGISTRY
UNIVERSITY HOUSE
WINSTON CHURCHILL AVENUE
PORTSMOUTH PO1 2UP
t: 023 9284 8484 f: 023 9284 3082
e: admissions@port.ac.uk
// www.port.ac.uk

QP33 BA English and Media Studies
Duration: 3FT Hon
Entry Requirements: *GCE:* 240-300. *BTEC Dip:* DD. *BTEC ExtDip:* DMM.

P5P3 BA Journalism with Media Studies
Duration: 3FT Hon
Entry Requirements: *GCE:* 240-300. *BTEC Dip:* DD. *BTEC ExtDip:* DMM.

P300 BA Media Studies
Duration: 3FT Hon
Entry Requirements: *GCE:* 240-300. *IB:* 25. *BTEC SubDip:* P. *BTEC Dip:* DD. *BTEC ExtDip:* DMM.

PW36 BA Media Studies and Entertainment Technology
Duration: 3FT Hon
Entry Requirements: *GCE:* 240-300. *IB:* 25. *BTEC SubDip:* P. *BTEC Dip:* DD. *BTEC ExtDip:* DMM.

LP33 BA Sociology and Media Studies
Duration: 3FT Hon
Entry Requirements: *GCE:* 240-300. *BTEC Dip:* DD. *BTEC ExtDip:* DMM.

Q25 QUEEN MARGARET UNIVERSITY, EDINBURGH
QUEEN MARGARET UNIVERSITY DRIVE
EDINBURGH EH21 6UU
t: 0131474 0000 f: 0131 474 0001
e: admissions@qmu.ac.uk
// www.qmu.ac.uk

P303 BA Film and Media
Duration: 4FT Hon
Entry Requirements: *GCE:* 260. *IB:* 28.

P301 BA Media
Duration: 4FT Hon
Entry Requirements: *GCE:* 260. *IB:* 28.

R06 RAVENSBOURNE
6 PENROSE WAY
GREENWICH PENINSULA
LONDON SE10 0EW
t: 020 3040 3998
e: info@rave.ac.uk
// www.rave.ac.uk

NP53 BA Fashion Promotion
Duration: 3FT Hon
Entry Requirements: *Foundation:* Pass. *GCE:* AA-CC. *IB:* 28.
Interview required. Portfolio required.

WP3H BA Music Production for Media (with Foundation Year)
Duration: 4FT Hon
Entry Requirements: Contact the institution for details.

PN32 BA Web Media
Duration: 3FT Hon
Entry Requirements: *Foundation:* Pass. *GCE:* AA-CC. *IB:* 28.
Interview required. Portfolio required.

PP53 BA Web Media (Fast-Track)
Duration: 2FT Hon
Entry Requirements: Contact the institution for details.

P304 BA Web Media (with Foundation Year)
Duration: 4FT Hon
Entry Requirements: Contact the institution for details.

R18 REGENT'S COLLEGE, LONDON (INCORPORATING REGENT'S BUSINESS SCHOOL, LONDON)
INNER CIRCLE, REGENT'S COLLEGE
REGENT'S PARK
LONDON NW1 4NS
t: +44(0)20 7487 7505 f: +44(0)20 7487 7425
e: exrel@regents.ac.uk
// www.regents.ac.uk/

W6P3 BA Film, Television and Digital Media Production
Duration: 3FT Hon
Entry Requirements: *SQAH:* BBCC. *SQAAH:* CC.

R20 RICHMOND, THE AMERICAN INTERNATIONAL UNIVERSITY IN LONDON
QUEENS ROAD
RICHMOND
SURREY TW10 6JP
t: 020 8332 9000 f: 020 8332 1596
e: enroll@richmond.ac.uk
// www.richmond.ac.uk

PP53 BA International Journalism and Media
Duration: 4FT Hon
Entry Requirements: Contact the institution for details.

R36 ROBERT GORDON UNIVERSITY
ROBERT GORDON UNIVERSITY
SCHOOLHILL
ABERDEEN
SCOTLAND AB10 1FR
t: 01224 26 27 28 f: 01224 26 21 47
e: UGOffice@rgu.ac.uk
// www.rgu.ac.uk

P300 BA Media
Duration: 4FT Hon
Entry Requirements: *GCE:* CCC. *SQAH:* BBCC. *IB:* 26.

R48 ROEHAMPTON UNIVERSITY
ROEHAMPTON LANE
LONDON SW15 5PU
t: 020 8392 3232 f: 020 8392 3470
e: enquiries@roehampton.ac.uk
// www.roehampton.ac.uk

PL33 BA Media & Culture
Duration: 3FT Hon
Entry Requirements: *GCE:* 300. *IB:* 26. *BTEC ExtDip:* DDM. *OCR NED:* D2 Interview required.

NP23 BSc Business Management and Digital Media
Duration: 3FT Hon
Entry Requirements: *GCE:* 320. *IB:* 27. *BTEC ExtDip:* DDM. *OCR NED:* D2 Interview required.

R72 ROYAL HOLLOWAY, UNIVERSITY OF LONDON
ROYAL HOLLOWAY, UNIVERSITY OF LONDON
EGHAM
SURREY TW20 0EX
t: 01784 414944 f: 01784 473662
e: Admissions@rhul.ac.uk
// www.rhul.ac.uk

R1P3 BA French with Film Studies
Duration: 4FT Hon
Entry Requirements: *GCE:* ABB-BBB. *SQAH:* AABBB-BBBBB.
SQAAH: ABB-BBB. *IB:* 32.

R4P3 BA Spanish with Film Studies
Duration: 4FT Hon
Entry Requirements: *GCE:* ABB-BBB. *SQAH:* AABBB-BBBBB.
SQAAH: ABB-BBB. *IB:* 32.

S03 THE UNIVERSITY OF SALFORD
SALFORD M5 4WT
t: 0161 295 4545 f: 0161 295 4646
e: ug-admissions@salford.ac.uk
// www.salford.ac.uk

PP53 BA Journalism: Broadcast
Duration: 3FT Hon
Entry Requirements: *GCE:* 280. *IB:* 31. *OCR NED:* M2 Interview required.

S21 SHEFFIELD HALLAM UNIVERSITY
CITY CAMPUS
HOWARD STREET
SHEFFIELD S1 1WB
t: 0114 225 5555 f: 0114 225 2167
e: admissions@shu.ac.uk
// www.shu.ac.uk

P300 BA Media
Duration: 3FT Hon
Entry Requirements: *GCE:* 280.

WP23 BA Media (Extended degree programme)
Duration: 4FT Hon
Entry Requirements: *GCE:* 220.

S30 SOUTHAMPTON SOLENT UNIVERSITY
EAST PARK TERRACE
SOUTHAMPTON
HAMPSHIRE SO14 0RT
t: +44 (0) 23 8031 9039 f: + 44 (0)23 8022 2259
e: admissions@solent.ac.uk
// www.solent.ac.uk/

QP33 BA English and Film
Duration: 3FT Hon
Entry Requirements: *Foundation:* Distinction. *GCE:* 240. *SQAAH:* AA-CCD. *IB:* 24. *BTEC ExtDip:* MMM. *OCR ND:* D *OCR NED:* M3

QP3H BA English and Media
Duration: 3FT Hon
Entry Requirements: *Foundation:* Distinction. *GCE:* 240. *SQAAH:* AA-CCD. *IB:* 24. *BTEC ExtDip:* MMM. *OCR ND:* D *OCR NED:* M3

QPH3 BA English and Media
Duration: 4SW Hon
Entry Requirements: *Foundation:* Distinction. *GCE:* 240. *SQAAH:* AA-CCD. *IB:* 24. *BTEC ExtDip:* MMM. *OCR ND:* D *OCR NED:* M3

PP35 BA Media Writing (Top-Up)
Duration: 1FT Hon
Entry Requirements: Interview required. HND required.

P902 BA Media, Communications and Culture (Top-Up)
Duration: 1FT Hon
Entry Requirements: Interview required. HND required.

HP63 BSc Media Technology
Duration: 3FT Hon
Entry Requirements: *GCE:* 160.

HP6H BSc Media Technology (with foundation)
Duration: 4FT Hon
Entry Requirements: *GCE:* 40.

P304 BSc Media Technology with International Foundation Year (Intl only, Jan)
Duration: 4FT Hon
Entry Requirements: Contact the institution for details.

S43 SOUTH ESSEX COLLEGE OF FURTHER & HIGHER EDUCATION
LUKER ROAD
SOUTHEND-ON-SEA
ESSEX SS1 1ND
t: 0845 52 12345 f: 01702 432320
e: Admissions@southessex.ac.uk
// www.southessex.ac.uk

WP83 BA Creative Writing for Media
Duration: 3FT Hon
Entry Requirements: *GCE:* 160. *IB:* 24. Interview required.

S64 ST MARY'S UNIVERSITY COLLEGE, TWICKENHAM
WALDEGRAVE ROAD
STRAWBERRY HILL
MIDDLESEX TW1 4SX
t: 020 8240 4029 f: 020 8240 2361
e: admit@smuc.ac.uk
// www.smuc.ac.uk

PQ33 BA English and Media Arts
Duration: 3FT Hon
Entry Requirements: *GCE:* 240. *SQAH:* BBBC. *IB:* 28. *OCR ND:* D *OCR NED:* M3 Interview required.

VP13 BA History and Media Arts
Duration: 3FT Hon
Entry Requirements: *GCE:* 240. *SQAH:* BBBC. *IB:* 28. *OCR ND:* D *OCR NED:* M3 Interview required.

PQ35 BA Irish Studies and Media Arts
Duration: 3FT Hon
Entry Requirements: *GCE:* 240. *SQAH:* BBBC. *IB:* 28. *OCR ND:* D *OCR NED:* M3 Interview required.

NP23 BA Management Studies and Media Arts
Duration: 3FT Hon
Entry Requirements: *GCE:* 240. *SQAH:* BBBC. *IB:* 28. *OCR ND:* D *OCR NED:* M3 Interview required.

P300 BA Media Arts
Duration: 3FT Hon
Entry Requirements: *GCE:* 240. *SQAH:* BBBC. *IB:* 28. *OCR ND:* D *OCR NED:* M3 Interview required.

PW38 BA Media Arts and Creative & Professional Writing
Duration: 3FT Hon
Entry Requirements: *GCE:* 240. *SQAH:* BBBC. *IB:* 28. *OCR ND:* D *OCR NED:* M3 Interview required.

LP33 BA Media Arts and Sociology
Duration: 3FT Hon
Entry Requirements: *GCE:* 240. *SQAH:* BBBC. *IB:* 28. *OCR ND:* D *OCR NED:* M3 Interview required.

PN38 BA Media Arts and Tourism
Duration: 3FT Hon
Entry Requirements: *GCE:* 240. *SQAH:* BBBC. *IB:* 28. *OCR ND:* D *OCR NED:* M3 Interview required.

PHR4 BA Media and Spanish
Duration: 3FT Hon
Entry Requirements: Contact the institution for details.

CP63 BA/BSc Media Arts and Sport Science
Duration: 3FT Hon
Entry Requirements: *GCE:* 240. *SQAH:* BBBC. *IB:* 28. *OCR ND:* D *OCR NED:* M3 Interview required.

S72 STAFFORDSHIRE UNIVERSITY
COLLEGE ROAD
STOKE ON TRENT ST4 2DE
t: 01782 292753 f: 01782 292740
e: admissions@staffs.ac.uk
// www.staffs.ac.uk

W8P3 BA Screenwriting with Film Studies
Duration: 3FT Hon
Entry Requirements: *GCE:* 200-240. *IB:* 24. *BTEC Dip:* DD. *BTEC ExtDip:* MMM.

PJ39 BSc Film Production and Music Technology
Duration: 3FT/4SW Hon
Entry Requirements: *GCE:* 240-280. *IB:* 24.

P390 FdA Creative and Cultural Industries (Digital Media Production)
Duration: 2FT Hon
Entry Requirements: *GCE:* 80. Interview required.

S74 STRATFORD UPON AVON COLLEGE
THE WILLOWS NORTH
ALCESTER ROAD
STRATFORD-UPON-AVON
WARWICKSHIRE CV37 9QR
t: 01789 266245 f: 01789 267524
e: college@stratford.ac.uk
// www.stratford.ac.uk

003P HND Creative Media Production
Duration: 2FT HND
Entry Requirements: *GCE:* 200. Interview required. Portfolio required.

S75 THE UNIVERSITY OF STIRLING
STUDENT RECRUITMENT & ADMISSIONS SERVICE
UNIVERSITY OF STIRLING
STIRLING
SCOTLAND FK9 4LA
t: 01786 467044 f: 01786 466800
e: admissions@stir.ac.uk
// www.stir.ac.uk

NP13 BA Business Studies and Film & Media
Duration: 4FT Hon
Entry Requirements: *GCE:* BBC. *SQAH:* BBBB. *SQAAH:* AAA-CCC. *IB:* 32. *BTEC ExtDip:* DMM.

QP33 BA English Studies and Film & Media
Duration: 4FT Hon
Entry Requirements: *GCE:* BBC. *SQAH:* BBBB. *SQAAH:* AAA-CCC. *IB:* 32. *BTEC ExtDip:* DMM.

P3R1 BA European Film and Media
Duration: 4FT Hon
Entry Requirements: *GCE:* BBC. *SQAH:* BBBB. *SQAAH:* AAA-CCC. *IB:* 32. *BTEC ExtDip:* DMM.

P300 BA Film & Media
Duration: 4FT Hon
Entry Requirements: *GCE:* BBC. *SQAH:* BBBB. *SQAAH:* AAA-CCC.
IB: 32. *BTEC ExtDip:* DMM.

RP13 BA Film & Media and French
Duration: 4FT Hon
Entry Requirements: *GCE:* BBC. *SQAH:* BBBB. *SQAAH:* AAA-CCC.
IB: 32. *BTEC ExtDip:* DMM.

PV31 BA Film & Media and History
Duration: 4FT Hon
Entry Requirements: *GCE:* BBC. *SQAH:* BBBB. *SQAAH:* AAA-CCC.
IB: 32. *BTEC ExtDip:* DMM.

PP35 BA Film & Media and Journalism Studies
Duration: 4FT Hon
Entry Requirements: *GCE:* BBC. *SQAH:* BBBB. *SQAAH:* AAA-CCC.
IB: 32. *BTEC ExtDip:* DMM.

PN35 BA Film & Media and Marketing
Duration: 4FT Hon
Entry Requirements: *GCE:* BBC. *SQAH:* BBBB. *SQAAH:* AAA-CCC.
IB: 32. *BTEC ExtDip:* DMM.

VP53 BA Film & Media and Philosophy
Duration: 4FT Hon
Entry Requirements: *GCE:* BBC. *SQAH:* BBBB. *SQAAH:* AAA-CCC.
IB: 32. *BTEC ExtDip:* DMM.

PL32 BA Film & Media and Politics
Duration: 4FT Hon
Entry Requirements: *GCE:* BBC. *SQAH:* BBBB. *SQAAH:* AAA-CCC.
IB: 32. *BTEC ExtDip:* DMM.

CP83 BA Film & Media and Psychology
Duration: 4FT Hon
Entry Requirements: *GCE:* BBC. *SQAH:* BBBB. *SQAAH:* AAA-CCC.
IB: 32. *BTEC ExtDip:* DMM.

VP63 BA Film & Media and Religion
Duration: 4FT Hon
Entry Requirements: *GCE:* BBC. *SQAH:* BBBB. *SQAAH:* AAA-CCC.
IB: 32. *BTEC ExtDip:* DMM.

LP33 BA Film & Media and Sociology
Duration: 4FT Hon
Entry Requirements: *GCE:* BBC. *SQAH:* BBBB. *SQAAH:* AAA-CCC.
IB: 32. *BTEC ExtDip:* DMM.

RP43 BA Film & Media and Spanish
Duration: 4FT Hon
Entry Requirements: *GCE:* BBC. *SQAH:* BBBB. *SQAAH:* AAA-CCC.
IB: 32. *BTEC ExtDip:* DMM.

CP63 BA Film & Media and Sports Studies
Duration: 4FT Hon
Entry Requirements: *GCE:* BBC. *SQAH:* BBBB. *SQAAH:* AAA-CCC.
IB: 32. *BTEC ExtDip:* DMM.

S82 UNIVERSITY CAMPUS SUFFOLK (UCS)
WATERFRONT BUILDING
NEPTUNE QUAY
IPSWICH
SUFFOLK IP4 1QJ
t: 01473 338833 f: 01473 339900
e: info@ucs.ac.uk
// www.ucs.ac.uk

P300 BA Film
Duration: 3FT Hon
Entry Requirements: *GCE:* 240-280. *IB:* 28. *BTEC ExtDip:* DMM.
Admissions Test required.

P391 FdA Visual Media Production
Duration: 2FT Fdg
Entry Requirements: *GCE:* 200. *IB:* 28. *BTEC ExtDip:* DMM.
Interview required.

S84 UNIVERSITY OF SUNDERLAND
STUDENT HELPLINE
THE STUDENT GATEWAY
CHESTER ROAD
SUNDERLAND SR1 3SD
t: 0191 515 3000 f: 0191 515 3805
e: student.helpline@sunderland.ac.uk
// www.sunderland.ac.uk

NP13 BA Business Management and Media Studies
Duration: 3FT Hon
Entry Requirements: *GCE:* 260-360. *IB:* 31. *OCR ND:* D *OCR NED:* M3

N1P3 BA Business Management with Media Studies
Duration: 3FT Hon
Entry Requirements: *GCE:* 260-360. *IB:* 31. *OCR ND:* D *OCR NED:* M3

XPH3 BA Childhood Studies and Media Studies
Duration: 3FT Hon
Entry Requirements: *GCE:* 260-360.

X3P3 BA Childhood Studies with Media Studies
Duration: 3FT Hon
Entry Requirements: *GCE:* 260-360.

MP9H BA Criminology and Media Studies
Duration: 3FT Hon
Entry Requirements: *GCE:* 260-360. *OCR ND:* D *OCR NED:* M3

M9P3 BA Criminology with Media Studies
Duration: 3FT Hon
Entry Requirements: *GCE:* 260-360. *OCR ND:* D *OCR NED:* M3

PW35 BA Dance and Media Studies
Duration: 3FT Hon
Entry Requirements: *GCE:* 260-360. *IB:* 31. *OCR ND:* D *OCR NED:* M3

W5P3 BA Dance with Media Studies
Duration: 3FT Hon
Entry Requirements: *GCE:* 260-360. *IB:* 31. *OCR ND:* D *OCR NED:* M3

W4P3 BA Drama with Media Studies
Duration: 3FT Hon
Entry Requirements: *GCE:* 260-360. *OCR ND:* D *OCR NED:* M3

Q1P3 BA English Language & Linguistics with Media Studies
Duration: 3FT Hon
Entry Requirements: *GCE:* 260-360. *OCR ND:* D *OCR NED:* M3

QP33 BA English and Media Studies
Duration: 3FT Hon
Entry Requirements: *GCE:* 260-360. *IB:* 31. *OCR ND:* D *OCR NED:* M3

Q3P3 BA English with Media Studies
Duration: 3FT Hon
Entry Requirements: *GCE:* 260-360. *IB:* 31. *OCR ND:* D *OCR NED:* M3

PW36 BA Film and Media
Duration: 3FT Hon
Entry Requirements: *GCE:* 260-360. *IB:* 30.

LP53 BA Health & Social Care and Media Studies
Duration: 3FT Hon
Entry Requirements: *GCE:* 260-360.

L5P3 BA Health & Social Care with Media Studies
Duration: 3FT Hon
Entry Requirements: *GCE:* 260-360.

VP13 BA History and Media Studies
Duration: 3FT Hon
Entry Requirements: *GCE:* 260-360. *IB:* 31. *OCR ND:* D *OCR NED:* M3

V1P3 BA History with Media Studies
Duration: 3FT Hon
Entry Requirements: *GCE:* 260-360. *IB:* 31. *OCR ND:* D *OCR NED:* M3

MP13 BA Law and Media Studies
Duration: 3FT Hon
Entry Requirements: *GCE:* 260-360. *OCR ND:* D *OCR NED:* M3

HP63 BA Media Production (Television and Radio)
Duration: 3FT Hon
Entry Requirements: *GCE:* 260-360. *IB:* 30. Interview required.

PH36 BA Media Production (Video and New Media)
Duration: 3FT Hon
Entry Requirements: *GCE:* 260-360. *IB:* 30. Interview required.

PW34 BA Media Studies and Drama
Duration: 3FT Hon
Entry Requirements: *GCE:* 260-360. *OCR ND:* D *OCR NED:* M3

PX33 BA Media Studies and Education
Duration: 3FT Hon
Entry Requirements: *GCE:* 220-360. *IB:* 32. *OCR ND:* D *OCR NED:* M3

PQ31 BA Media Studies and English Language/Linguistics
Duration: 3FT Hon
Entry Requirements: *GCE:* 260-360. *IB:* 32. *OCR ND:* D *OCR NED:* M3

WP63 BA Media Studies and Photography
Duration: 3FT Hon
Entry Requirements: *GCE:* 260-360. *IB:* 32. *OCR ND:* D *OCR NED:* M3

PL32 BA Media Studies and Politics
Duration: 3FT Hon
Entry Requirements: *GCE:* 260-360. *IB:* 32. *OCR ND:* D *OCR NED:* M3

PL33 BA Media Studies and Sociology
Duration: 3FT Hon
Entry Requirements: *GCE:* 260-360. *IB:* 32. *OCR ND:* D *OCR NED:* M3

PX31 BA Media Studies and TESOL
Duration: 3FT Hon
Entry Requirements: *GCE:* 260-360. *OCR ND:* D *OCR NED:* M3

P3N1 BA Media Studies with Business Management
Duration: 3FT Hon
Entry Requirements: *GCE:* 260-360. *IB:* 32. *OCR ND:* D *OCR NED:* M3

P3XH BA Media Studies with Childhood Studies
Duration: 3FT Hon
Entry Requirements: *GCE:* 260-360.

P3M9 BA Media Studies with Criminology
Duration: 3FT Hon
Entry Requirements: *GCE:* 260-360. *IB:* 32. *OCR ND:* D *OCR NED:* M3

P3W5 BA Media Studies with Dance
Duration: 3FT Hon
Entry Requirements: *GCE:* 260-360. *IB:* 31. *OCR ND:* D *OCR NED:* M3

P3W4 BA Media Studies with Drama
Duration: 3FT Hon
Entry Requirements: *GCE:* 260-360. *OCR ND:* D *OCR NED:* M3

P3X3 BA Media Studies with Education
Duration: 3FT Hon
Entry Requirements: *GCE:* 260-360. *IB:* 32. *OCR ND:* D *OCR NED:* M3

P3Q1 BA Media Studies with English Language/Linguistics
Duration: 3FT Hon
Entry Requirements: *GCE:* 260-360. *IB:* 32. *OCR ND:* D *OCR NED:* M3

P3Q3 BA Media Studies with English Studies
Duration: 3FT Hon
Entry Requirements: *GCE:* 260-360. *IB:* 32. *OCR ND:* D *OCR NED:* M3

P3L5 BA Media Studies with Health & Social Care
Duration: 3FT Hon
Entry Requirements: *GCE:* 260-360.

P3V1 BA Media Studies with History
Duration: 3FT Hon
Entry Requirements: *GCE:* 260-360. *IB:* 32. *OCR ND:* D *OCR NED:* M3

P3R2 BA Media Studies with MFL (German)
Duration: 3FT Hon
Entry Requirements: *GCE:* 260-360. *OCR ND:* D *OCR NED:* M3

P3R1 BA Media Studies with Modern Foreign Language (French)
Duration: 3FT Hon
Entry Requirements: *GCE:* 260-360. *OCR ND:* D *OCR NED:* M3

P3R4 BA Media Studies with Modern Foreign Language (Spanish)
Duration: 3FT Hon
Entry Requirements: *GCE:* 260-360. *OCR ND:* D *OCR NED:* M3

P3W6 BA Media Studies with Photography
Duration: 3FT Hon
Entry Requirements: *GCE:* 260-360. *IB:* 32. *OCR ND:* D *OCR NED:* M3

P3L2 BA Media Studies with Politics
Duration: 3FT Hon
Entry Requirements: *GCE:* 260-360. *IB:* 32. *OCR ND:* D *OCR NED:* M3

P3C8 BA Media Studies with Psychology
Duration: 3FT Hon
Entry Requirements: *GCE:* 260-360. *IB:* 32. *OCR ND:* D *OCR NED:* M3

P3L3 BA Media Studies with Sociology
Duration: 3FT Hon
Entry Requirements: *GCE:* 260-360. *IB:* 32. *OCR ND:* D *OCR NED:* M3

P3C6 BA Media Studies with Sport
Duration: 3FT Hon
Entry Requirements: *GCE:* 260-360. *OCR ND:* D *OCR NED:* M3

P3X1 BA Media Studies with TESOL
Duration: 3FT Hon
Entry Requirements: *GCE:* 260-360. *OCR ND:* D *OCR NED:* M3

P3N8 BA Media Studies with Tourism
Duration: 3FT Hon
Entry Requirements: *GCE:* 260-360. *OCR ND:* D *OCR NED:* M3

PP39 BA Media, Culture and Communication
Duration: 3FT Hon
Entry Requirements: *GCE:* 260-360. *IB:* 30.

RP13 BA Modern Foreign Languages (French) and Media
Duration: 3FT Hon
Entry Requirements: *GCE:* 260-360. *IB:* 31. *OCR ND:* D *OCR NED:* M3

PR32 BA Modern Foreign Languages (German) and Media Studies
Duration: 3FT Hon
Entry Requirements: *GCE:* 260-360. *IB:* 31. *OCR ND:* D *OCR NED:* M3

PR34 BA Modern Foreign Languages (Spanish) and Media Studies
Duration: 3FT Hon
Entry Requirements: *GCE:* 260-360. *IB:* 31. *OCR ND:* D *OCR NED:* M3

L2P3 BA Politics with Media Studies
Duration: 3FT Hon
Entry Requirements: *GCE:* 260-360. *IB:* 31. *OCR ND:* D *OCR NED:* M3

L3P3 BA Sociology with Media Studies
Duration: 3FT Hon
Entry Requirements: *GCE:* 260-360. *IB:* 31. *OCR ND:* D *OCR NED:* M3

X1P3 BA TESOL with Media Studies
Duration: 3FT Hon
Entry Requirements: *GCE:* 260-360. *OCR ND:* D *OCR NED:* M3

NP83 BA Tourism and Media Studies
Duration: 3FT Hon
Entry Requirements: *GCE:* 260-360. *IB:* 31. *OCR ND:* D *OCR NED:* M3

N8P3 BA Tourism with Media Studies
Duration: 3FT Hon
Entry Requirements: *GCE:* 220-360. *IB:* 31. *OCR ND:* D *OCR NED:* M3

PC38 BA/BSc Media Studies and Psychology
Duration: 3FT Hon
Entry Requirements: *GCE:* 260-360. *IB:* 32. *OCR ND:* D *OCR NED:* M3

CP63 BA/BSc Sport and Media Studies
Duration: 3FT Hon
Entry Requirements: *GCE:* 260-360. *OCR ND:* D *OCR NED:* M3

C8P3 BSc Psychology with Media Studies
Duration: 3FT Hon
Entry Requirements: *GCE:* 260-360. *IB:* 32. *OCR ND:* D *OCR NED:* M3

C6P3 BSc Sport with Media Studies
Duration: 3FT Hon
Entry Requirements: *GCE:* 260-360. *OCR ND:* D *OCR NED:* M3

S85 UNIVERSITY OF SURREY
STAG HILL
GUILDFORD
SURREY GU2 7XH
t: +44(0)1483 689305 f: +44(0)1483 689388
e: ugteam@surrey.ac.uk
// www.surrey.ac.uk

P306 BA Media Studies (3 or 4 years)
Duration: 3FT/4SW Hon
Entry Requirements: *GCE:* 300-320.

LP33 BSc Sociology, Culture and Media (3 years)
Duration: 3FT Hon
Entry Requirements: *GCE:* ABB. *SQAH:* BBBB. *IB:* 34.

LP3H BSc Sociology, Culture and Media (4 years)
Duration: 4SW Hon
Entry Requirements: *GCE:* 300-320.

S90 UNIVERSITY OF SUSSEX
UNDERGRADUATE ADMISSIONS
SUSSEX HOUSE
UNIVERSITY OF SUSSEX
BRIGHTON BN1 9RH
t: 01273 678416 f: 01273 678545
e: ug.applicants@sussex.ac.uk
// www.sussex.ac.uk

TP73 BA American Studies and Film Studies
Duration: 4FT Hon
Entry Requirements: *GCE:* AAB. *SQAH:* AAABB. *IB:* 35. *BTEC SubDip:* D. *BTEC Dip:* DD. *BTEC ExtDip:* DDD. *OCR ND:* D *OCR NED:* D1

QP33 BA English and Media Studies
Duration: 3FT Hon
Entry Requirements: *GCE:* AAA-AAB. *SQAH:* AAAAA-AAABB. *SQAAH:* AAA-AAB. *IB:* 35. *BTEC SubDip:* D. *BTEC Dip:* DD. *BTEC ExtDip:* DDD. *OCR ND:* M1 *OCR NED:* D1

P300 BA Film Studies
Duration: 3FT Hon
Entry Requirements: *GCE:* AAB-ABB. *SQAH:* AAABB-AABBB. *BTEC SubDip:* D. *BTEC Dip:* DM. *BTEC ExtDip:* DDM. *OCR ND:* M1 *OCR NED:* D2

PRH9 BA Media Studies and a Language (French/Italian/Spanish)
Duration: 4FT Hon
Entry Requirements: *GCE:* ABB. *SQAH:* AABBB. *SQAAH:* ABB. *IB:* 34. *BTEC SubDip:* D. *BTEC Dip:* DD. *BTEC ExtDip:* DDM. *OCR ND:* D *OCR NED:* D2

P306 BA Media and Communications
Duration: 3FT Hon
Entry Requirements: *GCE:* ABB. *SQAH:* AABBB. *IB:* 34. *BTEC SubDip:* D. *BTEC Dip:* DD. *BTEC ExtDip:* DDM. *OCR ND:* D *OCR NED:* D2

PR39 BA Media and Cultural Studies
Duration: 3FT Hon
Entry Requirements: *GCE:* ABB. *SQAH:* AABBB. *IB:* 34. *BTEC SubDip:* D. *BTEC Dip:* DD. *BTEC ExtDip:* DDM. *OCR ND:* D *OCR NED:* D2

LP33 BA Sociology and Media Studies
Duration: 3FT Hon
Entry Requirements: *GCE:* ABB. *SQAH:* AABBB. *IB:* 34. *BTEC SubDip:* D. *BTEC Dip:* DD. *BTEC ExtDip:* DDD. *OCR ND:* M1 *OCR NED:* D2

S93 SWANSEA UNIVERSITY
SINGLETON PARK
SWANSEA SA2 8PP
t: 01792 295111 f: 01792 295110
e: admissions@swansea.ac.uk
// www.swansea.ac.uk

QP53 BA Cymraeg a'r Cyfryngau
Duration: 3FT Hon
Entry Requirements: Contact the institution for details.

P300 BA Media Studies
Duration: 3FT Hon
Entry Requirements: *GCE:* BBB. *IB:* 32.

QP33 BA Media Studies and English
Duration: 3FT Hon
Entry Requirements: *GCE:* ABB-BBB.

PR31 BA Media Studies and French
Duration: 4FT Hon
Entry Requirements: *GCE:* BBB. *IB:* 32.

PR32 BA Media Studies and German
Duration: 4FT Hon
Entry Requirements: *GCE:* BBB. *IB:* 32.

PR33 BA Media Studies and Italian
Duration: 4FT Hon
Entry Requirements: *GCE:* BBB. *IB:* 32.

PR34 BA Media Studies and Spanish
Duration: 4FT Hon
Entry Requirements: *GCE:* BBB. *IB:* 32.

PQ35 BA Media Studies and Welsh
Duration: 3FT Hon
Entry Requirements: *GCE:* BBB. *IB:* 32.

T20 TEESSIDE UNIVERSITY
MIDDLESBROUGH TS1 3BA
t: 01642 218121 f: 01642 384201
e: registry@tees.ac.uk
// www.tees.ac.uk

P300 BA Media Studies
Duration: 3FT Hon
Entry Requirements: *GCE:* 280. *IB:* 24.

T80 UNIVERSITY OF WALES TRINITY SAINT DAVID
COLLEGE ROAD
CARMARTHEN SA31 3EP
t: 01267 676767 f: 01267 676766
e: registry@trinitysaintdavid.ac.uk
// www.tsd.ac.uk

PW33 BA Cerdd a'r Cyfryngau
Duration: 3FT Hon
Entry Requirements: *GCE:* 160-360. *IB:* 26. Interview required.

P306 BA Y Cyfryngau Creadigol
Duration: 3FT Hon
Entry Requirements: *GCE:* 160-360. *IB:* 26. Interview required.

T85 TRURO AND PENWITH COLLEGE
TRURO COLLEGE
COLLEGE ROAD
TRURO
CORNWALL TR1 3XX
t: 01872 267122 f: 01872 267526
e: heinfo@trurocollege.ac.uk
// www.truro-penwith.ac.uk

P300 BA Applied Media
Duration: 1FT Hon
Entry Requirements: Contact the institution for details.

U20 UNIVERSITY OF ULSTER
COLERAINE
CO. LONDONDERRY
NORTHERN IRELAND BT52 1SA
t: 028 7012 4221 f: 028 7012 4908
e: online@ulster.ac.uk
// www.ulster.ac.uk

PQ33 BA English and Media Studies
Duration: 3FT Hon
Entry Requirements: *GCE:* 280. *IB:* 24.

Q3PH BA English with Media Studies
Duration: 3FT Hon
Entry Requirements: *GCE:* 280. *IB:* 24.

P391 BA Film Studies and Media Studies
Duration: 3FT Hon
Entry Requirements: *GCE:* BBC. *IB:* 24.

P392 BA Film Studies with Media Studies
Duration: 3FT Hon
Entry Requirements: *GCE:* BBC. *IB:* 24.

RP13 BA French and Media Studies
Duration: 3FT Hon
Entry Requirements: *GCE:* 260. *IB:* 24.

R1PH BA French with Media Studies
Duration: 4FT Hon
Entry Requirements: *GCE:* 260. *IB:* 24.

RP23 BA German and Media Studies
Duration: 3FT Hon
Entry Requirements: *GCE:* 260. *IB:* 24.

R2PH BA German with Media Studies
Duration: 4FT Hon
Entry Requirements: *GCE:* 260. *IB:* 24.

VP13 BA History and Media Studies
Duration: 3FT Hon
Entry Requirements: *GCE:* 280. *IB:* 24.

V1PH BA History with Media Studies
Duration: 3FT Hon
Entry Requirements: *GCE:* 280. *IB:* 24.

P300 BA Media Studies and Production
Duration: 3FT Hon
Entry Requirements: *GCE:* 280-300.

PRH4 BA Media Studies and Spanish
Duration: 3FT Hon
Entry Requirements: *GCE:* 260. *IB:* 24. Interview required.

P3N1 BA Media Studies with Business
Duration: 3FT Hon
Entry Requirements: *GCE:* 280. *IB:* 24.

P3G4 BA Media Studies with Computing
Duration: 3FT Hon
Entry Requirements: *GCE:* 280. *IB:* 24.

P3Q3 BA Media Studies with English
Duration: 3FT Hon
Entry Requirements: *GCE:* 280. *IB:* 24.

P390 BA Media Studies with Film Studies
Duration: 3FT Hon
Entry Requirements: *GCE:* 280. *IB:* 24.

P3R1 BA Media Studies with French
Duration: 3FT Hon
Entry Requirements: *GCE:* 280. *IB:* 24.

P3F8 BA Media Studies with Geography
Duration: 3FT Hon
Entry Requirements: *GCE:* 280. *IB:* 24.

P3R2 BA Media Studies with German
Duration: 3FT Hon
Entry Requirements: *GCE:* 280. *IB:* 24.

P3V1 BA Media Studies with History
Duration: 3FT Hon
Entry Requirements: *GCE:* 280. *IB:* 24.

P3LX BA Media Studies with International Development
Duration: 4SW Hon
Entry Requirements: *GCE:* 280. *IB:* 24.

P3N5 BA Media Studies with Marketing
Duration: 4SW Hon
Entry Requirements: *GCE:* 280. *IB:* 24.

P3WP BA Media Studies with Photo-Imaging
Duration: 3FT Hon
Entry Requirements: *GCE:* 280. *IB:* 24.

P3C8 BA Media Studies with Psychology
Duration: 3FT Hon
Entry Requirements: *GCE:* 280. *IB:* 24.

P3N2 BA Media Studies with Retail Studies
Duration: 4SW Hon
Entry Requirements: *GCE:* 280. *IB:* 24.

P3R4 BA Media Studies with Spanish
Duration: 3FT Hon
Entry Requirements: *GCE:* 280. *IB:* 24.

R4PH BA Spanish with Media Studies
Duration: 4SW Hon
Entry Requirements: *GCE:* 260. *IB:* 24.

N1PH BSc Business with Media Studies
Duration: 4SW Hon
Entry Requirements: *GCE:* 240-280. *IB:* 24.

U40 UNIVERSITY OF THE WEST OF SCOTLAND
PAISLEY
RENFREWSHIRE
SCOTLAND PA1 2BE
t: 0141 848 3727 f: 0141 848 3623
e: admissions@uws.ac.uk
// www.uws.ac.uk

GP43 BSc Multimedia Technology
Duration: 3FT/4FT Ord/Hon
Entry Requirements: *GCE:* CC. *SQAH:* BBC.

U65 UNIVERSITY OF THE ARTS LONDON
272 HIGH HOLBORN
LONDON WC1V 7EY
t: 020 7514 6000x6197 f: 020 7514 6198
e: c.anderson@arts.ac.uk
// www.arts.ac.uk

WPF3 BA Illustration and Visual Media
Duration: 3FT Hon
Entry Requirements: Contact the institution for details.

P302 BA Media Communications
Duration: 3FT Hon
Entry Requirements: Contact the institution for details.

P306 BA Media Practice (Top-Up)
Duration: 1FT Hon
Entry Requirements: Contact the institution for details.

P300 BA Media and Cultural Studies
Duration: 3FT Hon
Entry Requirements: *IB:* 28. Foundation Course required. Interview required. Portfolio required.

P305 BA Print Media Management (Top-Up)
Duration: 1FT Hon
Entry Requirements: Contact the institution for details.

W05 THE UNIVERSITY OF WEST LONDON
ST MARY'S ROAD
EALING
LONDON W5 5RF
t: 0800 036 8888 f: 020 8566 1353
e: learning.advice@uwl.ac.uk
// www.uwl.ac.uk

P306 BA Media Studies
Duration: 3FT Hon
Entry Requirements: *GCE:* 240. Interview required.

W50 UNIVERSITY OF WESTMINSTER
2ND FLOOR, CAVENDISH HOUSE
101 NEW CAVENDISH STREET,
LONDON W1W 6XH
t: 020 7915 5511
e: course-enquiries@westminster.ac.uk
// www.westminster.ac.uk

WP23 BA Mixed Media Fine Art
Duration: 3FT Hon
Entry Requirements: *GCE:* CC. *IB:* 28. Interview required. Portfolio required.

GP43 BSc Multimedia Computing
Duration: 3FT/4SW Hon
Entry Requirements: *GCE:* AA-CCC. *SQAH:* BCCC-CCCCC. *IB:* 28. *OCR ND:* M1 *OCR NED:* M1 Interview required.

W52 WESTMINSTER KINGSWAY COLLEGE
VICTORIA CENTRE
VINCENT SQUARE
LONDON SW1P 2PD
t: 0870 060 9800 f: 020 7931 6969
e: courseinfo@westking.ac.uk
// www.westking.ac.uk

P300 HND Creative Media Production
Duration: 1FT Hon
Entry Requirements: Contact the institution for details.

W75 UNIVERSITY OF WOLVERHAMPTON
ADMISSIONS UNIT
MX207, CAMP STREET
WOLVERHAMPTON
WEST MIDLANDS WV1 1AD
t: 01902 321000 f: 01902 321896
e: admissions@wlv.ac.uk
// www.wlv.ac.uk

WP8H BA Creative & Professional Writing and Media & Communication Studies
Duration: 3FT Hon
Entry Requirements: *GCE:* 160-220.

QP3H BA English Language and Media & Communication Studies
Duration: 3FT Hon
Entry Requirements: *GCE:* 160-220.

QPH3 BA English and Media & Cultural Studies
Duration: 3FT Hon
Entry Requirements: *GCE:* 160-220. *IB:* 24.

WPQ3 BA Film Studies and Media & Cultural Studies
Duration: 3FT Hon
Entry Requirements: *GCE:* 160-220. *IB:* 24.

PWH6 BA Media & Communication Studies and Film Studies
Duration: 3FT Hon
Entry Requirements: *GCE:* 160-220. *IB:* 28.

PQ33 BA Media & Cultural Studies and English Language
Duration: 3FT Hon
Entry Requirements: *GCE:* 160-220.

PL33 BA Media & Cultural Studies and Sociology
Duration: 3FT Hon
Entry Requirements: *GCE:* 160-220. *IB:* 24.

PP93 BA Media and Communication Studies
Duration: 3FT Hon
Entry Requirements: *GCE:* 160-220. *IB:* 28.

PL36 BA Media and Cultural Studies
Duration: 3FT Hon
Entry Requirements: *GCE:* 160-220. *IB:* 24.

LP23 BA Politics and Media & Communication Studies
Duration: 3FT Hon
Entry Requirements: *GCE:* 160-220. *IB:* 28.

W76 UNIVERSITY OF WINCHESTER
WINCHESTER
HANTS SO22 4NR
t: 01962 827234 f: 01962 827288
e: course.enquiries@winchester.ac.uk
// www.winchester.ac.uk

PT37 BA American Studies and Media Studies
Duration: 3FT Hon
Entry Requirements: *Foundation:* Distinction. *GCE:* 260-300. *IB:* 25. *OCR ND:* D *OCR NED:* M2

FP43 BA Archaeology and Media Studies
Duration: 3FT Hon
Entry Requirements: *Foundation:* Distinction. *GCE:* 260-300. *IB:* 25. *OCR ND:* D *OCR NED:* M2

NP13 BA Business Management and Media Studies
Duration: 3FT Hon
Entry Requirements: *Foundation:* Distinction. *GCE:* 260-300. *IB:* 25. *OCR ND:* D *OCR NED:* M2

LPMH BA Childhood,Youth & Community Studies and Media Studies
Duration: 3FT Hon
Entry Requirements: *Foundation:* Distinction. *GCE:* 260-300. *IB:* 25. *OCR ND:* D *OCR NED:* M2

PWJ5 BA Choreography & Dance and Media Studies
Duration: 3FT Hon
Entry Requirements: *Foundation:* Distinction. *GCE:* 260-300. *IB:* 25. *OCR ND:* D *OCR NED:* M2

WPV3 BA Creative Writing and Media Studies
Duration: 3FT Hon
Entry Requirements: *Foundation:* Distinction. *GCE:* 260-300. *IB:* 25. *OCR ND:* D *OCR NED:* M2

LP3H BA Criminology and Media Studies
Duration: 3FT Hon
Entry Requirements: *Foundation:* Distinction. *GCE:* 260-300. *IB:* 24. *OCR ND:* D *OCR NED:* M2

PW34 BA Drama and Media Studies
Duration: 3FT Hon
Entry Requirements: *Foundation:* Distinction. *GCE:* 260-300. *IB:* 25. *OCR ND:* D *OCR NED:* M2

QPJ3 BA English Language Studies and Media Studies
Duration: 3FT Hon
Entry Requirements: *Foundation:* Distinction. *GCE:* 260-300. *IB:* 25. *OCR ND:* D *OCR NED:* M2

PQ33 BA English and Media Studies
Duration: 3FT Hon
Entry Requirements: *Foundation:* Distinction. *GCE:* 260-300. *IB:* 25. *OCR ND:* D *OCR NED:* M2

NP8J BA Event Management and Media Studies
Duration: 3FT Hon
Entry Requirements: *Foundation:* Distinction. *GCE:* 260-300. *IB:* 25. *OCR ND:* D *OCR NED:* M2

WP63 BA Film & Cinema Technologies and Media Studies
Duration: 3FT Hon
Entry Requirements: *Foundation:* Distinction. *GCE:* 260-300. *IB:* 25. *OCR ND:* D *OCR NED:* M2

WPQ3 BA Film and Cinema Technologies
Duration: 3FT Hon
Entry Requirements: *Foundation:* Distinction. *GCE:* 260-300. *IB:* 24. *OCR ND:* D *OCR NED:* M2

PL3N BA Health, Community & Social Care Studies and Media Studies
Duration: 3FT Hon
Entry Requirements: Contact the institution for details.

VP13 BA History and Media Studies
Duration: 3FT Hon
Entry Requirements: *Foundation:* Distinction. *GCE:* 260-300. *IB:* 25. *OCR ND:* D *OCR NED:* M2

PPM3 BA Journalism Studies and Media Studies
Duration: 3FT Hon
Entry Requirements: *Foundation:* Distinction. *GCE:* 260-300. *IB:* 25. *OCR ND:* D *OCR NED:* M2

MPC3 BA Law and Media Studies
Duration: 3FT Hon
Entry Requirements: *Foundation:* Distinction. *GCE:* 260-300. *IB:* 25. *OCR ND:* D *OCR NED:* M2

P39C BA Media Production and Media Studies
Duration: 3FT Hon
Entry Requirements: Contact the institution for details.

P3W6 BA Media Studies
Duration: 3FT Hon
Entry Requirements: *Foundation:* Distinction. *GCE:* 260-300. *IB:* 25. *OCR ND:* D *OCR NED:* M2

PW39 BA Media Studies and Modern Liberal Arts
Duration: 3FT Hon
Entry Requirements: *Foundation:* Distinction. *GCE:* 260-300. *IB:* 25. *OCR ND:* D *OCR NED:* M2

CP83 BA Media Studies and Psychology
Duration: 3FT Hon
Entry Requirements: *Foundation:* Distinction. *GCE:* 260-300. *IB:* 25. *OCR ND:* D *OCR NED:* M2

PL3J BA Media Studies and Sociology
Duration: 3FT Hon
Entry Requirements: *Foundation:* Distinction. *GCE:* 260-300. *IB:* 25. *OCR ND:* D *OCR NED:* M2

PNH8 BA Media Studies and Sports Management
Duration: 3FT Hon
Entry Requirements: *Foundation:* Distinction. *GCE:* 260-300. *IB:* 25. *OCR ND:* D

CP63 BA Media Studies and Sports Studies
Duration: 3FT Hon
Entry Requirements: *Foundation:* Merit. *GCE:* 260-300. *IB:* 25.

PVH6 BA Media Studies and Theology & Religious Studies
Duration: 3FT Hon
Entry Requirements: *Foundation:* Distinction. *GCE:* 260-300. *IB:* 25. *OCR ND:* D *OCR NED:* M2

PWH3 BA Media Studies and Vocal & Choral Studies
Duration: 3FT Hon
Entry Requirements: *Foundation:* Distinction. *GCE:* 260-300. *IB:* 25. *OCR ND:* D *OCR NED:* M2

LPF3 BA Politics & Global Studies and Media Studies
Duration: 3FT Hon
Entry Requirements: *Foundation:* Distinction. *GCE:* 260-300. *IB:* 25. *OCR ND:* D *OCR NED:* M2

W80 UNIVERSITY OF WORCESTER
HENWICK GROVE
WORCESTER WR2 6AJ
t: 01905 855111 f: 01905 855377
e: admissions@worc.ac.uk
// www.worcester.ac.uk

WP13 BA Art & Design and Media & Cultural Studies
Duration: 3FT Hon
Entry Requirements: *GCE:* 240-260. *IB:* 24. *OCR ND:* D Interview required. Portfolio required.

WP83 BA Creative & Professional Writing and Media & Cultural Studies
Duration: 3FT Hon
Entry Requirements: Contact the institution for details.

P393 BA Creative Digital Media and Digital Film Production
Duration: 3FT Hon
Entry Requirements: Contact the institution for details.

PW3G BA Creative Digital Media and Graphic Design & Multimedia
Duration: 3FT Hon
Entry Requirements: Contact the institution for details.

PQ33 BA English Language Studies and Media & Cultural Studies
Duration: 3FT Hon
Entry Requirements: *GCE:* 240-260. *IB:* 24. *OCR ND:* D *OCR NED:* M3

QP33 BA English Literary Studies and Media & Cultural Studies
Duration: 3FT Hon
Entry Requirements: *GCE:* 240-300. *IB:* 24. *OCR ND:* D *OCR NED:* M3

WPFH BA Graphic Design & Multimedia and Media & Cultural Studies
Duration: 3FT Hon
Entry Requirements: Contact the institution for details.

LP33 BA Media & Cultural Studies and Sociology
Duration: 3FT Hon
Entry Requirements: *GCE:* 240-300. *IB:* 24. *OCR ND:* D *OCR NED:* M3

Y75 YORK ST JOHN UNIVERSITY
LORD MAYOR'S WALK
YORK YO31 7EX
t: 01904 876598 f: 01904 876940/876921
e: admissions@yorksj.ac.uk
// w3.yorksj.ac.uk

WP83 BA Creative Writing and Media
Duration: 3FT Hon
Entry Requirements: *GCE:* 220-260. *IB:* 24.

P391 BA Film Studies and Media
Duration: 3FT Hon
Entry Requirements: *GCE:* 220-260. *IB:* 24.

P305 BA Media
Duration: 3FT Hon
Entry Requirements: *Foundation:* Pass. *GCE:* 220-260. *IB:* 24.

P301 BA Media (for international applicants only)
Duration: 4FT Hon
Entry Requirements: *Foundation:* Pass. *GCE:* 220-260. *IB:* 24.

PQH3 BA Media and English Literature
Duration: 3FT Hon
Entry Requirements: *GCE:* 220-260. *IB:* 24.

QP33 BA Media and English Literature (for international applicants only)
Duration: 4FT Hon
Entry Requirements: *Foundation:* Pass. *GCE:* 220-260. *IB:* 24.

TELEVISION, FILM AND RADIO

A60 ANGLIA RUSKIN UNIVERSITY
BISHOP HALL LANE
CHELMSFORD
ESSEX CM1 1SQ
t: 0845 271 3333 f: 01245 251789
e: answers@anglia.ac.uk
// www.anglia.ac.uk

WP4H BA Drama and Film Studies
Duration: 3FT Hon
Entry Requirements: *GCE:* 220-260. *SQAH:* BBCC. *SQAAH:* BB.
IB: 24.

P303 BA Film Studies
Duration: 3FT Hon
Entry Requirements: *GCE:* 220-260. *SQAH:* BBCC. *SQAAH:* BC.
IB: 24.

WP83 BA Writing and Film Studies
Duration: 3FT Hon
Entry Requirements: *GCE:* 220-260. *SQAH:* BBBC. *SQAAH:* BC.
IB: 28.

B06 BANGOR UNIVERSITY
BANGOR UNIVERSITY
BANGOR
GWYNEDD LL57 2DG
t: 01248 388484 f: 01248 370451
e: admissions@bangor.ac.uk
// www.bangor.ac.uk

QP13 BA English Language and Film Studies
Duration: 3FT Hon
Entry Requirements: Contact the institution for details.

QP33 BA English and Film Studies
Duration: 3FT Hon
Entry Requirements: Contact the institution for details.

P3V4 BA Film Studies and Archaeology
Duration: 3FT Hon
Entry Requirements: Contact the institution for details.

P3W8 BA Film Studies and Creative Writing
Duration: 3FT Hon
Entry Requirements: Contact the institution for details.

PR31 BA Film Studies and French
Duration: 4FT Hon
Entry Requirements: *GCE:* 260-300. *IB:* 28.

PR32 BA Film Studies and German
Duration: 4FT Hon
Entry Requirements: *GCE:* 260-300. *IB:* 28.

P3V1 BA Film Studies and History
Duration: 3FT Hon
Entry Requirements: Contact the institution for details.

P0R3 BA Film Studies and Italian
Duration: 4FT Hon
Entry Requirements: Contact the institution for details.

PR34 BA Film Studies and Spanish
Duration: 4FT Hon
Entry Requirements: *GCE:* 260-300. *IB:* 28.

P3W4 BA Film Studies with Theatre
Duration: 3FT Hon
Entry Requirements: *GCE:* 260-300. *IB:* 28.

VP23 BA Welsh History and Film Studies
Duration: 3FT Hon
Entry Requirements: *GCE:* 240-280. *IB:* 28.

V2P3 BA Welsh History with Film Studies
Duration: 3FT Hon
Entry Requirements: *GCE:* 240-280. *IB:* 28.

B20 BATH SPA UNIVERSITY
NEWTON PARK
NEWTON ST LOE
BATH BA2 9BN
t: 01225 875875 f: 01225 875444
e: enquiries@bathspa.ac.uk
// www.bathspa.ac.uk/clearing

P3V1 BA Film & Screen Studies/History
Duration: 3FT Hon
Entry Requirements: *GCE:* 220-280.

B24 BIRKBECK, UNIVERSITY OF LONDON
MALET STREET
LONDON WC1E 7HX
t: 020 7631 6316
e: webform: www.bbk.ac.uk/ask
// www.bbk.ac.uk/ask

P390 BA Film and Media
Duration: 3FT Hon
Entry Requirements: *GCE:* ABC. *SQAH:* AAAA-AABB. *IB:* 30.
Interview required.

B32 THE UNIVERSITY OF BIRMINGHAM
EDGBASTON
BIRMINGHAM B15 2TT
t: 0121 415 8900 f: 0121 414 7159
e: admissions@bham.ac.uk
// www.birmingham.ac.uk

TP73 BA American & Canadian Studies and Film Studies
Duration: 3FT Hon
Entry Requirements: *GCE:* ABB. *SQAH:* ABBBB. *SQAAH:* AB. *IB:* 34.

R9P3 BA Modern Languages with Film Studies
Duration: 4FT Hon
Entry Requirements: *GCE:* ABB. *SQAH:* ABBBB. *SQAAH:* AB. *IB:* 32.

B56 THE UNIVERSITY OF BRADFORD
RICHMOND ROAD
BRADFORD
WEST YORKSHIRE BD7 1DP
t: 0800 073 1225 f: 01274 235585
e: course-enquiries@bradford.ac.uk
// www.bradford.ac.uk

P303 BA Film Studies
Duration: 3FT Hon
Entry Requirements: *GCE:* 240. *IB:* 24.

P301 BA Media Studies with Television
Duration: 3FT Hon
Entry Requirements: *GCE:* 240. *IB:* 24.

B80 UNIVERSITY OF THE WEST OF ENGLAND, BRISTOL
FRENCHAY CAMPUS
COLDHARBOUR LANE
BRISTOL BS16 1QY
t: +44 (0)117 32 83333 f: +44 (0)117 32 82810
e: admissions@uwe.ac.uk
// www.uwe.ac.uk

P303 BA Film Studies
Duration: 3FT Hon
Entry Requirements: *GCE:* 300.

PW38 BA Film Studies and Screenwriting
Duration: 3FT/4SW Hon
Entry Requirements: *GCE:* 300.

C10 CANTERBURY CHRIST CHURCH UNIVERSITY
NORTH HOLMES ROAD
CANTERBURY
KENT CT1 1QU
t: 01227 782900 f: 01227 782888
e: admissions@canterbury.ac.uk
// www.canterbury.ac.uk

NP13 BA Entrepreneurship and Film, Radio & Television Studies
Duration: 3FT Hon
Entry Requirements: *GCE:* 240. *IB:* 24.

P3NC BA Film, Radio & Television Studies with Entrepreneurship
Duration: 3FT Hon
Entry Requirements: *GCE:* 240. *IB:* 24.

P3GA BA Film, Radio & Television Studies with Internet Computing
Duration: 3FT Hon
Entry Requirements: *GCE:* 240. *IB:* 24.

GP4H BA Internet Computing and Film, Radio & Television
Duration: 3FT Hon
Entry Requirements: *GCE:* 240. *IB:* 24.

G4PJ BA Internet Computing with Film, Radio & Television
Duration: 3FT Hon
Entry Requirements: *GCE:* 240. *IB:* 24.

R1P3 BA/BSc French with Film, Radio & Television Studies
Duration: 3FT Hon
Entry Requirements: Contact the institution for details.

C55 UNIVERSITY OF CHESTER
PARKGATE ROAD
CHESTER CH1 4BJ
t: 01244 511000 f: 01244 511300
e: enquiries@chester.ac.uk
// www.chester.ac.uk

NPFJ BA Business Management and Film Studies
Duration: 3FT Hon
Entry Requirements: *GCE:* 240-280. *SQAH:* BBBB. *IB:* 26.

WP63 BA Digital Photography and Film Studies
Duration: 3FT Hon
Entry Requirements: *GCE:* 240-280. *SQAH:* BBBB. *IB:* 26.

NP8H BA Events Management and Film Studies
Duration: 3FT Hon
Entry Requirements: *GCE:* 240-280. *SQAH:* BBBB. *IB:* 26.

PNH5 BA Film Studies and Advertising
Duration: 3FT Hon
Entry Requirements: *GCE:* 240-280. *SQAH:* BBBB. *IB:* 26.

P392 BA Film Studies and Commercial Music Production
Duration: 3FT Hon
Entry Requirements: *Foundation:* Pass. *GCE:* 260-300. *SQAH:* BBBB. *IB:* 28.

PPH5 BA Film Studies and Journalism
Duration: 3FT Hon
Entry Requirements: *GCE:* 240-280. *SQAH:* BBBB. *IB:* 26.

P393 BA Film Studies and Radio Production
Duration: 3FT Hon
Entry Requirements: *Foundation:* Pass. *GCE:* 260-300. *SQAH:* BBBB. *IB:* 28.

PC3Q BA Film Studies and Sport Development
Duration: 3FT Hon
Entry Requirements: *GCE:* 240-280. *SQAH:* BBBB. *IB:* 26.

P394 BA Film Studies and TV Production
Duration: 3FT Hon
Entry Requirements: *GCE:* 260-300. *SQAH:* BBBB. *IB:* 24.

D26 DE MONTFORT UNIVERSITY
THE GATEWAY
LEICESTER LE1 9BH
t: 0116 255 1551 f: 0116 250 6204
e: enquiries@dmu.ac.uk
// www.dmu.ac.uk

WP83 BA Creative Writing and Film Studies
Duration: 3FT Hon
Entry Requirements: *GCE:* 260. *IB:* 28. *BTEC Dip:* D*D*. *BTEC ExtDip:* DMM.

P303 BA Film Studies
Duration: 3FT Hon
Entry Requirements: *GCE:* 260. *IB:* 28. *BTEC Dip:* D*D*. *BTEC ExtDip:* DMM.

PP35 BA Film Studies and Journalism
Duration: 3FT Hon
Entry Requirements: *GCE:* 260. *IB:* 28. *BTEC Dip:* D*D*. *BTEC ExtDip:* DMM.

D39 UNIVERSITY OF DERBY
KEDLESTON ROAD
DERBY DE22 1GB
t: 01332 591167 f: 01332 597724
e: askadmissions@derby.ac.uk
// www.derby.ac.uk

MP2H BA Applied Criminology and Film & Television Studies
Duration: 3FT Hon
Entry Requirements: *Foundation:* Distinction. *GCE:* 260-300. *IB:* 28. *BTEC Dip:* D*D*. *BTEC ExtDip:* DMM. *OCR NED:* M2

PV31 BA Film & Television Studies and History
Duration: 3FT Hon
Entry Requirements: *Foundation:* Distinction. *GCE:* 260-300. *IB:* 28. *BTEC Dip:* D*D*. *BTEC ExtDip:* DMM. *OCR NED:* M2

PW3V BA Film & Television Studies and Professional Writing
Duration: 3FT Hon
Entry Requirements: *Foundation:* Distinction. *GCE:* 260-300. *IB:* 28. *BTEC Dip:* D*D*. *BTEC ExtDip:* DMM. *OCR NED:* M2

PK32 BA Film & Television Studies and Property Development
Duration: 3FT Hon
Entry Requirements: *Foundation:* Distinction. *GCE:* 260-300. *IB:* 28. *BTEC Dip:* D*D*. *BTEC ExtDip:* DMM. *OCR NED:* M2

PC36 BA Film & Television Studies and Sport & Exercise Studies
Duration: 3FT Hon
Entry Requirements: *Foundation:* Distinction. *GCE:* 260-300. *IB:* 28. *BTEC Dip:* D*D*. *BTEC ExtDip:* DMM. *OCR NED:* M2

CP1H BA/BSc Biology and Film & Television Studies
Duration: 3FT Hon
Entry Requirements: *Foundation:* Distinction. *GCE:* 260-300. *IB:* 28. *BTEC Dip:* D*D*. *BTEC ExtDip:* DMM. *OCR NED:* M2

PL39 BA/BSc Film & Television Studies and Third World Development
Duration: 3FT Hon
Entry Requirements: *Foundation:* Distinction. *GCE:* 260-300. *IB:* 28. *BTEC Dip:* D*D*. *BTEC ExtDip:* DMM. *OCR NED:* M2

CP3H BA/BSc Zoology and Film & Television Studies
Duration: 3FT Hon
Entry Requirements: *Foundation:* Distinction. *GCE:* 260-300. *IB:* 28. *BTEC Dip:* D*D*. *BTEC ExtDip:* DMM. *OCR NED:* M2

D65 UNIVERSITY OF DUNDEE
NETHERGATE
DUNDEE DD1 4HN
t: 01382 383838 f: 01382 388150
e: contactus@dundee.ac.uk
// www.dundee.ac.uk/admissions/undergraduate/

VP53 MA Philosophy and Film
Duration: 4FT Hon
Entry Requirements: *GCE:* BCC. *SQAH:* ABBB. *IB:* 30.

E14 UNIVERSITY OF EAST ANGLIA
NORWICH NR4 7TJ
t: 01603 591515 f: 01603 591523
e: admissions@uea.ac.uk
// www.uea.ac.uk

VP53 BA Philosophy and Film Studies
Duration: 3FT Hon   CRB Check: Required
Entry Requirements: *GCE:* AAB. *SQAAH:* AAB. *IB:* 33. *BTEC ExtDip:* DDD. Interview required.

E28 UNIVERSITY OF EAST LONDON
DOCKLANDS CAMPUS
UNIVERSITY WAY
LONDON E16 2RD
t: 020 8223 3333 f: 020 8223 2978
e: study@uel.ac.uk
// www.uel.ac.uk

LP13 BA Business Economics/Film Studies
Duration: 3FT Hon
Entry Requirements: *GCE:* 240. *IB:* 24.

W2P3 BA Computer Games Design with Film Studies
Duration: 3FT Hon
Entry Requirements: *GCE:* 280. *IB:* 24.

W8P3 BA Creative & Professional Writing with Film Studies
Duration: 3FT Hon
Entry Requirements: *GCE:* 240. *IB:* 24.

Q3P3 BA English Literature with Film Studies
Duration: 3FT Hon
Entry Requirements: *GCE:* 240. *IB:* 24.

P3P9 BA Film Studies with Communication Studies
Duration: 3FT Hon
Entry Requirements: *GCE:* 240. *IB:* 24.

P3I1 BA Film Studies with Computing
Duration: 3FT Hon
Entry Requirements: *GCE:* 240. *IB:* 24.

P3W8 BA Film Studies with Creative & Professional Writing
Duration: 3FT Hon
Entry Requirements: *GCE:* 240. *IB:* 24.

P3L6 BA Film Studies with Cultural Studies
Duration: 3FT Hon
Entry Requirements: *GCE:* 240. *IB:* 24.

P3QH BA Film Studies with English Literature
Duration: 3FT Hon
Entry Requirements: *GCE:* 240. *IB:* 24.

P3N5 BA Film Studies with Marketing
Duration: 3FT Hon
Entry Requirements: *GCE:* 240. *IB:* 24.

P3W3 BA Film Studies with Music Culture
Duration: 3FT Hon
Entry Requirements: *GCE:* 240. *IB:* 24.

P3WP BA Film Studies with Photography
Duration: 3FT Hon
Entry Requirements: *GCE:* 240. *IB:* 24.

P3WK BA Film Studies with Theatre Studies
Duration: 3FT Hon
Entry Requirements: *GCE:* 240. *IB:* 24.

PW38 BA Film Studies/Creative & Professional Writing
Duration: 3FT Hon
Entry Requirements: *GCE:* 240. *IB:* 24.

PL36 BA Film Studies/Cultural Studies
Duration: 3FT Hon
Entry Requirements: *GCE:* 240. *IB:* 24.

V000 BA Media & Creative Industries option - Film Studies
Duration: 3FT Hon
Entry Requirements: *GCE:* 240. *IB:* 24.

P301 BA Media Studies (Extended)
Duration: 4FT Hon
Entry Requirements: *GCE:* 120. *IB:* 24.

PHW8 BA Media Studies with Creative and Professional Writing
Duration: 3FT Hon
Entry Requirements: *GCE:* 240. *IB:* 24.

GP5H BA/BSc Business Information Systems/Film Studies
Duration: 3FT Hon
Entry Requirements: *GCE:* 240. *IB:* 24.

QP33 BA/BSc Film Studies/English Literature
Duration: 3FT Hon
Entry Requirements: *GCE:* 240. *IB:* 24.

G4P3 BSc Computer Networks with Film Studies
Duration: 3FT Hon
Entry Requirements: *GCE:* 240. *IB:* 24.

WP23 BSc/BA Multimedia Design Technology/Film Studies
Duration: 3FT Hon
Entry Requirements: *GCE:* 240.

E42 EDGE HILL UNIVERSITY
ORMSKIRK
LANCASHIRE L39 4QP
t: 01695 657000 f: 01695 584355
e: study@edgehill.ac.uk
// www.edgehill.ac.uk

QP33 BA English Language and Film Studies
Duration: 3FT Hon
Entry Requirements: *GCE:* 280. *IB:* 26. *OCR ND:* D *OCR NED:* M2

QP3J BA English Literature and Film Studies
Duration: 3FT Hon
Entry Requirements: *GCE:* 280. *IB:* 26. *OCR ND:* D *OCR NED:* M2

P303 BA Film Studies
Duration: 3FT Hon
Entry Requirements: *GCE:* 280. *IB:* 26. *OCR ND:* D *OCR NED:* M2

P3W9 BA Film Studies with Creative Writing
Duration: 3FT Hon
Entry Requirements: *GCE:* 280. *IB:* 26. *OCR ND:* D *OCR NED:* M2

E56 THE UNIVERSITY OF EDINBURGH
STUDENT RECRUITMENT & ADMISSIONS
57 GEORGE SQUARE
EDINBURGH EH8 9JU
t: 0131 650 4360 f: 0131 651 1236
e: sra.enquiries@ed.ac.uk
// www.ed.ac.uk/studying/undergraduate/

P390 BA Film and Television
Duration: 4FT Hon
Entry Requirements: *Foundation:* Merit. *GCE:* BBB. *SQAH:* BBBB. *IB:* 34. Portfolio required.

E59 EDINBURGH NAPIER UNIVERSITY
CRAIGLOCKHART CAMPUS
EDINBURGH EH14 1DJ
t: +44 (0)8452 60 60 40 f: 0131 455 6464
e: info@napier.ac.uk
// www.napier.ac.uk

QP33 BA English and Film
Duration: 3FT/4FT Ord/Hon
Entry Requirements: *GCE:* 220.

P301 BA Television
Duration: 2FT Hon
Entry Requirements: Contact the institution for details.

E70 THE UNIVERSITY OF ESSEX
WIVENHOE PARK
COLCHESTER
ESSEX CO4 3SQ
t: 01206 873666 f: 01206 874477
e: admit@essex.ac.uk
// www.essex.ac.uk

T7P3 BA American (United States) Studies with Film (term abroad)
Duration: 3FT Hon
Entry Requirements: *GCE:* ABB-BBB. *SQAH:* AAAB-AABB. Interview required.

P303 BA Film Studies (Including Year Abroad)
Duration: 4FT Hon
Entry Requirements: Contact the institution for details.

PQ32 BA Film Studies and Literature (Including Year Abroad)
Duration: 4FT Hon
Entry Requirements: Contact the institution for details.

PW38 BA Film and Creative Writing
Duration: 3FT Hon
Entry Requirements: *GCE:* ABB-BBB. *SQAH:* AAAB-AABB. *BTEC ExtDip:* DDM.

PWH8 BA Film and Creative Writing (Including Year Abroad)
Duration: 4FT Hon
Entry Requirements: Contact the institution for details.

E84 UNIVERSITY OF EXETER
LAVER BUILDING
NORTH PARK ROAD
EXETER
DEVON EX4 4QE
t: 01392 723044 f: 01392 722479
e: admissions@exeter.ac.uk
// www.exeter.ac.uk

Q3W7 BA English and Film Studies with Study Abroad (4 years)
Duration: 4FT Hon
Entry Requirements: Contact the institution for details.

W600 BA Film Studies
Duration: 3FT Hon
Entry Requirements: *GCE:* AAB-ABB. *SQAH:* AAABB-AABBB. *SQAAH:* ABB-BBB.

W601 BA Film Studies with Study Abroad (4 years)
Duration: 4FT Hon
Entry Requirements: Contact the institution for details.

F66 FARNBOROUGH COLLEGE OF TECHNOLOGY
BOUNDARY ROAD
FARNBOROUGH
HAMPSHIRE GU14 6SB
t: 01252 407028 f: 01252 407041
e: admissions@farn-ct.ac.uk
// www.farn-ct.ac.uk

P396 BSc Media Production (Film and Television)
Duration: 3FT Hon
Entry Requirements: *GCE:* 180-200. *OCR ND:* M2 *OCR NED:* M3 Admissions Test required.

P395 BSc Media Production (Radio)
Duration: 3FT Hon
Entry Requirements: *GCE:* 180-200. *OCR ND:* M2 *OCR NED:* M3 Admissions Test required.

P302 BSc Media Production (Radio) (Top Up)
Duration: 1FT Hon
Entry Requirements: Contact the institution for details.

P392 BSc Media Production (Television and Film) (Top Up)
Duration: 1FT Hon
Entry Requirements: Contact the institution for details.

P390 FdSc Film and Television Production
Duration: 2FT Fdg
Entry Requirements: *GCE:* 160.

P393 FdSc Radio & Television Production
Duration: 2FT Fdg
Entry Requirements: *GCE:* 160.

G14 UNIVERSITY OF GLAMORGAN, CARDIFF AND PONTYPRIDD
ENQUIRIES AND ADMISSIONS UNIT
PONTYPRIDD CF37 1DL
t: 08456 434030 f: 01443 654050
e: enquiries@glam.ac.uk
// www.glam.ac.uk

PH03 BA Creative Industries (Film and Video Top-Up)
Duration: 1FT Hon
Entry Requirements: Contact the institution for details.

P301 BA Media Production (Photography/Radio/New Media)
Duration: 3FT Hon
Entry Requirements: *GCE:* BBC. *IB:* 25. *BTEC SubDip:* M. *BTEC Dip:* D*D*. *BTEC ExtDip:* DMM. *OCR NED:* M2

G28 UNIVERSITY OF GLASGOW
71 SOUTHPARK AVENUE
UNIVERSITY OF GLASGOW
GLASGOW G12 8QQ
t: 0141 330 6062 f: 0141 330 2961
e: student.recruitment@glasgow.ac.uk
// www.glasgow.ac.uk

QP83 MA Classics/Film & Television Studies
Duration: 4FT Hon
Entry Requirements: *GCE:* ABB. *SQAH:* AAAB-ABBB. *IB:* 34.

GP53 MA Digital Media & Information Studies/Film & Television Studies
Duration: 4FT Hon
Entry Requirements: *GCE:* ABB. *SQAH:* AAAB-ABBB. *IB:* 34.

G50 THE UNIVERSITY OF GLOUCESTERSHIRE
PARK CAMPUS
THE PARK
CHELTENHAM GL50 2RH
t: 01242 714501 f: 01242 714869
e: admissions@glos.ac.uk
// www.glos.ac.uk

P30H BA Film
Duration: 3FT Hon
Entry Requirements: Interview required. Portfolio required.

P30I BA Film
Duration: 2FT Hon
Entry Requirements: Interview required. Portfolio required.

G53 GLYNDWR UNIVERSITY
PLAS COCH
MOLD ROAD
WREXHAM LL11 2AW
t: 01978 293439 f: 01978 290008
e: sid@glyndwr.ac.uk
// www.glyndwr.ac.uk

PP93 BA Media Communications and Screen Studies
Duration: 3FT Hon
Entry Requirements: *GCE:* 240.

WP43 BA Theatre, Television and Performance
Duration: 3FT Hon
Entry Requirements: *GCE:* 240. Interview required.

G70 UNIVERSITY OF GREENWICH
GREENWICH CAMPUS
OLD ROYAL NAVAL COLLEGE
PARK ROW
LONDON SE10 9LS
t: 020 8331 9000 f: 020 8331 8145
e: courseinfo@gre.ac.uk
// www.gre.ac.uk

P303 BA Film Studies
Duration: 3FT Hon
Entry Requirements: *GCE:* 240. *IB:* 24.

H60 THE UNIVERSITY OF HUDDERSFIELD
QUEENSGATE
HUDDERSFIELD HD1 3DH
t: 01484 473969 f: 01484 472765
e: admissionsandrecords@hud.ac.uk
// www.hud.ac.uk

PW43 BA(Hons) Film Studies and Drama
Duration: 3FT Hon
Entry Requirements: *GCE:* 280.

PQ32 BA(Hons) Film Studies and English Literature
Duration: 3FT Hon
Entry Requirements: *GCE:* 280.

PV13 BA(Hons) Film Studies and History
Duration: 3FT Hon
Entry Requirements: *GCE:* 280.

H72 THE UNIVERSITY OF HULL
THE UNIVERSITY OF HULL
COTTINGHAM ROAD
HULL HU6 7RX
t: 01482 466100 f: 01482 442290
e: admissions@hull.ac.uk
// www.hull.ac.uk

WP43 BA Drama and Film Studies
Duration: 3FT Hon
Entry Requirements: *GCE:* 280-320. *IB:* 28. *BTEC ExtDip:* DDM.

VP13 BA History and Film Studies
Duration: 3FT Hon
Entry Requirements: *GCE:* 280-320. *IB:* 30. *BTEC ExtDip:* DMM.

WP33 BA Music and Film Studies
Duration: 3FT Hon
Entry Requirements: *GCE:* 280-320. *IB:* 28. *BTEC ExtDip:* DDM.
Interview required.

VP63 BA Religion and Film Studies
Duration: 3FT Hon
Entry Requirements: *GCE:* 280-320. *IB:* 28. *BTEC ExtDip:* DMM.

LP33 BA Sociology and Film Studies
Duration: 3FT Hon
Entry Requirements: *GCE:* 280-320. *IB:* 28. *BTEC ExtDip:* DMM.

K12 KEELE UNIVERSITY
KEELE UNIVERSITY
STAFFORDSHIRE ST5 5BG
t: 01782 734005 f: 01782 632343
e: undergraduate@keele.ac.uk
// www.keele.ac.uk

NP43 BA Accounting and Film Studies
Duration: 3FT Hon
Entry Requirements: *GCE:* ABB.

TP73 BA American Studies and Film Studies
Duration: 3FT Hon
Entry Requirements: *GCE:* BBB.

NP23 BA Business Management and Film Studies
Duration: 3FT Hon
Entry Requirements: *GCE:* ABB.

MP93 BA Criminology and Film Studies
Duration: 3FT Hon
Entry Requirements: *GCE:* BBB.

LP13 BA Economics and Film Studies
Duration: 3FT Hon
Entry Requirements: *GCE:* ABB.

XP33 BA Educational Studies and Film Studies
Duration: 3FT Hon
Entry Requirements: *GCE:* BBB.

QP33 BA English and Film Studies
Duration: 3FT Hon
Entry Requirements: *GCE:* BBB.

PV3C BA Film Studies and History
Duration: 3FT Hon
Entry Requirements: *GCE:* BBB.

PN3P BA Film Studies and Human Resource Management
Duration: 3FT Hon
Entry Requirements: *GCE:* ABB.

PN3C BA Film Studies and International Business
Duration: 3FT Hon
Entry Requirements: *GCE:* ABB.

PN3M BA Film Studies and Marketing
Duration: 3FT Hon
Entry Requirements: *GCE:* ABB.

PP39 BA Film Studies and Media, Communications & Culture
Duration: 3FT Hon
Entry Requirements: *GCE:* BBB.

PW3H BA Film Studies and Music
Duration: 3FT Hon
Entry Requirements: *GCE:* BBB.

PJ3X BA Film Studies and Music Technology
Duration: 3FT Hon
Entry Requirements: *GCE:* BBB.

PV3M BA Film Studies and Philosophy
Duration: 3FT Hon
Entry Requirements: *GCE:* BBB.

PL3F BA Film Studies and Politics
Duration: 3FT Hon
Entry Requirements: *GCE:* BBB.

PL3H BA Film Studies and Sociology
Duration: 3FT Hon
Entry Requirements: *GCE:* BBB.

P3V0 BA Film Studies with Humanities Foundation Year
Duration: 4FT Hon
Entry Requirements: *GCE:* CC.

FP73 BSc Applied Environmental Science and Film Studies
Duration: 3FT Hon
Entry Requirements: *GCE:* BBB.

CP73 BSc Biochemistry and Film Studies
Duration: 3FT Hon
Entry Requirements: *GCE:* BBB.

CP13 BSc Biology and Film Studies
Duration: 3FT Hon
Entry Requirements: *GCE:* BBB.

FP13 BSc Chemistry and Film Studies
Duration: 3FT Hon
Entry Requirements: *GCE:* BBB.

GP43 BSc Computer Science and Film Studies
Duration: 3FT Hon
Entry Requirements: *GCE:* BBB.

GP4H BSc Creative Computing and Film Studies
Duration: 3FT Hon
Entry Requirements: *GCE:* BBB.

PF3P BSc Film Studies and Geology
Duration: 3FT Hon
Entry Requirements: *GCE:* BBB.

PB3C BSc Film Studies and Human Biology
Duration: 3FT Hon
Entry Requirements: *GCE:* BBB.

PG35 BSc Film Studies and Information Systems
Duration: 3FT Hon
Entry Requirements: *GCE:* BBB.

PG3C BSc Film Studies and Mathematics
Duration: 3FT Hon
Entry Requirements: *GCE:* BBB.

PF31 BSc Film Studies and Medicinal Chemistry
Duration: 3FT Hon
Entry Requirements: *GCE:* BBB.

PB3D BSc Film Studies and Neuroscience
Duration: 3FT Hon
Entry Requirements: *GCE:* BBB.

PG37 BSc Film Studies and Smart Systems
Duration: 3FT Hon
Entry Requirements: *GCE:* BBB.

K24 THE UNIVERSITY OF KENT
RECRUITMENT & ADMISSIONS OFFICE
REGISTRY
UNIVERSITY OF KENT
CANTERBURY, KENT CT2 7NZ
t: 01227 827272 f: 01227 827077
e: information@kent.ac.uk
// www.kent.ac.uk

W611 BA Film Studies with a Placement Year
Duration: 4FT Hon
Entry Requirements: *GCE:* AAB-ABB. *SQAH:* AAAAB-AAABB. *SQAAH:* AAB-ABB. *IB:* 33. *OCR ND:* D *OCR NED:* D1 Interview required.

K60 KING'S COLLEGE LONDON (UNIVERSITY OF LONDON)
STRAND
LONDON WC2R 2LS
t: 020 7836 5454 f: 020 7848 7171
e: prospective@kcl.ac.uk
// www.kcl.ac.uk/prospectus

Q2P3 BA Comparative Literature with Film Studies
Duration: 3FT Hon
Entry Requirements: *GCE:* AAAc. *SQAH:* AAAAB. *IB:* 38.

P303 BA Film Studies
Duration: 3FT Hon
Entry Requirements: *GCE:* AABc. *SQAH:* AAABB. *IB:* 36.

K84 KINGSTON UNIVERSITY
STUDENT INFORMATION & ADVICE CENTRE
COOPER HOUSE
40-46 SURBITON ROAD
KINGSTON UPON THAMES KT1 2HX
t: 0844 8552177 f: 020 8547 7080
e: aps@kingston.ac.uk
// www.kingston.ac.uk

WPH3 BA Creative Music Technologies and Film Studies
Duration: 3FT Hon
Entry Requirements: *GCE:* 260-280. Interview required.

WPG3 BA Creative Music Technologies and TV & New Broadcasting Media
Duration: 3FT Hon
Entry Requirements: *GCE:* 260-280. Interview required.

WP83 BA Creative Writing and Film Studies
Duration: 3FT Hon
Entry Requirements: *GCE:* 220-360. *IB:* 30.

WPW3 BA Creative Writing and Television & New Broadcasting Media
Duration: 3FT Hon
Entry Requirements: *GCE:* 220-360.

LP33 BA Criminology and Film Studies
Duration: 3FT Hon
Entry Requirements: *GCE:* 240-320. *SQAH:* BBCCC. *SQAAH:* BBC.

PW35 BA Dance and Film Studies
Duration: 3FT Hon
Entry Requirements: *GCE:* 300-360. Interview required.

WPM3 BA Dance and Television & New Broadcasting Media
Duration: 3FT Hon
Entry Requirements: *GCE:* 300-360. Interview required.

WP43 BA Drama and Film Studies
Duration: 3FT Hon
Entry Requirements: *GCE:* 300-360. *SQAH:* BBCCC. *SQAAH:* BBC.

LPC3 BA Economics (Applied) and Television & New Broadcasting Media
Duration: 3FT Hon
Entry Requirements: *GCE:* 240-320. *IB:* 24.

QP33 BA English Language & Communications and Film Studies
Duration: 3FT Hon
Entry Requirements: *GCE:* 240-360.

QPH3 BA English Language & Communications and Television & New Broadcasting Media
Duration: 3FT Hon
Entry Requirements: *GCE:* 240-360.

QPJ3 BA English Literature and Film Studies
Duration: 3FT Hon
Entry Requirements: *GCE:* 280-360.

QP3J BA English Literature and Television & New Broadcasting Media
Duration: 3FT Hon
Entry Requirements: *GCE:* 280-360.

Q3PH BA English Literature with Television & New Broadcasting Media
Duration: 3FT Hon
Entry Requirements: *GCE:* 240-360.

PV31 BA Film Studies and History
Duration: 3FT Hon
Entry Requirements: *GCE:* 240-360. *IB:* 30.

PV33 BA Film Studies and History of Art, Design & Film
Duration: 3FT Hon
Entry Requirements: *GCE:* 240-360. *IB:* 30.

PP35 BA Film Studies and Journalism
Duration: 3FT Hon
Entry Requirements: *GCE:* 340.

PM31 BA Film Studies and Law
Duration: 3FT Hon
Entry Requirements: *GCE:* 280.

PW33 BA Film Studies and Music
Duration: 3FT Hon
Entry Requirements: *GCE:* 260-280.

PL33 BA Film Studies and Sociology
Duration: 3FT Hon
Entry Requirements: *GCE:* 240-360. *IB:* 30.

P396 BA Film Studies andTelevision & New Broadcasting Media
Duration: 3FT Hon
Entry Requirements: *GCE:* 220-360.

VP13 BA History and Television & New Broadcasting Media
Duration: 3FT Hon
Entry Requirements: *GCE:* 240-360.

LPG3 BA Human Rights and Television & New Broadcasting Media
Duration: 3FT Hon
Entry Requirements: *GCE:* 240-360.

MPC3 BA Law and Television & New Broadcasting Media
Duration: 3FT Hon
Entry Requirements: *GCE:* 280.

LPFH BA Politics and Television & New Broadcasting Media
Duration: 3FT Hon
Entry Requirements: *GCE:* 240-360.

CP83 BA Psychology and Television & New Broadcasting Media
Duration: 3FT Hon
Entry Requirements: *GCE:* 240-360.

C8PH BA Psychology with Television & New Broadcasting Media
Duration: 3FT Hon
Entry Requirements: *GCE:* 240-360.

LPJ3 BA Sociology and Television & New Broadcasting Media
Duration: 3FT Hon
Entry Requirements: *GCE:* 240-360.

P3RC BA Television & New Broadcasting Media with French
Duration: 3FT Hon
Entry Requirements: *GCE:* 240-360.

P3CV BA Television & New Broadcasting Media with Psychology
Duration: 3FT Hon
Entry Requirements: *GCE:* 240-360.

LP2J BSc International Relations and Television & New Broadcasting Media
Duration: 3FT Hon
Entry Requirements: *GCE:* 240-360.

P301 BSc Television and Video Technology (including Foundation Year)
Duration: 4FT Hon
Entry Requirements: Contact the institution for details.

L14 LANCASTER UNIVERSITY
THE UNIVERSITY
LANCASTER
LANCASHIRE LA1 4YW
t: 01524 592029 f: 01524 846243
e: ugadmissions@lancaster.ac.uk
// www.lancs.ac.uk

RP93 BA European Languages and Film Studies (4 years)
Duration: 4FT Hon
Entry Requirements: *GCE:* AAB. *SQAH:* ABBBB. *SQAAH:* AAB. *IB:* 35.

P303 BA Film Studies
Duration: 3FT Hon
Entry Requirements: *GCE:* AAB. *SQAH:* ABBBB. *SQAAH:* AAB. *IB:* 35.

PQ33 BA Film Studies and English Literature
Duration: 3FT Hon
Entry Requirements: *GCE:* AAA. *SQAH:* AAABB. *SQAAH:* AAA. *IB:* 36.

L24 LEEDS TRINITY UNIVERSITY COLLEGE
BROWNBERRIE LANE
HORSFORTH
LEEDS LS18 5HD
t: 0113 283 7150 f: 0113 283 7222
e: enquiries@leedstrinity.ac.uk
// www.leedstrinity.ac.uk

QP3H BA English and Film Studies
Duration: 3FT Hon
Entry Requirements: *GCE:* 240. *IB:* 24.

P303 BA Film Studies
Duration: 3FT Hon
Entry Requirements: *GCE:* 280. *IB:* 25. *OCR NED:* M2

P391 BA Film and Television Studies
Duration: 3FT Hon
Entry Requirements: *GCE:* 280. *IB:* 25. *OCR NED:* M2

P301 BA Television
Duration: 3FT Hon
Entry Requirements: *GCE:* 280. *IB:* 25. *OCR NED:* M2

L34 UNIVERSITY OF LEICESTER
UNIVERSITY ROAD
LEICESTER LE1 7RH
t: 0116 252 5281 f: 0116 252 2447
e: admissions@le.ac.uk
// www.le.ac.uk

PQ33 BA Film Studies and English
Duration: 3FT Hon
Entry Requirements: *GCE:* BBB. *SQAH:* BBBBB. *SQAAH:* BBB. *IB:* 30.

R8P3 BA Modern Languages with Film Studies
Duration: 4FT Hon
Entry Requirements: *GCE:* ABB. *SQAH:* AABBB. *SQAAH:* ABB. *IB:* 32.

L39 UNIVERSITY OF LINCOLN
ADMISSIONS
BRAYFORD POOL
LINCOLN LN6 7TS
t: 01522 886097 f: 01522 886146
e: admissions@lincoln.ac.uk
// www.lincoln.ac.uk

PW36 BA Film & Television
Duration: 3FT Hon
Entry Requirements: *GCE:* 280.

P301 BA Media Production
Duration: 3FT Hon
Entry Requirements: *GCE:* 300.

L41 THE UNIVERSITY OF LIVERPOOL
THE FOUNDATION BUILDING
BROWNLOW HILL
LIVERPOOL L69 7ZX
t: 0151 794 2000 f: 0151 708 6502
e: ugrecruitment@liv.ac.uk
// www.liv.ac.uk

PR39 BA Film Studies (European) and a Modern Language
Duration: 4FT Hon
Entry Requirements: *GCE:* ABB. *SQAH:* AABBB. *SQAAH:* ABB. *IB:* 33.

L51 LIVERPOOL JOHN MOORES UNIVERSITY
KINGSWAY HOUSE
HATTON GARDEN
LIVERPOOL L3 2AJ
t: 0151 231 5090 f: 0151 904 6368
e: courses@ljmu.ac.uk
// www.ljmu.ac.uk

P303 BA Film Studies
Duration: 3FT Hon
Entry Requirements: *GCE:* 280. *IB:* 29.

L68 LONDON METROPOLITAN UNIVERSITY
166-220 HOLLOWAY ROAD
LONDON N7 8DB
t: 020 7133 4200
e: admissions@londonmet.ac.uk
// www.londonmet.ac.uk

P303 BA Film and Television Studies
Duration: 3FT Hon
Entry Requirements: *GCE:* 260. *IB:* 28.

PPM3 BA Journalism, Film and Television Studies
Duration: 3FT Hon
Entry Requirements: *GCE:* 260. *IB:* 28.

M40 THE MANCHESTER METROPOLITAN UNIVERSITY
ADMISSIONS OFFICE
ALL SAINTS (GMS)
ALL SAINTS
MANCHESTER M15 6BH
t: 0161 247 2000
// www.mmu.ac.uk

PW32 BA Filmmaking
Duration: 3FT Hon
Entry Requirements: *GCE:* 280. *IB:* 27. Interview required. Portfolio required.

P303 BA Studies in Film (Top-up)
Duration: 1FT Hon
Entry Requirements: Contact the institution for details.

M80 MIDDLESEX UNIVERSITY
MIDDLESEX UNIVERSITY
THE BURROUGHS
LONDON NW4 4BT
t: 020 8411 5555 f: 020 8411 5649
e: enquiries@mdx.ac.uk
// www.mdx.ac.uk

P303 BA Film
Duration: 3FT Hon
Entry Requirements: Contact the institution for details.

N38 UNIVERSITY OF NORTHAMPTON
PARK CAMPUS
BOUGHTON GREEN ROAD
NORTHAMPTON NN2 7AL
t: 0800 358 2232 f: 01604 722083
e: admissions@northampton.ac.uk
// www.northampton.ac.uk

W6D4 BA Film & Television Studies with Equine Studies
Duration: 3FT Hon
Entry Requirements: *GCE:* 260-280. *SQAH:* AAA-BBBB. *IB:* 24. *BTEC Dip:* DD. *BTEC ExtDip:* DMM. *OCR ND:* D *OCR NED:* M2

N77 NORTHUMBRIA UNIVERSITY
TRINITY BUILDING
NORTHUMBERLAND ROAD
NEWCASTLE UPON TYNE NE1 8ST
t: 0191 243 7420 f: 0191 227 4561
e: er.admissions@northumbria.ac.uk
// www.northumbria.ac.uk

P391 BA Film and Television Studies
Duration: 3FT Hon
Entry Requirements: *GCE:* 300. *SQAH:* BBBBC. *SQAAH:* BBC. *IB:* 26. Portfolio required.

N84 THE UNIVERSITY OF NOTTINGHAM
THE ADMISSIONS OFFICE
THE UNIVERSITY OF NOTTINGHAM
UNIVERSITY PARK
NOTTINGHAM NG7 2RD
t: 0115 951 5151 f: 0115 951 4668
// www.nottingham.ac.uk

PL33 BA Film & Television Studies and Cultural Sociology
Duration: 3FT Hon
Entry Requirements: *GCE:* ABC-BBB. *SQAAH:* ABC-BBB. *IB:* 30.

RP23 BA Film & Television Studies and German (Beginners)
Duration: 4FT Hon
Entry Requirements: *GCE:* ABC-BBB. *SQAAH:* ABC-BBB. *IB:* 30.

P3T1 BA Film & Television Studies with Chinese Studies
Duration: 3FT Hon
Entry Requirements: *GCE:* ABC-BBB. *SQAAH:* ABC-BBB. *IB:* 30.

PR3K BA Film/Television Studies and Beginners' Spanish
Duration: 4FT Hon
Entry Requirements: *GCE:* ABC-BBB. *SQAAH:* ABC-BBB. *IB:* 30.

PR31 BA Film/Television Studies and French
Duration: 4FT Hon
Entry Requirements: *GCE:* ABB. *SQAAH:* ABB. *IB:* 32.

PR32 BA Film/Television Studies and German
Duration: 4FT Hon
Entry Requirements: *GCE:* ABC-BBB. *SQAAH:* ABC-BBB. *IB:* 30.

PR34 BA Film/Television Studies and Hispanic Studies
Duration: 4FT Hon
Entry Requirements: *GCE:* ABC-BBB. *SQAAH:* ABC-BBB. *IB:* 30.

PR37 BA Film/Television Studies and Russian
Duration: 4FT Hon
Entry Requirements: *GCE:* ABB. *SQAAH:* ABB. *IB:* 32.

PRH7 BA Film/Television Studies and Russian Beginners
Duration: 4FT Hon
Entry Requirements: *GCE:* ABB. *SQAAH:* ABB. *IB:* 32.

N91 NOTTINGHAM TRENT UNIVERSITY
DRYDEN BUILDING
BURTON STREET
NOTTINGHAM NG1 4BU
t: +44 (0) 115 848 4200 f: +44 (0) 115 848 8869
e: applications@ntu.ac.uk
// www.ntu.ac.uk

PP93 BA Communication & Society and Film &TV
Duration: 3FT Hon
Entry Requirements: *GCE:* 260. *BTEC ExtDip:* DMM. *OCR NED:* M2

QP33 BA English and Film & TV
Duration: 3FT Hon
Entry Requirements: *GCE:* 260. *BTEC ExtDip:* DMM. *OCR NED:* M2

RP83 BA European Studies and Film & TV
Duration: 3FT Hon
Entry Requirements: *GCE:* 260. *BTEC ExtDip:* DMM. *OCR NED:* M2

PL39 BA Film & TV and Global Studies
Duration: 3FT Hon
Entry Requirements: *GCE:* 260. *BTEC ExtDip:* DMM. *OCR NED:* M2

PV3C BA Film & TV and History
Duration: 3FT Hon
Entry Requirements: *GCE:* 260. *BTEC ExtDip:* DMM. *OCR NED:* M2

PL32 BA Film & TV and International Relations
Duration: 3FT Hon
Entry Requirements: *GCE:* 260. *BTEC ExtDip:* DMM. *OCR NED:* M2

PR33 BA Film & TV and Italian
Duration: 3FT Hon
Entry Requirements: *GCE:* 260. *BTEC ExtDip:* DMM. *OCR NED:* M2

PQ3C BA Film & TV and Linguistics
Duration: 3FT Hon
Entry Requirements: *GCE:* 260. *BTEC ExtDip:* DMM. *OCR NED:* M2

PV35 BA Film & TV and Philosophy
Duration: 3FT Hon
Entry Requirements: *GCE:* 260. *BTEC ExtDip:* DMM. *OCR NED:* M2

PR34 BA Film & TV and Spanish
Duration: 3FT Hon
Entry Requirements: *GCE:* 260. *BTEC ExtDip:* DMM. *OCR NED:* M2

TP13 BA Mandarin Chinese and Film and TV
Duration: 3FT Hon
Entry Requirements: *GCE:* 260. *BTEC ExtDip:* DMM. *OCR NED:* M2

O66 OXFORD BROOKES UNIVERSITY
ADMISSIONS OFFICE
HEADINGTON CAMPUS
GIPSY LANE
OXFORD OX3 0BP
t: 01865 483040 f: 01865 483983
e: admissions@brookes.ac.uk
// www.brookes.ac.uk

QP33 BA English/Film Studies
Duration: 3FT Hon
Entry Requirements: *GCE:* BBB.

P303 BA Film Studies
Duration: 3FT Hon
Entry Requirements: *GCE:* BBC.

NP23 BA/BSc Business Management/Film Studies
Duration: 3FT Hon
Entry Requirements: *GCE:* BBB.

PP39 BA/BSc Communications, Media and Culture/Film Studies
Duration: 3FT Hon
Entry Requirements: *GCE:* BBC.

WP43 BA/BSc Drama/Film Studies
Duration: 3FT Hon
Entry Requirements: *GCE:* BBC.

QP9H BA/BSc English Language and Communication/Film Studies
Duration: 3FT Hon
Entry Requirements: Contact the institution for details.

P3R4 BA/BSc Film Studies with Spanish (Minor)
Duration: 4SW Hon
Entry Requirements: *GCE:* BBC. *IB:* 31.

PV31 BA/BSc Film Studies/History
Duration: 3FT Hon
Entry Requirements: *GCE:* BBC.

PV33 BA/BSc Film Studies/History of Art
Duration: 3FT Hon
Entry Requirements: *GCE:* BBC.

PW33 BA/BSc Film Studies/Music
Duration: 3FT Hon
Entry Requirements: *GCE:* BCC.

PV35 BA/BSc Film Studies/Philosophy
Duration: 3FT Hon
Entry Requirements: *GCE:* BBC.

W1P3 BA/BSc Fine Art/Film Studies
Duration: 3FT Hon
Entry Requirements: Contact the institution for details.

TP23 BA/BSc Japanese Studies/Film Studies
Duration: 4SW Hon
Entry Requirements: *GCE:* BBB.

P80 UNIVERSITY OF PORTSMOUTH
ACADEMIC REGISTRY
UNIVERSITY HOUSE
WINSTON CHURCHILL AVENUE
PORTSMOUTH PO1 2UP
t: 023 9284 8484 f: 023 9284 3082
e: admissions@port.ac.uk
// www.port.ac.uk

PW38 BA Film Studies and Creative Writing
Duration: 3FT Hon
Entry Requirements: *GCE:* 240-300. *IB:* 26. *BTEC SubDip:* P.
BTEC Dip: DD. *BTEC ExtDip:* DMM.

P391 BA Film and Television Studies
Duration: 3FT Hon
Entry Requirements: *GCE:* 240-300. *IB:* 25. *BTEC SubDip:* P.
BTEC Dip: DD. *BTEC ExtDip:* DMM.

P301 BSc Digital Media
Duration: 3FT/4SW Hon
Entry Requirements: *GCE:* 240-300. *IB:* 28. *BTEC SubDip:* P.
BTEC Dip: DD. *BTEC ExtDip:* DMM.

P30C BSc Television and Broadcasting
Duration: 3FT/4SW Hon
Entry Requirements: *GCE:* 240-300. *IB:* 28. *BTEC Dip:* DD.
BTEC ExtDip: DMM.

Q50 QUEEN MARY, UNIVERSITY OF LONDON
QUEEN MARY, UNIVERSITY OF LONDON
MILE END ROAD
LONDON E1 4NS
t: 020 7882 5555 f: 020 7882 5500
e: admissions@qmul.ac.uk
// www.qmul.ac.uk

QP23 BA Comparative Literature and Film Studies
Duration: 3FT Hon
Entry Requirements: *GCE:* 340. *IB:* 34.

P303 BA Film Studies
Duration: 3FT Hon
Entry Requirements: *GCE:* 340. *IB:* 34.

R48 ROEHAMPTON UNIVERSITY
ROEHAMPTON LANE
LONDON SW15 5PU
t: 020 8392 3232 f: 020 8392 3470
e: enquiries@roehampton.ac.uk
// www.roehampton.ac.uk

PW38 BA Film and Creative Writing
Duration: 3FT Hon
Entry Requirements: *GCE:* 300. *IB:* 26. *BTEC ExtDip:* DDM. *OCR*
NED: D2 Interview required.

PWH4 BA Film and Drama, Theatre & Performance Studies
Duration: 3FT Hon
Entry Requirements: *GCE:* 300. *IB:* 26. *BTEC ExtDip:* DDM. *OCR*
NED: D2 Interview required.

QP3H BA Film and English Literature
Duration: 3FT Hon
Entry Requirements: *GCE:* 300. *IB:* 26. *BTEC ExtDip:* DDM. *OCR*
NED: D2 Interview required.

PR39 BA Film and French
Duration: 4FT Hon
Entry Requirements: *GCE:* 300. *IB:* 26. *BTEC ExtDip:* DDM. *OCR*
NED: D2 Interview required.

RP43 BA Film and Spanish
Duration: 4FT Hon
Entry Requirements: *GCE:* 300. *IB:* 26. *BTEC ExtDip:* DDM. *OCR*
NED: D2 Interview required.

WP63 BA Photography and Film
Duration: 3FT Hon
Entry Requirements: *GCE:* 300. *IB:* 26. *BTEC ExtDip:* DDM. *OCR*
NED: D2 Interview required.

PP53 BA/BSc Journalism and Film
Duration: 3FT Hon
Entry Requirements: *GCE:* 300. *IB:* 26. *BTEC ExtDip:* DDM. *OCR*
NED: D2 Interview required.

P391 BA/BSc Media & Culture and Film
Duration: 3FT Hon
Entry Requirements: *GCE:* 300. *IB:* 26. *BTEC ExtDip:* DDM. *OCR*
NED: D2 Interview required.

R72 ROYAL HOLLOWAY, UNIVERSITY OF LONDON
ROYAL HOLLOWAY, UNIVERSITY OF LONDON
EGHAM
SURREY TW20 0EX
t: 01784 414944 f: 01784 473662
e: Admissions@rhul.ac.uk
// www.rhul.ac.uk

Q2P3 BA Comparative Literature & Culture with Film Studies
Duration: 3FT Hon
Entry Requirements: *GCE:* ABB-BBB. *SQAH:* AAABB-BBBBB. *SQAAH:* ABB-BBB. *IB:* 34.

QW36 BA English and Film Studies
Duration: 3FT Hon
Entry Requirements: Contact the institution for details.

S03 THE UNIVERSITY OF SALFORD
SALFORD M5 4WT
t: 0161 295 4545 f: 0161 295 4646
e: ug-admissions@salford.ac.uk
// www.salford.ac.uk

QP33 BA English and Film Studies
Duration: 3FT Hon
Entry Requirements: *GCE:* 300. *IB:* 31.

P303 BA Film Studies
Duration: 3FT Hon
Entry Requirements: *GCE:* 300. *IB:* 31. *OCR NED:* M2

S21 SHEFFIELD HALLAM UNIVERSITY
CITY CAMPUS
HOWARD STREET
SHEFFIELD S1 1WB
t: 0114 225 5555 f: 0114 225 2167
e: admissions@shu.ac.uk
// www.shu.ac.uk

P303 BA Film Studies
Duration: 3FT Hon
Entry Requirements: *GCE:* 240.

QP33 BA Film Studies and English
Duration: 3FT Hon
Entry Requirements: *GCE:* 240.

W8P3 BA Film and Screenwriting
Duration: 3FT Hon
Entry Requirements: *GCE:* 240.

S27 UNIVERSITY OF SOUTHAMPTON
HIGHFIELD
SOUTHAMPTON SO17 1BJ
t: 023 8059 4732 f: 023 8059 3037
e: admissions@soton.ac.uk
// www.southampton.ac.uk

P303 BA Film
Duration: 3FT Hon
Entry Requirements: *GCE:* AAB. *IB:* 34.

S30 SOUTHAMPTON SOLENT UNIVERSITY
EAST PARK TERRACE
SOUTHAMPTON
HAMPSHIRE SO14 0RT
t: +44 (0) 23 8031 9039 f: + 44 (0)23 8022 2259
e: admissions@solent.ac.uk
// www.solent.ac.uk/

QP3J BA English and Film
Duration: 4SW Hon
Entry Requirements: *Foundation:* Distinction. *GCE:* 240. *SQAAH:* AA-CCD. *IB:* 24. *BTEC ExtDip:* MMM. *OCR ND:* D *OCR NED:* M3

P901 BA Film and Television (Top-Up)
Duration: 1FT Hon
Entry Requirements: Interview required. HND required.

P303 BA Film and Television Studies
Duration: 3FT Hon
Entry Requirements: *Foundation:* Distinction. *GCE:* 240. *SQAAH:* AA-CCD. *IB:* 24. *BTEC ExtDip:* MMM. *OCR ND:* D *OCR NED:* M3 Interview required.

P301 BA Media Culture and Production
Duration: 3FT Hon
Entry Requirements: *Foundation:* Distinction. *GCE:* 240. *SQAAH:* AA-CCD. *IB:* 24. *BTEC ExtDip:* MMM. *OCR ND:* D *OCR NED:* M3

PP34 BA Television and Video Production with IFY
Duration: 4FT Hon
Entry Requirements: Contact the institution for details.

S36 UNIVERSITY OF ST ANDREWS
ST KATHARINE'S WEST
16 THE SCORES
ST ANDREWS
FIFE KY16 9AX
t: 01334 462150 f: 01334 463330
e: admissions@st-andrews.ac.uk
// www.st-andrews.ac.uk

VP13 MA Ancient History and Film Studies
Duration: 4FT Hon
Entry Requirements: *GCE:* AAB. *SQAH:* AABB. *IB:* 35.

TP63 MA Arabic and Film Studies
Duration: 4FT Hon
Entry Requirements: *GCE:* AAB. *SQAH:* AABB. *IB:* 35.

TPP3 MA Arabic and Film Studies (year abroad)
Duration: 5FT Hon
Entry Requirements: *GCE:* AAB. *SQAH:* AABB. *IB:* 35.

VP33 MA Art History and Film Studies
Duration: 4FT Hon
Entry Requirements: *GCE:* AAB. *SQAH:* AABB. *IB:* 35.

VP63 MA Biblical Studies and Film Studies
Duration: 4FT Hon
Entry Requirements: *GCE:* AAA. *SQAH:* AAAB. *IB:* 36.

QP83 MA Classical Studies and Film Studies
Duration: 4FT Hon
Entry Requirements: *GCE:* AAB. *SQAH:* AABB. *IB:* 35.

LP13 MA Economics and Film Studies
Duration: 4FT Hon
Entry Requirements: *GCE:* AAA. *SQAH:* AAAB. *IB:* 38.

PQ33 MA English and Film Studies
Duration: 4FT Hon
Entry Requirements: *GCE:* AAA. *SQAH:* AAAB. *IB:* 36.

PR31 MA Film Studies and French
Duration: 4FT Hon
Entry Requirements: *GCE:* AAB. *SQAH:* AABB. *IB:* 35.

PR3C MA Film Studies and French (year abroad)
Duration: 5FT Hon
Entry Requirements: *GCE:* AAB. *SQAH:* AABB. *IB:* 35.

LP73 MA Film Studies and Geography
Duration: 4FT Hon
Entry Requirements: *GCE:* AAA. *SQAH:* AAAB. *IB:* 36.

PR32 MA Film Studies and German
Duration: 4FT Hon
Entry Requirements: *GCE:* AAB. *SQAH:* AABB. *IB:* 35.

PR3F MA Film Studies and German (year abroad)
Duration: 5FT Hon
Entry Requirements: *GCE:* AAB. *SQAH:* AABB. *IB:* 35.

LP23 MA Film Studies and International Relations
Duration: 4FT Hon
Entry Requirements: *GCE:* AAA. *SQAH:* AAAA. *IB:* 38.

PR33 MA Film Studies and Italian
Duration: 4FT Hon
Entry Requirements: *GCE:* AAB. *SQAH:* AABB. *IB:* 35.

PR3H MA Film Studies and Italian (year abroad)
Duration: 5FT Hon
Entry Requirements: *GCE:* AAB. *SQAH:* AABB. *IB:* 35.

PV31 MA Film Studies and Modern History
Duration: 4FT Hon
Entry Requirements: *GCE:* AAA. *SQAH:* AABB. *IB:* 36.

PV35 MA Film Studies and Philosophy
Duration: 4FT Hon
Entry Requirements: *GCE:* AAB. *SQAH:* AABB. *IB:* 35.

CP83 MA Film Studies and Psychology
Duration: 4FT Hon
Entry Requirements: *GCE:* AAA. *SQAH:* AAAB. *IB:* 36.

PR37 MA Film Studies and Russian
Duration: 4FT Hon
Entry Requirements: *GCE:* AAB. *SQAH:* AABB. *IB:* 35.

PRH7 MA Film Studies and Russian (year abroad)
Duration: 5FT Hon
Entry Requirements: *GCE:* AAB. *SQAH:* AABB. *IB:* 35.

PV32 MA Film Studies and Scottish History
Duration: 4FT Hon
Entry Requirements: *GCE:* AAA. *SQAH:* AABB. *IB:* 36.

PL36 MA Film Studies and Social Anthropology
Duration: 4FT Hon
Entry Requirements: *GCE:* AAB. *SQAH:* AABB. *IB:* 35.

PR34 MA Film Studies and Spanish
Duration: 4FT Hon
Entry Requirements: *GCE:* AAB. *SQAH:* AABB. *IB:* 35.

PR3K MA Film Studies and Spanish (year abroad)
Duration: 5FT Hon
Entry Requirements: *GCE:* AAB. *SQAH:* AABB. *IB:* 35.

PV36 MA Film Studies and Theological Studies
Duration: 4FT Hon
Entry Requirements: *GCE:* AAA. *SQAH:* AAAB. *IB:* 36.

C8P3 MA Psychology with Film Studies
Duration: 4FT Hon
Entry Requirements: *GCE:* AAA. *SQAH:* AAAB. *IB:* 36.

QP23 MA Hons Comparative Literature and Film Studies
Duration: 4FT Hon
Entry Requirements: *GCE:* AAB. *SQAH:* AABB. *IB:* 35.

S43 SOUTH ESSEX COLLEGE OF FURTHER & HIGHER EDUCATION
LUKER ROAD
SOUTHEND-ON-SEA
ESSEX SS1 1ND
t: 0845 52 12345 f: 01702 432320
e: Admissions@southessex.ac.uk
// www.southessex.ac.uk

P320 BA Television Production and Screen Media
Duration: 3FT Hon
Entry Requirements: *GCE:* 160. *IB:* 24. Interview required.

S64 ST MARY'S UNIVERSITY COLLEGE, TWICKENHAM
WALDEGRAVE ROAD
STRAWBERRY HILL
MIDDLESEX TW1 4SX
t: 020 8240 4029 f: 020 8240 2361
e: admit@smuc.ac.uk
// www.smuc.ac.uk

XP93 BA Education & Social Science and Film & Popular Culture
Duration: 3FT Hon
Entry Requirements: *GCE:* 240. *SQAH:* BBBC. *IB:* 28. *OCR ND:* D *OCR NED:* M3 Interview required.

QP33 BA English and Film & Popular Culture
Duration: 3FT Hon
Entry Requirements: *GCE:* 240. *SQAH:* BBBC. *IB:* 28. *OCR ND:* D *OCR NED:* M3 Interview required.

P303 BA Film & Popular Culture
Duration: 3FT Hon
Entry Requirements: *GCE:* 240. *SQAH:* BBBC. *IB:* 28. *OCR ND:* D *OCR NED:* M3 Interview required.

PW3V BA Film & Popular Culture and Creative & Professional Writing
Duration: 3FT Hon
Entry Requirements: *GCE:* 240. *SQAH:* BBBC. *IB:* 28. *OCR ND:* D *OCR NED:* M3 Interview required.

PW3P BA Film & Popular Culture and Media Arts
Duration: 3FT Hon
Entry Requirements: *GCE:* 240. *SQAH:* BBBC. *IB:* 28. *OCR ND:* D *OCR NED:* M3 Interview required.

PV35 BA Film & Popular Culture and Philosophy
Duration: 3FT Hon
Entry Requirements: *GCE:* 240. *SQAH:* BBBC. *IB:* 28. *OCR ND:* D *OCR NED:* M3 Interview required.

PL33 BA Film & Popular Culture and Sociology
Duration: 3FT Hon
Entry Requirements: *GCE:* 240. *SQAH:* BBBC. *IB:* 28. *OCR ND:* D *OCR NED:* M3 Interview required.

S72 STAFFORDSHIRE UNIVERSITY
COLLEGE ROAD
STOKE ON TRENT ST4 2DE
t: 01782 292753 f: 01782 292740
e: admissions@staffs.ac.uk
// www.staffs.ac.uk

P301 BSc Television Production Technology
Duration: 3FT/4SW Hon
Entry Requirements: Contact the institution for details.

S75 THE UNIVERSITY OF STIRLING
STUDENT RECRUITMENT & ADMISSIONS SERVICE
UNIVERSITY OF STIRLING
STIRLING
SCOTLAND FK9 4LA
t: 01786 467044 f: 01786 466800
e: admissions@stir.ac.uk
// www.stir.ac.uk

P390 BA Global Cinema
Duration: 4FT Hon
Entry Requirements: *GCE:* BBC. *SQAH:* BBBB. *SQAAH:* AAA-CCC. *IB:* 32. *BTEC ExtDip:* DMM.

S84 UNIVERSITY OF SUNDERLAND
STUDENT HELPLINE
THE STUDENT GATEWAY
CHESTER ROAD
SUNDERLAND SR1 3SD
t: 0191 515 3000 f: 0191 515 3805
e: student.helpline@sunderland.ac.uk
// www.sunderland.ac.uk

QP3H BA English and Film
Duration: 3FT Hon
Entry Requirements: *GCE:* 260-360. *OCR ND:* D *OCR NED:* M3

P302 FdA Community Radio
Duration: 2FT Fdg
Entry Requirements: *GCE:* 80-360. *IB:* 22. Interview required.

S90 UNIVERSITY OF SUSSEX
UNDERGRADUATE ADMISSIONS
SUSSEX HOUSE
UNIVERSITY OF SUSSEX
BRIGHTON BN1 9RH
t: 01273 678416 f: 01273 678545
e: ug.applicants@sussex.ac.uk
// www.sussex.ac.uk

VP33 BA Art History and Film Studies
Duration: 3FT Hon
Entry Requirements: *GCE:* AAB. *SQAH:* AAABB. *IB:* 35. *BTEC SubDip:* D. *BTEC Dip:* DD. *BTEC ExtDip:* DDD. *OCR ND:* D *OCR NED:* D1

WP43 BA Drama Studies and Film Studies
Duration: 3FT Hon
Entry Requirements: *GCE:* AAB. *SQAH:* AAABB. *IB:* 35. *BTEC SubDip:* D. *BTEC Dip:* DD. *BTEC ExtDip:* DDD. *OCR ND:* M1 *OCR NED:* D1

QP3H BA English and Film Studies
Duration: 3FT Hon
Entry Requirements: *GCE:* AAA-AAB. *SQAH:* AAAAA-AAABB. *SQAAH:* AAA-AAB. *IB:* 35. *BTEC SubDip:* D. *BTEC Dip:* DD. *BTEC ExtDip:* DDD. *OCR ND:* M1 *OCR NED:* D1

PRJ9 BA Film Studies and a Language (French/Italian/Spanish)
Duration: 4FT Hon
Entry Requirements: *GCE:* AAB-ABB. *SQAH:* AAABB-AABBB. *SQAAH:* ABB. *BTEC SubDip:* D. *BTEC Dip:* DD. *BTEC ExtDip:* DDD. *OCR ND:* M1 *OCR NED:* D2

VP13 BA History and Film Studies
Duration: 3FT Hon
Entry Requirements: *GCE:* AAB. *SQAH:* AAABB. *IB:* 35. *BTEC SubDip:* D. *BTEC Dip:* DD. *BTEC ExtDip:* DDD. *OCR ND:* D *OCR NED:* D1

T80 UNIVERSITY OF WALES TRINITY SAINT DAVID
COLLEGE ROAD
CARMARTHEN SA31 3EP
t: 01267 676767 f: 01267 676766
e: registry@trinitysaintdavid.ac.uk
// www.tsd.ac.uk

P30H BA Film and Visual Culture
Duration: 3FT Hon
Entry Requirements: Contact the institution for details.

U20 UNIVERSITY OF ULSTER
COLERAINE
CO. LONDONDERRY
NORTHERN IRELAND BT52 1SA
t: 028 7012 4221 f: 028 7012 4908
e: online@ulster.ac.uk
// www.ulster.ac.uk

QP33 BA English and Film Studies
Duration: 3FT Hon
Entry Requirements: *GCE:* 280. *IB:* 24.

Q3P3 BA English with Film Studies
Duration: 3FT Hon
Entry Requirements: *GCE:* 280. *IB:* 24.

PR31 BA Film Studies and French
Duration: 3FT Hon
Entry Requirements: *GCE:* CCC. *IB:* 24. Interview required.

PR32 BA Film Studies and German
Duration: 3FT Hon
Entry Requirements: *GCE:* 260. *IB:* 24. Interview required.

PV31 BA Film Studies and History
Duration: 3FT Hon
Entry Requirements: *GCE:* BBC. *IB:* 24.

PR34 BA Film Studies and Spanish
Duration: 3FT Hon
Entry Requirements: *GCE:* 260. *IB:* 24. Interview required.

P3QH BA Film Studies with English
Duration: 3FT Hon
Entry Requirements: *GCE:* BBC. *IB:* 24.

P3RC BA Film Studies with French
Duration: 3FT Hon
Entry Requirements: *GCE:* BBC. *IB:* 24.

P3RF BA Film Studies with German
Duration: 3FT Hon
Entry Requirements: *GCE:* BBC. *IB:* 24.

P3VC BA Film Studies with History
Duration: 3FT Hon
Entry Requirements: *GCE:* BBC. *IB:* 24.

P3L9 BA Film Studies with International Development
Duration: 3FT Hon
Entry Requirements: *GCE:* BBC. *IB:* 24.

P3W6 BA Film Studies with Photo-Imaging
Duration: 3FT Hon
Entry Requirements: *GCE:* BBC. *IB:* 24.

P3RK BA Film Studies with Spanish
Duration: 3FT Hon
Entry Requirements: *GCE:* BBC. *IB:* 24.

R1P3 BA French with Film Studies
Duration: 4FT Hon
Entry Requirements: *GCE:* 260. *IB:* 24.

R2P3 BA German with Film Studies
Duration: 4FT Hon
Entry Requirements: *GCE:* 260. *IB:* 24.

V1P3 BA History with Film Studies
Duration: 3FT Hon
Entry Requirements: *GCE:* 280. *IB:* 24.

P5P3 BA Journalism with Film Studies
Duration: 3FT Hon
Entry Requirements: *GCE:* 280-300.

R4P3 BA Spanish with Film Studies
Duration: 4SW Hon
Entry Requirements: *GCE:* 260. *IB:* 24.

W05 THE UNIVERSITY OF WEST LONDON
ST MARY'S ROAD
EALING
LONDON W5 5RF
t: 0800 036 8888 f: 020 8566 1353
e: learning.advice@uwl.ac.uk
// www.uwl.ac.uk

PH03 BA Film: Video Production and Film Studies
Duration: 3FT Hon
Entry Requirements: *GCE:* 240. Interview required.

P303 BA (Hons) Film
Duration: 3FT Hon
Entry Requirements: *GCE:* 240. Interview required.

W75 UNIVERSITY OF WOLVERHAMPTON
ADMISSIONS UNIT
MX207, CAMP STREET
WOLVERHAMPTON
WEST MIDLANDS WV1 1AD
t: 01902 321000 f: 01902 321896
e: admissions@wlv.ac.uk
// www.wlv.ac.uk

WP83 BA Creative & Professional Writing and Film Studies
Duration: 3FT Hon
Entry Requirements: *GCE:* 160-220.

WP4H BA Drama and Film Studies
Duration: 3FT Hon   **CRB Check:** Required
Entry Requirements: *GCE:* 200. *IB:* 24. *BTEC Dip:* DM. *BTEC ExtDip:* MMP. *OCR ND:* M1 *OCR NED:* P1 Interview required.

P303 BA Film Studies
Duration: 3FT Hon
Entry Requirements: *GCE:* 160-220. *IB:* 24.

PV35 BA Film Studies and Philosophy
Duration: 3FT Hon
Entry Requirements: Contact the institution for details.

W76 UNIVERSITY OF WINCHESTER
WINCHESTER
HANTS SO22 4NR
t: 01962 827234 f: 01962 827288
e: course.enquiries@winchester.ac.uk
// www.winchester.ac.uk

TP73 BA American Studies and Film Studies
Duration: 3FT Hon
Entry Requirements: *Foundation:* Distinction. *GCE:* 260-300. *IB:* 24. *OCR ND:* D *OCR NED:* M2

NPC3 BA Business Management and Film Studies
Duration: 3FT Hon
Entry Requirements: *Foundation:* Distinction. *GCE:* 260-300. *IB:* 24. *OCR ND:* D *OCR NED:* M2

LP5H BA Childhood,Youth & Community Studies and Film Studies
Duration: 3FT Hon
Entry Requirements: *GCE:* 260-300. *IB:* 24.

PW35 BA Choreography & Dance and Film Studies
Duration: 3FT Hon
Entry Requirements: *Foundation:* Distinction. *GCE:* 260-300. *IB:* 25. *OCR ND:* D *OCR NED:* M2

PWH8 BA Creative Writing and Film Studies
Duration: 3FT Hon
Entry Requirements: *Foundation:* Distinction. *GCE:* 260-300. *IB:* 25. *OCR ND:* D *OCR NED:* M2

XP33 BA Education Studies (Early Childhood) and Film Studies
Duration: 3FT Hon
Entry Requirements: *Foundation:* Distinction. *GCE:* 260-300. *IB:* 24. *OCR ND:* D *OCR NED:* M2

XPH3 BA Education Studies and Film Studies
Duration: 3FT Hon
Entry Requirements: *Foundation:* Distinction. *GCE:* 260-300. *IB:* 24. *OCR ND:* D *OCR NED:* M2

QPH3 BA English and Film Studies
Duration: 3FT Hon
Entry Requirements: *Foundation:* Distinction. *GCE:* 260-300. *IB:* 25. *OCR ND:* D *OCR NED:* M2

NP8H BA Event Management and Film Studies
Duration: 3FT Hon
Entry Requirements: *Foundation:* Distinction. *GCE:* 260-300. *IB:* 24. *OCR ND:* D *OCR NED:* M2

PL53 BA Film & Cinema Technologies and Health, Community & Social Care Studies
Duration: 3FT Hon
Entry Requirements: Contact the institution for details.

P303 BA Film Studies
Duration: 3FT Hon
Entry Requirements: *Foundation:* Distinction. *GCE:* 260-300. *IB:* 25. *OCR ND:* D *OCR NED:* M2

PW36 BA Film Studies and Film & Cinema Technologies
Duration: 3FT Hon
Entry Requirements: *Foundation:* Distinction. *GCE:* 260-300. *IB:* 24. *OCR ND:* D *OCR NED:* M2

PL5H BA Film Studies and Health, Community & Social Care Studies
Duration: 3FT Hon
Entry Requirements: Contact the institution for details.

PV31 BA Film Studies and History
Duration: 3FT Hon
Entry Requirements: *Foundation:* Distinction. *GCE:* 260-300. *IB:* 24. *OCR ND:* D *OCR NED:* M2

PP35 BA Film Studies and Journalism Studies
Duration: 3FT Hon
Entry Requirements: *Foundation:* Distinction. *GCE:* 260-300. *IB:* 24. *OCR ND:* D *OCR NED:* M2

P392 BA Film Studies and Media Production
Duration: 3FT Hon
Entry Requirements: *Foundation:* Distinction. *GCE:* 260-300. *IB:* 24. *OCR ND:* D *OCR NED:* M2

PW3K BA Film Studies and Performing Arts (Contemporary Performance)
Duration: 3FT Hon
Entry Requirements: *Foundation:* Distinction. *GCE:* 260-300. *IB:* 24. *OCR ND:* D *OCR NED:* M2

CPX3 BA Film Studies and Psychology
Duration: 3FT Hon
Entry Requirements: *Foundation:* Distinction. *GCE:* 260-300. *IB:* 25. *OCR ND:* D *OCR NED:* M2

PLJ3 BA Film Studies and Sociology
Duration: 3FT Hon
Entry Requirements: *Foundation:* Distinction. *GCE:* 260-300. *IB:* 24. *OCR ND:* D *OCR NED:* M2

PV36 BA Film Studies and Theology & Religious Studies
Duration: 3FT Hon
Entry Requirements: *Foundation:* Distinction. *GCE:* 260-300. *IB:* 25. *OCR ND:* D *OCR NED:* M2

PW33 BA Film Studies and Vocal & Choral Studies
Duration: 3FT Hon
Entry Requirements: *Foundation:* Distinction. *GCE:* 260-300. *IB:* 24. *OCR ND:* D *OCR NED:* M2

MP13 BA Law and Film Studies
Duration: 3FT Hon
Entry Requirements: *Foundation:* Distinction. *GCE:* 260-300. *IB:* 25. *OCR ND:* D *OCR NED:* M2

LP23 BA Politics & Global Studies and Film Studies
Duration: 3FT Hon
Entry Requirements: *Foundation:* Distinction. *GCE:* 260-300. *IB:* 24. *OCR ND:* D

QP3I BA (Hons) English Language Studies and Film Studies
Duration: 3FT Hon
Entry Requirements: Contact the institution for details.

W80 UNIVERSITY OF WORCESTER
HENWICK GROVE
WORCESTER WR2 6AJ
t: 01905 855111 f: 01905 855377
e: admissions@worc.ac.uk
// www.worcester.ac.uk

PW36 BA Digital Film Production and Film Studies
Duration: 3FT Hon
Entry Requirements: *GCE:* 240-260. *IB:* 24. *OCR ND:* D Interview required. Portfolio required.

WP4H BA Drama & Performance and Film Studies
Duration: 3FT Hon
Entry Requirements: *GCE:* 240-260. *IB:* 24. *OCR ND:* D *OCR NED:* M3

QP3J BA English Language Studies and Film Studies
Duration: 3FT Hon
Entry Requirements: *GCE:* 240-260. *IB:* 24. *OCR ND:* D *OCR NED:* M3

QP3H BA English Literary Studies and Film Studies
Duration: 3FT Hon
Entry Requirements: *GCE:* 240-260. *IB:* 24. *OCR ND:* D *OCR NED:* M3

P303 BA Film Studies
Duration: 3FT Hon
Entry Requirements: Contact the institution for details.

P390 BA Film Studies and Media & Cultural Studies
Duration: 3FT Hon
Entry Requirements: *GCE:* 240-300. *IB:* 24. *OCR ND:* D *OCR NED:* M3

PW38 BA Film Studies and Screen Writing
Duration: 3FT Hon
Entry Requirements: *GCE:* 240-300. *IB:* 24. *OCR ND:* D *OCR NED:* M3

Y75 YORK ST JOHN UNIVERSITY
LORD MAYOR'S WALK
YORK YO31 7EX
t: 01904 876598 f: 01904 876940/876921
e: admissions@yorksj.ac.uk
// w3.yorksj.ac.uk

TP7H BA American Studies and Film Studies
Duration: 3FT Hon
Entry Requirements: *GCE:* 220-260. *IB:* 24.

TPR3 BA American Studies and Film Studies (international only)
Duration: 4FT Hon
Entry Requirements: *GCE:* 220-260. *IB:* 24.

QP3H BA English Literature and Film Studies
Duration: 3FT Hon
Entry Requirements: *GCE:* 220-260. *IB:* 24.

MEDIA PRODUCTION

A40 ABERYSTWYTH UNIVERSITY
ABERYSTWYTH UNIVERSITY, WELCOME CENTRE
PENGLAIS CAMPUS
ABERYSTWYTH
CEREDIGION SY23 3FB
t: 01970 622021 f: 01970 627410
e: ug-admissions@aber.ac.uk
// www.aber.ac.uk

W620 BA Film & Television Studies
Duration: 3FT Hon
Entry Requirements: *GCE:* 300-320.

WW64 BA Film & Television Studies/Drama & Theatre Studies
Duration: 3FT Hon
Entry Requirements: *GCE:* 300-320. *IB:* 32.

WX63 BA Film & Television Studies/Education
Duration: 3FT Hon
Entry Requirements: *GCE:* 300-320. *IB:* 32.

QW36 BA Film & Television Studies/English Literature
Duration: 3FT Hon
Entry Requirements: *GCE:* 300-320. *IB:* 32.

WW16 BA Film & Television Studies/Fine Art
Duration: 3FT Hon
Entry Requirements: *GCE:* 300-320. *IB:* 32. Portfolio required.

RW16 BA French/Film & Television Studies (4 years)
Duration: 4FT Hon
Entry Requirements: *GCE:* 300-320. *IB:* 32.

QP53 BA Gwyddeleg: Iaith a Lln/Astudiaethau Ffilm a Theledu
Duration: 4FT Hon
Entry Requirements: *GCE:* 300-320. *IB:* 32.

VW26 BA Hanes Cymru ac Astudiaethau Ffilm a Theledu
Duration: 3FT Hon
Entry Requirements: *GCE:* 300-320. *IB:* 29.

VW16 BA History/Film & Television Studies
Duration: 3FT Hon
Entry Requirements: *GCE:* 300-320. *IB:* 29.

LW26 BA International Politics/Film & Television Studies
Duration: 3FT Hon
Entry Requirements: *GCE:* 300-320. *IB:* 29.

GW16 BA Mathematics/Film & Television Studies
Duration: 3FT Hon
Entry Requirements: *GCE:* 320. *IB:* 27.

LWF6 BA Politics/Film & Television Studies
Duration: 3FT Hon
Entry Requirements: *GCE:* 300-320. *IB:* 29.

WP43 BA Scenography & Theatre Design/Film & Television Studies
Duration: 3FT Hon
Entry Requirements: *GCE:* 300-320. *IB:* 32.

RW46 BA Spanish/Film & Television Studies (4 years)
Duration: 4FT Hon
Entry Requirements: *GCE:* 300-320. *IB:* 32.

VWF6 BA Welsh History/Film & Television Studies
Duration: 3FT Hon
Entry Requirements: *GCE:* 300-320. *IB:* 29.

A44 ACCRINGTON & ROSSENDALE COLLEGE
BROAD OAK ROAD,
ACCRINGTON,
LANCASHIRE, BB5 2AW.
t: 01254 389933 f: 01254 354001
e: info@accross.ac.uk
// www.accrosshighereducation.co.uk/

WP63 BA (Hons) Film and Digital Media
Duration: 3FT Hon
Entry Requirements: *GCE:* 160. Interview required.

A66 THE ARTS UNIVERSITY COLLEGE AT BOURNEMOUTH (FORMERLY ARTS INSTITUTE AT BOURNEMOUTH)
WALLISDOWN
POOLE
DORSET BH12 5HH
t: 01202 363228 f: 01202 537729
e: admissions@aucb.ac.uk
// www.aucb.ac.uk

P310 BA Digital Media Production
Duration: 3FT Hon
Entry Requirements: *Foundation:* Pass. *GCE:* BCC. *IB:* 24. *OCR ND:* M1 *OCR NED:* M1 Interview required. Portfolio required.

B11 BARKING AND DAGENHAM COLLEGE
DAGENHAM ROAD
ROMFORD
ESSEX RM7 0XU
t: 020 8090 3020 f: 020 8090 3021
e: engagement.services@barkingdagenhamcollege.ac.uk
// www.barkingdagenhamcollege.ac.uk

013P HND Creative Media Production
Duration: 2FT HND
Entry Requirements: Contact the institution for details.

B20 BATH SPA UNIVERSITY
NEWTON PARK
NEWTON ST LOE
BATH BA2 9BN
t: 01225 875875 f: 01225 875444
e: enquiries@bathspa.ac.uk
// www.bathspa.ac.uk/clearing

WP93 BA Creative Media Practice
Duration: 3FT Hon
Entry Requirements: *GCE:* 220-280. *IB:* 24. Interview required. Portfolio required.

B22 UNIVERSITY OF BEDFORDSHIRE
PARK SQUARE
LUTON
BEDS LU1 3JU
t: 0844 8482234 f: 01582 489323
e: admissions@beds.ac.uk
// www.beds.ac.uk

P310 BA Media Production
Duration: 3FT Hon
Entry Requirements: *Foundation:* Pass. *GCE:* 200. *SQAH:* BCC.
SQAAH: BCC. *IB:* 24. *OCR ND:* M1 *OCR NED:* P1

PW36 BA Media Production (Moving Image)
Duration: 3FT Hon
Entry Requirements: *Foundation:* Pass. *GCE:* 200. *SQAH:* BCC.
SQAAH: BCC. *IB:* 24. *OCR ND:* M1 *OCR NED:* P1

PW3G BA Media Production (New Media)
Duration: 3FT Hon
Entry Requirements: *Foundation:* Pass. *GCE:* 200. *SQAH:* BCC.
SQAAH: BCC. *IB:* 24. *OCR ND:* M1 *OCR NED:* P1

P312 BA Media Production (Radio)
Duration: 3FT Hon
Entry Requirements: *Foundation:* Pass. *GCE:* 200. *SQAH:* BCC.
SQAAH: BCC. *IB:* 24. *OCR ND:* M1 *OCR NED:* P1

P314 FdA Media Production
Duration: 2FT Fdg
Entry Requirements: Contact the institution for details.

B25 BIRMINGHAM CITY UNIVERSITY
PERRY BARR
BIRMINGHAM B42 2SU
t: 0121 331 5595 f: 0121 331 7994
// www.bcu.ac.uk

PN38 BA Media and Communication (Event and Exhibition Industries)
Duration: 3FT Hon
Entry Requirements: *Foundation:* Pass. *GCE:* BBC. *SQAH:* ABBB.
SQAAH: BBC. *IB:* 30.

PJ39 BA Media and Communication (Music Industries)
Duration: 3FT Hon
Entry Requirements: *Foundation:* Pass. *GCE:* BBC. *SQAH:* ABBB.
SQAAH: BBC. *IB:* 30.

P9P3 BA Media and Communication (Radio)
Duration: 3FT Hon
Entry Requirements: *Foundation:* Pass. *GCE:* BBC. *SQAH:* ABBB.
SQAAH: BBC. *IB:* 30.

W614 BSc Film Technology and Special Effects
Duration: 3FT/4SW Hon
Entry Requirements: *GCE:* 300. *IB:* 32.

WP63 BSc Film, Production and Technology
Duration: 3FT/4SW Hon
Entry Requirements: *GCE:* 300. *IB:* 30.

P310 BSc Multimedia Technology
Duration: 3FT/4SW Hon
Entry Requirements: *GCE:* 280. *IB:* 30.

P312 FdA Radio Production
Duration: 2FT Fdg
Entry Requirements: Contact the institution for details.

B41 BLACKPOOL AND THE FYLDE COLLEGE AN ASSOCIATE COLLEGE OF LANCASTER UNIVERSITY
ASHFIELD ROAD
BISPHAM
BLACKPOOL
LANCS FY2 0HB
t: 01253 504346 f: 01253 504198
e: admissions@blackpool.ac.uk
// www.blackpool.ac.uk

P310 BA Hons Media Writing and Production (Top-Up)
Duration: 1FT Hon
Entry Requirements: Contact the institution for details.

WP83 FdA Media Writing with Production
Duration: 2FT Fdg
Entry Requirements: *GCE:* 120.

B44 UNIVERSITY OF BOLTON
DEANE ROAD
BOLTON BL3 5AB
t: 01204 903903 f: 01204 399074
e: enquiries@bolton.ac.uk
// www.bolton.ac.uk

P3C0 BA Media Production
Duration: 1FT Hon
Entry Requirements: Interview required. Portfolio required.

PWH8 BA Media, Writing & Production
Duration: 3FT Hon
Entry Requirements: *GCE:* 240. Interview required. Portfolio required.

P310 FdA Media Production
Duration: 2FT Fdg
Entry Requirements: *GCE:* 120. Interview required. Portfolio required.

B50 BOURNEMOUTH UNIVERSITY
TALBOT CAMPUS
FERN BARROW
POOLE
DORSET BH12 5BB
t: 01202 524111
// www.bournemouth.ac.uk

PW36 BA Film Production and Cinematography
Duration: 3FT Hon
Entry Requirements: *GCE:* 340. *IB:* 33. *BTEC SubDip:* D. *BTEC Dip:* DD. *BTEC ExtDip:* DDD. Interview required.

PH10 BA Media Production
Duration: 3FT Hon
Entry Requirements: *GCE:* 340. *IB:* 33. *BTEC SubDip:* D. *BTEC Dip:* DD. *BTEC ExtDip:* DDD.

P31F BA Radio
Duration: 3FT Hon
Entry Requirements: *GCE:* 300. *IB:* 31. *BTEC SubDip:* M. *BTEC Dip:* DM. *BTEC ExtDip:* DDM.

P314 FdA Commercial Video with Multimedia
Duration: 2FT Fdg
Entry Requirements: *GCE:* 120.

P391 FdA Digital Media Practice
Duration: 2FT Fdg
Entry Requirements: *GCE:* 240.

JP93 FdA Radio Production
Duration: 2FT Fdg
Entry Requirements: *GCE:* 120. *IB:* 24. Interview required.

B56 THE UNIVERSITY OF BRADFORD
RICHMOND ROAD
BRADFORD
WEST YORKSHIRE BD7 1DP
t: 0800 073 1225 f: 01274 235585
e: course-enquiries@bradford.ac.uk
// www.bradford.ac.uk

P311 BA Television Production
Duration: 3FT Hon
Entry Requirements: *GCE:* 240. *IB:* 24. Interview required.

B72 UNIVERSITY OF BRIGHTON
MITHRAS HOUSE 211
LEWES ROAD
BRIGHTON BN2 4AT
t: 01273 644644 f: 01273 642607
e: admissions@brighton.ac.uk
// www.brighton.ac.uk

P314 BA Broadcast Media (Top-Up)
Duration: 1FT Hon
Entry Requirements: HND required.

P313 BA Digital Film Production
Duration: 3FT Hon
Entry Requirements: Contact the institution for details.

P310 FdA Broadcast Media
Duration: 2FT Fdg
Entry Requirements: *GCE:* 160. *IB:* 24.

P312 FdA Radio Production
Duration: 2FT Fdg
Entry Requirements: *GCE:* 160. *IB:* 24.

P311 FdA Television Production
Duration: 2FT Fdg
Entry Requirements: *GCE:* 160. *IB:* 24.

B77 BRISTOL, CITY OF BRISTOL COLLEGE
SOUTH BRISTOL SKILLS ACADEMY
CITY OF BRISTOL COLLEGE
PO BOX 2887 BS2 2BB
t: 0117 312 5000
e: HEAdmissions@cityofbristol.ac.uk
// www.cityofbristol.ac.uk

P310 FdA Digital Media Production
Duration: 2FT Fdg
Entry Requirements: *GCE:* 140. Interview required. Portfolio required.

B94 BUCKINGHAMSHIRE NEW UNIVERSITY
QUEEN ALEXANDRA ROAD
HIGH WYCOMBE
BUCKINGHAMSHIRE HP11 2JZ
t: 0800 0565 660 f: 01494 605 023
e: admissions@bucks.ac.uk
// bucks.ac.uk

PW36 BA Film and TV Production
Duration: 3FT Hon
Entry Requirements: *GCE:* 200-240. *IB:* 24. *OCR ND:* M1 *OCR NED:* M3

P312 FdA Radio Production
Duration: 2FT Fdg
Entry Requirements: *GCE:* 100-140. *IB:* 24. *OCR ND:* P2 *OCR NED:* P3 Interview required.

P311 FdA Television Production
Duration: 2FT Fdg
Entry Requirements: *GCE:* 100-140. *IB:* 24. *OCR ND:* P2 *OCR NED:* P3 Interview required.

C10 CANTERBURY CHRIST CHURCH UNIVERSITY
NORTH HOLMES ROAD
CANTERBURY
KENT CT1 1QU
t: 01227 782900 f: 01227 782888
e: admissions@canterbury.ac.uk
// www.canterbury.ac.uk

P310 BA Film, Radio & Television Studies (Broadcasting)
Duration: 3FT Hon   CRB Check: Required
Entry Requirements: *GCE:* 260. *IB:* 24. Interview required.

P314 BA Film, Radio & Television Studies (Film)
Duration: 3FT Hon   CRB Check: Required
Entry Requirements: *GCE:* 260. *IB:* 24. Interview required.

P312 BA Film, Radio & Television Studies (Radio)
Duration: 3FT Hon   CRB Check: Required
Entry Requirements: *GCE:* 260. *IB:* 24. Interview required.

P311 BA Film, Radio & Television Studies (Television)
Duration: 3FT Hon   CRB Check: Required
Entry Requirements: *GCE:* 260. *IB:* 24. Interview required.

N1PH BSc Business Studies with Film, Radio & Television 'International Only'
Duration: 4FT FYr
Entry Requirements: Interview required.

C30 UNIVERSITY OF CENTRAL LANCASHIRE
PRESTON
LANCS PR1 2HE
t: 01772 201201 f: 01772 894954
e: uadmissions@uclan.ac.uk
// www.uclan.ac.uk

PW3P BA Film & Media and Film Production
Duration: 3FT Hon
Entry Requirements: *GCE:* 260-300. *IB:* 28. *BTEC Dip:* D*D*. *BTEC ExtDip:* DMM. *OCR ND:* D *OCR NED:* M2

WP6J BA Film Production
Duration: 3FT Hon
Entry Requirements: *GCE:* 240-260. *IB:* 28. *OCR ND:* D *OCR NED:* M3 Portfolio required.

PWH6 BA Film Production and Media Production & Technology
Duration: 3FT Hon
Entry Requirements: *GCE:* 260-300. *IB:* 28. *BTEC Dip:* D*D*. *BTEC ExtDip:* DMM. *OCR ND:* D *OCR NED:* M2

PW38 BA Film Production and Screenwriting
Duration: 3FT Hon
Entry Requirements: *GCE:* 260-300. *IB:* 28. *BTEC Dip:* D*D*. *BTEC ExtDip:* DMM. *OCR ND:* D *OCR NED:* M2 Interview required.

P311 BSc TV Production
Duration: 3FT Hon
Entry Requirements: *GCE:* 300. *SQAH:* AAAB. *IB:* 30. *OCR ND:* D *OCR NED:* D2

C55 UNIVERSITY OF CHESTER
PARKGATE ROAD
CHESTER CH1 4BJ
t: 01244 511000 f: 01244 511300
e: enquiries@chester.ac.uk
// www.chester.ac.uk

NP5H BA Advertising and Commercial Music Production
Duration: 3FT Hon
Entry Requirements: *GCE:* 240-280. *SQAH:* BBBB. *IB:* 26.

NP5J BA Advertising and Radio Production
Duration: 3FT Hon
Entry Requirements: *Foundation:* Pass. *GCE:* 260-300. *SQAH:* BBBB. *IB:* 28.

NPMH BA Advertising and TV Production
Duration: 3FT Hon
Entry Requirements: *Foundation:* Pass. *GCE:* 260-300. *SQAH:* BBBB. *IB:* 28.

NPC3 BA Business Management and Commercial Music Production
Duration: 3FT Hon
Entry Requirements: *Foundation:* Pass. *GCE:* 260-300. *SQAH:* BBBB. *IB:* 28.

NPD3 BA Business Management and Radio Production
Duration: 3FT Hon
Entry Requirements: *Foundation:* Pass. *GCE:* 260-300. *SQAH:* BBBB. *IB:* 28.

NPCH BA Business Management and TV Production
Duration: 3FT Hon
Entry Requirements: *Foundation:* Pass. *GCE:* 260-300. *SQAH:* BBBB. *IB:* 28.

WP6J BA Digital Photography and Radio Production
Duration: 3FT Hon
Entry Requirements: *Foundation:* Pass. *GCE:* 260-300. *SQAH:* BBBB. *IB:* 28.

WPP3 BA Digital Photography and TV Production
Duration: 3FT Hon
Entry Requirements: *Foundation:* Pass. *GCE:* 260-300. *SQAH:* BBBB. *IB:* 28.

NPV3 BA Events Management and Radio Production
Duration: 3FT Hon
Entry Requirements: *Foundation:* Pass. *GCE:* 260-300. *SQAH:* BBBB. *IB:* 28.

NPVH BA Events Management and TV Production
Duration: 3FT Hon
Entry Requirements: *Foundation:* Pass. *GCE:* 260-300. *SQAH:* BBBB. *IB:* 28.

PPM3 BA Journalism and Commercial Music Production
Duration: 3FT Hon
Entry Requirements: *Foundation:* Pass. *GCE:* 260-300. *SQAH:* BBBB. *IB:* 28.

PPN3 BA Journalism and Radio Production
Duration: 3FT Hon
Entry Requirements: *Foundation:* Pass. *GCE:* 260-300. *SQAH:* BBBB. *IB:* 28.

PPMJ BA Journalism and TV Production
Duration: 3FT Hon
Entry Requirements: *Foundation:* Pass. *GCE:* 260-300. *SQAH:* BBBB. *IB:* 28.

P314 BA Radio Production and Commercial Music Production
Duration: 3FT Hon
Entry Requirements: *Foundation:* Pass. *GCE:* 260-300. *SQAH:* BBBB. *IB:* 28.

P317 BA TV Production and Commercial Music Production
Duration: 3FT Hon
Entry Requirements: *Foundation:* Pass. *GCE:* 260-300. *SQAH:* BBBB. *IB:* 28.

P310 BA TV Production and Media Studies
Duration: 3FT Hon
Entry Requirements: *Foundation:* Pass. *GCE:* 260-300. *SQAH:* BBBB. *IB:* 28.

P318 BA TV Production and Radio Production
Duration: 3FT Hon
Entry Requirements: *Foundation:* Pass. *GCE:* 260-300. *SQAH:* BBBB. *IB:* 28.

C57 CHICHESTER COLLEGE
WESTGATE FIELDS
CHICHESTER
WEST SUSSEX PO19 1SB
t: 01243 786321 x2127 f: 01243 539481
e: sally.billingham@chichester.ac.uk
// www.chichester.ac.uk

36PW HND Film Making
Duration: 2FT/1FT HND/HNC
Entry Requirements: *Foundation:* Merit. *GCE:* AA-DD. *SQAH:* AAAAA-DDDDD. *SQAAH:* AAA-CCC. *OCR ND:* M2 *OCR NED:* M3 Interview required. Portfolio required.

C75 COLCHESTER INSTITUTE
SHEEPEN ROAD
COLCHESTER
ESSEX CO3 3LL
t: 01206 712777 f: 01206 712800
e: info@colchester.ac.uk
// www.colchester.ac.uk

013P HNC Creative Media Production (Moving Image)
Duration: 1FT HNC
Entry Requirements: Contact the institution for details.

01HP HND Creative Media Production (Moving Image)
Duration: 2FT HND
Entry Requirements: Contact the institution for details.

C78 CORNWALL COLLEGE
POOL
REDRUTH
CORNWALL TR15 3RD
t: 01209 616161 f: 01209 611612
e: he.admissions@cornwall.ac.uk
// www.cornwall.ac.uk

36WP HNC Creative Media Production
Duration: 1FT HNC CRB Check: Required
Entry Requirements: Contact the institution for details.

63PW HND Creative Media Production
Duration: 2FT HND CRB Check: Required
Entry Requirements: Contact the institution for details.

C85 COVENTRY UNIVERSITY
THE STUDENT CENTRE
COVENTRY UNIVERSITY
1 GULSON RD
COVENTRY CV1 2JH
t: 024 7615 2222 f: 024 7615 2223
e: studentenquiries@coventry.ac.uk
// www.coventry.ac.uk

P310 BA Media Production
Duration: 3FT/4SW Hon
Entry Requirements: *GCE:* BCC. *SQAH:* BCCCC. *IB:* 27. *BTEC ExtDip:* DMM. *OCR NED:* M2 Interview required. Portfolio required.

C92 CROYDON COLLEGE
COLLEGE ROAD
CROYDON CR9 1DX
t: 020 8760 5934 f: 020 8760 5880
e: admissions@croydon.ac.uk
// www.croydon.ac.uk

P313 BA Digital Film Production
Duration: 1FT Hon
Entry Requirements: Contact the institution for details.

PWJ4 BA Digital Film Production Design
Duration: 1FT Hon
Entry Requirements: Contact the institution for details.

PW34 FdA Digital Film Production Design
Duration: 2FT Fdg
Entry Requirements: Contact the institution for details.

C99 UNIVERSITY OF CUMBRIA
FUSEHILL STREET
CARLISLE
CUMBRIA CA1 2HH
t: 01228 616234 f: 01228 616235
// www.cumbria.ac.uk

P311 BA Film & Television Production
Duration: 3FT Hon
Entry Requirements: *Foundation:* Pass. *GCE:* 240. *SQAH:* BBC.
SQAAH: CC. *IB:* 30. *OCR ND:* D Interview required. Portfolio
required.

P314 BA Film and Television Production (with Year 0)
Duration: 4FT Hon
Entry Requirements: *Foundation:* Pass. *GCE:* C-cccc. *SQAH:* CC.
SQAAH: C. *IB:* 25. Interview required. Portfolio required.

P3C0 BA Mass Communication (Top-up)
Duration: 1FT Hon
Entry Requirements: Contact the institution for details.

D26 DE MONTFORT UNIVERSITY
THE GATEWAY
LEICESTER LE1 9BH
t: 0116 255 1551 f: 0116 250 6204
e: enquiries@dmu.ac.uk
// www.dmu.ac.uk

P310 BSc Media Production
Duration: 3FT/4SW Hon
Entry Requirements: *GCE:* 300. *IB:* 30. *BTEC ExtDip:* DDM.

WP63 FdSc Digital Video and Broadcast Production
Duration: 2FT Fdg
Entry Requirements: *GCE:* 120. *IB:* 24. *OCR NED:* P2

D39 UNIVERSITY OF DERBY
KEDLESTON ROAD
DERBY DE22 1GB
t: 01332 591167 f: 01332 597724
e: askadmissions@derby.ac.uk
// www.derby.ac.uk

P310 BA Media Production
Duration: 3FT Hon
Entry Requirements: *Foundation:* Distinction. *GCE:* 280. *IB:* 28.
BTEC Dip: D*D*. *BTEC ExtDip:* DMM. *OCR NED:* M2 Interview
required.

E14 UNIVERSITY OF EAST ANGLIA
NORWICH NR4 7TJ
t: 01603 591515 f: 01603 591523
e: admissions@uea.ac.uk
// www.uea.ac.uk

RP9H BA Honours Language and Film & Television
Duration: 4FT Hon CRB Check: Required
Entry Requirements: *GCE:* ABB. *SQAAH:* ABB. *IB:* 32. *BTEC
ExtDip:* DDM. Interview required.

E28 UNIVERSITY OF EAST LONDON
DOCKLANDS CAMPUS
UNIVERSITY WAY
LONDON E16 2RD
t: 020 8223 3333 f: 020 8223 2978
e: study@uel.ac.uk
// www.uel.ac.uk

V000 BA Media & Creative Industries
Duration: 3FT Hon
Entry Requirements: *GCE:* 240.

LPV0 BA Media & Creative Industries (Extended)
Duration: 4FT Hon
Entry Requirements: *GCE:* 80.

E42 EDGE HILL UNIVERSITY
ORMSKIRK
LANCASHIRE L39 4QP
t: 01695 657000 f: 01695 584355
e: study@edgehill.ac.uk
// www.edgehill.ac.uk

P311 BA Television Production Management
Duration: 3FT Hon
Entry Requirements: *GCE:* 280. *IB:* 26. *OCR ND:* D *OCR NED:* M2
Interview required. Portfolio required.

E81 EXETER COLLEGE
HELE ROAD
EXETER
DEVON EX4 4JS
t: 0845 111 6000
e: info@exe-coll.ac.uk
// www.exe-coll.ac.uk/he

P310 FdA Creative Digital Video
Duration: 2FT Fdg
Entry Requirements: *GCE:* 160.

P311 FdA Television Production
Duration: 2FT Fdg
Entry Requirements: *GCE:* 160.

F66 FARNBOROUGH COLLEGE OF TECHNOLOGY
BOUNDARY ROAD
FARNBOROUGH
HAMPSHIRE GU14 6SB
t: 01252 407028 f: 01252 407041
e: admissions@farn-ct.ac.uk
// www.farn-ct.ac.uk

HP63 BA Media Production
Duration: 3FT Hon
Entry Requirements: *GCE:* 180-200. *OCR ND:* M2 *OCR NED:* M3 Admissions Test required.

PW3J BA Media Production (Performance)
Duration: 3FT Hon
Entry Requirements: *GCE:* 180-200. *OCR ND:* M2 *OCR NED:* M3 Admissions Test required.

PW34 BA Media Production (Performance) (Top Up)
Duration: 1FT Hon
Entry Requirements: Contact the institution for details.

PW36 BA Media Production (Photography)
Duration: 3FT Hon
Entry Requirements: *GCE:* 180-200. *OCR ND:* M2 *OCR NED:* M3 Admissions Test required.

WP33 BSc Media Production (Music)
Duration: 3FT Hon
Entry Requirements: *GCE:* 180-200. *OCR ND:* M2 *OCR NED:* M3 Admissions Test required.

PW33 BSc Media Production (Music, Top-Up)
Duration: 1FT Hon
Entry Requirements: Contact the institution for details.

P311 BSc Media Production (Top-Up)
Duration: 1FT Hon
Entry Requirements: Contact the institution for details.

P314 FdSc Studio Engineering and Media Technology
Duration: 2FT Fdg
Entry Requirements: *GCE:* 160.

G14 UNIVERSITY OF GLAMORGAN, CARDIFF AND PONTYPRIDD
ENQUIRIES AND ADMISSIONS UNIT
PONTYPRIDD CF37 1DL
t: 08456 434030 f: 01443 654050
e: enquiries@glam.ac.uk
// www.glam.ac.uk

P310 BA Cynhyrchu yn y Cyfryngau - Cwrs Dwyieithog
Duration: 3FT Hon
Entry Requirements: *GCE:* ABB. *BTEC SubDip:* M. *BTEC Dip:* D*D*. *BTEC ExtDip:* DMM. *OCR NED:* M2

PW36 BA Photography
Duration: 3FT Hon
Entry Requirements: *GCE:* BBB. *IB:* 26. *BTEC SubDip:* M. *BTEC Dip:* DD. *BTEC ExtDip:* DDM. *OCR NED:* M2 Interview required. Portfolio required.

P312 BA Radio
Duration: 3FT Hon
Entry Requirements: *GCE:* BBC. *IB:* 25. *BTEC SubDip:* M. *BTEC Dip:* D*D*. *BTEC ExtDip:* DDM. *OCR NED:* M2 Interview required.

PH10 BSc Creative Industries (Popular Music Technology) (Top-Up)
Duration: 1FT Hon
Entry Requirements: Contact the institution for details.

P3C0 BSc Media Technology
Duration: 4SW Hon
Entry Requirements: *GCE:* BBB. *IB:* 26. *BTEC SubDip:* M. *BTEC Dip:* DD. *BTEC ExtDip:* DDM. *OCR NED:* M1 Interview required. Portfolio required.

G50 THE UNIVERSITY OF GLOUCESTERSHIRE
PARK CAMPUS
THE PARK
CHELTENHAM GL50 2RH
t: 01242 714501 f: 01242 714869
e: admissions@glos.ac.uk
// www.glos.ac.uk

P302 BA Creative Media
Duration: 2FT Hon
Entry Requirements: Contact the institution for details.

P313 BA Film Production
Duration: 3FT Hon
Entry Requirements: Interview required. Portfolio required.

P310 BA Media Production
Duration: 1FT Hon
Entry Requirements: Interview required. Portfolio required.

P312 BA Radio Production
Duration: 3FT Hon
Entry Requirements: *GCE:* 280-300. Interview required.

P311 BA Television Production
Duration: 3FT Hon
Entry Requirements: *GCE:* 280-300. Interview required.

G70 UNIVERSITY OF GREENWICH
GREENWICH CAMPUS
OLD ROYAL NAVAL COLLEGE
PARK ROW
LONDON SE10 9LS
t: 020 8331 9000 f: 020 8331 8145
e: courseinfo@gre.ac.uk
// www.gre.ac.uk

P315 BA Media Arts Production
Duration: 3FT Hon
Entry Requirements: *GCE:* 240. *IB:* 24.

PG34 BSc Digital Television and Interactive Media
Duration: 3FT Hon
Entry Requirements: *GCE:* 240. *IB:* 24.

P311 BSc Film & TV Production
Duration: 3FT Hon
Entry Requirements: *GCE:* 280. *IB:* 24.

P314 BSc Media Arts Production
Duration: 3FT Hon
Entry Requirements: *GCE:* 240. *IB:* 24.

P310 FdA Moving Image Production
Duration: 2FT Fdg
Entry Requirements: *IB:* 24.

G80 GRIMSBY INSTITUTE OF FURTHER AND HIGHER EDUCATION
NUNS CORNER
GRIMSBY
NE LINCOLNSHIRE DN34 5BQ
t: 0800 328 3631
e: headmissions@grimsby.ac.uk
// www.grimsby.ac.uk

P314 BA Digital Film and Television Production
Duration: 3FT Hon
Entry Requirements: Interview required.

H14 HAVERING COLLEGE OF FURTHER AND HIGHER EDUCATION
ARDLEIGH GREEN ROAD
HORNCHURCH
ESSEX RM11 2LL
t: 01708 462793 f: 01708 462736
e: HE@havering-college.ac.uk
// www.havering-college.ac.uk

013P HNC Creative Media Production
Duration: 1FT HNC
Entry Requirements: Interview required. Portfolio required.

H36 UNIVERSITY OF HERTFORDSHIRE
UNIVERSITY ADMISSIONS SERVICE
COLLEGE LANE
HATFIELD
HERTS AL10 9AB
t: 01707 284800
// www.herts.ac.uk

WP63 BA Film and Television Entertainment
Duration: 3FT Hon
Entry Requirements: *GCE:* 300. Interview required. Portfolio required.

P310 BSc Multimedia Technology
Duration: 3FT/4SW Hon
Entry Requirements: *GCE:* 240.

H73 HULL COLLEGE
QUEEN'S GARDENS
HULL HU1 3DG
t: 01482 329943 f: 01482 598733
e: info@hull-college.ac.uk
// www.hull-college.ac.uk/higher-education

P314 BA Broadcast Media (Top-Up)
Duration: 1FT Hon
Entry Requirements: Contact the institution for details.

P310 FdA Broadcast Media
Duration: 2FT Fdg
Entry Requirements: *GCE:* 200. *OCR NED:* P2 Interview required. Portfolio required.

K84 KINGSTON UNIVERSITY
STUDENT INFORMATION & ADVICE CENTRE
COOPER HOUSE
40-46 SURBITON ROAD
KINGSTON UPON THAMES KT1 2HX
t: 0844 8552177 f: 020 8547 7080
e: aps@kingston.ac.uk
// www.kingston.ac.uk

WP63 BA Film Making
Duration: 3FT Hon
Entry Requirements: *Foundation:* Pass. *GCE:* 240. Interview required. Portfolio required.

P310 BSc Media Technology
Duration: 3FT Hon
Entry Requirements: *GCE:* 240-280.

P314 BSc Media Technology
Duration: 4SW Hon
Entry Requirements: *GCE:* 240-280.

P318 BSc Media Technology (Foundation)
Duration: 4FT Hon
Entry Requirements: *GCE:* 60.

L27 LEEDS METROPOLITAN UNIVERSITY
COURSE ENQUIRIES OFFICE
CITY CAMPUS
LEEDS LS1 3HE
t: 0113 81 23113 f: 0113 81 23129
// www.leedsmet.ac.uk

P314 BA Film & Moving Image Production
Duration: 3FT Hon
Entry Requirements: *GCE:* 240. *IB:* 24. Interview required.
Portfolio required.

HP63 BSc Broadcast Media Technologies
Duration: 3FT Hon
Entry Requirements: *GCE:* 200. *IB:* 24. Interview required.

L43 LIVERPOOL COMMUNITY COLLEGE
LIVERPOOL COMMUNITY COLLEGE
CLARENCE STREET
LIVERPOOL L3 5TP
t: 0151 252 3352 f: 0151 252 3351
e: enquiry@liv-coll.ac.uk
// www.liv-coll.ac.uk

W212 FdA Media Production Practice
Duration: 2FT Fdg
Entry Requirements: *GCE:* C. *SQAAH:* C. Interview required.
Portfolio required.

L53 COLEG LLANDRILLO CYMRU
LLANDUDNO ROAD
RHOS-ON-SEA
COLWYN BAY
NORTH WALES LL28 4HZ
t: 01492 542338/339 f: 01492 543052
e: degrees@llandrillo.ac.uk
// www.llandrillo.ac.uk

WP63 FdA Digital Media and Television Production
Duration: 2FT Fdg
Entry Requirements: *GCE:* 180. Interview required.

L62 THE LONDON COLLEGE, UCK
VICTORIA GARDENS
NOTTING HILL GATE
LONDON W11 3PE
t: 020 7243 4000 f: 020 7243 1484
e: admissions@lcuck.ac.uk
// www.lcuck.ac.uk

013P HNC Creative Media Production
Duration: 1FT HNC
Entry Requirements: Contact the institution for details.

113P HND Creative Media Production
Duration: 2FT HND
Entry Requirements: Contact the institution for details.

L68 LONDON METROPOLITAN UNIVERSITY
166-220 HOLLOWAY ROAD
LONDON N7 8DB
t: 020 7133 4200
e: admissions@londonmet.ac.uk
// www.londonmet.ac.uk

P313 BA Media Practice (Film and Broadcast Production)
Duration: 3FT Hon
Entry Requirements: Contact the institution for details.

M10 THE MANCHESTER COLLEGE
OPENSHAW CAMPUS
ASHTON OLD ROAD
OPENSHAW
MANCHESTER M11 2WH
t: 0800 068 8585 f: 0161 920 4103
e: enquiries@themanchestercollege.ac.uk
// www.themanchestercollege.ac.uk

P313 BA TV and Film Production
Duration: 2FT Hon
Entry Requirements: Contact the institution for details.

P312 FdA Radio Production
Duration: 2FT Fdg
Entry Requirements: *GCE:* 160. *BTEC ExtDip:* MPP.

P301 FdSc Broadcast Television
Duration: 2FT Fdg
Entry Requirements: *GCE:* 160. *BTEC ExtDip:* MPP.

M80 MIDDLESEX UNIVERSITY
MIDDLESEX UNIVERSITY
THE BURROUGHS
LONDON NW4 4BT
t: 020 8411 5555 f: 020 8411 5649
e: enquiries@mdx.ac.uk
// www.mdx.ac.uk

P311 BA Television Production
Duration: 3FT Hon
Entry Requirements: *GCE:* 200-300. *IB:* 28.

P314 BA Television Production - Technical Arts
Duration: 3FT Hon
Entry Requirements: *GCE:* 200-300. *IB:* 28.

N23 NEWCASTLE COLLEGE
STUDENT SERVICES
RYE HILL CAMPUS
SCOTSWOOD ROAD
NEWCASTLE UPON TYNE NE4 7SA
t: 0191 200 4110 f: 0191 200 4349
e: enquiries@ncl-coll.ac.uk
// www.newcastlecollege.co.uk

WP63 BA Television & Media Practice (Top-up)
Duration: 1FT Hon
Entry Requirements: Interview required. Portfolio required. HND required.

N30 NEW COLLEGE NOTTINGHAM
ADAMS BUILDING
STONEY STREET
THE LACE MARKET
NOTTINGHAM NG1 1NG
t: 0115 910 0100 f: 0115 953 4349
e: he.team@ncn.ac.uk
// www.ncn.ac.uk

PP35 FdA Broadcast Media
Duration: 2FT Fdg
Entry Requirements: GCE: 100-240. Interview required.

P310 FdA Broadcast Media (Audio Production)
Duration: 2FT Fdg
Entry Requirements: Contact the institution for details.

P311 FdA Broadcast Media (Video Production)
Duration: 2FT Fdg
Entry Requirements: Contact the institution for details.

N36 NEWMAN UNIVERSITY COLLEGE, BIRMINGHAM
GENNERS LANE
BARTLEY GREEN
BIRMINGHAM B32 3NT
t: 0121 476 1181 f: 0121 476 1196
e: Admissions@newman.ac.uk
// www.newman.ac.uk

NP13 FdA Business and Media Production
Duration: 2FT Fdg
Entry Requirements: Contact the institution for details.

N38 UNIVERSITY OF NORTHAMPTON
PARK CAMPUS
BOUGHTON GREEN ROAD
NORTHAMPTON NN2 7AL
t: 0800 358 2232 f: 01604 722083
e: admissions@northampton.ac.uk
// www.northampton.ac.uk

N4P3 BA Accounting/Media Production
Duration: 3FT Hon
Entry Requirements: GCE: 260-280. SQAH: AAA-BBBB. IB: 24.
BTEC Dip: DD. BTEC ExtDip: DMM. OCR ND: D OCR NED: M2

C1PH BA Biological Conservation/Media Production
Duration: 3FT Hon
Entry Requirements: GCE: 260-280. SQAH: AAA-BBBB. IB: 24.
BTEC Dip: DD. BTEC ExtDip: DMM. OCR ND: D OCR NED: M2

N1PH BA Business Entrepreneurship/Media Production
Duration: 3FT Hon
Entry Requirements: GCE: 260-280. SQAH: AAA-BBBB. IB: 24.
BTEC Dip: DD. BTEC ExtDip: DMM. OCR ND: D OCR NED: M2

N1PJ BA Business/Media Production
Duration: 3FT Hon
Entry Requirements: GCE: 260-280. SQAH: AAA-BBBB. IB: 24.
BTEC Dip: DD. BTEC ExtDip: DMM. OCR ND: D OCR NED: M2

W8PH BA Creative Writing/Media Production
Duration: 3FT Hon
Entry Requirements: GCE: 260-280. SQAH: AAA-BBBB. IB: 24.
BTEC Dip: DD. BTEC ExtDip: DMM. OCR ND: D OCR NED: M2

M9PH BA Criminology/Media Production
Duration: 3FT Hon
Entry Requirements: GCE: 260-280. SQAH: AAA-BBBB. IB: 24.
BTEC Dip: DD. BTEC ExtDip: DMM. OCR ND: D OCR NED: M2

W5PH BA Dance/Media Production
Duration: 3FT Hon
Entry Requirements: GCE: 260-280. SQAH: AAA-BBBB. IB: 24.
BTEC Dip: DD. BTEC ExtDip: DMM. OCR ND: D OCR NED: M2
Interview required.

W4PJ BA Drama/Media Production
Duration: 3FT Hon
Entry Requirements: GCE: 260-280. SQAH: AAA-BBBB. IB: 24.
BTEC Dip: DD. BTEC ExtDip: DMM. OCR ND: D OCR NED: M2
Interview required.

L1PH BA Economics/Media Production
Duration: 3FT Hon
Entry Requirements: GCE: 260-280. SQAH: AAA-BBBB. IB: 24.
BTEC Dip: DD. BTEC ExtDip: DMM. OCR ND: D OCR NED: M2

X3PH BA Education Studies/Media Production
Duration: 3FT Hon
Entry Requirements: GCE: 260-280. SQAH: AAA-BBBB. IB: 24.
BTEC Dip: DD. BTEC ExtDip: DMM. OCR ND: D OCR NED: M2

N8PJ BA Events Management/Media Production
Duration: 3FT Hon
Entry Requirements: *GCE:* 260-280. *SQAH:* AAA-BBBB. *IB:* 24.
BTEC Dip: DD. *BTEC ExtDip:* DMM. *OCR ND:* D *OCR NED:* M2

W6PH BA Film & Television Studies/Media Production
Duration: 3FT Hon
Entry Requirements: *GCE:* 260-280. *SQAH:* AAA-BBBB. *IB:* 24.
BTEC Dip: DD. *BTEC ExtDip:* DMM. *OCR ND:* D *OCR NED:* M2

W1PH BA Fine Art Painting & Drawing/Media Production
Duration: 3FT Hon
Entry Requirements: *GCE:* 260-280. *SQAH:* AAA-BBBB. *IB:* 24.
BTEC Dip: DD. *BTEC ExtDip:* DMM. *OCR ND:* D *OCR NED:* M2

R1PH BA French/Media Production
Duration: 3FT Hon
Entry Requirements: *GCE:* 260-280. *SQAH:* AAA-BBBB. *IB:* 24.
BTEC Dip: DD. *BTEC ExtDip:* DMM. *OCR ND:* D *OCR NED:* M2

L4PH BA Health Studies/Media Production
Duration: 3FT Hon
Entry Requirements: *GCE:* 260-280. *SQAH:* AAA-BBBB. *IB:* 24.
BTEC Dip: DD. *BTEC ExtDip:* DMM. *OCR ND:* D *OCR NED:* M2

V1PH BA History/Media Production
Duration: 3FT Hon
Entry Requirements: *GCE:* 260-280. *SQAH:* AAA-BBBB. *IB:* 24.
BTEC Dip: DD. *BTEC ExtDip:* DMM. *OCR ND:* D *OCR NED:* M2

L7P3 BA Human Geography/Media Production
Duration: 3FT Hon
Entry Requirements: *GCE:* 260-280. *SQAH:* AAA-BBBB. *IB:* 24.
BTEC Dip: DD. *BTEC ExtDip:* DMM. *OCR ND:* D *OCR NED:* M2

N6PH BA Human Resource Management/Media Production
Duration: 3FT Hon
Entry Requirements: *GCE:* 260-280. *SQAH:* AAA-BBBB. *IB:* 24.
BTEC Dip: DD. *BTEC ExtDip:* DMM. *OCR ND:* D *OCR NED:* M2

P5P3 BA Journalism/Media Production
Duration: 3FT Hon
Entry Requirements: *GCE:* 260-280. *SQAH:* AAA-BBBB. *IB:* 24.
BTEC Dip: DD. *BTEC ExtDip:* DMM. *OCR ND:* D *OCR NED:* M2

N2PJ BA Management/Media Production
Duration: 3FT Hon
Entry Requirements: *GCE:* 260-280. *SQAH:* AAA-BBBB. *IB:* 24.
BTEC Dip: DD. *BTEC ExtDip:* DMM. *OCR ND:* D *OCR NED:* M2

P390 BA Media Production
Duration: 3FT Hon
Entry Requirements: *GCE:* 260-280. *SQAH:* AAA-BBBB. *IB:* 24.
BTEC Dip: DD. *BTEC ExtDip:* DMM. *OCR ND:* D *OCR NED:* M2

P3DK BA Media Production with Applied Equine Studies
Duration: 3FT Hon
Entry Requirements: *GCE:* 260-280. *SQAH:* AAA-BBBB. *IB:* 24.
BTEC Dip: DD. *BTEC ExtDip:* DMM. *OCR ND:* D *OCR NED:* M2

P3NB BA Media Production with Applied Management
Duration: 3FT Hon
Entry Requirements: *GCE:* 260-280. *SQAH:* AAA-BBBB. *IB:* 24.
BTEC Dip: DD. *BTEC ExtDip:* DMM. *OCR ND:* D *OCR NED:* M2

P3NK BA Media Production/Accounting
Duration: 3FT Hon
Entry Requirements: *GCE:* 260-280. *SQAH:* AAA-BBBB. *IB:* 24.
BTEC Dip: DD. *BTEC ExtDip:* DMM. *OCR ND:* D *OCR NED:* M2

P3CC BA Media Production/Biological Conservation
Duration: 3FT Hon
Entry Requirements: *GCE:* 260-280. *SQAH:* AAA-BBBB. *IB:* 24.
BTEC Dip: DD. *BTEC ExtDip:* DMM. *OCR ND:* D *OCR NED:* M2

P3ND BA Media Production/Business
Duration: 3FT Hon
Entry Requirements: *GCE:* 260-280. *SQAH:* AAA-BBBB. *IB:* 24.
BTEC Dip: DD. *BTEC ExtDip:* DMM. *OCR ND:* D *OCR NED:* M2

P3GM BA Media Production/Business Computing Systems
Duration: 3FT Hon
Entry Requirements: *GCE:* 260-280. *SQAH:* AAA-BBBB. *IB:* 24.
BTEC Dip: DD. *BTEC ExtDip:* DMM. *OCR ND:* D *OCR NED:* M2

P3NC BA Media Production/Business Entrepreneurship
Duration: 3FT Hon
Entry Requirements: *GCE:* 260-280. *SQAH:* AAA-BBBB. *IB:* 24.
BTEC Dip: DD. *BTEC ExtDip:* DMM. *OCR ND:* D *OCR NED:* M2

P3WV BA Media Production/Creative Writing
Duration: 3FT Hon
Entry Requirements: *GCE:* 260-280. *SQAH:* AAA-BBBB. *IB:* 24.
BTEC Dip: DD. *BTEC ExtDip:* DMM. *OCR ND:* D *OCR NED:* M2

P3MX BA Media Production/Criminology
Duration: 3FT Hon
Entry Requirements: *GCE:* 260-280. *SQAH:* AAA-BBBB. *IB:* 24.
BTEC Dip: DD. *BTEC ExtDip:* DMM. *OCR ND:* D *OCR NED:* M2

P3WM BA Media Production/Dance
Duration: 3FT Hon
Entry Requirements: *GCE:* 260-280. *SQAH:* AAA-BBBB. *IB:* 24.
BTEC Dip: DD. *BTEC ExtDip:* DMM. *OCR ND:* D *OCR NED:* M2
Interview required.

P3WL BA Media Production/Drama
Duration: 3FT Hon
Entry Requirements: *GCE:* 260-280. *SQAH:* AAA-BBBB. *IB:* 24.
BTEC Dip: DD. *BTEC ExtDip:* DMM. *OCR ND:* D *OCR NED:* M2
Interview required.

P3LC BA Media Production/Economics
Duration: 3FT Hon
Entry Requirements: *GCE:* 260-280. *SQAH:* AAA-BBBB. *IB:* 24.
BTEC Dip: DD. *BTEC ExtDip:* DMM. *OCR ND:* D *OCR NED:* M2

P3XJ BA Media Production/Education Studies
Duration: 3FT Hon
Entry Requirements: *GCE:* 260-280. *SQAH:* AAA-BBBB. *IB:* 24.
BTEC Dip: DD. *BTEC ExtDip:* DMM. *OCR ND:* D *OCR NED:* M2

P3NW BA Media Production/Events Management
Duration: 3FT Hon
Entry Requirements: *GCE:* 260-280. *SQAH:* AAA-BBBB. *IB:* 24.
BTEC Dip: DD. *BTEC ExtDip:* DMM. *OCR ND:* D *OCR NED:* M2

P3WP BA Media Production/Film & Television Studies
Duration: 3FT Hon
Entry Requirements: *GCE:* 260-280. *SQAH:* AAA-BBBB. *IB:* 24.
BTEC Dip: DD. *BTEC ExtDip:* DMM. *OCR ND:* D *OCR NED:* M2

P3WC BA Media Production/Fine Art Painting & Drawing
Duration: 3FT Hon
Entry Requirements: *GCE:* 260-280. *SQAH:* AAA-BBBB. *IB:* 24.
BTEC Dip: DD. *BTEC ExtDip:* DMM. *OCR ND:* D *OCR NED:* M2

P3RC BA Media Production/French
Duration: 3FT Hon
Entry Requirements: *GCE:* 260-280. *SQAH:* AAA-BBBB. *IB:* 24.
BTEC Dip: DD. *BTEC ExtDip:* DMM. *OCR ND:* D *OCR NED:* M2

P3LL BA Media Production/Health Studies
Duration: 3FT Hon
Entry Requirements: *GCE:* 260-280. *SQAH:* AAA-BBBB. *IB:* 24.
BTEC Dip: DD. *BTEC ExtDip:* DMM. *OCR ND:* D *OCR NED:* M2

P3VC BA Media Production/History
Duration: 3FT Hon
Entry Requirements: *GCE:* 260-280. *SQAH:* AAA-BBBB. *IB:* 24.
BTEC Dip: DD. *BTEC ExtDip:* DMM. *OCR ND:* D *OCR NED:* M2

P3B1 BA Media Production/Human Bioscience
Duration: 3FT Hon
Entry Requirements: *GCE:* 260-280. *SQAH:* AAA-BBBB. *IB:* 24.
BTEC Dip: DD. *BTEC ExtDip:* DMM. *OCR ND:* D *OCR NED:* M2

P3L7 BA Media Production/Human Geography
Duration: 3FT Hon
Entry Requirements: *GCE:* 260-280. *SQAH:* AAA-BBBB. *IB:* 24.
BTEC Dip: DD. *BTEC ExtDip:* DMM. *OCR ND:* D *OCR NED:* M2

P3NP BA Media Production/Human Resource Management
Duration: 3FT Hon
Entry Requirements: *GCE:* 260-280. *SQAH:* AAA-BBBB. *IB:* 24.
BTEC Dip: DD. *BTEC ExtDip:* DMM. *OCR ND:* D *OCR NED:* M2

P3P5 BA Media Production/Journalism
Duration: 3FT Hon
Entry Requirements: *GCE:* 260-280. *SQAH:* AAA-BBBB. *IB:* 24.
BTEC Dip: DD. *BTEC ExtDip:* DMM. *OCR ND:* D *OCR NED:* M2

P3NA BA Media Production/Management
Duration: 3FT Hon
Entry Requirements: *GCE:* 260-280. *SQAH:* AAA-BBBB. *IB:* 24.
BTEC Dip: DD. *BTEC ExtDip:* DMM. *OCR ND:* D *OCR NED:* M2

P3FW BA Media Production/Physical Geography
Duration: 3FT Hon
Entry Requirements: *GCE:* 260-280. *SQAH:* AAA-BBBB. *IB:* 24.
BTEC Dip: DD. *BTEC ExtDip:* DMM. *OCR ND:* D *OCR NED:* M2

P3LF BA Media Production/Politics
Duration: 3FT Hon
Entry Requirements: *GCE:* 260-280. *SQAH:* AAA-BBBB. *IB:* 24.
BTEC Dip: DD. *BTEC ExtDip:* DMM. *OCR ND:* D *OCR NED:* M2

P3WH BA Media Production/Popular Music
Duration: 3FT Hon
Entry Requirements: *GCE:* 260-280. *SQAH:* AAA-BBBB. *IB:* 24.
BTEC Dip: DD. *BTEC ExtDip:* DMM. *OCR ND:* D *OCR NED:* M2
Interview required.

P3CV BA Media Production/Psychology
Duration: 3FT Hon
Entry Requirements: *GCE:* 260-280. *SQAH:* AAA-BBBB. *IB:* 24.
BTEC Dip: DD. *BTEC ExtDip:* DMM. *OCR ND:* D *OCR NED:* M2

P3L5 BA Media Production/Social Care
Duration: 3FT Hon
Entry Requirements: *GCE:* 260-280. *SQAH:* AAA-BBBB. *IB:* 24.
BTEC Dip: DD. *BTEC ExtDip:* DMM. *OCR ND:* D *OCR NED:* M2

P3LH BA Media Production/Sociology
Duration: 3FT Hon
Entry Requirements: *GCE:* 260-280. *SQAH:* AAA-BBBB. *IB:* 24.
BTEC Dip: DD. *BTEC ExtDip:* DMM. *OCR ND:* D *OCR NED:* M2

P3GL BA Media Production/Web Design
Duration: 3FT Hon
Entry Requirements: *GCE:* 260-280. *SQAH:* AAA-BBBB. *IB:* 24.
BTEC Dip: DD. *BTEC ExtDip:* DMM. *OCR ND:* D *OCR NED:* M2

L2PH BA Politics/Media Production
Duration: 3FT Hon
Entry Requirements: *GCE:* 260-280. *SQAH:* AAA-BBBB. *IB:* 24.
BTEC Dip: DD. *BTEC ExtDip:* DMM. *OCR ND:* D *OCR NED:* M2

W3PH BA Popular Music/Media Production
Duration: 3FT Hon
Entry Requirements: *GCE:* 260-280. *SQAH:* AAA-BBBB. *IB:* 24.
BTEC Dip: DD. *BTEC ExtDip:* DMM. *OCR ND:* D *OCR NED:* M2

C8PH BA Psychology/Media Production
Duration: 3FT Hon
Entry Requirements: *GCE:* 260-280. *SQAH:* AAA-BBBB. *IB:* 24.
BTEC Dip: DD. *BTEC ExtDip:* DMM. *OCR ND:* D *OCR NED:* M2

L5P3 BA Social Care/Media Production
Duration: 3FT Hon
Entry Requirements: *GCE:* 260-280. *SQAH:* AAA-BBBB. *IB:* 24.
BTEC Dip: DD. *BTEC ExtDip:* DMM. *OCR ND:* D *OCR NED:* M2

L3PH BA Sociology/Media Production
Duration: 3FT Hon
Entry Requirements: *GCE:* 260-280. *SQAH:* AAA-BBBB. *IB:* 24.
BTEC Dip: DD. *BTEC ExtDip:* DMM. *OCR ND:* D *OCR NED:* M2

X3PI BA Special Educational Needs & Inclusion/Media Production
Duration: 3FT Hon
Entry Requirements: *GCE:* 260-280. *SQAH:* AAA-BBBB. *IB:* 24.
BTEC Dip: DD. *BTEC ExtDip:* DMM. *OCR ND:* D *OCR NED:* M2

G5PH BSc Business Computing Systems/Media Production
Duration: 3FT Hon
Entry Requirements: *GCE:* 260-280. *SQAH:* AAA-BBBB. *IB:* 24.
BTEC Dip: DD. *BTEC ExtDip:* DMM. *OCR ND:* D *OCR NED:* M2

B1P3 BSc Human Bioscience/Media Production
Duration: 3FT Hon
Entry Requirements: *GCE:* 260-280. *SQAH:* AAA-BBBB. *IB:* 24.
BTEC Dip: DD. *BTEC ExtDip:* DMM. *OCR ND:* D *OCR NED:* M2

F8PJ BSc Physical Geography/Media Production
Duration: 3FT Hon
Entry Requirements: *GCE:* 260-280. *SQAH:* AAA-BBBB. *IB:* 24.
BTEC Dip: DD. *BTEC ExtDip:* DMM. *OCR ND:* D *OCR NED:* M2

N77 NORTHUMBRIA UNIVERSITY
TRINITY BUILDING
NORTHUMBERLAND ROAD
NEWCASTLE UPON TYNE NE1 8ST
t: 0191 243 7420 f: 0191 227 4561
e: er.admissions@northumbria.ac.uk
// www.northumbria.ac.uk

P310 BA Media Production
Duration: 3FT Hon
Entry Requirements: *GCE:* 300. *SQAH:* BBBBC. *SQAAH:* BBC. *IB:* 26.

N82 NORWICH CITY COLLEGE OF FURTHER AND HIGHER EDUCATION (AN ASSOCIATE COLLEGE OF UEA)
IPSWICH ROAD
NORWICH
NORFOLK NR2 2LJ
t: 01603 773012 f: 01603 773301
e: he_office@ccn.ac.uk
// www.ccn.ac.uk

P310 FdA Media Practice
Duration: 2FT Fdg
Entry Requirements: Contact the institution for details.

P63 UCP MARJON - UNIVERSITY COLLEGE PLYMOUTH ST MARK & ST JOHN
DERRIFORD ROAD
PLYMOUTH PL6 8BH
t: 01752 636890 f: 01752 636819
e: admissions@marjon.ac.uk
// www.ucpmarjon.ac.uk

P310 BA Media Production
Duration: 3FT Hon
Entry Requirements: *GCE:* 220.

P314 BA Sports Media and Journalism
Duration: 3FT Hon   CRB Check: Required
Entry Requirements: *GCE:* 220.

P65 PLYMOUTH COLLEGE OF ART (FORMERLY PLYMOUTH COLLEGE OF ART AND DESIGN)
TAVISTOCK PLACE
PLYMOUTH PL4 8AT
t: 01752 203434 f: 01752 203444
e: infoservices@plymouthart.ac.uk
// www.plymouthart.ac.uk

PW34 BA Production for Stage and Screen
Duration: 3FT Hon
Entry Requirements: Contact the institution for details.

R06 RAVENSBOURNE
6 PENROSE WAY
GREENWICH PENINSULA
LONDON SE10 0EW
t: 020 3040 3998
e: info@rave.ac.uk
// www.rave.ac.uk

P313 BA Digital Film Production
Duration: 3FT Hon
Entry Requirements: Contact the institution for details.

PH13 BA Digital Film Production (Fast-Track)
Duration: 2FT Hon
Entry Requirements: Contact the institution for details.

WP33 BA Music Production for Media
Duration: 3FT Hon
Entry Requirements: *Foundation:* Pass. *GCE:* AA-CC. *IB:* 28.

HP63 BA Production (Top-Up)
Duration: 1FT Hon
Entry Requirements: Interview required. Portfolio required.

R36 ROBERT GORDON UNIVERSITY
ROBERT GORDON UNIVERSITY
SCHOOLHILL
ABERDEEN
SCOTLAND AB10 1FR
t: 01224 26 27 28 f: 01224 26 21 47
e: UGOffice@rgu.ac.uk
// www.rgu.ac.uk

PI31 BSc Digital Media (Design, Production and Development)
Duration: 4FT Hon
Entry Requirements: Contact the institution for details.

R52 ROTHERHAM COLLEGE OF ARTS AND TECHNOLOGY
EASTWOOD LANE
ROTHERHAM
SOUTH YORKSHIRE S65 1EG
t: 08080 722777 f: 01709 373053
e: info@rotherham.ac.uk
// www.rotherham.ac.uk

P990 FdA Film and Media Production
Duration: 2FT Fdg
Entry Requirements: GCE: 120. Interview required. Portfolio required.

S21 SHEFFIELD HALLAM UNIVERSITY
CITY CAMPUS
HOWARD STREET
SHEFFIELD S1 1WB
t: 0114 225 5555 f: 0114 225 2167
e: admissions@shu.ac.uk
// www.shu.ac.uk

P391 MArt Film and Media Production
Duration: 4FT Hon
Entry Requirements: GCE: 300.

S22 SHEFFIELD COLLEGE
THE SHEFFIELD COLLEGE
HE UNIT
HILLSBOROUGH COLLEGE AT THE BARRACKS
SHEFFIELD S6 2LR
t: 0114 260 2597
e: heunit@sheffcol.ac.uk
// www.sheffcol.ac.uk

P310 FdA Media Production
Duration: 2FT Fdg
Entry Requirements: GCE: 120.

S30 SOUTHAMPTON SOLENT UNIVERSITY
EAST PARK TERRACE
SOUTHAMPTON
HAMPSHIRE SO14 0RT
t: +44 (0) 23 8031 9039 f: + 44 (0)23 8022 2259
e: admissions@solent.ac.uk
// www.solent.ac.uk/

P319 BA Media Production (Top-Up)
Duration: 1FT Hon
Entry Requirements: Interview required. HND required.

P390 BA Television & Video Production
Duration: 3FT Hon
Entry Requirements: Foundation: Distinction. GCE: 240. SQAAH: AA-CCD. IB: 24. BTEC ExtDip: MMM. OCR ND: D OCR NED: M3 Interview required.

P318 BA Television Post-Production
Duration: 3FT Hon
Entry Requirements: Foundation: Distinction. GCE: 240. SQAAH: AA-CCD. IB: 24. BTEC ExtDip: MMM. OCR ND: D OCR NED: M3 Interview required.

P311 BA Television Studio Production
Duration: 3FT Hon
Entry Requirements: Foundation: Distinction. GCE: 240. SQAAH: AA-CCD. IB: 24. BTEC ExtDip: MMM. OCR ND: D OCR NED: M3 Interview required.

P310 BSc Outside Broadcast (Production Operations)
Duration: 3FT Hon
Entry Requirements: GCE: 160.

P316 BSc Outside Broadcast (Production Operations) with fdn
Duration: 4FT Hon
Entry Requirements: GCE: 40.

S32 SOUTH DEVON COLLEGE
LONG ROAD
PAIGNTON
DEVON TQ4 7EJ
t: 08000 213181 f: 01803 540541
e: university@southdevon.ac.uk
// www.southdevon.ac.uk/
welcome-to-university-level

WP33 FdA Creative Digital Media
Duration: 2FT Fdg
Entry Requirements: Contact the institution for details.

S72 STAFFORDSHIRE UNIVERSITY
COLLEGE ROAD
STOKE ON TRENT ST4 2DE
t: 01782 292753 f: 01782 292740
e: admissions@staffs.ac.uk
// www.staffs.ac.uk

P310 BA Music Broadcasting
Duration: 3FT Hon
Entry Requirements: *GCE:* 200-240. *IB:* 24. *BTEC Dip:* DD.
BTEC ExtDip: MMM. Interview required.

P312 BA Radio Production
Duration: 3FT Hon
Entry Requirements: *GCE:* 200-240. *IB:* 24. *BTEC Dip:* DD.
BTEC ExtDip: MMM. Interview required.

P391 FdA Film and Television Production Technology and Management
Duration: 2FT Fdg
Entry Requirements: Interview required.

P392 FdSc Film and Television Production Technology
Duration: 2FT Fdg
Entry Requirements: *GCE:* 120. Interview required.

N2P3 FdSc Film and Television Production Technology with Management
Duration: 2FT Fdg
Entry Requirements: *GCE:* 120. Interview required.

P3W6 FdSc Film and Television Production Technology with Sound
Duration: 2FT Fdg
Entry Requirements: *GCE:* 120. Interview required.

S76 STOCKPORT COLLEGE
WELLINGTON ROAD SOUTH
STOCKPORT SK1 3UQ
t: 0161 958 3143 f: 0161 958 3663
e: susan.kelly@stockport.ac.uk
// www.stockport.ac.uk

P311 FdA Television Production
Duration: 2FT Fdg
Entry Requirements: Interview required.

S84 UNIVERSITY OF SUNDERLAND
STUDENT HELPLINE
THE STUDENT GATEWAY
CHESTER ROAD
SUNDERLAND SR1 3SD
t: 0191 515 3000 f: 0191 515 3805
e: student.helpline@sunderland.ac.uk
// www.sunderland.ac.uk

P391 BA Mass Communications
Duration: 3FT Hon
Entry Requirements: Contact the institution for details.

P312 BA Radio (Top-up)
Duration: 1FT Hon
Entry Requirements: Interview required. HND required.

P310 BA Television and Video (Top-up)
Duration: 1FT Hon
Entry Requirements: Interview required. HND required.

S90 UNIVERSITY OF SUSSEX
UNDERGRADUATE ADMISSIONS
SUSSEX HOUSE
UNIVERSITY OF SUSSEX
BRIGHTON BN1 9RH
t: 01273 678416 f: 01273 678545
e: ug.applicants@sussex.ac.uk
// www.sussex.ac.uk

P310 BA Media Practice
Duration: 3FT Hon
Entry Requirements: *GCE:* ABB. *SQAH:* AABBB. *IB:* 34. *BTEC SubDip:* D. *BTEC Dip:* DD. *BTEC ExtDip:* DDM. *OCR ND:* D *OCR NED:* D2

S96 SWANSEA METROPOLITAN UNIVERSITY
MOUNT PLEASANT CAMPUS
SWANSEA SA1 6ED
t: 01792 481000 f: 01792 481061
e: gemma.green@smu.ac.uk
// www.smu.ac.uk

013P HND Technical Theatre
Duration: 2FT HND
Entry Requirements: *GCE:* 80-360. *IB:* 24. Interview required.

T20 TEESSIDE UNIVERSITY
MIDDLESBROUGH TS1 3BA
t: 01642 218121 f: 01642 384201
e: registry@tees.ac.uk
// www.tees.ac.uk

P314 BA Broadcast Media Production
Duration: 3FT Hon
Entry Requirements: *GCE:* 280. *IB:* 25. Interview required. Portfolio required.

WP43 BA Performance for Live & Recorded Media
Duration: 3FT Hon
Entry Requirements: *GCE:* 280. *IB:* 25. Interview required.

P331 BA Television and Film Production
Duration: 3FT Hon
Entry Requirements: *GCE:* 280. *IB:* 25. Interview required. Portfolio required.

T80 UNIVERSITY OF WALES TRINITY SAINT DAVID
COLLEGE ROAD
CARMARTHEN SA31 3EP
t: 01267 676767 f: 01267 676766
e: registry@trinitysaintdavid.ac.uk
// www.tsd.ac.uk

PH10 BA New Media Production
Duration: 3FT Hon
Entry Requirements: Contact the institution for details.

U20 UNIVERSITY OF ULSTER
COLERAINE
CO. LONDONDERRY
NORTHERN IRELAND BT52 1SA
t: 028 7012 4221 f: 028 7012 4908
e: online@ulster.ac.uk
// www.ulster.ac.uk

P310 BA Interactive Media Arts
Duration: 3FT Hon
Entry Requirements: GCE: 260. IB: 24.

U65 UNIVERSITY OF THE ARTS LONDON
272 HIGH HOLBORN
LONDON WC1V 7EY
t: 020 7514 6000x6197 f: 020 7514 6198
e: c.anderson@arts.ac.uk
// www.arts.ac.uk

P311 BA Production for Live Events and Television (Top-Up)
Duration: 1FT Hon
Entry Requirements: Contact the institution for details.

W05 THE UNIVERSITY OF WEST LONDON
ST MARY'S ROAD
EALING
LONDON W5 5RF
t: 0800 036 8888 f: 020 8566 1353
e: learning.advice@uwl.ac.uk
// www.uwl.ac.uk

P315 BA Broadcasting
Duration: 3FT Hon
Entry Requirements: GCE: 240. Interview required.

W12 WALSALL COLLEGE
WALSALL COLLEGE
LITTLETON STREET WEST
WALSALL
WEST MIDLANDS WS2 8ES
t: 01922 657000 f: 01922 657083
e: ckemp@walsallcollege.ac.uk
// www.walsallcollege.ac.uk

013P HNC Media
Duration: 1FT HNC
Entry Requirements: Contact the institution for details.

01HP HND Media
Duration: 2FT HND
Entry Requirements: Contact the institution for details.

W50 UNIVERSITY OF WESTMINSTER
2ND FLOOR, CAVENDISH HOUSE
101 NEW CAVENDISH STREET,
LONDON W1W 6XH
t: 020 7915 5511
e: course-enquiries@westminster.ac.uk
// www.westminster.ac.uk

P312 BA Radio Production
Duration: 3FT Hon
Entry Requirements: GCE: BBB. SQAH: AAAAA-BBBBB. SQAAH: AAA-BBB. IB: 30. OCR ND: D OCR NED: D2 Interview required.

P311 BA Television Production
Duration: 3FT Hon
Entry Requirements: GCE: BBB. SQAH: AAAAA-BBBBB. SQAAH: AAA-BBB. IB: 30. OCR ND: D OCR NED: D2 Interview required.

W65 WEST THAMES COLLEGE
LONDON ROAD
ISLEWORTH
MIDDLESEX TW7 4HS
t: 020 8326 2000 f: 020 8326 2001
e: info@west-thames.ac.uk
// www.west-thames.ac.uk/en/ higher-education/

JP93 HND Media Production
Duration: 2FT HND
Entry Requirements: Contact the institution for details.

W73 WIRRAL METROPOLITAN COLLEGE
CONWAY PARK CAMPUS
EUROPA BOULEVARD
BIRKENHEAD, WIRRAL
MERSEYSIDE CH41 4NT
t: 0151 551 7777 f: 0151 551 7001
// www.wmc.ac.uk

P300 BA Media Production
Duration: 3FT Hon
Entry Requirements: GCE: DD. Interview required.

W75 UNIVERSITY OF WOLVERHAMPTON
ADMISSIONS UNIT
MX207, CAMP STREET
WOLVERHAMPTON
WEST MIDLANDS WV1 1AD
t: 01902 321000 f: 01902 321896
e: admissions@wlv.ac.uk
// www.wlv.ac.uk

PP35 BA Broadcasting and Journalism
Duration: 3FT Hon
Entry Requirements: Contact the institution for details.

W76 UNIVERSITY OF WINCHESTER
WINCHESTER
HANTS SO22 4NR
t: 01962 827234 f: 01962 827288
e: course.enquiries@winchester.ac.uk
// www.winchester.ac.uk

TP7H BA American Studies and Media Production
Duration: 3FT Hon
Entry Requirements: *Foundation:* Distinction. *GCE:* 260-300. *IB:* 24. *OCR ND:* D *OCR NED:* M2

VP4H BA Archaeology and Media Production
Duration: 3FT Hon
Entry Requirements: *Foundation:* Distinction. *GCE:* 260-300. *IB:* 24. *OCR ND:* D *OCR NED:* M2

NPFJ BA Business Management and Media Production
Duration: 3FT Hon
Entry Requirements: *Foundation:* Distinction. *GCE:* 260-300. *IB:* 24. *OCR ND:* D *OCR NED:* M2

LP5J BA Childhood,Youth & Community Studies and Media Production
Duration: 3FT Hon
Entry Requirements: *GCE:* 260-300. *IB:* 24.

WP53 BA Choreography & Dance and Media Production
Duration: 3FT Hon
Entry Requirements: *Foundation:* Distinction. *GCE:* 260-300. *IB:* 25. *OCR ND:* D *OCR NED:* M2

WP8H BA Creative Writing and Media Production
Duration: 3FT Hon
Entry Requirements: *Foundation:* Distinction. *GCE:* 260-300. *IB:* 25. *OCR ND:* D *OCR NED:* M2

LP33 BA Criminology and Media Production
Duration: 3FT Hon
Entry Requirements: *Foundation:* Distinction. *GCE:* 260-300. *IB:* 24. *OCR ND:* D *OCR NED:* M2

WP43 BA Drama and Media Production
Duration: 3FT Hon
Entry Requirements: *Foundation:* Distinction. *GCE:* 260-300. *IB:* 25. *OCR ND:* D *OCR NED:* M2

QP3J BA English Language Studies and Media Production
Duration: 3FT Hon
Entry Requirements: *Foundation:* Distinction. *GCE:* 260-300. *IB:* 25. *OCR ND:* D *OCR NED:* M2

QP3H BA English and Media Production
Duration: 3FT Hon
Entry Requirements: *Foundation:* Distinction. *GCE:* 260-300. *IB:* 25. *OCR ND:* D *OCR NED:* M2

NPV3 BA Event Management and Media Production
Duration: 3FT Hon
Entry Requirements: *Foundation:* Distinction. *GCE:* 260-300. *IB:* 24. *OCR ND:* D *OCR NED:* M2

WP6H BA Film & Cinema Technologies and Media Production
Duration: 3FT Hon
Entry Requirements: *Foundation:* Distinction. *GCE:* 260-300. *IB:* 24. *OCR ND:* D *OCR NED:* M2

PL5J BA Health, Community & Social Care Studies and Media Production
Duration: 3FT Hon
Entry Requirements: Contact the institution for details.

VPC3 BA History and Media Production
Duration: 3FT Hon
Entry Requirements: *Foundation:* Distinction. *GCE:* 260-300. *IB:* 24. *OCR ND:* D *OCR NED:* M2

PP53 BA Journalism Studies and Media Production
Duration: 3FT Hon
Entry Requirements: *Foundation:* Distinction. *GCE:* 260-300. *IB:* 24. *OCR ND:* D *OCR NED:* M2

MP1H BA Law and Media Production
Duration: 3FT Hon
Entry Requirements: *Foundation:* Distinction. *GCE:* 260-300. *IB:* 25. *OCR ND:* D *OCR NED:* M2

P310 BA Media Production
Duration: 3FT Hon
Entry Requirements: *Foundation:* Distinction. *GCE:* 260-300. *IB:* 25. *OCR ND:* D *OCR NED:* M2

PW3Y BA Media Production and Modern Liberal Arts
Duration: 3FT Hon
Entry Requirements: *Foundation:* Distinction. *GCE:* 260-300. *IB:* 25. *OCR ND:* D *OCR NED:* M2

PC38 BA Media Production and Psychology
Duration: 3FT Hon
Entry Requirements: *Foundation:* Distinction. *GCE:* 260-300. *IB:* 25. *OCR ND:* D *OCR NED:* M2

PLHJ BA Media Production and Sociology
Duration: 3FT Hon
Entry Requirements: *Foundation:* Distinction. *GCE:* 260-300. *IB:* 24. *OCR ND:* D *OCR NED:* M2

PN3V BA Media Production and Sports Management
Duration: 3FT Hon
Entry Requirements: *Foundation:* Pass. *GCE:* 260-300. *IB:* 24. *OCR ND:* D

PC36 BA Media Production and Sports Studies
Duration: 3FT Hon
Entry Requirements: *Foundation:* Merit. *GCE:* 260-300. *IB:* 24.

PV3P BA Media Production and Theology & Religious Studies
Duration: 3FT Hon
Entry Requirements: *Foundation:* Distinction. *GCE:* 260-300. *IB:* 25. *OCR ND:* D *OCR NED:* M2

PWHH BA Media Production and Vocal & Choral Studies
Duration: 3FT Hon
Entry Requirements: *Foundation:* Distinction. *GCE:* 260-300. *IB:* 24. *OCR ND:* D *OCR NED:* M2

LP2H BA Politics & Global Studies and Media Production
Duration: 3FT Hon
Entry Requirements: *Foundation:* Distinction. *GCE:* 260-300. *IB:* 24. *OCR ND:* D

PWJ4 BA Theatre Production (Stage and Arts Management)
Duration: 3FT Hon
Entry Requirements: *Foundation:* Distinction. *GCE:* 260-300. *IB:* 26. *OCR ND:* D Interview required.

JOURNALISM

A60 ANGLIA RUSKIN UNIVERSITY
BISHOP HALL LANE
CHELMSFORD
ESSEX CM1 1SQ
t: 0845 271 3333 f: 01245 251789
e: answers@anglia.ac.uk
// www.anglia.ac.uk

P500 BA Journalism
Duration: 3FT Hon
Entry Requirements: *GCE:* 180. *SQAH:* CCCC. *SQAAH:* BC. *IB:* 24.

P501 FdA Sports Journalism
Duration: 2FT Fdg
Entry Requirements: *GCE:* 80.

B06 BANGOR UNIVERSITY
BANGOR UNIVERSITY
BANGOR
GWYNEDD LL57 2DG
t: 01248 388484 f: 01248 370451
e: admissions@bangor.ac.uk
// www.bangor.ac.uk

Q5P5 BA Cymraeg gyda Newyddiaduraeth
Duration: 3FT Hon
Entry Requirements: *GCE:* 220-260. *IB:* 28.

Q5PM BA Cymraeg gyda Newyddiaduraeth
Duration: 4FT Hon
Entry Requirements: Contact the institution for details.

PQ53 BA English Language and Journalism
Duration: 3FT Hon
Entry Requirements: *GCE:* 260-300. *IB:* 28.

Q3P5 BA English with Journalism
Duration: 3FT Hon
Entry Requirements: *GCE:* 240-300. *IB:* 28.

R1P5 BA French with Journalism
Duration: 4FT Hon
Entry Requirements: *GCE:* 240-260. *IB:* 28.

R2P5 BA German with Journalism
Duration: 4FT Hon
Entry Requirements: *GCE:* 240-260. *IB:* 28.

V1PM BA Hanes gyda Newyddiaduraeth
Duration: 3FT Hon
Entry Requirements: *GCE:* 240-280. *IB:* 28.

V1P5 BA History with Journalism
Duration: 3FT Hon
Entry Requirements: *GCE:* 240-280. *IB:* 28.

R4P5 BA Spanish with Journalism
Duration: 4FT Hon
Entry Requirements: *GCE:* 240-260. *IB:* 28.

B22 UNIVERSITY OF BEDFORDSHIRE
PARK SQUARE
LUTON
BEDS LU1 3JU
t: 0844 8482234 f: 01582 489323
e: admissions@beds.ac.uk
// www.beds.ac.uk

P503 BA Broadcast Journalism
Duration: 3FT Hon
Entry Requirements: *Foundation:* Pass. *GCE:* 240. *SQAH:* BBBB-BBBC. *SQAAH:* BCC. *IB:* 24. *OCR ND:* D *OCR NED:* M3 Interview required.

WP85 BA Creative Writing and Journalism
Duration: 3FT Hon
Entry Requirements: *GCE:* 200.

P500 BA Journalism
Duration: 3FT Hon
Entry Requirements: *Foundation:* Pass. *GCE:* 200. *SQAH:* BCC.
SQAAH: BCC. *IB:* 24. *OCR ND:* M1 *OCR NED:* P1 Interview required.

P501 BA Magazine Journalism
Duration: 3FT Hon
Entry Requirements: *Foundation:* Pass. *GCE:* 200. *SQAH:* BCC.
SQAAH: BCC. *IB:* 24. *OCR ND:* M1 *OCR NED:* P1 Interview required.

P504 BA Multimedia Journalism
Duration: 3FT Hon
Entry Requirements: *Foundation:* Pass. *GCE:* 240. *SQAH:* BBBB-BBBC. *SQAAH:* BCC. *IB:* 24. *OCR ND:* D *OCR NED:* M3 Interview required.

P590 BA Sport Journalism
Duration: 3FT Hon
Entry Requirements: *Foundation:* Pass. *GCE:* 200. *SQAH:* BCC.
SQAAH: BCC. *IB:* 24. *OCR ND:* M1 *OCR NED:* P1

P502 FdA Journalism
Duration: 2FT Fdg
Entry Requirements: Contact the institution for details.

B25 BIRMINGHAM CITY UNIVERSITY
PERRY BARR
BIRMINGHAM B42 2SU
t: 0121 331 5595 f: 0121 331 7994
// www.bcu.ac.uk

P9P5 BA Media and Communication (Journalism)
Duration: 3FT Hon
Entry Requirements: *Foundation:* Pass. *GCE:* BBC. *SQAH:* ABBB.
SQAAH: BBC. *IB:* 30. Interview required. Portfolio required.

B40 BLACKBURN COLLEGE
FEILDEN STREET
BLACKBURN BB2 1LH
t: 01254 292594 f: 01254 679647
e: he-admissions@blackburn.ac.uk
// www.blackburn.ac.uk

P501 BA Journalism (Top-Up)
Duration: 1FT Hon
Entry Requirements: Contact the institution for details.

P500 FdA Journalism
Duration: 2FT Fdg
Entry Requirements: Contact the institution for details.

B50 BOURNEMOUTH UNIVERSITY
TALBOT CAMPUS
FERN BARROW
POOLE
DORSET BH12 5BB
t: 01202 524111
// www.bournemouth.ac.uk

P500 BA Multimedia Journalism
Duration: 3FT Hon
Entry Requirements: *GCE:* 340. *IB:* 33. *BTEC SubDip:* D. *BTEC Dip:* DD. *BTEC ExtDip:* DDD. Interview required.

B72 UNIVERSITY OF BRIGHTON
MITHRAS HOUSE 211
LEWES ROAD
BRIGHTON BN2 4AT
t: 01273 644644 f: 01273 642607
e: admissions@brighton.ac.uk
// www.brighton.ac.uk

P501 BA Broadcast Journalism
Duration: 3FT/4SW Hon
Entry Requirements: *GCE:* BBB. *IB:* 24.

P500 BA Sport Journalism
Duration: 3FT Hon
Entry Requirements: *GCE:* ABB. *IB:* 32.

B80 UNIVERSITY OF THE WEST OF ENGLAND, BRISTOL
FRENCHAY CAMPUS
COLDHARBOUR LANE
BRISTOL BS16 1QY
t: +44 (0)117 32 83333 f: +44 (0)117 32 82810
e: admissions@uwe.ac.uk
// www.uwe.ac.uk

QP3M BA English and Journalism
Duration: 3FT Hon
Entry Requirements: *GCE:* 320.

P500 BA (Hons) Journalism
Duration: 3FT Hon
Entry Requirements: *GCE:* 280-320.

B84 BRUNEL UNIVERSITY
UXBRIDGE
MIDDLESEX UB8 3PH
t: 01895 265265 f: 01895 269790
e: admissions@brunel.ac.uk
// www.brunel.ac.uk

P500 BA Journalism
Duration: 3FT Hon
Entry Requirements: *GCE:* AAB. *SQAAH:* AAB. *IB:* 35. *BTEC ExtDip:* D*D*D. *OCR NED:* D1 Interview required. Admissions Test required.

B90 THE UNIVERSITY OF BUCKINGHAM
YEOMANRY HOUSE
HUNTER STREET
BUCKINGHAM MK18 1EG
t: 01280 820313 f: 01280 822245
e: info@buckingham.ac.uk
// www.buckingham.ac.uk

QP35 BA Communication, Media and Journalism
Duration: 2FT Hon
Entry Requirements: *GCE:* CCC. *SQAH:* BBCC. *SQAAH:* CCC. *IB:* 30.

Q3P5 BA English Literature with Journalism
Duration: 2FT Hon
Entry Requirements: *GCE:* BBB. *SQAH:* ABBB. *SQAAH:* BBB. *IB:* 34. *OCR NED:* M2

Q3PM BA English Studies with Journalism
Duration: 2FT Hon
Entry Requirements: *GCE:* BBC-BCC. *SQAH:* BBBB-BBBC. *SQAAH:* BBC-BCC. *IB:* 33.

V2P5 BA History with Journalism
Duration: 2FT Hon
Entry Requirements: *GCE:* BCC. *SQAH:* BBBC. *SQAAH:* BCC. *IB:* 31.

L9P5 BA International Studies with Journalism
Duration: 2FT Hon
Entry Requirements: *GCE:* BCC. *SQAH:* BBBC. *SQAAH:* BCC. *IB:* 31.

P5P9 BA Journalism with Communication Studies
Duration: 2FT Hon
Entry Requirements: *GCE:* BBC-BCC. *SQAH:* BBBB-BBBC. *SQAAH:* BBC-BCC. *IB:* 33.

P5Q3 BA Journalism with English Literature
Duration: 2FT Hon
Entry Requirements: *GCE:* BBC-BCC. *SQAH:* BBBB-BBBC. *SQAAH:* BBC-BCC. *IB:* 33.

P5L2 BA Journalism with International Studies
Duration: 2FT Hon
Entry Requirements: *GCE:* BBC-BCC. *SQAH:* BBBB-BBBC. *SQAAH:* BBC-BCC. *IB:* 33.

L1P5 BSc Economics with Journalism
Duration: 2FT Hon
Entry Requirements: *GCE:* BBB. *SQAH:* ABBB. *SQAAH:* BBB. *IB:* 34.

C10 CANTERBURY CHRIST CHURCH UNIVERSITY
NORTH HOLMES ROAD
CANTERBURY
KENT CT1 1QU
t: 01227 782900 f: 01227 782888
e: admissions@canterbury.ac.uk
// www.canterbury.ac.uk

P501 BA Journalism: Multimedia Journalism
Duration: 3FT Hon   CRB Check: Required
Entry Requirements: *GCE:* 260. *IB:* 24. Interview required.

C15 CARDIFF UNIVERSITY
PO BOX 927
30-36 NEWPORT ROAD
CARDIFF CF24 0DE
t: 029 2087 9999 f: 029 2087 6138
e: admissions@cardiff.ac.uk
// www.cardiff.ac.uk

LP35 BA Journalism, Media and Sociology
Duration: 3FT Hon
Entry Requirements: *GCE:* ABB. *SQAAH:* AAABB. *IB:* 36. Admissions Test required.

C30 UNIVERSITY OF CENTRAL LANCASHIRE
PRESTON
LANCS PR1 2HE
t: 01772 201201 f: 01772 894954
e: uadmissions@uclan.ac.uk
// www.uclan.ac.uk

W8P5 BA Creative Writing and Journalism
Duration: 3FT Hon
Entry Requirements: *GCE:* 260-300. *IB:* 28. *BTEC Dip:* D*D*. *BTEC ExtDip:* DMM. *OCR ND:* D *OCR NED:* M2

QP35 BA English Language and Journalism
Duration: 3FT Hon
Entry Requirements: *GCE:* 260-280. *IB:* 28. *OCR NED:* M2

N5P5 BA Fashion & Brand Promotion and Journalism
Duration: 3FT Hon
Entry Requirements: *Foundation:* Distinction. *GCE:* 260-300. *IB:* 25. *BTEC Dip:* D*D*. *BTEC ExtDip:* DMM. *OCR NED:* M2 Interview required.

P502 BA International Journalism
Duration: 3FT Hon
Entry Requirements: *GCE:* BCC. *IB:* 28. *OCR ND:* D *OCR NED:* M2

P500 BA Journalism
Duration: 3FT Hon
Entry Requirements: *GCE:* ABB. *IB:* 32. *OCR ND:* D *OCR NED:* D2

P503 BA Journalism (Foundation Entry)
Duration: 4FT Hon
Entry Requirements: Contact the institution for details.

PQ53 BA Journalism and English Literature
Duration: 3FT Hon
Entry Requirements: *GCE:* BCC. *IB:* 28. *OCR ND:* D *OCR NED:* M2

P5W8 BA Screenwriting and Journalism
Duration: 3FT Hon
Entry Requirements: *GCE:* 260-300. *IB:* 28. *BTEC Dip:* D*D*.
BTEC ExtDip: DMM. *OCR ND:* D *OCR NED:* M2 Interview required.

P501 BA Sports Journalism
Duration: 3FT Hon
Entry Requirements: *GCE:* ABB. *SQAH:* AAAB. *IB:* 30. *OCR ND:* D
OCR NED: D2

P5P4 BA/BSc Journalism and Web & Multimedia
Duration: 3FT Hon
Entry Requirements: *GCE:* 260-300. *IB:* 28. *BTEC Dip:* D*D*.
BTEC ExtDip: DMM. *OCR ND:* D *OCR NED:* M2

C55 UNIVERSITY OF CHESTER
PARKGATE ROAD
CHESTER CH1 4BJ
t: 01244 511000 f: 01244 511300
e: enquiries@chester.ac.uk
// www.chester.ac.uk

NPM5 BA Advertising and Journalism
Duration: 3FT Hon
Entry Requirements: *GCE:* 240-280. *SQAH:* BBBB. *IB:* 26.

NP2M BA Business Management and Journalism
Duration: 3FT Hon
Entry Requirements: *GCE:* 240-280. *SQAH:* BBBB. *IB:* 26.

WP85 BA Creative Writing and Journalism
Duration: 3FT Hon
Entry Requirements: *Foundation:* Merit. *GCE:* 260-300. *SQAH:*
BBBB. *IB:* 28.

WP6M BA Digital Photography and Journalism
Duration: 3FT Hon
Entry Requirements: *GCE:* 240-280. *SQAH:* BBBB. *IB:* 26.

QP35 BA English Language and Journalism
Duration: 3FT Hon
Entry Requirements: *Foundation:* Merit. *GCE:* 260-300. *SQAH:*
BBBB. *IB:* 28.

NP8M BA Events Management and Journalism
Duration: 3FT Hon
Entry Requirements: *GCE:* 240-280. *SQAH:* BBBB. *IB:* 26.

P500 BA Journalism
Duration: 3FT Hon
Entry Requirements: *Foundation:* Pass. *GCE:* 260-300. *SQAH:*
BBBB. *IB:* 28.

MP95 BA Journalism and Criminology
Duration: 3FT Hon
Entry Requirements: *GCE:* 240-280. *SQAH:* BBBB. *IB:* 26.

PW54 BA Journalism and Drama & Theatre Studies
Duration: 3FT Hon
Entry Requirements: *Foundation:* Pass. *GCE:* 260-300. *SQAH:*
BBBB. *IB:* 28.

PQ53 BA Journalism and English
Duration: 3FT Hon
Entry Requirements: *Foundation:* Merit. *GCE:* 260-300. *SQAH:*
BBBB. *IB:* 28.

PR51 BA Journalism and French
Duration: 4FT Hon
Entry Requirements: *GCE:* 240-280. *SQAH:* BBBB. *IB:* 26.

PV51 BA Journalism and History
Duration: 3FT Hon
Entry Requirements: *GCE:* 260-300. *SQAH:* BBBB. *IB:* 28.

PR54 BA Journalism and Spanish
Duration: 4FT Hon
Entry Requirements: *GCE:* 240-280. *SQAH:* BBBB. *IB:* 26.

PC56 BA Journalism and Sport Development
Duration: 3FT Hon
Entry Requirements: *GCE:* 240-280. *SQAH:* BBBB. *IB:* 26.

MP15 BA Law and Journalism
Duration: 3FT Hon
Entry Requirements: *GCE:* 240-280. *SQAH:* BBBB. *IB:* 26.

FP75 BA Natural Hazard Management and Journalism
Duration: 3FT Hon
Entry Requirements: *GCE:* 240-280. *SQAH:* BBBB. *IB:* 26.

PW5P BA Photography and Journalism
Duration: 3FT Hon
Entry Requirements: *Foundation:* Pass. *GCE:* 240-280. *SQAH:*
BBBB. *IB:* 26. Interview required. Portfolio required.

P590 BA Sports Journalism
Duration: 3FT Hon
Entry Requirements: *Foundation:* Pass. *GCE:* 260-300. *SQAH:*
BBBB. *IB:* 28.

C60 CITY UNIVERSITY
NORTHAMPTON SQUARE
LONDON EC1V 0HB
t: 020 7040 5060 f: 020 7040 8995
e: ugadmissions@city.ac.uk
// www.city.ac.uk

P500 BA Journalism (3 years or 4 year SW)
Duration: 3FT Hon
Entry Requirements: *GCE:* AAA. *IB:* 35.

LP15 BA Journalism and Economics (3 years or 4 year SW)
Duration: 3FT Hon
Entry Requirements: *GCE:* AAA. *IB:* 35.

CP85 BA Journalism and Psychology (3 years or 4 year SW)
Duration: 3FT Hon
Entry Requirements: *GCE:* AAA. *IB:* 35.

LP35 BA Journalism and Sociology (3 years or 4 year SW)
Duration: 3FT Hon
Entry Requirements: *GCE:* AAA. *IB:* 35.

P501 Cert International Foundation (Journalism)
Duration: 1FT FYr
Entry Requirements: Contact the institution for details.

C78 CORNWALL COLLEGE
POOL
REDRUTH
CORNWALL TR15 3RD
t: 01209 616161 f: 01209 611612
e: he.admissions@cornwall.ac.uk
// www.cornwall.ac.uk

P500 FdA Newspaper & Magazine Journalism
Duration: 2FT Fdg **CRB Check:** Required
Entry Requirements: *GCE:* 120. Interview required.

C85 COVENTRY UNIVERSITY
THE STUDENT CENTRE
COVENTRY UNIVERSITY
1 GULSON RD
COVENTRY CV1 2JH
t: 024 7615 2222 f: 024 7615 2223
e: studentenquiries@coventry.ac.uk
// www.coventry.ac.uk

QP35 BA English and Journalism
Duration: 3FT/4SW Hon
Entry Requirements: *GCE:* BCC. *SQAH:* BCCCC. *IB:* 28. *BTEC ExtDip:* DMM. *OCR NED:* M2

C93 UNIVERSITY FOR THE CREATIVE ARTS
FALKNER ROAD
FARNHAM
SURREY GU9 7DS
t: 01252 892960
e: admissions@ucreative.ac.uk
// www.ucreative.ac.uk

WP25 BA Fashion Journalism
Duration: 3FT Hon
Entry Requirements: *GCE:* 220. *IB:* 24. *BTEC ExtDip:* PPP. Interview required. Portfolio required.

WP35 BA Music Journalism
Duration: 3FT Hon
Entry Requirements: *GCE:* 220. *IB:* 24. *BTEC ExtDip:* PPP. Interview required. Portfolio required.

C99 UNIVERSITY OF CUMBRIA
FUSEHILL STREET
CARLISLE
CUMBRIA CA1 2HH
t: 01228 616234 f: 01228 616235
// www.cumbria.ac.uk

P500 BA Journalism
Duration: 3FT Hon
Entry Requirements: *Foundation:* Merit. *GCE:* 240. *SQAH:* BBC. *SQAAH:* CC. *IB:* 30. *OCR ND:* D Interview required. Portfolio required.

D26 DE MONTFORT UNIVERSITY
THE GATEWAY
LEICESTER LE1 9BH
t: 0116 255 1551 f: 0116 250 6204
e: enquiries@dmu.ac.uk
// www.dmu.ac.uk

WP85 BA Creative Writing and Journalism
Duration: 3FT Hon
Entry Requirements: *GCE:* 260. *IB:* 28. *BTEC Dip:* D*D*. *BTEC ExtDip:* DMM.

QP35 BA English Language and Journalism
Duration: 3FT Hon
Entry Requirements: *GCE:* 260. *IB:* 28. *BTEC Dip:* D*D*. *BTEC ExtDip:* DMM.

PQ53 BA English and Journalism
Duration: 3FT Hon
Entry Requirements: *GCE:* 260. *IB:* 28. *BTEC Dip:* D*D*. *BTEC ExtDip:* DMM.

PV51 BA History and Journalism
Duration: 3FT Hon
Entry Requirements: *GCE:* 260. *IB:* 28. *BTEC Dip:* D*D*. *BTEC ExtDip:* DMM.

LP25 BA International Relations and Journalism
Duration: 3FT Hon
Entry Requirements: *GCE:* 260. *IB:* 28. *BTEC Dip:* D*D*. *BTEC ExtDip:* DMM.

P500 BA Journalism
Duration: 3FT Hon
Entry Requirements: *GCE:* 260. *IB:* 28. *BTEC Dip:* D*D*. *BTEC ExtDip:* DMM. Admissions Test required.

LPF5 BA Journalism and Politics
Duration: 3FT Hon
Entry Requirements: *GCE:* 260. *IB:* 28. *BTEC Dip:* D*D*. *BTEC ExtDip:* DMM.

D39 UNIVERSITY OF DERBY
KEDLESTON ROAD
DERBY DE22 1GB
t: 01332 591167 f: 01332 597724
e: askadmissions@derby.ac.uk
// www.derby.ac.uk

P500 BA Journalism
Duration: 3FT Hon
Entry Requirements: *Foundation:* Distinction. *GCE:* 260. *IB:* 28.
BTEC Dip: D*D*. *BTEC ExtDip:* DMM. *OCR NED:* M2 Interview required.

E28 UNIVERSITY OF EAST LONDON
DOCKLANDS CAMPUS
UNIVERSITY WAY
LONDON E16 2RD
t: 020 8223 3333 f: 020 8223 2978
e: study@uel.ac.uk
// www.uel.ac.uk

W8P5 BA Creative & Professional Writing with Journalism Studies
Duration: 3FT Hon
Entry Requirements: *GCE:* 240. *IB:* 24.

NP65 BA Human Resource Management/Journalism Studies
Duration: 3FT Hon
Entry Requirements: *GCE:* 240. *IB:* 24.

NP15 BA International Business/Journalism Studies
Duration: 3FT Hon
Entry Requirements: *GCE:* 240. *IB:* 24.

P500 BA Journalism
Duration: 3FT Hon
Entry Requirements: *GCE:* 240. *IB:* 24.

P501 BA Journalism (Extended)
Duration: 4FT Hon
Entry Requirements: *GCE:* 80. *IB:* 24.

P5W6 BA Journalism Studies with Animation
Duration: 3FT Hon
Entry Requirements: *GCE:* 240. *IB:* 24.

P5P9 BA Journalism Studies with Communication Studies
Duration: 3FT Hon
Entry Requirements: *GCE:* 240. *IB:* 24.

P5I1 BA Journalism Studies with Computing
Duration: 3FT Hon
Entry Requirements: *GCE:* 240. *IB:* 24.

P5W8 BA Journalism Studies with Creative & Professional Writing
Duration: 3FT Hon
Entry Requirements: *GCE:* 240. *IB:* 24.

P5Q3 BA Journalism Studies with English Literature
Duration: 3FT Hon
Entry Requirements: *GCE:* 240. *IB:* 24.

PW58 BA Journalism Studies/Creative & Professional Writing
Duration: 3FT Hon
Entry Requirements: *GCE:* 240. *IB:* 24.

PL52 BA Journalism Studies/International Politics
Duration: 3FT Hon
Entry Requirements: *GCE:* 240. *IB:* 24.

LP35 BA Journalism Studies/Sociology
Duration: 3FT Hon
Entry Requirements: *GCE:* 240. *IB:* 24.

V000 BA Media & Creative Industries option - Journalism Studies
Duration: 3FT Hon
Entry Requirements: *GCE:* 240. *IB:* 24.

N2P5 BA Music Industry Management with Journalism Studies
Duration: 3FT Hon
Entry Requirements: *GCE:* 240. *IB:* 24.

P502 BA Sports Journalism
Duration: 3FT Hon
Entry Requirements: *GCE:* 280. *IB:* 24.

P503 BA Sports Journalism (Extended)
Duration: 4FT Hon
Entry Requirements: *GCE:* 120.

GP55 BA/BSc Business Information Systems/Journalism Studies
Duration: 3FT Hon
Entry Requirements: *GCE:* 240. *IB:* 24.

CP65 BA/BSc Sports Coaching/Journalism Studies
Duration: 3FT Hon
Entry Requirements: *GCE:* 240. *IB:* 24.

CP6M BSc Fitness & Health and Sport Journalism
Duration: 3FT Hon
Entry Requirements: *GCE:* 280.

C6P5 BSc Fitness & Health with Sport Journalism
Duration: 3FT Hon
Entry Requirements: *GCE:* 280. *IB:* 24.

CP6N BSc Sports & Exercise Science and Sport Journalism
Duration: 3FT Hon
Entry Requirements: *GCE:* 240. *IB:* 24.

C6PM BSc Sports & Exercise Science with Sport Journalism
Duration: 3FT Hon
Entry Requirements: *GCE:* 280. *IB:* 24.

CPP5 BSc Sports Development and Sport Journalism
Duration: 3FT Hon
Entry Requirements: *GCE:* 280. *IB:* 24.

C6PN BSc Sports Development with Sport Journalism
Duration: 3FT Hon
Entry Requirements: *GCE:* 280. *IB:* 24.

E59 EDINBURGH NAPIER UNIVERSITY
CRAIGLOCKHART CAMPUS
EDINBURGH EH14 1DJ
t: +44 (0)8452 60 60 40 f: 0131 455 6464
e: info@napier.ac.uk
// www.napier.ac.uk

P500 BA Journalism
Duration: 3FT/4FT Ord/Hon
Entry Requirements: *GCE:* 240. Interview required.

F33 UNIVERSITY COLLEGE FALMOUTH
WOODLANE
FALMOUTH
CORNWALL TR11 4RH
t: 01326213730
e: admissions@falmouth.ac.uk
// www.falmouth.ac.uk

P500 BA(Hons) Journalism
Duration: 3FT Hon
Entry Requirements: *GCE:* 220. *IB:* 24. Interview required. Portfolio required.

WP65 BA(Hons) Press & Editorial Photography
Duration: 3FT Hon
Entry Requirements: *GCE:* 220. *IB:* 24. Interview required. Portfolio required.

G14 UNIVERSITY OF GLAMORGAN, CARDIFF AND PONTYPRIDD
ENQUIRIES AND ADMISSIONS UNIT
PONTYPRIDD CF37 1DL
t: 08456 434030 f: 01443 654050
e: enquiries@glam.ac.uk
// www.glam.ac.uk

P500 BA Journalism
Duration: 3FT Hon
Entry Requirements: *GCE:* BBB. *IB:* 26. *BTEC SubDip:* M. *BTEC Dip:* DD. *BTEC ExtDip:* DDM. *OCR NED:* M1 Interview required. Admissions Test required.

G42 GLASGOW CALEDONIAN UNIVERSITY
STUDENT RECRUITMENT & ADMISSIONS SERVICE
CITY CAMPUS
COWCADDENS ROAD
GLASGOW G4 0BA
t: 0141 331 3000 f: 0141 331 8676
e: undergraduate@gcu.ac.uk
// www.gcu.ac.uk

P500 BA Multimedia Journalism
Duration: 4FT Hon
Entry Requirements: *GCE:* BBC. *SQAH:* ABBB-BBBB. *IB:* 25. Interview required. Admissions Test required.

G50 THE UNIVERSITY OF GLOUCESTERSHIRE
PARK CAMPUS
THE PARK
CHELTENHAM GL50 2RH
t: 01242 714501 f: 01242 714869
e: admissions@glos.ac.uk
// www.glos.ac.uk

P500 BA Journalism
Duration: 2FT Hon
Entry Requirements: Interview required. Portfolio required.

P502 BA Journalism
Duration: 3FT Hon
Entry Requirements: *GCE:* 280-300. Interview required.

WP65 BA Photojournalism and Documentary Photography
Duration: 3FT Hon
Entry Requirements: *GCE:* 280-300. Interview required. Portfolio required.

G53 GLYNDWR UNIVERSITY
PLAS COCH
MOLD ROAD
WREXHAM LL11 2AW
t: 01978 293439 f: 01978 290008
e: sid@glyndwr.ac.uk
// www.glyndwr.ac.uk

PP35 BA Broadcasting, Journalism and Media Communications
Duration: 3FT Hon
Entry Requirements: *GCE:* 240.

G80 GRIMSBY INSTITUTE OF FURTHER AND HIGHER EDUCATION
NUNS CORNER
GRIMSBY
NE LINCOLNSHIRE DN34 5BQ
t: 0800 328 3631
e: headmissions@grimsby.ac.uk
// www.grimsby.ac.uk

P502 BA Multi-Platform Journalism
Duration: 3FT Hon
Entry Requirements: Interview required.

H36 UNIVERSITY OF HERTFORDSHIRE
UNIVERSITY ADMISSIONS SERVICE
COLLEGE LANE
HATFIELD
HERTS AL10 9AB
t: 01707 284800
// www.herts.ac.uk

Q1P5 BA English Language & Communication with Journalism
Duration: 3FT Hon
Entry Requirements: GCE: 300.

Q3P5 BA English Literature with Journalism
Duration: 3FT Hon
Entry Requirements: GCE: 300.

V1P5 BA History with Journalism
Duration: 3FT Hon
Entry Requirements: GCE: 300.

V5P5 BA Philosophy with Journalism
Duration: 3FT Hon
Entry Requirements: GCE: 300.

N1P5 BSc Business/Journalism & Media Cultures
Duration: 3FT/4SW Hon
Entry Requirements: GCE: 300.

Q1PM BSc English Language & Communication/Journalism & Media Cultures
Duration: 3FT/4SW Hon
Entry Requirements: GCE: 220.

B9P5 BSc Health Studies/Journalism & Media Cultures
Duration: 3FT/4SW Hon
Entry Requirements: GCE: 300.

B1P5 BSc Human Biology/Journalism & Media Cultures
Duration: 3FT/4SW Hon
Entry Requirements: GCE: 300.

L7P5 BSc Human Geography/Journalism & Media Cultures
Duration: 3FT/4SW Hon
Entry Requirements: GCE: 300.

P5N1 BSc Journalism & Media Cultures/Business
Duration: 3FT/4SW Hon
Entry Requirements: GCE: 300.

P5Q1 BSc Journalism & Media Cultures/English Language & Communication
Duration: 3FT/4SW Hon
Entry Requirements: GCE: 260.

P5B9 BSc Journalism & Media Cultures/Health Studies
Duration: 3FT/4SW Hon
Entry Requirements: GCE: 300.

P5B1 BSc Journalism & Media Cultures/Human Biology
Duration: 3FT/4SW Hon
Entry Requirements: GCE: 300.

P5L7 BSc Journalism & Media Cultures/Human Geography
Duration: 3FT/4SW Hon
Entry Requirements: GCE: 300.

P5M1 BSc Journalism & Media Cultures/Law
Duration: 3FT/4SW Hon
Entry Requirements: GCE: 320.

P5G1 BSc Journalism & Media Cultures/Mathematics
Duration: 3FT/4SW Hon
Entry Requirements: GCE: 300.

P5V5 BSc Journalism & Media Cultures/Philosophy
Duration: 3FT/4SW Hon
Entry Requirements: GCE: 260.

P5C6 BSc Journalism & Media Cultures/Sports Studies
Duration: 3FT/4SW Hon
Entry Requirements: GCE: 300.

M1P5 BSc Law/Journalism & Media Cultures
Duration: 3FT/4SW Hon
Entry Requirements: GCE: 320.

G1P5 BSc Mathematics/Journalism & Media Cultures
Duration: 3FT/4SW Hon
Entry Requirements: GCE: 300.

V5PM BSc Philosophy/Journalism & Media Cultures
Duration: 3FT/4SW Hon
Entry Requirements: GCE: 220.

C6P5 BSc Sports Studies/Journalism & Media Cultures
Duration: 3FT/4SW Hon
Entry Requirements: GCE: 300.

H60 THE UNIVERSITY OF HUDDERSFIELD
QUEENSGATE
HUDDERSFIELD HD1 3DH
t: 01484 473969 f: 01484 472765
e: admissionsandrecords@hud.ac.uk
// www.hud.ac.uk

P501 BA Broadcast Journalism
Duration: 3FT Hon
Entry Requirements: *GCE:* 280. Interview required.

NP15 BA Business and Journalism
Duration: 3FT/4SW Hon
Entry Requirements: *GCE:* 300.

P500 BA Journalism
Duration: 3FT Hon
Entry Requirements: *GCE:* 280. Interview required.

P502 BA Music Journalism
Duration: 3FT Hon
Entry Requirements: *GCE:* 280. Interview required.

P503 BA Sports Journalism
Duration: 3FT Hon
Entry Requirements: *GCE:* 280. Interview required.

H73 HULL COLLEGE
QUEEN'S GARDENS
HULL HU1 3DG
t: 01482 329943 f: 01482 598733
e: info@hull-college.ac.uk
// www.hull-college.ac.uk/higher-education

P500 FdA Digital Media Journalism
Duration: 2FT Fdg
Entry Requirements: *GCE:* 200. Foundation Course required.
Interview required. Portfolio required.

K24 THE UNIVERSITY OF KENT
RECRUITMENT & ADMISSIONS OFFICE
REGISTRY
UNIVERSITY OF KENT
CANTERBURY, KENT CT2 7NZ
t: 01227 827272 f: 01227 827077
e: information@kent.ac.uk
// www.kent.ac.uk

P500 BA Journalism
Duration: 3FT Hon
Entry Requirements: *GCE:* ABB. *IB:* 33. *OCR ND:* M1 *OCR NED:*
M2 Interview required. Admissions Test required.

K84 KINGSTON UNIVERSITY
STUDENT INFORMATION & ADVICE CENTRE
COOPER HOUSE
40-46 SURBITON ROAD
KINGSTON UPON THAMES KT1 2HX
t: 0844 8552177 f: 020 8547 7080
e: aps@kingston.ac.uk
// www.kingston.ac.uk

WP85 BA Creative Writing and Journalism
Duration: 3FT Hon
Entry Requirements: *GCE:* 340.

LP15 BA Economics (Applied) and Journalism
Duration: 3FT Hon
Entry Requirements: *GCE:* 340.

QP35 BA English Language & Communications and Journalism
Duration: 3FT Hon
Entry Requirements: *GCE:* 340.

QPH5 BA English Literature and Journalism
Duration: 3FT Hon
Entry Requirements: *GCE:* 340.

VP15 BA History and Journalism
Duration: 3FT Hon
Entry Requirements: *GCE:* 340.

VP35 BA History of Art, Design & Film and Journalism
Duration: 3FT Hon
Entry Requirements: *GCE:* 340.

LP25 BA Human Rights and Journalism
Duration: 3FT Hon
Entry Requirements: *GCE:* 340.

LPF5 BA International Relations and Journalism
Duration: 3FT Hon
Entry Requirements: *GCE:* 340.

P500 BA Journalism
Duration: 3FT Hon
Entry Requirements: *GCE:* 340. *SQAH:* BBCCC. *SQAAH:* BBC. *IB:* 25.

PL52 BA Journalism and Politics
Duration: 3FT Hon
Entry Requirements: *GCE:* 340. *SQAH:* BBCCC. *SQAAH:* BBC. *IB:* 25.

PC58 BA Journalism and Psychology
Duration: 3FT Hon
Entry Requirements: *GCE:* 340. *SQAH:* BBCCC. *SQAAH:* BBC. *IB:* 25.

PL53 BA Journalism and Sociology
Duration: 3FT Hon
Entry Requirements: *GCE:* 340. *SQAH:* BBCCC. *SQAAH:* BBC. *IB:* 25.

P5R1 BA Journalism with French
Duration: 3FT Hon
Entry Requirements: *GCE:* 340. *SQAH:* BBCCC. *SQAAH:* BBC. *IB:* 25.

P5C8 BA Journalism with Psychology
Duration: 3FT Hon
Entry Requirements: *GCE:* 340. *SQAH:* BBCCC. *SQAAH:* BBC. *IB:* 25.

C8P5 BA Psychology with Journalism
Duration: 3FT Hon
Entry Requirements: *GCE:* 340.

P5R4 BA (Hons) Journalism with Spanish
Duration: 3FT Hon
Entry Requirements: *GCE:* 340. *SQAH:* BBCCC. *SQAAH:* BBC. *IB:* 25.

L23 UNIVERSITY OF LEEDS
THE UNIVERSITY OF LEEDS
WOODHOUSE LANE
LEEDS LS2 9JT
t: 0113 343 3999
e: admissions@leeds.ac.uk
// www.leeds.ac.uk

PJ59 BA Broadcast Journalism
Duration: 3FT Hon
Entry Requirements: *GCE:* ABB. *SQAH:* AAABB. *SQAAH:* ABB. *IB:* 34.

L24 LEEDS TRINITY UNIVERSITY COLLEGE
BROWNBERRIE LANE
HORSFORTH
LEEDS LS18 5HD
t: 0113 283 7150 f: 0113 283 7222
e: enquiries@leedstrinity.ac.uk
// www.leedstrinity.ac.uk

P501 BA Journalism
Duration: 3FT Hon
Entry Requirements: *GCE:* 280. *IB:* 25. *OCR NED:* M2

P591 BA Sports Journalism
Duration: 3FT Hon
Entry Requirements: *GCE:* 280. *IB:* 25. *OCR NED:* M2

L27 LEEDS METROPOLITAN UNIVERSITY
COURSE ENQUIRIES OFFICE
CITY CAMPUS
LEEDS LS1 3HE
t: 0113 81 23113 f: 0113 81 23129
// www.leedsmet.ac.uk

P500 BA Journalism
Duration: 3FT Hon
Entry Requirements: *GCE:* 280. *IB:* 28. Portfolio required.

WP65 BSc Photographic Journalism
Duration: 3FT Hon
Entry Requirements: *GCE:* 200. *IB:* 24. Interview required.

L39 UNIVERSITY OF LINCOLN
ADMISSIONS
BRAYFORD POOL
LINCOLN LN6 7TS
t: 01522 886097 f: 01522 886146
e: admissions@lincoln.ac.uk
// www.lincoln.ac.uk

PQ53 BA English and Journalism
Duration: 3FT Hon
Entry Requirements: *GCE:* 280.

P500 BA Journalism
Duration: 3FT Hon
Entry Requirements: *GCE:* 280.

P590 BA Journalism (Investigative)
Duration: 3FT Hon
Entry Requirements: *GCE:* 280.

L51 LIVERPOOL JOHN MOORES UNIVERSITY
KINGSWAY HOUSE
HATTON GARDEN
LIVERPOOL L3 2AJ
t: 0151 231 5090 f: 0151 904 6368
e: courses@ljmu.ac.uk
// www.ljmu.ac.uk

P510 BA International Journalism
Duration: 3FT Hon
Entry Requirements: *GCE:* 260. *IB:* 28.

P500 BA Journalism
Duration: 3FT Hon
Entry Requirements: *GCE:* 280. *IB:* 29.

L62 THE LONDON COLLEGE, UCK
VICTORIA GARDENS
NOTTING HILL GATE
LONDON W11 3PE
t: 020 7243 4000 f: 020 7243 1484
e: admissions@lcuck.ac.uk
// www.lcuck.ac.uk

105P HNC Creative Media Production (Journalism)
Duration: 1FT HNC
Entry Requirements: Contact the institution for details.

205P HND Creative Media Production (Journalism)
Duration: 2FT HND
Entry Requirements: Contact the institution for details.

L68 LONDON METROPOLITAN UNIVERSITY
166-220 HOLLOWAY ROAD
LONDON N7 8DB
t: 020 7133 4200
e: admissions@londonmet.ac.uk
// www.londonmet.ac.uk

NP5M BA Fashion Marketing and Journalism
Duration: 3FT Hon
Entry Requirements: *GCE:* 280. *IB:* 28.

P502 BA Journalism
Duration: 3FT Hon
Entry Requirements: *GCE:* 280. *IB:* 28.

L75 LONDON SOUTH BANK UNIVERSITY
ADMISSIONS AND RECRUITMENT CENTRE
90 LONDON ROAD
LONDON SE1 6LN
t: 0800 923 8888 f: 020 7815 8273
e: course.enquiry@lsbu.ac.uk
// www.lsbu.ac.uk

P590 BA Communications
Duration: 3FT Hon
Entry Requirements: *GCE:* 240. *IB:* 24.

P501 BA Multimedia Journalism
Duration: 3FT Hon
Entry Requirements: *GCE:* 240. *IB:* 24.

M80 MIDDLESEX UNIVERSITY
MIDDLESEX UNIVERSITY
THE BURROUGHS
LONDON NW4 4BT
t: 020 8411 5555 f: 020 8411 5649
e: enquiries@mdx.ac.uk
// www.mdx.ac.uk

WP85 BA Creative Writing and Journalism Studies
Duration: 3FT Hon
Entry Requirements: *GCE:* 200-300. *IB:* 28.

PP59 BA Journalism and Communication Studies
Duration: 3FT Hon
Entry Requirements: *GCE:* 200-300. *IB:* 28.

PP54 BA Journalism and Publishing Studies
Duration: 3FT Hon
Entry Requirements: *GCE:* 200-300. *IB:* 28.

PP45 BA Publishing, Journalism and Media
Duration: 3FT Hon
Entry Requirements: *GCE:* 200-300. *IB:* 28.

N30 NEW COLLEGE NOTTINGHAM
ADAMS BUILDING
STONEY STREET
THE LACE MARKET
NOTTINGHAM NG1 1NG
t: 0115 910 0100 f: 0115 953 4349
e: he.team@ncn.ac.uk
// www.ncn.ac.uk

P500 FdA Broadcast Media (Journalism)
Duration: 2FT Fdg
Entry Requirements: Contact the institution for details.

N38 UNIVERSITY OF NORTHAMPTON
PARK CAMPUS
BOUGHTON GREEN ROAD
NORTHAMPTON NN2 7AL
t: 0800 358 2232 f: 01604 722083
e: admissions@northampton.ac.uk
// www.northampton.ac.uk

N5PM BA Advertising/Journalism
Duration: 3FT Hon
Entry Requirements: *GCE:* 260-280. *SQAH:* AAA-BBBB. *IB:* 24.
BTEC Dip: DD. *BTEC ExtDip:* DMM. *OCR ND:* D *OCR NED:* M2

N1P5 BA Business/Journalism
Duration: 3FT Hon
Entry Requirements: *GCE:* 260-280. *SQAH:* AAA-BBBB. *IB:* 24.
BTEC Dip: DD. *BTEC ExtDip:* DMM. *OCR ND:* D *OCR NED:* M2

W8P5 BA Creative Writing/Journalism
Duration: 3FT Hon
Entry Requirements: *GCE:* 260-280. *SQAH:* AAA-BBBB. *IB:* 24.
BTEC Dip: DD. *BTEC ExtDip:* DMM. *OCR ND:* D *OCR NED:* M2

W4P5 BA Drama/Journalism
Duration: 3FT Hon
Entry Requirements: *GCE:* 260-280. *SQAH:* AAA-BBBB. *IB:* 24.
BTEC Dip: DD. *BTEC ExtDip:* DMM. *OCR ND:* D *OCR NED:* M2
Interview required.

L1P5 BA Economics/Journalism
Duration: 3FT Hon
Entry Requirements: *GCE:* 260-280. *SQAH:* AAA-BBBB. *IB:* 24.
BTEC Dip: DD. *BTEC ExtDip:* DMM. *OCR ND:* D *OCR NED:* M2

X3P5 BA Education Studies/Journalism
Duration: 3FT Hon
Entry Requirements: *GCE:* 260-280. *SQAH:* AAA-BBBB. *IB:* 24.
BTEC Dip: DD. *BTEC ExtDip:* DMM. *OCR ND:* D *OCR NED:* M2

Q3P5 BA English/Journalism
Duration: 3FT Hon
Entry Requirements: *GCE:* 260-280. *SQAH:* AAA-BBBB. *IB:* 24.
BTEC Dip: DD. *BTEC ExtDip:* DMM. *OCR ND:* D *OCR NED:* M2

N8PN BA Events Management/Journalism
Duration: 3FT Hon
Entry Requirements: *GCE:* 260-280. *SQAH:* AAA-BBBB. *IB:* 24.
BTEC Dip: DD. *BTEC ExtDip:* DMM. *OCR ND:* D *OCR NED:* M2

W6P5 BA Film & Television Studies/Journalism
Duration: 3FT Hon
Entry Requirements: **GCE:** 260-280. **SQAH:** AAA-BBBB. **IB:** 24.
BTEC Dip: DD. **BTEC ExtDip:** DMM. **OCR ND:** D **OCR NED:** M2

L4P5 BA Health Studies/Journalism
Duration: 3FT Hon
Entry Requirements: **GCE:** 260-280. **SQAH:** AAA-BBBB. **IB:** 24.
BTEC Dip: DD. **BTEC ExtDip:** DMM. **OCR ND:** D **OCR NED:** M2

L9P5 BA International Development/Journalism
Duration: 3FT Hon
Entry Requirements: **GCE:** 260-280. **SQAH:** AAA-BBBB. **IB:** 24.
BTEC Dip: DD. **BTEC ExtDip:** DMM. **OCR ND:** D **OCR NED:** M2

P500 BA Journalism
Duration: 3FT Hon
Entry Requirements: **GCE:** 260-280. **SQAH:** AAA-BBBB. **IB:** 24.
BTEC Dip: DD. **BTEC ExtDip:** DMM. **OCR ND:** D **OCR NED:** M2

P5D4 BA Journalism with Applied Equine Studies
Duration: 3FT Hon
Entry Requirements: **GCE:** 260-280. **SQAH:** AAA-BBBB. **IB:** 24.
BTEC Dip: DD. **BTEC ExtDip:** DMM. **OCR ND:** D **OCR NED:** M2

P5NF BA Journalism with Applied Management
Duration: 3FT Hon
Entry Requirements: **GCE:** 260-280. **SQAH:** AAA-BBBB. **IB:** 24.
BTEC Dip: DD. **BTEC ExtDip:** DMM. **OCR ND:** D **OCR NED:** M2

P5NM BA Journalism/Advertising
Duration: 3FT Hon
Entry Requirements: **GCE:** 260-280. **SQAH:** AAA-BBBB. **IB:** 24.
BTEC Dip: DD. **BTEC ExtDip:** DMM. **OCR ND:** D **OCR NED:** M2

P5C1 BA Journalism/Biological Conservation
Duration: 3FT Hon
Entry Requirements: **GCE:** 260-280. **SQAH:** AAA-BBBB. **IB:** 24.
BTEC Dip: DD. **BTEC ExtDip:** DMM. **OCR ND:** D **OCR NED:** M2

P5N1 BA Journalism/Business
Duration: 3FT Hon
Entry Requirements: **GCE:** 260-280. **SQAH:** AAA-BBBB. **IB:** 24.
BTEC Dip: DD. **BTEC ExtDip:** DMM. **OCR ND:** D **OCR NED:** M2

P5G5 BA Journalism/Business Computing Systems
Duration: 3FT Hon
Entry Requirements: **GCE:** 260-280. **SQAH:** AAA-BBBB. **IB:** 24.
BTEC Dip: DD. **BTEC ExtDip:** DMM. **OCR ND:** D **OCR NED:** M2

P5G4 BA Journalism/Computing
Duration: 3FT Hon
Entry Requirements: **GCE:** 260-280. **SQAH:** AAA-BBBB. **IB:** 24.
BTEC Dip: DD. **BTEC ExtDip:** DMM. **OCR ND:** D **OCR NED:** M2

P5W8 BA Journalism/Creative Writing
Duration: 3FT Hon
Entry Requirements: **GCE:** 260-280. **SQAH:** AAA-BBBB. **IB:** 24.
BTEC Dip: DD. **BTEC ExtDip:** DMM. **OCR ND:** D **OCR NED:** M2

P5W4 BA Journalism/Drama
Duration: 3FT Hon
Entry Requirements: **GCE:** 260-280. **SQAH:** AAA-BBBB. **IB:** 24.
BTEC Dip: DD. **BTEC ExtDip:** DMM. **OCR ND:** D **OCR NED:** M2

P5L1 BA Journalism/Economics
Duration: 3FT Hon
Entry Requirements: **GCE:** 260-280. **SQAH:** AAA-BBBB. **IB:** 24.
BTEC Dip: DD. **BTEC ExtDip:** DMM. **OCR ND:** D **OCR NED:** M2

P5X3 BA Journalism/Education Studies
Duration: 3FT Hon
Entry Requirements: **GCE:** 260-280. **SQAH:** AAA-BBBB. **IB:** 24.
BTEC Dip: DD. **BTEC ExtDip:** DMM. **OCR ND:** D **OCR NED:** M2

P5Q3 BA Journalism/English
Duration: 3FT Hon
Entry Requirements: **GCE:** 260-280. **SQAH:** AAA-BBBB. **IB:** 24.
BTEC Dip: DD. **BTEC ExtDip:** DMM. **OCR ND:** D **OCR NED:** M2

P5NV BA Journalism/Events Management
Duration: 3FT Hon
Entry Requirements: **GCE:** 260-280. **SQAH:** AAA-BBBB. **IB:** 24.
BTEC Dip: DD. **BTEC ExtDip:** DMM. **OCR ND:** D **OCR NED:** M2

P5W6 BA Journalism/Film & Television Studies
Duration: 3FT Hon
Entry Requirements: **GCE:** 260-280. **SQAH:** AAA-BBBB. **IB:** 24.
BTEC Dip: DD. **BTEC ExtDip:** DMM. **OCR ND:** D **OCR NED:** M2

P5L4 BA Journalism/Health Studies
Duration: 3FT Hon
Entry Requirements: **GCE:** 260-280. **SQAH:** AAA-BBBB. **IB:** 24.
BTEC Dip: DD. **BTEC ExtDip:** DMM. **OCR ND:** D **OCR NED:** M2

P5L9 BA Journalism/International Development
Duration: 3FT Hon
Entry Requirements: **GCE:** 260-280. **SQAH:** AAA-BBBB. **IB:** 24.
BTEC Dip: DD. **BTEC ExtDip:** DMM. **OCR ND:** D **OCR NED:** M2

P5M1 BA Journalism/Law
Duration: 3FT Hon
Entry Requirements: **GCE:** 260-280. **SQAH:** AAA-BBBB. **IB:** 24.
BTEC Dip: DD. **BTEC ExtDip:** DMM. **OCR ND:** D **OCR NED:** M2

P5N2 BA Journalism/Management
Duration: 3FT Hon
Entry Requirements: **GCE:** 260-280. **SQAH:** AAA-BBBB. **IB:** 24.
BTEC Dip: DD. **BTEC ExtDip:** DMM. **OCR ND:** D **OCR NED:** M2

P5N5 BA Journalism/Marketing
Duration: 3FT Hon
Entry Requirements: **GCE:** 260-280. **SQAH:** AAA-BBBB. **IB:** 24.
BTEC Dip: DD. **BTEC ExtDip:** DMM. **OCR ND:** D **OCR NED:** M2

P5F8 BA Journalism/Physical Geography
Duration: 3FT Hon
Entry Requirements: *GCE:* 260-280. *SQAH:* AAA-BBBB. *IB:* 24.
BTEC Dip: DD. *BTEC ExtDip:* DMM. *OCR ND:* D *OCR NED:* M2

P5L2 BA Journalism/Politics
Duration: 3FT Hon
Entry Requirements: *GCE:* 260-280. *SQAH:* AAA-BBBB. *IB:* 24.
BTEC Dip: DD. *BTEC ExtDip:* DMM. *OCR ND:* D *OCR NED:* M2

P5W3 BA Journalism/Popular Music
Duration: 3FT Hon
Entry Requirements: *GCE:* 260-280. *SQAH:* AAA-BBBB. *IB:* 24.
BTEC Dip: DD. *BTEC ExtDip:* DMM. *OCR ND:* D *OCR NED:* M2
Interview required.

P5C8 BA Journalism/Psychology
Duration: 3FT Hon
Entry Requirements: *GCE:* 260-280. *SQAH:* AAA-BBBB. *IB:* 24.
BTEC Dip: DD. *BTEC ExtDip:* DMM. *OCR ND:* D *OCR NED:* M2

P5L3 BA Journalism/Sociology
Duration: 3FT Hon
Entry Requirements: *GCE:* 260-280. *SQAH:* AAA-BBBB. *IB:* 24.
BTEC Dip: DD. *BTEC ExtDip:* DMM. *OCR ND:* D *OCR NED:* M2

P5C6 BA Journalism/Sport Studies
Duration: 3FT Hon
Entry Requirements: *GCE:* 260-280. *SQAH:* AAA-BBBB. *IB:* 24.
BTEC Dip: DD. *BTEC ExtDip:* DMM. *OCR ND:* D *OCR NED:* M2

P5N8 BA Journalism/Tourism
Duration: 3FT Hon
Entry Requirements: *GCE:* 260-280. *SQAH:* AAA-BBBB. *IB:* 24.
BTEC Dip: DD. *BTEC ExtDip:* DMM. *OCR ND:* D *OCR NED:* M2

P5FV BA Journalism/Wastes Management
Duration: 3FT Hon
Entry Requirements: *GCE:* 260-280. *SQAH:* AAA-BBBB. *IB:* 24.
BTEC Dip: DD. *BTEC ExtDip:* DMM. *OCR ND:* D *OCR NED:* M2

P5GK BA Journalism/Web Design
Duration: 3FT Hon
Entry Requirements: *GCE:* 260-280. *SQAH:* AAA-BBBB. *IB:* 24.
BTEC Dip: DD. *BTEC ExtDip:* DMM. *OCR ND:* D *OCR NED:* M2

M1P5 BA Law/Journalism
Duration: 3FT Hon
Entry Requirements: *GCE:* 260-280. *SQAH:* AAA-BBBB. *IB:* 24.
BTEC Dip: DD. *BTEC ExtDip:* DMM. *OCR ND:* D *OCR NED:* M2

N2P5 BA Management/Journalism
Duration: 3FT Hon
Entry Requirements: *GCE:* 260-280. *SQAH:* AAA-BBBB. *IB:* 24.
BTEC Dip: DD. *BTEC ExtDip:* DMM. *OCR ND:* D *OCR NED:* M2

N5P5 BA Marketing/Journalism
Duration: 3FT Hon
Entry Requirements: *GCE:* 260-280. *SQAH:* AAA-BBBB. *IB:* 24.
BTEC Dip: DD. *BTEC ExtDip:* DMM. *OCR ND:* D *OCR NED:* M2

L2P5 BA Politics/Journalism
Duration: 3FT Hon
Entry Requirements: *GCE:* 260-280. *SQAH:* AAA-BBBB. *IB:* 24.
BTEC Dip: DD. *BTEC ExtDip:* DMM. *OCR ND:* D *OCR NED:* M2

W3P5 BA Popular Music/Journalism
Duration: 3FT Hon
Entry Requirements: *GCE:* 260-280. *SQAH:* AAA-BBBB. *IB:* 24.
BTEC Dip: DD. *BTEC ExtDip:* DMM. *OCR ND:* D *OCR NED:* M2
Interview required.

C8P5 BA Psychology/Journalism
Duration: 3FT Hon
Entry Requirements: *GCE:* 260-280. *SQAH:* AAA-BBBB. *IB:* 24.
BTEC Dip: DD. *BTEC ExtDip:* DMM. *OCR ND:* D *OCR NED:* M2

L3P5 BA Sociology/Journalism
Duration: 3FT Hon
Entry Requirements: *GCE:* 260-280. *SQAH:* AAA-BBBB. *IB:* 24.
BTEC Dip: DD. *BTEC ExtDip:* DMM. *OCR ND:* D *OCR NED:* M2

XP35 BA Special Educational Needs & Inclusion/Journalism
Duration: 3FT Hon
Entry Requirements: *GCE:* 260-280. *SQAH:* AAA-BBBB. *IB:* 24.
BTEC Dip: DD. *BTEC ExtDip:* DMM. *OCR ND:* D *OCR NED:* M2

C6P5 BA Sport Studies/Journalism
Duration: 3FT Hon
Entry Requirements: *GCE:* 260-280. *SQAH:* AAA-BBBB. *IB:* 24.
BTEC Dip: DD. *BTEC ExtDip:* DMM. *OCR ND:* D *OCR NED:* M2

N8P5 BA Tourism/Journalism
Duration: 3FT Hon
Entry Requirements: *GCE:* 260-280. *SQAH:* AAA-BBBB. *IB:* 24.
BTEC Dip: DD. *BTEC ExtDip:* DMM. *OCR ND:* D *OCR NED:* M2

C1P5 BSc Biological Conservation/Journalism
Duration: 3FT Hon
Entry Requirements: *GCE:* 260-280. *SQAH:* AAA-BBBB. *IB:* 24.
BTEC Dip: DD. *BTEC ExtDip:* DMM. *OCR ND:* D *OCR NED:* M2

G5P5 BSc Business Computing Systems/Journalism
Duration: 3FT Hon
Entry Requirements: *GCE:* 260-280. *SQAH:* AAA-BBBB. *IB:* 24.
BTEC Dip: DD. *BTEC ExtDip:* DMM. *OCR ND:* D *OCR NED:* M2

G4P5 BSc Computing/Journalism
Duration: 3FT Hon
Entry Requirements: *GCE:* 260-280. *SQAH:* AAA-BBBB. *IB:* 24.
BTEC Dip: DD. *BTEC ExtDip:* DMM. *OCR ND:* D *OCR NED:* M2

F8P5 BSc Physical Geography/Journalism
Duration: 3FT Hon
Entry Requirements: *GCE:* 260-280. *SQAH:* AAA-BBBB. *IB:* 24.
BTEC Dip: DD. *BTEC ExtDip:* DMM. *OCR ND:* D *OCR NED:* M2

F8PM BSc Wastes Management/Journalism
Duration: 3FT Hon
Entry Requirements: *GCE:* 260-280. *SQAH:* AAA-BBBB. *IB:* 24.
BTEC Dip: DD. *BTEC ExtDip:* DMM. *OCR ND:* D *OCR NED:* M2

G4PM BSc Web Design/Journalism
Duration: 3FT Hon
Entry Requirements: *GCE:* 260-280. *SQAH:* AAA-BBBB. *IB:* 24.
BTEC Dip: DD. *BTEC ExtDip:* DMM. *OCR ND:* D *OCR NED:* M2

N77 NORTHUMBRIA UNIVERSITY
TRINITY BUILDING
NORTHUMBERLAND ROAD
NEWCASTLE UPON TYNE NE1 8ST
t: 0191 243 7420 f: 0191 227 4561
e: er.admissions@northumbria.ac.uk
// www.northumbria.ac.uk

P500 BA Journalism
Duration: 3FT Hon
Entry Requirements: *GCE:* 300. *SQAH:* BBBBC. *SQAAH:* BBC. *IB:* 26.

PQ53 BA Journalism and English Literature
Duration: 3FT Hon
Entry Requirements: *GCE:* 320. *SQAH:* BBBBB. *SQAAH:* BBB. *IB:* 27.

N82 NORWICH CITY COLLEGE OF FURTHER AND HIGHER EDUCATION (AN ASSOCIATE COLLEGE OF UEA)
IPSWICH ROAD
NORWICH
NORFOLK NR2 2LJ
t: 01603 773012 f: 01603 773301
e: he_office@ccn.ac.uk
// www.ccn.ac.uk

P500 FdA Journalism
Duration: 2FT Fdg
Entry Requirements: Contact the institution for details.

N91 NOTTINGHAM TRENT UNIVERSITY
DRYDEN BUILDING
BURTON STREET
NOTTINGHAM NG1 4BU
t: +44 (0) 115 848 4200 f: +44 (0) 115 848 8869
e: applications@ntu.ac.uk
// www.ntu.ac.uk

P500 BA Broadcast Journalism
Duration: 3FT Hon
Entry Requirements: *GCE:* 300. *BTEC ExtDip:* DMM.

P501 BA Print Journalism
Duration: 3FT Hon
Entry Requirements: *GCE:* 300. *BTEC ExtDip:* DMM.

P56 UNIVERSITY CENTRE PETERBOROUGH
PARK CRESCENT
PETERBOROUGH PE1 4DZ
t: 0845 1965750 f: 01733 767986
e: UCPenquiries@anglia.ac.uk
// www.anglia.ac.uk/ucp

P500 BA Journalism
Duration: 3FT Hon
Entry Requirements: *GCE:* 120. Interview required.

P63 UCP MARJON - UNIVERSITY COLLEGE PLYMOUTH ST MARK & ST JOHN
DERRIFORD ROAD
PLYMOUTH PL6 8BH
t: 01752 636890 f: 01752 636819
e: admissions@marjon.ac.uk
// www.ucpmarjon.ac.uk

P500 BA Journalism
Duration: 3FT Hon
Entry Requirements: *GCE:* 220.

P80 UNIVERSITY OF PORTSMOUTH
ACADEMIC REGISTRY
UNIVERSITY HOUSE
WINSTON CHURCHILL AVENUE
PORTSMOUTH PO1 2UP
t: 023 9284 8484 f: 023 9284 3082
e: admissions@port.ac.uk
// www.port.ac.uk

P500 BA Journalism
Duration: 3FT Hon
Entry Requirements: *GCE:* 240-300. *BTEC Dip:* DD. *BTEC ExtDip:* DMM. Admissions Test required. Portfolio required.

P5Q3 BA Journalism with English Language
Duration: 3FT Hon
Entry Requirements: *GCE:* 240-300. *BTEC Dip:* DD. *BTEC ExtDip:* DMM.

P5QJ BA Journalism with English Literature
Duration: 3FT Hon
Entry Requirements: *GCE:* 240-300. *BTEC Dip:* DD. *BTEC ExtDip:* DMM.

R36 ROBERT GORDON UNIVERSITY
ROBERT GORDON UNIVERSITY
SCHOOLHILL
ABERDEEN
SCOTLAND AB10 1FR
t: 01224 26 27 28 f: 01224 26 21 47
e: UGOffice@rgu.ac.uk
// www.rgu.ac.uk

P500 BA Journalism
Duration: 4FT Hon
Entry Requirements: *GCE:* CCC. *SQAH:* BBCC. *IB:* 26. Interview required.

R48 ROEHAMPTON UNIVERSITY
ROEHAMPTON LANE
LONDON SW15 5PU
t: 020 8392 3232 f: 020 8392 3470
e: enquiries@roehampton.ac.uk
// www.roehampton.ac.uk

RP95 BA French and Journalism
Duration: 4FT Hon
Entry Requirements: *GCE:* 300. *IB:* 26. *BTEC ExtDip:* DDM. *OCR NED:* D2 Interview required.

P500 BA Journalism
Duration: 3FT Hon
Entry Requirements: *GCE:* 300. *IB:* 26. *BTEC ExtDip:* DDM. *OCR NED:* D2 Interview required.

PR54 BA Journalism and Spanish
Duration: 4FT Hon
Entry Requirements: *GCE:* 300. *IB:* 26. *BTEC ExtDip:* DDM. *OCR NED:* D2 Interview required.

WP65 BA Photography and Journalism
Duration: 3FT Hon
Entry Requirements: *GCE:* 300. *IB:* 26. *BTEC ExtDip:* DDM. *OCR NED:* D2 Interview required.

PP3M BA,BSc Media & Culture and Journalism
Duration: 3FT Hon
Entry Requirements: *GCE:* 300. *IB:* 26. *BTEC ExtDip:* DDM. *OCR NED:* D2 Interview required.

PW58 BA/BSc Journalism and Creative Writing
Duration: 3FT Hon
Entry Requirements: *GCE:* 300. *IB:* 26. *BTEC ExtDip:* DDM. *OCR NED:* D2 Interview required.

PM52 BA/BSc Journalism and Criminology
Duration: 3FT Hon
Entry Requirements: *GCE:* 300. *IB:* 26. *BTEC ExtDip:* DDM. *OCR NED:* D2 Interview required.

PW54 BA/BSc Journalism and Drama, Theatre & Performance Studies
Duration: 3FT Hon
Entry Requirements: *GCE:* 300. *IB:* 26. *BTEC ExtDip:* DDM. *OCR NED:* D2 Interview required.

PQ5J BA/BSc Journalism and English Language & Linguistics
Duration: 3FT Hon
Entry Requirements: *GCE:* 300. *IB:* 26. *BTEC ExtDip:* DDM. *OCR NED:* D2 Interview required.

PQM3 BA/BSc Journalism and English Literature
Duration: 3FT Hon
Entry Requirements: *GCE:* 300. *IB:* 26. *BTEC ExtDip:* DDM. *OCR NED:* D2 Interview required.

PL5H BA/BSc Journalism and Sociology
Duration: 3FT Hon
Entry Requirements: *GCE:* 300. *IB:* 26. *BTEC ExtDip:* DDM. *OCR NED:* D2 Interview required.

S03 THE UNIVERSITY OF SALFORD
SALFORD M5 4WT
t: 0161 295 4545 f: 0161 295 4646
e: ug-admissions@salford.ac.uk
// www.salford.ac.uk

PQ53 BA Journalism: Journalism and English
Duration: 3FT Hon
Entry Requirements: *GCE:* 280. *IB:* 31. *OCR NED:* M2 Interview required.

P50Y BA Journalism: Multimedia
Duration: 3FT Hon
Entry Requirements: Contact the institution for details.

P50V BA Journalism: News
Duration: 3FT Hon
Entry Requirements: Contact the institution for details.

S18 THE UNIVERSITY OF SHEFFIELD
THE UNIVERSITY OF SHEFFIELD
LEVEL 2, ARTS TOWER
WESTERN BANK
SHEFFIELD S10 2TN
t: 0114 222 8030 f: 0114 222 8032
// www.sheffield.ac.uk

P500 BA Journalism Studies
Duration: 3FT Hon
Entry Requirements: *GCE:* AAB. *SQAH:* AAABB. *SQAAH:* A. *IB:* 35. *BTEC ExtDip:* DDD.

PR51 BA Journalism and French
Duration: 4FT Hon
Entry Requirements: *GCE:* AAB. *SQAH:* AAABB. *SQAAH:* B. *IB:* 35. *BTEC ExtDip:* DDD.

PR52 BA Journalism and Germanic Studies
Duration: 4FT Hon
Entry Requirements: *GCE:* AAB. *SQAH:* AAABB. *SQAAH:* B. *IB:* 35. *BTEC ExtDip:* DDD.

PR54 BA Journalism and Hispanic Studies
Duration: 4FT Hon
Entry Requirements: *GCE:* AAB. *SQAH:* AAABB. *SQAAH:* B. *IB:* 35. *BTEC ExtDip:* DDD.

PR57 BA Journalism and Russian
Duration: 4FT Hon
Entry Requirements: *GCE:* AAB. *SQAH:* AAABB. *SQAAH:* B. *IB:* 35. *BTEC ExtDip:* DDD.

S21 SHEFFIELD HALLAM UNIVERSITY
CITY CAMPUS
HOWARD STREET
SHEFFIELD S1 1WB
t: 0114 225 5555 f: 0114 225 2167
e: admissions@shu.ac.uk
// www.shu.ac.uk

P500 BA Journalism
Duration: 3FT Hon
Entry Requirements: *GCE:* 280.

S30 SOUTHAMPTON SOLENT UNIVERSITY
EAST PARK TERRACE
SOUTHAMPTON
HAMPSHIRE SO14 0RT
t: +44 (0) 23 8031 9039 f: + 44 (0)23 8022 2259
e: admissions@solent.ac.uk
// www.solent.ac.uk/

QP35 BA English and Magazine Journalism
Duration: 3FT Hon
Entry Requirements: *Foundation:* Distinction. *GCE:* 240. *SQAAH:* AA-CCD. *IB:* 24. *BTEC ExtDip:* MMM. *OCR ND:* D *OCR NED:* M3

QP3M BA English and Magazine Journalism
Duration: 4SW Hon
Entry Requirements: *Foundation:* Distinction. *GCE:* 240. *SQAAH:* AA-CCD. *IB:* 24. *BTEC ExtDip:* MMM. *OCR ND:* D *OCR NED:* M3

P500 BA Journalism
Duration: 3FT Hon
Entry Requirements: *Foundation:* Distinction. *GCE:* 260. *SQAAH:* AA-CCC. *IB:* 24. *BTEC ExtDip:* DDM. *OCR NED:* M2 Interview required.

P501 BA Journalism
Duration: 4SW Hon
Entry Requirements: *Foundation:* Distinction. *GCE:* 260. *SQAAH:* AA-CCC. *IB:* 24. *BTEC ExtDip:* DDM. *OCR NED:* M2 Interview required.

P502 BA Journalism (Top-Up)
Duration: 1FT Hon
Entry Requirements: Interview required. HND required.

PW58 BA Magazine Journalism and Feature Writing
Duration: 3FT Hon
Entry Requirements: *Foundation:* Distinction. *GCE:* 260. *SQAAH:* AA-CCC. *IB:* 24. *BTEC ExtDip:* DDM. *OCR NED:* M2 Interview required.

P5Q3 BA Magazine Journalism and Feature Writing with International Foundation Year
Duration: 4FT Hon
Entry Requirements: *GCE:* 240. Interview required.

P593 BA Multimedia Journalism
Duration: 3FT Hon
Entry Requirements: *Foundation:* Distinction. *GCE:* 240. *SQAAH:* AA-CCD. *IB:* 24. *BTEC ExtDip:* MMM. *OCR ND:* D *OCR NED:* M3 Interview required.

P594 BA Photojournalism
Duration: 3FT Hon
Entry Requirements: Contact the institution for details.

P592 BA Popular Music Journalism
Duration: 3FT Hon
Entry Requirements: *Foundation:* Distinction. *GCE:* 240. *SQAAH:* AA-CCD. *IB:* 24. *BTEC ExtDip:* MMM. *OCR ND:* D *OCR NED:* M3 Interview required.

P590 BA Sport Journalism
Duration: 3FT Hon
Entry Requirements: *Foundation:* Distinction. *GCE:* 240. *SQAAH:* AA-CCD. *IB:* 24. *BTEC ExtDip:* MMM. *OCR ND:* D *OCR NED:* M3 Interview required.

P5QH BA Sport Journalism with International Foundation Year
Duration: 4FT Hon
Entry Requirements: *GCE:* 240. Interview required.

P509 BA Writing Fashion and Culture
Duration: 3FT Hon
Entry Requirements: *Foundation:* Distinction. *GCE:* 260. *SQAAH:* AA-CCC. *IB:* 24. *BTEC ExtDip:* DDM. *OCR NED:* M2 Interview required.

S43 SOUTH ESSEX COLLEGE OF FURTHER & HIGHER EDUCATION
LUKER ROAD
SOUTHEND-ON-SEA
ESSEX SS1 1ND
t: 0845 52 12345 f: 01702 432320
e: Admissions@southessex.ac.uk
// www.southessex.ac.uk

P500 BA Journalism
Duration: 3FT Hon
Entry Requirements: *GCE:* 160. *IB:* 24. Interview required.

S72 STAFFORDSHIRE UNIVERSITY
COLLEGE ROAD
STOKE ON TRENT ST4 2DE
t: 01782 292753 f: 01782 292740
e: admissions@staffs.ac.uk
// www.staffs.ac.uk

PL52 BA Broadcast Journalism
Duration: 3FT Hon
Entry Requirements: *GCE:* 240-300. *IB:* 24. *BTEC ExtDip:* DDM. Interview required.

WP85 BA Creative Writing and Journalism
Duration: 3FT Hon
Entry Requirements: *GCE:* 220-260. *IB:* 24.

PQ53 BA English Literature and Journalism
Duration: 3FT Hon
Entry Requirements: *GCE:* 220-260. *IB:* 24.

P500 BA Journalism
Duration: 3FT Hon
Entry Requirements: *GCE:* 240-300. *IB:* 24. Interview required.

PJ59 BA Music Journalism and Broadcasting
Duration: 3FT Hon
Entry Requirements: *GCE:* 220-260. *IB:* 24.

WP65 BA Photojournalism
Duration: 3FT/4FT Hon
Entry Requirements: *Foundation:* Merit. *GCE:* 200-240. *IB:* 24.
BTEC Dip: DD. *BTEC ExtDip:* MMM. Interview required. Portfolio
required.

P501 BA Sports Journalism
Duration: 3FT Hon
Entry Requirements: *GCE:* 240-300. *IB:* 24.

S75 THE UNIVERSITY OF STIRLING
STUDENT RECRUITMENT & ADMISSIONS SERVICE
UNIVERSITY OF STIRLING
STIRLING
SCOTLAND FK9 4LA
t: 01786 467044 f: 01786 466800
e: admissions@stir.ac.uk
// www.stir.ac.uk

**QP35 BA English Studies and Journalism
Studies**
Duration: 4FT Hon
Entry Requirements: *GCE:* BBC. *SQAH:* BBBB. *SQAAH:* AAA-CCC.
IB: 32. *BTEC ExtDip:* DMM.

RP15 BA French and Journalism Studies
Duration: 4FT Hon
Entry Requirements: *GCE:* BBC. *SQAH:* BBBB. *SQAAH:* AAA-CCC.
IB: 32. *BTEC ExtDip:* DMM.

VP15 BA History and Journalism Studies
Duration: 4FT Hon
Entry Requirements: *GCE:* BBC. *SQAH:* BBBB. *SQAAH:* AAA-CCC.
IB: 32. *BTEC ExtDip:* DMM.

P500 BA Journalism Studies
Duration: 4FT Hon
Entry Requirements: *GCE:* BBC. *SQAH:* BBBB. *SQAAH:* AAA-CCC.
IB: 32. *BTEC ExtDip:* DMM.

PL52 BA Journalism Studies and Politics
Duration: 4FT Hon
Entry Requirements: *GCE:* BBC. *SQAH:* BBBB. *SQAAH:* AAA-CCC.
IB: 32. *BTEC ExtDip:* DMM.

PR54 BA Journalism Studies and Spanish
Duration: 4FT Hon
Entry Requirements: *GCE:* BBC. *SQAH:* BBBB. *SQAAH:* AAA-CCC.
IB: 32. *BTEC ExtDip:* DMM.

**PC56 BA Journalism Studies and Sports
Studies**
Duration: 4FT Hon
Entry Requirements: *GCE:* BBC. *SQAH:* BBBB. *SQAAH:* AAA-CCC.
IB: 32. *BTEC ExtDip:* DMM.

S78 THE UNIVERSITY OF STRATHCLYDE
GLASGOW G1 1XQ
t: 0141 552 4400 f: 0141 552 0775
// www.strath.ac.uk

**QP35 BA English and Journalism & Creative
Writing**
Duration: 4FT Hon
Entry Requirements: *GCE:* ABB. *SQAH:* AAABB-AAAB. *IB:* 34.
Portfolio required.

**RP15 BA French and Journalism & Creative
Writing**
Duration: 5FT Hon
Entry Requirements: *GCE:* ABB. *SQAH:* AAABB-AAAB. *IB:* 34.
Portfolio required.

**VP15 BA History and Journalism & Creative
Writing**
Duration: 4FT Hon
Entry Requirements: *GCE:* ABB. *SQAH:* AAABB-AAAB. *IB:* 34.
Portfolio required.

**RP35 BA Italian and Journalism & Creative
Writing**
Duration: 5FT Hon
Entry Requirements: *GCE:* ABB. *SQAH:* AAABB-AAAB. *IB:* 34.
Portfolio required.

**PL51 BA Journalism & Creative Writing and
Economics**
Duration: 4FT Hon
Entry Requirements: *GCE:* ABB. *SQAH:* AAABB-AAAB. *IB:* 34.
Portfolio required.

**PN56 BA Journalism & Creative Writing and
Human Resource Management**
Duration: 4FT Hon
Entry Requirements: *GCE:* ABB. *SQAH:* AAABB-AAAB. *IB:* 34.
Portfolio required.

**PM51 BA Journalism & Creative Writing and
Law**
Duration: 4FT Hon
Entry Requirements: *GCE:* ABB. *SQAH:* AAABB-AAAB. *IB:* 34.
Portfolio required.

**PR54 BA Journalism & Creative Writing and
Spanish**
Duration: 5FT Hon
Entry Requirements: *GCE:* ABB. *SQAH:* AAABB-AAAB. *IB:* 34.
Portfolio required.

PX53 BA Journalism and Creative Writing and Education
Duration: 4FT Hon
Entry Requirements: Contact the institution for details.

LP25 BA Politics and Journalism & Creative Writing
Duration: 4FT Hon
Entry Requirements: *GCE:* ABB. *SQAH:* AAABB-AAAB. *IB:* 34. Portfolio required.

S84 UNIVERSITY OF SUNDERLAND
STUDENT HELPLINE
THE STUDENT GATEWAY
CHESTER ROAD
SUNDERLAND SR1 3SD
t: 0191 515 3000 f: 0191 515 3805
e: student.helpline@sunderland.ac.uk
// www.sunderland.ac.uk

P501 BA Broadcast Journalism
Duration: 3FT Hon
Entry Requirements: *GCE:* 260-360. *IB:* 30. Interview required.

NP15 BA Business Management and Journalism
Duration: 3FT Hon
Entry Requirements: *GCE:* 260-360. *IB:* 31. *OCR ND:* D *OCR NED:* M3

N2P5 BA Business Management with Journalism
Duration: 3FT Hon
Entry Requirements: *GCE:* 220-360. *IB:* 31. *OCR ND:* D *OCR NED:* M3

XPH5 BA Childhood Studies and Journalism
Duration: 3FT Hon
Entry Requirements: *GCE:* 260-360.

X3P5 BA Childhood Studies with Journalism
Duration: 3FT Hon
Entry Requirements: *GCE:* 260-360.

MP95 BA Criminology and Journalism
Duration: 3FT Hon
Entry Requirements: *GCE:* 260-360. *OCR ND:* D *OCR NED:* M3

M9P5 BA Criminology with Journalism
Duration: 3FT Hon
Entry Requirements: *GCE:* 260-360. *OCR ND:* D *OCR NED:* M3

PW55 BA Dance and Journalism
Duration: 3FT Hon
Entry Requirements: *GCE:* 260-360. *IB:* 31. *OCR ND:* D *OCR NED:* M3

W5P5 BA Dance with Journalism
Duration: 3FT Hon
Entry Requirements: *GCE:* 260-360. *IB:* 31. *OCR ND:* D *OCR NED:* M3

W4P5 BA Drama with Journalisim
Duration: 3FT Hon
Entry Requirements: *GCE:* 260-360. *OCR ND:* D *OCR NED:* M3

Q1P5 BA English Language & Linguistics with Journalism
Duration: 3FT Hon
Entry Requirements: *GCE:* 260-360. *OCR ND:* D *OCR NED:* M3

PQ53 BA English and Journalism
Duration: 3FT Hon
Entry Requirements: *GCE:* 260-360. *IB:* 31. *OCR ND:* D *OCR NED:* M3

Q3P5 BA English with Journalism
Duration: 3FT Hon
Entry Requirements: *GCE:* 260-360. *IB:* 31. *OCR ND:* D *OCR NED:* M3

P507 BA Fashion Journalism
Duration: 3FT Hon
Entry Requirements: *GCE:* 260-360. *IB:* 30.

L5P5 BA Health & Social Care with Journalism
Duration: 3FT Hon
Entry Requirements: *GCE:* 260-360.

PV51 BA History and Journalism
Duration: 3FT Hon
Entry Requirements: *GCE:* 260-360. *IB:* 31. *OCR ND:* D *OCR NED:* M3

V1P5 BA History with Journalism
Duration: 3FT Hon
Entry Requirements: *GCE:* 260-360. *IB:* 31. *OCR ND:* D *OCR NED:* M3

P500 BA Journalism
Duration: 3FT Hon
Entry Requirements: *GCE:* 260-360. *IB:* 30.

PW54 BA Journalism and Drama
Duration: 3FT Hon
Entry Requirements: *GCE:* 260-360. *OCR ND:* D *OCR NED:* M3

PX53 BA Journalism and Education
Duration: 3FT Hon
Entry Requirements: *GCE:* 260-360. *IB:* 32. *OCR ND:* D *OCR NED:* M3

PQ51 BA Journalism and English Language/Linguistics
Duration: 3FT Hon
Entry Requirements: *GCE:* 260-360. *IB:* 32. *OCR ND:* D *OCR NED:* M3

PW56 BA Journalism and Photography
Duration: 3FT Hon
Entry Requirements: *GCE:* 260-360. *IB:* 32. *OCR ND:* D *OCR NED:* M3

LP25 BA Journalism and Politics
Duration: 3FT Hon
Entry Requirements: *GCE:* 260-360. *IB:* 32. *OCR ND:* D *OCR NED:* M3

CP85 BA Journalism and Psychology
Duration: 3FT Hon
Entry Requirements: *GCE:* 260-360. *IB:* 32. *OCR ND:* D *OCR NED:* M3

LP35 BA Journalism and Sociology
Duration: 3FT Hon
Entry Requirements: *GCE:* 260-360. *IB:* 32. *OCR ND:* D *OCR NED:* M3

PX51 BA Journalism and TESOL
Duration: 3FT Hon
Entry Requirements: *GCE:* 260-360. *OCR ND:* D *OCR NED:* M3

P5N1 BA Journalism with Business Management
Duration: 3FT Hon
Entry Requirements: *GCE:* 260-360. *IB:* 32. *OCR ND:* D *OCR NED:* M3

P5XH BA Journalism with Childhood Studies
Duration: 3FT Hon
Entry Requirements: *GCE:* 260-360.

P5M9 BA Journalism with Criminology
Duration: 3FT Hon
Entry Requirements: *GCE:* 260-360. *IB:* 32. *OCR ND:* D *OCR NED:* M3

P5W5 BA Journalism with Dance
Duration: 3FT Hon
Entry Requirements: *GCE:* 260-360. *IB:* 31. *OCR ND:* D *OCR NED:* M3

P5W4 BA Journalism with Drama
Duration: 3FT Hon
Entry Requirements: *GCE:* 260-360. *OCR ND:* D *OCR NED:* M3

P5X3 BA Journalism with Education
Duration: 3FT Hon
Entry Requirements: *GCE:* 260-360. *IB:* 32. *OCR ND:* D *OCR NED:* M3

P5Q1 BA Journalism with English Language/Linguistics
Duration: 3FT Hon
Entry Requirements: *GCE:* 260-360. *IB:* 32. *OCR ND:* D *OCR NED:* M3

P5Q3 BA Journalism with English Studies
Duration: 3FT Hon
Entry Requirements: *GCE:* 260-360. *IB:* 32. *OCR ND:* D *OCR NED:* M3

P5L5 BA Journalism with Health & Social Care
Duration: 3FT Hon
Entry Requirements: *GCE:* 260-360.

P5V1 BA Journalism with History
Duration: 3FT Hon
Entry Requirements: *GCE:* 260-360. *IB:* 32. *OCR ND:* D *OCR NED:* M3

P5M1 BA Journalism with Law
Duration: 3FT Hon
Entry Requirements: *GCE:* 260-360. *OCR ND:* D *OCR NED:* M3

P5R1 BA Journalism with MFL (French)
Duration: 3FT Hon
Entry Requirements: *GCE:* 260-360. *OCR ND:* D *OCR NED:* M3

P5R2 BA Journalism with MFL (German)
Duration: 3FT Hon
Entry Requirements: *GCE:* 260-360. *OCR ND:* D *OCR NED:* M3

P5R4 BA Journalism with MFL (Spanish)
Duration: 3FT Hon
Entry Requirements: *GCE:* 260-360. *OCR ND:* D *OCR NED:* M3

P5W6 BA Journalism with Photography
Duration: 3FT Hon
Entry Requirements: *GCE:* 260-360. *IB:* 32. *OCR ND:* D *OCR NED:* M3

P5L2 BA Journalism with Politics
Duration: 3FT Hon
Entry Requirements: *GCE:* 260-360. *IB:* 32. *OCR ND:* D *OCR NED:* M3

P5C8 BA Journalism with Psychology
Duration: 3FT Hon
Entry Requirements: *GCE:* 260-360. *IB:* 32. *OCR ND:* D *OCR NED:* M3

P5L3 BA Journalism with Sociology
Duration: 3FT Hon
Entry Requirements: *GCE:* 260-360. *IB:* 32. *OCR ND:* D *OCR NED:* M3

P5C6 BA Journalism with Sport
Duration: 3FT Hon
Entry Requirements: *GCE:* 260-360. *OCR ND:* D *OCR NED:* M3

P5X1 BA Journalism with TESOL
Duration: 3FT Hon
Entry Requirements: *GCE:* 260-360. *OCR ND:* D *OCR NED:* M3

MP15 BA Law and Journalism
Duration: 3FT Hon
Entry Requirements: *GCE:* 260-360. *OCR ND:* D *OCR NED:* M3

P503 BA Magazine Journalism
Duration: 3FT Hon
Entry Requirements: *GCE:* 260-360. *IB:* 30.

RP15 BA Modern Foreign Languages (French) and Journalism
Duration: 3FT Hon
Entry Requirements: *GCE:* 260-360. *IB:* 31. *OCR ND:* D *OCR NED:* M3

PR52 BA Modern Foreign Languages (German) and Journalism
Duration: 3FT Hon
Entry Requirements: *GCE:* 260-360. *IB:* 31. *OCR ND:* D *OCR NED:* M3

PR54 BA Modern Foreign Languages (Spanish) and Journalism
Duration: 3FT Hon
Entry Requirements: *GCE:* 260-360. *IB:* 31. *OCR ND:* D *OCR NED:* M3

P504 BA News Journalism
Duration: 3FT Hon
Entry Requirements: *GCE:* 260-360. *IB:* 30.

L2P5 BA Politics with Journalism
Duration: 3FT Hon
Entry Requirements: *GCE:* 260-360. *IB:* 31. *OCR ND:* D *OCR NED:* M3

L3P5 BA Sociology with Journalism
Duration: 3FT Hon
Entry Requirements: *GCE:* 260-360. *IB:* 31. *OCR ND:* D *OCR NED:* M3

P505 BA Sports Journalism
Duration: 3FT Hon
Entry Requirements: *GCE:* 260-360. *IB:* 30.

X1P5 BA TESOL with Journalism
Duration: 3FT Hon
Entry Requirements: *GCE:* 260-360. *OCR ND:* D *OCR NED:* M3

NP85 BA Tourism and Journalism
Duration: 3FT Hon
Entry Requirements: *GCE:* 260-360. *IB:* 31. *OCR ND:* D *OCR NED:* M3

N8P5 BA Tourism with Journalism
Duration: 3FT Hon
Entry Requirements: *GCE:* 260-360. *IB:* 31. *OCR ND:* D *OCR NED:* M3

C8P5 BSc Psychology with Journalism
Duration: 3FT Hon
Entry Requirements: *GCE:* 260-360. *OCR ND:* D *OCR NED:* M3

CP65 BSc Sport and Journalism
Duration: 3FT Hon
Entry Requirements: *GCE:* 260-360. *OCR ND:* D *OCR NED:* M3

S96 SWANSEA METROPOLITAN UNIVERSITY
MOUNT PLEASANT CAMPUS
SWANSEA SA1 6ED
t: 01792 481000 f: 01792 481061
e: gemma.green@smu.ac.uk
// www.smu.ac.uk

W6P5 BA Photojournalism
Duration: 3FT Hon
Entry Requirements: *Foundation:* Pass. *GCE:* 200-360. *IB:* 24. Interview required. Portfolio required.

WP65 BA Photojournalism (4 Year Programme)
Duration: 4FT Hon
Entry Requirements: *Foundation:* Pass. *GCE:* 200-360. *IB:* 24. Interview required. Portfolio required.

T20 TEESSIDE UNIVERSITY
MIDDLESBROUGH TS1 3BA
t: 01642 218121 f: 01642 384201
e: registry@tees.ac.uk
// www.tees.ac.uk

P590 BA Journalism and News Practice
Duration: 1FT Hon
Entry Requirements: Contact the institution for details.

P502 BA Multimedia Journalism Professional Practice
Duration: 3FT Hon
Entry Requirements: *GCE:* 280. *IB:* 25. Interview required. Portfolio required.

P500 FdA Journalism
Duration: 2FT Fdg
Entry Requirements: *GCE:* 80-100. *IB:* 24.

U20 UNIVERSITY OF ULSTER
COLERAINE
CO. LONDONDERRY
NORTHERN IRELAND BT52 1SA
t: 028 7012 4221 f: 028 7012 4908
e: online@ulster.ac.uk
// www.ulster.ac.uk

P5N1 BA Journalism with Business
Duration: 3FT Hon
Entry Requirements: *GCE:* 280-300.

P5G4 BA Journalism with Computing
Duration: 3FT Hon
Entry Requirements: *GCE:* 280-300.

P5X3 BA Journalism with Education
Duration: 3FT Hon
Entry Requirements: *GCE:* 280-300.

P5Q3 BA Journalism with English
Duration: 3FT Hon
Entry Requirements: *GCE:* 280-300.

P5R1 BA Journalism with French
Duration: 3FT Hon
Entry Requirements: *GCE:* 280-300.

P5FV BA Journalism with Geography
Duration: 3FT Hon
Entry Requirements: *GCE:* 280-300.

P5R2 BA Journalism with German
Duration: 3FT Hon
Entry Requirements: *GCE:* 280-300.

P5V1 BA Journalism with History
Duration: 3FT Hon
Entry Requirements: *GCE:* 280-300.

P5L9 BA Journalism with International Development
Duration: 3FT Hon
Entry Requirements: *GCE:* 280-300.

P5N5 BA Journalism with Marketing
Duration: 3FT Hon
Entry Requirements: *GCE:* 280-300.

P5W6 BA Journalism with Photo Imaging
Duration: 3FT Hon
Entry Requirements: *GCE:* 280-300.

P5C8 BA Journalism with Psychology
Duration: 3FT Hon
Entry Requirements: *GCE:* 280-300.

P5R4 BA Journalism with Spanish
Duration: 3FT Hon
Entry Requirements: *GCE:* 280-300.

U40 UNIVERSITY OF THE WEST OF SCOTLAND
PAISLEY
RENFREWSHIRE
SCOTLAND PA1 2BE
t: 0141 848 3727 f: 0141 848 3623
e: admissions@uws.ac.uk
// www.uws.ac.uk

P500 BA Journalism
Duration: 3FT/4FT Ord/Hon
Entry Requirements: *GCE:* BC. *SQAH:* BBC. Interview required. Portfolio required.

P501 BA Sports Journalism
Duration: 3FT/4FT Ord/Hon
Entry Requirements: *GCE:* CC. *SQAH:* BBC. Interview required.

U65 UNIVERSITY OF THE ARTS LONDON
272 HIGH HOLBORN
LONDON WC1V 7EY
t: 020 7514 6000x6197 f: 020 7514 6198
e: c.anderson@arts.ac.uk
// www.arts.ac.uk

P507 BA Fashion Journalism (Print, Broadcast)
Duration: 3FT Hon
Entry Requirements: Interview required.

P500 BA Journalism
Duration: 3FT Hon
Entry Requirements: *GCE:* 80. *IB:* 28. Foundation Course required. Interview required. Portfolio required.

P503 BA Photojournalism
Duration: 3FT Hon
Entry Requirements: *GCE:* 80. *IB:* 28. Foundation Course required. Interview required. Portfolio required.

P506 BA Sports Journalism (Top-Up)
Duration: 1FT Hon
Entry Requirements: Contact the institution for details.

W05 THE UNIVERSITY OF WEST LONDON
ST MARY'S ROAD
EALING
LONDON W5 5RF
t: 0800 036 8888 f: 020 8566 1353
e: learning.advice@uwl.ac.uk
// www.uwl.ac.uk

P500 BA Broadcast Journalism
Duration: 3FT Hon
Entry Requirements: *GCE:* 240. Interview required.

W50 UNIVERSITY OF WESTMINSTER
2ND FLOOR, CAVENDISH HOUSE
101 NEW CAVENDISH STREET,
LONDON W1W 6XH
t: 020 7915 5511
e: course-enquiries@westminster.ac.uk
// www.westminster.ac.uk

P500 BA Journalism
Duration: 3FT Hon
Entry Requirements: *GCE:* BBB. *SQAH:* AAAAA-BBBBB. *SQAAH:* AAA-BBB. *IB:* 30. *OCR ND:* D *OCR NED:* D2 Interview required.

W75 UNIVERSITY OF WOLVERHAMPTON
ADMISSIONS UNIT
MX207, CAMP STREET
WOLVERHAMPTON
WEST MIDLANDS WV1 1AD
t: 01902 321000 f: 01902 321896
e: admissions@wlv.ac.uk
// www.wlv.ac.uk

P500 FdA Broadcast Journalism
Duration: 2FT Fdg
Entry Requirements: *GCE:* 80-140.

W76 UNIVERSITY OF WINCHESTER
WINCHESTER
HANTS SO22 4NR
t: 01962 827234 f: 01962 827288
e: course.enquiries@winchester.ac.uk
// www.winchester.ac.uk

TP7M BA American Studies and Journalism Studies
Duration: 3FT Hon
Entry Requirements: *Foundation:* Distinction. *GCE:* 260-300. *IB:* 24. *OCR ND:* D *OCR NED:* M2

VP45 BA Archaeology and Journalism Studies
Duration: 3FT Hon
Entry Requirements: *Foundation:* Distinction. *GCE:* 260-300. *IB:* 24. *OCR ND:* D *OCR NED:* M2

WP55 BA Choreography & Dance and Journalism Studies
Duration: 3FT Hon
Entry Requirements: *Foundation:* Distinction. *GCE:* 260-300. *IB:* 25. *OCR ND:* D *OCR NED:* M2

WP85 BA Creative Writing and Journalism Studies
Duration: 3FT Hon
Entry Requirements: *Foundation:* Distinction. *GCE:* 260-300. *IB:* 25. *OCR ND:* D *OCR NED:* M2

LP35 BA Criminology and Journalism Studies
Duration: 3FT Hon
Entry Requirements: *Foundation:* Distinction. *GCE:* 260-300. *IB:* 24. *OCR ND:* D *OCR NED:* M2

WP45 BA Drama and Journalism Studies
Duration: 3FT Hon
Entry Requirements: *Foundation:* Distinction. *GCE:* 260-300. *IB:* 25. *OCR ND:* D *OCR NED:* M2

XP35 BA Education Studies (Early Childhood) and Journalism Studies
Duration: 3FT Hon
Entry Requirements: *Foundation:* Distinction. *GCE:* 260-300. *IB:* 24. *OCR ND:* D *OCR NED:* M2

XPH5 BA Education Studies and Journalism Studies
Duration: 3FT Hon
Entry Requirements: *Foundation:* Distinction. *GCE:* 260-300. *IB:* 24. *OCR ND:* D *OCR NED:* M2

QP3N BA English Language Studies and Journalism Studies
Duration: 3FT Hon
Entry Requirements: *Foundation:* Distinction. *GCE:* 260-300. *IB:* 25. *OCR ND:* D *OCR NED:* M2

QP35 BA English and Journalism Studies
Duration: 3FT Hon
Entry Requirements: *Foundation:* Distinction. *GCE:* 260-300. *IB:* 25. *OCR ND:* D *OCR NED:* M2

NP85 BA Event Management and Journalism Studies
Duration: 3FT Hon
Entry Requirements: *Foundation:* Distinction. *GCE:* 260-300. *IB:* 24. *OCR ND:* D *OCR NED:* M2

WP65 BA Film & Cinema Technologies and Journalism Studies
Duration: 3FT Hon
Entry Requirements: Contact the institution for details.

LP55 BA Health, Community & Social Care Studies and Journalism Studies
Duration: 3FT Hon
Entry Requirements: Contact the institution for details.

P500 BA Journalism
Duration: 3FT Hon
Entry Requirements: *Foundation:* Distinction. *GCE:* 260-300. *IB:* 26. *OCR ND:* D Interview required.

MP15 BA Journalism Studies and Law
Duration: 3FT Hon
Entry Requirements: *Foundation:* Distinction. *GCE:* 260-300. *IB:* 25. *OCR ND:* D *OCR NED:* M2

PW5X BA Journalism Studies and Modern Liberal Arts
Duration: 3FT Hon
Entry Requirements: *Foundation:* Distinction. *GCE:* 260-300. *IB:* 25. *OCR ND:* D *OCR NED:* M2

PW54 BA Journalism Studies and Performing Arts (Contemporary Performance)
Duration: 3FT Hon
Entry Requirements: *Foundation:* Distinction. *GCE:* 260-300. *IB:* 24. *OCR ND:* D *OCR NED:* M2

LP25 BA Journalism Studies and Politics & Global Studies
Duration: 3FT Hon
Entry Requirements: *Foundation:* Distinction. *GCE:* 260-300. *IB:* 24. *OCR ND:* D

PC58 BA Journalism Studies and Psychology
Duration: 3FT Hon
Entry Requirements: *Foundation:* Distinction. *GCE:* 260-300. *IB:*
25. *OCR ND:* D *OCR NED:* M2

**PNM8 BA Journalism Studies and Sports
Management**
Duration: 3FT Hon
Entry Requirements: *Foundation:* Pass. *GCE:* 260-300. *IB:* 24.
OCR ND: D

**PCM6 BA Journalism Studies and Sports
Studies**
Duration: 3FT Hon
Entry Requirements: *Foundation:* Merit. *GCE:* 260-300. *IB:* 24.

**PV56 BA Journalism Studies and Theology &
Religious Studies**
Duration: 3FT Hon
Entry Requirements: *Foundation:* Distinction. *GCE:* 260-300. *IB:*
25. *OCR ND:* D *OCR NED:* M2

**PW5H BA Journalism Studies and Vocal &
Choral Studies**
Duration: 3FT Hon
Entry Requirements: *Foundation:* Distinction. *GCE:* 260-300. *IB:*
24. *OCR ND:* D *OCR NED:* M2

W80 UNIVERSITY OF WORCESTER
HENWICK GROVE
WORCESTER WR2 6AJ
t: 01905 855111 f: 01905 855377
e: admissions@worc.ac.uk
// www.worcester.ac.uk

**GP45 BA Creative Digital Media and
Journalism**
Duration: 3FT Hon
Entry Requirements: *GCE:* 240-260. *IB:* 24. *OCR ND:* D Interview
required. Portfolio required.

**PQ53 BA English Language Studies and
Journalism**
Duration: 3FT Hon
Entry Requirements: *GCE:* 240-260. *IB:* 24. *OCR ND:* D *OCR
NED:* M3

P500 BA Journalism
Duration: 3FT Hon
Entry Requirements: *GCE:* 280-300. *IB:* 25. *OCR ND:* D *OCR
NED:* M3

**PP53 BA Journalism and Media & Cultural
Studies**
Duration: 3FT Hon
Entry Requirements: *GCE:* 240-300. *IB:* 24. *OCR ND:* D *OCR
NED:* M3

**PL52 BA Journalism and Politics: People and
Power**
Duration: 3FT Hon
Entry Requirements: *GCE:* 240-300. *IB:* 24. *OCR ND:* D *OCR
NED:* M3

**PCM6 BA/BSc Journalism and Sports
Coaching Science**
Duration: 3FT Hon CRB Check: Required
Entry Requirements: Contact the institution for details.

PC5P BA/BSc Journalism and Sports Studies
Duration: 3FT Hon
Entry Requirements: *GCE:* 240-300. *IB:* 24. *OCR ND:* D Interview
required. Portfolio required.

MUSIC

A20 THE UNIVERSITY OF ABERDEEN
UNIVERSITY OFFICE
KING'S COLLEGE
ABERDEEN AB24 3FX
t: +44 (0) 1224 273504 f: +44 (0) 1224 272034
e: sras@abdn.ac.uk
// www.abdn.ac.uk/sras

W300 BMus Music
Duration: 4FT Hon
Entry Requirements: *SQAH:* BBB. *SQAAH:* B. *IB:* 30. Interview
required.

XW13 BMus Music Education
Duration: 4FT Hon CRB Check: Required
Entry Requirements: *SQAH:* BBB. *SQAAH:* B. *IB:* 30. Interview
required.

W390 BMus Music and Communities
Duration: 4FT Hon
Entry Requirements: *SQAH:* BBB. *SQAAH:* B. *IB:* 30. Interview
required.

M1W3 LLB Law with options in Music
Duration: 4FT Hon
Entry Requirements: *GCE:* BBB. *SQAH:* AABB-ABBBB. *SQAAH:*
BBB. *IB:* 34.

V6W3 MA Divinity with Music Studies
Duration: 4FT Hon
Entry Requirements: *GCE:* BBB. *SQAH:* BBBB. *IB:* 30.

Q3W3 MA English with Music Studies
Duration: 4FT Hon
Entry Requirements: *GCE:* BBB. *SQAH:* BBBB. *IB:* 30.

R1W3 MA French with Music Studies
Duration: 5FT Hon
Entry Requirements: *GCE:* BBB. *SQAH:* BBBB. *IB:* 30.

R1WH MA French with Music Studies
Duration: 4FT Hon
Entry Requirements: *GCE:* BBB. *SQAH:* BBBB. *IB:* 30.

R2W3 MA German with Music Studies
Duration: 5FT Hon
Entry Requirements: *GCE:* BBB. *SQAH:* BBBB. *IB:* 30.

R2WH MA German with Music Studies
Duration: 4FT Hon
Entry Requirements: *GCE:* BBB. *SQAH:* BBBB. *IB:* 30.

R4W3 MA Hispanic Studies with Music Studies
Duration: 5FT Hon
Entry Requirements: *GCE:* BBB. *SQAH:* BBBB. *IB:* 30.

R4WH MA Hispanic Studies with Music Studies
Duration: 4FT Hon
Entry Requirements: *GCE:* BBB. *SQAH:* BBBB. *IB:* 30.

V3W3 MA History of Art with Music Studies
Duration: 4FT Hon
Entry Requirements: *GCE:* BBB. *SQAH:* BBBB. *IB:* 30.

V1W3 MA History with Music Studies
Duration: 4FT Hon
Entry Requirements: *GCE:* BBB. *SQAH:* BBBB. *IB:* 30.

V5W3 MA Philosophy with Music Studies
Duration: 4FT Hon
Entry Requirements: *GCE:* BBB. *SQAH:* BBBB. *IB:* 30.

V6WH MA Religious Studies with Music Studies
Duration: 4FT Hon
Entry Requirements: *GCE:* BBB. *SQAH:* BBBB. *IB:* 30.

A30 UNIVERSITY OF ABERTAY DUNDEE
BELL STREET
DUNDEE DD1 1HG
t: 01382 308080 f: 01382 308081
e: sro@abertay.ac.uk
// www.abertay.ac.uk

JG94 BA Creative Sound Production (Top-Up)
Duration: 2FT Hon
Entry Requirements: Interview required. HND required.

A44 ACCRINGTON & ROSSENDALE COLLEGE
BROAD OAK ROAD,
ACCRINGTON,
LANCASHIRE, BB5 2AW.
t: 01254 389933 f: 01254 354001
e: info@accross.ac.uk
// www.accrosshighereducation.co.uk/

J930 FdA Music Production
Duration: 2FT Fdg
Entry Requirements: Interview required.

A60 ANGLIA RUSKIN UNIVERSITY
BISHOP HALL LANE
CHELMSFORD
ESSEX CM1 1SQ
t: 0845 271 3333 f: 01245 251789
e: answers@anglia.ac.uk
// www.anglia.ac.uk

WJ39 BA Creative Music Technology
Duration: 3FT Hon
Entry Requirements: *GCE:* 220-260. *SQAH:* BBCC. *SQAAH:* BB. *IB:* 26.

W300 BA Music
Duration: 3FT Hon
Entry Requirements: *GCE:* 220-260. *SQAH:* BBCC. *SQAAH:* BB. *IB:* 26.

W34C BA (Hons) Popular Music
Duration: 3FT Hon
Entry Requirements: *GCE:* 220-260. Interview required.

B06 BANGOR UNIVERSITY
BANGOR UNIVERSITY
BANGOR
GWYNEDD LL57 2DG
t: 01248 388484 f: 01248 370451
e: admissions@bangor.ac.uk
// www.bangor.ac.uk

QW5H BA Cymraeg Creadigol gyda Cherddoriaeth Boblogaidd
Duration: 3FT Hon
Entry Requirements: *GCE:* 260-300. *IB:* 28.

QW53 BA Cymraeg/Music
Duration: 3FT Hon
Entry Requirements: *GCE:* 260-300. *IB:* 28.

QW33 BA English and Music
Duration: 3FT Hon
Entry Requirements: *GCE:* 260-300. *IB:* 28.

Q3W8 BA English with Songwriting
Duration: 3FT Hon
Entry Requirements: *GCE:* 240-300. *IB:* 28.

VW23 BA Hanes Cymru a Cherddoriaeth
Duration: 3FT Hon
Entry Requirements: *GCE:* 260-300. *IB:* 28.

VW13 BA History and Music
Duration: 3FT Hon
Entry Requirements: *GCE:* 260-300. *IB:* 28.

WQ35 BA Llenyddiaeth Gymraeg a Llenyddiaeth y Cyfryngau a Cherdd
Duration: 3FT Hon
Entry Requirements: *GCE:* 260-300. *IB:* 28.

W300 BA Music
Duration: 3FT Hon
Entry Requirements: *GCE:* 260-300. *IB:* 28.

JH9P BA Music Technology and Electronics
Duration: 3FT Hon
Entry Requirements: *GCE:* 280. *IB:* 28.

WW38 BA Music and Creative Writing
Duration: 3FT Hon
Entry Requirements: *GCE:* 260-300. *IB:* 28.

WW36 BA Music and Film Studies
Duration: 3FT Hon
Entry Requirements: *GCE:* 260-300. *IB:* 28.

WV32 BA Music and History & Welsh History
Duration: 3FT Hon
Entry Requirements: *GCE:* 260-300. *IB:* 28.

RW13 BA Music/French
Duration: 4FT Hon
Entry Requirements: *GCE:* 260-300. *IB:* 28.

WR32 BA Music/German
Duration: 4FT Hon
Entry Requirements: *GCE:* 260-300. *IB:* 28.

WR33 BA Music/Italian
Duration: 4FT Hon
Entry Requirements: *GCE:* 260-300. *IB:* 28.

WR34 BA Music/Spanish
Duration: 4FT Hon
Entry Requirements: *GCE:* 260-300. *IB:* 28.

VW2H BA Welsh History and Music
Duration: 3FT Hon
Entry Requirements: *GCE:* 260-300. *IB:* 28.

W302 BMus Music
Duration: 3FT Hon
Entry Requirements: *GCE:* 260-300. *IB:* 28.

JH96 BSc Music Technology and Electronics
Duration: 3FT Hon
Entry Requirements: *GCE:* 280. *IB:* 28.

B20 BATH SPA UNIVERSITY
NEWTON PARK
NEWTON ST LOE
BATH BA2 9BN
t: 01225 875875 f: 01225 875444
e: enquiries@bathspa.ac.uk
// www.bathspa.ac.uk/clearing

WW13 BA Art/Music
Duration: 3FT Hon
Entry Requirements: *Foundation:* Pass. *GCE:* 220-280. *IB:* 24.
Interview required.

NW13 BA Business & Management/Music
Duration: 3FT Hon
Entry Requirements: *GCE:* 220-280. *IB:* 24. Interview required.

WW2H BA Ceramics/Music
Duration: 3FT Hon
Entry Requirements: *Foundation:* Pass. *GCE:* 220-280. *IB:* 24.
Interview required.

W304 BA Commercial Music
Duration: 3FT Hon
Entry Requirements: *GCE:* 220-280. *IB:* 24. Interview required.

J931 BA Creative Music Technology
Duration: 3FT Hon
Entry Requirements: *GCE:* 220-280. *IB:* 24. Interview required.
Portfolio required.

WW93 BA Creative Writing/Music
Duration: 3FT Hon
Entry Requirements: *GCE:* 220-280. *IB:* 24. Interview required.

WW53 BA Dance/Music
Duration: 3FT Hon
Entry Requirements: *GCE:* 220-280. *IB:* 24. Interview required.

WW3K BA Drama Studies/Music
Duration: 3FT Hon
Entry Requirements: *GCE:* 220-280. *IB:* 24. Interview required.

XW13 BA Education/Music
Duration: 3FT Hon   CRB Check: Required
Entry Requirements: *GCE:* 220-280. *IB:* 24. Interview required.

XW33 BA Education/Music
Duration: 3FT Hon   CRB Check: Required
Entry Requirements: *GCE:* 220-280. *IB:* 24. Interview required.

QW33 BA English Literature/Music
Duration: 3FT Hon
Entry Requirements: *GCE:* 220-280. *IB:* 24. Interview required.

VW13 BA History/Music
Duration: 3FT Hon
Entry Requirements: *GCE:* 220-280. *IB:* 24. Interview required.

W300 BA Music
Duration: 3FT Hon
Entry Requirements: *GCE:* 220-280. *IB:* 24. Interview required.

WV36 BA Music/Study of Religions
Duration: 3FT Hon
Entry Requirements: *GCE:* 220-280. *IB:* 24. Interview required.

WWH2 BA Music/Textile Design Studies
Duration: 3FT Hon
Entry Requirements: *GCE:* 220-280. *IB:* 24. Interview required.
Portfolio required.

WW32 BA Music/Visual Design
Duration: 3FT Hon
Entry Requirements: *Foundation:* Pass. *GCE:* 220-280. *IB:* 24.
Interview required.

WW3L BA Musical Theatre
Duration: 1FT Hon
Entry Requirements: Interview required.

CW13 BA/BSc Biology/Music
Duration: 3FT Hon
Entry Requirements: *GCE:* 220-280. *IB:* 24. Interview required.

WW63 BA/BSc Film & Screen Studies/Music
Duration: 3FT Hon
Entry Requirements: *GCE:* 220-280. *IB:* 24. Interview required.

DW63 BA/BSc Food & Nutrition/Music
Duration: 3FT Hon
Entry Requirements: *GCE:* 220-280. *IB:* 24.

FW83 BA/BSc Geography/Music
Duration: 3FT Hon
Entry Requirements: *GCE:* 220-280. *IB:* 24. Interview required.

LW43 BA/BSc Health Studies/Music
Duration: 3FT Hon
Entry Requirements: *GCE:* 220-280. *IB:* 24. Interview required.

WV3M BA/BSc Music/Philosophy & Ethics
Duration: 3FT Hon
Entry Requirements: *GCE:* 220-280. *IB:* 24. Interview required.

WC38 BA/BSc Music/Psychology
Duration: 3FT Hon
Entry Requirements: *GCE:* 220-280. *IB:* 24. Interview required.

WL33 BA/BSc Music/Sociology
Duration: 3FT Hon
Entry Requirements: *GCE:* 220-280. *IB:* 24. Interview required.

CW83 DipHE Music/Psychology
Duration: 2FT Dip
Entry Requirements: *GCE:* 220-280. *IB:* 24.

VW63 DipHE Music/Study of Religions
Duration: 2FT Dip
Entry Requirements: *GCE:* 220-280. *IB:* 24.

WW34 FdA Musical Theatre
Duration: 2FT Fdg
Entry Requirements: *GCE:* 220-280. *IB:* 24. Interview required.

J930 FdMus Music Production
Duration: 2FT Fdg
Entry Requirements: *GCE:* 220-280. *IB:* 24. Interview required.

W340 FdMus Popular Music
Duration: 2FT Fdg
Entry Requirements: *GCE:* 220-280. *IB:* 24. Interview required.
Portfolio required.

W310 FdMus Professional Musicianship
Duration: 2FT Fdg
Entry Requirements: *GCE:* 220-280. *IB:* 24. Interview required.

B22 UNIVERSITY OF BEDFORDSHIRE
PARK SQUARE
LUTON
BEDS LU1 3JU
t: 0844 8482234 f: 01582 489323
e: admissions@beds.ac.uk
// www.beds.ac.uk

W370 BSc Music Technology
Duration: 3FT Hon
Entry Requirements: Contact the institution for details.

B25 BIRMINGHAM CITY UNIVERSITY
PERRY BARR
BIRMINGHAM B42 2SU
t: 0121 331 5595 f: 0121 331 7994
// www.bcu.ac.uk

W350 BSc Music Technology
Duration: 3FT/4SW Hon
Entry Requirements: *GCE:* 300. *IB:* 30.

143W HND Popular Music Practice
Duration: 2FT HND
Entry Requirements: *GCE:* 80. *SQAH:* CCC. Interview required.

B32 THE UNIVERSITY OF BIRMINGHAM
EDGBASTON
BIRMINGHAM B15 2TT
t: 0121 415 8900 f: 0121 414 7159
e: admissions@bham.ac.uk
// www.birmingham.ac.uk

QW83 BA Classical Literature & Civilisation and Music
Duration: 3FT Hon
Entry Requirements: *GCE:* ABB. *SQAH:* AAAAA-ABBBB. *SQAAH:* AB. *IB:* 34.

WW34 BA Drama and Music
Duration: 3FT Hon
Entry Requirements: *GCE:* AAB. *SQAH:* AABBB. *SQAAH:* AA. *IB:* 36.

QW33 BA English Language and Music
Duration: 3FT Hon
Entry Requirements: *GCE:* AAB. *SQAH:* AABBB. *SQAAH:* AA. *IB:* 36.

QW3H BA English Literature and Music
Duration: 3FT Hon
Entry Requirements: *GCE:* AAB. *SQAH:* AABBB. *SQAAH:* AA. *IB:* 36.

RW13 BA French Studies and Music (4 years)
Duration: 4FT Hon
Entry Requirements: *GCE:* ABB. *SQAH:* ABBBB. *SQAAH:* AB. *IB:* 32.

RW23 BA German Studies and Music (4 years)
Duration: 4FT Hon
Entry Requirements: *GCE:* ABB. *SQAH:* ABBBB. *SQAAH:* AB. *IB:* 32.

RW43 BA Hispanic Studies and Music (4 years)
Duration: 4FT Hon
Entry Requirements: *GCE:* ABB. *SQAH:* AABBB. *SQAAH:* AB. *IB:* 34.

VW13 BA History and Music
Duration: 3FT Hon
Entry Requirements: *GCE:* AAB. *SQAH:* AABBB. *SQAAH:* AB.

RW33 BA Italian Studies and Music (4 years)
Duration: 4FT Hon
Entry Requirements: *GCE:* ABB. *SQAH:* ABBBB. *SQAAH:* AB. *IB:*
34.

GW13 BA Mathematics and Music
Duration: 3FT Hon
Entry Requirements: *GCE:* AAB. *SQAH:* AAAAA-AABBB. *SQAAH:*
AA-AB. *IB:* 34.

R9W3 BA Modern Languages with Music (4 years)
Duration: 4FT Hon
Entry Requirements: *GCE:* ABB. *SQAH:* AAABB. *SQAAH:* AB. *IB:*
32.

RW73 BA Music and Russian Studies (4 years)
Duration: 4FT Hon
Entry Requirements: *GCE:* ABB. *SQAH:* ABBBB. *SQAAH:* AB. *IB:*
34.

VW63 BA Music and Theology
Duration: 3FT Hon
Entry Requirements: *GCE:* ABB. *SQAH:* AABBB. *SQAAH:* AB. *IB:*
34.

W302 BMus Music
Duration: 3FT Hon
Entry Requirements: *GCE:* AAA-AAB. *SQAH:* AAABB-AABBB.
SQAAH: AA.

B38 BISHOP GROSSETESTE UNIVERSITY COLLEGE LINCOLN
BISHOP GROSSETESTE UNIVERSITY COLLEGE
LINCOLN LN1 3DY
t: 01522 583658 f: 01522 530243
e: admissions@bishopg.ac.uk
// www.bishopg.ac.uk/courses

WW43 BA Applied Drama and Music
Duration: 3FT Hon CRB Check: Required
Entry Requirements: Contact the institution for details.

W4W3 BA Applied Drama with Music
Duration: 3FT Hon CRB Check: Required
Entry Requirements: Contact the institution for details.

XW33 BA Early Childhood Studies and Music
Duration: 3FT Hon CRB Check: Required
Entry Requirements: *GCE:* 220. *IB:* 24.

X3W3 BA Early Childhood Studies with Music
Duration: 3FT Hon CRB Check: Required
Entry Requirements: *GCE:* 220. *IB:* 24.

X1W3 BA Education Studies and Music
Duration: 3FT Hon CRB Check: Required
Entry Requirements: *GCE:* 220.

X3WC BA Education Studies with Music
Duration: 3FT Hon CRB Check: Required
Entry Requirements: Contact the institution for details.

QW33 BA English and Music
Duration: 3FT Hon CRB Check: Required
Entry Requirements: Contact the institution for details.

Q3W3 BA English with Music
Duration: 3FT Hon CRB Check: Required
Entry Requirements: Contact the institution for details.

VW13 BA History and Music
Duration: 3FT Hon CRB Check: Required
Entry Requirements: Contact the institution for details.

XW3H BA Special Educational Needs & Inclusion and Music
Duration: 3FT Hon CRB Check: Required
Entry Requirements: Contact the institution for details.

B41 BLACKPOOL AND THE FYLDE COLLEGE AN ASSOCIATE COLLEGE OF LANCASTER UNIVERSITY
ASHFIELD ROAD
BISPHAM
BLACKPOOL
LANCS FY2 0HB
t: 01253 504346 f: 01253 504198
e: admissions@blackpool.ac.uk
// www.blackpool.ac.uk

WW34 BA Musical Theatre
Duration: 3FT Hon
Entry Requirements: *Foundation:* Merit. *GCE:* 220. *IB:* 24.
Interview required.

B44 UNIVERSITY OF BOLTON
DEANE ROAD
BOLTON BL3 5AB
t: 01204 903903 f: 01204 399074
e: enquiries@bolton.ac.uk
// www.bolton.ac.uk

WN35 BSc Music & Creative Industries Business
Duration: 3FT Hon
Entry Requirements: *GCE:* 260. Interview required.

WN36 FdSc Music & Creative Industries Business
Duration: 2FT Fdg
Entry Requirements: *GCE:* 160. Interview required. Portfolio
required.

B50 BOURNEMOUTH UNIVERSITY
TALBOT CAMPUS
FERN BARROW
POOLE
DORSET BH12 5BB
t: 01202 524111
// www.bournemouth.ac.uk

WW34 FdA Performing Arts: Music Theatre
Duration: 2FT Fdg
Entry Requirements: *GCE:* 120. *IB:* 24. Interview required.

W340 FdA Popular Music
Duration: 2FT Fdg
Entry Requirements: *GCE:* 120. *IB:* 24. Interview required.

B60 BRADFORD COLLEGE: AN ASSOCIATE COLLEGE OF LEEDS METROPOLITAN UNIVERSITY
GREAT HORTON ROAD
BRADFORD
WEST YORKSHIRE BD7 1AY
t: 01274 433008 f: 01274 431652
e: heregistry@bradfordcollege.ac.uk
// www.bradfordcollege.ac.uk/university-centre

W300 HND Music
Duration: 2FT HND
Entry Requirements: Contact the institution for details.

B72 UNIVERSITY OF BRIGHTON
MITHRAS HOUSE 211
LEWES ROAD
BRIGHTON BN2 4AT
t: 01273 644644 f: 01273 642607
e: admissions@brighton.ac.uk
// www.brighton.ac.uk

WJ39 BA Creative Music Production (Top-Up)
Duration: 1FT Hon
Entry Requirements: Interview required. Portfolio required. HND required.

W390 BA Digital Music and Sound Arts
Duration: 3FT Hon
Entry Requirements: *GCE:* BBC. Interview required. Portfolio required.

W301 BA Music Production and Creative Recording (Top-Up)
Duration: 1FT Hon
Entry Requirements: Interview required. Portfolio required. HND required.

WW31 BA Music and Visual Art
Duration: 3FT Hon
Entry Requirements: *GCE:* BBC. Foundation Course required. Interview required. Portfolio required.

W391 MFA Digital Music and Sound Arts
Duration: 4FT Hon
Entry Requirements: *GCE:* BBC. Interview required. Portfolio required.

B78 UNIVERSITY OF BRISTOL
UNDERGRADUATE ADMISSIONS OFFICE
SENATE HOUSE
TYNDALL AVENUE
BRISTOL BS8 1TH
t: 0117 928 9000 f: 0117 331 7391
e: ug-admissions@bristol.ac.uk
// www.bristol.ac.uk

W300 BA Music
Duration: 3FT Hon
Entry Requirements: *GCE:* ABB. *SQAH:* AABBB. *SQAAH:* BB. *IB:* 33.

WR31 BA Music and French (4 years)
Duration: 4FT Hon
Entry Requirements: *GCE:* ABB. *SQAH:* AABBB. *SQAAH:* AB. *IB:* 33.

WR32 BA Music and German (4 years)
Duration: 4FT Hon
Entry Requirements: *GCE:* ABB. *SQAH:* AABBB. *SQAAH:* AB. *IB:* 33.

WR33 BA Music and Italian (4 years)
Duration: 4FT Hon
Entry Requirements: *GCE:* ABB. *SQAH:* AABBB. *SQAAH:* AB. *IB:* 33.

B79 BRISTOL FILTON COLLEGE
FILTON AVENUE
BRISTOL BS34 7AT
t: 0117 909 2255 f: 0117 931 2233
e: info@filton.ac.uk
// www.filton.ac.uk

43WW HND Performing Arts (Acting and Theatre Making)
Duration: 2FT HND
Entry Requirements: Interview required. Portfolio required.

34WW HND Performing Arts (Musical Theatre)
Duration: 2FT HND
Entry Requirements: Contact the institution for details.

B80 UNIVERSITY OF THE WEST OF ENGLAND, BRISTOL
FRENCHAY CAMPUS
COLDHARBOUR LANE
BRISTOL BS16 1QY
t: +44 (0)117 32 83333 f: +44 (0)117 32 82810
e: admissions@uwe.ac.uk
// www.uwe.ac.uk

WJ39 BSc Creative Music Technology
Duration: 3FT/4SW Hon
Entry Requirements: *GCE:* 300. Interview required.

B84 BRUNEL UNIVERSITY
UXBRIDGE
MIDDLESEX UB8 3PH
t: 01895 265265 f: 01895 269790
e: admissions@brunel.ac.uk
// www.brunel.ac.uk

WW2H BA Games Design and Sonic Arts
Duration: 3FT Hon
Entry Requirements: *GCE:* BBB. *SQAAH:* BBB. *IB:* 32. *BTEC ExtDip:* DDM. Admissions Test required.

W300 BA Music
Duration: 3FT Hon
Entry Requirements: *GCE:* BBB. *SQAAH:* BBB. *IB:* 32. *BTEC ExtDip:* DDM. Admissions Test required.

WJ39 BA Sonic Arts
Duration: 3FT Hon
Entry Requirements: *GCE:* BBB. *SQAAH:* BBB. *IB:* 32. *BTEC ExtDip:* DDM. Admissions Test required.

W302 BMus Musical Composition
Duration: 3FT Hon
Entry Requirements: *GCE:* BBB. *SQAAH:* BBB. *IB:* 32. *BTEC ExtDip:* DDM. Admissions Test required.

W312 BMus Musical Performance
Duration: 3FT Hon
Entry Requirements: *GCE:* BBB. *SQAAH:* BBB. *IB:* 32. *BTEC ExtDip:* DDM. Admissions Test required.

B92 BROOKSBY MELTON COLLEGE
MELTON CAMPUS
ASFORDBY ROAD
MELTON MOWBRAY
LEICESTERSHIRE LE13 0HJ
t: 01664 850850 f: 01664 855355
e: heenquiries@brooksbymelton.ac.uk
// www.brooksbymelton.ac.uk

W345 BA Performing Arts
Duration: 3FT Hon
Entry Requirements: Contact the institution for details.

W310 HND Contemporary Performance
Duration: 2FT HND
Entry Requirements: *GCE:* 160.

B94 BUCKINGHAMSHIRE NEW UNIVERSITY
QUEEN ALEXANDRA ROAD
HIGH WYCOMBE
BUCKINGHAMSHIRE HP11 2JZ
t: 0800 0565 660 f: 01494 605 023
e: admissions@bucks.ac.uk
// bucks.ac.uk

NW23 BA Music Management and Artist Development
Duration: 3FT Hon
Entry Requirements: *GCE:* 200-240. *IB:* 24. *OCR ND:* M1 *OCR NED:* M3

WW43 BA Musical Theatre (Top-Up)
Duration: 1FT Hon
Entry Requirements: Interview required. HND required.

W391 FdA Commercial Music Performance & Production
Duration: 2FT Fdg
Entry Requirements: *GCE:* 100-140. *IB:* 24. *OCR ND:* P2 *OCR NED:* P3 Interview required.

WW4H FdA Musical Theatre
Duration: 2FT Fdg
Entry Requirements: *GCE:* 100-140. *IB:* 24. *OCR ND:* P2 *OCR NED:* P3 Interview required.

C05 UNIVERSITY OF CAMBRIDGE
CAMBRIDGE ADMISSIONS OFFICE
FITZWILLIAM HOUSE
32 TRUMPINGTON STREET
CAMBRIDGE CB2 1QY
t: 01223 333 308 f: 01223 746 868
e: admissions@cam.ac.uk
// www.study.cam.ac.uk/undergraduate/

X3W3 BA Education with Music
Duration: 3FT Hon
Entry Requirements: *GCE:* A*AA. *SQAAH:* AAA-AAB. Interview required.

W300 BA Music
Duration: 3FT Hon
Entry Requirements: *GCE:* A*AA. *SQAAH:* AAA-AAB. Interview required.

C10 CANTERBURY CHRIST CHURCH
UNIVERSITY
NORTH HOLMES ROAD
CANTERBURY
KENT CT1 1QU
t: 01227 782900 f: 01227 782888
e: admissions@canterbury.ac.uk
// www.canterbury.ac.uk

GW53 BA Business Computing and Music
Duration: 3FT Hon
Entry Requirements: *GCE:* 240. *IB:* 24.

G5WH BA Business Computing with Music
Duration: 3FT Hon
Entry Requirements: *GCE:* 240. *IB:* 24.

W340 BA Commercial Music
Duration: 3FT Hon
Entry Requirements: *GCE:* 200. *IB:* 24. Interview required.

W341 BA Commercial Music 'International only'
Duration: 4FT Hon
Entry Requirements: Interview required.

QW33 BA English Language & Communication and Music
Duration: 3FT Hon
Entry Requirements: *GCE:* 240. *IB:* 24. Interview required.

Q3WH BA English Language & Communication with Music
Duration: 3FT Hon
Entry Requirements: *GCE:* 240. *IB:* 24. Interview required.

BW93 BA Health Studies and Music
Duration: 3FT Hon
Entry Requirements: *GCE:* 240. *IB:* 24.

GW4J BA Internet Computing and Music
Duration: 3FT Hon
Entry Requirements: *GCE:* 240. *IB:* 24.

W3GM BA Music with Business Computing
Duration: 3FT Hon
Entry Requirements: *GCE:* 240. *IB:* 24.

W3QH BA Music with English Language & Communication
Duration: 3FT Hon
Entry Requirements: *GCE:* 240. *IB:* 24.

W3W1 BA Music with Fine & Applied Arts
Duration: 3FT Hon
Entry Requirements: *GCE:* 240. *IB:* 24.

W3B9 BA Music with Health Studies
Duration: 3FT Hon
Entry Requirements: *GCE:* 240. *IB:* 24.

W3GL BA Music with Internet Computing
Duration: 3FT Hon
Entry Requirements: *GCE:* 240. *IB:* 24.

W310 BA Performing Arts (Vocal Studies)
Duration: 3FT Hon
Entry Requirements: *GCE:* 200. *IB:* 24. Interview required.

WN31 BA/BSc Business Studies and Music
Duration: 3FT Hon
Entry Requirements: *GCE:* 240. *IB:* 24. Interview required.

WG35 BA/BSc Computing and Music
Duration: 3FT Hon
Entry Requirements: *GCE:* 240. *IB:* 24.

XW3H BA/BSc Education Studies and Music
Duration: 3FT Hon   CRB Check: Required
Entry Requirements: *GCE:* 240. *IB:* 24. Interview required.

X3WH BA/BSc Education Studies with Music
Duration: 3FT Hon   CRB Check: Required
Entry Requirements: *GCE:* 240. *IB:* 24.

WQ33 BA/BSc English Literature and Music
Duration: 3FT Hon
Entry Requirements: *GCE:* 240. *IB:* 24. Interview required.

Q3W3 BA/BSc English Literature with Music
Duration: 3FT Hon
Entry Requirements: *GCE:* 240. *IB:* 24. Interview required.

W6W3 BA/BSc Film, Radio & Television Studies with Music
Duration: 3FT Hon
Entry Requirements: *GCE:* 240. *IB:* 24. Interview required.

WW13 BA/BSc Fine & Applied Arts and Music
Duration: 3FT Hon
Entry Requirements: *GCE:* 240. *IB:* 24.

W1W3 BA/BSc Fine & Applied Arts with Music
Duration: 3FT Hon
Entry Requirements: *GCE:* 240. *IB:* 24. Interview required.

RW13 BA/BSc French and Music
Duration: 3FT Hon
Entry Requirements: *GCE:* 240. *IB:* 24.

R1W3 BA/BSc French with Music
Duration: 3FT Hon
Entry Requirements: Contact the institution for details.

B9W3 BA/BSc Health Studies with Music
Duration: 3FT Hon
Entry Requirements: *GCE:* 240. *IB:* 24.

VW13 BA/BSc History and Music
Duration: 3FT Hon
Entry Requirements: *GCE:* 240. *IB:* 24. Interview required.

MW23 BA/BSc Legal Studies and Music
Duration: 3FT Hon
Entry Requirements: *GCE:* 240. *IB:* 24. Interview required.

M2W3 BA/BSc Legal Studies with Music
Duration: 3FT Hon
Entry Requirements: *GCE:* 240. *IB:* 24.

GWK3 BA/BSc Multimedia Design and Music Production
Duration: 3FT Hon
Entry Requirements: *GCE:* 240. *IB:* 24.

WW63 BA/BSc Music and Film, Radio & Television Studies
Duration: 3FT Hon
Entry Requirements: *GCE:* 240. *IB:* 24.

CW83 BA/BSc Music and Psychology
Duration: 3FT Hon
Entry Requirements: *GCE:* 260. *IB:* 24.

VW63 BA/BSc Music and Religious Studies
Duration: 3FT Hon
Entry Requirements: *GCE:* 240. *IB:* 24. Interview required.

LW33 BA/BSc Music and Sociology & Social Science
Duration: 3FT Hon
Entry Requirements: *GCE:* 240. *IB:* 24.

NW83 BA/BSc Music and Tourism & Leisure Studies
Duration: 3FT Hon
Entry Requirements: *GCE:* 240. *IB:* 24.

W3C1 BA/BSc Music with Biosciences
Duration: 3FT Hon
Entry Requirements: *GCE:* 240. *IB:* 24.

W3N1 BA/BSc Music with Business Studies
Duration: 3FT Hon
Entry Requirements: *GCE:* 240. *IB:* 24.

W3G5 BA/BSc Music with Computing
Duration: 3FT Hon
Entry Requirements: *GCE:* 240. *IB:* 24.

W3XJ BA/BSc Music with Education Studies
Duration: 3FT Hon   CRB Check: Required
Entry Requirements: *GCE:* 240. *IB:* 24.

W3Q3 BA/BSc Music with English Literature
Duration: 3FT Hon
Entry Requirements: *GCE:* 240. *IB:* 24.

W3W6 BA/BSc Music with Film, Radio & Television Studies
Duration: 3FT Hon
Entry Requirements: *GCE:* 240. *IB:* 24.

W3R1 BA/BSc Music with French
Duration: 3FT Hon
Entry Requirements: *GCE:* 240. *IB:* 24.

W3V1 BA/BSc Music with History
Duration: 3FT Hon
Entry Requirements: *GCE:* 240. *IB:* 24.

W3M2 BA/BSc Music with Legal Studies
Duration: 3FT Hon
Entry Requirements: *GCE:* 240. *IB:* 24.

W3C8 BA/BSc Music with Psychology
Duration: 3FT Hon
Entry Requirements: *GCE:* 260. *IB:* 24.

W3V6 BA/BSc Music with Religious Studies
Duration: 3FT Hon
Entry Requirements: *GCE:* 240. *IB:* 24.

W3L3 BA/BSc Music with Sociology & Social Science
Duration: 3FT Hon
Entry Requirements: *GCE:* 240. *IB:* 24.

W3VP BA/BSc Music with Theology
Duration: 3FT Hon
Entry Requirements: *GCE:* 240. *IB:* 24.

W3N8 BA/BSc Music with Tourism & Leisure Studies
Duration: 3FT Hon
Entry Requirements: *GCE:* 240. *IB:* 24.

C8W3 BA/BSc Psychology with Music
Duration: 3FT Hon
Entry Requirements: *GCE:* 260. *IB:* 24.

V6W3 BA/BSc Religious Studies with Music
Duration: 3FT Hon
Entry Requirements: *GCE:* 240. *IB:* 24.

L3W3 BA/BSc Sociology & Social Science with Music
Duration: 3FT Hon
Entry Requirements: *GCE:* 240. *IB:* 24.

VW6H BA/BSc Theology and Music
Duration: 3FT Hon
Entry Requirements: *GCE:* 240. *IB:* 24.

V6WH BA/BSc Theology with Music
Duration: 3FT Hon
Entry Requirements: *GCE:* 240. *IB:* 24.

N8W3 BA/BSc Tourism & Leisure Studies with Music
Duration: 3FT Hon
Entry Requirements: *GCE:* 240. *IB:* 24.

W302 BMus International Foundation Music
Duration: 4FT Hon
Entry Requirements: Interview required.

W300 BMus Music
Duration: 3FT Hon
Entry Requirements: *GCE:* 240. *IB:* 24. Interview required.

N1W3 BSc Business Studies with Music
Duration: 3FT Hon
Entry Requirements: *GCE:* 240. *IB:* 24.

CW13 BSc/BA Biosciences and Music
Duration: 3FT Hon
Entry Requirements: *GCE:* 240. *IB:* 24.

C1W3 BSc/BA Biosciences with Music
Duration: 3FT Hon
Entry Requirements: *GCE:* 240. *IB:* 24.

G5W3 BSc/BA Computing with Music
Duration: 3FT Hon
Entry Requirements: *GCE:* 240. *IB:* 24.

V1W3 BSc/BA History with Music
Duration: 3FT Hon
Entry Requirements: *GCE:* 240. *IB:* 24.

W342 FdA Church Music
Duration: 2FT Fdg
Entry Requirements: *GCE:* 120.

003W HNC Music Production
Duration: 1FT HNC
Entry Requirements: Contact the institution for details.

093W HNC Music Production
Duration: 1FT HNC
Entry Requirements: *GCE:* 100. Interview required.

013W HND Music Performance
Duration: 2FT HND
Entry Requirements: *GCE:* 100. Interview required.

C15 CARDIFF UNIVERSITY
PO BOX 927
30-36 NEWPORT ROAD
CARDIFF CF24 0DE
t: 029 2087 9999 f: 029 2087 6138
e: admissions@cardiff.ac.uk
// www.cardiff.ac.uk

WQ33 BA English Literature/Music
Duration: 3FT Hon
Entry Requirements: *GCE:* AAB. *SQAH:* AAABB. *SQAAH:* AAB. *IB:* 35. Interview required.

WR31 BA French/Music (4 years)
Duration: 4FT Hon
Entry Requirements: *GCE:* ABB. *SQAAH:* ABB. *IB:* 34.

WR32 BA German/Music (4 years)
Duration: 4FT Hon
Entry Requirements: *GCE:* BBB. *IB:* 32.

WV31 BA History/Music
Duration: 3FT Hon
Entry Requirements: *GCE:* ABB. *SQAH:* AABBB. *SQAAH:* ABB. *IB:* 34. Interview required.

WR33 BA Italian/Music (4 years)
Duration: 4FT Hon
Entry Requirements: *GCE:* BBB. *IB:* 32.

GW13 BA Mathematics/Music
Duration: 3FT Hon
Entry Requirements: *GCE:* AAB. *SQAH:* AAABB. *SQAAH:* AAB. *IB:* 35.

W300 BA Music
Duration: 3FT Hon   CRB Check: Required
Entry Requirements: *GCE:* AAB-BBB. *SQAH:* AAABB. *SQAAH:* AABBB. *IB:* 32. Interview required. Admissions Test required.

VW53 BA Music/Philosophy
Duration: 3FT Hon
Entry Requirements: *GCE:* AAB. *SQAH:* AAABB. *SQAAH:* AAB. *IB:* 35.

VW63 BA Music/Religious Studies
Duration: 3FT Hon
Entry Requirements: *GCE:* BBB. *IB:* 32.

QW53 BA Music/Welsh
Duration: 3FT Hon
Entry Requirements: *GCE:* ABB-BBB. *IB:* 32.

W302 BMus Music
Duration: 3FT Hon   CRB Check: Required
Entry Requirements: *GCE:* AAB-BBB. *SQAH:* AAABB. *SQAAH:* AABBB. *IB:* 32. Interview required. Admissions Test required.

FW33 BSc Physics and Music
Duration: 3FT Hon
Entry Requirements: *GCE:* ABB. *SQAAH:* BBB. *IB:* 30. Interview required. Admissions Test required.

C20 CARDIFF METROPOLITAN UNIVERSITY (UWIC)
ADMISSIONS UNIT
LLANDAFF CAMPUS
WESTERN AVENUE
CARDIFF CF5 2YB
t: 029 2041 6070 f: 029 2041 6286
e: admissions@cardiffmet.ac.uk
// www.cardiffmet.ac.uk

XW33 BA Secondary Education Music leading to QTS (3 Years)
Duration: 2FT/3FT Hon   CRB Check: Required
Entry Requirements: *GCE:* 280. *IB:* 25. *BTEC ExtDip:* DMM. Interview required.

C30 UNIVERSITY OF CENTRAL LANCASHIRE
PRESTON
LANCS PR1 2HE
t: 01772 201201 f: 01772 894954
e: uadmissions@uclan.ac.uk
// www.uclan.ac.uk

W300 BA Music Practice
Duration: 3FT Hon
Entry Requirements: *GCE:* 260-300. *IB:* 26. Interview required.

WJ39 BA Music Production
Duration: 3FT Hon
Entry Requirements: *GCE:* 260-300. *IB:* 26. Interview required.

W310 BA Music Theatre
Duration: 3FT Hon
Entry Requirements: *GCE:* 260-300. *IB:* 26. Interview required.

W301 FdA Music
Duration: 2FT Fdg
Entry Requirements: *GCE:* 160.

**C35 CENTRAL SCHOOL OF SPEECH AND
DRAMA, UNIVERSITY OF LONDON**
EMBASSY THEATRE
64 ETON AVENUE
LONDON NW3 3HY
t: 0207 722 8183 f: 0207 722 4132
e: enquiries@cssd.ac.uk
// www.cssd.ac.uk

WW34 BA Theatre Practice: Theatre Sound
Duration: 3FT Hon
Entry Requirements: *GCE:* BBC. Interview required. Portfolio
required.

C55 UNIVERSITY OF CHESTER
PARKGATE ROAD
CHESTER CH1 4BJ
t: 01244 511000 f: 01244 511300
e: enquiries@chester.ac.uk
// www.chester.ac.uk

W340 BA Popular Music Performance
Duration: 3FT Hon
Entry Requirements: *GCE:* 260-300. *SQAH:* BBBB. *IB:* 28.
Interview required.

C57 CHICHESTER COLLEGE
WESTGATE FIELDS
CHICHESTER
WEST SUSSEX PO19 1SB
t: 01243 786321 x2127 f: 01243 539481
e: sally.billingham@chichester.ac.uk
// www.chichester.ac.uk

W314 HND Music Performance in Jazz
Duration: 2FT HND
Entry Requirements: *Foundation:* Merit. *GCE:* AA-CC. *SQAH:*
AAAAAA-CCCCCC. *SQAAH:* AAA-CCC. *OCR ND:* M1 *OCR NED:* M1
Interview required.

C58 UNIVERSITY OF CHICHESTER
BISHOP OTTER CAMPUS
COLLEGE LANE
CHICHESTER
WEST SUSSEX PO19 6PE
t: 01243 816002 f: 01243 816161
e: admissions@chi.ac.uk
// www.chiuni.ac.uk

W340 BA Commercial Music
Duration: 3FT Hon
Entry Requirements: *GCE:* 240-280. *IB:* 28. *BTEC ExtDip:* MMM.
Interview required.

W341 BA Commercial Music
Duration: 1FT Hon
Entry Requirements: Interview required.

**WW83 BA English & Creative Writing and
Music**
Duration: 3FT Hon
Entry Requirements: *GCE:* BCD-CCC. *SQAAH:* CCC. *IB:* 28. *BTEC
SubDip:* M. *BTEC Dip:* DD.

**W8WH BA English & Creative Writing with
Music**
Duration: 3FT Hon
Entry Requirements: *GCE:* BCD-CCC. *SQAAH:* CCC. *IB:* 28. *BTEC
SubDip:* M. *BTEC Dip:* DD.

QW33 BA English and Music
Duration: 3FT Hon
Entry Requirements: *GCE:* BCD-CCC. *SQAAH:* CCC. *IB:* 28. *BTEC
SubDip:* M. *BTEC Dip:* DD.

Q3W3 BA English with Music
Duration: 3FT Hon
Entry Requirements: *GCE:* BCD-CCC. *SQAAH:* CCC. *IB:* 28. *BTEC
SubDip:* M. *BTEC Dip:* DD.

VW13 BA History and Music
Duration: 3FT Hon
Entry Requirements: *GCE:* BCD-CCC. *SQAAH:* CCC. *IB:* 28. *BTEC
SubDip:* M. *BTEC Dip:* DD.

**QW3H BA International English Studies and
Music**
Duration: 3FT Hon
Entry Requirements: *GCE:* 160-200. *IB:* 28. *BTEC ExtDip:* MMM.
Interview required.

W300 BA Music
Duration: 3FT Hon
Entry Requirements: *GCE:* CCD. *SQAAH:* CCC-CCD. *IB:* 28. *BTEC
ExtDip:* MMM. *OCR ND:* D *OCR NED:* M1 Interview required.

W312 BA Music Performance
Duration: 3FT Hon
Entry Requirements: Interview required.

W392 BA Music and Musical Theatre
Duration: 3FT Hon
Entry Requirements: Interview required.

W390 BA Music with Community Music
Duration: 3FT Hon
Entry Requirements: *GCE:* CCD. *SQAAH:* CCC-CCD. *IB:* 28. *BTEC
ExtDip:* MMM. *OCR ND:* D *OCR NED:* M1 Interview required.

W3Q3 BA Music with English
Duration: 3FT Hon
Entry Requirements: *GCE:* CCD. *SQAAH:* CCC-CCD. *IB:* 28. *BTEC
ExtDip:* MMM. *OCR ND:* D *OCR NED:* M1 Interview required.

W3V1 BA Music with History
Duration: 3FT Hon
Entry Requirements: *GCE:* CCD. *SQAAH:* CCC-CCD. *IB:* 28. *BTEC ExtDip:* MMM. *OCR ND:* D *OCR NED:* M1 Interview required.

W3XD BA Music with Instrumental/Vocal Teaching
Duration: 3FT Hon
Entry Requirements: *GCE:* CCD. *SQAAH:* CCC-CCD. *IB:* 28. *BTEC ExtDip:* MMM. *OCR ND:* D *OCR NED:* M1 Interview required.

W3QH BA Music with International English Studies
Duration: 3FT Hon
Entry Requirements: *GCE:* CCD. *SQAAH:* CCC-CCD. *IB:* 28. *BTEC ExtDip:* MMM. *OCR ND:* D *OCR NED:* M1 Interview required.

W3N5 BA Music with Music, Marketing & Administration
Duration: 3FT Hon
Entry Requirements: *GCE:* CCD. *SQAAH:* CCC-CCD. *IB:* 28. *BTEC ExtDip:* MMM. *OCR ND:* D *OCR NED:* M1 Interview required.

W391 BA Music with Musical Theatre
Duration: 3FT Hon
Entry Requirements: *GCE:* CCD. *SQAAH:* CCC-CCD. *IB:* 28. *BTEC ExtDip:* MMM. *OCR ND:* D *OCR NED:* M1 Interview required.

W3V6 BA Music with Theology & Religion
Duration: 3FT Hon
Entry Requirements: *GCE:* CCD. *SQAAH:* CCC-CCD. *IB:* 28. *BTEC ExtDip:* MMM. *OCR ND:* D *OCR NED:* M1 Interview required.

WW34 BA Musical Theatre
Duration: 3FT Hon CRB Check: Required
Entry Requirements: *GCE:* CCD. *SQAAH:* CCC-CCD. *IB:* 28. *BTEC ExtDip:* MMM. *OCR ND:* D *OCR NED:* M1 Interview required.

WW3K BA Musical Theatre
Duration: 1FT Hon CRB Check: Required
Entry Requirements: Interview required.

WW4J BA Performing Arts (Theatre Performance and Music)
Duration: 3FT Hon
Entry Requirements: *GCE:* BBC-BCC. *SQAAH:* BBC-BCC. *IB:* 28. *BTEC Dip:* DD. *BTEC ExtDip:* DMM. Interview required.

W311 BMus Performance
Duration: 4FT Hon
Entry Requirements: *GCE:* CCD. *SQAAH:* CCC-CCD. *IB:* 28. *BTEC ExtDip:* MMM. *OCR ND:* D *OCR NED:* M1 Interview required.

C60 CITY UNIVERSITY
NORTHAMPTON SQUARE
LONDON EC1V 0HB
t: 020 7040 5060 f: 020 7040 8995
e: ugadmissions@city.ac.uk
// www.city.ac.uk

W300 BMus Music
Duration: 3FT Hon
Entry Requirements: *GCE:* AAB. *SQAH:* AABB. *SQAAH:* BBC-BCC. *IB:* 32.

C64 CITY COLLEGE COVENTRY
SWANSWELL
50 SWANSWELL STREET
COVENTRY CV1 5DG
t: 0800 616 202 f: 024 7622 3390
e: courses@covcollege.ac.uk
// www.covcollege.ac.uk

W374 HND Music Production
Duration: 2FT HND
Entry Requirements: Contact the institution for details.

C75 COLCHESTER INSTITUTE
SHEEPEN ROAD
COLCHESTER
ESSEX CO3 3LL
t: 01206 712777 f: 01206 712800
e: info@colchester.ac.uk
// www.colchester.ac.uk

W301 BA Film Music and Soundtrack Production
Duration: 3FT Hon
Entry Requirements: Contact the institution for details.

W300 BA Music
Duration: 3FT Hon
Entry Requirements: *GCE:* 160. *SQAH:* CCCC. Interview required.

W300 BA Music option - Arts Business
Duration: 3FT Hon
Entry Requirements: *GCE:* 160. Interview required.

W300 BA Music option - Performance Studies
Duration: 3FT Hon
Entry Requirements: *GCE:* 160. Interview required.

W300 BA Music option - Composition
Duration: 3FT Hon
Entry Requirements: *GCE:* 160. Interview required.

W300 BA Music option - Education
Duration: 3FT Hon
Entry Requirements: *GCE:* 160. Interview required.

WW34 BA Musical Theatre
Duration: 3FT Hon
Entry Requirements: *GCE:* 160. Interview required.

W341 BA Popular Music
Duration: 3FT Hon
Entry Requirements: *GCE:* 160. Interview required.

W390 FdA Musical Theatre
Duration: 2FT Fdg
Entry Requirements: *GCE:* 80. Interview required.

W340 FdA Popular Music
Duration: 2FT Fdg
Entry Requirements: *GCE:* 80. Interview required.

C78 CORNWALL COLLEGE
POOL
REDRUTH
CORNWALL TR15 3RD
t: 01209 616161 f: 01209 611612
e: he.admissions@cornwall.ac.uk
// www.cornwall.ac.uk

383W HNC Music (DJ and Electronic Music Production)
Duration: 1FT HNC   CRB Check: Required
Entry Requirements: Contact the institution for details.

093W HNC Music (Performance and Technology)
Duration: 1FT HNC   CRB Check: Required
Entry Requirements: Contact the institution for details.

243W HNC Music (for Film and Television)
Duration: 1FT HNC   CRB Check: Required
Entry Requirements: Contact the institution for details.

38HW HND Music (DJ and Electronic Music Production)
Duration: 2FT HND   CRB Check: Required
Entry Requirements: Contact the institution for details.

039W HND Music (Performance and Technology)
Duration: 2FT HND   CRB Check: Required
Entry Requirements: Contact the institution for details.

24HW HND Music (for Film and Television)
Duration: 2FT HND   CRB Check: Required
Entry Requirements: Contact the institution for details.

C85 COVENTRY UNIVERSITY
THE STUDENT CENTRE
COVENTRY UNIVERSITY
1 GULSON RD
COVENTRY CV1 2JH
t: 024 7615 2222 f: 024 7615 2223
e: studentenquiries@coventry.ac.uk
// www.coventry.ac.uk

W303 BA Music Composition
Duration: 3FT/4SW Hon
Entry Requirements: *GCE:* CCC. *SQAH:* CCCCC. *IB:* 27. *BTEC ExtDip:* MMM. *OCR NED:* M3 Interview required.

W304 BA Music Performance
Duration: 3FT/4SW Hon
Entry Requirements: *GCE:* CCC. *SQAH:* CCCCC. *IB:* 27. *BTEC ExtDip:* MMM. *OCR NED:* M3 Interview required.

C99 UNIVERSITY OF CUMBRIA
FUSEHILL STREET
CARLISLE
CUMBRIA CA1 2HH
t: 01228 616234 f: 01228 616235
// www.cumbria.ac.uk

WW53 BA Dance Performance and Musical Theatre Performance
Duration: 3FT Hon
Entry Requirements: *GCE:* 280. *IB:* 30. *OCR ND:* D Interview required.

WW43 BA Drama Performance and Musical Theatre Performance
Duration: 3FT Hon
Entry Requirements: *GCE:* 280. *IB:* 30. *OCR ND:* D Interview required.

D26 DE MONTFORT UNIVERSITY
THE GATEWAY
LEICESTER LE1 9BH
t: 0116 255 1551 f: 0116 250 6204
e: enquiries@dmu.ac.uk
// www.dmu.ac.uk

JW93 BA Music, Technology and Performance
Duration: 3FT Hon
Entry Requirements: *GCE:* 260. *IB:* 28. *BTEC Dip:* D*D*. *BTEC ExtDip:* DMM.

JW9H BSc Music Technology
Duration: 3FT Hon
Entry Requirements: *GCE:* 300. *IB:* 28. *BTEC ExtDip:* DDM. Interview required.

D39 UNIVERSITY OF DERBY
KEDLESTON ROAD
DERBY DE22 1GB
t: 01332 591167 f: 01332 597724
e: askadmissions@derby.ac.uk
// www.derby.ac.uk

TW73 BA American Studies and Popular Music (Production)
Duration: 3FT Hon
Entry Requirements: *Foundation:* Distinction. *GCE:* 260-300. *IB:* 28. *BTEC Dip:* D*D*. *BTEC ExtDip:* DMM. *OCR NED:* M2

W391 BA Creative Expressive Therapies (Music)
Duration: 3FT Hon   CRB Check: Required
Entry Requirements: *Foundation:* Distinction. *GCE:* 280. *IB:* 28. *BTEC Dip:* D*D*. *BTEC ExtDip:* DMM. *OCR NED:* M2 Interview required.

WW35 BA Dance & Movement Studies and Popular Music (Production)
Duration: 3FT Hon
Entry Requirements: *Foundation:* Distinction. *GCE:* 260-300. *IB:* 28. *BTEC Dip:* D*D*. *BTEC ExtDip:* DMM. *OCR NED:* M2

WX33 BA Education Studies and Popular Music (Production)
Duration: 3FT Hon
Entry Requirements: *Foundation:* Distinction. *GCE:* 260-300. *IB:* 28. *BTEC Dip:* D*D*. *BTEC ExtDip:* DMM. *OCR NED:* M2

NW53 BA Marketing and Popular Music (Production)
Duration: 3FT Hon
Entry Requirements: *Foundation:* Distinction. *GCE:* 260-300. *IB:* 28. *BTEC Dip:* D*D*. *BTEC ExtDip:* DMM. *OCR NED:* M2

LW33 BA Popular Music Production and Sociology
Duration: 3FT Hon
Entry Requirements: *Foundation:* Distinction. *GCE:* 260-300. *IB:* 28. *BTEC Dip:* D*D*. *BTEC ExtDip:* DMM. *OCR NED:* M2

WC36 BA Popular Music Production and Sport & Exercise Studies
Duration: 3FT Hon
Entry Requirements: *Foundation:* Distinction. *GCE:* 260-300. *IB:* 28. *BTEC Dip:* D*D*. *BTEC ExtDip:* DMM. *OCR NED:* M2

WW34 BA Popular Music Production and Theatre Arts
Duration: 3FT Hon
Entry Requirements: *Foundation:* Distinction. *GCE:* 260-300. *IB:* 28. *BTEC Dip:* D*D*. *BTEC ExtDip:* DMM. *OCR NED:* M2

W340 BA Popular Music with Music Technology
Duration: 3FT Hon
Entry Requirements: *GCE:* 260. *IB:* 28. *BTEC Dip:* D*D*. *BTEC ExtDip:* DMM. *OCR NED:* M2

WP33 BA Professional Writing and Popular Music Production
Duration: 3FT Hon
Entry Requirements: *Foundation:* Distinction. *GCE:* 260-300. *IB:* 28. *BTEC Dip:* D*D*. *BTEC ExtDip:* DMM. *OCR NED:* M2

LW73 BA/BSc Geography and Popular Music Production
Duration: 3FT Hon
Entry Requirements: *Foundation:* Distinction. *GCE:* 260-300. *IB:* 28. *BTEC Dip:* D*D*. *BTEC ExtDip:* DMM. *OCR NED:* M2

CW13 BSc Biology and Popular Music (Production)
Duration: 3FT Hon
Entry Requirements: *Foundation:* Distinction. *GCE:* 260-300. *IB:* 28. *BTEC Dip:* D*D*. *BTEC ExtDip:* DMM. *OCR NED:* M2

CW83 BSc Psychology and Popular Music (Production)
Duration: 3FT Hon
Entry Requirements: *Foundation:* Distinction. *GCE:* 260-300. *IB:* 28. *BTEC Dip:* D*D*. *BTEC ExtDip:* DMM. *OCR NED:* M2

W3J9 FYr Popular Music with Music Technology Foundation
Duration: 1FT FYr
Entry Requirements: *Foundation:* Pass. *GCE:* 160. *IB:* 24. *BTEC Dip:* D*D*. *BTEC ExtDip:* DMM. *OCR ND:* M2 *OCR NED:* P2

D52 DONCASTER COLLEGE
THE HUB
CHAPPELL DRIVE
SOUTH YORKSHIRE DN1 2RF
t: 01302 553610
e: he@don.ac.uk
// www.don.ac.uk

W391 BA Creative Music Technology
Duration: 3FT Hon
Entry Requirements: *GCE:* 180-240.

D86 DURHAM UNIVERSITY
DURHAM UNIVERSITY
UNIVERSITY OFFICE
DURHAM DH1 3HP
t: 0191 334 2000 f: 0191 334 6055
e: admissions@durham.ac.uk
// www.durham.ac.uk

X1W3 BA Education Studies (Music)
Duration: 3FT Hon
Entry Requirements: *GCE:* AAB. *SQAH:* AAABB. *SQAAH:* AAB. *IB:* 36.

W300 BA Music
Duration: 3FT Hon
Entry Requirements: *GCE:* AAB. *SQAH:* AAABB. *SQAAH:* AAB. *IB:* 36.

W301 BA Music with Foundation
Duration: 4FT Hon
Entry Requirements: Contact the institution for details.

E28 UNIVERSITY OF EAST LONDON
DOCKLANDS CAMPUS
UNIVERSITY WAY
LONDON E16 2RD
t: 020 8223 3333 f: 020 8223 2978
e: study@uel.ac.uk
// www.uel.ac.uk

NW63 BA Human Resource Management/Music Cultures
Duration: 3FT Hon
Entry Requirements: *GCE:* 240. *IB:* 24.

W3P9 BA Music Culture with Communication Studies
Duration: 3FT Hon
Entry Requirements: *GCE:* 240. *IB:* 24.

W3L6 BA Music Culture with Cultural Studies
Duration: 3FT Hon
Entry Requirements: *GCE:* 240. *IB:* 24.

W3C6 BA Music Culture with Sports Development
Duration: 3FT Hon
Entry Requirements: *GCE:* 240. *IB:* 24.

W3WK BA Music Culture with Theatre Studies
Duration: 3FT Hon
Entry Requirements: *GCE:* 240. *IB:* 24.

WR39 BA Music Culture/Cultural Studies
Duration: 3FT Hon
Entry Requirements: *GCE:* 240. *IB:* 24.

WJ39 BA Music Culture: Theory and Production
Duration: 3FT Hon
Entry Requirements: *GCE:* 240. *IB:* 24.

N2W3 BA Music Industry Management with Music Culture
Duration: 3FT Hon
Entry Requirements: *GCE:* 240. *IB:* 24.

W4W3 BA Theatre Studies with Music Culture
Duration: 3FT Hon
Entry Requirements: *GCE:* 240. *IB:* 24. Interview required.

GW53 BA/BSc Business Information Systems/Music Culture
Duration: 3FT Hon
Entry Requirements: *GCE:* 240. *IB:* 24. Interview required.

IW13 BA/BSc Computing and Music Industry Management
Duration: 3FT Hon
Entry Requirements: *GCE:* 240. *IB:* 24.

W310 BMus Popular Music Performance
Duration: 3FT Hon
Entry Requirements: *GCE:* 200. *IB:* 27. Interview required.

G4W3 BSc Computer Networks with Music Culture
Duration: 3FT Hon
Entry Requirements: *GCE:* 240. *IB:* 24. Interview required.

L3W3 BSc Sociology (Professional Development) with Music Culture
Duration: 3FT Hon
Entry Requirements: *GCE:* 240. *IB:* 24. Interview required.

W391 FdA Music and Production
Duration: 2FT Fdg
Entry Requirements: *GCE:* 200.

E42 EDGE HILL UNIVERSITY
ORMSKIRK
LANCASHIRE L39 4QP
t: 01695 657000 f: 01695 584355
e: study@edgehill.ac.uk
// www.edgehill.ac.uk

WJ39 BA Music and Sound with Drama
Duration: 3FT Hon
Entry Requirements: *GCE:* 280. *IB:* 26. *OCR ND:* D *OCR NED:* M2
Interview required.

W390 BA Music, Sound and Enterprise
Duration: 3FT Hon
Entry Requirements: *GCE:* 280. *IB:* 26. *OCR ND:* D *OCR NED:* M2
Interview required.

E56 THE UNIVERSITY OF EDINBURGH
STUDENT RECRUITMENT & ADMISSIONS
57 GEORGE SQUARE
EDINBURGH EH8 9JU
t: 0131 650 4360 f: 0131 651 1236
e: sra.enquiries@ed.ac.uk
// www.ed.ac.uk/studying/undergraduate/

W302 BMus Music
Duration: 4FT Hon
Entry Requirements: *GCE:* BBB. *SQAH:* ABBB-ABBC. *IB:* 34.
Interview required.

W351 BMus Music Technology
Duration: 4FT Hon
Entry Requirements: *GCE:* BBB. *SQAH:* ABBB-ABBC. *IB:* 34.
Interview required.

GW13 BSc Mathematics and Music
Duration: 4FT Hon
Entry Requirements: *GCE:* AAA-ABB. *SQAH:* AAAA-ABBB.

FW33 BSc Physics and Music
Duration: 4FT Hon
Entry Requirements: *GCE:* AAA-ABB. *SQAH:* AAAA-ABBB.

VW33 MA History of Art and History of Music
Duration: 4FT Hon
Entry Requirements: **GCE:** AAA-BBB. **SQAH:** AAAA-BBBB. **IB:** 34.

E59 EDINBURGH NAPIER UNIVERSITY
CRAIGLOCKHART CAMPUS
EDINBURGH EH14 1DJ
t: +44 (0)8452 60 60 40 f: 0131 455 6464
e: info@napier.ac.uk
// www.napier.ac.uk

W341 BA Popular Music
Duration: 3FT/4FT Ord/Hon
Entry Requirements: **GCE:** 240. Interview required.

W302 BMus Music
Duration: 3FT/4FT Ord/Hon
Entry Requirements: **GCE:** 240. Interview required.

E81 EXETER COLLEGE
HELE ROAD
EXETER
DEVON EX4 4JS
t: 0845 111 6000
e: info@exe-coll.ac.uk
// www.exe-coll.ac.uk/he

WW34 FdA Performance Production
Duration: 2FT Fdg
Entry Requirements: **GCE:** 160.

W300 HND Music
Duration: 2FT HND
Entry Requirements: Contact the institution for details.

F33 UNIVERSITY COLLEGE FALMOUTH
WOODLANE
FALMOUTH
CORNWALL TR11 4RH
t: 01326213730
e: admissions@falmouth.ac.uk
// www.falmouth.ac.uk

W390 BA(Hons) Creative Music Technology
Duration: 3FT Hon
Entry Requirements: **GCE:** 220. **IB:** 24. Interview required.
Portfolio required.

W300 BA(Hons) Music
Duration: 3FT Hon
Entry Requirements: **GCE:** 220. **IB:** 24. Interview required.
Portfolio required.

WW34 BA(Hons) Music Theatre
Duration: 3FT Hon
Entry Requirements: **GCE:** 220. **IB:** 24. Interview required.

W340 BA(Hons) Popular Music
Duration: 3FT Hon
Entry Requirements: **GCE:** 220. **IB:** 24. Interview required.
Portfolio required.

F66 FARNBOROUGH COLLEGE OF TECHNOLOGY
BOUNDARY ROAD
FARNBOROUGH
HAMPSHIRE GU14 6SB
t: 01252 407028 f: 01252 407041
e: admissions@farn-ct.ac.uk
// www.farn-ct.ac.uk

W300 FdSc Music Production
Duration: 2FT Fdg
Entry Requirements: **GCE:** 160.

G14 UNIVERSITY OF GLAMORGAN, CARDIFF AND PONTYPRIDD
ENQUIRIES AND ADMISSIONS UNIT
PONTYPRIDD CF37 1DL
t: 08456 434030 f: 01443 654050
e: enquiries@glam.ac.uk
// www.glam.ac.uk

W340 BA Cerddoriaeth Boblogaidd - Cwrs Dwyieithog
Duration: 3FT Hon
Entry Requirements: **GCE:** BBB. **IB:** 24. **BTEC SubDip:** M. **BTEC Dip:** DD. **BTEC ExtDip:** DDM. **OCR NED:** M2 Interview required.

W300 BA Popular Music
Duration: 3FT Hon
Entry Requirements: **GCE:** BBB. **IB:** 26. **BTEC SubDip:** M. **BTEC Dip:** DD. **BTEC ExtDip:** DDM. **OCR NED:** M1 Interview required.

WJ39 FdA Creative Industries (Popular Music Technology)
Duration: 2FT Fdg
Entry Requirements: **GCE:** CCC. **BTEC SubDip:** M. **BTEC Dip:** DD. **BTEC ExtDip:** MMM.

G28 UNIVERSITY OF GLASGOW
71 SOUTHPARK AVENUE
UNIVERSITY OF GLASGOW
GLASGOW G12 8QQ
t: 0141 330 6062 f: 0141 330 2961
e: student.recruitment@glasgow.ac.uk
// www.glasgow.ac.uk

H6W3 BEng Electronics with Music
Duration: 4FT Hon
Entry Requirements: **GCE:** ABB. **SQAH:** AAAB-BBB. **IB:** 32.

W302 BMus Music
Duration: 4FT Hon
Entry Requirements: **GCE:** ABB. **SQAH:** ABBB. **IB:** 32. Interview required.

VW43 MA Archaeology/Music
Duration: 4FT Hon
Entry Requirements: **GCE:** ABB. **SQAH:** AAAB-ABBB. **IB:** 34.

NW23 MA Business & Management/Music
Duration: 4FT Hon
Entry Requirements: **GCE:** ABB. **SQAH:** AAAB-ABBB. **IB:** 34.

QW53 MA Celtic Studies/Music
Duration: 4FT Hon
Entry Requirements: *GCE:* ABB. *SQAH:* AAAB-ABBB. *IB:* 34.

RWR3 MA Central & East European Studies/Music
Duration: 4FT Hon
Entry Requirements: *GCE:* ABB. *SQAH:* AAAB-ABBB. *IB:* 34.

QW83 MA Classics/Music
Duration: 4FT Hon
Entry Requirements: *GCE:* ABB. *SQAH:* AAAB-ABBB. *IB:* 34.

QWF3 MA Comparative Literature/Music
Duration: 4FT Hon
Entry Requirements: *GCE:* ABB. *SQAH:* AAAB-ABBB. *IB:* 34.

GW43 MA Computing/Music
Duration: 4FT Hon
Entry Requirements: *GCE:* ABB. *SQAH:* AAAB-ABBB. *IB:* 36.

GW5H MA Digital Media & Information Studies/Music
Duration: 4FT Hon
Entry Requirements: *GCE:* ABB. *SQAH:* AAAB-ABBB. *IB:* 34.

VW33 MA Economic & Social History/Music
Duration: 4FT Hon
Entry Requirements: *GCE:* ABB. *SQAH:* AAAB-ABBB. *IB:* 36.

LW13 MA Economics/Music
Duration: 4FT Hon
Entry Requirements: *GCE:* ABB. *SQAH:* AAAB-ABBB. *IB:* 36.

QW3J MA English Language/Music
Duration: 4FT Hon
Entry Requirements: *GCE:* ABB. *SQAH:* AAAB-ABBB. *IB:* 36.

QW3H MA English Literature/Music
Duration: 4FT Hon
Entry Requirements: *GCE:* ABB. *SQAH:* AAAB-ABBB. *IB:* 36.

WW36 MA Film & Television Studies/Music
Duration: 4FT Hon
Entry Requirements: *GCE:* ABB. *SQAH:* AAAB-ABBB. *IB:* 36.

RW13 MA French/Music
Duration: 5FT Hon
Entry Requirements: *GCE:* ABB. *SQAH:* AAAB-ABBB. *IB:* 36.

LW73 MA Geography/Music
Duration: 4FT Hon
Entry Requirements: *GCE:* ABB. *SQAH:* AAAB-ABBB. *IB:* 36.

RW23 MA German/Music
Duration: 5FT Hon
Entry Requirements: *GCE:* ABB. *SQAH:* AAAB-ABBB. *IB:* 36.

QW73 MA Greek/Music
Duration: 4FT Hon
Entry Requirements: *GCE:* ABB. *SQAH:* AAAB-ABBB. *IB:* 36.

VWH3 MA History of Art/Music
Duration: 4FT Hon
Entry Requirements: *GCE:* ABB. *SQAH:* AAAB-ABBB. *IB:* 36.

VW13 MA History/Music
Duration: 4FT Hon
Entry Requirements: *GCE:* ABB. *SQAH:* AAAB-ABBB. *IB:* 36.

RW33 MA Italian/Music
Duration: 5FT Hon
Entry Requirements: *GCE:* ABB. *SQAH:* AAAB-ABBB. *IB:* 36.

QW63 MA Latin/Music
Duration: 4FT Hon
Entry Requirements: *GCE:* ABB. *SQAH:* AAAB-ABBB. *IB:* 36.

GW13 MA Mathematics/Music
Duration: 4FT Hon
Entry Requirements: *GCE:* ABB. *SQAH:* AAAB-ABBB. *IB:* 36.

W300 MA Music
Duration: 4FT Hon
Entry Requirements: *GCE:* ABB. *SQAH:* AAAB-ABBB. *IB:* 36.

VW53 MA Music/Philosophy
Duration: 4FT Hon
Entry Requirements: *GCE:* ABB. *SQAH:* AAAB-ABBB. *IB:* 36.

FW33 MA Music/Physics
Duration: 4FT Hon
Entry Requirements: *GCE:* ABB. *SQAH:* AAAB-ABBB. *IB:* 36.

LW23 MA Music/Politics
Duration: 4FT Hon
Entry Requirements: *GCE:* ABB. *SQAH:* AAAB-ABBB. *IB:* 36.

CW83 MA Music/Psychology
Duration: 4FT Hon
Entry Requirements: *GCE:* ABB. *SQAH:* AAAB-ABBB. *IB:* 36.

LW43 MA Music/Public Policy
Duration: 4FT Hon
Entry Requirements: *GCE:* ABB. *SQAH:* AAAB-ABBB. *IB:* 36.

RW73 MA Music/Russian
Duration: 5FT Hon
Entry Requirements: *GCE:* ABB. *SQAH:* AAAB-ABBB. *IB:* 36.

VWF3 MA Music/Scottish History
Duration: 4FT Hon
Entry Requirements: *GCE:* ABB. *SQAH:* AAAB-ABBB. *IB:* 36.

QW23 MA Music/Scottish Literature
Duration: 4FT Hon
Entry Requirements: *GCE:* ABB. *SQAH:* AAAB-ABBB. *IB:* 36.

WW34 MA Music/Theatre Studies
Duration: 4FT Hon
Entry Requirements: *GCE:* ABB. *SQAH:* AAAB-ABBB. *IB:* 36.

WV36 MA Music/Theology & Religious Studies
Duration: 4FT Hon
Entry Requirements: *GCE:* ABB. *SQAH:* AAAB-ABBB. *IB:* 36.

RW4H MA Spanish/Music
Duration: 5FT Hon
Entry Requirements: *GCE:* ABB. *SQAH:* AAAB-ABBB. *IB:* 36.

H6WJ MEng Electronics with Music
Duration: 5FT Hon
Entry Requirements: *GCE:* AAB. *SQAH:* AAAA-AAABB. *IB:* 34.

G45 GLOUCESTERSHIRE COLLEGE
PRINCESS ELIZABETH WAY
CHELTENHAM GL51 7SJ
t: 01242 532008 f: 01242 532023
e: admissions@gloscol.ac.uk
// www.gloscol.ac.uk

W374 HNC Music Production
Duration: 1FT HNC
Entry Requirements: Contact the institution for details.

G50 THE UNIVERSITY OF GLOUCESTERSHIRE
PARK CAMPUS
THE PARK
CHELTENHAM GL50 2RH
t: 01242 714501 f: 01242 714869
e: admissions@glos.ac.uk
// www.glos.ac.uk

W300 BA Popular Music
Duration: 3FT Hon
Entry Requirements: GCE: 280-300. Interview required. Portfolio required.

G53 GLYNDWR UNIVERSITY
PLAS COCH
MOLD ROAD
WREXHAM LL11 2AW
t: 01978 293439 f: 01978 290008
e: sid@glyndwr.ac.uk
// www.glyndwr.ac.uk

HWP3 BSc Studio Recording and Performance Technology
Duration: 3FT Hon
Entry Requirements: GCE: 240.

G56 GOLDSMITHS, UNIVERSITY OF LONDON
GOLDSMITHS, UNIVERSITY OF LONDON
NEW CROSS
LONDON SE14 6NW
t: 020 7048 5300 f: 020 7919 7509
e: admissions@gold.ac.uk
// www.gold.ac.uk

W302 BMus Music
Duration: 3FT Hon
Entry Requirements: GCE: ABB. SQAH: AABBB. SQAAH: ABB. IB: 32. Interview required.

W303 BMus Music (4-year extension degree)
Duration: 4FT Hon
Entry Requirements: Interview required.

WG34 BMus Music Computing
Duration: 3FT Hon
Entry Requirements: GCE: BBB. SQAH: BBBBB. SQAAH: BBB. Interview required.

W340 BMus Popular Music
Duration: 3FT Hon
Entry Requirements: GCE: BBB. SQAH: BBBBB. SQAAH: BBB. IB: 32. Interview required.

G80 GRIMSBY INSTITUTE OF FURTHER AND HIGHER EDUCATION
NUNS CORNER
GRIMSBY
NE LINCOLNSHIRE DN34 5BQ
t: 0800 328 3631
e: headmissions@grimsby.ac.uk
// www.grimsby.ac.uk

W390 BA Creative Music
Duration: 3FT Hon
Entry Requirements: GCE: 160. Interview required.

H14 HAVERING COLLEGE OF FURTHER AND HIGHER EDUCATION
ARDLEIGH GREEN ROAD
HORNCHURCH
ESSEX RM11 2LL
t: 01708 462793 f: 01708 462736
e: HE@havering-college.ac.uk
// www.havering-college.ac.uk

WJ3X BA Contemporary Music and Technology
Duration: 3FT Hon
Entry Requirements: Interview required. Portfolio required.

H36 UNIVERSITY OF HERTFORDSHIRE
UNIVERSITY ADMISSIONS SERVICE
COLLEGE LANE
HATFIELD
HERTS AL10 9AB
t: 01707 284800
// www.herts.ac.uk

W374 BSc Audio Recording & Production
Duration: 3FT Hon
Entry Requirements: Contact the institution for details.

W392 BSc Music Composition & Technology for Film and Games
Duration: 3FT Hon
Entry Requirements: Contact the institution for details.

W300 BSc Music Composition and Technology
Duration: 3FT Hon
Entry Requirements: GCE: 240.

W352 BSc Music Technology
Duration: 3FT Hon
Entry Requirements: GCE: 220.

W390 BSc Music: Commercial Composition and Technology
Duration: 3FT Hon
Entry Requirements: *GCE:* 240.

W3T4 BSc Songwriting & Music Production
Duration: 3FT Hon
Entry Requirements: Contact the institution for details.

W391 BSc Sound Design Technology
Duration: 3FT Hon
Entry Requirements: *GCE:* 220.

WN32 BSc/BA Music and Entertainment Industry Management
Duration: 3FT Hon
Entry Requirements: *GCE:* 300.

H49 UNIVERSITY OF THE HIGHLANDS AND ISLANDS
UHI EXECUTIVE OFFICE
NESS WALK
INVERNESS
SCOTLAND IV3 5SQ
t: 01463 279000 f: 01463 279001
e: info@uhi.ac.uk
// www.uhi.ac.uk

W301 BA Applied Music
Duration: 4FT Hon
Entry Requirements: *GCE:* BB. *SQAH:* ABB. Interview required.

QW53 BA Gaelic and Traditional Music
Duration: 4FT Hon
Entry Requirements: *GCE:* C. *SQAH:* CCC. Interview required.

W310 BA Popular Music
Duration: 3FT Hon
Entry Requirements: Interview required.

W3N1 BA Hons Music Business
Duration: 3FT Hon
Entry Requirements: Interview required.

103W HNC Music
Duration: 1FT HNC
Entry Requirements: *GCE:* D. *SQAH:* C. Interview required.

31WN HNC Music Business
Duration: 1FT HNC
Entry Requirements: *GCE:* D. *SQAH:* C. Interview required.

H60 THE UNIVERSITY OF HUDDERSFIELD
QUEENSGATE
HUDDERSFIELD HD1 3DH
t: 01484 473969 f: 01484 472765
e: admissionsandrecords@hud.ac.uk
// www.hud.ac.uk

WW63 BA Film, Animation, Music and Enterprise
Duration: 3FT/4SW Hon
Entry Requirements: *GCE:* 260.

WJ3X BA Music Production and Sound Recording
Duration: 3FT Hon
Entry Requirements: *GCE:* 240. *BTEC ExtDip:* MMM.

HW63 BA Music Technology
Duration: 3FT/4SW Hon
Entry Requirements: *GCE:* 300.

JWX3 BA Music Technology and Popular Music
Duration: 3FT/4SW Hon
Entry Requirements: *GCE:* 300.

W3W4 BA Music with Drama
Duration: 3FT/4SW Hon
Entry Requirements: *GCE:* 320. Interview required.

W3Q3 BA Music with English
Duration: 3FT/4SW Hon
Entry Requirements: *GCE:* 320. Interview required.

W3R9 BA Music with a Modern Language
Duration: 3FT/4SW Hon
Entry Requirements: *GCE:* 320. Interview required.

W340 BA Popular Music
Duration: 3FT Hon
Entry Requirements: *GCE:* 240. Interview required.

WJ39 BA Popular Music Production
Duration: 3FT/4SW Hon
Entry Requirements: *GCE:* 300.

W300 BMus Music
Duration: 3FT/4SW Hon
Entry Requirements: *GCE:* 320. Interview required.

H6W3 BSc Music Technology and Audio Systems
Duration: 3FT/4SW Hon
Entry Requirements: *GCE:* 300.

JW93 BSc Popular Music Production
Duration: 3FT/4SW Hon
Entry Requirements: *GCE:* 300.

H72 THE UNIVERSITY OF HULL
THE UNIVERSITY OF HULL
COTTINGHAM ROAD
HULL HU6 7RX
t: 01482 466100 f: 01482 442290
e: admissions@hull.ac.uk
// www.hull.ac.uk

W3N2 BA Creative Music Technology with Business Management
Duration: 3FT Hon
Entry Requirements: *GCE:* 260-300. *IB:* 24. *BTEC ExtDip:* DMM.

WW34 BA Drama and Music
Duration: 3FT Hon
Entry Requirements: *GCE:* 280-320. *IB:* 28. *BTEC ExtDip:* DDM.
Interview required.

QW33 BA English and Music
Duration: 3FT Hon
Entry Requirements: *GCE:* 280-320. *IB:* 30. *BTEC ExtDip:* DDM.
Interview required.

W340 BA Jazz and Popular Music
Duration: 3FT Hon
Entry Requirements: *GCE:* 280-320. *IB:* 28. *BTEC ExtDip:* DDM.
Interview required.

W300 BA Music
Duration: 3FT Hon
Entry Requirements: *GCE:* 280-320. *IB:* 28. *BTEC ExtDip:* DDM.
Interview required.

W3Q3 BA Music (including Foundation English Language)
Duration: 4FT Hon
Entry Requirements: *GCE:* 280-320. *IB:* 28. *BTEC ExtDip:* DDM.

W301 BA Music (with Foundation Year)
Duration: 4FT Hon
Entry Requirements: Interview required.

WR31 BA Music and French
Duration: 4FT Hon
Entry Requirements: *GCE:* 280-320. *IB:* 28. *BTEC ExtDip:* DDM.
Interview required.

WR32 BA Music and German
Duration: 4FT Hon
Entry Requirements: *GCE:* 280-320. *IB:* 28. *BTEC ExtDip:* DDM.
Interview required.

WR33 BA Music and Italian
Duration: 4FT Hon
Entry Requirements: *GCE:* 280-320. *IB:* 28. *BTEC ExtDip:* DDM.
Interview required.

WR34 BA Music and Spanish
Duration: 4FT Hon
Entry Requirements: *GCE:* 280-320. *IB:* 28. *BTEC ExtDip:* DDM.
Interview required.

WW3K BA Music and Theatre
Duration: 3FT Hon
Entry Requirements: *GCE:* 280-320. *IB:* 28. *BTEC ExtDip:* DDM.
Interview required.

W341 BA Popular Music
Duration: 3FT Hon
Entry Requirements: *GCE:* 260-300. *IB:* 24. *BTEC ExtDip:* DMM.

W302 BMus Music
Duration: 3FT Hon
Entry Requirements: *GCE:* 280-320. *IB:* 28. *BTEC ExtDip:* DDM.
Interview required.

H73 HULL COLLEGE
QUEEN'S GARDENS
HULL HU1 3DG
t: 01482 329943 f: 01482 598733
e: info@hull-college.ac.uk
// www.hull-college.ac.uk/higher-education

W313 BA Music Performance
Duration: 1FT Hon
Entry Requirements: Interview required. Admissions Test required. Portfolio required. HND required.

WJ39 BA Music Production (Top-Up)
Duration: 1FT Hon
Entry Requirements: Interview required. Admissions Test required. Portfolio required. HND required.

WW3K BA Musical Theatre
Duration: 1FT Hon
Entry Requirements: Interview required. HND required.

W312 FdA Music Performance
Duration: 2FT Fdg
Entry Requirements: *GCE:* 180-200. Interview required. Admissions Test required. Portfolio required.

WJ3X FdA Music Production
Duration: 2FT Fdg
Entry Requirements: *GCE:* 180-200. Interview required. Admissions Test required. Portfolio required.

WW34 FdA Musical Theatre
Duration: 2FT Fdg
Entry Requirements: *GCE:* 240. Interview required. Admissions Test required. Portfolio required.

I50 IMPERIAL COLLEGE LONDON
REGISTRY
SOUTH KENSINGTON CAMPUS
IMPERIAL COLLEGE LONDON
LONDON SW7 2AZ
t: 020 7589 5111 f: 020 7594 8004
// www.imperial.ac.uk

F3W3 BSc Physics and Music Performance
Duration: 4FT Hon
Entry Requirements: *GCE:* A*AA. *SQAAH:* AAA. *IB:* 39. Interview required.

K12 KEELE UNIVERSITY
KEELE UNIVERSITY
STAFFORDSHIRE ST5 5BG
t: 01782 734005 f: 01782 632343
e: undergraduate@keele.ac.uk
// www.keele.ac.uk

NW43 BA Accounting and Music
Duration: 3FT Hon
Entry Requirements: *GCE:* ABB.

TW73 BA American Studies and Music
Duration: 3FT Hon
Entry Requirements: *GCE:* BBB.

TWR3 BA American Studies and Music Technology
Duration: 3FT Hon
Entry Requirements: *GCE:* BBB.

NW23 BA Business Management and Music Technology
Duration: 3FT Hon
Entry Requirements: *GCE:* ABB.

MWX3 BA Criminology and Music
Duration: 3FT Hon
Entry Requirements: *GCE:* BBC.

LW13 BA Economics and Music
Duration: 3FT Hon
Entry Requirements: *GCE:* ABB.

LWC3 BA Economics and Music Technology
Duration: 3FT Hon
Entry Requirements: *GCE:* ABB.

WX33 BA Educational Studies and Music
Duration: 3FT Hon
Entry Requirements: *GCE:* BBC.

WXH3 BA Educational Studies and Music Technology
Duration: 3FT Hon
Entry Requirements: *GCE:* BBC.

QW33 BA English and Music
Duration: 3FT Hon
Entry Requirements: *GCE:* BBB.

NW33 BA Finance and Music
Duration: 3FT Hon
Entry Requirements: *GCE:* ABB.

NWH3 BA Finance and Music Technology
Duration: 3FT Hon
Entry Requirements: *GCE:* ABB.

LW73 BA Geography and Music
Duration: 3FT Hon
Entry Requirements: *GCE:* BBC.

LWT3 BA Geography and Music Technology
Duration: 3FT Hon
Entry Requirements: *GCE:* BBC.

VW13 BA History and Music
Duration: 3FT Hon
Entry Requirements: *GCE:* BBB.

WV31 BA History and Music Technology
Duration: 3FT Hon
Entry Requirements: *GCE:* BBB.

LWR3 BA Human Geography and Music
Duration: 3FT Hon
Entry Requirements: *GCE:* BBC.

WL37 BA Human Geography and Music Technology
Duration: 3FT Hon
Entry Requirements: *GCE:* BBC.

NW63 BA Human Resource Management and Music
Duration: 3FT Hon
Entry Requirements: *GCE:* ABB.

LWG3 BA International Relations and Music
Duration: 3FT Hon
Entry Requirements: *GCE:* BBB.

LWF3 BA International Relations and Music Technology
Duration: 3FT Hon
Entry Requirements: *GCE:* BBB.

MW13 BA Law and Music
Duration: 3FT Hon
Entry Requirements: *GCE:* ABB.

MWD3 BA Law and Music Technology
Duration: 3FT Hon
Entry Requirements: *GCE:* ABB.

NW53 BA Marketing and Music Technology
Duration: 3FT Hon
Entry Requirements: *GCE:* ABB.

W301 BA Music
Duration: 3FT Hon
Entry Requirements: *GCE:* BCC.

WJ39 BA Music Technology
Duration: 3FT Hon
Entry Requirements: *GCE:* BCC.

WV35 BA Music Technology and Philosophy
Duration: 3FT Hon
Entry Requirements: *GCE:* BBB.

LW33 BA Music Technology and Sociology
Duration: 3FT Hon
Entry Requirements: *GCE:* BBC.

LW23 BA Music and Politics
Duration: 3FT Hon
Entry Requirements: *GCE:* BBB.

W300 BA Music with Humanities foundation year
Duration: 4FT Hon
Entry Requirements: *GCE:* CC. Interview required.

FW73 BSc Applied Environmental Science and Music
Duration: 3FT Hon
Entry Requirements: *GCE:* BBC.

CW8H BSc Applied Psychology and Music
Duration: 4FT Deg
Entry Requirements: *GCE:* BBC.

FW53 BSc Astrophysics and Music
Duration: 3FT Hon
Entry Requirements: *GCE:* BBC.

FWM3 BSc Astrophysics and Music Technology
Duration: 3FT Hon
Entry Requirements: *GCE:* BBC.

CW73 BSc Biochemistry and Music
Duration: 3FT Hon
Entry Requirements: *GCE:* BBC.

CW13 BSc Biology and Music Technology
Duration: 3FT Hon
Entry Requirements: *GCE:* BBC.

FW13 BSc Chemistry and Music
Duration: 3FT Hon
Entry Requirements: *GCE:* BBC.

FW1J BSc Chemistry and Music Technology
Duration: 3FT Hon
Entry Requirements: *GCE:* BBC.

GW43 BSc Computer Science and Music
Duration: 3FT Hon
Entry Requirements: *GCE:* BBC.

GWK3 BSc Computer Science and Music Technology
Duration: 3FT Hon
Entry Requirements: *GCE:* BBC.

GW4H BSc Creative Computing and Music
Duration: 3FT Hon
Entry Requirements: *GCE:* BBC.

FW43 BSc Forensic Science and Music
Duration: 3FT Hon
Entry Requirements: *GCE:* BBC.

FW4H BSc Forensic Science and Music Technology
Duration: 3FT Hon
Entry Requirements: *GCE:* BBC.

FW63 BSc Geology and Music
Duration: 3FT Hon
Entry Requirements: *GCE:* BBC.

WG34 BSc Information Systems and Music
Duration: 3FT Hon
Entry Requirements: *GCE:* BBC.

GW13 BSc Mathematics and Music
Duration: 3FT Hon
Entry Requirements: *GCE:* BBC.

FWD3 BSc Medicinal Chemistry and Music
Duration: 3FT Hon
Entry Requirements: *GCE:* BBC.

FWC3 BSc Medicinal Chemistry and Music Technology
Duration: 3FT Hon
Entry Requirements: *GCE:* BBC.

BW13 BSc Music Technology and Neuroscience
Duration: 3FT Hon
Entry Requirements: *GCE:* BBC.

WF38 BSc Music Technology and Physical Geography
Duration: 3FT Hon
Entry Requirements: *GCE:* BBC.

FWH3 BSc Music Technology and Physics
Duration: 3FT Hon
Entry Requirements: *GCE:* BBC.

CWV3 BSc Music Technology and Psychology
Duration: 3FT Hon
Entry Requirements: *GCE:* BBC.

FW83 BSc Music and Physical Geography
Duration: 3FT Hon
Entry Requirements: *GCE:* BBC.

FW33 BSc Music and Physics
Duration: 3FT Hon
Entry Requirements: *GCE:* BBC.

CW83 BSc Music and Psychology
Duration: 3FT Hon
Entry Requirements: *GCE:* BBC.

GW73 BSc Smart Systems and Music
Duration: 3FT Hon
Entry Requirements: *GCE:* BBC.

K24 THE UNIVERSITY OF KENT
RECRUITMENT & ADMISSIONS OFFICE
REGISTRY
UNIVERSITY OF KENT
CANTERBURY, KENT CT2 7NZ
t: 01227 827272 f: 01227 827077
e: information@kent.ac.uk
// www.kent.ac.uk

W311 BA Popular Music Performance (Top-up)
Duration: 1FT Hon
Entry Requirements: Interview required. Portfolio required.

W301 BMus Music
Duration: 3FT Hon
Entry Requirements: *GCE:* ABB-BBB. *SQAH:* AABBB-ABBBB. *SQAAH:* ABB-BBB. *IB:* 33. *OCR ND:* D *OCR NED:* D2 Interview required.

W300 BMus Popular Music
Duration: 3FT Hon
Entry Requirements: *GCE:* ABB-BBB. *SQAH:* AABBB-ABBBB. *SQAAH:* ABB-BBB. *IB:* 33. *OCR ND:* D *OCR NED:* D2 Interview required.

W351 BSc Music Technology
Duration: 3FT Hon
Entry Requirements: *GCE:* ABB-BBB. *SQAH:* AABBB-ABBBB. *SQAAH:* ABB-BBB. *IB:* 33. *OCR ND:* D *OCR NED:* D2 Interview required.

W310 FdA Popular Music Performance
Duration: 2FT Fdg
Entry Requirements: *GCE:* 100. *OCR NED:* M2 Interview required. Portfolio required.

K60 KING'S COLLEGE LONDON (UNIVERSITY OF LONDON)
STRAND
LONDON WC2R 2LS
t: 020 7836 5454 f: 020 7848 7171
e: prospective@kcl.ac.uk
// www.kcl.ac.uk/prospectus

RW23 BA German and Music (4 years)
Duration: 4FT Hon
Entry Requirements: *GCE:* AAAc. *SQAH:* AAAAB. *IB:* 38.

W302 BMus Music
Duration: 3FT Hon
Entry Requirements: *GCE:* AAAc. *SQAH:* AAB. *SQAAH:* AA. *IB:* 38.

K84 KINGSTON UNIVERSITY
STUDENT INFORMATION & ADVICE CENTRE
COOPER HOUSE
40-46 SURBITON ROAD
KINGSTON UPON THAMES KT1 2HX
t: 0844 8552177 f: 020 8547 7080
e: aps@kingston.ac.uk
// www.kingston.ac.uk

WWH4 BA Creative Music Technologies and Dance
Duration: 3FT Hon
Entry Requirements: *GCE:* 260-360. Interview required.

WWG4 BA Creative Music Technologies and Drama
Duration: 3FT Hon
Entry Requirements: *GCE:* 260-360. Interview required.

WW53 BA Dance and Music
Duration: 3FT Hon
Entry Requirements: *GCE:* 300-360. Interview required.

WW43 BA Drama and Music
Duration: 3FT Hon
Entry Requirements: *GCE:* 300-360. Interview required.

VW33 BA History of Art, Design & Film and Music
Duration: 3FT Hon
Entry Requirements: *GCE:* 260-280. Interview required.

W301 BMus Creative Music Technologies
Duration: 3FT Hon
Entry Requirements: *GCE:* 260-280. Interview required.

W300 BMus Music
Duration: 3FT Hon
Entry Requirements: *GCE:* 260-280. Interview required.

L14 LANCASTER UNIVERSITY
THE UNIVERSITY
LANCASTER
LANCASHIRE LA1 4YW
t: 01524 592029 f: 01524 846243
e: ugadmissions@lancaster.ac.uk
// www.lancs.ac.uk

WQ33 BA English Literature and Music
Duration: 3FT Hon
Entry Requirements: *GCE:* AAA. *SQAH:* AAABB. *SQAAH:* AAA. *IB:* 36.

WR31 BA French Studies and Music
Duration: 4SW Hon
Entry Requirements: *GCE:* AAB. *SQAH:* ABBBB. *SQAAH:* AAB. *IB:* 35.

WR32 BA German Studies and Music
Duration: 4SW Hon
Entry Requirements: *GCE:* AAB. *SQAH:* ABBBB. *SQAAH:* AAB. *IB:* 35.

WV31 BA History and Music
Duration: 3FT Hon
Entry Requirements: *GCE:* AAB. *SQAH:* ABBBB. *SQAAH:* AAB. *IB:* 35.

W300 BA Music
Duration: 3FT Hon
Entry Requirements: *GCE:* ABB. *SQAH:* BBBBB. *SQAAH:* BBB. *IB:* 32.

WR34 BA Spanish Studies and Music
Duration: 4SW Hon
Entry Requirements: *GCE:* AAB. *SQAH:* ABBBB. *SQAAH:* AAB. *IB:* 35.

GW43 BSc Computer Science and Music
Duration: 3FT Hon
Entry Requirements: *GCE:* ABB. *SQAH:* BBBBB. *SQAAH:* BBB. *IB:* 32.

L23 UNIVERSITY OF LEEDS
THE UNIVERSITY OF LEEDS
WOODHOUSE LANE
LEEDS LS2 9JT
t: 0113 343 3999
e: admissions@leeds.ac.uk
// www.leeds.ac.uk

QW33 BA English and Music
Duration: 3FT Hon
Entry Requirements: *GCE:* ABB. *SQAAH:* ABB. *IB:* 34.

RW13 BA French and Music
Duration: 4FT Hon
Entry Requirements: *GCE:* ABB. *SQAAH:* ABB. *IB:* 34.

RW23 BA German and Music
Duration: 4FT Hon
Entry Requirements: *GCE:* ABB. *SQAAH:* ABB. *IB:* 34.

VW13 BA History and Music
Duration: 3FT Hon
Entry Requirements: *GCE:* ABB. *SQAAH:* ABB. *IB:* 34.

RW33 BA Italian A and Music
Duration: 4FT Hon
Entry Requirements: *GCE:* ABB. *SQAAH:* ABB. *IB:* 34.

RWH3 BA Italian B and Music
Duration: 4FT Hon
Entry Requirements: *GCE:* ABB. *SQAAH:* ABB. *IB:* 34.

W300 BA Music
Duration: 3FT/4FT Hon
Entry Requirements: *GCE:* ABB. *SQAH:* AAABB. *SQAAH:* ABB. *IB:* 33.

VW53 BA Music and Philosophy
Duration: 3FT Hon
Entry Requirements: *GCE:* ABB. *SQAAH:* ABB. *IB:* 34.

WR34 BA Music and Spanish
Duration: 4FT Hon
Entry Requirements: Contact the institution for details.

VW63 BA Music and Theology & Religious Studies
Duration: 3FT Hon
Entry Requirements: *GCE:* ABB. *SQAAH:* ABB. *IB:* 34.

GW13 BSc Mathematics and Music
Duration: 3FT Hon
Entry Requirements: *GCE:* AAB. *SQAAH:* AAB.

WGH4 BSc Music, Multimedia and Electronics
Duration: 3FT Hon
Entry Requirements: *GCE:* AAB. *SQAAH:* AAB. *IB:* 36.

L27 LEEDS METROPOLITAN UNIVERSITY
COURSE ENQUIRIES OFFICE
CITY CAMPUS
LEEDS LS1 3HE
t: 0113 81 23113 f: 0113 81 23129
// www.leedsmet.ac.uk

W3W1 BA Music Production and Performance
Duration: 3FT Hon
Entry Requirements: Contact the institution for details.

WJ3X BA Music Production
Duration: 3FT/4SW Hon
Entry Requirements: *GCE:* 240. *IB:* 24. Interview required.

L30 LEEDS COLLEGE OF MUSIC
3 QUARRY HILL
LEEDS
WEST YORKSHIRE LS2 7PD
t: 0113 222 3416 f: 0113 243 8798
e: enquiries@lcm.ac.uk
// www.lcm.ac.uk

W307 BA Music (Accelerated Degree)
Duration: 2FT Hon
Entry Requirements: *GCE:* 240. Interview required. Portfolio required.

W300 BA Music (Classical Music)
Duration: 3FT Hon
Entry Requirements: *GCE:* 240. Interview required. Portfolio required.

W341 BA Music (Jazz)
Duration: 3FT Hon
Entry Requirements: *GCE:* 240. Interview required. Portfolio required.

W302 BA Music (Popular Music)
Duration: 3FT Hon
Entry Requirements: *GCE:* 240. Interview required. Portfolio required.

W301 BA Music (Production)
Duration: 3FT Hon
Entry Requirements: *GCE:* 240. Interview required. Portfolio required.

W303 BA Music (combined)
Duration: 3FT Hon
Entry Requirements: *GCE:* 240. Interview required. Portfolio required.

W304 BA Music Production (Top-up)
Duration: 1FT Hon
Entry Requirements: Contact the institution for details.

W305 BA Popular Music (Top-Up)
Duration: 1FT Hon
Entry Requirements: Contact the institution for details.

W308 FYr Music Year 0
Duration: 1FT FYr
Entry Requirements: *GCE:* 240. Interview required. Portfolio required.

W306 FdA Music Production
Duration: 2FT Fdg
Entry Requirements: Interview required.

L31 LEEDS COLLEGE OF MUSIC
3 QUARRY HILL
LEEDS
WEST YORKSHIRE LS2 7PD
t: 0113 222 3416 f: 0113 243 8798
e: enquiries.assistant@lcm.ac.uk
// www.lcm.ac.uk

720F MA/MMus MA/MMus Music (Composition)
Duration: 1FT PMD
Entry Requirements: Interview required.

L41 THE UNIVERSITY OF LIVERPOOL
THE FOUNDATION BUILDING
BROWNLOW HILL
LIVERPOOL L69 7ZX
t: 0151 794 2000 f: 0151 708 6502
e: ugrecruitment@liv.ac.uk
// www.liv.ac.uk

W300 BA Music
Duration: 3FT Hon
Entry Requirements: *GCE:* ABB. *SQAAH:* ABB. *IB:* 33. Interview required.

W301 BA (Hons) Music/Popular Music
Duration: 3FT Hon
Entry Requirements: *GCE:* ABB. *SQAAH:* ABB. *IB:* 33. Interview required.

W340 BA (Hons) Popular Music
Duration: 3FT Hon
Entry Requirements: *GCE:* ABB. *SQAAH:* ABB. *IB:* 33. Interview required.

L43 LIVERPOOL COMMUNITY COLLEGE
LIVERPOOL COMMUNITY COLLEGE
CLARENCE STREET
LIVERPOOL L3 5TP
t: 0151 252 3352 f: 0151 252 3351
e: enquiry@liv-coll.ac.uk
// www.liv-coll.ac.uk

W341 FdA Popular Music
Duration: 2FT Fdg
Entry Requirements: Contact the institution for details.

L46 LIVERPOOL HOPE UNIVERSITY
HOPE PARK
LIVERPOOL L16 9JD
t: 0151 291 3331 f: 0151 291 3434
e: administration@hope.ac.uk
// www.hope.ac.uk

GW4J BA Computing and Music
Duration: 3FT Hon
Entry Requirements: *GCE:* 300-320.

WX33 BA Education and Music
Duration: 3FT Hon CRB Check: Required
Entry Requirements: *GCE:* 300-320. *IB:* 25.

QW33 BA English Literature and Music
Duration: 3FT Hon
Entry Requirements: *GCE:* 300-320. *IB:* 25.

WW1H BA Fine Art and Music
Duration: 3FT Hon
Entry Requirements: *GCE:* 300-320. *IB:* 25. Interview required. Portfolio required.

VW13 BA History and Music
Duration: 3FT Hon
Entry Requirements: *GCE:* 300-320. *IB:* 25.

W300 BA Music
Duration: 3FT Hon
Entry Requirements: *GCE:* 300-320. *IB:* 25. Interview required.

WVH5 BA Music and Philosophy & Ethics
Duration: 3FT Hon
Entry Requirements: *GCE:* 300-320. *IB:* 25. Interview required.

WLH2 BA Music and Politics
Duration: 3FT Hon
Entry Requirements: *GCE:* 300-320. *IB:* 25. Interview required.

WC38 BA Music and Psychology
Duration: 3FT Hon
Entry Requirements: *GCE:* 300-320. *IB:* 25. Interview required.

X1WJ BA Primary Teaching with Music
Duration: 4FT Hon CRB Check: Required
Entry Requirements: *GCE:* 300-320. *IB:* 25. Interview required. Admissions Test required.

L48 THE LIVERPOOL INSTITUTE FOR PERFORMING ARTS
MOUNT STREET
LIVERPOOL L1 9HF
t: 0151 330 3000 f: 0151 330 3131
e: admissions@lipa.ac.uk
// www.lipa.ac.uk

W300 BA Music
Duration: 3FT Hon
Entry Requirements: *GCE:* 300. Interview required.

HW63 BA Sound Technology
Duration: 3FT Hon
Entry Requirements: *GCE:* 280. Interview required.

L51 LIVERPOOL JOHN MOORES UNIVERSITY
KINGSWAY HOUSE
HATTON GARDEN
LIVERPOOL L3 2AJ
t: 0151 231 5090 f: 0151 904 6368
e: courses@ljmu.ac.uk
// www.ljmu.ac.uk

W340 BA Popular Music Studies
Duration: 3FT Hon
Entry Requirements: *GCE:* 260. *IB:* 28.

L68 LONDON METROPOLITAN UNIVERSITY
166-220 HOLLOWAY ROAD
LONDON N7 8DB
t: 020 7133 4200
e: admissions@londonmet.ac.uk
// www.londonmet.ac.uk

W300 BA Music Industry Management
Duration: 3FT Hon
Entry Requirements: *GCE:* 240. *IB:* 28.

WN39 BA Music Industry and Media Business Management
Duration: 3FT/4SW Hon
Entry Requirements: *GCE:* 240. *IB:* 28.

W390 BSc Music Technology (Music Production)
Duration: 3FT Hon
Entry Requirements: *GCE:* 240. *IB:* 28.

L75 LONDON SOUTH BANK UNIVERSITY
ADMISSIONS AND RECRUITMENT CENTRE
90 LONDON ROAD
LONDON SE1 6LN
t: 0800 923 8888 f: 020 7815 8273
e: course.enquiry@lsbu.ac.uk
// www.lsbu.ac.uk

WW43 BA Drama and Performance Studies
Duration: 3FT Hon
Entry Requirements: *GCE:* 240. *IB:* 24.

M10 THE MANCHESTER COLLEGE
OPENSHAW CAMPUS
ASHTON OLD ROAD
OPENSHAW
MANCHESTER M11 2WH
t: 0800 068 8585 f: 0161 920 4103
e: enquiries@themanchestercollege.ac.uk
// www.themanchestercollege.ac.uk

W315 FdA Popular Music and Performance
Duration: 2FT Fdg
Entry Requirements: Contact the institution for details.

WJ39 FdA Popular Music and Production
Duration: 2FT Fdg
Entry Requirements: *GCE:* 160. *BTEC ExtDip:* MPP. Interview required.

WN38 FdSc Music Industries Management
Duration: 2FT Fdg
Entry Requirements: *GCE:* 160. *BTEC ExtDip:* MPP. Interview required.

M20 THE UNIVERSITY OF MANCHESTER
RUTHERFORD BUILDING
OXFORD ROAD
MANCHESTER M13 9PL
t: 0161 275 2077 f: 0161 275 2106
e: ug-admissions@manchester.ac.uk
// www.manchester.ac.uk

WW34 BA Music and Drama
Duration: 3FT Hon
Entry Requirements: *GCE:* AAB. *SQAAH:* AAB. Interview required.

W302 BMus Music
Duration: 3FT Hon
Entry Requirements: *GCE:* AAB. *SQAAH:* AAB.

M40 THE MANCHESTER METROPOLITAN UNIVERSITY
ADMISSIONS OFFICE
ALL SAINTS (GMS)
ALL SAINTS
MANCHESTER M15 6BH
t: 0161 247 2000
// www.mmu.ac.uk

NW13 BA Business/Music
Duration: 3FT Hon
Entry Requirements: *GCE:* 280. *IB:* 28. *BTEC Dip:* D*D*. *BTEC ExtDip:* DMM. Interview required.

NW1H BA Business/Popular Music
Duration: 3FT Hon
Entry Requirements: *GCE:* 280. *IB:* 28. *BTEC Dip:* D*D*. *BTEC ExtDip:* DMM. Interview required.

WX3H BA Childhood & Youth Studies/Popular Music
Duration: 3FT Hon
Entry Requirements: *GCE:* 280. *IB:* 28. *BTEC Dip:* D*D*. *BTEC ExtDip:* DMM. Interview required.

W394 BA Creative Music Production
Duration: 3FT Hon
Entry Requirements: *GCE:* 280. *IB:* 28. *BTEC Dip:* D*D*. *BTEC ExtDip:* DMM. Interview required.

WW3W BA Creative Music Production/Creative Writing
Duration: 3FT Hon
Entry Requirements: *GCE:* 280. *IB:* 28. *BTEC Dip:* D*D*. *BTEC ExtDip:* DMM. Interview required.

WWH5 BA Creative Music Production/Dance
Duration: 3FT Hon
Entry Requirements: *GCE:* 280. *IB:* 28. *BTEC Dip:* D*D*. *BTEC ExtDip:* DMM. Interview required.

QW39 BA Creative Music Production/English
Duration: 3FT Hon
Entry Requirements: *GCE:* 280. *IB:* 28. *BTEC Dip:* D*D*. *BTEC ExtDip:* DMM. Interview required.

WW3Q BA Creative Music Production/Film & Television Studies
Duration: 3FT Hon
Entry Requirements: *GCE:* 280. *IB:* 28. *BTEC Dip:* D*D*. *BTEC ExtDip:* DMM. Interview required.

WN33 BA Creative Music Production/Financial Management
Duration: 3FT Hon
Entry Requirements: *GCE:* 280. *IB:* 28. *BTEC Dip:* D*D*. *BTEC ExtDip:* DMM. Interview required.

WN35 BA Creative Music Production/Marketing
Duration: 3FT Hon
Entry Requirements: *GCE:* 280. *IB:* 28. *BTEC Dip:* D*D*. *BTEC ExtDip:* DMM. Interview required.

W396 BA Creative Music Production/Popular Music
Duration: 3FT Hon
Entry Requirements: *GCE:* 280. *IB:* 28. *BTEC Dip:* D*D*. *BTEC ExtDip:* DMM. Interview required.

WW38 BA Creative Writing/Popular Music
Duration: 3FT Hon
Entry Requirements: *GCE:* 280. *IB:* 28. *BTEC Dip:* D*D*. *BTEC ExtDip:* DMM. Interview required. Portfolio required.

WW35 BA Dance/Music
Duration: 3FT Hon
Entry Requirements: *GCE:* 280. *IB:* 28. *BTEC Dip:* D*D*. *BTEC ExtDip:* DMM. Interview required.

WW34 BA Drama/Music
Duration: 3FT Hon
Entry Requirements: *GCE:* 280. *IB:* 28. *BTEC Dip:* D*D*. *BTEC ExtDip:* DMM. Interview required.

WW3K BA Drama/Popular Music
Duration: 3FT Hon
Entry Requirements: *GCE:* 280. *IB:* 28. *BTEC Dip:* D*D*. *BTEC ExtDip:* DMM. Interview required.

WX33 BA Education Studies/Music
Duration: 3FT Hon
Entry Requirements: *GCE:* 280. *IB:* 28. *BTEC Dip:* D*D*. *BTEC ExtDip:* DMM. Interview required.

QW3H BA English/Popular Music
Duration: 3FT Hon
Entry Requirements: *GCE:* 280. *IB:* 28. *BTEC Dip:* D*D*. *BTEC ExtDip:* DMM.

WW36 BA Film & Television Studies/Music
Duration: 3FT Hon
Entry Requirements: *GCE:* 280. *IB:* 28. *BTEC Dip:* D*D*. *BTEC ExtDip:* DMM. Interview required.

W301 BA Music
Duration: 3FT Hon
Entry Requirements: *GCE:* 280. *IB:* 28. *BTEC Dip:* D*D*. *BTEC ExtDip:* DMM. Interview required.

VW53 BA Music/Philosophy
Duration: 3FT Hon
Entry Requirements: *GCE:* 280. *IB:* 28. *BTEC Dip:* D*D*. *BTEC ExtDip:* DMM. Interview required.

W391 BA Music/Popular Music
Duration: 3FT Hon
Entry Requirements: *GCE:* 280. *IB:* 28. *BTEC Dip:* D*D*. *BTEC ExtDip:* DMM. Interview required.

VW5H BA Philosophy/Popular Music
Duration: 3FT Hon
Entry Requirements: *GCE:* 280. *IB:* 28. *BTEC Dip:* D*D*. *BTEC ExtDip:* DMM. Interview required.

W340 BA Popular Music
Duration: 3FT Hon
Entry Requirements: *GCE:* 280. *IB:* 28. *BTEC Dip:* D*D*. *BTEC ExtDip:* DMM. Interview required.

LWHJ BA Popular Music/Sociology
Duration: 3FT Hon
Entry Requirements: *GCE:* 280. *IB:* 28. *BTEC Dip:* D*D*. *BTEC ExtDip:* DMM. Interview required.

WC3Q BA/BSc Creative Music Production/Outdoor Studies
Duration: 3FT Hon
Entry Requirements: *GCE:* 280. *IB:* 28. *BTEC Dip:* D*D*. *BTEC ExtDip:* DMM. Interview required.

WC38 BA/BSc Music/Psychology
Duration: 3FT Hon
Entry Requirements: *GCE:* 280. *IB:* 28. *BTEC Dip:* D*D*. *BTEC ExtDip:* DMM. Interview required.

M80 MIDDLESEX UNIVERSITY
MIDDLESEX UNIVERSITY
THE BURROUGHS
LONDON NW4 4BT
t: 020 8411 5555 f: 020 8411 5649
e: enquiries@mdx.ac.uk
// www.mdx.ac.uk

W340 BA Jazz
Duration: 3FT Hon
Entry Requirements: *GCE:* 200-300. *IB:* 28. Interview required.

W301 BA Music
Duration: 3FT Hon
Entry Requirements: Contact the institution for details.

W3N2 BA Music and Arts Management
Duration: 3FT Hon
Entry Requirements: *GCE:* 200-300. *IB:* 28. Interview required.

W341 BMUS Popular Music
Duration: 3FT Hon
Entry Requirements: *GCE:* 200-300. *IB:* 28. Interview required.

N13 NEATH PORT TALBOT COLLEGE
NEATH CAMPUS
DWR-Y-FELIN ROAD
NEATH
NEATH PORT TALBOT BOROUGH SA10 7RF
t: 01639 648000 f: 01639 648077
e: admissions@nptc.ac.uk
// www.nptc.ac.uk

W300 FdA Popular Music
Duration: 2FT Fdg
Entry Requirements: Contact the institution for details.

N21 NEWCASTLE UNIVERSITY
KING'S GATE
NEWCASTLE UPON TYNE NE1 7RU
t: 01912083333
// www.ncl.ac.uk

W300 BA Music
Duration: 3FT Hon
Entry Requirements: *GCE:* AAB. *SQAH:* AAAABB. *IB:* 35. *BTEC ExtDip:* DDD. Interview required.

W340 BMus Folk and Traditional Music
Duration: 4FT Hon
Entry Requirements: *GCE:* AAB-BBB. *SQAH:* AAABB-AAAB. Interview required.

W304 BMus Music
Duration: 4FT Hon
Entry Requirements: *GCE:* AAA-AAB. *SQAH:* AAAAA-AAABB. *IB:* 35. *BTEC ExtDip:* D*DD. Interview required.

W301 BMus Popular and Contemporary Music
Duration: 2FT Hon
Entry Requirements: Interview required.

N23 NEWCASTLE COLLEGE
STUDENT SERVICES
RYE HILL CAMPUS
SCOTSWOOD ROAD
NEWCASTLE UPON TYNE NE4 7SA
t: 0191 200 4110 f: 0191 200 4349
e: enquiries@ncl-coll.ac.uk
// www.newcastlecollege.co.uk

W392 BA Music Enterprise (Top-up)
Duration: 1FT Hon
Entry Requirements: Interview required. HND required.

WW34 FdA Live Music and Theatre Production
Duration: 2FT Fdg   CRB Check: Required
Entry Requirements: *GCE:* 120-160. *OCR ND:* P2 *OCR NED:* P3 Interview required.

W300 FdA Music Production
Duration: 2FT Fdg   CRB Check: Required
Entry Requirements: *GCE:* 120-160. *OCR ND:* P2 *OCR NED:* P3 Interview required.

W391 FdA Musical Theatre
Duration: 2FT Fdg   CRB Check: Required
Entry Requirements: *GCE:* 120-160. *OCR ND:* P2 *OCR NED:* P3
Interview required.

W341 FdA Popular Music
Duration: 2FT Fdg   CRB Check: Required
Entry Requirements: *GCE:* 120-160. *OCR ND:* P2 *OCR NED:* P3
Interview required.

N30 NEW COLLEGE NOTTINGHAM
ADAMS BUILDING
STONEY STREET
THE LACE MARKET
NOTTINGHAM NG1 1NG
t: 0115 910 0100 f: 0115 953 4349
e: he.team@ncn.ac.uk
// www.ncn.ac.uk

W390 BA Sonic Arts (Top-up)
Duration: 1FT Hon
Entry Requirements: Interview required. Portfolio required.

WJ3X FdA Music and Sonic Arts (Music Performance)
Duration: 2FT Fdg
Entry Requirements: *GCE:* 120-240. Interview required. Portfolio required.

WJ39 FdA Music and Sonic Arts (Music Technology)
Duration: 2FT Fdg
Entry Requirements: *GCE:* 120-240. Interview required. Portfolio required.

N37 UNIVERSITY OF WALES, NEWPORT
ADMISSIONS
LODGE ROAD
CAERLEON
NEWPORT NP18 3QT
t: 01633 432030 f: 01633 432850
e: admissions@newport.ac.uk
// www.newport.ac.uk

W000 BA Performing Arts
Duration: 3FT Hon
Entry Requirements: *Foundation:* Merit. *GCE:* 240-260. *IB:* 24.
Interview required. Portfolio required.

N38 UNIVERSITY OF NORTHAMPTON
PARK CAMPUS
BOUGHTON GREEN ROAD
NORTHAMPTON NN2 7AL
t: 0800 358 2232 f: 01604 722083
e: admissions@northampton.ac.uk
// www.northampton.ac.uk

N4W3 BA Accounting/Popular Music
Duration: 3FT Hon
Entry Requirements: *GCE:* 260-280. *SQAH:* AAA-BBBB. *IB:* 24.
BTEC Dip: DD. *BTEC ExtDip:* DMM. *OCR ND:* D *OCR NED:* M2
Interview required.

N5WH BA Advertising/Popular Music
Duration: 3FT Hon
Entry Requirements: *GCE:* 260-280. *SQAH:* AAA-BBBB. *IB:* 24.
BTEC Dip: DD. *BTEC ExtDip:* DMM. *OCR ND:* D *OCR NED:* M2
Interview required.

N1WH BA Business Entrepreneurship/Popular Music
Duration: 3FT Hon
Entry Requirements: *GCE:* 260-280. *SQAH:* AAA-BBBB. *IB:* 24.
BTEC Dip: DD. *BTEC ExtDip:* DMM. *OCR ND:* D *OCR NED:* M2
Interview required.

N1W3 BA Business/Popular Music
Duration: 3FT Hon
Entry Requirements: *GCE:* 260-280. *SQAH:* AAA-BBBB. *IB:* 24.
BTEC Dip: DD. *BTEC ExtDip:* DMM. *OCR ND:* D *OCR NED:* M2

M9W3 BA Criminology/Popular Music
Duration: 3FT Hon
Entry Requirements: *GCE:* 260-280. *SQAH:* AAA-BBBB. *IB:* 24.
BTEC Dip: DD. *BTEC ExtDip:* DMM. *OCR ND:* D *OCR NED:* M2

W5W3 BA Dance/Popular Music
Duration: 3FT Hon
Entry Requirements: *GCE:* 260-280. *SQAH:* AAA-BBBB. *IB:* 24.
BTEC Dip: DD. *BTEC ExtDip:* DMM. *OCR ND:* D *OCR NED:* M2
Interview required.

W4W3 BA Drama/Popular Music
Duration: 3FT Hon
Entry Requirements: *GCE:* 260-280. *SQAH:* AAA-BBBB. *IB:* 24.
BTEC Dip: DD. *BTEC ExtDip:* DMM. *OCR ND:* D *OCR NED:* M2
Interview required.

X3W3 BA Education Studies/Popular Music
Duration: 3FT Hon
Entry Requirements: *GCE:* 260-280. *SQAH:* AAA-BBBB. *IB:* 24.
BTEC Dip: DD. *BTEC ExtDip:* DMM. *OCR ND:* D *OCR NED:* M2
Interview required.

Q3W3 BA English/Popular Music
Duration: 3FT Hon
Entry Requirements: *GCE:* 260-280. *SQAH:* AAA-BBBB. *IB:* 24.
BTEC Dip: DD. *BTEC ExtDip:* DMM. *OCR ND:* D *OCR NED:* M2
Interview required.

N8WH BA Events Management/Popular Music
Duration: 3FT Hon
Entry Requirements: *GCE:* 260-280. *SQAH:* AAA-BBBB. *IB:* 24.
BTEC Dip: DD. *BTEC ExtDip:* DMM. *OCR ND:* D *OCR NED:* M2
Interview required.

W6W3 BA Film & Television Studies/Popular Music
Duration: 3FT Hon
Entry Requirements: *GCE:* 260-280. *SQAH:* AAA-BBBB. *IB:* 24.
BTEC Dip: DD. *BTEC ExtDip:* DMM. *OCR ND:* D *OCR NED:* M2
Interview required.

W1W3 BA Fine Art Painting & Drawing/Popular Music
Duration: 3FT Hon
Entry Requirements: *GCE:* 260-280. *SQAH:* AAA-BBBB. *IB:* 24.
BTEC Dip: DD. *BTEC ExtDip:* DMM. *OCR ND:* D *OCR NED:* M2
Interview required.

R1W3 BA French/Popular Music
Duration: 3FT Hon
Entry Requirements: *GCE:* 260-280. *SQAH:* AAA-BBBB. *IB:* 24.
BTEC Dip: DD. *BTEC ExtDip:* DMM. *OCR ND:* D *OCR NED:* M2
Interview required.

L4W3 BA Health Studies/Popular Music
Duration: 3FT Hon
Entry Requirements: *GCE:* 260-280. *SQAH:* AAA-BBBB. *IB:* 24.
BTEC Dip: DD. *BTEC ExtDip:* DMM. *OCR ND:* D *OCR NED:* M2

V1W3 BA History/Popular Music
Duration: 3FT Hon
Entry Requirements: *GCE:* 260-280. *SQAH:* AAA-BBBB. *IB:* 24.
BTEC Dip: DD. *BTEC ExtDip:* DMM. *OCR ND:* D *OCR NED:* M2

L7W3 BA Human Geography/Popular Music
Duration: 3FT Hon
Entry Requirements: *GCE:* 260-280. *SQAH:* AAA-BBBB. *IB:* 24.
BTEC Dip: DD. *BTEC ExtDip:* DMM. *OCR ND:* D *OCR NED:* M2

N6W3 BA Human Resource Management/Popular Music
Duration: 3FT Hon
Entry Requirements: *GCE:* 260-280. *SQAH:* AAA-BBBB. *IB:* 24.
BTEC Dip: DD. *BTEC ExtDip:* DMM. *OCR ND:* D *OCR NED:* M2

L9WH BA International Development/Popular Music
Duration: 3FT Hon
Entry Requirements: *GCE:* 260-280. *SQAH:* AAA-BBBB. *IB:* 24.
BTEC Dip: DD. *BTEC ExtDip:* DMM. *OCR ND:* D *OCR NED:* M2

M1W3 BA Law/Popular Music
Duration: 3FT Hon
Entry Requirements: *GCE:* 260-280. *SQAH:* AAA-BBBB. *IB:* 24.
BTEC Dip: DD. *BTEC ExtDip:* DMM. *OCR ND:* D *OCR NED:* M2

N2W3 BA Management/Popular Music
Duration: 3FT Hon
Entry Requirements: *GCE:* 260-280. *SQAH:* AAA-BBBB. *IB:* 24.
BTEC Dip: DD. *BTEC ExtDip:* DMM. *OCR ND:* D *OCR NED:* M2

N5W3 BA Marketing/Popular Music
Duration: 3FT Hon
Entry Requirements: *GCE:* 260-280. *SQAH:* AAA-BBBB. *IB:* 24.
BTEC Dip: DD. *BTEC ExtDip:* DMM. *OCR ND:* D *OCR NED:* M2
Interview required.

W301 BA Music Practice (top-up)
Duration: 1FT Hon
Entry Requirements: Contact the institution for details.

W391 BA Music Production (top-up)
Duration: 1FT Hon
Entry Requirements: Interview required. HND required.

W340 BA Popular Music
Duration: 3FT Hon
Entry Requirements: *GCE:* 260-280. *SQAH:* AAA-BBBB. *IB:* 24.
BTEC Dip: DD. *BTEC ExtDip:* DMM. *OCR ND:* D *OCR NED:* M2
Interview required.

W3NA BA Popular Music with Applied Management
Duration: 3FT Hon
Entry Requirements: *GCE:* 260-280. *SQAH:* AAA-BBBB. *IB:* 24.
BTEC Dip: DD. *BTEC ExtDip:* DMM. *OCR ND:* D *OCR NED:* M2
Interview required.

W3N4 BA Popular Music/Accounting
Duration: 3FT Hon
Entry Requirements: *GCE:* 260-280. *SQAH:* AAA-BBBB. *IB:* 24.
BTEC Dip: DD. *BTEC ExtDip:* DMM. *OCR ND:* D *OCR NED:* M2

W3NM BA Popular Music/Advertising
Duration: 3FT Hon
Entry Requirements: *GCE:* 260-280. *SQAH:* AAA-BBBB. *IB:* 24.
BTEC Dip: DD. *BTEC ExtDip:* DMM. *OCR ND:* D *OCR NED:* M2
Interview required.

W3C1 BA Popular Music/Biological Conservation
Duration: 3FT Hon
Entry Requirements: *GCE:* 260-280. *SQAH:* AAA-BBBB. *IB:* 24.
BTEC Dip: DD. *BTEC ExtDip:* DMM. *OCR ND:* D *OCR NED:* M2

W3N1 BA Popular Music/Business
Duration: 3FT Hon
Entry Requirements: *GCE:* 260-280. *SQAH:* AAA-BBBB. *IB:* 24.
BTEC Dip: DD. *BTEC ExtDip:* DMM. *OCR ND:* D *OCR NED:* M2
Interview required.

W3NF BA Popular Music/Business Entrepreneurship
Duration: 3FT Hon
Entry Requirements: *GCE:* 260-280. *SQAH:* AAA-BBBB. *IB:* 24.
BTEC Dip: DD. *BTEC ExtDip:* DMM. *OCR ND:* D *OCR NED:* M2
Interview required.

W3G4 BA Popular Music/Computing
Duration: 3FT Hon
Entry Requirements: *GCE:* 260-280. *SQAH:* AAA-BBBB. *IB:* 24.
BTEC Dip: DD. *BTEC ExtDip:* DMM. *OCR ND:* D *OCR NED:* M2

W3M9 BA Popular Music/Criminology
Duration: 3FT Hon
Entry Requirements: *GCE:* 260-280. *SQAH:* AAA-BBBB. *IB:* 24.
BTEC Dip: DD. *BTEC ExtDip:* DMM. *OCR ND:* D *OCR NED:* M2

W3W5 BA Popular Music/Dance
Duration: 3FT Hon
Entry Requirements: *GCE:* 260-280. *SQAH:* AAA-BBBB. *IB:* 24.
BTEC Dip: DD. *BTEC ExtDip:* DMM. *OCR ND:* D *OCR NED:* M2
Interview required.

W3W4 BA Popular Music/Drama
Duration: 3FT Hon
Entry Requirements: *GCE:* 260-280. *SQAH:* AAA-BBBB. *IB:* 24.
BTEC Dip: DD. *BTEC ExtDip:* DMM. *OCR ND:* D *OCR NED:* M2
Interview required.

W3X3 BA Popular Music/Education Studies
Duration: 3FT Hon
Entry Requirements: *GCE:* 260-280. *SQAH:* AAA-BBBB. *IB:* 24.
BTEC Dip: DD. *BTEC ExtDip:* DMM. *OCR ND:* D *OCR NED:* M2
Interview required.

W3Q3 BA Popular Music/English
Duration: 3FT Hon
Entry Requirements: *GCE:* 260-280. *SQAH:* AAA-BBBB. *IB:* 24.
BTEC Dip: DD. *BTEC ExtDip:* DMM. *OCR ND:* D *OCR NED:* M2
Interview required.

W3NV BA Popular Music/Events Management
Duration: 3FT Hon
Entry Requirements: *GCE:* 260-280. *SQAH:* AAA-BBBB. *IB:* 24.
BTEC Dip: DD. *BTEC ExtDip:* DMM. *OCR ND:* D *OCR NED:* M2
Interview required.

W3W6 BA Popular Music/Film & Television Studies
Duration: 3FT Hon
Entry Requirements: *GCE:* 260-280. *SQAH:* AAA-BBBB. *IB:* 24.
BTEC Dip: DD. *BTEC ExtDip:* DMM. *OCR ND:* D *OCR NED:* M2
Interview required.

W3W1 BA Popular Music/Fine Art Painting & Drawing
Duration: 3FT Hon
Entry Requirements: *GCE:* 260-280. *SQAH:* AAA-BBBB. *IB:* 24.
BTEC Dip: DD. *BTEC ExtDip:* DMM. *OCR ND:* D *OCR NED:* M2
Interview required.

W3R1 BA Popular Music/French
Duration: 3FT Hon
Entry Requirements: *GCE:* 260-280. *SQAH:* AAA-BBBB. *IB:* 24.
BTEC Dip: DD. *BTEC ExtDip:* DMM. *OCR ND:* D *OCR NED:* M2
Interview required.

W3L4 BA Popular Music/Health Studies
Duration: 3FT Hon
Entry Requirements: *GCE:* 260-280. *SQAH:* AAA-BBBB. *IB:* 24.
BTEC Dip: DD. *BTEC ExtDip:* DMM. *OCR ND:* D *OCR NED:* M2

W3V1 BA Popular Music/History
Duration: 3FT Hon
Entry Requirements: *GCE:* 260-280. *SQAH:* AAA-BBBB. *IB:* 24.
BTEC Dip: DD. *BTEC ExtDip:* DMM. *OCR ND:* D *OCR NED:* M2

W3B1 BA Popular Music/Human Biology
Duration: 3FT Hon
Entry Requirements: *GCE:* 260-280. *SQAH:* AAA-BBBB. *IB:* 24.
BTEC Dip: DD. *BTEC ExtDip:* DMM. *OCR ND:* D *OCR NED:* M2
Interview required.

W3L7 BA Popular Music/Human Geography
Duration: 3FT Hon
Entry Requirements: *GCE:* 260-280. *SQAH:* AAA-BBBB. *IB:* 24.
BTEC Dip: DD. *BTEC ExtDip:* DMM. *OCR ND:* D *OCR NED:* M2

W3N6 BA Popular Music/Human Resource Management
Duration: 3FT Hon
Entry Requirements: *GCE:* 260-280. *SQAH:* AAA-BBBB. *IB:* 24.
BTEC Dip: DD. *BTEC ExtDip:* DMM. *OCR ND:* D *OCR NED:* M2

W3LX BA Popular Music/International Development
Duration: 3FT Hon
Entry Requirements: *GCE:* 260-280. *SQAH:* AAA-BBBB. *IB:* 24.
BTEC Dip: DD. *BTEC ExtDip:* DMM. *OCR ND:* D *OCR NED:* M2

W3M1 BA Popular Music/Law
Duration: 3FT Hon
Entry Requirements: *GCE:* 260-280. *SQAH:* AAA-BBBB. *IB:* 24.
BTEC Dip: DD. *BTEC ExtDip:* DMM. *OCR ND:* D *OCR NED:* M2

W3N2 BA Popular Music/Management
Duration: 3FT Hon
Entry Requirements: *GCE:* 260-280. *SQAH:* AAA-BBBB. *IB:* 24.
BTEC Dip: DD. *BTEC ExtDip:* DMM. *OCR ND:* D *OCR NED:* M2

W3N5 BA Popular Music/Marketing
Duration: 3FT Hon
Entry Requirements: *GCE:* 260-280. *SQAH:* AAA-BBBB. *IB:* 24.
BTEC Dip: DD. *BTEC ExtDip:* DMM. *OCR ND:* D *OCR NED:* M2

W3L5 BA Popular Music/Social Care
Duration: 3FT Hon
Entry Requirements: *GCE:* 260-280. *SQAH:* AAA-BBBB. *IB:* 24.
BTEC Dip: DD. *BTEC ExtDip:* DMM. *OCR ND:* D *OCR NED:* M2

W3L3 BA Popular Music/Sociology
Duration: 3FT Hon
Entry Requirements: *GCE:* 260-280. *SQAH:* AAA-BBBB. *IB:* 24.
BTEC Dip: DD. *BTEC ExtDip:* DMM. *OCR ND:* D *OCR NED:* M2

W3C6 BA Popular Music/Sport Studies
Duration: 3FT Hon
Entry Requirements: *GCE:* 260-280. *SQAH:* AAA-BBBB. *IB:* 24.
BTEC Dip: DD. *BTEC ExtDip:* DMM. *OCR ND:* D *OCR NED:* M2

W3N8 BA Popular Music/Tourism
Duration: 3FT Hon
Entry Requirements: *GCE:* 260-280. *SQAH:* AAA-BBBB. *IB:* 24.
BTEC Dip: DD. *BTEC ExtDip:* DMM. *OCR ND:* D *OCR NED:* M2
Interview required.

L5W3 BA Social Care/Popular Music
Duration: 3FT Hon
Entry Requirements: *GCE:* 260-280. *SQAH:* AAA-BBBB. *IB:* 24.
BTEC Dip: DD. *BTEC ExtDip:* DMM. *OCR ND:* D *OCR NED:* M2

L3W3 BA Sociology/Popular Music
Duration: 3FT Hon
Entry Requirements: *GCE:* 260-280. *SQAH:* AAA-BBBB. *IB:* 24.
BTEC Dip: DD. *BTEC ExtDip:* DMM. *OCR ND:* D *OCR NED:* M2

XW33 BA Special Educational Needs & Inclusion/Popular Music
Duration: 3FT Hon
Entry Requirements: *GCE:* 260-280. *SQAH:* AAA-BBBB. *IB:* 24.
BTEC Dip: DD. *BTEC ExtDip:* DMM. *OCR ND:* D *OCR NED:* M2
Interview required.

C6W3 BA Sport Studies/Popular Music
Duration: 3FT Hon
Entry Requirements: *GCE:* 260-280. *SQAH:* AAA-BBBB. *IB:* 24.
BTEC Dip: DD. *BTEC ExtDip:* DMM. *OCR ND:* D *OCR NED:* M2

N8W3 BA Tourism/Popular Music
Duration: 3FT Hon
Entry Requirements: *GCE:* 260-280. *SQAH:* AAA-BBBB. *IB:* 24.
BTEC Dip: DD. *BTEC ExtDip:* DMM. *OCR ND:* D *OCR NED:* M2

C1W3 BSc Biological Conservation/Popular Music
Duration: 3FT Hon
Entry Requirements: *GCE:* 260-280. *SQAH:* AAA-BBBB. *IB:* 24.
BTEC Dip: DD. *BTEC ExtDip:* DMM. *OCR ND:* D *OCR NED:* M2

G4W3 BSc Computing/Popular Music
Duration: 3FT Hon
Entry Requirements: *GCE:* 260-280. *SQAH:* AAA-BBBB. *IB:* 24.
BTEC Dip: DD. *BTEC ExtDip:* DMM. *OCR ND:* D *OCR NED:* M2
Interview required.

B1W3 BSc Human Bioscience/Popular Music
Duration: 3FT Hon
Entry Requirements: *GCE:* 260-280. *SQAH:* AAA-BBBB. *IB:* 24.
BTEC Dip: DD. *BTEC ExtDip:* DMM. *OCR ND:* D *OCR NED:* M2
Interview required.

003W HND Music Practice
Duration: 2FT HND
Entry Requirements: *GCE:* 140-160. *SQAH:* BC-CCC. *IB:* 24.
BTEC Dip: MP. *BTEC ExtDip:* MPP. *OCR ND:* P1 *OCR NED:* P2
Interview required.

093W HND Music Production
Duration: 2FT HND
Entry Requirements: *GCE:* 140-160. *SQAH:* BC-CCC. *IB:* 24.
BTEC Dip: MP. *BTEC ExtDip:* MPP. *OCR ND:* P1 *OCR NED:* P2
Interview required.

N41 NORTHBROOK COLLEGE SUSSEX
LITTLEHAMPTON ROAD
WORTHING
WEST SUSSEX BN12 6NU
t: 0845 155 6060 f: 01903 606073
e: enquiries@nbcol.ac.uk
// www.northbrook.ac.uk

JN91 BA Music Business and Management (Top-Up)
Duration: 1FT Hon
Entry Requirements: Interview required.

W393 BA Music Composition for Film and Media (Top-Up)
Duration: 1FT Hon
Entry Requirements: Interview required.

W310 BA Music Performance (Top-Up)
Duration: 1FT Hon
Entry Requirements: Interview required.

W361 BA Music Production (Top-Up)
Duration: 1FT Hon
Entry Requirements: Interview required.

WW24 FdA Lighting and Sound Design
Duration: 2FT Fdg
Entry Requirements: *GCE:* 160. Interview required.

N190 FdA Music Business and Management
Duration: 2FT Fdg
Entry Requirements: *GCE:* 160. Interview required.

W300 FdA Music Composition for Film and Media
Duration: 2FT Fdg
Entry Requirements: *GCE:* 160. Interview required.

W313 FdA Music Performance
Duration: 2FT Fdg
Entry Requirements: *GCE:* 160. Interview required.

J931 FdA Music Production
Duration: 2FT Fdg
Entry Requirements: *GCE:* 160. Interview required.

W392 FdA Theatre Arts - Musical Theatre
Duration: 2FT Fdg
Entry Requirements: *GCE:* 160. Interview required.

N82 NORWICH CITY COLLEGE OF FURTHER AND HIGHER EDUCATION (AN ASSOCIATE COLLEGE OF UEA)
IPSWICH ROAD
NORWICH
NORFOLK NR2 2LJ
t: 01603 773012 f: 01603 773301
e: he_office@ccn.ac.uk
// www.ccn.ac.uk

W390 FdA Popular Music Performance and Production
Duration: 2FT Fdg
Entry Requirements: Interview required.

N84 THE UNIVERSITY OF NOTTINGHAM
THE ADMISSIONS OFFICE
THE UNIVERSITY OF NOTTINGHAM
UNIVERSITY PARK
NOTTINGHAM NG7 2RD
t: 0115 951 5151 f: 0115 951 4668
// www.nottingham.ac.uk

RW2H BA German (Beginners) and Music
Duration: 4FT Hon
Entry Requirements: *GCE:* ABB. *SQAAH:* ABB. *IB:* 32.

RW23 BA German and Music
Duration: 4FT Hon
Entry Requirements: *GCE:* ABB. *SQAAH:* ABB. *IB:* 32.

W300 BA Music
Duration: 3FT Hon
Entry Requirements: *GCE:* AAB. *SQAAH:* AAB. *IB:* 34.

WV35 BA Music and Philosophy
Duration: 3FT Hon
Entry Requirements: *GCE:* ABB. *SQAAH:* ABB. *IB:* 32.

O33 OXFORD UNIVERSITY
UNDERGRADUATE ADMISSIONS OFFICE
UNIVERSITY OF OXFORD
WELLINGTON SQUARE
OXFORD OX1 2JD
t: 01865 288000 f: 01865 270212
e: undergraduate.admissions@admin.ox.ac.uk
// www.admissions.ox.ac.uk

W300 BA Music
Duration: 3FT Hon
Entry Requirements: *GCE:* AAA. *SQAH:* AAAAA-AAAAB. *SQAAH:* AAB. Interview required. Admissions Test required.

O66 OXFORD BROOKES UNIVERSITY
ADMISSIONS OFFICE
HEADINGTON CAMPUS
GIPSY LANE
OXFORD OX3 0BP
t: 01865 483040 f: 01865 483983
e: admissions@brookes.ac.uk
// www.brookes.ac.uk

QW3H BA English/Music
Duration: 3FT Hon
Entry Requirements: *GCE:* BBC.

W300 BA Music
Duration: 3FT Hon
Entry Requirements: *GCE:* BBC.

GW4H BA/BSc Computer Science/Music
Duration: 3FT Hon
Entry Requirements: *GCE:* BCC.

WW43 BA/BSc Drama/Music
Duration: 3FT Hon
Entry Requirements: *GCE:* BBC.

XW33 BA/BSc Education Studies/Music
Duration: 3FT Hon
Entry Requirements: *GCE:* BCC.

QW93 BA/BSc English Language and Communication/Music
Duration: 3FT Hon
Entry Requirements: *GCE:* BCC.

W1W3 BA/BSc Fine Art/Music
Duration: 3FT Hon
Entry Requirements: *GCE:* BCC.

RW13 BA/BSc French Studies/Music
Duration: 4SW Hon
Entry Requirements: *GCE:* BBC.

VW33 BA/BSc History of Art/Music
Duration: 3FT Hon
Entry Requirements: *GCE:* BCC.

VW13 BA/BSc History/Music
Duration: 3FT Hon
Entry Requirements: *GCE:* BCC.

TW2H BA/BSc Japanese Studies/Music
Duration: 4SW Hon
Entry Requirements: *GCE:* BBC.

GW13 BA/BSc Mathematics/Music
Duration: 3FT Hon
Entry Requirements: *GCE:* BCC.

W3R4 BA/BSc Music with Spanish (Minor)
Duration: 4SW Hon
Entry Requirements: *GCE:* BBC. *IB:* 31.

VW53 BA/BSc Music/Philosophy
Duration: 3FT Hon
Entry Requirements: *GCE:* BCC.

CW83 BA/BSc Music/Psychology
Duration: 3FT Hon
Entry Requirements: *GCE:* BBB.

PW4H BA/BSc Publishing Media/Music
Duration: 3FT Hon
Entry Requirements: *GCE:* BBC.

P51 PETROC
OLD STICKLEPATH HILL
BARNSTAPLE
NORTH DEVON EX31 2BQ
t: 01271 852365 f: 01271 338121
e: he@petroc.ac.uk
// www.petroc.ac.uk

W310 FdA Music Performance
Duration: 2FT Fdg
Entry Requirements: Contact the institution for details.

P60 PLYMOUTH UNIVERSITY
DRAKE CIRCUS
PLYMOUTH PL4 8AA
t: 01752 585858 f: 01752 588055
e: admissions@plymouth.ac.uk
// www.plymouth.ac.uk

W300 BA Music
Duration: 3FT Hon
Entry Requirements: *GCE:* 260. *IB:* 25. *BTEC ExtDip:* DMM.

X1W3 BEd Primary (Music)
Duration: 3FT Hon   CRB Check: Required
Entry Requirements: *GCE:* 240. *IB:* 26. *OCR ND:* D Interview required.

W391 FdA Community Music
Duration: 2FT Fdg
Entry Requirements: *GCE:* 80. *IB:* 24. *OCR ND:* P3 *OCR NED:* P3

P63 UCP MARJON - UNIVERSITY COLLEGE PLYMOUTH ST MARK & ST JOHN
DERRIFORD ROAD
PLYMOUTH PL6 8BH
t: 01752 636890 f: 01752 636819
e: admissions@marjon.ac.uk
// www.ucpmarjon.ac.uk

W390 BA Live Music
Duration: 1FT Hon
Entry Requirements: *GCE:* 220. Portfolio required.

W310 BA Live Music (accelerated)
Duration: 2FT Hon
Entry Requirements: Contact the institution for details.

Q75 QUEEN'S UNIVERSITY BELFAST
UNIVERSITY ROAD
BELFAST BT7 1NN
t: 028 9097 3838 f: 028 9097 5151
e: admissions@qub.ac.uk
// www.qub.ac.uk

W302 BMus Music
Duration: 3FT Hon
Entry Requirements: *GCE:* BBB-BBCb. *SQAH:* ABBBC. *SQAAH:* BBB. *IB:* 32.

R06 RAVENSBOURNE
6 PENROSE WAY
GREENWICH PENINSULA
LONDON SE10 0EW
t: 020 3040 3998
e: info@rave.ac.uk
// www.rave.ac.uk

WPH3 BA Music Production for Media (Fast-Track)
Duration: 2FT Hon
Entry Requirements: Contact the institution for details.

R12 THE UNIVERSITY OF READING
THE UNIVERSITY OF READING
PO BOX 217
READING RG6 6AH
t: 0118 378 8619 f: 0118 378 8924
e: student.recruitment@reading.ac.uk
// www.reading.ac.uk

X1W3 BA Primary Education with Music
Duration: 3FT Deg   CRB Check: Required
Entry Requirements: *GCE:* 180. *SQAH:* BBC. *SQAAH:* BD. *BTEC Dip:* DM. *BTEC ExtDip:* MMP. Interview required.

R48 ROEHAMPTON UNIVERSITY
ROEHAMPTON LANE
LONDON SW15 5PU
t: 020 8392 3232 f: 020 8392 3470
e: enquiries@roehampton.ac.uk
// www.roehampton.ac.uk

XWC3 BA Primary Education Foundation Stage & Key Stage 1 (Music)
Duration: 3FT Hon   CRB Check: Required
Entry Requirements: *GCE:* 320. *IB:* 27. *BTEC ExtDip:* DDM. *OCR NED:* D2 Interview required.

XW1H BA Primary Education Key Stage 2 (Music Education)
Duration: 3FT Hon   CRB Check: Required
Entry Requirements: *GCE:* 320. *IB:* 27. *BTEC ExtDip:* DDM. *OCR NED:* D2 Interview required.

R51 ROSE BRUFORD COLLEGE
LAMORBEY PARK
BURNT OAK LANE
SIDCUP
KENT DA15 9DF
t: 0208 308 2600 f: 020 8308 0542
e: enquiries@bruford.ac.uk
// www.bruford.ac.uk

W4W3 BA Actor Musician
Duration: 3FT Hon
Entry Requirements: *GCE:* 160-280.

R52 ROTHERHAM COLLEGE OF ARTS AND TECHNOLOGY
EASTWOOD LANE
ROTHERHAM
SOUTH YORKSHIRE S65 1EG
t: 08080 722777 f: 01709 373053
e: info@rotherham.ac.uk
// www.rotherham.ac.uk

W300 FdA Performing Arts Music
Duration: 2FT Fdg
Entry Requirements: *GCE:* 120. Interview required.

R72 ROYAL HOLLOWAY, UNIVERSITY OF LONDON
ROYAL HOLLOWAY, UNIVERSITY OF LONDON
EGHAM
SURREY TW20 0EX
t: 01784 414944 f: 01784 473662
e: Admissions@rhul.ac.uk
// www.rhul.ac.uk

WW43 BA Drama and Music
Duration: 3FT Hon
Entry Requirements: *GCE:* ABB. *SQAH:* AABBB. *SQAAH:* ABB. *IB:* 34.

L1W3 BA Economics with Music
Duration: 3FT Hon
Entry Requirements: *GCE:* AAA-ABB. *SQAH:* AAAAA-AABBB. *SQAAH:* AAA-ABB. *IB:* 32.

RW13 BA French and Music
Duration: 4FT Hon
Entry Requirements: *GCE:* ABB. *SQAH:* AABBB. *SQAAH:* ABB. *IB:* 33.

R1W3 BA French with Music
Duration: 4FT Hon
Entry Requirements: *GCE:* ABB-BBB. *SQAH:* AABBB-BBBBB. *SQAAH:* ABB-BBB. *IB:* 32.

RW23 BA German and Music
Duration: 4FT Hon
Entry Requirements: *GCE:* ABB. *SQAH:* AABBB. *SQAAH:* ABB. *IB:* 34.

VW13 BA History and Music
Duration: 3FT Hon
Entry Requirements: *GCE:* ABB. *SQAH:* AABBB. *SQAAH:* ABB. *IB:* 34.

RW33 BA Italian and Music
Duration: 4FT Hon
Entry Requirements: *GCE:* ABB. *SQAH:* AABBB. *SQAAH:* ABB. *IB:* 34.

GW13 BA Mathematics and Music
Duration: 3FT Hon
Entry Requirements: *GCE:* 340. *SQAH:* AAAAB. *SQAAH:* A. *IB:* 35

WV35 BA Music and Philosophy
Duration: 3FT Hon
Entry Requirements: *GCE:* AAB. *SQAH:* AAAAB. *IB:* 35.

W3R1 BA Music with French
Duration: 3FT Hon
Entry Requirements: *GCE:* ABB. *SQAH:* AABBB. *SQAAH:* ABB. *IB:* 34.

W3R2 BA Music with German
Duration: 3FT Hon
Entry Requirements: *GCE:* ABB. *SQAH:* AABBB. *SQAAH:* ABB. *IB:* 34.

W3R3 BA Music with Italian
Duration: 3FT Hon
Entry Requirements: *GCE:* ABB. *SQAH:* AABBB. *SQAAH:* ABB. *IB:* 34.

W3V5 BA Music with Philosophy
Duration: 3FT Hon
Entry Requirements: *GCE:* AAB. *SQAH:* AAAAB. *IB:* 35.

W3L2 BA Music with Political Studies
Duration: 3FT Hon
Entry Requirements: *GCE:* AAB. *SQAH:* AAAAB. *IB:* 35.

W3R4 BA Music with Spanish
Duration: 3FT Hon
Entry Requirements: *GCE:* ABB. *SQAH:* AABBB. *SQAAH:* ABB. *IB:* 34.

R4W3 BA Spanish with Music
Duration: 4FT Hon
Entry Requirements: *GCE:* ABB-BBB. *SQAH:* AABBB-BBBBB. *SQAAH:* ABB-BBB. *IB:* 32.

W302 BMus Music
Duration: 3FT Hon
Entry Requirements: *GCE:* AAB. *SQAH:* AAAAB. *IB:* 35.

F3W3 BSc Physics with Music
Duration: 3FT Hon
Entry Requirements: *GCE:* 320-340. *IB:* 34.

S03 THE UNIVERSITY OF SALFORD
SALFORD M5 4WT
t: 0161 295 4545 f: 0161 295 4646
e: ug-admissions@salford.ac.uk
// www.salford.ac.uk

W304 BA Music
Duration: 3FT Hon
Entry Requirements: *GCE:* 300. *IB:* 31. *OCR ND:* D *OCR NED:* M2
Interview required.

W374 BA Music: Interactive Music and Studio Production
Duration: 3FT Hon
Entry Requirements: Contact the institution for details.

W350 BA Music: Popular Musicology
Duration: 3FT Hon
Entry Requirements: *GCE:* 280. *IB:* 31. *OCR ND:* D *OCR NED:* M2
Interview required.

S09 SCHOOL OF ORIENTAL AND AFRICAN STUDIES (UNIVERSITY OF LONDON)
THORNHAUGH STREET
RUSSELL SQUARE
LONDON WC1H 0XG
t: 020 7898 4301 f: 020 7898 4039
e: undergradadmissions@soas.ac.uk
// www.soas.ac.uk

VW33 BA History of Art/Archaeology and Music
Duration: 3FT Hon
Entry Requirements: *GCE:* ABB.

TW2H BA Japanese Studies and Music
Duration: 3FT Hon
Entry Requirements: *GCE:* AAB.

QW33 BA Linguistics and Music
Duration: 3FT Hon
Entry Requirements: *GCE:* AAB.

TW6H BA Middle Eastern Studies and Music
Duration: 3FT Hon
Entry Requirements: *GCE:* AAB.

W300 BA Music
Duration: 3FT Hon
Entry Requirements: *GCE:* BBB.

WT35 BA Music and African Studies
Duration: 3FT Hon
Entry Requirements: *GCE:* AAB.

TW63 BA Music and Arabic
Duration: 4FT Hon
Entry Requirements: *GCE:* AAB.

TWH3 BA Music and Burmese
Duration: 3FT Hon
Entry Requirements: *GCE:* AAB.

TW13 BA Music and Chinese
Duration: 4FT Hon
Entry Requirements: *GCE:* AAB.

LW93 BA Music and Development Studies
Duration: 3FT Hon
Entry Requirements: *GCE:* AAA.

LW73 BA Music and Geography
Duration: 3FT Hon
Entry Requirements: *GCE:* AAB.

TW93 BA Music and Georgian
Duration: 3FT Hon
Entry Requirements: *GCE:* AAB.

TWM3 BA Music and Hausa
Duration: 4FT Hon
Entry Requirements: *GCE:* AAB.

QW43 BA Music and Hebrew
Duration: 4FT Hon
Entry Requirements: *GCE:* AAB.

VW13 BA Music and History
Duration: 3FT Hon
Entry Requirements: *GCE:* AAB.

TWHH BA Music and Indonesian
Duration: 3FT Hon
Entry Requirements: *GCE:* AAB.

TW23 BA Music and Japanese
Duration: 4FT Hon
Entry Requirements: *GCE:* AAB.

TWLH BA Music and Korean
Duration: 4FT Hon
Entry Requirements: *GCE:* AAB.

WTHH BA Music and South-East Asian Studies
Duration: 3FT Hon
Entry Requirements: *GCE:* AAB.

TWQ3 BA Persian and Music
Duration: 3FT Hon
Entry Requirements: *GCE:* AAB.

LW63 BA Social Anthropology and Music
Duration: 3FT Hon
Entry Requirements: *GCE:* AAA.

WTH3 BA South Asian Studies and Music
Duration: 3FT Hon
Entry Requirements: *GCE:* AAB.

TW33 BA South Asian Studies and Music (including year abroad)
Duration: 4FT Hon
Entry Requirements: *GCE:* AAB.

VW63 BA Study of Religions and Music
Duration: 3FT Hon
Entry Requirements: *GCE:* ABB.

TWN3 BA Swahili and Music
Duration: 4FT Hon
Entry Requirements: *GCE:* AAB.

WT33 BA Thai and Music
Duration: 3FT Hon
Entry Requirements: *GCE:* AAB.

TWP3 BA Turkish and Music
Duration: 4FT Hon
Entry Requirements: *GCE:* AAB.

WTJ3 BA Vietnamese and Music
Duration: 3FT Hon
Entry Requirements: *GCE:* AAB.

S18 THE UNIVERSITY OF SHEFFIELD
THE UNIVERSITY OF SHEFFIELD
LEVEL 2, ARTS TOWER
WESTERN BANK
SHEFFIELD S10 2TN
t: 0114 222 8030 f: 0114 222 8032
// www.sheffield.ac.uk

QW33 BA English and Music
Duration: 3FT Hon
Entry Requirements: *GCE:* ABB. *SQAH:* AABBB. *SQAAH:* B. *IB:* 33.
BTEC ExtDip: DDM.

RW13 BA French and Music
Duration: 4FT Hon
Entry Requirements: *GCE:* BBB. *SQAH:* BBBBB. *SQAAH:* B. *IB:* 32.
BTEC ExtDip: DDM.

RW23 BA German and Music
Duration: 4FT Hon
Entry Requirements: *GCE:* BBB. *SQAH:* BBBBB. *SQAAH:* B. *IB:* 32.
BTEC ExtDip: DDM.

WT31 BA Music and Chinese Studies
Duration: 4FT Hon
Entry Requirements: *GCE:* ABB. *SQAH:* AAABB. *IB:* 33. *BTEC ExtDip:* DDM.

WT34 BA Music and East Asian Studies
Duration: 3FT Hon
Entry Requirements: *GCE:* ABB. *SQAH:* AAABB. *IB:* 33. *BTEC ExtDip:* DDM.

RW43 BA Music and Hispanic Studies
Duration: 4FT Hon
Entry Requirements: *GCE:* BBB. *SQAH:* BBBBB. *SQAAH:* B. *IB:* 32.
BTEC ExtDip: DDM.

WTH4 BA Music and Korean Studies
Duration: 3FT Hon
Entry Requirements: *GCE:* ABB. *SQAH:* AAABB. *IB:* 33. *BTEC ExtDip:* DDM.

VW53 BA Music and Philosophy
Duration: 3FT Hon
Entry Requirements: *GCE:* ABB. *SQAH:* AAABB. *IB:* 33. *BTEC ExtDip:* DDM.

RW73 BA Russian and Music
Duration: 4FT Hon
Entry Requirements: *GCE:* BBB. *SQAH:* BBBBB. *SQAAH:* B. *IB:* 32.
BTEC ExtDip: DDM.

VW63 BA Theology and Music
Duration: 3FT Hon
Entry Requirements: *GCE:* ABB. *SQAH:* AAABB. *IB:* 33. *BTEC ExtDip:* DDM.

W302 BMus Music
Duration: 3FT Hon
Entry Requirements: *GCE:* ABB. *SQAH:* AAABB. *IB:* 33. *BTEC ExtDip:* DDM.

S27 UNIVERSITY OF SOUTHAMPTON
HIGHFIELD
SOUTHAMPTON SO17 1BJ
t: 023 8059 4732 f: 023 8059 3037
e: admissions@soton.ac.uk
// www.southampton.ac.uk

QW33 BA English and Music
Duration: 3FT Hon
Entry Requirements: *GCE:* ABB. *SQAH:* AABBB. *IB:* 32.

RW13 BA French and Music (4 years)
Duration: 4FT Hon
Entry Requirements: *GCE:* AAB. *IB:* 34.

RW23 BA German and Music (4 years)
Duration: 4FT Hon
Entry Requirements: *GCE:* AAB. *IB:* 34.

W300 BA Music
Duration: 3FT Hon
Entry Requirements: *GCE:* ABB. *IB:* 32.

WN32 BA Music and Management Sciences
Duration: 3FT Hon
Entry Requirements: *GCE:* ABB. *IB:* 32.

VW53 BA Philosophy and Music
Duration: 3FT Hon
Entry Requirements: Contact the institution for details.

HW73 BSc Acoustics and Music
Duration: 3FT Hon
Entry Requirements: *GCE:* AAA-BBB. *IB:* 35. Interview required.

G1W3 BSc Mathematics with Music
Duration: 3FT Hon
Entry Requirements: *GCE:* AAA-AAB. *SQAH:* AAAAA. *SQAAH:* AA. *IB:* 36.

S30 SOUTHAMPTON SOLENT UNIVERSITY
EAST PARK TERRACE
SOUTHAMPTON
HAMPSHIRE SO14 0RT
t: +44 (0) 23 8031 9039 f: + 44 (0)23 8022 2259
e: admissions@solent.ac.uk
// www.solent.ac.uk/

WJ39 BA Digital Music
Duration: 3FT Hon
Entry Requirements: *Foundation:* Merit. *GCE:* 200. *SQAAH:* AC-DDD. *IB:* 24. *BTEC ExtDip:* MMP. *OCR ND:* M1 *OCR NED:* P1
Interview required. Portfolio required.

WN35 BA Music Promotion
Duration: 3FT Hon
Entry Requirements: *Foundation:* Distinction. *GCE:* 240. *SQAAH:* AA-CCD. *IB:* 24. *BTEC ExtDip:* MMM. *OCR ND:* D *OCR NED:* M3
Interview required.

W310 BA Popular Music Performance
Duration: 3FT Hon
Entry Requirements: *Foundation:* Distinction. *GCE:* 240. *SQAAH:* AA-CCD. *IB:* 24. *BTEC ExtDip:* MMM. *OCR ND:* D *OCR NED:* M3
Interview required.

W313 BA Popular Music Performance (Top-Up)
Duration: 1FT Hon
Entry Requirements: Interview required. HND required.

W390 BA Popular Music Production (Top-Up)
Duration: 1FT Hon
Entry Requirements: Interview required. HND required.

W300 BA Popular Music and Record Production
Duration: 3FT Hon
Entry Requirements: *Foundation:* Distinction. *GCE:* 240. *SQAAH:* AA-CCD. *IB:* 24. *BTEC ExtDip:* MMM. *OCR ND:* D *OCR NED:* M3
Interview required.

JW93 BA Popular Music and Record Production with IFY
Duration: 4FT Hon
Entry Requirements: Contact the institution for details.

WH36 BSc Audio Technology
Duration: 3FT Hon
Entry Requirements: *GCE:* 160.

WHH6 BSc Audio Technology (with foundation)
Duration: 4FT Hon
Entry Requirements: *GCE:* 40.

S32 SOUTH DEVON COLLEGE
LONG ROAD
PAIGNTON
DEVON TQ4 7EJ
t: 08000 213181 f: 01803 540541
e: university@southdevon.ac.uk
// www.southdevon.ac.uk/
welcome-to-university-level

W310 FdA Modern Music Practice (Performance and Technology)
Duration: 2FT Fdg
Entry Requirements: Contact the institution for details.

S42 SOUTH DOWNS COLLEGE
COLLEGE ROAD
WATERLOOVILLE
HAMPSHIRE PO7 8AA
t: 023 9279 7979 f: 023 9279 4609
e: college@southdowns.ac.uk
// www.southdowns.ac.uk

503W HND Music Performance
Duration: 2FT HND
Entry Requirements: *GCE:* 80. Interview required.

S43 SOUTH ESSEX COLLEGE OF FURTHER & HIGHER EDUCATION
LUKER ROAD
SOUTHEND-ON-SEA
ESSEX SS1 1ND
t: 0845 52 12345 f: 01702 432320
e: Admissions@southessex.ac.uk
// www.southessex.ac.uk

W312 BA Music Performance, Production and Composition
Duration: 3FT Hon
Entry Requirements: Contact the institution for details.

W310 BA Music Production
Duration: 3FT Hon
Entry Requirements: *GCE:* 160. *IB:* 24. Interview required.

013W CertHE Music Performance, Production and Composition
Duration: 1FT Cer
Entry Requirements: Contact the institution for details.

213W CertHE Music Production
Duration: 1FT Cer
Entry Requirements: Contact the institution for details.

113W DipHE Music Performance, Production and Composition
Duration: 2FT Dip
Entry Requirements: Contact the institution for details.

313W DipHE Music Production
Duration: 2FT Dip
Entry Requirements: Contact the institution for details.

S51 ST HELENS COLLEGE
WATER STREET
ST HELENS
MERSEYSIDE WA10 1PP
t: 01744 733766 f: 01744 623400
e: enquiries@sthelens.ac.uk
// www.sthelens.ac.uk

HW63 FdA Music Production and Sound Design
Duration: 2FT Fdg
Entry Requirements: *GCE:* 40-80. *IB:* 18. Interview required. Admissions Test required.

S72 STAFFORDSHIRE UNIVERSITY
COLLEGE ROAD
STOKE ON TRENT ST4 2DE
t: 01782 292753 f: 01782 292740
e: admissions@staffs.ac.uk
// www.staffs.ac.uk

JW93 BSc Creative Music Technology
Duration: 3FT/4SW Hon
Entry Requirements: *GCE:* 240-280. *IB:* 24.

W3N2 BSc Music Technology with Management
Duration: 3FT/4SW Hon
Entry Requirements: *GCE:* 240-280. *IB:* 24.

J9H0 FdA Music Technology
Duration: 2FT Fdg
Entry Requirements: Interview required.

193W HND Music Production
Duration: 2FT HND
Entry Requirements: Interview required.

S74 STRATFORD UPON AVON COLLEGE
THE WILLOWS NORTH
ALCESTER ROAD
STRATFORD-UPON-AVON
WARWICKSHIRE CV37 9QR
t: 01789 266245 f: 01789 267524
e: college@stratford.ac.uk
// www.stratford.ac.uk

003W HND Music Practice
Duration: 2FT HND
Entry Requirements: *GCE:* 200. Interview required.

S82 UNIVERSITY CAMPUS SUFFOLK (UCS)
WATERFRONT BUILDING
NEPTUNE QUAY
IPSWICH
SUFFOLK IP4 1QJ
t: 01473 338833 f: 01473 339900
e: info@ucs.ac.uk
// www.ucs.ac.uk

JW93 BA Music Production (Level 3 entry only)
Duration: 1FT Hon
Entry Requirements: Interview required.

W300 FdA Creative Music
Duration: 2FT Fdg
Entry Requirements: *GCE:* 200. *IB:* 28. *BTEC ExtDip:* DMM. Interview required. Portfolio required.

S84 UNIVERSITY OF SUNDERLAND
STUDENT HELPLINE
THE STUDENT GATEWAY
CHESTER ROAD
SUNDERLAND SR1 3SD
t: 0191 515 3000 f: 0191 515 3805
e: student.helpline@sunderland.ac.uk
// www.sunderland.ac.uk

WX39 BA Community Music
Duration: 3FT Hon   CRB Check: Required
Entry Requirements: *GCE:* 220. *OCR ND:* D *OCR NED:* M3 Interview required.

W301 BA Music (Top-up)
Duration: 1FT Hon
Entry Requirements: Interview required. HND required.

L2W3 BA Politics with Music
Duration: 3FT Hon
Entry Requirements: *GCE:* 260-360. *IB:* 31. *OCR ND:* D *OCR NED:* M3

L3W3 BA Sociology with Music
Duration: 3FT Hon
Entry Requirements: *GCE:* 260-360. *IB:* 31. *OCR ND:* D *OCR NED:* M3

W340 BMus Jazz, Popular and Commercial Music
Duration: 3FT Hon
Entry Requirements: Contact the institution for details.

W390 FdA Applied Music Practice
Duration: 2FT Fdg
Entry Requirements: *GCE:* 80-220. *SQAH:* CCCC. *IB:* 22. Interview required.

S85 UNIVERSITY OF SURREY
STAG HILL
GUILDFORD
SURREY GU2 7XH
t: +44(0)1483 689305 f: +44(0)1483 689388
e: ugteam@surrey.ac.uk
// www.surrey.ac.uk

W3G5 BMus Creative Music Technology (3 years)
Duration: 3FT Hon
Entry Requirements: *GCE:* ABB. *SQAH:* ABBB. *SQAAH:* ABB. *IB:* 34. Interview required.

W300 BMus Music (3 years)
Duration: 3FT Hon
Entry Requirements: *GCE:* 320. *SQAH:* ABBB. *IB:* 32.

W301 BMus Music (4 years)
Duration: 4SW Hon
Entry Requirements: *GCE:* 320. *SQAH:* ABBB. *IB:* 32.

G1W3 BSc Mathematics with Music (3 years)
Duration: 3FT Hon
Entry Requirements: *GCE:* 340. Interview required.

G1WH BSc Mathematics with Music (4 years)
Duration: 4SW Hon
Entry Requirements: *GCE:* 340. Interview required.

S90 UNIVERSITY OF SUSSEX
UNDERGRADUATE ADMISSIONS
SUSSEX HOUSE
UNIVERSITY OF SUSSEX
BRIGHTON BN1 9RH
t: 01273 678416 f: 01273 678545
e: ug.applicants@sussex.ac.uk
// www.sussex.ac.uk

W300 BA Music
Duration: 3FT Hon
Entry Requirements: *GCE:* ABB. *SQAH:* AABBB. *SQAAH:* ABB. *IB:* 34. *BTEC SubDip:* D. *BTEC Dip:* DD. *BTEC ExtDip:* DDM. *OCR ND:* D *OCR NED:* D2

WG34 BA Music Informatics
Duration: 3FT Hon
Entry Requirements: *GCE:* ABB. *SQAH:* AABBB. *SQAAH:* ABB. *IB:* 34. *BTEC SubDip:* D. *BTEC Dip:* DD. *BTEC ExtDip:* DDD. *OCR ND:* M1 *OCR NED:* D2

VW53 BA Philosophy and Music
Duration: 3FT Hon
Entry Requirements: *GCE:* AAB. *SQAH:* AAABB. *SQAAH:* AAB. *IB:* 35. *BTEC SubDip:* D. *BTEC Dip:* DD. *BTEC ExtDip:* DDD. *OCR ND:* D *OCR NED:* D1

WGH4 BSc Music Informatics
Duration: 3FT Hon
Entry Requirements: *GCE:* ABB. *SQAH:* AABBB. *IB:* 34. *BTEC SubDip:* D. *BTEC Dip:* DD. *BTEC ExtDip:* DDD. *OCR ND:* M1 *OCR NED:* D2

T80 UNIVERSITY OF WALES TRINITY SAINT DAVID
COLLEGE ROAD
CARMARTHEN SA31 3EP
t: 01267 676767 f: 01267 676766
e: registry@trinitysaintdavid.ac.uk
// www.tsd.ac.uk

W390 BA Cerddoriaeth Broffesiynol
Duration: 3FT Hon
Entry Requirements: *GCE:* 160-360. *IB:* 26. Interview required.

T85 TRURO AND PENWITH COLLEGE
TRURO COLLEGE
COLLEGE ROAD
TRURO
CORNWALL TR1 3XX
t: 01872 267122 f: 01872 267526
e: heinfo@trurocollege.ac.uk
// www.truro-penwith.ac.uk

W341 BA (Hons) Contemporary World Jazz
Duration: 3FT Hon
Entry Requirements: *GCE:* 160. *IB:* 24. *BTEC Dip:* MP. *BTEC ExtDip:* PPP. Interview required.

W340 FdA Commercial Music Performance and Production
Duration: 2FT Fdg
Entry Requirements: *GCE:* 60. *IB:* 24. *BTEC Dip:* MP. *BTEC ExtDip:* PPP. Interview required.

W310 FdA Music Performance
Duration: 2FT Fdg
Entry Requirements: *GCE:* 60. *IB:* 24. *BTEC Dip:* MP. *BTEC ExtDip:* PPP. Interview required.

U20 UNIVERSITY OF ULSTER
COLERAINE
CO. LONDONDERRY
NORTHERN IRELAND BT52 1SA
t: 028 7012 4221 f: 028 7012 4908
e: online@ulster.ac.uk
// www.ulster.ac.uk

W5W3 BA Dance with Music
Duration: 3FT Hon
Entry Requirements: *GCE:* CCD. *IB:* 24. Interview required.

W4W3 BA Drama with Music
Duration: 3FT Hon
Entry Requirements: *GCE:* BBC. *IB:* 24. Interview required.

Q5W3 BA Irish with Music
Duration: 3FT/4SW Hon
Entry Requirements: *GCE:* 260. *IB:* 24.

W3W5 BA Music with Dance
Duration: 3FT Hon
Entry Requirements: *GCE:* CCC. *IB:* 24. Interview required.

W3W4 BA Music with Drama
Duration: 3FT Hon
Entry Requirements: *GCE:* CCC. *IB:* 24. Interview required.

W3Q5 BA Music with Irish
Duration: 3FT Hon
Entry Requirements: *GCE:* BCD. *IB:* 24. Interview required.

W3C8 BA Music with Psychology
Duration: 3FT Hon
Entry Requirements: *GCE:* CCC. *IB:* 24. Interview required.

W302 BMus Music
Duration: 3FT Hon
Entry Requirements: *GCE:* BBC. *IB:* 24. Interview required.

U40 UNIVERSITY OF THE WEST OF SCOTLAND
PAISLEY
RENFREWSHIRE
SCOTLAND PA1 2BE
t: 0141 848 3727 f: 0141 848 3623
e: admissions@uws.ac.uk
// www.uws.ac.uk

W340 BA Commercial Music
Duration: 3FT/4FT Ord/Hon
Entry Requirements: *GCE:* CC. *SQAH:* BBC. Interview required.
Portfolio required.

WW34 BA Musical Theatre
Duration: 1FT/2FT Ord/Hon
Entry Requirements: Interview required.

W350 BSc Music Technology
Duration: 3FT/4FT Ord/Hon
Entry Requirements: *GCE:* CC. *SQAH:* BBC.

U65 UNIVERSITY OF THE ARTS LONDON
272 HIGH HOLBORN
LONDON WC1V 7EY
t: 020 7514 6000x6197 f: 020 7514 6198
e: c.anderson@arts.ac.uk
// www.arts.ac.uk

W390 BA Sound Arts and Design
Duration: 3FT Hon
Entry Requirements: *GCE:* 80. *IB:* 28. Foundation Course required.
Interview required. Portfolio required.

W05 THE UNIVERSITY OF WEST LONDON
ST MARY'S ROAD
EALING
LONDON W5 5RF
t: 0800 036 8888 f: 020 8566 1353
e: learning.advice@uwl.ac.uk
// www.uwl.ac.uk

W351 BA Music Technology Specialist
Duration: 3FT Hon
Entry Requirements: *GCE:* 200. *IB:* 28. Interview required.
Portfolio required.

JW9J BA Music Technology and Pop Music Performance
Duration: 3FT Hon
Entry Requirements: *GCE:* 200. *IB:* 28. Interview required.
Portfolio required.

W394 BA (Hons) Music Technology and Music Composition
Duration: 3FT Hon
Entry Requirements: Contact the institution for details.

W396 BA (Hons) Music Technology and Music Performance
Duration: 3FT Hon
Entry Requirements: Contact the institution for details.

WHV8 BA (Hons) Song Writing
Duration: 3FT Hon
Entry Requirements: Contact the institution for details.

W388 BMus Music Composition
Duration: 3FT Hon
Entry Requirements: Contact the institution for details.

WC90 BMus Music Composition with Music Management
Duration: 3FT Hon
Entry Requirements: Contact the institution for details.

WD90 BMus Music Composition with Music Technology
Duration: 3FT Hon
Entry Requirements: Contact the institution for details.

WJ88 BMus Music Performance
Duration: 3FT Hon
Entry Requirements: Contact the institution for details.

W300 BMus Music Performance and Recording
Duration: 3FT Hon
Entry Requirements: *GCE:* 200. *IB:* 28. Interview required.

W393 BMus Music Performance with Music Technology
Duration: 3FT Hon
Entry Requirements: Contact the institution for details.

W315 BMus Music with Foundation
Duration: 4FT Hon
Entry Requirements: Contact the institution for details.

W392 BMus(Hons) Music Performance with Music Management
Duration: 3FT Hon
Entry Requirements: Contact the institution for details.

J931 DipHE Music Technology
Duration: 2FT Hon
Entry Requirements: Contact the institution for details.

W08 WAKEFIELD COLLEGE
MARGARET STREET
WAKEFIELD
WEST YORKSHIRE WF1 2DH
t: 01924 789111 f: 01924 789281
e: courseinfo@wakefield.ac.uk
// www.wakefield.ac.uk/highereducation

113W HND Music Performance (Popular Music)
Duration: 2FT HND
Entry Requirements: *GCE:* 240. Interview required.

W50 UNIVERSITY OF WESTMINSTER
2ND FLOOR, CAVENDISH HOUSE
101 NEW CAVENDISH STREET,
LONDON W1W 6XH
t: 020 7915 5511
e: course-enquiries@westminster.ac.uk
// www.westminster.ac.uk

W304 BA Commercial Music
Duration: 3FT Hon
Entry Requirements: *GCE:* CC. *SQAH:* CCCC. *IB:* 26. Interview required.

W310 BMus Commercial Music Performance
Duration: 3FT Hon
Entry Requirements: *GCE:* CC. *SQAH:* CCCC. *IB:* 26. Interview required.

W51 CITY OF WESTMINSTER COLLEGE
CITY OF WESTMINSTER COLLEGE
PADDINGTON GREEN CAMPUS
25 PADDINGTON GREEN
LONDON W2 1NB
t: 020 7723 8826
e: customer.services@cwc.ac.uk
// www.cwc.ac.uk

W37L HND Music Production
Duration: 2FT HND
Entry Requirements: Contact the institution for details.

W75 UNIVERSITY OF WOLVERHAMPTON
ADMISSIONS UNIT
MX207, CAMP STREET
WOLVERHAMPTON
WEST MIDLANDS WV1 1AD
t: 01902 321000 f: 01902 321896
e: admissions@wlv.ac.uk
// www.wlv.ac.uk

WJ3X BA Music Technology
Duration: 3FT Hon
Entry Requirements: *GCE:* 200. *IB:* 24. *BTEC Dip:* DM. *BTEC ExtDip:* MMP. *OCR ND:* M1 *OCR NED:* P1 Interview required.

W391 BA Music Technology and Popular Music
Duration: 3FT Hon
Entry Requirements: *GCE:* 200. *IB:* 24. *BTEC Dip:* DM. *BTEC ExtDip:* MMP. *OCR ND:* M1 *OCR NED:* P1 Interview required.

W312 BA Musical Theatre
Duration: 3FT Hon **CRB Check:** Required
Entry Requirements Contact the institution for details.

W300 BMus Music
Duration: 3FT Hon
Entry Requirements: *GCE:* 200. *IB:* 24. *BTEC Dip:* DM. *BTEC ExtDip:* MMP. *OCR ND:* M1 *OCR NED:* P1 Interview required.

WW33 BMus Music and Popular Music
Duration: 3FT Hon
Entry Requirements: *GCE:* 200. *IB:* 24. *BTEC Dip:* DM. *BTEC ExtDip:* MMP. *OCR ND:* M1 *OCR NED:* P1 Interview required.

W390 BMus Popular Music
Duration: 3FT Hon
Entry Requirements: *GCE:* 200. *IB:* 24. *BTEC Dip:* DM. *BTEC ExtDip:* MMP. *OCR ND:* M1 *OCR NED:* P1 Interview required.

WJ39 FdA Creative Music Production
Duration: 2FT Fdg
Entry Requirements: *GCE:* 100. *IB:* 24. *BTEC Dip:* MP. *BTEC ExtDip:* PPP. *OCR NED:* P3 Interview required.

W310 FdA Music Performance
Duration: 2FT Fdg
Entry Requirements: *GCE:* 100. *IB:* 24. *BTEC Dip:* MP. *BTEC ExtDip:* PPP. *OCR NED:* P3 Interview required.

W76 UNIVERSITY OF WINCHESTER
WINCHESTER
HANTS SO22 4NR
t: 01962 827234 f: 01962 827288
e: course.enquiries@winchester.ac.uk
// www.winchester.ac.uk

TW7J BA American Studies and Vocal & Choral Studies
Duration: 3FT Hon
Entry Requirements: *Foundation:* Distinction. *GCE:* 260-300. *IB:* 24. *OCR ND:* D *OCR NED:* M2

VW4J BA Archaeology and Vocal & Choral Studies
Duration: 3FT Hon
Entry Requirements: *Foundation:* Distinction. *GCE:* 260-300. *IB:* 24. *OCR ND:* D *OCR NED:* M2

NW23 BA Business Management and Vocal & Choral Studies
Duration: 3FT Hon
Entry Requirements: *Foundation:* Distinction. *GCE:* 260-300. *IB:* 24. *OCR ND:* D *OCR NED:* M2

LW5H BA Childhood Youth & Community Studies and Vocal & Choral Studies
Duration: 3FT Hon
Entry Requirements: *Foundation:* Distinction. *GCE:* 260-300. *IB:* 24. *OCR ND:* D

WW53 BA Choreography & Dance and Vocal & Choral Studies
Duration: 3FT Hon
Entry Requirements: *Foundation:* Distinction. *GCE:* 260-300. *IB:* 25. *OCR ND:* D *OCR NED:* M2

LW3J BA Criminology and Vocal & Choral Studies
Duration: 3FT Hon
Entry Requirements: *Foundation:* Distinction. *GCE:* 260-300. *IB:* 24. *OCR ND:* D *OCR NED:* M2

WW43 BA Drama and Vocal & Choral Studies
Duration: 3FT Hon
Entry Requirements: *Foundation:* Distinction. *GCE:* 260-300. *IB:* 25. *OCR ND:* D *OCR NED:* M2

XW3H BA Education Studies (Early Childhood) and Vocal & Choral Studies
Duration: 3FT Hon
Entry Requirements: *Foundation:* Distinction. *GCE:* 260-300. *IB:* 24. *OCR ND:* D *OCR NED:* M2

XWH3 BA Education Studies and Vocal & Choral Studies
Duration: 3FT Hon
Entry Requirements: *Foundation:* Distinction. *GCE:* 260-300. *IB:* 24. *OCR ND:* D *OCR NED:* M2

QW3J BA English Language Studies and Vocal & Choral Studies
Duration: 3FT Hon
Entry Requirements: *Foundation:* Distinction. *GCE:* 260-300. *IB:* 25. *OCR ND:* D *OCR NED:* M2

QW33 BA English and Vocal & Choral Studies
Duration: 3FT Hon
Entry Requirements: *Foundation:* Distinction. *GCE:* 260-300. *IB:* 25. *OCR ND:* D *OCR NED:* M2

WW6H BA Film & Cinema Technology and Vocal & Choral Studies
Duration: 3FT Hon
Entry Requirements: *Foundation:* Distinction. *GCE:* 260-300. *IB:* 24. *OCR ND:* D *OCR NED:* M2

WL35 BA Health, Community & Social Care and Performing Arts (Contemporary Performance)
Duration: 3FT Hon
Entry Requirements: Contact the institution for details.

VW1H BA History and Vocal & Choral Studies
Duration: 3FT Hon
Entry Requirements: *Foundation:* Distinction. *GCE:* 260-300. *IB:* 24. *OCR ND:* D *OCR NED:* M2

MW1H BA Law and Vocal & Choral Studies
Duration: 3FT Hon
Entry Requirements: *Foundation:* Distinction. *GCE:* 260-300. *IB:* 25. *OCR ND:* D *OCR NED:* M2

WW93 BA Modern Liberal Arts and Vocal & Choral Studies
Duration: 3FT Hon
Entry Requirements: *Foundation:* Distinction. *GCE:* 260-300. *IB:* 25. *OCR ND:* D *OCR NED:* M2

WW4J BA Performing Arts (Contemporary Performance) and Vocal & Choral Studies
Duration: 3FT Hon
Entry Requirements: *Foundation:* Distinction. *GCE:* 260-300. *IB:* 24. *OCR ND:* D

LW23 BA Politics & Global Studies and Vocal & Choral Studies
Duration: 3FT Hon
Entry Requirements: *Foundation:* Distinction. *GCE:* 260-300. *IB:* 24. *OCR ND:* D

LW33 BA Sociology and Vocal & Choral Studies
Duration: 3FT Hon
Entry Requirements: *Foundation:* Distinction. *GCE:* 260-300. *IB:* 24. *OCR ND:* D *OCR NED:* M2

NW83 BA Sports Management and Vocal & Choral Studies
Duration: 3FT Hon
Entry Requirements: *Foundation:* Pass. *GCE:* 260-300. *IB:* 24. *OCR ND:* D

CW6H BA Sports Studies and Vocal & Choral Studies
Duration: 3FT Hon
Entry Requirements: *Foundation:* Pass. *GCE:* 260-300. *IB:* 24. *OCR ND:* D

VW6J BA Theology & Religious Studies and Vocal & Choral Studies
Duration: 3FT Hon
Entry Requirements: *Foundation:* Distinction. *GCE:* 260-300. *IB:* 25. *OCR ND:* D *OCR NED:* M2

W311 BA Vocal & Choral Studies
Duration: 3FT Hon
Entry Requirements: Contact the institution for details.

W80 UNIVERSITY OF WORCESTER
HENWICK GROVE
WORCESTER WR2 6AJ
t: 01905 855111 f: 01905 855377
e: admissions@worc.ac.uk
// www.worcester.ac.uk

043W HND Urban & Electronic Music
Duration: 2FT HND
Entry Requirements: *GCE:* 60. *IB:* 24.

W81 WORCESTER COLLEGE OF TECHNOLOGY
DEANSWAY
WORCESTER WR1 2JF
t: 01905 725555 f: 01905 28906
// www.wortech.ac.uk

WJ39 FdSc Popular Music Technology
Duration: 2FT Fdg
Entry Requirements: *GCE:* 80.

Y50 THE UNIVERSITY OF YORK
STUDENT RECRUITMENT AND ADMISSIONS
UNIVERSITY OF YORK
HESLINGTON
YORK YO10 5DD
t: 01904 324000 f: 01904 323538
e: ug-admissions@york.ac.uk
// www.york.ac.uk

W300 BA Music
Duration: 3FT Hon
Entry Requirements: *GCE:* AAB-ABB. *SQAH:* AAAAB-AABBB. *SQAAH:* AB. *IB:* 35. Interview required.

Y75 YORK ST JOHN UNIVERSITY
LORD MAYOR'S WALK
YORK YO31 7EX
t: 01904 876598 f: 01904 876940/876921
e: admissions@yorksj.ac.uk
// w3.yorksj.ac.uk

W300 BA Music
Duration: 3FT Hon
Entry Requirements: *Foundation:* Pass. *GCE:* 200-240. *IB:* 24.

W301 BA Music (for international applicants only)
Duration: 4FT Hon
Entry Requirements: *Foundation:* Pass. *GCE:* 200-240. *IB:* 24.

PRACTICE-BASED MUSIC, DANCE AND DRAMA COURSES - CUKAS

B34 BIRMINGHAM CONSERVATOIRE
BIRMINGHAM CONSERVATOIRE
PARADISE PLACE
BIRMINGHAM B3 3HG
t: +44 (0)121 331 5901 f: +44 (0)121 331 5906
e: conservatoire.admissions@bcu.ac.uk
// www.conservatoire.bcu.ac.uk

602F AdvPGDip Professional Performance (Instrumental/Vocal/Accompaniment/Repetiteur)
Duration: 1FT PMD
Entry Requirements: Interview required.

602P AdvPgDip Professional Performance (Instrumental/Vocal/Accompaniment/Repetiteur)
Duration: 2PT PMD
Entry Requirements: Interview required.

310F BMus BMus (Hons) Jazz
Duration: 4FT Hon
Entry Requirements: *IB:* 24. Interview required. Admissions Test required.

300F BMus BMus (Hons) Music
Duration: 4FT Hon
Entry Requirements: *IB:* 24. Interview required. Admissions Test required.

802F MMus Choral Conducting/Orchestral Conducting
Duration: 2FT PMD
Entry Requirements: Interview required.

802P MMus Choral Conducting/Orchestral Conducting
Duration: 3PT PMD
Entry Requirements: Interview required.

807F MMus Choral Conducting/Orchestral Conducting
Duration: 1FT PMD
Entry Requirements: Interview required.

800F MMus Instrumental Performance/Composition/Music Technology/Musicology
Duration: 2FT PMD
Entry Requirements: Interview required.

800P MMus Instrumental Performance/Composition/Music Technology/Musicology
Duration: 3PT PMD
Entry Requirements: Interview required.

805F MMus Instrumental Performance/Composition/Music Technology/Musicology
Duration: 1FT PMD
Entry Requirements: Interview required.

803F MMus Jazz Performance/Jazz Composition
Duration: 2FT PMD
Entry Requirements: Interview required.

803P MMus Jazz Performance/Jazz Composition
Duration: 3PT PMD
Entry Requirements: Interview required.

808F MMus Jazz Performance/Jazz Composition
Duration: 1FT PMD
Entry Requirements: Interview required.

809F MMus Orchestral Performance
Duration: 2FT PMD
Entry Requirements: Interview required.

810F MMus Orchestral Performance
Duration: 1FT PMD
Entry Requirements: Interview required.

804F MMus Performance and Pedagogy
Duration: 2FT PMD
Entry Requirements: Interview required.

804P MMus Performance and Pedagogy
Duration: 3PT PMD
Entry Requirements: Interview required.

801F MMus Vocal Performance
Duration: 2FT PMD
Entry Requirements: Interview required.

801P MMus Vocal Performance
Duration: 3PT PMD
Entry Requirements: Interview required.

806F MMus Vocal Performance
Duration: 1FT PMD
Entry Requirements: Interview required.

500P PGCert Instrumental/Jazz Performance
Duration: 1PT PMD
Entry Requirements: Interview required.

501F PGCert Specialist Performance (Instrumental/Jazz)
Duration: 1FT PMD
Entry Requirements: Interview required.

600F PGDip Instrumental Performance/Composition/Music Technology
Duration: 1FT PMD
Entry Requirements: Interview required.

503F PgCert Specialist Performance (Vocal)
Duration: 1FT PMD
Entry Requirements: Interview required.

502P PgCert Vocal Performance
Duration: 1PT PMD
Entry Requirements: Interview required.

603F PgDip Choral Conducting/Orchestral Conducting
Duration: 1FT PMD
Entry Requirements: Interview required.

603P PgDip Choral Conducting/Orchestral Conducting
Duration: 2PT PMD
Entry Requirements: Interview required.

600P PgDip Instrumental Performance/Composition/Music Technology
Duration: 2PT PMD
Entry Requirements: Interview required.

604F PgDip Jazz Performance/Jazz Composition
Duration: 1FT PMD
Entry Requirements: Interview required.

604P PgDip Jazz Performance/Jazz Composition
Duration: 2PT PMD
Entry Requirements: Interview required.

605F PgDip Orchestral Performance
Duration: 1FT PMD
Entry Requirements: Interview required.

605P PgDip Orchestral Performance
Duration: 2PT PMD
Entry Requirements: Interview required.

601F PgDip Vocal Performance
Duration: 1FT PMD
Entry Requirements: Interview required.

601P PgDip Vocal Performance
Duration: 2PT PMD
Entry Requirements: Interview required.

L31 LEEDS COLLEGE OF MUSIC
3 QUARRY HILL
LEEDS
WEST YORKSHIRE LS2 7PD
t: 0113 222 3416 f: 0113 243 8798
e: enquiries.assistant@lcm.ac.uk
// www.lcm.ac.uk

720F MA/MMus MA/MMus Music (Composition)
Duration: 1FT PMD
Entry Requirements: Interview required.

720P MA/MMus MA/MMus Music (Composition)
Duration: 2.5PT PMD
Entry Requirements: Interview required.

791F MA/MMus MA/MMus Music (Performance)
Duration: 1FT PMD
Entry Requirements: Interview required.

791P MA/MMus MA/MMus Music (Performance)
Duration: 2.5PT Hon
Entry Requirements: Interview required.

620F PGDip Postgraduate Diploma in Music (Composition)
Duration: 1FT PMD
Entry Requirements: Interview required.

620P PGDip Postgraduate Diploma in Music (Composition)
Duration: 1.5PT PMD
Entry Requirements: Interview required.

601F PGDip Postgraduate Diploma in Music (Performance)
Duration: 1FT PMD
Entry Requirements: Interview required.

601P PGDip Postgraduate Diploma in Music (Performance) Part-Time
Duration: 1.5PT PMD
Entry Requirements: Interview required.

R56 ROYAL COLLEGE OF MUSIC
PRINCE CONSORT ROAD
LONDON SW7 2BS
t: +44 (0)20 7591 4362 f: +44 (0)20 7591 4737
e: admissions@rcm.ac.uk
// www.rcm.ac.uk

851F ArtDip Artist Diploma in Opera
Duration: 2FT/1FT PMD
Entry Requirements: Interview required.

603F ArtDip Artist Diploma in Performance
Duration: 1FT Oth
Entry Requirements: Contact the institution for details.

300F BMus Bachelor of Music (Honours)
Duration: 4FT Hon
Entry Requirements: *GCE:* 120. Portfolio required.

420F GradDip Graduate Diploma in Vocal Performance
Duration: 1FT Oth
Entry Requirements: Contact the institution for details.

821F MComp Master of Composition
Duration: 2FT PMD
Entry Requirements: Interview required. Portfolio required.

705F MComp Master of Composition in Composition for Screen
Duration: 2FT PMD
Entry Requirements: Interview required.

822F MMus Fast-Track Master of Music in Composition
Duration: 1FT PMD
Entry Requirements: Interview required. Portfolio required.

802F MMus Fast-Track Master of Music in Performance
Duration: 1FT PMD
Entry Requirements: Interview required.

807F MMus Master of Music in Composition
Duration: 2FT PMD
Entry Requirements: Interview required. Portfolio required.

808F MMus Master of Music in Composition for Screen
Duration: 2FT PMD
Entry Requirements: Interview required. Portfolio required.

804F MMus Master of Music in Conducting
Duration: 2FT PMD
Entry Requirements: Interview required.

810F MMus Master of Music in Contemporary Piano
Duration: 2FT PMD
Entry Requirements: Interview required.

800F MMus Master of Music in Historical Performance
Duration: 2FT PMD
Entry Requirements: Contact the institution for details.

803F MMus Master of Music in Performance
Duration: 2FT PMD
Entry Requirements: Contact the institution for details.

805F MMus Master of Music in Piano Accompaniment
Duration: 2FT PMD
Entry Requirements: Contact the institution for details.

806F MMus Master of Music in Vocal Performance
Duration: 2FT PMD
Entry Requirements: Contact the institution for details.

801F MPerf Master of Performance
Duration: 2FT PMD
Entry Requirements: Contact the institution for details.

701F MPerf Master of Performance in Conducting
Duration: 2FT PMD
Entry Requirements: Interview required.

809F MPerf Master of Performance in Contemporary Piano
Duration: 2FT PMD
Entry Requirements: Interview required.

702F MPerf Master of Performance in Historical Performance
Duration: 2FT PMD
Entry Requirements: Contact the institution for details.

703F MPerf Master of Performance in Orchestral Performance
Duration: 2FT PMD
Entry Requirements: Contact the institution for details.

704F MPerf Master of Performance in Piano Accompaniment
Duration: 2FT PMD
Entry Requirements: Contact the institution for details.

850F MPerf Master of Performance in Vocal Performance
Duration: 2FT PMD
Entry Requirements: Contact the institution for details.

700P MSc Master of Science in Performance Science
Duration: 2PT PMD
Entry Requirements: Interview required.

706F MSc Master of Science in Performance Science
Duration: 1FT PMD
Entry Requirements: Interview required.

100F Non-award Gap Year Experience Programme
Duration: 1FT Oth
Entry Requirements: *GCE:* 120. Portfolio required.

102F Non-award Junior Year Experience Programme
Duration: 1FT Oth
Entry Requirements: *GCE:* 120. Portfolio required.

101F Non-award Semester Experience Programme
Duration: 0.5FT Oth
Entry Requirements: *GCE:* 160-240. Portfolio required.

R57 ROYAL NORTHERN COLLEGE OF MUSIC
124 OXFORD ROAD
MANCHESTER M13 9RD
t: +44 (0) 161 907 5260 f: +44 (0) 161 273 7611
e: admissions@rncm.ac.uk
// www.rncm.ac.uk

201F BA BA (Hons) Popular Music Performance
Duration: 3FT Hon
Entry Requirements: *GCE:* A-E. *SQAH:* AA-DD. *SQAAH:* A-D. *BTEC SubDip:* P. *BTEC Dip:* PP. *BTEC ExtDip:* PPP. *OCR ND:* P3 *OCR NED:* P3 Interview required. Portfolio required.

300F BMus BMus (Hons) Performance/Composition
Duration: 4FT Hon
Entry Requirements: *GCE:* A-E. *SQAH:* AA-DD. *SQAAH:* A-D. *BTEC SubDip:* P. *BTEC Dip:* PP. *BTEC ExtDip:* PPP. *OCR ND:* P3 *OCR NED:* P3 Interview required. Portfolio required.

811F MMus MMus Chamber Music
Duration: 1FT PMD
Entry Requirements: Interview required. Portfolio required.

820F MMus MMus Composition
Duration: 2FT PMD
Entry Requirements: Interview required. Portfolio required.

823F MMus MMus Composition
Duration: 1FT PMD
Entry Requirements: Interview required. Portfolio required.

841F MMus MMus Orchestral Studies
Duration: 1FT PMD
Entry Requirements: Interview required. Portfolio required.

801F MMus MMus Solo Performance
Duration: 2FT PMD
Entry Requirements: Interview required. Portfolio required.

805F MMus MMus Solo Performance
Duration: 1FT PMD
Entry Requirements: Interview required. Portfolio required.

W310 MPerf Master of Performance
Duration: 1FT PMD
Entry Requirements: Interview required. Portfolio required.

399F MusB GradDip/MusB (Hons) Performance/Composition
Duration: 4FT Hon
Entry Requirements: *GCE:* AAB. *SQAH:* AAAAA-AAAAB. *SQAAH:* AAA-AAB. Interview required. Portfolio required.

611F PGDip PGDip Chamber Music
Duration: 1FT PMD
Entry Requirements: Interview required.

620F PGDip PGDip Composition
Duration: 1FT PMD
Entry Requirements: Interview required. Portfolio required.

641F PGDip PGDip Orchestral Studies
Duration: 1FT PMD
Entry Requirements: Interview required.

601F PGDip PGDip Solo Performance
Duration: 1FT PMD
Entry Requirements: Interview required.

R58 ROYAL CONSERVATOIRE OF SCOTLAND
100 RENFREW STREET
GLASGOW G2 3DB
t: 0141 332 4101 f: 0141 332 8901
e: registry@rsamd.ac.uk
// www.rsamd.ac.uk

W310 BA BA (Hons) Contemporary Performance Practice
Duration: 4FT Hon
Entry Requirements: Interview required.

251F BA BA (Hons) Scottish Music - Piping
Duration: 4FT Hon
Entry Requirements: Interview required.

W410 BA BA Acting
Duration: 3FT Ord
Entry Requirements: Interview required.

200F BA BA Digital Film and Television
Duration: 3FT Ord
Entry Requirements: Interview required.

201F BA BA Modern Ballet
Duration: 3FT Ord
Entry Requirements: Interview required.

202F BA BA Musical Theatre
Duration: 3FT Ord
Entry Requirements: Interview required.

203F BA BA Technical and Production Arts (Applied Arts and Construction)
Duration: 3FT Ord
Entry Requirements: Interview required.

204F BA BA Technical and Production Arts (Management and Technology)
Duration: 3FT Ord
Entry Requirements: Interview required.

205F BA Technical and Production Arts (Design)
Duration: 3FT Ord
Entry Requirements: Interview required.

250F BAScotMus BA (Hons) Scottish Music
Duration: 4FT Hon
Entry Requirements: Interview required.

WX33 BEd BEd (Hons) Music
Duration: 4FT Hon
Entry Requirements: Interview required. Admissions Test required.

301F BMus Bachelor of Music (Hons) - Joint Principal Study
Duration: 4FT Hon
Entry Requirements: Interview required.

302F BMus Bachelor of Music (Hons) Composition
Duration: 4FT Hon
Entry Requirements: Interview required. Portfolio required.

303F BMus Bachelor of Music (Hons) Jazz
Duration: 4FT Hon
Entry Requirements: Interview required.

300F BMus Bachelor of Music (Hons) Performance
Duration: 4FT Hon
Entry Requirements: Interview required.

700F MA MA Classical and Contemporary Text (Acting)
Duration: 1FT PMD
Entry Requirements: Interview required.

701F MA MA Classical and Contemporary Text (Directing)
Duration: 1FT PMD
Entry Requirements: Interview required.

702F MA MA Musical Theatre (Musical Directing)
Duration: 1FT PMD
Entry Requirements: Interview required.

703F MA MA Musical Theatre (Performance)
Duration: 1FT PMD
Entry Requirements: Interview required.

893F MMus Master of Music (Accompaniment)
Duration: 2FT PMD
Entry Requirements: Interview required.

831F MMus Master of Music (Accompaniment) APEL
Duration: 1FT PMD
Entry Requirements: Interview required. Portfolio required.

891F MMus Master of Music (Composition)
Duration: 2FT PMD
Entry Requirements: Interview required. Portfolio required.

820F MMus Master of Music (Composition) APEL
Duration: 1FT PMD
Entry Requirements: Interview required. Portfolio required.

892F MMus Master of Music (Conducting)
Duration: 2FT PMD
Entry Requirements: Interview required.

840F MMus Master of Music (Conducting) APEL
Duration: 1FT PMD
Entry Requirements: Interview required. Portfolio required.

808F MMus Master of Music (Jazz)
Duration: 2FT PMD
Entry Requirements: Interview required.

807F MMus Master of Music (Jazz) APEL
Duration: 1FT PMD
Entry Requirements: Interview required. Portfolio required.

851F MMus Master of Music (Opera)
Duration: 2FT PMD
Entry Requirements: Interview required.

800F MMus Master of Music (Opera) APEL
Duration: 1FT PMD
Entry Requirements: Interview required. Portfolio required.

890F MMus Master of Music (Performance)
Duration: 2FT PMD
Entry Requirements: Interview required.

801F MMus Master of Music (Performance) APEL
Duration: 1FT PMD
Entry Requirements: Interview required. Portfolio required.

803F MMus Master of Music (Piano for Dance)
Duration: 2FT PMD
Entry Requirements: Interview required.

802F MMus Master of Music (Piano for Dance) APEL
Duration: 1FT PMD
Entry Requirements: Interview required. Portfolio required.

894F MMus Master of Music (Repetiteurship)
Duration: 2FT PMD
Entry Requirements: Interview required.

860F MMus Master of Music (Repetiteurship) APEL
Duration: 1FT PMD
Entry Requirements: Interview required. Portfolio required.

806F MMus Master of Music (Scottish Music)
Duration: 2FT PMD
Entry Requirements: Interview required.

805F MMus Master of Music (Scottish Music) APEL
Duration: 1FT PMD
Entry Requirements: Interview required. Portfolio required.

R59 ROYAL WELSH COLLEGE OF MUSIC AND DRAMA
CASTLE GROUNDS
CATHAYS PARK
CARDIFF CF10 3ER
t: +44 (0)29 2039 1361 f: +44 (0)29 2039 1301
e: admissions@rwcmd.ac.uk
// www.rwcmd.ac.uk

200F BA (Hons) Acting
Duration: 3FT Hon
Entry Requirements: Interview required.

310F BMus Bachelor of Music (Honors) Jazz
Duration: 4FT Hon
Entry Requirements: Contact the institution for details.

300F BMus Bachelor of Music (Honours)
Duration: 4FT Hon
Entry Requirements: Interview required.

704F MA Acting for Stage, Screen & Radio
Duration: 1FT PMD
Entry Requirements: Interview required.

700P MA Arts Management
Duration: 2PT PMD
Entry Requirements: Interview required.

705F MA Arts Management
Duration: 1FT PMD
Entry Requirements: Interview required.

706F MA Brass Band Conducting
Duration: 2FT PMD
Entry Requirements: Interview required. Portfolio required.

714F MA Brass Band Conducting
Duration: 1FT PMD
Entry Requirements: Interview required. Portfolio required.

715F MA Choral Conducting
Duration: 1FT PMD
Entry Requirements: Interview required. Portfolio required.

741F MA Choral Conducting
Duration: 2FT PMD
Entry Requirements: Interview required. Portfolio required.

700F MA Composition
Duration: 2FT PMD
Entry Requirements: Interview required. Portfolio required.

716F MA Composition
Duration: 1FT PMD
Entry Requirements: Interview required. Portfolio required.

707F MA Creative Audio & New Media
Duration: 2FT PMD
Entry Requirements: Interview required. Portfolio required.

717F MA Creative Audio and New Media
Duration: 1FT PMD
Entry Requirements: Interview required. Portfolio required.

701F MA Historical Performance
Duration: 2FT PMD
Entry Requirements: Interview required. Portfolio required.

722F MA Historical Performance
Duration: 1FT PMD
Entry Requirements: Interview required. Portfolio required.

710F MA Jazz
Duration: 2FT PMD
Entry Requirements: Contact the institution for details.

702F MA Music Performance
Duration: 2FT PMD
Entry Requirements: Interview required. Portfolio required.

718F MA Music Performance
Duration: 1FT PMD
Entry Requirements: Interview required. Portfolio required.

713F MA Musical Theatre
Duration: 1FT PMD
Entry Requirements: Interview required.

752F MA Opera Performance
Duration: 2FT PMD
Entry Requirements: Interview required.

708F MA Orchestral Conducting
Duration: 2FT PMD
Entry Requirements: Interview required. Portfolio required.

719F MA Orchestral Conducting
Duration: 1FT PMD
Entry Requirements: Interview required. Portfolio required.

703F MA Orchestral Performance
Duration: 2FT PMD
Entry Requirements: Interview required. Portfolio required.

720F MA Orchestral Performance
Duration: 1FT PMD
Entry Requirements: Interview required. Portfolio required.

709F MA Repetiteurship
Duration: 2FT PMD
Entry Requirements: Interview required. Portfolio required.

721F MA Repetiteurship
Duration: 1FT PMD
Entry Requirements: Interview required. Portfolio required.

711F MA Scenic Art & Construction for Stage & Screen
Duration: 2FT PMD
Entry Requirements: Interview required.

712F MA Theatre Design
Duration: 2FT PMD
Entry Requirements: Interview required.

809F MMus Brass Band Conducting
Duration: 1FT PMD
Entry Requirements: Interview required. Portfolio required.

810F MMus Brass Band Conducting
Duration: 2FT PMD
Entry Requirements: Interview required. Portfolio required.

811F MMus Choral Conducting
Duration: 1FT PMD
Entry Requirements: Interview required. Portfolio required.

812F MMus Choral Conducting
Duration: 2FT PMD
Entry Requirements: Interview required. Portfolio required.

802F MMus Composition
Duration: 1FT PMD
Entry Requirements: Interview required. Portfolio required.

803F MMus Composition
Duration: 2FT PMD
Entry Requirements: Interview required. Portfolio required.

813F MMus Creative Audio & New Media
Duration: 1FT PMD
Entry Requirements: Interview required. Portfolio required.

814F MMus Creative Audio & New Media
Duration: 2FT PMD
Entry Requirements: Interview required. Portfolio required.

801F MMus Historical Performance
Duration: 2FT PMD
Entry Requirements: Interview required. Portfolio required.

804F MMus Historical Performance
Duration: 1FT PMD
Entry Requirements: Interview required. Portfolio required.

805F MMus Music Performance
Duration: 2FT PMD
Entry Requirements: Interview required. Portfolio required.

806F MMus Music Performance
Duration: 1FT PMD
Entry Requirements: Interview required. Portfolio required.

815F MMus Orchestral Conducting
Duration: 1FT PMD
Entry Requirements: Interview required. Portfolio required.

816F MMus Orchestral Conducting
Duration: 2FT PMD
Entry Requirements: Interview required. Portfolio required.

807F MMus Orchestral Performance
Duration: 1FT PMD
Entry Requirements: Interview required. Portfolio required.

808F MMus Orchestral Performance
Duration: 2FT PMD
Entry Requirements: Interview required. Portfolio required.

817F MMus Repetiteurship
Duration: 1FT PMD
Entry Requirements: Interview required. Portfolio required.

818F MMus Repetiteurship
Duration: 2FT PMD
Entry Requirements: Interview required. Portfolio required.

611F PGDip Brass Band Conducting
Duration: 2FT PMD
Entry Requirements: Interview required.

612F PGDip Brass Band Conducting
Duration: 1FT PMD
Entry Requirements: Interview required.

613F PGDip Choral Conducting
Duration: 1FT PMD
Entry Requirements: Interview required.

614F PGDip Choral Conducting
Duration: 2FT PMD
Entry Requirements: Interview required.

603F PGDip Composition
Duration: 2FT PMD
Entry Requirements: Interview required. Portfolio required.

604F PGDip Composition
Duration: 1FT PMD
Entry Requirements: Interview required. Portfolio required.

615F PGDip Creative Audio & New Media
Duration: 2FT PMD
Entry Requirements: Foundation Course required. Interview required.

616F PGDip Creative Audio & New Media
Duration: 1FT PMD
Entry Requirements: Foundation Course required. Interview required.

605F PGDip Historical Performance
Duration: 2FT PMD
Entry Requirements: Interview required.

606F PGDip Historical Performance
Duration: 1FT PMD
Entry Requirements: Interview required.

607F PGDip Music Performance
Duration: 2FT PMD
Entry Requirements: Interview required.

608F PGDip Music Performance
Duration: 1FT PMD
Entry Requirements: Interview required.

617F PGDip Orchestral Conducting
Duration: 1FT PMD
Entry Requirements: Interview required.

618F PGDip Orchestral Conducting
Duration: 2FT PMD
Entry Requirements: Interview required.

609F PGDip Orchestral Performance
Duration: 1FT PMD
Entry Requirements: Interview required.

610F PGDip Orchestral Performance
Duration: 2FT PMD
Entry Requirements: Interview required.

619F PGDip Repetiteurship
Duration: 2FT PMD
Entry Requirements: Interview required.

620F PGDip Repetiteurship
Duration: 1FT PMD
Entry Requirements: Interview required.

T75 TRINITY LABAN CONSERVATOIRE OF MUSIC AND DANCE
KING CHARLES COURT
OLD ROYAL NAVAL COLLEGE
GREENWICH
LONDON SE10 9JF
t: +44 (0)20 8305 4444
e: admissions@trinitylaban.ac.uk
// www.trinitylaban.ac.uk

230F BA BA (Hons) Musical Theatre Performance
Duration: 3FT Hon
Entry Requirements: Interview required.

300F BMus BMus (Hons) Performance
Duration: 4FT Hon
Entry Requirements: Admissions Test required.

310F BMus BMus (Hons) Performance Jazz Studies
Duration: 4FT Hon
Entry Requirements: Admissions Test required.

190F FPS Flexible Programmes of Study
Duration: 1FT Oth
Entry Requirements: Contact the institution for details.

801P MFA MFA Creative Practice (Music)
Duration: 2PT PMD
Entry Requirements: Contact the institution for details.

804F MFA MFA Creative Practice (Music)
Duration: 1FT PMD
Entry Requirements: Contact the institution for details.

800F MMus MMus (Performance/Composition/Jazz/Creative Practice)
Duration: 1FT PMD
Entry Requirements: Contact the institution for details.

800P MMus MMus (Performance/Composition/Jazz/Creative Practice)
Duration: 2PT PMD
Entry Requirements: Contact the institution for details.

802P MMus MMus Education Programme
Duration: 2PT PMD
Entry Requirements: Contact the institution for details.

805F MMus MMus Education Programme
Duration: 1FT PMD
Entry Requirements: Contact the institution for details.

803P MSc MSc in Performance Science
Duration: 2PT PMD
Entry Requirements: Contact the institution for details.

806F MSc MSc in Performance Science
Duration: 1FT PMD
Entry Requirements: Contact the institution for details.

602F PGA Postgraduate Artist Diploma (Performance Studies/Composition/Jazz)
Duration: 1FT PMD
Entry Requirements: Contact the institution for details.

602P PGA Postgraduate Artist Diploma (Performance Studies/Composition/Jazz)
Duration: 2PT PMD
Entry Requirements: Contact the institution for details.

600F PGDip Postgraduate Diploma (Performance, Composition, Jazz)
Duration: 1FT PMD
Entry Requirements: Contact the institution for details.

600P PGDip Postgraduate Diploma (Performance, Composition, Jazz)
Duration: 2PT PMD
Entry Requirements: Contact the institution for details.

DRAMA AND ACTING

A40 ABERYSTWYTH UNIVERSITY
ABERYSTWYTH UNIVERSITY, WELCOME CENTRE
PENGLAIS CAMPUS
ABERYSTWYTH
CEREDIGION SY23 3FB
t: 01970 622021 f: 01970 627410
e: ug-admissions@aber.ac.uk
// www.aber.ac.uk

W400 BA Drama & Theatre Studies
Duration: 3FT Hon
Entry Requirements: *GCE:* 300-320.

WW14 BA Drama & Theatre Studies/Fine Art
Duration: 3FT Hon
Entry Requirements: *GCE:* 300-320. *IB:* 32. Portfolio required.

WV41 BA Drama & Theatre Studies/History
Duration: 3FT Hon
Entry Requirements: *GCE:* 300-320. *IB:* 29.

LW24 BA Drama & Theatre Studies/International Politics
Duration: 3FT Hon
Entry Requirements: *GCE:* 300-320. *IB:* 29.

LWFK BA Drama & Theatre Studies/Politics
Duration: 3FT Hon
Entry Requirements: *GCE:* 300-320. *IB:* 29.

W401 BA Drama ac Astudiaethau Theatr
Duration: 3FT Hon
Entry Requirements: *GCE:* 300-320. *IB:* 32.

WWP4 BA Drama ac Astudiaethau Theatr/Astudiaethau Ffilm a Theledu
Duration: 3FT Hon
Entry Requirements: *GCE:* 300-320. *IB:* 32.

WVK1 BA Drama ac Astudiaethau Theatr/Hanes
Duration: 3FT Hon
Entry Requirements: *GCE:* 300-320. *IB:* 29.

VW24 BA Drama ac Astudiaethau Theatr/Hanes Cymru
Duration: 3FT Hon
Entry Requirements: *GCE:* 300-320. *IB:* 29.

WX43 BA Education/Drama & Theatre Studies
Duration: 3FT Hon
Entry Requirements: *GCE:* 300-320. *IB:* 32.

QW34 BA English Literature/Drama & Theatre Studies
Duration: 3FT Hon
Entry Requirements: *GCE:* 300-320. *IB:* 32.

RW14 BA French/Drama & Theatre Studies
Duration: 4FT Hon
Entry Requirements: *GCE:* 300-320. *IB:* 32.

GW14 BA Mathematics/Drama & Theatre Studies
Duration: 3FT Hon
Entry Requirements: *GCE:* 320. *IB:* 27.

W432 BA Scenography & Theatre Design/Drama & Theatre Studies
Duration: 3FT Hon
Entry Requirements: *GCE:* 300-320. *IB:* 32.

RW44 BA Spanish/Drama & Theatre Studies
Duration: 4FT Hon
Entry Requirements: *GCE:* 300-320. *IB:* 32.

VWF4 BA Welsh History/Drama & Theatre Studies
Duration: 3FT Hon
Entry Requirements: *GCE:* 300-320. *IB:* 29.

B20 BATH SPA UNIVERSITY
NEWTON PARK
NEWTON ST LOE
BATH BA2 9BN
t: 01225 875875 f: 01225 875444
e: enquiries@bathspa.ac.uk
// www.bathspa.ac.uk/clearing

WW4Y BA Creative Writing/Drama Studies
Duration: 3FT Hon
Entry Requirements: *GCE:* 220-280. *IB:* 24.

WW5K BA Dance/Drama Studies
Duration: 3FT Hon
Entry Requirements: *GCE:* 220-280. *IB:* 24. Interview required.

WW4X DipHE Creative Writing/Drama Studies
Duration: 2FT Dip
Entry Requirements: *GCE:* 220-280. *IB:* 24.

B24 BIRKBECK, UNIVERSITY OF LONDON
MALET STREET
LONDON WC1E 7HX
t: 020 7631 6316
e: webform: www.bbk.ac.uk/ask
// www.bbk.ac.uk/ask

W490 BA Theatre and Drama
Duration: 3FT Hon
Entry Requirements: *GCE:* BBB. *SQAH:* BBBBB-BBBCC. *IB:* 30.
Interview required.

B80 UNIVERSITY OF THE WEST OF ENGLAND, BRISTOL
FRENCHAY CAMPUS
COLDHARBOUR LANE
BRISTOL BS16 1QY
t: +44 (0)117 32 83333 f: +44 (0)117 32 82810
e: admissions@uwe.ac.uk
// www.uwe.ac.uk

W4W8 BA (Hons) Drama with Creative Writing
Duration: 3FT Hon
Entry Requirements: *GCE:* 320.

C10 CANTERBURY CHRIST CHURCH UNIVERSITY
NORTH HOLMES ROAD
CANTERBURY
KENT CT1 1QU
t: 01227 782900 f: 01227 782888
e: admissions@canterbury.ac.uk
// www.canterbury.ac.uk

WW45 FdA Performing Arts 'International Only'
Duration: 4FT Fdg
Entry Requirements: Interview required.

C58 UNIVERSITY OF CHICHESTER
BISHOP OTTER CAMPUS
COLLEGE LANE
CHICHESTER
WEST SUSSEX PO19 6PE
t: 01243 816002 f: 01243 816161
e: admissions@chi.ac.uk
// www.chiuni.ac.uk

WW4N BA Performing Arts (Theatre Performance and Dance)
Duration: 3FT Hon
Entry Requirements: *GCE:* BBC-BCC. *SQAAH:* BBC-BCC. *IB:* 28.
BTEC Dip: DD. *BTEC ExtDip:* DMM. Interview required.

C99 UNIVERSITY OF CUMBRIA
FUSEHILL STREET
CARLISLE
CUMBRIA CA1 2HH
t: 01228 616234 f: 01228 616235
// www.cumbria.ac.uk

WW54 BA Dance Performance and Drama Performance
Duration: 3FT Hon
Entry Requirements: *GCE:* 280. *IB:* 30. *OCR ND:* D Interview
required.

D26 DE MONTFORT UNIVERSITY
THE GATEWAY
LEICESTER LE1 9BH
t: 0116 255 1551 f: 0116 250 6204
e: enquiries@dmu.ac.uk
// www.dmu.ac.uk

WW84 BA Creative Writing and Drama Studies
Duration: 3FT Hon
Entry Requirements: *GCE:* 260. *IB:* 28. *BTEC Dip:* D*D*. *BTEC ExtDip:* DMM.

E14 UNIVERSITY OF EAST ANGLIA
NORWICH NR4 7TJ
t: 01603 591515 f: 01603 591523
e: admissions@uea.ac.uk
// www.uea.ac.uk

WW84 BA Scriptwriting and Performance
Duration: 3FT Hon   CRB Check: Required
Entry Requirements: *GCE:* AAB. *SQAAH:* AAB. *IB:* 33. *BTEC ExtDip:* DDD. Interview required. Portfolio required.

E42 EDGE HILL UNIVERSITY
ORMSKIRK
LANCASHIRE L39 4QP
t: 01695 657000 f: 01695 584355
e: study@edgehill.ac.uk
// www.edgehill.ac.uk

WW45 BA Dance and Drama with Physical Theatres
Duration: 3FT Hon
Entry Requirements: *GCE:* 280. *IB:* 26. *OCR ND:* D *OCR NED:* M2
Interview required.

W490 BA Visual Theatre
Duration: 3FT Hon
Entry Requirements: *GCE:* 280. *IB:* 26. *OCR ND:* D *OCR NED:* M2
Interview required.

E70 THE UNIVERSITY OF ESSEX
WIVENHOE PARK
COLCHESTER
ESSEX CO4 3SQ
t: 01206 873666 f: 01206 874477
e: admit@essex.ac.uk
// www.essex.ac.uk

W441 BA Acting and Contemporary Theatre
Duration: 3FT Hon
Entry Requirements: *GCE:* EE. *IB:* 24. Interview required.

F66 FARNBOROUGH COLLEGE OF TECHNOLOGY
BOUNDARY ROAD
FARNBOROUGH
HAMPSHIRE GU14 6SB
t: 01252 407028 f: 01252 407041
e: admissions@farn-ct.ac.uk
// www.farn-ct.ac.uk

WW54 FdA Theatre, Dance and Film Acting
Duration: 2FT Fdg
Entry Requirements: *GCE:* 160.

H14 HAVERING COLLEGE OF FURTHER AND HIGHER EDUCATION
ARDLEIGH GREEN ROAD
HORNCHURCH
ESSEX RM11 2LL
t: 01708 462793 f: 01708 462736
e: HE@havering-college.ac.uk
// www.havering-college.ac.uk

54WW HNC Performing Arts (Dance/Drama)
Duration: 1FT HNC
Entry Requirements: Contact the institution for details.

45WW HND Performing Arts (Dance/Drama)
Duration: 1FT HND
Entry Requirements: Contact the institution for details.

H36 UNIVERSITY OF HERTFORDSHIRE
UNIVERSITY ADMISSIONS SERVICE
COLLEGE LANE
HATFIELD
HERTS AL10 9AB
t: 01707 284800
// www.herts.ac.uk

WW45 FdA Performing Arts
Duration: 2FT Fdg
Entry Requirements: *GCE:* 80. Interview required.

H60 THE UNIVERSITY OF HUDDERSFIELD
QUEENSGATE
HUDDERSFIELD HD1 3DH
t: 01484 473969 f: 01484 472765
e: admissionsandrecords@hud.ac.uk
// www.hud.ac.uk

W444 BA(Hons) Technical Theatre
Duration: 3FT Hon
Entry Requirements: Interview required. Portfolio required.

K84 KINGSTON UNIVERSITY
STUDENT INFORMATION & ADVICE CENTRE
COOPER HOUSE
40-46 SURBITON ROAD
KINGSTON UPON THAMES KT1 2HX
t: 0844 8552177 f: 020 8547 7080
e: aps@kingston.ac.uk
// www.kingston.ac.uk

WW84 BA Creative Writing and Drama
Duration: 3FT Hon
Entry Requirements: *GCE:* 300-360. *IB:* 30.

WW45 BA Dance and Drama
Duration: 3FT Hon
Entry Requirements: *GCE:* 300-360. *SQAH:* BBCCC. *SQAAH:* BBC.
Interview required.

L39 UNIVERSITY OF LINCOLN
ADMISSIONS
BRAYFORD POOL
LINCOLN LN6 7TS
t: 01522 886097 f: 01522 886146
e: admissions@lincoln.ac.uk
// www.lincoln.ac.uk

WW45 BA Dance and Drama
Duration: 3FT Hon
Entry Requirements: *GCE:* 280. Interview required.

L46 LIVERPOOL HOPE UNIVERSITY
HOPE PARK
LIVERPOOL L16 9JD
t: 0151 291 3331 f: 0151 291 3434
e: administration@hope.ac.uk
// www.hope.ac.uk

WW54 BA Dance and Drama & Theatre Studies
Duration: 3FT Hon
Entry Requirements: *GCE:* 300-320. *IB:* 25. Interview required.

L51 LIVERPOOL JOHN MOORES UNIVERSITY
KINGSWAY HOUSE
HATTON GARDEN
LIVERPOOL L3 2AJ
t: 0151 231 5090 f: 0151 904 6368
e: courses@ljmu.ac.uk
// www.ljmu.ac.uk

WW48 BA Drama and Creative Writing
Duration: 3FT Hon
Entry Requirements: *GCE:* 260. *IB:* 28. Interview required.

M40 THE MANCHESTER METROPOLITAN UNIVERSITY
ADMISSIONS OFFICE
ALL SAINTS (GMS)
ALL SAINTS
MANCHESTER M15 6BH
t: 0161 247 2000
// www.mmu.ac.uk

W431 BA Contemporary Theatre and Performance
Duration: 3FT Hon
Entry Requirements: *GCE:* 280. *IB:* 28. *BTEC Dip:* D*D*. *BTEC ExtDip:* DMM. Interview required.

WW84 BA Creative Writing/Drama
Duration: 3FT Hon
Entry Requirements: *GCE:* 280. *IB:* 28. *BTEC Dip:* D*D*. *BTEC ExtDip:* DMM. Interview required. Portfolio required.

WW54 BA Dance/Drama
Duration: 3FT Hon
Entry Requirements: *GCE:* 280. *IB:* 28. *BTEC Dip:* D*D*. *BTEC ExtDip:* DMM. Interview required.

N36 NEWMAN UNIVERSITY COLLEGE, BIRMINGHAM
GENNERS LANE
BARTLEY GREEN
BIRMINGHAM B32 3NT
t: 0121 476 1181 f: 0121 476 1196
e: Admissions@newman.ac.uk
// www.newman.ac.uk

W4W8 BA Drama with Creative Writing
Duration: 3FT Hon
Entry Requirements: *Foundation:* Distinction. *GCE:* 260. *IB:* 24. *BTEC ExtDip:* DMM. *OCR ND:* M2 *OCR NED:* M2

N37 UNIVERSITY OF WALES, NEWPORT
ADMISSIONS
LODGE ROAD
CAERLEON
NEWPORT NP18 3QT
t: 01633 432030 f: 01633 432850
e: admissions@newport.ac.uk
// www.newport.ac.uk

W4W8 BA Applied Drama with Creative Writing
Duration: 3FT Hon
Entry Requirements: *GCE:* 260. *IB:* 24. Interview required.

N38 UNIVERSITY OF NORTHAMPTON
PARK CAMPUS
BOUGHTON GREEN ROAD
NORTHAMPTON NN2 7AL
t: 0800 358 2232 f: 01604 722083
e: admissions@northampton.ac.uk
// www.northampton.ac.uk

W8W4 BA Creative Writing/Drama
Duration: 3FT Hon
Entry Requirements: *GCE:* 260-280. *SQAH:* AAA-BBBB. *IB:* 24. *BTEC Dip:* DD. *BTEC ExtDip:* DMM. *OCR ND:* D *OCR NED:* M2 Interview required.

W5W4 BA Dance/Drama
Duration: 3FT Hon
Entry Requirements: *GCE:* 260-280. *SQAH:* AAA-BBBB. *IB:* 24. *BTEC Dip:* DD. *BTEC ExtDip:* DMM. *OCR ND:* D *OCR NED:* M2 Interview required.

W4W8 BA Drama/Creative Writing
Duration: 3FT Hon
Entry Requirements: *GCE:* 260-280. *SQAH:* AAA-BBBB. *IB:* 24. *BTEC Dip:* DD. *BTEC ExtDip:* DMM. *OCR ND:* D *OCR NED:* M2 Interview required.

W4W5 BA Drama/Dance
Duration: 3FT Hon
Entry Requirements: *GCE:* 260-280. *SQAH:* AAA-BBBB. *IB:* 24. *BTEC Dip:* DD. *BTEC ExtDip:* DMM. *OCR ND:* D *OCR NED:* M2 Interview required.

N77 NORTHUMBRIA UNIVERSITY
TRINITY BUILDING
NORTHUMBERLAND ROAD
NEWCASTLE UPON TYNE NE1 8ST
t: 0191 243 7420 f: 0191 227 4561
e: er.admissions@northumbria.ac.uk
// www.northumbria.ac.uk

WW84 BA Drama and Scriptwriting
Duration: 3FT Hon
Entry Requirements: *GCE:* 300. *SQAH:* BBBBC. *SQAAH:* BBC. *IB:*
26. Portfolio required.

R18 REGENT'S COLLEGE, LONDON (INCORPORATING REGENT'S BUSINESS SCHOOL, LONDON)
INNER CIRCLE, REGENT'S COLLEGE
REGENT'S PARK
LONDON NW1 4NS
t: +44(0)20 7487 7505 f: +44(0)20 7487 7425
e: exrel@regents.ac.uk
// www.regents.ac.uk/

W490 BA Acting and Global Theatre
Duration: 3FT Hon
Entry Requirements: *SQAH:* BBCC. *SQAAH:* CC.

R48 ROEHAMPTON UNIVERSITY
ROEHAMPTON LANE
LONDON SW15 5PU
t: 020 8392 3232 f: 020 8392 3470
e: enquiries@roehampton.ac.uk
// www.roehampton.ac.uk

WW84 BA Creative Writing and Drama, Theatre & Performance Studies
Duration: 3FT Hon
Entry Requirements: *GCE:* 300. *IB:* 26. *BTEC ExtDip:* DDM. *OCR NED:* D2 Interview required.

WW45 BA Dance Studies and Drama, Theatre & Performance Studies
Duration: 3FT Hon
Entry Requirements: *GCE:* 340. *IB:* 28. *BTEC ExtDip:* DDD. *OCR NED:* D1 Interview required.

R72 ROYAL HOLLOWAY, UNIVERSITY OF LONDON
ROYAL HOLLOWAY, UNIVERSITY OF LONDON
EGHAM
SURREY TW20 0EX
t: 01784 414944 f: 01784 473662
e: Admissions@rhul.ac.uk
// www.rhul.ac.uk

WW48 BA Drama and Creative Writing
Duration: 3FT Hon
Entry Requirements: *GCE:* AAB. *SQAH:* AAAAB. *SQAAH:* AAB. *IB:* 35.

S03 THE UNIVERSITY OF SALFORD
SALFORD M5 4WT
t: 0161 295 4545 f: 0161 295 4646
e: ug-admissions@salford.ac.uk
// www.salford.ac.uk

WW48 BA Drama and Creative Writing
Duration: 3FT Hon
Entry Requirements: *GCE:* 280. *IB:* 25.

S22 SHEFFIELD COLLEGE
THE SHEFFIELD COLLEGE
HE UNIT
HILLSBOROUGH COLLEGE AT THE BARRACKS
SHEFFIELD S6 2LR
t: 0114 260 2597
e: heunit@sheffcol.ac.uk
// www.sheffcol.ac.uk

WW45 FdA Performing Arts
Duration: 2FT Fdg
Entry Requirements: Contact the institution for details.

S64 ST MARY'S UNIVERSITY COLLEGE, TWICKENHAM
WALDEGRAVE ROAD
STRAWBERRY HILL
MIDDLESEX TW1 4SX
t: 020 8240 4029 f: 020 8240 2361
e: admit@smuc.ac.uk
// www.smuc.ac.uk

WW84 BA Drama and Creative and Professional Writing
Duration: 3FT Hon
Entry Requirements: *GCE:* 260. *SQAH:* BBBC. *IB:* 28. *OCR ND:* D *OCR NED:* M3 Interview required.

W499 BA Drama and Physical Theatre
Duration: 3FT Hon
Entry Requirements: *GCE:* 260. *SQAH:* BBBC. *IB:* 28. *OCR ND:* D *OCR NED:* M3 Interview required.

W400 BA Drama and Theatre Arts
Duration: 3FT Hon
Entry Requirements: *GCE:* 260. *SQAH:* BBBC. *IB:* 28. *OCR ND:* D *OCR NED:* M3 Interview required.

S72 STAFFORDSHIRE UNIVERSITY
COLLEGE ROAD
STOKE ON TRENT ST4 2DE
t: 01782 292753 f: 01782 292740
e: admissions@staffs.ac.uk
// www.staffs.ac.uk

WW54 FdA Creative & Cultural Industries (Dance and Theatre Arts)
Duration: 2FT Hon
Entry Requirements: Interview required.

S84 UNIVERSITY OF SUNDERLAND
STUDENT HELPLINE
THE STUDENT GATEWAY
CHESTER ROAD
SUNDERLAND SR1 3SD
t: 0191 515 3000 f: 0191 515 3805
e: student.helpline@sunderland.ac.uk
// www.sunderland.ac.uk

WW45 BA Dance and Drama
Duration: 3FT Hon
Entry Requirements: *GCE:* 260-360. *OCR ND:* D *OCR NED:* M3

W5W4 BA Dance with Drama
Duration: 3FT Hon
Entry Requirements: *GCE:* 260-360. *OCR ND:* D *OCR NED:* M3

W4W5 BA Drama with Dance
Duration: 3FT Hon
Entry Requirements: *GCE:* 260-360. *OCR ND:* D *OCR NED:* M3

U20 UNIVERSITY OF ULSTER
COLERAINE
CO. LONDONDERRY
NORTHERN IRELAND BT52 1SA
t: 028 7012 4221 f: 028 7012 4908
e: online@ulster.ac.uk
// www.ulster.ac.uk

W5W4 BA Dance with Drama
Duration: 3FT Hon
Entry Requirements: *GCE:* CCD. *IB:* 24. Interview required.

W4W5 BA Drama with Dance
Duration: 3FT Hon
Entry Requirements: *GCE:* BBC. *IB:* 24. Interview required.

W05 THE UNIVERSITY OF WEST LONDON
ST MARY'S ROAD
EALING
LONDON W5 5RF
t: 0800 036 8888 f: 020 8566 1353
e: learning.advice@uwl.ac.uk
// www.uwl.ac.uk

W490 CertHE Performing Arts
Duration: 1FT Cer
Entry Requirements: Contact the institution for details.

W75 UNIVERSITY OF WOLVERHAMPTON
ADMISSIONS UNIT
MX207, CAMP STREET
WOLVERHAMPTON
WEST MIDLANDS WV1 1AD
t: 01902 321000 f: 01902 321896
e: admissions@wlv.ac.uk
// www.wlv.ac.uk

WW54 BA Dance and Drama
Duration: 3FT Hon CRB Check: Required
Entry Requirements: *GCE:* 200. *IB:* 24. *BTEC Dip:* DM. *BTEC ExtDip:* MMP. *OCR ND:* M1 *OCR NED:* P1 Interview required.

WW48 BA Drama and Creative Professional Writing
Duration: 3FT Hon CRB Check: Required
Entry Requirements: *GCE:* 200. *IB:* 24. *BTEC Dip:* DM. *BTEC ExtDip:* MMP. *OCR ND:* M1 *OCR NED:* P1 Interview required.

W76 UNIVERSITY OF WINCHESTER
WINCHESTER
HANTS SO22 4NR
t: 01962 827234 f: 01962 827288
e: course.enquiries@winchester.ac.uk
// www.winchester.ac.uk

WW45 BA Choreography & Dance and Drama
Duration: 3FT Hon
Entry Requirements: *Foundation:* Distinction. *GCE:* 260-300. *IB:* 25. *OCR ND:* D *OCR NED:* M2

WWK5 BA Choreography & Dance and Performing Arts (Contemporary Performance)
Duration: 3FT Hon
Entry Requirements: *Foundation:* Distinction. *GCE:* 260-300. *IB:* 25. *OCR ND:* D *OCR NED:* M2

WW48 BA Creative Writing and Drama
Duration: 3FT Hon
Entry Requirements: *Foundation:* Distinction. *GCE:* 260-300. *IB:* 25. *OCR ND:* D *OCR NED:* M2

W80 UNIVERSITY OF WORCESTER
HENWICK GROVE
WORCESTER WR2 6AJ
t: 01905 855111 f: 01905 855377
e: admissions@worc.ac.uk
// www.worcester.ac.uk

WW48 BA Drama & Performance and Screen Writing
Duration: 3FT Hon
Entry Requirements: *GCE:* 240-260. *IB:* 24. *OCR ND:* D *OCR NED:* M3

DIRECTING, PRODUCING AND STAGE MANAGEMENT

B25 BIRMINGHAM CITY UNIVERSITY
PERRY BARR
BIRMINGHAM B42 2SU
t: 0121 331 5595 f: 0121 331 7994
// www.bcu.ac.uk

W450 BA Stage Management
Duration: 3FT Hon
Entry Requirements: *GCE:* 240. Interview required.

C35 CENTRAL SCHOOL OF SPEECH AND DRAMA, UNIVERSITY OF LONDON
EMBASSY THEATRE
64 ETON AVENUE
LONDON NW3 3HY
t: 0207 722 8183 f: 0207 722 4132
e: enquiries@cssd.ac.uk
// www.cssd.ac.uk

W451 BA Theatre Practice: Production Lighting
Duration: 3FT Hon
Entry Requirements: *GCE:* BBC. Interview required. Portfolio required.

W450 BA Theatre Practice: Theatre Lighting Design
Duration: 3FT Hon
Entry Requirements: *GCE:* BBC. Interview required. Portfolio required.

C99 UNIVERSITY OF CUMBRIA
FUSEHILL STREET
CARLISLE
CUMBRIA CA1 2HH
t: 01228 616234 f: 01228 616235
// www.cumbria.ac.uk

W450 FdA Stage Management
Duration: 2FT Fdg
Entry Requirements: *Foundation:* Pass. *GCE:* C-cccc. *SQAH:* CC. *SQAAH:* C. *IB:* 25. Interview required. Portfolio required.

E70 THE UNIVERSITY OF ESSEX
WIVENHOE PARK
COLCHESTER
ESSEX CO4 3SQ
t: 01206 873666 f: 01206 874477
e: admit@essex.ac.uk
// www.essex.ac.uk

W450 BA Stage Management and Technical Theatre (Top-up)
Duration: 1FT Hon
Entry Requirements: Interview required. Portfolio required.

W453 FdA Stage Management and Technical Theatre
Duration: 2FT Fdg
Entry Requirements: *GCE:* E. *SQAH:* CCCC. *SQAAH:* CCC. *IB:* 24. Interview required. Admissions Test required.

G70 UNIVERSITY OF GREENWICH
GREENWICH CAMPUS
OLD ROYAL NAVAL COLLEGE
PARK ROW
LONDON SE10 9LS
t: 020 8331 9000 f: 020 8331 8145
e: courseinfo@gre.ac.uk
// www.gre.ac.uk

W450 FdA Stage Management and Technical Theatre (ALRA)
Duration: 2FT Fdg
Entry Requirements: *GCE:* 60.

L23 UNIVERSITY OF LEEDS
THE UNIVERSITY OF LEEDS
WOODHOUSE LANE
LEEDS LS2 9JT
t: 0113 343 3999
e: admissions@leeds.ac.uk
// www.leeds.ac.uk

W450 BA Managing Performance
Duration: 3FT Hon
Entry Requirements: *GCE:* BBB. *SQAAH:* BBB. *IB:* 32.

W462 BA Performance Design
Duration: 3FT Hon
Entry Requirements: *GCE:* BBB. *SQAAH:* BBB. *IB:* 32. Interview required.

L48 THE LIVERPOOL INSTITUTE FOR PERFORMING ARTS
MOUNT STREET
LIVERPOOL L1 9HF
t: 0151 330 3000 f: 0151 330 3131
e: admissions@lipa.ac.uk
// www.lipa.ac.uk

W450 BA Music, Theatre and Entertainment Management
Duration: 3FT Hon
Entry Requirements: *GCE:* 240. Interview required.

N30 NEW COLLEGE NOTTINGHAM
ADAMS BUILDING
STONEY STREET
THE LACE MARKET
NOTTINGHAM NG1 1NG
t: 0115 910 0100 f: 0115 953 4349
e: he.team@ncn.ac.uk
// www.ncn.ac.uk

W450 FdA Theatre Arts (Technical Theatre)
Duration: 2FT Fdg
Entry Requirements: *GCE:* 120-240. Interview required.

N41 NORTHBROOK COLLEGE SUSSEX
LITTLEHAMPTON ROAD
WORTHING
WEST SUSSEX BN12 6NU
t: 0845 155 6060 f: 01903 606073
e: enquiries@nbcol.ac.uk
// www.northbrook.ac.uk

W490 FdA Prop Making and Special Effects
Duration: 2FT Fdg
Entry Requirements: *GCE:* 160. Interview required. Portfolio required.

W450 FdA Theatre Arts - Stage and Production Management
Duration: 2FT Fdg
Entry Requirements: *GCE:* 160. Interview required.

R51 ROSE BRUFORD COLLEGE
LAMORBEY PARK
BURNT OAK LANE
SIDCUP
KENT DA15 9DF
t: 0208 308 2600 f: 020 8308 0542
e: enquiries@bruford.ac.uk
// www.bruford.ac.uk

WG46 BA Creative Lighting Control
Duration: 3FT Hon
Entry Requirements: Contact the institution for details.

W450 BA Stage Management
Duration: 3FT Hon
Entry Requirements: *GCE:* 160-280.

R86 ROYAL WELSH COLLEGE OF MUSIC AND DRAMA (COLEG BRENHINOL CERDD A DRAMA CYMRU)
CASTLE GROUNDS
CATHAYS PARK
CARDIFF CF10 3ER
t: 029 2039 1361 f: 029 2039 1301
e: admissions@rwcmd.ac.uk
// www.rwcmd.ac.uk

W450 BA Stage Management
Duration: 3FT Hon
Entry Requirements: *GCE:* 240-360. Interview required.

THEATRE STUDIES

A44 ACCRINGTON & ROSSENDALE COLLEGE
BROAD OAK ROAD,
ACCRINGTON,
LANCASHIRE, BB5 2AW.
t: 01254 389933 f: 01254 354001
e: info@accross.ac.uk
// www.accrosshighereducation.co.uk/

W440 FdA Theatre and Performance
Duration: 2FT Fdg
Entry Requirements: Interview required.

B06 BANGOR UNIVERSITY
BANGOR UNIVERSITY
BANGOR
GWYNEDD LL57 2DG
t: 01248 388484 f: 01248 370451
e: admissions@bangor.ac.uk
// www.bangor.ac.uk

Q3WX BA English with Theatre and Performance
Duration: 3FT Hon
Entry Requirements: Contact the institution for details.

B22 UNIVERSITY OF BEDFORDSHIRE
PARK SQUARE
LUTON
BEDS LU1 3JU
t: 0844 8482234 f: 01582 489323
e: admissions@beds.ac.uk
// www.beds.ac.uk

WQ43 BA English and Theatre Studies
Duration: 3FT Hon
Entry Requirements: *GCE:* 180-220. Interview required.

B32 THE UNIVERSITY OF BIRMINGHAM
EDGBASTON
BIRMINGHAM B15 2TT
t: 0121 415 8900 f: 0121 414 7159
e: admissions@bham.ac.uk
// www.birmingham.ac.uk

W440 BA Drama and Theatre Arts
Duration: 3FT Hon
Entry Requirements: *GCE:* AAB-ABB. *SQAH:* AABBB-ABBBB.
SQAAH: AA-AB.

B72 UNIVERSITY OF BRIGHTON
MITHRAS HOUSE 211
LEWES ROAD
BRIGHTON BN2 4AT
t: 01273 644644 f: 01273 642607
e: admissions@brighton.ac.uk
// www.brighton.ac.uk

W4WD BA Performance and Visual Arts (Theatre)
Duration: 3FT Hon
Entry Requirements: *GCE:* BBC. Foundation Course required.
Interview required. Portfolio required.

B77 BRISTOL, CITY OF BRISTOL COLLEGE
SOUTH BRISTOL SKILLS ACADEMY
CITY OF BRISTOL COLLEGE
PO BOX 2887 BS2 2BB
t: 0117 312 5000
e: HEAdmissions@cityofbristol.ac.uk
// www.cityofbristol.ac.uk

WW54 FdA Dance Theatre Performance
Duration: 2FT Fdg   CRB Check: Required
Entry Requirements: *GCE:* 140. Interview required.

B84 BRUNEL UNIVERSITY
UXBRIDGE
MIDDLESEX UB8 3PH
t: 01895 265265 f: 01895 269790
e: admissions@brunel.ac.uk
// www.brunel.ac.uk

W440 BA Theatre
Duration: 3FT Hon
Entry Requirements: *GCE:* BBB. *SQAAH:* BBB. *IB:* 32. *BTEC
ExtDip:* DDM.

W4WW BA Theatre and Creative Writing
Duration: 3FT Hon
Entry Requirements: *GCE:* ABB. *SQAAH:* ABB. *IB:* 33. *BTEC
ExtDip:* D*DD.

WQ43 BA Theatre and English
Duration: 3FT Hon
Entry Requirements: *GCE:* AAB. *SQAAH:* AAB. *IB:* 35. *BTEC
ExtDip:* D*D*D.

WW46 BA Theatre and Film & TV Studies
Duration: 3FT Hon
Entry Requirements: *GCE:* BBB. *SQAAH:* BBB. *IB:* 32. *BTEC
ExtDip:* DDM.

WW42 BA Theatre and Games Design
Duration: 3FT Hon
Entry Requirements: *GCE:* BBB. *SQAAH:* BBB. *IB:* 32. *BTEC
ExtDip:* DDM.

C10 CANTERBURY CHRIST CHURCH UNIVERSITY
NORTH HOLMES ROAD
CANTERBURY
KENT CT1 1QU
t: 01227 782900 f: 01227 782888
e: admissions@canterbury.ac.uk
// www.canterbury.ac.uk

W440 BA Technical Theatre
Duration: 3FT Hon
Entry Requirements: *GCE:* 240. *IB:* 24. Interview required.

C30 UNIVERSITY OF CENTRAL LANCASHIRE
PRESTON
LANCS PR1 2HE
t: 01772 201201 f: 01772 894954
e: uadmissions@uclan.ac.uk
// www.uclan.ac.uk

W441 BA Contemporary Theatre and Performance
Duration: 3FT Hon
Entry Requirements: *GCE:* 260-300. *IB:* 26. Interview required.

W440 FdA Theatre and Performance
Duration: 2FT Fdg
Entry Requirements: *GCE:* 80. *SQAH:* CC.

C35 CENTRAL SCHOOL OF SPEECH AND DRAMA, UNIVERSITY OF LONDON
EMBASSY THEATRE
64 ETON AVENUE
LONDON NW3 3HY
t: 0207 722 8183 f: 0207 722 4132
e: enquiries@cssd.ac.uk
// www.cssd.ac.uk

W440 BA Theatre Practice: Performance Arts
Duration: 3FT Hon
Entry Requirements: *GCE:* BBC. Interview required. Portfolio required.

W441 BA Theatre Practice: Puppetry
Duration: 3FT Hon
Entry Requirements: *GCE:* BBC. Interview required. Portfolio required.

C55 UNIVERSITY OF CHESTER
PARKGATE ROAD
CHESTER CH1 4BJ
t: 01244 511000 f: 01244 511300
e: enquiries@chester.ac.uk
// www.chester.ac.uk

WW84 BA Creative Writing and Drama & Theatre Studies
Duration: 3FT Hon
Entry Requirements: *Foundation:* Pass. *GCE:* 260-300. *SQAH:* BBBB. *IB:* 28.

C75 COLCHESTER INSTITUTE
SHEEPEN ROAD
COLCHESTER
ESSEX CO3 3LL
t: 01206 712777 f: 01206 712800
e: info@colchester.ac.uk
// www.colchester.ac.uk

W441 BA Technical Theatre
Duration: 3FT Hon
Entry Requirements: *GCE:* 160. Interview required.

W440 FdA Technical Theatre
Duration: 2FT Fdg
Entry Requirements: *GCE:* 80. Interview required.

C78 CORNWALL COLLEGE
POOL
REDRUTH
CORNWALL TR15 3RD
t: 01209 616161 f: 01209 611612
e: he.admissions@cornwall.ac.uk
// www.cornwall.ac.uk

04KW HNC Performing Arts (Small Scale Theatre)
Duration: 1FT HNC   CRB Check: Required
Entry Requirements: Contact the institution for details.

044W HND Performing Arts (Small Scale Theatre)
Duration: 2FT HND   CRB Check: Required
Entry Requirements: Contact the institution for details.

C85 COVENTRY UNIVERSITY
THE STUDENT CENTRE
COVENTRY UNIVERSITY
1 GULSON RD
COVENTRY CV1 2JH
t: 024 7615 2222 f: 024 7615 2223
e: studentenquiries@coventry.ac.uk
// www.coventry.ac.uk

W440 BA Theatre and Professional Practice
Duration: 3FT/4SW Hon
Entry Requirements: *GCE:* CCC. *SQAH:* CCCCC. *IB:* 27. *BTEC ExtDip:* MMM. *OCR NED:* M3 Interview required.

C93 UNIVERSITY FOR THE CREATIVE ARTS
FALKNER ROAD
FARNHAM
SURREY GU9 7DS
t: 01252 892960
e: admissions@ucreative.ac.uk
// www.ucreative.ac.uk

W440 BA Creative Arts for Theatre & Film
Duration: 3FT Hon
Entry Requirements: *GCE:* 220. *IB:* 24. *BTEC ExtDip:* PPP. Interview required. Portfolio required.

C99 UNIVERSITY OF CUMBRIA
FUSEHILL STREET
CARLISLE
CUMBRIA CA1 2HH
t: 01228 616234 f: 01228 616235
// www.cumbria.ac.uk

W440 BA Performing Arts
Duration: 3FT Hon
Entry Requirements: *GCE:* 280. *IB:* 30. *OCR ND:* D Interview required.

D39 UNIVERSITY OF DERBY
KEDLESTON ROAD
DERBY DE22 1GB
t: 01332 591167 f: 01332 597724
e: askadmissions@derby.ac.uk
// www.derby.ac.uk

MW24 BA Applied Criminology and Theatre Studies
Duration: 3FT Hon
Entry Requirements: *Foundation:* Distinction. *GCE:* 260-300. *IB:* 28. *BTEC Dip:* D*D*. *BTEC ExtDip:* DMM. *OCR NED:* M2

KW14 BA Architectural Design and Theatre Studies
Duration: 3FT Hon
Entry Requirements: *Foundation:* Distinction. *GCE:* 260-300. *IB:* 28. *BTEC Dip:* D*D*. *BTEC ExtDip:* DMM. *OCR NED:* M2

NW24 BA Business Management and Theatre Arts
Duration: 3FT Hon
Entry Requirements: *Foundation:* Distinction. *GCE:* 260-300. *IB:* 28. *BTEC Dip:* D*D*. *BTEC ExtDip:* DMM. *OCR NED:* M2

WW45 BA Dance & Movement Studies and Theatre Studies
Duration: 3FT Hon
Entry Requirements: *Foundation:* Distinction. *GCE:* 260-300. *IB:* 28. *BTEC Dip:* D*D*. *BTEC ExtDip:* DMM. *OCR NED:* M2

NW64 BA Human Resource Management and Theatre Studies
Duration: 3FT Hon
Entry Requirements: *Foundation:* Distinction. *GCE:* 260-300. *IB:* 28. *BTEC Dip:* D*D*. *BTEC ExtDip:* DMM. *OCR NED:* M2

NW5K BA Marketing and Theatre Studies
Duration: 3FT Hon
Entry Requirements: *Foundation:* Distinction. *GCE:* 260-300. *IB:* 28. *BTEC Dip:* D*D*. *BTEC ExtDip:* DMM. *OCR NED:* M2

W440 BA Theatre Arts
Duration: 3FT Hon
Entry Requirements: *Foundation:* Distinction. *GCE:* 260. *IB:* 26. *BTEC Dip:* D*D*. *BTEC ExtDip:* DMM. *OCR NED:* M2 Interview required.

LW74 BA/BSc Geography and Theatre Studies
Duration: 3FT Hon
Entry Requirements: *Foundation:* Distinction. *GCE:* 260-300. *IB:* 28. *BTEC Dip:* D*D*. *BTEC ExtDip:* DMM. *OCR NED:* M2

CW8K BA/BSc Psychology and Theatre Studies
Duration: 3FT Hon
Entry Requirements: *Foundation:* Distinction. *GCE:* 260-300. *IB:* 28. *BTEC Dip:* D*D*. *BTEC ExtDip:* DMM. *OCR NED:* M2

D52 DONCASTER COLLEGE
THE HUB
CHAPPELL DRIVE
SOUTH YORKSHIRE DN1 2RF
t: 01302 553610
e: he@don.ac.uk
// www.don.ac.uk

W441 BA Contemporary Performance Practice
Duration: 3FT Hon
Entry Requirements: Contact the institution for details.

E28 UNIVERSITY OF EAST LONDON
DOCKLANDS CAMPUS
UNIVERSITY WAY
LONDON E16 2RD
t: 020 8223 3333 f: 020 8223 2978
e: study@uel.ac.uk
// www.uel.ac.uk

L6W4 BA Cultural Studies with Theatre Studies
Duration: 3FT Hon
Entry Requirements: *GCE:* 240. *IB:* 24.

Q3WK BA English Literature with Theatre Studies
Duration: 3FT Hon
Entry Requirements: *GCE:* 240. *IB:* 24.

M1W4 BA Law with Theatre Studies
Duration: 3FT Hon
Entry Requirements: *GCE:* 240. *IB:* 28.

WW5K BA Professional Dance and Musical Theatre
Duration: 3FT Hon
Entry Requirements: *GCE:* 200. *IB:* 24. Interview required.

W442 BA Theatre Studies
Duration: 3FT Hon
Entry Requirements: *GCE:* 240. *IB:* 24. Interview required.

W443 BA Theatre Studies (International)
Duration: 3FT Hon
Entry Requirements: *GCE:* 240. *IB:* 24.

W4L9 BA Theatre Studies with Communication Studies
Duration: 3FT Hon
Entry Requirements: *GCE:* 240. *IB:* 24.

WX43 BA Theatre Studies with Education Studies
Duration: 3FT Hon
Entry Requirements: *GCE:* 240. *IB:* 24. Interview required.

W4QJ BA Theatre Studies with English Literature
Duration: 3FT Hon
Entry Requirements: *GCE:* 240. *IB:* 24. Interview required.

W4CP BA Theatre Studies with Sports & Exercise Science
Duration: 3FT Hon
Entry Requirements: *GCE:* 240. *IB:* 24. Interview required.

B9WK BSc Health Promotion with Theatre Studies
Duration: 3FT Hon
Entry Requirements: *GCE:* 240. *IB:* 24.

F33 UNIVERSITY COLLEGE FALMOUTH
WOODLANE
FALMOUTH
CORNWALL TR11 4RH
t: 01326213730
e: admissions@falmouth.ac.uk
// www.falmouth.ac.uk

W490 BA(Hons) Theatre
Duration: 3FT Hon
Entry Requirements: *GCE:* 220. *IB:* 24. Interview required.

G28 UNIVERSITY OF GLASGOW
71 SOUTHPARK AVENUE
UNIVERSITY OF GLASGOW
GLASGOW G12 8QQ
t: 0141 330 6062 f: 0141 330 2961
e: student.recruitment@glasgow.ac.uk
// www.glasgow.ac.uk

QWF4 MA Comparative Literature/Theatre Studies
Duration: 4FT Hon
Entry Requirements: *GCE:* ABB. *SQAH:* AAAB-ABBB. *IB:* 34.

LW44 MA Public Policy/Theatre Studies
Duration: 4FT Hon
Entry Requirements: *GCE:* ABB. *SQAH:* AAAB-ABBB. *IB:* 36.

LW34 MA Sociology/Theatre Studies
Duration: 4FT Hon
Entry Requirements: *GCE:* ABB. *SQAH:* AAAB-ABBB. *IB:* 36.

RW4K MA Spanish/Theatre Studies
Duration: 5FT Hon
Entry Requirements: *GCE:* ABB. *SQAH:* AAAB-ABBB. *IB:* 36.

W440 MA Theatre Studies
Duration: 4FT Hon
Entry Requirements: *GCE:* ABB. *SQAH:* AAAB-ABBB. *IB:* 36.

WQ46 MA Theatre Studies/Latin
Duration: 4FT Hon
Entry Requirements: *GCE:* ABB. *SQAH:* AAAB-ABBB. *IB:* 36.

VW64 MA Theology & Religious Studies/Theatre Studies
Duration: 4FT Hon
Entry Requirements: *GCE:* ABB. *SQAH:* AAAB-ABBB. *IB:* 36.

G56 GOLDSMITHS, UNIVERSITY OF LONDON
GOLDSMITHS, UNIVERSITY OF LONDON
NEW CROSS
LONDON SE14 6NW
t: 020 7048 5300 f: 020 7919 7509
e: admissions@gold.ac.uk
// www.gold.ac.uk

W440 BA Drama and Theatre Arts
Duration: 3FT Hon
Entry Requirements: *GCE:* ABB. *SQAH:* BBBBB. *SQAAH:* BBB. *IB:* 32. Interview required.

H54 HOPWOOD HALL COLLEGE
ROCHDALE ROAD
MIDDLETON
MANCHESTER M24 6XH
t: 0161 643 7560 f: 0161 643 2114
e: admissions@hopwood.ac.uk
// www.hopwood.ac.uk

W447 HND Performing Arts (Theatre in Education)
Duration: 2FT HND   CRB Check: Required
Entry Requirements: Contact the institution for details.

H60 THE UNIVERSITY OF HUDDERSFIELD
QUEENSGATE
HUDDERSFIELD HD1 3DH
t: 01484 473969 f: 01484 472765
e: admissionsandrecords@hud.ac.uk
// www.hud.ac.uk

W440 BA Drama
Duration: 3FT Hon
Entry Requirements: *GCE:* 280. Interview required.

H72 THE UNIVERSITY OF HULL
THE UNIVERSITY OF HULL
COTTINGHAM ROAD
HULL HU6 7RX
t: 01482 466100 f: 01482 442290
e: admissions@hull.ac.uk
// www.hull.ac.uk

Q3W4 BA English with Theatre & Performance
Duration: 3FT Hon
Entry Requirements: *GCE:* 260-300. *IB:* 26. *BTEC ExtDip:* DMM.

WQ43 BA Theatre and English
Duration: 3FT Hon
Entry Requirements: *GCE:* 260-300. *IB:* 26. *BTEC ExtDip:* DMM.

WWK5 BA Theatre and Performance
Duration: 3FT Hon
Entry Requirements: *GCE:* 260-300. *IB:* 24. *BTEC ExtDip:* DMM.

H73 HULL COLLEGE
QUEEN'S GARDENS
HULL HU1 3DG
t: 01482 329943 f: 01482 598733
e: info@hull-college.ac.uk
// www.hull-college.ac.uk/higher-education

W441 BA Stage Management and Technical Theatre
Duration: 1FT Hon
Entry Requirements: Interview required. Admissions Test required. Portfolio required. HND required.

W440 FdA Stage Management and Technical Theatre
Duration: 2FT Fdg
Entry Requirements: *GCE:* 240. Interview required. Admissions Test required. Portfolio required.

L14 LANCASTER UNIVERSITY
THE UNIVERSITY
LANCASTER
LANCASHIRE LA1 4YW
t: 01524 592029 f: 01524 846243
e: ugadmissions@lancaster.ac.uk
// www.lancs.ac.uk

W440 BA Theatre Studies
Duration: 3FT Hon
Entry Requirements: *GCE:* ABB. *SQAH:* BBBBB. *SQAAH:* BBB. *IB:* 32. Interview required.

L23 UNIVERSITY OF LEEDS
THE UNIVERSITY OF LEEDS
WOODHOUSE LANE
LEEDS LS2 9JT
t: 0113 343 3999
e: admissions@leeds.ac.uk
// www.leeds.ac.uk

QW34 BA English Literature and Theatre Studies
Duration: 3FT Hon
Entry Requirements: *GCE:* AAB. *SQAH:* AAAAB. *SQAAH:* AAB. *IB:* 35. Interview required.

W440 BA Theatre and Performance
Duration: 3FT Hon
Entry Requirements: *GCE:* ABB. *SQAAH:* ABB. *IB:* 36.

L42 LINCOLN COLLEGE
MONKS ROAD
LINCOLN LN2 5HQ
t: 01522 876000 f: 01522 876200
e: enquiries@lincolncollege.ac.uk
// www.lincolncollege.ac.uk

044W HND Theatre
Duration: 2FT HND
Entry Requirements: *GCE:* 120. Interview required.

L46 LIVERPOOL HOPE UNIVERSITY
HOPE PARK
LIVERPOOL L16 9JD
t: 0151 291 3331 f: 0151 291 3434
e: administration@hope.ac.uk
// www.hope.ac.uk

VW34 BA Art & Design History and Drama & Theatre Studies
Duration: 3FT Hon
Entry Requirements: *GCE:* 300-320. *IB:* 25. Interview required.

M10 THE MANCHESTER COLLEGE
OPENSHAW CAMPUS
ASHTON OLD ROAD
OPENSHAW
MANCHESTER M11 2WH
t: 0800 068 8585 f: 0161 920 4103
e: enquiries@themanchestercollege.ac.uk
// www.themanchestercollege.ac.uk

W440 FdA Contemporary Theatre Practice
Duration: 2FT Fdg
Entry Requirements: *GCE:* 180. *BTEC ExtDip:* MPP. Interview required.

M95 MOUNTVIEW ACADEMY OF THEATRE ARTS
RALPH RICHARDSON MEMORIAL STUDIOS
KINGFISHER PLACE
CLARENDON ROAD
LONDON N22 6XF
t: 020 8881 2201 f: 020 8829 0034
e: enquiries@mountview.ac.uk
// www.mountview.ac.uk

W440 BA Theatre Production Arts
Duration: 2FT Hon
Entry Requirements: Interview required. Portfolio required.

N38 UNIVERSITY OF NORTHAMPTON
PARK CAMPUS
BOUGHTON GREEN ROAD
NORTHAMPTON NN2 7AL
t: 0800 358 2232 f: 01604 722083
e: admissions@northampton.ac.uk
// www.northampton.ac.uk

044W HND Theatre
Duration: 2FT HND
Entry Requirements: *GCE:* 140-160. *SQAH:* BC-CCC. *IB:* 24.
BTEC Dip: MP. *BTEC ExtDip:* MPP. *OCR ND:* P1 *OCR NED:* P2
Interview required.

P51 PETROC
OLD STICKLEPATH HILL
BARNSTAPLE
NORTH DEVON EX31 2BQ
t: 01271 852365 f: 01271 338121
e: he@petroc.ac.uk
// www.petroc.ac.uk

W401 FdA Theatre: Performance and Production
Duration: 2FT Fdg
Entry Requirements: *GCE:* EE.

Q25 QUEEN MARGARET UNIVERSITY, EDINBURGH
QUEEN MARGARET UNIVERSITY DRIVE
EDINBURGH EH21 6UU
t: 0131474 0000 f: 0131 474 0001
e: admissions@qmu.ac.uk
// www.qmu.ac.uk

WW46 BA Theatre and Film Studies
Duration: 4FT Hon
Entry Requirements: *GCE:* 300. *IB:* 30.

R12 THE UNIVERSITY OF READING
THE UNIVERSITY OF READING
PO BOX 217
READING RG6 6AH
t: 0118 378 8619 f: 0118 378 8924
e: student.recruitment@reading.ac.uk
// www.reading.ac.uk

QW34 BA English Literature and Film & Theatre
Duration: 3FT Hon
Entry Requirements: *GCE:* AAC-ABB. *SQAH:* AAACC-ABBBB.
SQAAH: AAC-ABB.

W440 BA Theatre Arts Education and Deaf Studies
Duration: 3FT Hon
Entry Requirements: *GCE:* 160. *BTEC Dip:* MM. *BTEC ExtDip:*
MPP. Interview required.

R48 ROEHAMPTON UNIVERSITY
ROEHAMPTON LANE
LONDON SW15 5PU
t: 020 8392 3232 f: 020 8392 3470
e: enquiries@roehampton.ac.uk
// www.roehampton.ac.uk

W440 BA Drama, Theatre & Performance Studies
Duration: 3FT Hon
Entry Requirements: *GCE:* 300. *IB:* 26. *BTEC ExtDip:* DDM. *OCR*
NED: D2 Interview required.

R51 ROSE BRUFORD COLLEGE
LAMORBEY PARK
BURNT OAK LANE
SIDCUP
KENT DA15 9DF
t: 0208 308 2600 f: 020 8308 0542
e: enquiries@bruford.ac.uk
// www.bruford.ac.uk

WJ49 BA Performance Sound
Duration: 3FT Hon
Entry Requirements: Contact the institution for details.

R72 ROYAL HOLLOWAY, UNIVERSITY OF LONDON
ROYAL HOLLOWAY, UNIVERSITY OF LONDON
EGHAM
SURREY TW20 0EX
t: 01784 414944 f: 01784 473662
e: Admissions@rhul.ac.uk
// www.rhul.ac.uk

W440 BA Drama and Theatre Studies
Duration: 3FT Hon
Entry Requirements: *GCE:* AAB. *SQAH:* AAAAB. *SQAAH:* AAB. *IB:*
35.

S03 THE UNIVERSITY OF SALFORD
SALFORD M5 4WT
t: 0161 295 4545 f: 0161 295 4646
e: ug-admissions@salford.ac.uk
// www.salford.ac.uk

W440 BA Performance: Contemporary Practices
Duration: 3FT Hon
Entry Requirements: *GCE:* 300. *IB:* 31. *OCR ND:* D *OCR NED:* M1
Interview required.

WW54 BA Performance: Dance Theatre
Duration: 3FT Hon
Entry Requirements: *GCE:* 300. *IB:* 31. *OCR ND:* D *OCR NED:* M1
Interview required.

S18 THE UNIVERSITY OF SHEFFIELD
THE UNIVERSITY OF SHEFFIELD
LEVEL 2, ARTS TOWER
WESTERN BANK
SHEFFIELD S10 2TN
t: 0114 222 8030 f: 0114 222 8032
// www.sheffield.ac.uk

QW34 BA English and Theatre
Duration: 3FT Hon
Entry Requirements: *GCE:* AAB. *SQAH:* AAABB. *SQAAH:* A. *IB:* 35.
BTEC ExtDip: DDD.

W440 BA Theatre and Performance
Duration: 3FT Hon
Entry Requirements: *GCE:* AAB. *SQAH:* AAABB. *SQAAH:* A. *IB:* 35.
BTEC ExtDip: DDD.

S51 ST HELENS COLLEGE
WATER STREET
ST HELENS
MERSEYSIDE WA10 1PP
t: 01744 733766 f: 01744 623400
e: enquiries@sthelens.ac.uk
// www.sthelens.ac.uk

W440 FdA Theatre and Performance
Duration: 2FT Fdg
Entry Requirements: *GCE:* 120. *IB:* 20. Interview required.

S64 ST MARY'S UNIVERSITY COLLEGE, TWICKENHAM
WALDEGRAVE ROAD
STRAWBERRY HILL
MIDDLESEX TW1 4SX
t: 020 8240 4029 f: 020 8240 2361
e: admit@smuc.ac.uk
// www.smuc.ac.uk

W490 BA Drama and Applied Theatre
Duration: 3FT Hon
Entry Requirements: *GCE:* 260. *SQAH:* BBBC. *IB:* 28. *OCR ND:* D
OCR NED: M3 Interview required.

S72 STAFFORDSHIRE UNIVERSITY
COLLEGE ROAD
STOKE ON TRENT ST4 2DE
t: 01782 292753 f: 01782 292740
e: admissions@staffs.ac.uk
// www.staffs.ac.uk

W441 BA Theatre Studies and Technical Stage Production
Duration: 3FT Hon
Entry Requirements: *GCE:* 180-220. *IB:* 24. Interview required.

S85 UNIVERSITY OF SURREY
STAG HILL
GUILDFORD
SURREY GU2 7XH
t: +44(0)1483 689305 f: +44(0)1483 689388
e: ugteam@surrey.ac.uk
// www.surrey.ac.uk

W440 BA Theatre Studies
Duration: 3FT/4SW Hon
Entry Requirements: *GCE:* AAB-ABB. *SQAH:* BBBBC-BBBCC. *IB:* 34.

U20 UNIVERSITY OF ULSTER
COLERAINE
CO. LONDONDERRY
NORTHERN IRELAND BT52 1SA
t: 028 7012 4221 f: 028 7012 4908
e: online@ulster.ac.uk
// www.ulster.ac.uk

W440 BA Drama
Duration: 3FT Hon
Entry Requirements: *GCE:* BBC. *IB:* 24. Interview required.

W20 THE UNIVERSITY OF WARWICK
COVENTRY CV4 8UW
t: 024 7652 3723 f: 024 7652 4649
e: ugadmissions@warwick.ac.uk
// www.warwick.ac.uk

R1W4 BA French with Theatre Studies
Duration: 4FT Hon
Entry Requirements: *GCE:* AAB. *SQAAH:* AA. *IB:* 36.

W440 BA Theatre and Performance Studies
Duration: 3FT Hon
Entry Requirements: *GCE:* AABb. *SQAAH:* AA. *IB:* 36. Interview required.

W67 WIGAN AND LEIGH COLLEGE
PO BOX 53
PARSON'S WALK
WIGAN
GREATER MANCHESTER WN1 1RS
t: 01942 761605 f: 01942 761164
e: applications@wigan-leigh.ac.uk
// www.wigan-leigh.ac.uk

W440 FdA Theatre and Performance Studies
Duration: 2FT Fdg
Entry Requirements: Interview required.

W75 UNIVERSITY OF WOLVERHAMPTON
ADMISSIONS UNIT
MX207, CAMP STREET
WOLVERHAMPTON
WEST MIDLANDS WV1 1AD
t: 01902 321000 f: 01902 321896
e: admissions@wlv.ac.uk
// www.wlv.ac.uk

W440 FdA Musical Theatre
Duration: 2FT Fdg
Entry Requirements: *GCE:* 100. *IB:* 24. *BTEC Dip:* MP. *BTEC ExtDip:* PPP. *OCR NED:* P3 Interview required.

Y50 THE UNIVERSITY OF YORK
STUDENT RECRUITMENT AND ADMISSIONS
UNIVERSITY OF YORK
HESLINGTON
YORK YO10 5DD
t: 01904 324000 f: 01904 323538
e: ug-admissions@york.ac.uk
// www.york.ac.uk

W440 BA Writing, Directing and Performance
Duration: 3FT Hon
Entry Requirements: *GCE:* AAB. *SQAH:* AAAAB. *SQAAH:* AB. *IB:* 35. *BTEC ExtDip:* DDD.

Y75 YORK ST JOHN UNIVERSITY
LORD MAYOR'S WALK
YORK YO31 7EX
t: 01904 876598 f: 01904 876940/876921
e: admissions@yorksj.ac.uk
// w3.yorksj.ac.uk

WW64 BA Film & Television Production (for international applicants only)
Duration: 4FT Hon
Entry Requirements: *GCE:* 240-260. *IB:* 24.

W401 BA Theatre (for international applicants only)
Duration: 4FT Hon
Entry Requirements: *Foundation:* Pass. *GCE:* 200-240. *IB:* 24.

WARDROBE AND MAKE-UP

A66 THE ARTS UNIVERSITY COLLEGE AT BOURNEMOUTH (FORMERLY ARTS INSTITUTE AT BOURNEMOUTH)
WALLISDOWN
POOLE
DORSET BH12 5HH
t: 01202 363228 f: 01202 537729
e: admissions@aucb.ac.uk
// www.aucb.ac.uk

W451 BA Costume with Performance Design
Duration: 3FT Hon
Entry Requirements: *Foundation:* Pass. *GCE:* BBC. *IB:* 24. *OCR ND:* M1 *OCR NED:* M1 Interview required. Portfolio required.

W45G BA Make-Up for Media and Performance
Duration: 3FT Hon
Entry Requirements: *Foundation:* Pass. *GCE:* BBC. *IB:* 24. *OCR ND:* M1 *OCR NED:* M1 Interview required. Portfolio required.

B22 UNIVERSITY OF BEDFORDSHIRE
PARK SQUARE
LUTON
BEDS LU1 3JU
t: 0844 8482234 f: 01582 489323
e: admissions@beds.ac.uk
// www.beds.ac.uk

W901 FdA Specialist Make-up Design
Duration: 2FT Fdg
Entry Requirements: *GCE:* 80-120.

B25 BIRMINGHAM CITY UNIVERSITY
PERRY BARR
BIRMINGHAM B42 2SU
t: 0121 331 5595 f: 0121 331 7994
// www.bcu.ac.uk

W2W4 BA Fashion Design with Design for Performance
Duration: 3FT Hon
Entry Requirements: *GCE:* 280. *IB:* 28. Interview required. Portfolio required.

B35 UNIVERSITY COLLEGE BIRMINGHAM
SUMMER ROW
BIRMINGHAM B3 1JB
t: 0121 604 1040 f: 0121 604 1166
e: admissions@ucb.ac.uk
// www.ucb.ac.uk

W452 BA Specialist Hair and Media Make-Up
Duration: 3FT Hon
Entry Requirements: *GCE:* 200. *IB:* 24.

W45F FdA Specialist Hair and Media Make-Up
Duration: 2FT Fdg
Entry Requirements: *GCE:* 120.

B41 BLACKPOOL AND THE FYLDE COLLEGE AN ASSOCIATE COLLEGE OF LANCASTER UNIVERSITY
ASHFIELD ROAD
BISPHAM
BLACKPOOL
LANCS FY2 0HB
t: 01253 504346 f: 01253 504198
e: admissions@blackpool.ac.uk
// www.blackpool.ac.uk

W455 BA Fashion and Costume for Performance
Duration: 3FT Hon
Entry Requirements: *Foundation:* Merit. *GCE:* 220. *IB:* 24.
Interview required. Portfolio required.

B60 BRADFORD COLLEGE: AN ASSOCIATE COLLEGE OF LEEDS METROPOLITAN UNIVERSITY
GREAT HORTON ROAD
BRADFORD
WEST YORKSHIRE BD7 1AY
t: 01274 433008 f: 01274 431652
e: heregistry@bradfordcollege.ac.uk
// www.bradfordcollege.ac.uk/
university-centre

W453 BA Make-up Artistry & Special Make-up Effects
Duration: 1FT Hon
Entry Requirements: HND required.

W452 FdA Make-up Artistry & Special Make-up Effects
Duration: 2FT Fdg
Entry Requirements: *Foundation:* Pass. *GCE:* 60-80. Interview required.

B94 BUCKINGHAMSHIRE NEW UNIVERSITY
QUEEN ALEXANDRA ROAD
HIGH WYCOMBE
BUCKINGHAMSHIRE HP11 2JZ
t: 0800 0565 660 f: 01494 605 023
e: admissions@bucks.ac.uk
// bucks.ac.uk

W232 FdA Costume for Stage and Screen
Duration: 2FT Fdg
Entry Requirements: *GCE:* 100-140. *IB:* 24. *OCR ND:* P2 *OCR NED:* P3 Interview required.

C35 CENTRAL SCHOOL OF SPEECH AND DRAMA, UNIVERSITY OF LONDON
EMBASSY THEATRE
64 ETON AVENUE
LONDON NW3 3HY
t: 0207 722 8183 f: 0207 722 4132
e: enquiries@cssd.ac.uk
// www.cssd.ac.uk

W460 BA Theatre Practice: Costume Construction
Duration: 3FT Hon
Entry Requirements: *GCE:* BBC. Interview required. Portfolio required.

C71 CLEVELAND COLLEGE OF ART AND DESIGN
CHURCH SQUARE
HARTLEPOOL
CHURCH SQUARE TS24 7EX
t: 01642 288888 f: 01642 288828
e: studentrecruitment@ccad.ac.uk
// www.ccad.ac.uk

W451 FdA Costume Construction for Stage and Screen
Duration: 2FT Fdg
Entry Requirements: *Foundation:* Pass. *GCE:* 100. Interview required. Portfolio required.

C99 UNIVERSITY OF CUMBRIA
FUSEHILL STREET
CARLISLE
CUMBRIA CA1 2HH
t: 01228 616234 f: 01228 616235
// www.cumbria.ac.uk

W451 FdA Costume
Duration: 2FT Fdg
Entry Requirements: *Foundation:* Pass. *GCE:* C-cccc. *SQAH:* CC. *SQAAH:* C. *IB:* 25. Interview required. Portfolio required.

E56 THE UNIVERSITY OF EDINBURGH
STUDENT RECRUITMENT & ADMISSIONS
57 GEORGE SQUARE
EDINBURGH EH8 9JU
t: 0131 650 4360 f: 0131 651 1236
e: sra.enquiries@ed.ac.uk
// www.ed.ac.uk/studying/undergraduate/

W451 BA Performance Costume
Duration: 4FT Hon
Entry Requirements: *Foundation:* Merit. *GCE:* BBB. *SQAH:* BBBB. *IB:* 34. Portfolio required.

G14 UNIVERSITY OF GLAMORGAN, CARDIFF AND PONTYPRIDD
ENQUIRIES AND ADMISSIONS UNIT
PONTYPRIDD CF37 1DL
t: 08456 434030 f: 01443 654050
e: enquiries@glam.ac.uk
// www.glam.ac.uk

W453 BA Costume Construction for Screen and Stage (Top-Up)
Duration: 1FT Hon
Entry Requirements: Contact the institution for details.

W451 FdA Costume Construction for Screen and Stage
Duration: 2FT Fdg
Entry Requirements: *Foundation:* Pass. *GCE:* BBC. *IB:* 24. *BTEC SubDip:* M. *BTEC Dip:* D*D. *BTEC ExtDip:* DMM. *OCR ND:* M1 *OCR NED:* P1 Interview required. Portfolio required.

G80 GRIMSBY INSTITUTE OF FURTHER AND HIGHER EDUCATION
NUNS CORNER
GRIMSBY
NE LINCOLNSHIRE DN34 5BQ
t: 0800 328 3631
e: headmissions@grimsby.ac.uk
// www.grimsby.ac.uk

W452 BA Special Effects Make-Up Design for TV, Film & Theatre
Duration: 3FT Hon
Entry Requirements: Contact the institution for details.

H36 UNIVERSITY OF HERTFORDSHIRE
UNIVERSITY ADMISSIONS SERVICE
COLLEGE LANE
HATFIELD
HERTS AL10 9AB
t: 01707 284800
// www.herts.ac.uk

W452 BA Character Creation and Technical Effects
Duration: 3FT Hon
Entry Requirements: *GCE:* 240. Interview required. Portfolio required.

W451 BA Special Effects
Duration: 3FT Hon
Entry Requirements: *GCE:* 240. Interview required. Portfolio required.

H73 HULL COLLEGE
QUEEN'S GARDENS
HULL HU1 3DG
t: 01482 329943 f: 01482 598733
e: info@hull-college.ac.uk
// www.hull-college.ac.uk/higher-education

W451 FdA Costume Design and Interpretation
Duration: 2FT Fdg
Entry Requirements: *GCE:* 200. Foundation Course required. Interview required. Portfolio required.

L36 LEICESTER COLLEGE
FREEMEN'S PARK CAMPUS
AYLESTONE ROAD
LEICESTER LE2 7LW
t: 0116 224 2240 f: 0116 224 2041
e: info@leicestercollege.ac.uk
// www.leicestercollege.ac.uk

W452 FdA Artistic Make Up and Special Effects
Duration: 2FT Fdg
Entry Requirements: *GCE:* 80. Interview required.

M10 THE MANCHESTER COLLEGE
OPENSHAW CAMPUS
ASHTON OLD ROAD
OPENSHAW
MANCHESTER M11 2WH
t: 0800 068 8585 f: 0161 920 4103
e: enquiries@themanchestercollege.ac.uk
// www.themanchestercollege.ac.uk

B3W4 BA Make-up Artistry and Special Effects
Duration: 3FT Hon
Entry Requirements: Contact the institution for details.

W451 FdA Costume Design
Duration: 2FT Fdg
Entry Requirements: Contact the institution for details.

W453 FdA Make-up Artistry and Special Effects
Duration: 2FT Fdg
Entry Requirements: *GCE:* 160. *BTEC ExtDip:* MPP.

N41 NORTHBROOK COLLEGE SUSSEX
LITTLEHAMPTON ROAD
WORTHING
WEST SUSSEX BN12 6NU
t: 0845 155 6060 f: 01903 606073
e: enquiries@nbcol.ac.uk
// www.northbrook.ac.uk

W452 FdA Make Up & Hair for Theatre and Media
Duration: 2FT Fdg
Entry Requirements: *GCE:* 160. Interview required.

W451 FdA Theatre Arts - Costume Design and Realisation for Theatre, Film and Television
Duration: 2FT Fdg
Entry Requirements: *GCE:* 160. Interview required. Portfolio required.

N91 NOTTINGHAM TRENT UNIVERSITY
DRYDEN BUILDING
BURTON STREET
NOTTINGHAM NG1 4BU
t: +44 (0) 115 848 4200 f: +44 (0) 115 848 8869
e: applications@ntu.ac.uk
// www.ntu.ac.uk

W451 BA (Hons) Costume Design and Making
Duration: 3FT Hon
Entry Requirements: *GCE:* 280. *BTEC Dip:* D*D*. *BTEC ExtDip:* DMM. Interview required. Portfolio required.

Q25 QUEEN MARGARET UNIVERSITY, EDINBURGH
QUEEN MARGARET UNIVERSITY DRIVE
EDINBURGH EH21 6UU
t: 0131474 0000 f: 0131 474 0001
e: admissions@qmu.ac.uk
// www.qmu.ac.uk

W451 BA Costume Design and Construction
Duration: 4FT Hon
Entry Requirements: *GCE:* 220. *IB:* 28. Interview required.

R51 ROSE BRUFORD COLLEGE
LAMORBEY PARK
BURNT OAK LANE
SIDCUP
KENT DA15 9DF
t: 0208 308 2600 f: 020 8308 0542
e: enquiries@bruford.ac.uk
// www.bruford.ac.uk

W451 BA Costume Production
Duration: 3FT Hon
Entry Requirements: *GCE:* 160-280.

S28 SOMERSET COLLEGE OF ARTS AND TECHNOLOGY
WELLINGTON ROAD
TAUNTON
SOMERSET TA1 5AX
t: 01823 366331 f: 01823 366418
e: enquiries@somerset.ac.uk
// www.somerset.ac.uk/student-area/
considering-a-degree.html

W45B BA Media Make-Up
Duration: 1FT Hon
Entry Requirements: Contact the institution for details.

W452 FdA Media Make-Up
Duration: 2FT Fdg
Entry Requirements: *GCE:* 160. *IB:* 24. Interview required. Portfolio required.

S30 SOUTHAMPTON SOLENT UNIVERSITY
EAST PARK TERRACE
SOUTHAMPTON
HAMPSHIRE SO14 0RT
t: +44 (0) 23 8031 9039 f: + 44 (0)23 8022 2259
e: admissions@solent.ac.uk
// www.solent.ac.uk/

W453 BA Make-Up and Hair Design
Duration: 3FT Hon
Entry Requirements: *Foundation:* Merit. *GCE:* 200. *SQAAH:* AC-DDD. *IB:* 24. *BTEC ExtDip:* MMP. *OCR ND:* M1 *OCR NED:* P1 Interview required. Portfolio required.

S98 SWINDON COLLEGE
NORTH STAR AVENUE
SWINDON
WILTSHIRE SN2 1DY
t: 0800 731 2250 f: 01793 430503
e: headmissions@swindon-college.ac.uk
// www.swindon-college.ac.uk

W452 HND Performing Arts (Production) Media Make-up
Duration: 2FT HND
Entry Requirements: Interview required. Portfolio required.

U65 UNIVERSITY OF THE ARTS LONDON
272 HIGH HOLBORN
LONDON WC1V 7EY
t: 020 7514 6000x6197 f: 020 7514 6198
e: c.anderson@arts.ac.uk
// www.arts.ac.uk

W451 BA Costume for Performance
Duration: 3FT Hon
Entry Requirements: Foundation Course required. Interview required. Portfolio required.

W452 BA Make-up and Prosthetics for Performance
Duration: 3FT Hon
Entry Requirements: Interview required. Portfolio required.

W25 WARWICKSHIRE COLLEGE
WARWICK NEW ROAD
LEAMINGTON SPA
WARWICKSHIRE CV32 5JE
t: 01926 884223 f: 01926 318 111
e: kgooch@warkscol.ac.uk
// www.warwickshire.ac.uk

W451 FdA Costume for Performance
Duration: 2FT Fdg
Entry Requirements: Contact the institution for details.

W65 WEST THAMES COLLEGE
LONDON ROAD
ISLEWORTH
MIDDLESEX TW7 4HS
t: 020 8326 2000 f: 020 8326 2001
e: info@west-thames.ac.uk
// www.west-thames.ac.uk/en/
higher-education/

W452 BA Specialist Makeup (top up)
Duration: 1FT Hon
Entry Requirements: Interview required. Portfolio required. HND
required.

W451 FdA Costume in Practice
Duration: 2FT Fdg
Entry Requirements: *Foundation:* Pass. *GCE:* 40-120. Interview
required. Portfolio required.

254W HND Specialist Makeup
Duration: 2FT HND
Entry Requirements: *Foundation:* Pass. *GCE:* 40-120. Interview
required. Portfolio required.

W80 UNIVERSITY OF WORCESTER
HENWICK GROVE
WORCESTER WR2 6AJ
t: 01905 855111 f: 01905 855377
e: admissions@worc.ac.uk
// www.worcester.ac.uk

W453 BA Performance (Costume & Make-Up) (top-up)
Duration: 1FT Hon
Entry Requirements: Interview required. Portfolio required. HND
required.

Y70 YORK COLLEGE
SIM BALK LANE
YORK YO23 2BB
t: 01904 770448 f: 01904 770499
e: admissions.team@yorkcollege.ac.uk
// www.yorkcollege.ac.uk

W452 FdA Media Make-up and Hair Design for Film, TV and Theatre
Duration: 2FT Fdg
Entry Requirements: Contact the institution for details.

Y80 YORKSHIRE COAST COLLEGE OF FURTHER AND HIGHER EDUCATION
LADY EDITH'S DRIVE
SCARBOROUGH
NORTH YORKSHIRE YO12 5RN
t: 01723 372105 f: 01723 501918
e: admissions@ycoastco.ac.uk
// www.yorkshirecoastcollege.ac.uk

W451 BA Costume
Duration: 3FT Hon
Entry Requirements: *GCE:* 160. Interview required. Portfolio
required.

THEATRE AND STAGE DESIGN

A40 ABERYSTWYTH UNIVERSITY
ABERYSTWYTH UNIVERSITY, WELCOME CENTRE
PENGLAIS CAMPUS
ABERYSTWYTH
CEREDIGION SY23 3FB
t: 01970 622021 f: 01970 627410
e: ug-admissions@aber.ac.uk
// www.aber.ac.uk

W460 BA Scenography & Theatre Design
Duration: 3FT Hon
Entry Requirements: *GCE:* 300-320.

WQ43 BA Scenography & Theatre Design/English Literature
Duration: 3FT Hon
Entry Requirements: *GCE:* 300-320. *IB:* 32.

WW49 BA Scenography & Theatre Design/Performance Studies
Duration: 3FT Hon
Entry Requirements: *GCE:* 300-320. *IB:* 32.

B25 BIRMINGHAM CITY UNIVERSITY
PERRY BARR
BIRMINGHAM B42 2SU
t: 0121 331 5595 f: 0121 331 7994
// www.bcu.ac.uk

W460 BA Theatre, Performance and Event Design
Duration: 3FT Hon
Entry Requirements: *GCE:* 280. *IB:* 28. Interview required. Portfolio required.

C35 CENTRAL SCHOOL OF SPEECH AND DRAMA, UNIVERSITY OF LONDON
EMBASSY THEATRE
64 ETON AVENUE
LONDON NW3 3HY
t: 0207 722 8183 f: 0207 722 4132
e: enquiries@cssd.ac.uk
// www.cssd.ac.uk

W461 BA Theatre Practice: Design for the Stage
Duration: 3FT Hon
Entry Requirements: *GCE:* BBC. Interview required. Portfolio required.

W462 BA Theatre Practice: Props Making
Duration: 3FT Hon
Entry Requirements: *GCE:* BBC. Interview required. Portfolio required.

W463 BA Theatre Practice: Scenic Art
Duration: 3FT Hon
Entry Requirements: *GCE:* BBC. Interview required. Portfolio required.

W464 BA Theatre Practice: Scenic Construction
Duration: 3FT Hon
Entry Requirements: *GCE:* BBC. Interview required. Portfolio required.

E42 EDGE HILL UNIVERSITY
ORMSKIRK
LANCASHIRE L39 4QP
t: 01695 657000 f: 01695 584355
e: study@edgehill.ac.uk
// www.edgehill.ac.uk

W460 BA Design for Performance
Duration: 3FT Hon
Entry Requirements: *GCE:* 280. *IB:* 26. *OCR ND:* D *OCR NED:* M2 Interview required. Portfolio required.

G14 UNIVERSITY OF GLAMORGAN, CARDIFF AND PONTYPRIDD
ENQUIRIES AND ADMISSIONS UNIT
PONTYPRIDD CF37 1DL
t: 08456 434030 f: 01443 654050
e: enquiries@glam.ac.uk
// www.glam.ac.uk

W461 BA Television & Film Set Design
Duration: 3FT Hon
Entry Requirements: *Foundation:* Pass. *GCE:* BCC. *IB:* 24. *BTEC SubDip:* M. *BTEC Dip:* D*D. *BTEC ExtDip:* DMM. *OCR ND:* M1 *OCR NED:* M2 Interview required. Portfolio required.

L48 THE LIVERPOOL INSTITUTE FOR PERFORMING ARTS
MOUNT STREET
LIVERPOOL L1 9HF
t: 0151 330 3000 f: 0151 330 3131
e: admissions@lipa.ac.uk
// www.lipa.ac.uk

W460 BA Theatre and Performance Design
Duration: 3FT Hon
Entry Requirements: *GCE:* 180. Interview required.

W461 BA Theatre and Performance Technology
Duration: 3FT Hon
Entry Requirements: *GCE:* 180. Interview required.

N91 NOTTINGHAM TRENT UNIVERSITY
DRYDEN BUILDING
BURTON STREET
NOTTINGHAM NG1 4BU
t: +44 (0) 115 848 4200 f: +44 (0) 115 848 8869
e: applications@ntu.ac.uk
// www.ntu.ac.uk

W460 BA Theatre Design
Duration: 3FT Hon
Entry Requirements: *GCE:* 280. *BTEC Dip:* D*D*. *BTEC ExtDip:* DMM. Interview required. Portfolio required.

R51 ROSE BRUFORD COLLEGE
LAMORBEY PARK
BURNT OAK LANE
SIDCUP
KENT DA15 9DF
t: 0208 308 2600 f: 020 8308 0542
e: enquiries@bruford.ac.uk
// www.bruford.ac.uk

W4W2 BA Lighting Design
Duration: 3FT Hon
Entry Requirements: *GCE:* 160-280.

W4W7 BA Scenic Arts
Duration: 3FT Hon
Entry Requirements: *GCE:* 160-280.

W460 BA Theatre Design
Duration: 3FT Hon
Entry Requirements: *GCE:* 160-280.

R86 ROYAL WELSH COLLEGE OF MUSIC AND DRAMA (COLEG BRENHINOL CERDD A DRAMA CYMRU)
CASTLE GROUNDS
CATHAYS PARK
CARDIFF CF10 3ER
t: 029 2039 1361 f: 029 2039 1301
e: admissions@rwcmd.ac.uk
// www.rwcmd.ac.uk

W460 BA Theatre Design
Duration: 3FT Hon
Entry Requirements: *GCE:* AA-CC. Interview required. Portfolio required.

T80 UNIVERSITY OF WALES TRINITY SAINT DAVID
COLLEGE ROAD
CARMARTHEN SA31 3EP
t: 01267 676767 f: 01267 676766
e: registry@trinitysaintdavid.ac.uk
// www.tsd.ac.uk

W460 BA Theatre Design & Production
Duration: 3FT Hon
Entry Requirements: *Foundation:* Pass. *GCE:* 160-360. *IB:* 26. Interview required. Portfolio required.

U65 UNIVERSITY OF THE ARTS LONDON
272 HIGH HOLBORN
LONDON WC1V 7EY
t: 020 7514 6000x6197 f: 020 7514 6198
e: c.anderson@arts.ac.uk
// www.arts.ac.uk

W460 BA Performance Design and Practice
Duration: 3FT/4SW Hon
Entry Requirements: Interview required.

W462 BA Theatre and Screen : Theatre Design
Duration: 3FT Hon
Entry Requirements: *Foundation:* Pass. *GCE:* 80. *IB:* 28. Foundation Course required. Interview required. Portfolio required.

W461 BA Theatre and Screen: Set Design for Screen
Duration: 3FT Hon
Entry Requirements: *Foundation:* Pass. *GCE:* 80. *IB:* 28. Foundation Course required. Interview required. Portfolio required.

W05 THE UNIVERSITY OF WEST LONDON
ST MARY'S ROAD
EALING
LONDON W5 5RF
t: 0800 036 8888 f: 020 8566 1353
e: learning.advice@uwl.ac.uk
// www.uwl.ac.uk

W461 BA Theatre Production (Design & Management)
Duration: 3FT Hon
Entry Requirements: *GCE:* 200. *IB:* 28. Interview required. Portfolio required.

DANCE/CHOREOGRAPHY

B20 BATH SPA UNIVERSITY
NEWTON PARK
NEWTON ST LOE
BATH BA2 9BN
t: 01225 875875 f: 01225 875444
e: enquiries@bathspa.ac.uk
// www.bathspa.ac.uk/clearing

WW15 BA Art/Dance
Duration: 3FT Hon
Entry Requirements: *Foundation:* Pass. *GCE:* 220-280. *IB:* 24. Interview required.

NW15 BA Business & Management/Dance
Duration: 3FT Hon
Entry Requirements: *GCE:* 220-280. *IB:* 24. Interview required.

WW2M BA Ceramics/Dance
Duration: 3FT Hon
Entry Requirements: *Foundation:* Pass. *GCE:* 220-280. *IB:* 24. Interview required.

WW95 BA Creative Writing/Dance
Duration: 3FT Hon
Entry Requirements: *GCE:* 220-280. *IB:* 24. Interview required.

W500 BA Dance
Duration: 3FT Hon
Entry Requirements: *GCE:* 220-280. *IB:* 24. Interview required.

WX53 BA Dance/Education
Duration: 3FT Hon   CRB Check: Required
Entry Requirements: *GCE:* 220-280. *IB:* 24. Interview required.

WQ53 BA Dance/English Literature
Duration: 3FT Hon
Entry Requirements: *GCE:* 220-280. *IB:* 24. Interview required.

WV51 BA Dance/History
Duration: 3FT Hon
Entry Requirements: *GCE:* 220-280. *IB:* 24. Interview required.

WV56 BA Dance/Study of Religions
Duration: 3FT Hon
Entry Requirements: *GCE:* 220-280. *IB:* 24. Interview required.

WW52 BA Dance/Textile Design Studies
Duration: 3FT Hon
Entry Requirements: *Foundation:* Pass. *GCE:* 220-280. *IB:* 24.
Interview required.

WW5F BA Dance/Visual Design
Duration: 3FT Hon
Entry Requirements: *Foundation:* Pass. *GCE:* 220-280. *IB:* 24.
Interview required.

XW15 BA Education/Dance
Duration: 3FT Hon   CRB Check: Required
Entry Requirements   *GCE:* 220-280. *IB:* 24. Interview required.

WC51 BA/BSc Biology/Dance
Duration: 3FT Hon
Entry Requirements: *GCE:* 220-280. *IB:* 24. Interview required.

WW56 BA/BSc Dance/Film & Screen Studies
Duration: 3FT Hon
Entry Requirements: *GCE:* 220-280. *IB:* 24. Interview required.

WD56 BA/BSc Dance/Food & Nutrition
Duration: 3FT Hon
Entry Requirements: *GCE:* 220-280. *IB:* 24. Interview required.

WF58 BA/BSc Dance/Geography
Duration: 3FT Hon
Entry Requirements: *GCE:* 220-280. *IB:* 24. Interview required.

WL54 BA/BSc Dance/Health Studies
Duration: 3FT Hon
Entry Requirements: *GCE:* 220-280. *IB:* 24. Interview required.

WV55 BA/BSc Dance/Philosophy & Ethics
Duration: 3FT Hon
Entry Requirements: *GCE:* 220-280. *IB:* 24. Interview required.

WC58 BA/BSc Dance/Psychology
Duration: 3FT Hon
Entry Requirements: *GCE:* 220-280. *IB:* 24. Interview required.

CW85 DipHE Dance/Psychology
Duration: 2FT Dip
Entry Requirements: *GCE:* 220-280. *IB:* 24. Interview required.

VW65 DipHE Dance/Study of Religions
Duration: 2FT Dip
Entry Requirements: *GCE:* 220-280. *IB:* 24. Interview required.

B22 UNIVERSITY OF BEDFORDSHIRE
PARK SQUARE
LUTON
BEDS LU1 3JU
t: 0844 8482234 f: 01582 489323
e: admissions@beds.ac.uk
// www.beds.ac.uk

W590 BA Dance and Professional Practice
Duration: 3FT Hon
Entry Requirements: *Foundation:* Pass. *GCE:* 240. *SQAH:* BBBB-BBBC. *SQAAH:* BCC. *IB:* 24. *OCR ND:* D *OCR NED:* M3 Interview required.

B25 BIRMINGHAM CITY UNIVERSITY
PERRY BARR
BIRMINGHAM B42 2SU
t: 0121 331 5595 f: 0121 331 7994
// www.bcu.ac.uk

W590 BA Community and Applied Dance Theatre
Duration: 3FT Hon   CRB Check: Required
Entry Requirements: *GCE:* 240. Interview required.

B44 UNIVERSITY OF BOLTON
DEANE ROAD
BOLTON BL3 5AB
t: 01204 903903 f: 01204 399074
e: enquiries@bolton.ac.uk
// www.bolton.ac.uk

54WW HND Performing Arts
Duration: 2FT HND
Entry Requirements: *GCE:* 80. Interview required.

B50 BOURNEMOUTH UNIVERSITY
TALBOT CAMPUS
FERN BARROW
POOLE
DORSET BH12 5BB
t: 01202 524111
// www.bournemouth.ac.uk

WW45 FdA Performing Arts: Dance
Duration: 2FT Fdg
Entry Requirements: *GCE:* 120. *IB:* 24. Interview required.

B72 UNIVERSITY OF BRIGHTON
MITHRAS HOUSE 211
LEWES ROAD
BRIGHTON BN2 4AT
t: 01273 644644 f: 01273 642607
e: admissions@brighton.ac.uk
// www.brighton.ac.uk

W5W1 BA Performance and Visual Arts (Dance)
Duration: 3FT Hon
Entry Requirements: **GCE:** BBC. Foundation Course required. Interview required. Portfolio required.

B79 BRISTOL FILTON COLLEGE
FILTON AVENUE
BRISTOL BS34 7AT
t: 0117 909 2255 f: 0117 931 2233
e: info@filton.ac.uk
// www.filton.ac.uk

105W HND Performing Arts (Dance)
Duration: 2FT HND
Entry Requirements: Contact the institution for details.

B94 BUCKINGHAMSHIRE NEW UNIVERSITY
QUEEN ALEXANDRA ROAD
HIGH WYCOMBE
BUCKINGHAMSHIRE HP11 2JZ
t: 0800 0565 660 f: 01494 605 023
e: admissions@bucks.ac.uk
// bucks.ac.uk

WC56 BA Dance and Fitness
Duration: 3FT Hon
Entry Requirements: **GCE:** 200-240. **IB:** 24. **OCR ND:** M1 **OCR NED:** M3 Interview required.

W500 BA Dance and Performance
Duration: 3FT Hon
Entry Requirements: **GCE:** 200-240. **IB:** 24. **OCR ND:** M1 **OCR NED:** M3 Interview required.

WW45 BA Performing Arts (Film, TV & Stage)
Duration: 3FT Hon
Entry Requirements: **GCE:** 200-240. **IB:** 24. **OCR ND:** M1 **OCR NED:** M3 Interview required.

C10 CANTERBURY CHRIST CHURCH UNIVERSITY
NORTH HOLMES ROAD
CANTERBURY
KENT CT1 1QU
t: 01227 782900 f: 01227 782888
e: admissions@canterbury.ac.uk
// www.canterbury.ac.uk

WX53 BA Dance Education
Duration: 3FT Hon **CRB Check:** Required
Entry Requirements: **GCE:** 260. **IB:** 24. Interview required.

WX5H BA Dance Education 'International only'
Duration: 4FT Hon
Entry Requirements: Interview required.

W500 BA Performing Arts (Dance)
Duration: 3FT Hon
Entry Requirements: **GCE:** 240. **IB:** 24. Interview required.

C20 CARDIFF METROPOLITAN UNIVERSITY (UWIC)
ADMISSIONS UNIT
LLANDAFF CAMPUS
WESTERN AVENUE
CARDIFF CF5 2YB
t: 029 2041 6070 f: 029 2041 6286
e: admissions@cardiffmet.ac.uk
// www.cardiffmet.ac.uk

W500 BA Dance
Duration: 3FT Hon
Entry Requirements: **GCE:** 280. **IB:** 25. **BTEC Dip:** D*D*. **BTEC ExtDip:** DMM. **OCR ND:** D **OCR NED:** M3 Interview required.

C30 UNIVERSITY OF CENTRAL LANCASHIRE
PRESTON
LANCS PR1 2HE
t: 01772 201201 f: 01772 894954
e: uadmissions@uclan.ac.uk
// www.uclan.ac.uk

WX59 BA Dance, Performance and Teaching
Duration: 3FT Hon **CRB Check:** Required
Entry Requirements: **GCE:** 260-300. **IB:** 26. Interview required.

W500 FdA Professional Dance Practice
Duration: 2FT Fdg
Entry Requirements: Interview required.

C55 UNIVERSITY OF CHESTER
PARKGATE ROAD
CHESTER CH1 4BJ
t: 01244 511000 f: 01244 511300
e: enquiries@chester.ac.uk
// www.chester.ac.uk

W500 BA Dance
Duration: 3FT Hon
Entry Requirements: *GCE:* 260-300. *SQAH:* BBBB. *IB:* 28.
Interview required.

C57 CHICHESTER COLLEGE
WESTGATE FIELDS
CHICHESTER
WEST SUSSEX PO19 1SB
t: 01243 786321 x2127 f: 01243 539481
e: sally.billingham@chichester.ac.uk
// www.chichester.ac.uk

005W HNC Performing Arts (Dance)
Duration: 1FT/2FT HNC/HND
Entry Requirements: *Foundation:* Merit. *GCE:* A*-D. *SQAH:*
AAAAA-DDDDD. *SQAAH:* AAA-CCC. *BTEC SubDip:* M. *BTEC Dip:*
MM. *OCR ND:* M2 *OCR NED:* M3 Interview required.

C58 UNIVERSITY OF CHICHESTER
BISHOP OTTER CAMPUS
COLLEGE LANE
CHICHESTER
WEST SUSSEX PO19 6PE
t: 01243 816002 f: 01243 816161
e: admissions@chi.ac.uk
// www.chiuni.ac.uk

W500 BA Dance
Duration: 3FT Hon
Entry Requirements: *GCE:* BBC. *SQAAH:* BBC. *IB:* 30. *OCR NED:*
D2 Interview required.

WQ53 BA Dance and International English Studies
Duration: 3FT Hon
Entry Requirements: *GCE:* BBC. *SQAAH:* BBC. *IB:* 30. *BTEC Dip:*
DD. *BTEC ExtDip:* DDM. *OCR NED:* D2 Interview required.

W5Q3 BA Dance with International English Studies
Duration: 3FT Hon
Entry Requirements: *GCE:* BBC. *SQAAH:* BBC. *IB:* 30. *BTEC Dip:*
DD. *BTEC ExtDip:* DDM. *OCR NED:* D2 Interview required.

C64 CITY COLLEGE COVENTRY
SWANSWELL
50 SWANSWELL STREET
COVENTRY CV1 5DG
t: 0800 616 202 f: 024 7622 3390
e: courses@covcollege.ac.uk
// www.covcollege.ac.uk

005W HNC Dance
Duration: 1FT HNC
Entry Requirements: *Foundation:* Merit. *GCE:* 120-180. Interview required.

C69 CITY OF SUNDERLAND COLLEGE
BEDE CENTRE
DURHAM ROAD
SUNDERLAND
TYNE AND WEAR SR3 4AH
t: 0191 511 6260
e: highered.admissions@citysun.ac.uk
// www.citysun.ac.uk

W500 FdA Dance
Duration: 2FT Fdg
Entry Requirements: Contact the institution for details.

C85 COVENTRY UNIVERSITY
THE STUDENT CENTRE
COVENTRY UNIVERSITY
1 GULSON RD
COVENTRY CV1 2JH
t: 024 7615 2222 f: 024 7615 2223
e: studentenquiries@coventry.ac.uk
// www.coventry.ac.uk

W500 BA Dance Making and Performance
Duration: 3FT/4SW Hon
Entry Requirements: *GCE:* CCC. *SQAH:* CCCCC. *IB:* 27. *BTEC ExtDip:* MMM. *OCR NED:* M3 Interview required.

D26 DE MONTFORT UNIVERSITY
THE GATEWAY
LEICESTER LE1 9BH
t: 0116 255 1551 f: 0116 250 6204
e: enquiries@dmu.ac.uk
// www.dmu.ac.uk

WW59 BA Arts & Festivals Management and Dance
Duration: 3FT Hon
Entry Requirements: *GCE:* 260. *IB:* 28. *BTEC Dip:* D*D*. *BTEC ExtDip:* DMM.

W500 BA Dance
Duration: 3FT Hon
Entry Requirements: *GCE:* 260. *IB:* 28. *BTEC Dip:* D*D*. *BTEC ExtDip:* DMM.

WX53 BA Dance and Education Studies
Duration: 3FT Hon
Entry Requirements: *GCE:* 260. *IB:* 28. *BTEC Dip:* D*D*. *BTEC ExtDip:* DMM.

WW45 BA Performing Arts
Duration: 3FT Hon
Entry Requirements: *GCE:* 260. *IB:* 28. *BTEC Dip:* D*D*. *BTEC ExtDip:* DMM.

D39 UNIVERSITY OF DERBY
KEDLESTON ROAD
DERBY DE22 1GB
t: 01332 591167 f: 01332 597724
e: askadmissions@derby.ac.uk
// www.derby.ac.uk

W590 BA Creative Expressive Therapies (Dance)
Duration: 3FT Hon   CRB Check: Required
Entry Requirements: *Foundation:* Distinction. *GCE:* 280. *IB:* 28. *BTEC Dip:* D*D*. *BTEC ExtDip:* DMM. *OCR NED:* M2 Interview required.

WX53 BA Dance & Movement Studies and Education Studies
Duration: 3FT Hon
Entry Requirements: *Foundation:* Distinction. *GCE:* 260-300. *IB:* 28. *BTEC Dip:* D*D*. *BTEC ExtDip:* DMM. *OCR NED:* M2

QW35 BA Dance & Movement Studies and English
Duration: 3FT Hon
Entry Requirements: *Foundation:* Distinction. *GCE:* 260-300. *IB:* 28. *BTEC Dip:* D*D*. *BTEC ExtDip:* DMM. *OCR NED:* M2

WV51 BA Dance & Movement Studies and History
Duration: 3FT Hon
Entry Requirements: *Foundation:* Distinction. *GCE:* 260-300. *IB:* 28. *BTEC Dip:* D*D*. *BTEC ExtDip:* DMM. *OCR NED:* M2

NW65 BA Dance & Movement Studies and Human Resource Management
Duration: 3FT Hon
Entry Requirements: *Foundation:* Distinction. *GCE:* 260-300. *IB:* 28. *BTEC Dip:* D*D*. *BTEC ExtDip:* DMM. *OCR NED:* M2

NW55 BA Dance & Movement Studies and Marketing
Duration: 3FT Hon
Entry Requirements: *Foundation:* Distinction. *GCE:* 260-300. *IB:* 28. *BTEC Dip:* D*D*. *BTEC ExtDip:* DMM. *OCR NED:* M2

WL53 BA Dance & Movement Studies and Sociology
Duration: 3FT Hon
Entry Requirements: *Foundation:* Distinction. *GCE:* 260-300. *IB:* 28. *BTEC Dip:* D*D*. *BTEC ExtDip:* DMM. *OCR NED:* M2

WC56 BA Dance & Movement Studies and Sport & Exercise Studies
Duration: 3FT Hon
Entry Requirements: *Foundation:* Distinction. *GCE:* 260-300. *IB:* 28. *BTEC Dip:* D*D*. *BTEC ExtDip:* DMM. *OCR NED:* M2

WG51 BA/BSc Dance & Movement Studies and Mathematics
Duration: 3FT Hon
Entry Requirements: *Foundation:* Distinction. *GCE:* 260-300. *IB:* 28. *BTEC Dip:* D*D*. *BTEC ExtDip:* DMM. *OCR NED:* M2

WC58 BA/BSc Dance & Movement Studies and Psychology
Duration: 3FT Hon
Entry Requirements: *Foundation:* Distinction. *GCE:* 260-300. *IB:* 28. *BTEC Dip:* D*D*. *BTEC ExtDip:* DMM. *OCR NED:* M2

D52 DONCASTER COLLEGE
THE HUB
CHAPPELL DRIVE
SOUTH YORKSHIRE DN1 2RF
t: 01302 553610
e: he@don.ac.uk
// www.don.ac.uk

W500 BA Dance Practice
Duration: 3FT Hon
Entry Requirements: Contact the institution for details.

W590 BA Performing Arts Dance Pathway (top-up)
Duration: 1FT Hon
Entry Requirements: Contact the institution for details.

E28 UNIVERSITY OF EAST LONDON
DOCKLANDS CAMPUS
UNIVERSITY WAY
LONDON E16 2RD
t: 020 8223 3333 f: 020 8223 2978
e: study@uel.ac.uk
// www.uel.ac.uk

W590 BA Dance: Urban Practice
Duration: 3FT Hon
Entry Requirements: *GCE:* 240. *IB:* 24. Interview required.

V000 BA Media & Creative Industries option - Dance Studies
Duration: 3FT Hon
Entry Requirements: *GCE:* 240. *IB:* 24.

E42 EDGE HILL UNIVERSITY
ORMSKIRK
LANCASHIRE L39 4QP
t: 01695 657000 f: 01695 584355
e: study@edgehill.ac.uk
// www.edgehill.ac.uk

W500 BA Dance
Duration: 3FT Hon   CRB Check: Required
Entry Requirements: *GCE:* 300. *IB:* 26. *OCR ND:* D *OCR NED:* M1
Interview required.

WW54 BA Dance and Drama
Duration: 3FT Hon
Entry Requirements: *GCE:* 300. *IB:* 26. *OCR ND:* D *OCR NED:* M1
Interview required.

W5Q3 BA Film Studies with English
Duration: 3FT Hon
Entry Requirements: *GCE:* 280. *IB:* 26. *OCR ND:* D *OCR NED:* M2

F33 UNIVERSITY COLLEGE FALMOUTH
WOODLANE
FALMOUTH
CORNWALL TR11 4RH
t: 01326213730
e: admissions@falmouth.ac.uk
// www.falmouth.ac.uk

W511 BA(Hons) Choreography
Duration: 3FT Hon
Entry Requirements: *GCE:* 220. *IB:* 24. Interview required.
Portfolio required.

W501 BA(Hons) Dance
Duration: 3FT Hon
Entry Requirements: *GCE:* 220. *IB:* 24. Interview required.
Portfolio required.

G50 THE UNIVERSITY OF GLOUCESTERSHIRE
PARK CAMPUS
THE PARK
CHELTENHAM GL50 2RH
t: 01242 714501 f: 01242 714869
e: admissions@glos.ac.uk
// www.glos.ac.uk

XW35 BSc Sports Education and Dance
Duration: 3FT Hon
Entry Requirements: Contact the institution for details.

G80 GRIMSBY INSTITUTE OF FURTHER AND HIGHER EDUCATION
NUNS CORNER
GRIMSBY
NE LINCOLNSHIRE DN34 5BQ
t: 0800 328 3631
e: headmissions@grimsby.ac.uk
// www.grimsby.ac.uk

W500 BA Performance (Dance)
Duration: 3FT Hon
Entry Requirements: *GCE:* 160-240. Interview required.

H73 HULL COLLEGE
QUEEN'S GARDENS
HULL HU1 3DG
t: 01482 329943 f: 01482 598733
e: info@hull-college.ac.uk
// www.hull-college.ac.uk/higher-education

W501 BA Dance
Duration: 1FT Hon
Entry Requirements: Interview required. HND required.

W500 FdA Dance
Duration: 2FT Fdg
Entry Requirements: *GCE:* 240. Interview required. Admissions Test required. Portfolio required.

K84 KINGSTON UNIVERSITY
STUDENT INFORMATION & ADVICE CENTRE
COOPER HOUSE
40-46 SURBITON ROAD
KINGSTON UPON THAMES KT1 2HX
t: 0844 8552177 f: 020 8547 7080
e: aps@kingston.ac.uk
// www.kingston.ac.uk

W500 BA Dance
Duration: 3FT Hon
Entry Requirements: *GCE:* 300-360. Interview required.

WQ53 BA Dance and English Language & Communication
Duration: 3FT Hon
Entry Requirements: *GCE:* 300-360. Interview required.

QW35 BA Dance and English Literature
Duration: 3FT Hon
Entry Requirements: *GCE:* 280-360. Interview required.

L21 LEEDS CITY COLLEGE
TECHNOLOGY CAMPUS
COOKRIDGE STREET
LEEDS LS2 8BL
t: 0113 216 2406 f: 0113 216 2401
e: helen.middleton@leedscitycollege.ac.uk
// www.leedscitycollege.ac.uk

W500 FdA Creative Industries (Dance)
Duration: 2FT Fdg
Entry Requirements: Contact the institution for details.

L27 LEEDS METROPOLITAN UNIVERSITY
COURSE ENQUIRIES OFFICE
CITY CAMPUS
LEEDS LS1 3HE
t: 0113 81 23113 f: 0113 81 23129
// www.leedsmet.ac.uk

W540 BA Contemporary Dance Practices
Duration: 1FT Hon
Entry Requirements: Contact the institution for details.

W500 BA Dance
Duration: 3FT Hon
Entry Requirements: Contact the institution for details.

L36 LEICESTER COLLEGE
FREEMEN'S PARK CAMPUS
AYLESTONE ROAD
LEICESTER LE2 7LW
t: 0116 224 2240 f: 0116 224 2041
e: info@leicestercollege.ac.uk
// www.leicestercollege.ac.uk

W500 FdA Performing Arts (Dance)
Duration: 2FT Fdg
Entry Requirements: Contact the institution for details.

L39 UNIVERSITY OF LINCOLN
ADMISSIONS
BRAYFORD POOL
LINCOLN LN6 7TS
t: 01522 886097 f: 01522 886146
e: admissions@lincoln.ac.uk
// www.lincoln.ac.uk

W500 BA Dance
Duration: 3FT Hon
Entry Requirements: *GCE:* 280. Interview required.

L43 LIVERPOOL COMMUNITY COLLEGE
LIVERPOOL COMMUNITY COLLEGE
CLARENCE STREET
LIVERPOOL L3 5TP
t: 0151 252 3352 f: 0151 252 3351
e: enquiry@liv-coll.ac.uk
// www.liv-coll.ac.uk

500W HNC Performing Arts (Dance)
Duration: 1FT HNC
Entry Requirements: Contact the institution for details.

L46 LIVERPOOL HOPE UNIVERSITY
HOPE PARK
LIVERPOOL L16 9JD
t: 0151 291 3331 f: 0151 291 3434
e: administration@hope.ac.uk
// www.hope.ac.uk

V3W5 BA Art & Design History and Dance
Duration: 3FT Hon
Entry Requirements: *GCE:* 300-320. *IB:* 25.

XW35 BA Dance and Education
Duration: 3FT Hon   CRB Check: Required
Entry Requirements: *GCE:* 300-320. *IB:* 25. Interview required.

WQ35 BA Dance and English Language
Duration: 3FT Hon
Entry Requirements: *GCE:* 300-320. *IB:* 25. Interview required.

W5V5 BA Dance and Philosophy & Ethics
Duration: 3FT Hon
Entry Requirements: *GCE:* 300-320. *IB:* 25.

W5L2 BA Dance and Politics
Duration: 3FT Hon
Entry Requirements: *GCE:* 300-320. *IB:* 25.

W5C8 BA Dance and Psychology
Duration: 3FT Hon
Entry Requirements: *GCE:* 300-320. *IB:* 25.

L48 THE LIVERPOOL INSTITUTE FOR PERFORMING ARTS
MOUNT STREET
LIVERPOOL L1 9HF
t: 0151 330 3000 f: 0151 330 3131
e: admissions@lipa.ac.uk
// www.lipa.ac.uk

W500 BA Dance
Duration: 3FT Hon
Entry Requirements: *GCE:* 180. Interview required.

L51 LIVERPOOL JOHN MOORES UNIVERSITY
KINGSWAY HOUSE
HATTON GARDEN
LIVERPOOL L3 2AJ
t: 0151 231 5090 f: 0151 904 6368
e: courses@ljmu.ac.uk
// www.ljmu.ac.uk

W500 BA Dance Practices
Duration: 3FT Hon   CRB Check: Required
Entry Requirements: *GCE:* 280. Interview required.

L68 LONDON METROPOLITAN UNIVERSITY
166-220 HOLLOWAY ROAD
LONDON N7 8DB
t: 020 7133 4200
e: admissions@londonmet.ac.uk
// www.londonmet.ac.uk

CW65 BSc Sports and Dance Therapy
Duration: 3FT Hon
Entry Requirements: *GCE:* 240. *IB:* 28.

W500 FdA Dance
Duration: 2FT Fdg
Entry Requirements: *GCE:* 160. Interview required.

M10 THE MANCHESTER COLLEGE
OPENSHAW CAMPUS
ASHTON OLD ROAD
OPENSHAW
MANCHESTER M11 2WH
t: 0800 068 8585 f: 0161 920 4103
e: enquiries@themanchestercollege.ac.uk
// www.themanchestercollege.ac.uk

W542 FdA Dance Theatre
Duration: 2FT Fdg
Entry Requirements: Contact the institution for details.

W500 HNC Dance
Duration: 1FT HND
Entry Requirements: *GCE:* 120. *BTEC ExtDip:* PPP. Interview required.

M40 THE MANCHESTER METROPOLITAN UNIVERSITY
ADMISSIONS OFFICE
ALL SAINTS (GMS)
ALL SAINTS
MANCHESTER M15 6BH
t: 0161 247 2000
// www.mmu.ac.uk

LW55 BA Abuse Studies/Dance
Duration: 3FT Hon
Entry Requirements: *GCE:* 280. *IB:* 28. *BTEC Dip:* D*D*. *BTEC ExtDip:* DMM.

NW15 BA Business/Dance
Duration: 3FT Hon
Entry Requirements: *GCE:* 280. *IB:* 28. *BTEC Dip:* D*D*. *BTEC ExtDip:* DMM. Interview required.

XW35 BA Childhood & Youth Studies/Dance
Duration: 3FT Hon
Entry Requirements: *GCE:* 280. *IB:* 28. *BTEC Dip:* D*D*. *BTEC ExtDip:* DMM. Interview required.

WW85 BA Creative Writing/Dance
Duration: 3FT Hon
Entry Requirements: *GCE:* 280. *IB:* 28. *BTEC Dip:* D*D*. *BTEC ExtDip:* DMM. Interview required. Portfolio required.

LWJ5 BA Crime Studies/Dance
Duration: 3FT Hon
Entry Requirements: *GCE:* 280. *IB:* 28. *BTEC Dip:* D*D*. *BTEC ExtDip:* DMM. Interview required.

W500 BA Dance
Duration: 3FT Hon
Entry Requirements: *GCE:* 280. *IB:* 28. *BTEC Dip:* D*D*. *BTEC ExtDip:* DMM. Interview required.

QW35 BA Dance/English
Duration: 3FT Hon
Entry Requirements: *GCE:* 280. *IB:* 28. *BTEC Dip:* D*D*. *BTEC ExtDip:* DMM. Interview required.

NW55 BA Dance/Marketing
Duration: 3FT Hon
Entry Requirements: *GCE:* 280. *IB:* 28. *BTEC Dip:* D*D*. *BTEC ExtDip:* DMM. Interview required.

WL53 BA Dance/Sociology
Duration: 3FT Hon
Entry Requirements: *GCE:* 280. *IB:* 28. *BTEC Dip:* D*D*. *BTEC ExtDip:* DMM. Interview required.

CW65 BA/BSc Dance/Sport
Duration: 3FT Hon
Entry Requirements: *GCE:* 280. *IB:* 28. *BTEC Dip:* D*D*. *BTEC ExtDip:* DMM. Interview required.

M80 MIDDLESEX UNIVERSITY
MIDDLESEX UNIVERSITY
THE BURROUGHS
LONDON NW4 4BT
t: 020 8411 5555 f: 020 8411 5649
e: enquiries@mdx.ac.uk
// www.mdx.ac.uk

W500 BA Dance Performance
Duration: 3FT Hon
Entry Requirements: *GCE:* 200-300. *IB:* 28. Interview required.

W501 BA Dance Studies
Duration: 3FT Hon
Entry Requirements: *GCE:* 200-300. *IB:* 28. Interview required.

N23 NEWCASTLE COLLEGE
STUDENT SERVICES
RYE HILL CAMPUS
SCOTSWOOD ROAD
NEWCASTLE UPON TYNE NE4 7SA
t: 0191 200 4110 f: 0191 200 4349
e: enquiries@ncl-coll.ac.uk
// www.newcastlecollege.co.uk

W501 BA Contemporary Dance (Top-up)
Duration: 1FT Hon
Entry Requirements: Interview required. HND required.

W500 FdA Contemporary Dance
Duration: 2FT Fdg   CRB Check: Required
Entry Requirements: GCE: 120-160. OCR ND: P2 OCR NED: P3
Interview required.

N30 NEW COLLEGE NOTTINGHAM
ADAMS BUILDING
STONEY STREET
THE LACE MARKET
NOTTINGHAM NG1 1NG
t: 0115 910 0100 f: 0115 953 4349
e: he.team@ncn.ac.uk
// www.ncn.ac.uk

W500 FdA Theatre Arts (Dance)
Duration: 2FT Fdg
Entry Requirements: GCE: 120-240. Interview required.

N38 UNIVERSITY OF NORTHAMPTON
PARK CAMPUS
BOUGHTON GREEN ROAD
NORTHAMPTON NN2 7AL
t: 0800 358 2232 f: 01604 722083
e: admissions@northampton.ac.uk
// www.northampton.ac.uk

N5WM BA Advertising/Dance
Duration: 3FT Hon
Entry Requirements: GCE: 260-280. SQAH: AAA-BBBB. IB: 24.
BTEC Dip: DD. BTEC ExtDip: DMM. OCR ND: D OCR NED: M2
Interview required.

N1W5 BA Business/Dance
Duration: 3FT Hon
Entry Requirements: GCE: 260-280. SQAH: AAA-BBBB. IB: 24.
BTEC Dip: DD. BTEC ExtDip: DMM. OCR ND: D OCR NED: M2
Interview required.

W8W5 BA Creative Writing/Dance
Duration: 3FT Hon
Entry Requirements: GCE: 260-280. SQAH: AAA-BBBB. IB: 24.
BTEC Dip: DD. BTEC ExtDip: DMM. OCR ND: D OCR NED: M2
Interview required.

W500 BA Dance
Duration: 3FT Hon
Entry Requirements: GCE: 260-280. SQAH: AAA-BBBB. IB: 24.
BTEC Dip: DD. BTEC ExtDip: DMM. OCR ND: D OCR NED: M2
Interview required.

W5D4 BA Dance with Applied Equine Studies
Duration: 3FT Hon
Entry Requirements: GCE: 260-280. SQAH: AAA-BBBB. IB: 24.
BTEC Dip: DD. BTEC ExtDip: DMM. OCR ND: D OCR NED: M2
Interview required.

W5NA BA Dance with Applied Management
Duration: 3FT Hon
Entry Requirements: GCE: 260-280. SQAH: AAA-BBBB. IB: 24.
BTEC Dip: DD. BTEC ExtDip: DMM. OCR ND: D OCR NED: M2
Interview required.

W5NM BA Dance/Advertising
Duration: 3FT Hon
Entry Requirements: GCE: 260-280. SQAH: AAA-BBBB. IB: 24.
BTEC Dip: DD. BTEC ExtDip: DMM. OCR ND: D OCR NED: M2
Interview required.

W5C1 BA Dance/Biological Conservation
Duration: 3FT Hon
Entry Requirements: GCE: 260-280. SQAH: AAA-BBBB. IB: 24.
BTEC Dip: DD. BTEC ExtDip: DMM. OCR ND: D OCR NED: M2
Interview required.

W5N1 BA Dance/Business
Duration: 3FT Hon
Entry Requirements: GCE: 260-280. SQAH: AAA-BBBB. IB: 24.
BTEC Dip: DD. BTEC ExtDip: DMM. OCR ND: D OCR NED: M2
Interview required.

W5G5 BA Dance/Business Computing Systems
Duration: 3FT Hon
Entry Requirements: GCE: 260-280. SQAH: AAA-BBBB. IB: 24.
BTEC Dip: DD. BTEC ExtDip: DMM. OCR ND: D OCR NED: M2
Interview required.

W5G4 BA Dance/Computing
Duration: 3FT Hon
Entry Requirements: GCE: 260-280. SQAH: AAA-BBBB. IB: 24.
BTEC Dip: DD. BTEC ExtDip: DMM. OCR ND: D OCR NED: M2
Interview required.

W5W8 BA Dance/Creative Writing
Duration: 3FT Hon
Entry Requirements: GCE: 260-280. SQAH: AAA-BBBB. IB: 24.
BTEC Dip: DD. BTEC ExtDip: DMM. OCR ND: D OCR NED: M2
Interview required.

W5L1 BA Dance/Economics
Duration: 3FT Hon
Entry Requirements: GCE: 260-280. SQAH: AAA-BBBB. IB: 24.
BTEC Dip: DD. BTEC ExtDip: DMM. OCR ND: D OCR NED: M2
Interview required.

W5X3 BA Dance/Education Studies
Duration: 3FT Hon
Entry Requirements: *GCE:* 260-280. *SQAH:* AAA-BBBB. *IB:* 24.
BTEC Dip: DD. *BTEC ExtDip:* DMM. *OCR ND:* D *OCR NED:* M2
Interview required.

W5Q3 BA Dance/English
Duration: 3FT Hon
Entry Requirements: *GCE:* 260-280. *SQAH:* AAA-BBBB. *IB:* 24.
BTEC Dip: DD. *BTEC ExtDip:* DMM. *OCR ND:* D *OCR NED:* M2
Interview required.

W5NV BA Dance/Events Management
Duration: 3FT Hon
Entry Requirements: *GCE:* 260-280. *SQAH:* AAA-BBBB. *IB:* 24.
BTEC Dip: DD. *BTEC ExtDip:* DMM. *OCR ND:* D *OCR NED:* M2
Interview required.

W5W6 BA Dance/Film & Television Studies
Duration: 3FT Hon
Entry Requirements: *GCE:* 260-280. *SQAH:* AAA-BBBB. *IB:* 24.
BTEC Dip: DD. *BTEC ExtDip:* DMM. *OCR ND:* D *OCR NED:* M2
Interview required.

W5L4 BA Dance/Health Studies
Duration: 3FT Hon
Entry Requirements: *GCE:* 260-280. *SQAH:* AAA-BBBB. *IB:* 24.
BTEC Dip: DD. *BTEC ExtDip:* DMM. *OCR ND:* D *OCR NED:* M2
Interview required.

W5LX BA Dance/International Development
Duration: 3FT Hon
Entry Requirements: *GCE:* 260-280. *SQAH:* AAA-BBBB. *IB:* 24.
BTEC Dip: DD. *BTEC ExtDip:* DMM. *OCR ND:* D *OCR NED:* M2
Interview required.

W5M1 BA Dance/Law
Duration: 3FT Hon
Entry Requirements: *GCE:* 260-280. *SQAH:* AAA-BBBB. *IB:* 24.
BTEC Dip: DD. *BTEC ExtDip:* DMM. *OCR ND:* D *OCR NED:* M2
Interview required.

W5N2 BA Dance/Management
Duration: 3FT Hon
Entry Requirements: *GCE:* 260-280. *SQAH:* AAA-BBBB. *IB:* 24.
BTEC Dip: DD. *BTEC ExtDip:* DMM. *OCR ND:* D *OCR NED:* M2
Interview required.

W5N5 BA Dance/Marketing
Duration: 3FT Hon
Entry Requirements: *GCE:* 260-280. *SQAH:* AAA-BBBB. *IB:* 24.
BTEC Dip: DD. *BTEC ExtDip:* DMM. *OCR ND:* D *OCR NED:* M2
Interview required.

W5F8 BA Dance/Physical Geography
Duration: 3FT Hon
Entry Requirements: *GCE:* 260-280. *SQAH:* AAA-BBBB. *IB:* 24.
BTEC Dip: DD. *BTEC ExtDip:* DMM. *OCR ND:* D *OCR NED:* M2
Interview required.

W5L2 BA Dance/Politics
Duration: 3FT Hon
Entry Requirements: *GCE:* 260-280. *SQAH:* AAA-BBBB. *IB:* 24.
BTEC Dip: DD. *BTEC ExtDip:* DMM. *OCR ND:* D *OCR NED:* M2
Interview required.

W5C8 BA Dance/Psychology
Duration: 3FT Hon
Entry Requirements: *GCE:* 260-280. *SQAH:* AAA-BBBB. *IB:* 24.
BTEC Dip: DD. *BTEC ExtDip:* DMM. *OCR ND:* D *OCR NED:* M2
Interview required.

W5L3 BA Dance/Sociology
Duration: 3FT Hon
Entry Requirements: *GCE:* 260-280. *SQAH:* AAA-BBBB. *IB:* 24.
BTEC Dip: DD. *BTEC ExtDip:* DMM. *OCR ND:* D *OCR NED:* M2
Interview required.

W5C6 BA Dance/Sport Studies
Duration: 3FT Hon
Entry Requirements: *GCE:* 260-280. *SQAH:* AAA-BBBB. *IB:* 24.
BTEC Dip: DD. *BTEC ExtDip:* DMM. *OCR ND:* D *OCR NED:* M2
Interview required.

W5N8 BA Dance/Tourism
Duration: 3FT Hon
Entry Requirements: *GCE:* 260-280. *SQAH:* AAA-BBBB. *IB:* 24.
BTEC Dip: DD. *BTEC ExtDip:* DMM. *OCR ND:* D *OCR NED:* M2
Interview required.

W5GK BA Dance/Web Design
Duration: 3FT Hon
Entry Requirements: *GCE:* 260-280. *SQAH:* AAA-BBBB. *IB:* 24.
BTEC Dip: DD. *BTEC ExtDip:* DMM. *OCR ND:* D *OCR NED:* M2
Interview required.

L1W5 BA Economics/Dance
Duration: 3FT Hon
Entry Requirements: *GCE:* 260-280. *SQAH:* AAA-BBBB. *IB:* 24.
BTEC Dip: DD. *BTEC ExtDip:* DMM. *OCR ND:* D *OCR NED:* M2
Interview required.

X3W5 BA Education Studies/Dance
Duration: 3FT Hon
Entry Requirements: *GCE:* 260-280. *SQAH:* AAA-BBBB. *IB:* 24.
BTEC Dip: DD. *BTEC ExtDip:* DMM. *OCR ND:* D *OCR NED:* M2
Interview required.

Q3W5 BA English/Dance
Duration: 3FT Hon
Entry Requirements: *GCE:* 260-280. *SQAH:* AAA-BBBB. *IB:* 24.
BTEC Dip: DD. *BTEC ExtDip:* DMM. *OCR ND:* D *OCR NED:* M2
Interview required.

N8WM BA Events Management/Dance
Duration: 3FT Hon
Entry Requirements: *GCE:* 260-280. *SQAH:* AAA-BBBB. *IB:* 24.
BTEC Dip: DD. *BTEC ExtDip:* DMM. *OCR ND:* D *OCR NED:* M2
Interview required.

W6W5 BA Film & Television Studies/Dance
Duration: 3FT Hon
Entry Requirements: *GCE:* 260-280. *SQAH:* AAA-BBBB. *IB:* 24.
BTEC Dip: DD. *BTEC ExtDip:* DMM. *OCR ND:* D *OCR NED:* M2
Interview required.

L4W5 BA Health Studies/Dance
Duration: 3FT Hon
Entry Requirements: *GCE:* 260-280. *SQAH:* AAA-BBBB. *IB:* 24.
BTEC Dip: DD. *BTEC ExtDip:* DMM. *OCR ND:* D *OCR NED:* M2
Interview required.

L9WM BA International Development/Dance
Duration: 3FT Hon
Entry Requirements: *GCE:* 260-280. *SQAH:* AAA-BBBB. *IB:* 24.
BTEC Dip: DD. *BTEC ExtDip:* DMM. *OCR ND:* D *OCR NED:* M2
Interview required.

M1W5 BA Law/Dance
Duration: 3FT Hon
Entry Requirements: *GCE:* 260-280. *SQAH:* AAA-BBBB. *IB:* 24.
BTEC Dip: DD. *BTEC ExtDip:* DMM. *OCR ND:* D *OCR NED:* M2
Interview required.

N2W5 BA Management/Dance
Duration: 3FT Hon
Entry Requirements: *GCE:* 260-280. *SQAH:* AAA-BBBB. *IB:* 24.
BTEC Dip: DD. *BTEC ExtDip:* DMM. *OCR ND:* D *OCR NED:* M2
Interview required.

N5W5 BA Marketing/Dance
Duration: 3FT Hon
Entry Requirements: *GCE:* 260-280. *SQAH:* AAA-BBBB. *IB:* 24.
BTEC Dip: DD. *BTEC ExtDip:* DMM. *OCR ND:* D *OCR NED:* M2
Interview required.

L2W5 BA Politics/Dance
Duration: 3FT Hon
Entry Requirements: *GCE:* 260-280. *SQAH:* AAA-BBBB. *IB:* 24.
BTEC Dip: DD. *BTEC ExtDip:* DMM. *OCR ND:* D *OCR NED:* M2
Interview required.

C8W5 BA Psychology/Dance
Duration: 3FT Hon
Entry Requirements: *GCE:* 260-280. *SQAH:* AAA-BBBB. *IB:* 24.
BTEC Dip: DD. *BTEC ExtDip:* DMM. *OCR ND:* D *OCR NED:* M2
Interview required.

L3W5 BA Sociology/Dance
Duration: 3FT Hon
Entry Requirements: *GCE:* 260-280. *SQAH:* AAA-BBBB. *IB:* 24.
BTEC Dip: DD. *BTEC ExtDip:* DMM. *OCR ND:* D *OCR NED:* M2
Interview required.

XW53 BA Special Educational Needs & Inclusion/Dance
Duration: 3FT Hon
Entry Requirements: *GCE:* 260-280. *SQAH:* AAA-BBBB. *IB:* 24.
BTEC Dip: DD. *BTEC ExtDip:* DMM. *OCR ND:* D *OCR NED:* M2
Interview required.

C6W5 BA Sport Studies/Dance
Duration: 3FT Hon
Entry Requirements: *GCE:* 260-280. *SQAH:* AAA-BBBB. *IB:* 24.
BTEC Dip: DD. *BTEC ExtDip:* DMM. *OCR ND:* D *OCR NED:* M2
Interview required.

N8W5 BA Tourism/Dance
Duration: 3FT Hon
Entry Requirements: *GCE:* 260-280. *SQAH:* AAA-BBBB. *IB:* 24.
BTEC Dip: DD. *BTEC ExtDip:* DMM. *OCR ND:* D *OCR NED:* M2
Interview required.

W5NF BA. Dance/Business Entrepreneurship
Duration: 3FT Hon
Entry Requirements: *GCE:* 260-280. *SQAH:* AAA-BBBB. *IB:* 24.
BTEC Dip: DD. *BTEC ExtDip:* DMM. *OCR ND:* D *OCR NED:* M2
Interview required.

C1W5 BSc Biological Conservation/Dance
Duration: 3FT Hon
Entry Requirements: *GCE:* 260-280. *SQAH:* AAA-BBBB. *IB:* 24.
BTEC Dip: DD. *BTEC ExtDip:* DMM. *OCR ND:* D *OCR NED:* M2
Interview required.

G5W5 BSc Business Computing Systems/Dance
Duration: 3FT Hon
Entry Requirements: *GCE:* 260-280. *SQAH:* AAA-BBBB. *IB:* 24.
BTEC Dip: DD. *BTEC ExtDip:* DMM. *OCR ND:* D *OCR NED:* M2
Interview required.

G4W5 BSc Computing/Dance
Duration: 3FT Hon
Entry Requirements: *GCE:* 260-280. *SQAH:* AAA-BBBB. *IB:* 24.
BTEC Dip: DD. *BTEC ExtDip:* DMM. *OCR ND:* D *OCR NED:* M2
Interview required.

F8W5 BSc Physical Geography/Dance
Duration: 3FT Hon
Entry Requirements: *GCE:* 260-280. *SQAH:* AAA-BBBB. *IB:* 24.
BTEC Dip: DD. *BTEC ExtDip:* DMM. *OCR ND:* D *OCR NED:* M2
Interview required.

G4WM BSc Web Design/Dance
Duration: 3FT Hon
Entry Requirements: *GCE:* 260-280. *SQAH:* AAA-BBBB. *IB:* 24.
BTEC Dip: DD. *BTEC ExtDip:* DMM. *OCR ND:* D *OCR NED:* M2

N41 NORTHBROOK COLLEGE SUSSEX
LITTLEHAMPTON ROAD
WORTHING
WEST SUSSEX BN12 6NU
t: 0845 155 6060 f: 01903 606073
e: enquiries@nbcol.ac.uk
// www.northbrook.ac.uk

W540 FdA Dance
Duration: 2FT Fdg
Entry Requirements: *GCE:* 160. Interview required.

P51 PETROC
OLD STICKLEPATH HILL
BARNSTAPLE
NORTH DEVON EX31 2BQ
t: 01271 852365 f: 01271 338121
e: he@petroc.ac.uk
// www.petroc.ac.uk

W590 FdA Community Dance Practice
Duration: 2FT Fdg
Entry Requirements: Contact the institution for details.

P60 PLYMOUTH UNIVERSITY
DRAKE CIRCUS
PLYMOUTH PL4 8AA
t: 01752 585858 f: 01752 588055
e: admissions@plymouth.ac.uk
// www.plymouth.ac.uk

W501 BA Dance Theatre
Duration: 3FT Hon
Entry Requirements: *GCE:* 280. *IB:* 25. *BTEC ExtDip:* DMM.
Interview required.

R48 ROEHAMPTON UNIVERSITY
ROEHAMPTON LANE
LONDON SW15 5PU
t: 020 8392 3232 f: 020 8392 3470
e: enquiries@roehampton.ac.uk
// www.roehampton.ac.uk

W500 BA Dance Studies
Duration: 3FT Hon
Entry Requirements: *GCE:* 340. *IB:* 28. *BTEC ExtDip:* DDD. *OCR*
NED: D1 Interview required.

R55 ROYAL ACADEMY OF DANCE
ROYAL ACADEMY OF DANCE
FACULTY OF EDUCATION
36 BATTERSEA SQUARE
LONDON SW11 3RA
t: 020 7326 8086/8049 f: 020 7326 8040
e: faculty@rad.org.uk
// www.radeducation.org.uk

W540 BA Ballet Education
Duration: 3FT Hon   CRB Check: Required
Entry Requirements: *GCE:* 280. *IB:* 24. Interview required.

W541 BA Dance Education (Distance Learning)
Duration: 3FT Hon
Entry Requirements: *GCE:* 160. *IB:* 24.

W591 CertHE Dance Education (Distance Learning)
Duration: 1FT Cer
Entry Requirements: *GCE:* 160. *IB:* 24.

W590 DipHE Dance Education (Distance Learning)
Duration: 2FT Dip
Entry Requirements: *GCE:* 160. *IB:* 24.

S74 STRATFORD UPON AVON COLLEGE
THE WILLOWS NORTH
ALCESTER ROAD
STRATFORD-UPON-AVON
WARWICKSHIRE CV37 9QR
t: 01789 266245 f: 01789 267524
e: college@stratford.ac.uk
// www.stratford.ac.uk

005W HND Performing Arts (Dance)
Duration: 2FT HND
Entry Requirements: *GCE:* 200. Interview required.

S82 UNIVERSITY CAMPUS SUFFOLK (UCS)
WATERFRONT BUILDING
NEPTUNE QUAY
IPSWICH
SUFFOLK IP4 1QJ
t: 01473 338833 f: 01473 339900
e: info@ucs.ac.uk
// www.ucs.ac.uk

W590 BA Dance
Duration: 3FT Hon
Entry Requirements: *GCE:* 240-280. *IB:* 28. *BTEC ExtDip:* DMM.
Interview required.

S84 UNIVERSITY OF SUNDERLAND
STUDENT HELPLINE
THE STUDENT GATEWAY
CHESTER ROAD
SUNDERLAND SR1 3SD
t: 0191 515 3000 f: 0191 515 3805
e: student.helpline@sunderland.ac.uk
// www.sunderland.ac.uk

NW15 BA Business Management and Dance
Duration: 3FT Hon
Entry Requirements: *GCE:* 260-360. *IB:* 31. *OCR ND:* D *OCR*
NED: M3

N1W5 BA Business Management with Dance
Duration: 3FT Hon
Entry Requirements: *GCE:* 260-360. *IB:* 31. *OCR ND:* D *OCR*
NED: M3

XWH5 BA Childhood Studies and Dance
Duration: 3FT Hon
Entry Requirements: *GCE:* 260-360.

MW95 BA Criminology and Dance
Duration: 3FT Hon
Entry Requirements: *GCE:* 260-360. *IB:* 31. *OCR ND:* D *OCR*
NED: M3

M9W5 BA Criminology with Dance
Duration: 3FT Hon
Entry Requirements: *GCE:* 260-360. *IB:* 31. *OCR ND:* D *OCR NED:* M3

W502 BA Dance
Duration: 3FT Hon
Entry Requirements: *GCE:* 220. *OCR ND:* D *OCR NED:* M3
Interview required.

W501 BA Dance (Top-up)
Duration: 1FT Hon
Entry Requirements: Interview required. HND required.

WX53 BA Dance and Education
Duration: 3FT Hon
Entry Requirements: *GCE:* 260-360. *IB:* 31. *OCR ND:* D *OCR NED:* M3

QW15 BA Dance and English Language/Linguistics
Duration: 3FT Hon
Entry Requirements: *GCE:* 260-360. *IB:* 31. *OCR ND:* D *OCR NED:* M3

QW35 BA Dance and English Studies
Duration: 3FT Hon
Entry Requirements: *GCE:* 260-360. *IB:* 31. *OCR ND:* D *OCR NED:* M3

VW15 BA Dance and History
Duration: 3FT Hon
Entry Requirements: *GCE:* 260-360. *IB:* 31. *OCR ND:* D *OCR NED:* M3

WW56 BA Dance and Photography
Duration: 3FT Hon
Entry Requirements: *GCE:* 260-360. *IB:* 31. *OCR ND:* D *OCR NED:* M3

LW25 BA Dance and Politics
Duration: 3FT Hon
Entry Requirements: *GCE:* 260-360. *IB:* 31. *OCR ND:* D *OCR NED:* M3

WX51 BA Dance and TESOL
Duration: 3FT Hon
Entry Requirements: *GCE:* 260-360. *OCR ND:* D *OCR NED:* M3

W5NC BA Dance with Business Management
Duration: 3FT Hon
Entry Requirements: *GCE:* 260-360. *OCR ND:* D *OCR NED:* M3

W5XH BA Dance with Childhood Studies
Duration: 3FT Hon
Entry Requirements: *GCE:* 260-360.

W5M9 BA Dance with Criminology
Duration: 3FT Hon
Entry Requirements: *GCE:* 260-360. *IB:* 31. *OCR ND:* D *OCR NED:* M3

W5X3 BA Dance with Education
Duration: 3FT Hon
Entry Requirements: *GCE:* 260-360. *IB:* 31. *OCR ND:* D *OCR NED:* M3

W5Q1 BA Dance with English Language/Linguistics
Duration: 3FT Hon
Entry Requirements: *GCE:* 260-360. *IB:* 31. *OCR ND:* D *OCR NED:* M3

W5Q3 BA Dance with English Studies
Duration: 3FT Hon
Entry Requirements: *GCE:* 260-360. *IB:* 31. *OCR ND:* D *OCR NED:* M3

W5L5 BA Dance with Health & Social Care
Duration: 3FT Hon
Entry Requirements: *GCE:* 260-360.

W5V1 BA Dance with History
Duration: 3FT Hon
Entry Requirements: *GCE:* 260-360. *IB:* 31. *OCR ND:* D *OCR NED:* M3

W5R1 BA Dance with Modern Foreign Language (French)
Duration: 3FT Hon
Entry Requirements: *GCE:* 220-360. *OCR ND:* D *OCR NED:* M3

W5R2 BA Dance with Modern Foreign Language (German)
Duration: 3FT Hon
Entry Requirements: *GCE:* 260-360. *OCR ND:* D *OCR NED:* M3

W5R4 BA Dance with Modern Foreign Language (Spanish)
Duration: 3FT Hon
Entry Requirements: *GCE:* 260-360. *OCR ND:* D *OCR NED:* M3

W5W6 BA Dance with Photography
Duration: 3FT Hon
Entry Requirements: *GCE:* 220-360. *IB:* 31. *OCR ND:* D *OCR NED:* M3

W5L2 BA Dance with Politics
Duration: 3FT Hon
Entry Requirements: *GCE:* 260-360. *IB:* 31. *OCR ND:* D *OCR NED:* M3

W5C8 BA Dance with Psychology
Duration: 3FT Hon
Entry Requirements: *GCE:* 260-360. *IB:* 31. *OCR ND:* D *OCR NED:* M3

W5LH BA Dance with Sociology
Duration: 3FT Hon
Entry Requirements: *GCE:* 260-360. *IB:* 31. *OCR ND:* D *OCR NED:* M3

W5C6 BA Dance with Sport
Duration: 3FT Hon
Entry Requirements: *GCE:* 260-360. *OCR ND:* D *OCR NED:* M3

W5X1 BA Dance with TESOL
Duration: 3FT Hon
Entry Requirements: *GCE:* 260-360. *OCR ND:* D *OCR NED:* M3

Q1W5 BA English Language & Linguistics with Dance
Duration: 3FT Hon
Entry Requirements: *GCE:* 260-360. *OCR ND:* D *OCR NED:* M3

Q3W5 BA English with Dance
Duration: 3FT Hon
Entry Requirements: *GCE:* 260-360. *IB:* 31. *OCR ND:* D *OCR NED:* M3

WL55 BA Health & Social Care and Dance
Duration: 3FT Hon
Entry Requirements: *GCE:* 260-360.

L5W5 BA Health & Social Care with Dance
Duration: 3FT Hon
Entry Requirements: *GCE:* 260-360.

V1W5 BA History with Dance
Duration: 3FT Hon
Entry Requirements: *GCE:* 260-360. *IB:* 31. *OCR ND:* D *OCR NED:* M3

MW15 BA Law and Dance
Duration: 3FT Hon
Entry Requirements: *GCE:* 260-360. *OCR ND:* D *OCR NED:* M3

RW15 BA Modern Foreign Languages (French) and Dance
Duration: 3FT Hon
Entry Requirements: *GCE:* 260-360. *IB:* 31. *OCR ND:* D *OCR NED:* M3

RW25 BA Modern Foreign Languages (German) and Dance
Duration: 3FT Hon
Entry Requirements: *GCE:* 260-360. *IB:* 31. *OCR ND:* D *OCR NED:* M3

WR54 BA Modern Foreign Languages (Spanish) and Dance
Duration: 3FT Hon
Entry Requirements: *GCE:* 260-360. *IB:* 31. *OCR ND:* D *OCR NED:* M3

W6W5 BA Photography with Dance
Duration: 3FT Hon
Entry Requirements: *GCE:* 260-360.

L2W5 BA Politics with Dance
Duration: 3FT Hon
Entry Requirements: *GCE:* 260-360. *IB:* 31. *OCR ND:* D *OCR NED:* M3

L3W5 BA Sociology with Dance
Duration: 3FT Hon
Entry Requirements: *GCE:* 260-360. *IB:* 31. *OCR ND:* D *OCR NED:* M3

X1W5 BA TESOL with Dance
Duration: 3FT Hon
Entry Requirements: *GCE:* 260-360. *OCR ND:* D *OCR NED:* M3

NW85 BA Tourism and Dance
Duration: 3FT Hon
Entry Requirements: *GCE:* 260-360. *IB:* 31. *OCR ND:* D *OCR NED:* M3

N8W5 BA Tourism with Dance
Duration: 3FT Hon
Entry Requirements: *GCE:* 260-360. *IB:* 31. *OCR ND:* D *OCR NED:* M3

CW85 BA/BSc Dance and Psychology
Duration: 3FT Hon
Entry Requirements: *GCE:* 260-360. *IB:* 31. *OCR ND:* D *OCR NED:* M3

WL53 BA/BSc Dance and Sociology
Duration: 3FT Hon
Entry Requirements: *GCE:* 260-360. *IB:* 31. *OCR ND:* D *OCR NED:* M3

CW65 BA/BSc Sport and Dance
Duration: 3FT Hon
Entry Requirements: *GCE:* 260-360. *OCR ND:* D *OCR NED:* M3

C8W5 BSc Psychology with Dance
Duration: 3FT Hon
Entry Requirements: *GCE:* 260-360. *IB:* 31. *OCR ND:* D *OCR NED:* M3

C6W5 BSc Sport with Dance
Duration: 3FT Hon
Entry Requirements: *GCE:* 260-360. *OCR ND:* D *OCR NED:* M3

W503 FdA Dance
Duration: 2FT Fdg
Entry Requirements: *GCE:* 80-220. *SQAH:* CCCC. *IB:* 22.
Interview required.

S85 UNIVERSITY OF SURREY
STAG HILL
GUILDFORD
SURREY GU2 7XH
t: +44(0)1483 689305 f: +44(0)1483 689388
e: ugteam@surrey.ac.uk
// www.surrey.ac.uk

W552 BA Dance and Culture (3 years)
Duration: 3FT Hon
Entry Requirements: *GCE:* ABB. *SQAH:* ABBBB. *SQAAH:* ABB. *IB:* 34. Interview required.

W553 BA Dance and Culture (4 years)
Duration: 4SW Hon
Entry Requirements: *GCE:* ABB. *SQAH:* ABBBB. *SQAAH:* ABB. *IB:* 34. Interview required.

T20 TEESSIDE UNIVERSITY
MIDDLESBROUGH TS1 3BA
t: 01642 218121 f: 01642 384201
e: registry@tees.ac.uk
// www.tees.ac.uk

W590 BA Dance
Duration: 3FT Hon   CRB Check: Required
Entry Requirements: *GCE:* 280. *IB:* 25. Interview required.

T85 TRURO AND PENWITH COLLEGE
TRURO COLLEGE
COLLEGE ROAD
TRURO
CORNWALL TR1 3XX
t: 01872 267122 f: 01872 267526
e: heinfo@trurocollege.ac.uk
// www.truro-penwith.ac.uk

W500 FdA Dance
Duration: 2FT Fdg
Entry Requirements: *GCE:* 60. *IB:* 24. *BTEC Dip:* MP. *BTEC ExtDip:* PPP. Interview required.

U20 UNIVERSITY OF ULSTER
COLERAINE
CO. LONDONDERRY
NORTHERN IRELAND BT52 1SA
t: 028 7012 4221 f: 028 7012 4908
e: online@ulster.ac.uk
// www.ulster.ac.uk

W500 BA Dance
Duration: 3FT Hon
Entry Requirements: *GCE:* CCD. *IB:* 24. Interview required.

W5Q5 BA Dance with Irish
Duration: 3FT Hon
Entry Requirements: *GCE:* 220. *IB:* 24. Interview required.

W05 THE UNIVERSITY OF WEST LONDON
ST MARY'S ROAD
EALING
LONDON W5 5RF
t: 0800 036 8888 f: 020 8566 1353
e: learning.advice@uwl.ac.uk
// www.uwl.ac.uk

W501 BA Dance (top-up)
Duration: 1FT Hon
Entry Requirements: Interview required. HND required.

WW45 BA Musical Theatre
Duration: 3FT Hon
Entry Requirements: *GCE:* 200. *IB:* 28. Interview required.

W500 FdA Dance
Duration: 2FT Fdg
Entry Requirements: *GCE:* 100. *IB:* 24. Interview required.

W08 WAKEFIELD COLLEGE
MARGARET STREET
WAKEFIELD
WEST YORKSHIRE WF1 2DH
t: 01924 789111 f: 01924 789281
e: courseinfo@wakefield.ac.uk
// www.wakefield.ac.uk/highereducation

055W HND Performing Arts (Performance) Dance Pathway
Duration: 2FT HND
Entry Requirements: *GCE:* 240. Interview required.

W65 WEST THAMES COLLEGE
LONDON ROAD
ISLEWORTH
MIDDLESEX TW7 4HS
t: 020 8326 2000 f: 020 8326 2001
e: info@west-thames.ac.uk
// www.west-thames.ac.uk/en/higher-education/

005W HND Dance
Duration: 2FT HND
Entry Requirements: *GCE:* 40-120. Interview required.

W75 UNIVERSITY OF WOLVERHAMPTON
ADMISSIONS UNIT
MX207, CAMP STREET
WOLVERHAMPTON
WEST MIDLANDS WV1 1AD
t: 01902 321000 f: 01902 321896
e: admissions@wlv.ac.uk
// www.wlv.ac.uk

W500 BA Dance
Duration: 3FT Hon   CRB Check: Required
Entry Requirements: *GCE:* 200. *IB:* 24. *BTEC Dip:* DM. *BTEC ExtDip:* MMP. *OCR ND:* M1 *OCR NED:* P1 Interview required.

W76 UNIVERSITY OF WINCHESTER
WINCHESTER
HANTS SO22 4NR
t: 01962 827234 f: 01962 827288
e: course.enquiries@winchester.ac.uk
// www.winchester.ac.uk

VW4M BA Archaeology and Choreography & Dance
Duration: 3FT Hon
Entry Requirements: *Foundation:* Distinction. *GCE:* 260-300. *IB:* 25. *OCR ND:* D *OCR NED:* M2

NW15 BA Business Management and Choreography & Dance Studies
Duration: 3FT Hon
Entry Requirements: *Foundation:* Distinction. *GCE:* 260-300. *IB:* 25. *OCR ND:* D *OCR NED:* M2

LW55 BA Childhood,Youth & Community Studies and Choreography & Dance
Duration: 3FT Hon
Entry Requirements: *Foundation:* Distinction. *GCE:* 260-300. *IB:* 25. *OCR ND:* D *OCR NED:* M2

W500 BA Choreography & Dance
Duration: 3FT Hon
Entry Requirements: *Foundation:* Distinction. *GCE:* 260-300. *IB:* 26. *OCR ND:* D

WW58 BA Choreography & Dance and Creative Writing
Duration: 3FT Hon
Entry Requirements: *Foundation:* Distinction. *GCE:* 260-300. *IB:* 25. *OCR ND:* D *OCR NED:* M2

WLN3 BA Choreography & Dance and Criminology
Duration: 3FT Hon
Entry Requirements: *Foundation:* Distinction. *GCE:* 260-300. *IB:* 25. *OCR ND:* D *OCR NED:* M2

WXM3 BA Choreography & Dance and Education Studies
Duration: 3FT Hon
Entry Requirements: *Foundation:* Distinction. *GCE:* 260-300. *IB:* 25. *OCR ND:* D *OCR NED:* M2

WX53 BA Choreography & Dance and Education Studies (Modern Liberal Arts)
Duration: 3FT Hon
Entry Requirements: *Foundation:* Distinction. *GCE:* 260-300. *IB:* 25. *OCR ND:* D *OCR NED:* M2

WQ53 BA Choreography & Dance and English
Duration: 3FT Hon
Entry Requirements: *Foundation:* Distinction. *GCE:* 260-300. *IB:* 25. *OCR ND:* D *OCR NED:* M2

WQ5H BA Choreography & Dance and English Language Studies
Duration: 3FT Hon
Entry Requirements: *Foundation:* Distinction. *GCE:* 260-300. *IB:* 25. *OCR ND:* D *OCR NED:* M2

WN58 BA Choreography & Dance and Event Management
Duration: 3FT Hon
Entry Requirements: *Foundation:* Distinction. *GCE:* 260-300. *IB:* 25. *OCR ND:* D *OCR NED:* M2

WW56 BA Choreography & Dance and Film & Cinema Technologies
Duration: 3FT Hon
Entry Requirements: *Foundation:* Distinction. *GCE:* 260-300. *IB:* 25. *OCR ND:* D *OCR NED:* M2

WL5N BA Choreography & Dance and Health, Community & Social Care Studies
Duration: 3FT Hon
Entry Requirements: Contact the institution for details.

WV51 BA Choreography & Dance and History
Duration: 3FT Hon
Entry Requirements: *Foundation:* Distinction. *GCE:* 260-300. *IB:* 25. *OCR ND:* D *OCR NED:* M2

WW59 BA Choreography & Dance and Modern Liberal Arts
Duration: 3FT Hon
Entry Requirements: *Foundation:* Distinction. *GCE:* 260-300. *IB:* 25. *OCR ND:* D *OCR NED:* M2

CW85 BA Choreography & Dance and Psychology
Duration: 3FT Hon
Entry Requirements: *Foundation:* Distinction. *GCE:* 260-300. *IB:* 25. *OCR ND:* D *OCR NED:* M2

WL5H BA Choreography & Dance and Sociology
Duration: 3FT Hon
Entry Requirements: *Foundation:* Distinction. *GCE:* 260-300. *IB:* 25. *OCR ND:* D *OCR NED:* M2

WNM8 BA Choreography & Dance and Sports Management
Duration: 3FT Hon
Entry Requirements: *GCE:* 260-300. *IB:* 24.

WL53 BA Choreography & Dance and Sports Studies
Duration: 3FT Hon
Entry Requirements: *Foundation:* Merit. *GCE:* 260-300. *IB:* 24.

XWH5 BA Education Studies (Early Childhood) and Choreography & Dance Studies
Duration: 3FT Hon
Entry Requirements: *Foundation:* Distinction. *GCE:* 260-300. *IB:* 25. *OCR ND:* D *OCR NED:* M2

LW25 BA Politics & Global Studies and Choreography & Dance
Duration: 3FT Hon
Entry Requirements: *Foundation:* Distinction. *GCE:* 260-300. *IB:* 25. *OCR ND:* D *OCR NED:* M2

W80 UNIVERSITY OF WORCESTER
HENWICK GROVE
WORCESTER WR2 6AJ
t: 01905 855111 f: 01905 855377
e: admissions@worc.ac.uk
// www.worcester.ac.uk

005W HND Dance
Duration: 2FT HND
Entry Requirements: *GCE:* 60. *IB:* 24.

W81 WORCESTER COLLEGE OF TECHNOLOGY
DEANSWAY
WORCESTER WR1 2JF
t: 01905 725555 f: 01905 28906
// www.wortech.ac.uk

54WW HNC Performing Arts
Duration: 1FT HNC
Entry Requirements: Interview required.

Y75 YORK ST JOHN UNIVERSITY
LORD MAYOR'S WALK
YORK YO31 7EX
t: 01904 876598 f: 01904 876940/876921
e: admissions@yorksj.ac.uk
// w3.yorksj.ac.uk

W500 BA Dance
Duration: 3FT Hon
Entry Requirements: *Foundation:* Pass. *GCE:* 200-240. *IB:* 24.
Interview required.

W501 BA Dance (for international applicants only)
Duration: 4FT Hon
Entry Requirements: *Foundation:* Pass. *GCE:* 200-240. *IB:* 24.
Interview required.

IMAGINATIVE WRITING AND SCRIPTWRITING

A40 ABERYSTWYTH UNIVERSITY
ABERYSTWYTH UNIVERSITY, WELCOME CENTRE
PENGLAIS CAMPUS
ABERYSTWYTH
CEREDIGION SY23 3FB
t: 01970 622021 f: 01970 627410
e: ug-admissions@aber.ac.uk
// www.aber.ac.uk

QW38 BA English Literature and Creative Writing
Duration: 3FT Hon
Entry Requirements: *GCE:* 300. *IB:* 30.

A60 ANGLIA RUSKIN UNIVERSITY
BISHOP HALL LANE
CHELMSFORD
ESSEX CM1 1SQ
t: 0845 271 3333 f: 01245 251789
e: answers@anglia.ac.uk
// www.anglia.ac.uk

WQ83 BA Writing and English Literature
Duration: 3FT Hon
Entry Requirements: *GCE:* 220-260. *SQAH:* BBBC. *SQAAH:* BC.
IB: 28.

B06 BANGOR UNIVERSITY
BANGOR UNIVERSITY
BANGOR
GWYNEDD LL57 2DG
t: 01248 388484 f: 01248 370451
e: admissions@bangor.ac.uk
// www.bangor.ac.uk

W890 BA Creative and Professional Writing
Duration: 3FT Hon
Entry Requirements: Portfolio required.

Q3WL BA English Language with Creative Writing
Duration: 3FT Hon
Entry Requirements: *GCE:* 240-300. *IB:* 28.

Q3W4 BA English with Creative Writing
Duration: 3FT Hon
Entry Requirements: *GCE:* 240-300. *IB:* 28.

R1W8 BA French with Creative Writing
Duration: 4FT Hon
Entry Requirements: *GCE:* 240-260. *IB:* 28.

R2W8 BA German with Creative Writing
Duration: 4FT Hon
Entry Requirements: *GCE:* 240-260. *IB:* 28.

R4W8 BA Spanish with Creative Writing
Duration: 4FT Hon
Entry Requirements: *GCE:* 240-260. *IB:* 28.

B20 BATH SPA UNIVERSITY
NEWTON PARK
NEWTON ST LOE
BATH BA2 9BN
t: 01225 875875 f: 01225 875444
e: enquiries@bathspa.ac.uk
// www.bathspa.ac.uk/clearing

WW19 BA Art/Creative Writing
Duration: 3FT Hon
Entry Requirements: *Foundation:* Pass. *GCE:* 220-280. *IB:* 24.
Interview required.

NW19 BA Business & Management/Creative Writing
Duration: 3FT Hon
Entry Requirements: *GCE:* 220-280. *IB:* 24.

WW28 BA Ceramics/Creative Writing
Duration: 3FT Hon
Entry Requirements: *Foundation:* Pass. *GCE:* 220-280. *IB:* 24.
Interview required.

W800 BA Creative Writing
Duration: 3FT Hon
Entry Requirements: *GCE:* 220-280. *IB:* 24.

WX83 BA Creative Writing/Education
Duration: 3FT Hon   CRB Check: Required
Entry Requirements: *GCE:* 220-280. *IB:* 24.

WQ93 BA Creative Writing/English Literature
Duration: 3FT Hon
Entry Requirements: *GCE:* 220-280. *IB:* 24.

WW86 BA Creative Writing/Film & Screen Studies
Duration: 3FT Hon
Entry Requirements: *GCE:* 220-280. *IB:* 24.

WV91 BA Creative Writing/History
Duration: 3FT Hon
Entry Requirements: *GCE:* 220-280. *IB:* 24.

WP84 BA Creative Writing/Publishing
Duration: 3FT Hon
Entry Requirements: *GCE:* 220-280.

WV96 BA Creative Writing/Study of Religions
Duration: 3FT Hon
Entry Requirements: *GCE:* 220-280. *IB:* 24.

WWX2 BA Creative Writing/Textile Design Studies
Duration: 3FT Hon
Entry Requirements: *Foundation:* Pass. *GCE:* 220-280. *IB:* 24.
Interview required.

WW82 BA Creative Writing/Visual Design
Duration: 3FT Hon
Entry Requirements: *Foundation:* Pass. *GCE:* 220-280. *IB:* 24.
Interview required.

XW18 BA Education/Creative Writing
Duration: 3FT Hon   CRB Check: Required
Entry Requirements: *GCE:* 220-280. *IB:* 24.

WC91 BA/BSc Biology/Creative Writing
Duration: 3FT Hon
Entry Requirements: *GCE:* 220-280. *IB:* 24.

WF98 BA/BSc Creative Writing/Geography
Duration: 3FT Hon
Entry Requirements: *GCE:* 220-280. *IB:* 24.

WV85 BA/BSc Creative Writing/Philosophy & Ethics
Duration: 3FT Hon
Entry Requirements: *GCE:* 220-280. *IB:* 24.

WC88 BA/BSc Creative Writing/Psychology
Duration: 3FT Hon
Entry Requirements: *GCE:* 220-280. *IB:* 24.

WL93 BA/BSc Creative Writing/Sociology
Duration: 3FT Hon
Entry Requirements: *GCE:* 220-280. *IB:* 24.

WW91 DipHE Art/Creative Writing
Duration: 2FT Dip
Entry Requirements: *GCE:* 220-280. *IB:* 24.

CW19 DipHE Biology/Creative Writing
Duration: 2FT Dip
Entry Requirements: *GCE:* 220-280. *IB:* 24.

WN91 DipHE Business & Management/Creative Writing
Duration: 2FT Dip
Entry Requirements: *GCE:* 220-280. *IB:* 24.

W801 DipHE Creative Writing
Duration: 2FT Dip
Entry Requirements: *GCE:* 220-280. *IB:* 24.

VW99 DipHE Creative Writing/Cultural Studies
Duration: 2FT Dip
Entry Requirements: *GCE:* 220-280. *IB:* 24.

XW38 DipHE Creative Writing/Education
Duration: 2FT Dip
Entry Requirements: *GCE:* 220-280. *IB:* 24.

QW39 DipHE Creative Writing/English Literature
Duration: 2FT Dip
Entry Requirements: *GCE:* 220-280. *IB:* 24.

WW68 DipHE Creative Writing/Film & Screen Studies
Duration: 2FT Dip
Entry Requirements: *GCE:* 220-280. *IB:* 24.

FW89 DipHE Creative Writing/Geography
Duration: 2FT Dip
Entry Requirements: *GCE:* 220-280. *IB:* 24.

LW48 DipHE Creative Writing/Health Studies
Duration: 2FT Dip
Entry Requirements: *GCE:* 220-280. *IB:* 24.

VW19 DipHE Creative Writing/History
Duration: 2FT Dip
Entry Requirements: *GCE:* 220-280. *IB:* 24.

PW99 DipHE Creative Writing/Media Communications
Duration: 2FT Dip
Entry Requirements: *GCE:* 220-280. *IB:* 24.

WV8M DipHE Creative Writing/Philosophy & Ethics
Duration: 2FT Dip
Entry Requirements: *GCE:* 220-280.

LW39 DipHE Creative Writing/Sociology
Duration: 2FT Dip
Entry Requirements: *GCE:* 220-280. *IB:* 24.

VW69 DipHE Creative Writing/Study of Religions
Duration: 2FT Dip
Entry Requirements: *GCE:* 220-280. *IB:* 24.

B22 UNIVERSITY OF BEDFORDSHIRE
PARK SQUARE
LUTON
BEDS LU1 3JU
t: 0844 8482234 f: 01582 489323
e: admissions@beds.ac.uk
// www.beds.ac.uk

W800 BA Creative Writing
Duration: 3FT Hon
Entry Requirements: *Foundation:* Pass. *GCE:* 200. *SQAH:* BCC.
SQAAH: BCC. *IB:* 24. *OCR ND:* M1 *OCR NED:* P1

PW38 BA Media Production (Scriptwriting)
Duration: 3FT Hon
Entry Requirements: *Foundation:* Pass. *GCE:* 200. *SQAH:* BCC.
SQAAH: BCC. *IB:* 24. *OCR ND:* M1 *OCR NED:* P1

B25 BIRMINGHAM CITY UNIVERSITY
PERRY BARR
BIRMINGHAM B42 2SU
t: 0121 331 5595 f: 0121 331 7994
// www.bcu.ac.uk

QW38 BA English and Creative Writing
Duration: 3FT Hon
Entry Requirements: *GCE:* 300. *IB:* 26.

B32 THE UNIVERSITY OF BIRMINGHAM
EDGBASTON
BIRMINGHAM B15 2TT
t: 0121 415 8900 f: 0121 414 7159
e: admissions@bham.ac.uk
// www.birmingham.ac.uk

Q3W8 BA English with Creative Writing
Duration: 3FT Hon
Entry Requirements: *GCE:* AAA-AAB. *SQAH:* AAABB. *SQAAH:* AAB-AA.

B44 UNIVERSITY OF BOLTON
DEANE ROAD
BOLTON BL3 5AB
t: 01204 903903 f: 01204 399074
e: enquiries@bolton.ac.uk
// www.bolton.ac.uk

W800 BA Creative Writing
Duration: 3FT Hon
Entry Requirements: *GCE:* 240. Interview required.

QW38 BA Creative Writing and English
Duration: 3FT Hon
Entry Requirements: *GCE:* 240. Interview required.

B84 BRUNEL UNIVERSITY
UXBRIDGE
MIDDLESEX UB8 3PH
t: 01895 265265 f: 01895 269790
e: admissions@brunel.ac.uk
// www.brunel.ac.uk

W800 BA Creative Writing
Duration: 3FT Hon
Entry Requirements: *GCE:* ABB. *SQAAH:* ABB. *IB:* 33. *BTEC ExtDip:* D*DD.

Q3W8 BA English with Creative Writing
Duration: 3FT Hon
Entry Requirements: *GCE:* AAB. *SQAAH:* AAB. *IB:* 35. *BTEC ExtDip:* D*D*D.

WW28 BA Games Design and Creative Writing
Duration: 3FT Hon
Entry Requirements: *GCE:* ABB. *SQAAH:* ABB. *IB:* 33. *BTEC ExtDip:* D*DD.

C10 CANTERBURY CHRIST CHURCH UNIVERSITY
NORTH HOLMES ROAD
CANTERBURY
KENT CT1 1QU
t: 01227 782900 f: 01227 782888
e: admissions@canterbury.ac.uk
// www.canterbury.ac.uk

W800 BA Creative and Professional Writing
Duration: 3FT Hon
Entry Requirements: Interview required.

C20 CARDIFF METROPOLITAN UNIVERSITY (UWIC)
ADMISSIONS UNIT
LLANDAFF CAMPUS
WESTERN AVENUE
CARDIFF CF5 2YB
t: 029 2041 6070 f: 029 2041 6286
e: admissions@cardiffmet.ac.uk
// www.cardiffmet.ac.uk

QW38 BA English & Creative Writing
Duration: 3FT Hon
Entry Requirements: GCE: 260. IB: 24. BTEC ExtDip: DMM.
Interview required.

C30 UNIVERSITY OF CENTRAL LANCASHIRE
PRESTON
LANCS PR1 2HE
t: 01772 201201 f: 01772 894954
e: uadmissions@uclan.ac.uk
// www.uclan.ac.uk

W8W1 BA Creative Writing and Screenwriting
Duration: 3FT Hon
Entry Requirements: GCE: 260-300. IB: 28. BTEC Dip: D*D*.
BTEC ExtDip: DMM. OCR ND: D OCR NED: M2 Interview required.

Q3W8 BA English Literature and Creative Writing
Duration: 3FT Hon
Entry Requirements: GCE: 260-300. IB: 28. BTEC Dip: D*D*.
BTEC ExtDip: DMM. OCR ND: D OCR NED: M2

W810 BA Screenwriting
Duration: 3FT Hon
Entry Requirements: GCE: 240-260. IB: 28. OCR ND: D OCR NED: M3

C55 UNIVERSITY OF CHESTER
PARKGATE ROAD
CHESTER CH1 4BJ
t: 01244 511000 f: 01244 511300
e: enquiries@chester.ac.uk
// www.chester.ac.uk

WQ83 BA Creative Writing and English
Duration: 3FT Hon
Entry Requirements: Foundation: Merit. GCE: 260-300. SQAH: BBBB. IB: 28.

WV81 BA Creative Writing and History
Duration: 3FT Hon
Entry Requirements: Foundation: Merit. GCE: 260-300. SQAH: BBBB. IB: 28.

WR84 BA Creative Writing and Spanish
Duration: 4FT Hon
Entry Requirements: GCE: 240-280. SQAH: BBBB. IB: 26.

QW38 BA English Language and Creative Writing
Duration: 3FT Hon
Entry Requirements: Foundation: Merit. GCE: 260-300. SQAH: BBBB. IB: 28.

C58 UNIVERSITY OF CHICHESTER
BISHOP OTTER CAMPUS
COLLEGE LANE
CHICHESTER
WEST SUSSEX PO19 6PE
t: 01243 816002 f: 01243 816161
e: admissions@chi.ac.uk
// www.chiuni.ac.uk

QW38 BA English & Creative Writing
Duration: 3FT Hon
Entry Requirements: GCE: BCC. SQAH: BBBB-BBBC. SQAAH: BCC. IB: 30. BTEC ExtDip: DMM.

WV81 BA English & Creative Writing and History
Duration: 3FT Hon
Entry Requirements: GCE: BBC-BCC. SQAAH: BBC-BCC. IB: 30. BTEC ExtDip: DMM.

W8V6 BA English & Creative Writing and Theology & Religion
Duration: 3FT Hon
Entry Requirements: GCE: BCC. SQAH: BBBB-BBBC. SQAAH: BCC. IB: 30.

W8V1 BA English & Creative Writing with History
Duration: 3FT Hon
Entry Requirements: GCE: BCC. SQAH: BBBB-BBBC. SQAAH: BCC. IB: 30.

C85 COVENTRY UNIVERSITY
THE STUDENT CENTRE
COVENTRY UNIVERSITY
1 GULSON RD
COVENTRY CV1 2JH
t: 024 7615 2222 f: 024 7615 2223
e: studentenquiries@coventry.ac.uk
// www.coventry.ac.uk

QW38 BA English and Creative Writing
Duration: 3FT/4SW Hon
Entry Requirements: GCE: BCC. SQAH: BCCCC. IB: 28. BTEC ExtDip: DMM. OCR NED: M2

C93 UNIVERSITY FOR THE CREATIVE ARTS
FALKNER ROAD
FARNHAM
SURREY GU9 7DS
t: 01252 892960
e: admissions@ucreative.ac.uk
// www.ucreative.ac.uk

W803 BA Sports Journalism
Duration: 3FT Hon
Entry Requirements: *GCE:* 220. *IB:* 24. *BTEC ExtDip:* PPP.
Interview required. Portfolio required.

C99 UNIVERSITY OF CUMBRIA
FUSEHILL STREET
CARLISLE
CUMBRIA CA1 2HH
t: 01228 616234 f: 01228 616235
// www.cumbria.ac.uk

QW38 BA English and Creative Writing
Duration: 3FT Hon
Entry Requirements: *Foundation:* Merit. *GCE:* 200. *IB:* 28. *OCR ND:* M1 *OCR NED:* P1

QW3V DipHE English and Creative Writing
Duration: 2FT Dip
Entry Requirements: Contact the institution for details.

D26 DE MONTFORT UNIVERSITY
THE GATEWAY
LEICESTER LE1 9BH
t: 0116 255 1551 f: 0116 250 6204
e: enquiries@dmu.ac.uk
// www.dmu.ac.uk

WQ83 BA Creative Writing and English
Duration: 3FT Hon
Entry Requirements: *GCE:* 260. *IB:* 28. *BTEC Dip:* D*D*. *BTEC ExtDip:* DMM.

QW38 BA Creative Writing and English Language
Duration: 3FT Hon
Entry Requirements: *GCE:* 260. *IB:* 28. *BTEC Dip:* D*D*. *BTEC ExtDip:* DMM.

D39 UNIVERSITY OF DERBY
KEDLESTON ROAD
DERBY DE22 1GB
t: 01332 591167 f: 01332 597724
e: askadmissions@derby.ac.uk
// www.derby.ac.uk

KW18 BA Architectural Design and Creative Writing
Duration: 3FT Hon
Entry Requirements: *Foundation:* Distinction. *GCE:* 260-300. *IB:* 28. *BTEC Dip:* D*D*. *BTEC ExtDip:* DMM. *OCR NED:* M2

W800 BA Creative Writing
Duration: 3FT Hon
Entry Requirements: *Foundation:* Distinction. *GCE:* 260. *IB:* 28. *BTEC Dip:* D*D*. *BTEC ExtDip:* DMM. *OCR NED:* M2

WM81 BA Creative Writing and Law
Duration: 3FT Hon
Entry Requirements: *Foundation:* Distinction. *GCE:* 260-300. *IB:* 28. *BTEC Dip:* D*D*. *BTEC ExtDip:* DMM. *OCR NED:* M2

W890 BA Creative Writing and Professional Writing
Duration: 3FT Hon
Entry Requirements: *Foundation:* Distinction. *GCE:* 260-300. *IB:* 28. *BTEC Dip:* D*D*. *BTEC ExtDip:* DMM. *OCR NED:* M2

WL83 BA Creative Writing and Sociology
Duration: 3FT Hon
Entry Requirements: *Foundation:* Distinction. *GCE:* 260-300. *IB:* 28. *BTEC Dip:* D*D*. *BTEC ExtDip:* DMM. *OCR NED:* M2

L5W8 BA Early Childhood Studies and Creative Writing
Duration: 3FT Hon
Entry Requirements: *Foundation:* Distinction. *GCE:* 260-300. *IB:* 28. *BTEC Dip:* D*D*. *BTEC ExtDip:* DMM. *OCR NED:* M2

WX83 BA Education Studies and Creative Writing
Duration: 3FT Hon
Entry Requirements: *Foundation:* Distinction. *GCE:* 260-300. *IB:* 28. *BTEC Dip:* D*D*. *BTEC ExtDip:* DMM. *OCR NED:* M2

XW38 BA Education Studies and Professional Writing
Duration: 3FT Hon
Entry Requirements: *Foundation:* Distinction. *GCE:* 260-300. *IB:* 28. *BTEC Dip:* D*D*. *BTEC ExtDip:* DMM. *OCR NED:* M2

QW38 BA English and Creative Writing
Duration: 3FT Hon
Entry Requirements: *Foundation:* Distinction. *GCE:* 260-300. *IB:* 28. *BTEC Dip:* D*D*. *BTEC ExtDip:* DMM. *OCR NED:* M2

QW3V BA English and Professional Writing
Duration: 3FT Hon
Entry Requirements: *Foundation:* Distinction. *GCE:* 260-300. *IB:* 28. *BTEC Dip:* D*D*. *BTEC ExtDip:* DMM. *OCR NED:* M2

NW68 BA Human Resource Management and Professional Writing
Duration: 3FT Hon
Entry Requirements: *Foundation:* Distinction. *GCE:* 260-300. *IB:* 28. *BTEC Dip:* D*D*. *BTEC ExtDip:* DMM. *OCR NED:* M2

MW18 BA Law and Professional Writing
Duration: 3FT Hon
Entry Requirements: *Foundation:* Distinction. *GCE:* 260-300. *IB:* 28. *BTEC Dip:* D*D*. *BTEC ExtDip:* DMM. *OCR NED:* M2

NW58 BA Marketing and Professional Writing
Duration: 3FT Hon
Entry Requirements: *Foundation:* Distinction. *GCE:* 260-300. *IB:*
28. *BTEC Dip:* D*D*. *BTEC ExtDip:* DMM. *OCR NED:* M2

PWJ8 BA Media Studies and Professional Writing
Duration: 3FT Hon
Entry Requirements: *Foundation:* Distinction. *GCE:* 260-300. *IB:*
28. *BTEC Dip:* D*D*. *BTEC ExtDip:* DMM. *OCR NED:* M2

JW98 BA Popular Music Production and Creative Writing
Duration: 3FT Hon
Entry Requirements: *Foundation:* Distinction. *GCE:* 260-300. *IB:*
28. *BTEC Dip:* D*D*. *BTEC ExtDip:* DMM. *OCR NED:* M2

WL82 BA/BSc Creative Writing and International Relations & Global Development
Duration: 3FT Hon
Entry Requirements: *Foundation:* Distinction. *GCE:* 260-300. *IB:*
28. *BTEC Dip:* D*D*. *BTEC ExtDip:* DMM. *OCR NED:* M2

WG81 BA/BSc Creative Writing and Mathematics
Duration: 3FT Hon
Entry Requirements: *Foundation:* Distinction. *GCE:* 260-300. *IB:*
28. *BTEC Dip:* D*D*. *BTEC ExtDip:* DMM. *OCR NED:* M2

WL89 BA/BSc Creative Writing and Third World Development
Duration: 3FT Hon
Entry Requirements: *Foundation:* Distinction. *GCE:* 260-300. *IB:*
28. *BTEC Dip:* D*D*. *BTEC ExtDip:* DMM. *OCR NED:* M2

LW78 BA/BSc Geography and Professional Writing
Duration: 3FT Hon
Entry Requirements: *Foundation:* Distinction. *GCE:* 260-300. *IB:*
28. *BTEC Dip:* D*D*. *BTEC ExtDip:* DMM. *OCR NED:* M2

GW18 BA/BSc Mathematics and Professional Writing
Duration: 3FT Hon
Entry Requirements: *Foundation:* Distinction. *GCE:* 260-300. *IB:*
28. *BTEC Dip:* D*D*. *BTEC ExtDip:* DMM. *OCR NED:* M2

WC88 BA/BSc Professional Writing and Psychology
Duration: 3FT Hon
Entry Requirements: *Foundation:* Distinction. *GCE:* 260-300. *IB:*
28. *BTEC Dip:* D*D*. *BTEC ExtDip:* DMM. *OCR NED:* M2

D52 DONCASTER COLLEGE
THE HUB
CHAPPELL DRIVE
SOUTH YORKSHIRE DN1 2RF
t: 01302 553610
e: he@don.ac.uk
// www.don.ac.uk

W810 BA Scriptwriting
Duration: 3FT Hon
Entry Requirements: *GCE:* 160.

D65 UNIVERSITY OF DUNDEE
NETHERGATE
DUNDEE DD1 4HN
t: 01382 383838 f: 01382 388150
e: contactus@dundee.ac.uk
// www.dundee.ac.uk/admissions/
undergraduate/

QW38 MA English and Creative Writing
Duration: 4FT Hon
Entry Requirements: *GCE:* BCC. *SQAH:* ABBB. *IB:* 30.

E14 UNIVERSITY OF EAST ANGLIA
NORWICH NR4 7TJ
t: 01603 591515 f: 01603 591523
e: admissions@uea.ac.uk
// www.uea.ac.uk

T7W8 BA American Literature with Creative Writing with a Year Abroad
Duration: 4FT Hon CRB Check: Required
Entry Requirements: *GCE:* AAB. *SQAAH:* AAB. *IB:* 33. *BTEC ExtDip:* DDD. Interview required. Portfolio required.

Q3W8 BA English Literature with Creative Writing
Duration: 3FT Hon CRB Check: Required
Entry Requirements: *GCE:* AAA. *SQAAH:* AAA. *IB:* 34. *BTEC ExtDip:* DDD. Interview required. Portfolio required.

E28 UNIVERSITY OF EAST LONDON
DOCKLANDS CAMPUS
UNIVERSITY WAY
LONDON E16 2RD
t: 020 8223 3333 f: 020 8223 2978
e: study@uel.ac.uk
// www.uel.ac.uk

WQ83 BA Creative & Professional Writing / English Literature
Duration: 3FT Hon
Entry Requirements: *GCE:* 240. *IB:* 24.

W8Q3 BA Creative & Professional Writing with English Literature
Duration: 3FT Hon
Entry Requirements: *GCE:* 240. *IB:* 24.

W8W2 BA Creative & Professional Writing with Illustration
Duration: 3FT Hon
Entry Requirements: *GCE:* 240. *IB:* 24.

WM89 BA Creative & Professional Writing/Criminology
Duration: 3FT Hon
Entry Requirements: *GCE:* 240. *IB:* 24.

WN85 BA Creative & Professional Writing/Marketing
Duration: 3FT Hon
Entry Requirements: *GCE:* 240. *IB:* 24.

W800 BA Creative and Professional Writing
Duration: 3FT Hon
Entry Requirements: *GCE:* 240. *IB:* 24.

W801 BA Creative and Professional Writing (Extended)
Duration: 4FT Hon
Entry Requirements: *GCE:* 120. *IB:* 24.

W8W6 BA Creative and Professional Writing and Photography
Duration: 3FT Hon
Entry Requirements: *GCE:* 240. *IB:* 24.

W8P9 BA Creative and Professional Writing with Communication Studies
Duration: 3FT Hon
Entry Requirements: *GCE:* 240. *IB:* 24.

W8X3 BA Creative and Professional Writing with Early Childhood Studies
Duration: 3FT Hon
Entry Requirements: *GCE:* 240. *IB:* 24.

W8C8 BA Creative and Professional Writing with Psychology
Duration: 3FT Hon
Entry Requirements: *GCE:* 240. *IB:* 24.

W8L3 BA Creative and Professional Writing with Sociology (Professional Development)
Duration: 3FT Hon
Entry Requirements: *GCE:* 240. *IB:* 24.

XW38 BA Education Studies with Creative and Professional Writing
Duration: 3FT Hon
Entry Requirements: *GCE:* 240. *IB:* 24.

Q3W8 BA English Literature with Creative & Professional Writing
Duration: 3FT Hon
Entry Requirements: *GCE:* 240. *IB:* 24.

V1W8 BA History with Creative and Professional Writing
Duration: 3FT Hon
Entry Requirements: *GCE:* 240. *IB:* 24.

NW18 BA International Business/Creative & Professional Writing
Duration: 3FT Hon
Entry Requirements: *GCE:* 240. *IB:* 24.

LW28 BA International Politics with Creative and Professional Writing
Duration: 3FT Hon
Entry Requirements: *GCE:* 240. *IB:* 24.

V000 BA Media & Creative Industries option - Creative and Professional Writing
Duration: 3FT Hon
Entry Requirements: *GCE:* 240. *IB:* 24.

W6W8 BA Photography with Creative & Professional Writing
Duration: 3FT Hon
Entry Requirements: *GCE:* 200. *IB:* 24. Portfolio required.

C8W8 BA Psychosocial Studies with Creative and Professional Writing
Duration: 3FT Hon
Entry Requirements: *GCE:* 240. *IB:* 24.

L8W8 BA Third World Development with Creative and Professional Writing
Duration: 3FT Hon
Entry Requirements: *GCE:* 240. *IB:* 24.

GW58 BA/BSc Business Information Systems/Creative & Professional Writing
Duration: 3FT Hon
Entry Requirements: *GCE:* 240. *IB:* 24.

WL83 BA/BSc Creative & Professional Writing/Sociology (Professional Development)
Duration: 3FT Hon
Entry Requirements: *GCE:* 240. *IB:* 24.

BW98 BA/BSc Fitness & Health/Creative & Professional Writing
Duration: 3FT Hon
Entry Requirements: *GCE:* 240. *IB:* 24.

I1W8 BSc Computing with Creative and Professional Writing
Duration: 3FT Hon
Entry Requirements: *GCE:* 240. *IB:* 24.

I3W8 BSc Software Engineering with Creative and Professional Writing
Duration: 3FT Hon
Entry Requirements: *GCE:* 240. *IB:* 24.

M1W8 LLB Law with Creative and Professional Writing
Duration: 3FT Hon
Entry Requirements: *GCE:* 240. *IB:* 24.

E42 EDGE HILL UNIVERSITY
ORMSKIRK
LANCASHIRE L39 4QP
t: 01695 657000 f: 01695 584355
e: study@edgehill.ac.uk
// www.edgehill.ac.uk

W800 BA Creative Writing
Duration: 3FT Hon
Entry Requirements: *GCE:* 280. *IB:* 26. *OCR ND:* D *OCR NED:* M2

WQ83 BA Creative Writing and English Language
Duration: 3FT Hon
Entry Requirements: *GCE:* 280. *IB:* 26. *OCR ND:* D *OCR NED:* M2

QW38 BA Creative Writing and English Literature
Duration: 3FT Hon
Entry Requirements: *GCE:* 280. *IB:* 26. *OCR ND:* D *OCR NED:* M2

Q1W8 BA English Language with Creative Writing
Duration: 3FT Hon
Entry Requirements: *GCE:* 280. *IB:* 26. *OCR ND:* D *OCR NED:* M2

Q2W9 BA English Literature with Creative Writing
Duration: 3FT Hon
Entry Requirements: *GCE:* 280. *IB:* 26. *OCR ND:* D *OCR NED:* M2

Q3W8 BA English with Creative Writing
Duration: 3FT Hon
Entry Requirements: *GCE:* 280. *IB:* 26. *OCR ND:* D *OCR NED:* M2

V1W8 BA History with Creative Writing
Duration: 3FT Hon
Entry Requirements: *GCE:* 280. *IB:* 26. *OCR ND:* D *OCR NED:* M2

E70 THE UNIVERSITY OF ESSEX
WIVENHOE PARK
COLCHESTER
ESSEX CO4 3SQ
t: 01206 873666 f: 01206 874477
e: admit@essex.ac.uk
// www.essex.ac.uk

W800 BA Creative Writing
Duration: 3FT Hon
Entry Requirements: *GCE:* ABB. *SQAH:* AAAB. *IB:* 34.

W801 BA Creative Writing (Including Year Abroad)
Duration: 4FT Hon
Entry Requirements: Contact the institution for details.

E81 EXETER COLLEGE
HELE ROAD
EXETER
DEVON EX4 4JS
t: 0845 111 6000
e: info@exe-coll.ac.uk
// www.exe-coll.ac.uk/he

W800 BA Creative Writing
Duration: 3FT Hon   CRB Check: Required
Entry Requirements: Contact the institution for details.

WQ83 BA Creative Writing with English Literature
Duration: 3FT Hon   CRB Check: Required
Entry Requirements: Contact the institution for details.

Q3W8 BA English Literature with Creative Writing
Duration: 3FT Hon   CRB Check: Required
Entry Requirements: Contact the institution for details.

F33 UNIVERSITY COLLEGE FALMOUTH
WOODLANE
FALMOUTH
CORNWALL TR11 4RH
t: 01326213730
e: admissions@falmouth.ac.uk
// www.falmouth.ac.uk

W890 BA(Hons) Creative Writing
Duration: 3FT Hon
Entry Requirements: *GCE:* 220. *IB:* 24. Interview required.

Q3W8 BA(Hons) English with Creative Writing
Duration: 3FT Hon
Entry Requirements: *GCE:* 220. *IB:* 24. Interview required.

G14 UNIVERSITY OF GLAMORGAN, CARDIFF AND PONTYPRIDD
ENQUIRIES AND ADMISSIONS UNIT
PONTYPRIDD CF37 1DL
t: 08456 434030 f: 01443 654050
e: enquiries@glam.ac.uk
// www.glam.ac.uk

W800 BA Creative and Professional Writing
Duration: 3FT Hon
Entry Requirements: *GCE:* BBC. *IB:* 25. *BTEC SubDip:* M. *BTEC Dip:* D*D*. *BTEC ExtDip:* DMM. Interview required. Portfolio required.

G50 THE UNIVERSITY OF GLOUCESTERSHIRE
PARK CAMPUS
THE PARK
CHELTENHAM GL50 2RH
t: 01242 714501 f: 01242 714869
e: admissions@glos.ac.uk
// www.glos.ac.uk

W800 BA Creative Writing
Duration: 3FT Hon
Entry Requirements: *GCE:* 280-300.

QWH8 BA English Language and Creative Writing
Duration: 3FT Hon
Entry Requirements: *GCE:* 280-300.

QW38 BA English Literature and Creative Writing
Duration: 3FT Hon
Entry Requirements: *GCE:* 280-300.

G53 GLYNDWR UNIVERSITY
PLAS COCH
MOLD ROAD
WREXHAM LL11 2AW
t: 01978 293439 f: 01978 290008
e: sid@glyndwr.ac.uk
// www.glyndwr.ac.uk

WV81 BA Creative Writing and History
Duration: 3FT Hon
Entry Requirements: *GCE:* 240.

WQ83 BA English and Creative Writing
Duration: 3FT Hon
Entry Requirements: *GCE:* 240.

G56 GOLDSMITHS, UNIVERSITY OF LONDON
GOLDSMITHS, UNIVERSITY OF LONDON
NEW CROSS
LONDON SE14 6NW
t: 020 7048 5300 f: 020 7919 7509
e: admissions@gold.ac.uk
// www.gold.ac.uk

Q3W8 BA English with Creative Writing
Duration: 3FT Hon
Entry Requirements: *GCE:* AAB. *SQAH:* ABBBB. *SQAAH:* ABB. *IB:* 34. Interview required. Portfolio required.

G70 UNIVERSITY OF GREENWICH
GREENWICH CAMPUS
OLD ROYAL NAVAL COLLEGE
PARK ROW
LONDON SE10 9LS
t: 020 8331 9000 f: 020 8331 8145
e: courseinfo@gre.ac.uk
// www.gre.ac.uk

W801 BA Creative Writing
Duration: 3FT Hon
Entry Requirements: *GCE:* 280. *IB:* 24.

QW38 BA Creative Writing and English Literature
Duration: 3FT Hon
Entry Requirements: *GCE:* 240. *IB:* 24.

WV85 BA Creative Writing and Philosophy
Duration: 3FT Hon
Entry Requirements: *GCE:* 240. *IB:* 24.

Q3W8 BA English Literature with Creative Writing
Duration: 3FT Hon
Entry Requirements: *GCE:* 240. *IB:* 24.

W800 FdA Professional Writing
Duration: 2FT Fdg
Entry Requirements: Contact the institution for details.

G80 GRIMSBY INSTITUTE OF FURTHER AND HIGHER EDUCATION
NUNS CORNER
GRIMSBY
NE LINCOLNSHIRE DN34 5BQ
t: 0800 328 3631
e: headmissions@grimsby.ac.uk
// www.grimsby.ac.uk

W800 BA Professional Writing
Duration: 3FT Hon
Entry Requirements: *GCE:* 120-240. Interview required.

H36 UNIVERSITY OF HERTFORDSHIRE
UNIVERSITY ADMISSIONS SERVICE
COLLEGE LANE
HATFIELD
HERTS AL10 9AB
t: 01707 284800
// www.herts.ac.uk

Q1W8 BA English Language & Communication with Creative Writing
Duration: 3FT Hon
Entry Requirements: *GCE:* 300.

Q3W8 BA English Literature with Creative Writing
Duration: 3FT Hon
Entry Requirements: *GCE:* 300.

WW68 BA Film and Television Fiction
Duration: 3FT Hon
Entry Requirements: *GCE:* 300. Interview required. Portfolio required.

V1W8 BA History with Creative Writing
Duration: 3FT Hon
Entry Requirements: *GCE:* 300.

V5W8 BA Philosophy with Creative Writing
Duration: 3FT Hon
Entry Requirements: *GCE:* 300.

H60 THE UNIVERSITY OF HUDDERSFIELD
QUEENSGATE
HUDDERSFIELD HD1 3DH
t: 01484 473969 f: 01484 472765
e: admissionsandrecords@hud.ac.uk
// www.hud.ac.uk

Q3WV BA English Language with Creative Writing
Duration: 3FT Hon
Entry Requirements: *GCE:* 320.

Q3WW BA English Literature with Creative Writing
Duration: 3FT Hon
Entry Requirements: *GCE:* 320. *SQAH:* BBBB.

Q3W8 BA English with Creative Writing
Duration: 3FT Hon
Entry Requirements: *GCE:* 320.

H72 THE UNIVERSITY OF HULL
THE UNIVERSITY OF HULL
COTTINGHAM ROAD
HULL HU6 7RX
t: 01482 466100 f: 01482 442290
e: admissions@hull.ac.uk
// www.hull.ac.uk

T7W8 BA American Studies with Creative Writing
Duration: 3FT Hon
Entry Requirements: *GCE:* 280-320. *IB:* 28. *BTEC ExtDip:* DMM.

WT87 BA Creative Writing and American Studies
Duration: 3FT Hon
Entry Requirements: *GCE:* 280-320. *IB:* 30. *BTEC ExtDip:* DDM.

WQ83 BA Creative Writing and English
Duration: 3FT Hon
Entry Requirements: *GCE:* 300-340. *IB:* 30. *BTEC ExtDip:* DDM.

WW86 BA Creative Writing and Film Studies
Duration: 3FT Hon
Entry Requirements: *GCE:* 280-320. *IB:* 30. *BTEC ExtDip:* DDM.

WV85 BA Creative Writing and Philosophy
Duration: 3FT Hon
Entry Requirements: *GCE:* 280-320. *IB:* 30. *BTEC ExtDip:* DDM.

WV86 BA Creative Writing and Religion
Duration: 3FT Hon
Entry Requirements: *GCE:* 280-320. *IB:* 30. *BTEC ExtDip:* DDM.

V5W8 BA Philosophy with Creative Writing
Duration: 3FT Hon
Entry Requirements: *GCE:* 280-320. *IB:* 28. *BTEC ExtDip:* DMM.

K12 KEELE UNIVERSITY
KEELE UNIVERSITY
STAFFORDSHIRE ST5 5BG
t: 01782 734005 f: 01782 632343
e: undergraduate@keele.ac.uk
// www.keele.ac.uk

Q3W8 BA English with Creative Writing
Duration: 3FT Hon
Entry Requirements: Contact the institution for details.

K84 KINGSTON UNIVERSITY
STUDENT INFORMATION & ADVICE CENTRE
COOPER HOUSE
40-46 SURBITON ROAD
KINGSTON UPON THAMES KT1 2HX
t: 0844 8552177 f: 020 8547 7080
e: aps@kingston.ac.uk
// www.kingston.ac.uk

NW18 BA Business and Creative Writing
Duration: 3FT Hon
Entry Requirements: *GCE:* 280. *IB:* 30.

WL83 BA Creative Writing and Criminology
Duration: 3FT Hon
Entry Requirements: *GCE:* 240-320. *SQAH:* BBCCC. *SQAAH:* BBC. *IB:* 30.

WL81 BA Creative Writing and Economics (Applied)
Duration: 3FT Hon
Entry Requirements: *GCE:* 240-320. *IB:* 30.

WQ83 BA Creative Writing and English Language & Communications
Duration: 3FT Hon
Entry Requirements: *GCE:* 220-360.

WQV3 BA Creative Writing and English Literature
Duration: 3FT Hon
Entry Requirements: *GCE:* 280-360.

WV81 BA Creative Writing and History
Duration: 3FT Hon
Entry Requirements: *GCE:* 240-360. *IB:* 30.

WL82 BA Creative Writing and Human Rights
Duration: 3FT Hon
Entry Requirements: *GCE:* 240-360. *IB:* 30.

WLV2 BA Creative Writing and International Relations
Duration: 3FT Hon
Entry Requirements: *GCE:* 240-360. *IB:* 30.

WM81 BA Creative Writing and Law
Duration: 3FT Hon
Entry Requirements: *GCE:* 280.

WLW2 BA Creative Writing and Politics
Duration: 3FT Hon
Entry Requirements: *GCE:* 240-360.

WC88 BA Creative Writing and Psychology
Duration: 3FT Hon
Entry Requirements: *GCE:* 220-360.

W8C8 BA Creative Writing with Psychology
Duration: 3FT Hon
Entry Requirements: *GCE:* 220-360.

C8W8 BA Psychology with Creative Writing
Duration: 3FT Hon
Entry Requirements: *GCE:* 240-360.

L14 LANCASTER UNIVERSITY
THE UNIVERSITY
LANCASTER
LANCASHIRE LA1 4YW
t: 01524 592029 f: 01524 846243
e: ugadmissions@lancaster.ac.uk
// www.lancs.ac.uk

Q3WV BA English Language and Creative Writing
Duration: 3FT Hon
Entry Requirements: *GCE:* AAA. *SQAH:* AAABB. *SQAAH:* AAA. *IB:* 36.

Q3W8 BA English Literature with Creative Writing
Duration: 3FT Hon
Entry Requirements: *GCE:* AAA. *SQAH:* AAABB. *SQAAH:* AAA. *IB:* 36.

QW38 BA English Literature, Creative Writing and Practice
Duration: 3FT Hon
Entry Requirements: *GCE:* AAA. *SQAH:* AAABB. *SQAAH:* AAA. *IB:* 36.

L24 LEEDS TRINITY UNIVERSITY COLLEGE
BROWNBERRIE LANE
HORSFORTH
LEEDS LS18 5HD
t: 0113 283 7150 f: 0113 283 7222
e: enquiries@leedstrinity.ac.uk
// www.leedstrinity.ac.uk

QW38 BA English and Writing
Duration: 3FT Hon
Entry Requirements: *GCE:* 240. *IB:* 24.

L51 LIVERPOOL JOHN MOORES UNIVERSITY
KINGSWAY HOUSE
HATTON GARDEN
LIVERPOOL L3 2AJ
t: 0151 231 5090 f: 0151 904 6368
e: courses@ljmu.ac.uk
// www.ljmu.ac.uk

W800 BA Creative Writing
Duration: 3FT Hon
Entry Requirements: *GCE:* 260. *IB:* 28.

WW86 BA Creative Writing and Film Studies
Duration: 3FT Hon
Entry Requirements: *GCE:* 280. *IB:* 29.

WQ83 BA English and Creative Writing
Duration: 3FT Hon
Entry Requirements: *GCE:* 260.

L68 LONDON METROPOLITAN UNIVERSITY
166-220 HOLLOWAY ROAD
LONDON N7 8DB
t: 020 7133 4200
e: admissions@londonmet.ac.uk
// www.londonmet.ac.uk

W800 BA Creative Writing
Duration: 3FT Hon
Entry Requirements: *GCE:* 260. *IB:* 28. Portfolio required.

WQV3 BA Creative Writing and English Literature
Duration: 3FT Hon
Entry Requirements: *GCE:* 260. *IB:* 28. Portfolio required.

L75 LONDON SOUTH BANK UNIVERSITY
ADMISSIONS AND RECRUITMENT CENTRE
90 LONDON ROAD
LONDON SE1 6LN
t: 0800 923 8888 f: 020 7815 8273
e: course.enquiry@lsbu.ac.uk
// www.lsbu.ac.uk

W801 BA Creative Writing
Duration: 3FT Hon
Entry Requirements: *GCE:* 240. *IB:* 24.

Q3W8 BA English with Creative Writing
Duration: 3FT Hon
Entry Requirements: *GCE:* 240. *IB:* 24.

M10 THE MANCHESTER COLLEGE
OPENSHAW CAMPUS
ASHTON OLD ROAD
OPENSHAW
MANCHESTER M11 2WH
t: 0800 068 8585 f: 0161 920 4103
e: enquiries@themanchestercollege.ac.uk
// www.themanchestercollege.ac.uk

W800 HNC Creative Writing
Duration: 1FT HNC
Entry Requirements: *GCE:* 120. Interview required.

M40 THE MANCHESTER METROPOLITAN UNIVERSITY
ADMISSIONS OFFICE
ALL SAINTS (GMS)
ALL SAINTS
MANCHESTER M15 6BH
t: 0161 247 2000
// www.mmu.ac.uk

NW18 BA Business/Creative Writing
Duration: 3FT Hon
Entry Requirements: *GCE:* 280. *IB:* 28. *BTEC Dip:* D*D*. *BTEC ExtDip:* DMM. Portfolio required.

W800 BA Creative Writing
Duration: 3FT Hon
Entry Requirements: *GCE:* 280. *IB:* 28. *BTEC Dip:* D*D*. *BTEC ExtDip:* DMM. Interview required.

WQ83 BA Creative Writing/English
Duration: 3FT Hon
Entry Requirements: *GCE:* 280. *IB:* 28. *BTEC Dip:* D*D*. *BTEC ExtDip:* DMM. Portfolio required.

WW86 BA Creative Writing/Film & Television Studies
Duration: 3FT Hon
Entry Requirements: *GCE:* 280. *IB:* 28. *BTEC Dip:* D*D*. *BTEC ExtDip:* DMM. Portfolio required.

WV85 BA Creative Writing/Philosophy
Duration: 3FT Hon
Entry Requirements: *GCE:* 280. *IB:* 28. *BTEC Dip:* D*D*. *BTEC ExtDip:* DMM. Portfolio required.

QW38 BA English and Creative Writing
Duration: 3FT Hon
Entry Requirements: *GCE:* 280. *IB:* 28. Interview required. Portfolio required.

WC8P BA/BSc Creative Writing/Outdoor Studies
Duration: 3FT Hon
Entry Requirements: *GCE:* 280. *IB:* 28. *BTEC Dip:* D*D*. *BTEC ExtDip:* DMM. Portfolio required.

WC88 BA/BSc Creative Writing/Psychology
Duration: 3FT Hon
Entry Requirements: *GCE:* 280. *IB:* 28. *BTEC Dip:* D*D*. *BTEC ExtDip:* DMM. Portfolio required.

M80 MIDDLESEX UNIVERSITY
MIDDLESEX UNIVERSITY
THE BURROUGHS
LONDON NW4 4BT
t: 020 8411 5555 f: 020 8411 5649
e: enquiries@mdx.ac.uk
// www.mdx.ac.uk

WQ83 BA Creative Writing and English Literature
Duration: 3FT Hon
Entry Requirements: *GCE:* 200-300. *IB:* 28.

N36 NEWMAN UNIVERSITY COLLEGE, BIRMINGHAM
GENNERS LANE
BARTLEY GREEN
BIRMINGHAM B32 3NT
t: 0121 476 1181 f: 0121 476 1196
e: Admissions@newman.ac.uk
// www.newman.ac.uk

X3W8 BA Education Studies with Creative Writing
Duration: 3FT Hon
Entry Requirements: *Foundation:* Distinction. *GCE:* 260. *IB:* 24. *BTEC ExtDip:* DMM. *OCR ND:* M2 *OCR NED:* M2

V1W8 BA History with Creative Writing
Duration: 3FT Hon
Entry Requirements: *Foundation:* Distinction. *GCE:* 260. *IB:* 24. *BTEC ExtDip:* DMM. *OCR ND:* M2 *OCR NED:* M2

G5W8 BA IT with Creative Writing
Duration: 3FT Hon
Entry Requirements: *Foundation:* Distinction. *GCE:* 260. *IB:* 24. *BTEC ExtDip:* DMM. *OCR ND:* M2 *OCR NED:* M2

C8W8 BA Psychology with Creative Writing
Duration: 3FT Hon
Entry Requirements: *Foundation:* Distinction. *GCE:* 280. *IB:* 25. *BTEC ExtDip:* DMM. *OCR ND:* M2 *OCR NED:* M2

C6W8 BA Sports Studies with Creative Writing
Duration: 3FT Hon
Entry Requirements: *Foundation:* Distinction. *GCE:* 280. *IB:* 25. *BTEC ExtDip:* DMM. *OCR ND:* M2 *OCR NED:* M2

V6W8 BA Theology with Creative Writing
Duration: 3FT Hon
Entry Requirements: *Foundation:* Distinction. *GCE:* 260. *IB:* 24. *BTEC ExtDip:* DMM. *OCR ND:* M2 *OCR NED:* M2

L5W8 BA Working with Children Young People & Families with Creative Writing
Duration: 3FT Hon
Entry Requirements: *Foundation:* Distinction. *GCE:* 260. *IB:* 24.
BTEC ExtDip: DMM. *OCR ND:* M2 *OCR NED:* M2

N37 UNIVERSITY OF WALES, NEWPORT
ADMISSIONS
LODGE ROAD
CAERLEON
NEWPORT NP18 3QT
t: 01633 432030 f: 01633 432850
e: admissions@newport.ac.uk
// www.newport.ac.uk

VW68 BA Religious Studies and Creative Writing
Duration: 3FT Hon
Entry Requirements: *GCE:* 260. *IB:* 24.

Q3W8 BA/BSc English with Creative Writing
Duration: 3FT Hon
Entry Requirements: *GCE:* 260. *IB:* 24.

N38 UNIVERSITY OF NORTHAMPTON
PARK CAMPUS
BOUGHTON GREEN ROAD
NORTHAMPTON NN2 7AL
t: 0800 358 2232 f: 01604 722083
e: admissions@northampton.ac.uk
// www.northampton.ac.uk

N4W8 BA Accounting/Creative Writing
Duration: 3FT Hon
Entry Requirements: *GCE:* 260-280. *SQAH:* AAA-BBBB. *IB:* 24.
BTEC Dip: DD. *BTEC ExtDip:* DMM. *OCR ND:* D *OCR NED:* M2

N5WV BA Advertising/Creative Writing
Duration: 3FT Hon
Entry Requirements: *GCE:* 260-280. *SQAH:* AAA-BBBB. *IB:* 24.
BTEC Dip: DD. *BTEC ExtDip:* DMM. *OCR ND:* D *OCR NED:* M2

N1WV BA Business Entrepreneurship/Creative Writing
Duration: 3FT Hon
Entry Requirements: *GCE:* 260-280. *SQAH:* AAA-BBBB. *IB:* 24.
BTEC Dip: DD. *BTEC ExtDip:* DMM. *OCR ND:* D *OCR NED:* M2

N1W8 BA Business/Creative Writing
Duration: 3FT Hon
Entry Requirements: *GCE:* 260-280. *SQAH:* AAA-BBBB. *IB:* 24.
BTEC Dip: DD. *BTEC ExtDip:* DMM. *OCR ND:* D *OCR NED:* M2

W800 BA Creative Writing
Duration: 3FT Hon
Entry Requirements: *GCE:* 260-280. *SQAH:* AAA-BBBB. *IB:* 24.
BTEC Dip: DD. *BTEC ExtDip:* DMM. *OCR ND:* D *OCR NED:* M2

W8NA BA Creative Writing with Applied Management
Duration: 3FT Hon
Entry Requirements: *GCE:* 260-280. *SQAH:* AAA-BBBB. *IB:* 24.
BTEC Dip: DD. *BTEC ExtDip:* DMM. *OCR ND:* D *OCR NED:* M2

W8N4 BA Creative Writing/Accounting
Duration: 3FT Hon
Entry Requirements: *GCE:* 260-280. *SQAH:* AAA-BBBB. *IB:* 24.
BTEC Dip: DD. *BTEC ExtDip:* DMM. *OCR ND:* D *OCR NED:* M2

W8NM BA Creative Writing/Advertising
Duration: 3FT Hon
Entry Requirements: *GCE:* 260-280. *SQAH:* AAA-BBBB. *IB:* 24.
BTEC Dip: DD. *BTEC ExtDip:* DMM. *OCR ND:* D *OCR NED:* M2

W8C1 BA Creative Writing/Biological Conservation
Duration: 3FT Hon
Entry Requirements: *GCE:* 260-280. *SQAH:* AAA-BBBB. *IB:* 24.
BTEC Dip: DD. *BTEC ExtDip:* DMM. *OCR ND:* D *OCR NED:* M2

W8N1 BA Creative Writing/Business
Duration: 3FT Hon
Entry Requirements: *GCE:* 260-280. *SQAH:* AAA-BBBB. *IB:* 24.
BTEC Dip: DD. *BTEC ExtDip:* DMM. *OCR ND:* D *OCR NED:* M2

W8NF BA Creative Writing/Business Entrepreneurship
Duration: 3FT Hon
Entry Requirements: *GCE:* 260-280. *SQAH:* AAA-BBBB. *IB:* 24.
BTEC Dip: DD. *BTEC ExtDip:* DMM. *OCR ND:* D *OCR NED:* M2

W8G4 BA Creative Writing/Computing
Duration: 3FT Hon
Entry Requirements: *GCE:* 260-280. *SQAH:* AAA-BBBB. *IB:* 24.
BTEC Dip: DD. *BTEC ExtDip:* DMM. *OCR ND:* D *OCR NED:* M2

W8M9 BA Creative Writing/Criminology
Duration: 3FT Hon
Entry Requirements: *GCE:* 260-280. *SQAH:* AAA-BBBB. *IB:* 24.
BTEC Dip: DD. *BTEC ExtDip:* DMM. *OCR ND:* D *OCR NED:* M2

W8X3 BA Creative Writing/Education Studies
Duration: 3FT Hon
Entry Requirements: *GCE:* 260-280. *SQAH:* AAA-BBBB. *IB:* 24.
BTEC Dip: DD. *BTEC ExtDip:* DMM. *OCR ND:* D *OCR NED:* M2

W8Q3 BA Creative Writing/English
Duration: 3FT Hon
Entry Requirements: *GCE:* 260-280. *SQAH:* AAA-BBBB. *IB:* 24.
BTEC Dip: DD. *BTEC ExtDip:* DMM. *OCR ND:* D *OCR NED:* M2

W8NV BA Creative Writing/Events Management
Duration: 3FT Hon
Entry Requirements: *GCE:* 260-280. *SQAH:* AAA-BBBB. *IB:* 24.
BTEC Dip: DD. *BTEC ExtDip:* DMM. *OCR ND:* D *OCR NED:* M2

W8W6 BA Creative Writing/Film & Television Studies
Duration: 3FT Hon
Entry Requirements: *GCE:* 260-280. *SQAH:* AAA-BBBB. *IB:* 24.
BTEC Dip: DD. *BTEC ExtDip:* DMM. *OCR ND:* D *OCR NED:* M2

W8W1 BA Creative Writing/Fine Art Painting & Drawing
Duration: 3FT Hon
Entry Requirements: *GCE:* 260-280. *SQAH:* AAA-BBBB. *IB:* 24.
BTEC Dip: DD. *BTEC ExtDip:* DMM. *OCR ND:* D *OCR NED:* M2

W8R1 BA Creative Writing/French
Duration: 3FT Hon
Entry Requirements: *GCE:* 260-280. *SQAH:* AAA-BBBB. *IB:* 24.
BTEC Dip: DD. *BTEC ExtDip:* DMM. *OCR ND:* D *OCR NED:* M2

W8L4 BA Creative Writing/Health Studies
Duration: 3FT Hon
Entry Requirements: *GCE:* 260-280. *SQAH:* AAA-BBBB. *IB:* 24.
BTEC Dip: DD. *BTEC ExtDip:* DMM. *OCR ND:* D *OCR NED:* M2

W8V1 BA Creative Writing/History
Duration: 3FT Hon
Entry Requirements: *GCE:* 260-280. *SQAH:* AAA-BBBB. *IB:* 24.
BTEC Dip: DD. *BTEC ExtDip:* DMM. *OCR ND:* D *OCR NED:* M2

W8B1 BA Creative Writing/Human Bioscience
Duration: 3FT Hon
Entry Requirements: *GCE:* 260-280. *SQAH:* AAA-BBBB. *IB:* 24.
BTEC Dip: DD. *BTEC ExtDip:* DMM. *OCR ND:* D *OCR NED:* M2

W8L7 BA Creative Writing/Human Geography
Duration: 3FT Hon
Entry Requirements: *GCE:* 260-280. *SQAH:* AAA-BBBB. *IB:* 24.
BTEC Dip: DD. *BTEC ExtDip:* DMM. *OCR ND:* D *OCR NED:* M2

W8N6 BA Creative Writing/Human Resource Management
Duration: 3FT Hon
Entry Requirements: *GCE:* 260-280. *SQAH:* AAA-BBBB. *IB:* 24.
BTEC Dip: DD. *BTEC ExtDip:* DMM. *OCR ND:* D *OCR NED:* M2

W8L9 BA Creative Writing/International Development
Duration: 3FT Hon
Entry Requirements: *GCE:* 260-280. *SQAH:* AAA-BBBB. *IB:* 24.
BTEC Dip: DD. *BTEC ExtDip:* DMM. *OCR ND:* D *OCR NED:* M2

W8M1 BA Creative Writing/Law
Duration: 3FT Hon
Entry Requirements: *GCE:* 260-280. *SQAH:* AAA-BBBB. *IB:* 24.
BTEC Dip: DD. *BTEC ExtDip:* DMM. *OCR ND:* D *OCR NED:* M2

W8N2 BA Creative Writing/Management
Duration: 3FT Hon
Entry Requirements: *GCE:* 260-280. *SQAH:* AAA-BBBB. *IB:* 24.
BTEC Dip: DD. *BTEC ExtDip:* DMM. *OCR ND:* D *OCR NED:* M2

W8N5 BA Creative Writing/Marketing
Duration: 3FT Hon
Entry Requirements: *GCE:* 260-280. *SQAH:* AAA-BBBB. *IB:* 24.
BTEC Dip: DD. *BTEC ExtDip:* DMM. *OCR ND:* D *OCR NED:* M2

W8L5 BA Creative Writing/Social Care
Duration: 3FT Hon
Entry Requirements: *GCE:* 260-280. *SQAH:* AAA-BBBB. *IB:* 24.
BTEC Dip: DD. *BTEC ExtDip:* DMM. *OCR ND:* D *OCR NED:* M2

W8L3 BA Creative Writing/Sociology
Duration: 3FT Hon
Entry Requirements: *GCE:* 260-280. *SQAH:* AAA-BBBB. *IB:* 24.
BTEC Dip: DD. *BTEC ExtDip:* DMM. *OCR ND:* D *OCR NED:* M2

W8C6 BA Creative Writing/Sport Studies
Duration: 3FT Hon
Entry Requirements: *GCE:* 260-280. *SQAH:* AAA-BBBB. *IB:* 24.
BTEC Dip: DD. *BTEC ExtDip:* DMM. *OCR ND:* D *OCR NED:* M2

W8N8 BA Creative Writing/Tourism
Duration: 3FT Hon
Entry Requirements: *GCE:* 260-280. *SQAH:* AAA-BBBB. *IB:* 24.
BTEC Dip: DD. *BTEC ExtDip:* DMM. *OCR ND:* D *OCR NED:* M2

M9W8 BA Criminology/Creative Writing
Duration: 3FT Hon
Entry Requirements: *GCE:* 260-280. *SQAH:* AAA-BBBB. *IB:* 24.
BTEC Dip: DD. *BTEC ExtDip:* DMM. *OCR ND:* D *OCR NED:* M2

X3W8 BA Education Studies/Creative Writing
Duration: 3FT Hon
Entry Requirements: *GCE:* 260-280. *SQAH:* AAA-BBBB. *IB:* 24.
BTEC Dip: DD. *BTEC ExtDip:* DMM. *OCR ND:* D *OCR NED:* M2

Q3W8 BA English/Creative Writing
Duration: 3FT Hon
Entry Requirements: *GCE:* 260-280. *SQAH:* AAA-BBBB. *IB:* 24.
BTEC Dip: DD. *BTEC ExtDip:* DMM. *OCR ND:* D *OCR NED:* M2

N8WV BA Events Management/Creative Writing
Duration: 3FT Hon
Entry Requirements: *GCE:* 260-280. *SQAH:* AAA-BBBB. *IB:* 24.
BTEC Dip: DD. *BTEC ExtDip:* DMM. *OCR ND:* D *OCR NED:* M2

W6W8 BA Film & Television Studies/Creative Writing
Duration: 3FT Hon
Entry Requirements: *GCE:* 260-280. *SQAH:* AAA-BBBB. *IB:* 24.
BTEC Dip: DD. *BTEC ExtDip:* DMM. *OCR ND:* D *OCR NED:* M2

W1W8 BA Fine Art Painting & Drawing/Creative Writing
Duration: 3FT Hon
Entry Requirements: *GCE:* 260-280. *SQAH:* AAA-BBBB. *IB:* 24.
BTEC Dip: DD. *BTEC ExtDip:* DMM. *OCR ND:* D *OCR NED:* M2

R1W8 BA French/Creative Writing
Duration: 3FT Hon
Entry Requirements: *GCE:* 260-280. *SQAH:* AAA-BBBB. *IB:* 24.
BTEC Dip: DD. *BTEC ExtDip:* DMM. *OCR ND:* D *OCR NED:* M2

L4W8 BA Health Studies/Creative Writing
Duration: 3FT Hon
Entry Requirements: *GCE:* 260-280. *SQAH:* AAA-BBBB. *IB:* 24.
BTEC Dip: DD. *BTEC ExtDip:* DMM. *OCR ND:* D *OCR NED:* M2

V1W8 BA History/Creative Writing
Duration: 3FT Hon
Entry Requirements: *GCE:* 260-280. *SQAH:* AAA-BBBB. *IB:* 24.
BTEC Dip: DD. *BTEC ExtDip:* DMM. *OCR ND:* D *OCR NED:* M2

L7W8 BA Human Geography/Creative Writing
Duration: 3FT Hon
Entry Requirements: *GCE:* 260-280. *SQAH:* AAA-BBBB. *IB:* 24.
BTEC Dip: DD. *BTEC ExtDip:* DMM. *OCR ND:* D *OCR NED:* M2

N6W8 BA Human Resource Management/Creative Writing
Duration: 3FT Hon
Entry Requirements: *GCE:* 260-280. *SQAH:* AAA-BBBB. *IB:* 24.
BTEC Dip: DD. *BTEC ExtDip:* DMM. *OCR ND:* D *OCR NED:* M2

L9W8 BA International Development/Creative Writing
Duration: 3FT Hon
Entry Requirements: *GCE:* 260-280. *SQAH:* AAA-BBBB. *IB:* 24.
BTEC Dip: DD. *BTEC ExtDip:* DMM. *OCR ND:* D *OCR NED:* M2

M1W8 BA Law/Creative Writing
Duration: 3FT Hon
Entry Requirements: *GCE:* 260-280. *SQAH:* AAA-BBBB. *IB:* 24.
BTEC Dip: DD. *BTEC ExtDip:* DMM. *OCR ND:* D *OCR NED:* M2

N2W8 BA Management/Creative Writing
Duration: 3FT Hon
Entry Requirements: *GCE:* 260-280. *SQAH:* AAA-BBBB. *IB:* 24.
BTEC Dip: DD. *BTEC ExtDip:* DMM. *OCR ND:* D *OCR NED:* M2

N5W8 BA Marketing/Creative Writing
Duration: 3FT Hon
Entry Requirements: *GCE:* 260-280. *SQAH:* AAA-BBBB. *IB:* 24.
BTEC Dip: DD. *BTEC ExtDip:* DMM. *OCR ND:* D *OCR NED:* M2

L5W8 BA Social Care/Creative Writing
Duration: 3FT Hon
Entry Requirements: *GCE:* 260-280. *SQAH:* AAA-BBBB. *IB:* 24.
BTEC Dip: DD. *BTEC ExtDip:* DMM. *OCR ND:* D *OCR NED:* M2

L3W8 BA Sociology/Creative Writing
Duration: 3FT Hon
Entry Requirements: *GCE:* 260-280. *SQAH:* AAA-BBBB. *IB:* 24.
BTEC Dip: DD. *BTEC ExtDip:* DMM. *OCR ND:* D *OCR NED:* M2

XW83 BA Special Educational Needs & Inclusion/Creative Writing
Duration: 3FT Hon
Entry Requirements: *GCE:* 260-280. *SQAH:* AAA-BBBB. *IB:* 24.
BTEC Dip: DD. *BTEC ExtDip:* DMM. *OCR ND:* D *OCR NED:* M2

C6W8 BA Sport Studies/Creative Writing
Duration: 3FT Hon
Entry Requirements: *GCE:* 260-280. *SQAH:* AAA-BBBB. *IB:* 24.
BTEC Dip: DD. *BTEC ExtDip:* DMM. *OCR ND:* D *OCR NED:* M2

N8W8 BA Tourism/Creative Writing
Duration: 3FT Hon
Entry Requirements: *GCE:* 260-280. *SQAH:* AAA-BBBB. *IB:* 24.
BTEC Dip: DD. *BTEC ExtDip:* DMM. *OCR ND:* D *OCR NED:* M2

C1W8 BSc Biological Conservation/Creative Writing
Duration: 3FT Hon
Entry Requirements: *GCE:* 260-280. *SQAH:* AAA-BBBB. *IB:* 24.
BTEC Dip: DD. *BTEC ExtDip:* DMM. *OCR ND:* D *OCR NED:* M2

G4W8 BSc Computing/Creative Writing
Duration: 3FT Hon
Entry Requirements: *GCE:* 260-280. *SQAH:* AAA-BBBB. *IB:* 24.
BTEC Dip: DD. *BTEC ExtDip:* DMM. *OCR ND:* D *OCR NED:* M2

B1W8 BSc Human Bioscience/Creative Writing
Duration: 3FT Hon
Entry Requirements: *GCE:* 260-280. *SQAH:* AAA-BBBB. *IB:* 24.
BTEC Dip: DD. *BTEC ExtDip:* DMM. *OCR ND:* D *OCR NED:* M2

N77 NORTHUMBRIA UNIVERSITY
TRINITY BUILDING
NORTHUMBERLAND ROAD
NEWCASTLE UPON TYNE NE1 8ST
t: 0191 243 7420 f: 0191 227 4561
e: er.admissions@northumbria.ac.uk
// www.northumbria.ac.uk

QW38 BA English Literature and Creative Writing
Duration: 3FT Hon
Entry Requirements: *GCE:* 320. *SQAH:* BBBBB. *SQAAH:* BBB. *IB:* 27.

N84 THE UNIVERSITY OF NOTTINGHAM
THE ADMISSIONS OFFICE
THE UNIVERSITY OF NOTTINGHAM
UNIVERSITY PARK
NOTTINGHAM NG7 2RD
t: 0115 951 5151 f: 0115 951 4668
// www.nottingham.ac.uk

W800 BA Creative and Professional Writing
Duration: 3FT Hon
Entry Requirements: *GCE:* BCC. *SQAAH:* BCC. *IB:* 28.

Q3W8 BA English with Creative Writing
Duration: 3FT Hon
Entry Requirements: *GCE:* AAA-AAB. *SQAAH:* AAA-AAB. *IB:* 36.
Interview required.

N91 NOTTINGHAM TRENT UNIVERSITY
DRYDEN BUILDING
BURTON STREET
NOTTINGHAM NG1 4BU
t: +44 (0) 115 848 4200 f: +44 (0) 115 848 8869
e: applications@ntu.ac.uk
// www.ntu.ac.uk

Q3W8 BA English with Creative Writing
Duration: 3FT Hon
Entry Requirements: *GCE:* 280. *BTEC ExtDip:* DMM. *OCR NED:* D2

P60 PLYMOUTH UNIVERSITY
DRAKE CIRCUS
PLYMOUTH PL4 8AA
t: 01752 585858 f: 01752 588055
e: admissions@plymouth.ac.uk
// www.plymouth.ac.uk

WQ83 BA English and Creative Writing
Duration: 3FT Hon
Entry Requirements: *GCE:* 300. *IB:* 27. *BTEC ExtDip:* DDM.

P63 UCP MARJON - UNIVERSITY COLLEGE PLYMOUTH ST MARK & ST JOHN
DERRIFORD ROAD
PLYMOUTH PL6 8BH
t: 01752 636890 f: 01752 636819
e: admissions@marjon.ac.uk
// www.ucpmarjon.ac.uk

W800 BA Creative Writing
Duration: 3FT Hon
Entry Requirements: *GCE:* 220.

W8Q3 BA Creative Writing with English Literature
Duration: 3FT Hon
Entry Requirements: *GCE:* 220.

Q3W8 BA English Literature with Creative Writing
Duration: 3FT Hon
Entry Requirements: *GCE:* 220.

P80 UNIVERSITY OF PORTSMOUTH
ACADEMIC REGISTRY
UNIVERSITY HOUSE
WINSTON CHURCHILL AVENUE
PORTSMOUTH PO1 2UP
t: 023 9284 8484 f: 023 9284 3082
e: admissions@port.ac.uk
// www.port.ac.uk

W800 BA Creative and Media Writing
Duration: 3FT Hon
Entry Requirements: *GCE:* 240-300. *IB:* 26. *BTEC SubDip:* P. *BTEC Dip:* DD. *BTEC ExtDip:* DMM.

QW38 BA English and Creative Writing
Duration: 3FT Hon
Entry Requirements: *GCE:* 240-300. *IB:* 26. *BTEC SubDip:* P. *BTEC Dip:* DD. *BTEC ExtDip:* DMM.

Q75 QUEEN'S UNIVERSITY BELFAST
UNIVERSITY ROAD
BELFAST BT7 1NN
t: 028 9097 3838 f: 028 9097 5151
e: admissions@qub.ac.uk
// www.qub.ac.uk

Q3W8 BA English with Creative Writing
Duration: 3FT Hon
Entry Requirements: *GCE:* ABB-BBBb. *SQAH:* ABBBB. *SQAAH:* ABB. *IB:* 34.

R18 REGENT'S COLLEGE, LONDON (INCORPORATING REGENT'S BUSINESS SCHOOL, LONDON)
INNER CIRCLE, REGENT'S COLLEGE
REGENT'S PARK
LONDON NW1 4NS
t: +44(0)20 7487 7505 f: +44(0)20 7487 7425
e: exrel@regents.ac.uk
// www.regents.ac.uk/

WW86 BA Screen Writing and Producing
Duration: 3FT Hon
Entry Requirements: *SQAH:* BBCC. *SQAAH:* CC.

R48 ROEHAMPTON UNIVERSITY
ROEHAMPTON LANE
LONDON SW15 5PU
t: 020 8392 3232 f: 020 8392 3470
e: enquiries@roehampton.ac.uk
// www.roehampton.ac.uk

W801 BA Creative Writing
Duration: 3FT Hon
Entry Requirements: *GCE:* 300. *IB:* 26. *BTEC ExtDip:* DDM. *OCR NED:* D2 Interview required.

WQ83 BA Creative Writing and English Literature
Duration: 3FT Hon
Entry Requirements: *GCE:* 300. *IB:* 26. *BTEC ExtDip:* DDM. *OCR NED:* D2 Interview required.

WV85 BA Creative Writing and Philosophy
Duration: 3FT Hon
Entry Requirements: *GCE:* 300. *IB:* 26. *BTEC ExtDip:* DDM. *OCR NED:* D2 Interview required.

WW68 BA Photography and Creative Writing
Duration: 3FT Hon
Entry Requirements: *GCE:* 300. *IB:* 26. *BTEC ExtDip:* DDM. *OCR NED:* D2 Interview required.

R72 ROYAL HOLLOWAY, UNIVERSITY OF LONDON
ROYAL HOLLOWAY, UNIVERSITY OF LONDON
EGHAM
SURREY TW20 0EX
t: 01784 414944 f: 01784 473662
e: Admissions@rhul.ac.uk
// www.rhul.ac.uk

QW38 BA English and Creative Writing
Duration: 3FT Hon
Entry Requirements: *GCE:* AAB. *SQAH:* AAAAB. *SQAAH:* AAB. *IB:* 35.

R90 RUSKIN COLLEGE OXFORD
WALTON STREET
OXFORD OX1 2HE
t: 01865 759604 f: 01865 759640
e: admissions@ruskin.ac.uk
// www.ruskin.ac.uk

QW38 BA English Studies:Creative Writing & Critical Practice
Duration: 3FT Hon
Entry Requirements: Contact the institution for details.

W810 FdA Writing for Performance
Duration: 2FT Fdg
Entry Requirements: Contact the institution for details.

S03 THE UNIVERSITY OF SALFORD
SALFORD M5 4WT
t: 0161 295 4545 f: 0161 295 4646
e: ug-admissions@salford.ac.uk
// www.salford.ac.uk

QW38 BA English and Creative Writing
Duration: 3FT Hon
Entry Requirements: *GCE:* 280. *IB:* 31. Interview required.

W890 BA Performance: Comedy Practices
Duration: 3FT Hon
Entry Requirements: *GCE:* 300. *IB:* 31. *OCR ND:* D *OCR NED:* M1 Interview required.

S21 SHEFFIELD HALLAM UNIVERSITY
CITY CAMPUS
HOWARD STREET
SHEFFIELD S1 1WB
t: 0114 225 5555 f: 0114 225 2167
e: admissions@shu.ac.uk
// www.shu.ac.uk

W800 BA Creative Writing
Duration: 3FT Hon
Entry Requirements: *GCE:* 300.

S30 SOUTHAMPTON SOLENT UNIVERSITY
EAST PARK TERRACE
SOUTHAMPTON
HAMPSHIRE SO14 0RT
t: +44 (0) 23 8031 9039 f: + 44 (0)23 8022 2259
e: admissions@solent.ac.uk
// www.solent.ac.uk/

WW48 BA Comedy - Writing and Performance
Duration: 3FT Hon
Entry Requirements: *Foundation:* Distinction. *GCE:* 240. *SQAAH:* AA-CCD. *IB:* 24. *BTEC ExtDip:* MMM. *OCR ND:* D *OCR NED:* M3 Interview required.

QW3V BA English and Screenwriting
Duration: 3FT Hon
Entry Requirements: *Foundation:* Distinction. *GCE:* 240. *SQAAH:* AA-CCD. *IB:* 24. *BTEC ExtDip:* MMM. *OCR ND:* D *OCR NED:* M3

QWH8 BA English and Screenwriting
Duration: 4SW Hon
Entry Requirements: *Foundation:* Distinction. *GCE:* 240. *SQAAH:* AA-CCD. *IB:* 24. *BTEC ExtDip:* MMM. *OCR ND:* D *OCR NED:* M3

W810 BA Screenwriting
Duration: 3FT Hon
Entry Requirements: *Foundation:* Distinction. *GCE:* 240. *SQAAH:* AA-CCD. *IB:* 24. *BTEC ExtDip:* MMM. *OCR ND:* D *OCR NED:* M3

W8Q3 BA Screenwriting with International Foundation Year
Duration: 4FT Hon
Entry Requirements: *GCE:* 240.

S43 SOUTH ESSEX COLLEGE OF FURTHER & HIGHER EDUCATION
LUKER ROAD
SOUTHEND-ON-SEA
ESSEX SS1 1ND
t: 0845 52 12345 f: 01702 432320
e: Admissions@southessex.ac.uk
// www.southessex.ac.uk

W801 CertHE Creative Writing for Media
Duration: 1FT Cer
Entry Requirements: Contact the institution for details.

W800 DipHE Creative Writing for Media
Duration: 2FT Dip
Entry Requirements: *GCE:* 160. *IB:* 24. Interview required.

S64 ST MARY'S UNIVERSITY COLLEGE, TWICKENHAM
WALDEGRAVE ROAD
STRAWBERRY HILL
MIDDLESEX TW1 4SX
t: 020 8240 4029 f: 020 8240 2361
e: admit@smuc.ac.uk
// www.smuc.ac.uk

WV86 BA Creative & Professional Writing and Theology & Religious Studies
Duration: 3FT Hon
Entry Requirements: *GCE:* 240. *SQAH:* BBBC. *IB:* 28. *OCR ND:* D *OCR NED:* M3 Interview required.

W800 BA Creative and Professional Writing
Duration: 3FT Hon
Entry Requirements: *GCE:* 240. *SQAH:* BBBC. *IB:* 28. *OCR ND:* D *OCR NED:* M3 Interview required.

QW38 BA English and Creative & Professional Writing
Duration: 3FT Hon
Entry Requirements: *GCE:* 240. *SQAH:* BBBC. *IB:* 28. *OCR ND:* D *OCR NED:* M3 Interview required.

XW38 BA Physical & Sport Education and Creative & Professional Writing
Duration: 3FT Hon
Entry Requirements: *GCE:* 240. *SQAH:* BBBC. *IB:* 28. *OCR ND:* D *OCR NED:* M3 Interview required.

S72 STAFFORDSHIRE UNIVERSITY
COLLEGE ROAD
STOKE ON TRENT ST4 2DE
t: 01782 292753 f: 01782 292740
e: admissions@staffs.ac.uk
// www.staffs.ac.uk

W800 BA Creative Writing
Duration: 3FT Hon
Entry Requirements: *GCE:* 200-240. *IB:* 24. *BTEC Dip:* DD. *BTEC ExtDip:* MMM.

WV81 BA Creative Writing and Modern History
Duration: 3FT Hon
Entry Requirements: *GCE:* 200-240. *IB:* 24. *BTEC Dip:* DD. *BTEC ExtDip:* MMM.

WV85 BA Creative Writing and Philosophy
Duration: 3FT Hon
Entry Requirements: *GCE:* 200-240. *IB:* 24. *BTEC Dip:* DD. *BTEC ExtDip:* MMM.

QWH8 BA English Literature and Scriptwriting
Duration: 3FT Hon
Entry Requirements: *GCE:* 200-240. *IB:* 24. *BTEC Dip:* DD. *BTEC ExtDip:* MMM.

QW38 BA English and Creative Writing
Duration: 3FT Hon
Entry Requirements: *GCE:* 200-240. *IB:* 24. *BTEC Dip:* DD. *BTEC ExtDip:* MMM.

W810 BA Scriptwriting
Duration: 3FT Hon
Entry Requirements: *GCE:* 200-240. *IB:* 24. *BTEC Dip:* DD. *BTEC ExtDip:* MMM.

S84 UNIVERSITY OF SUNDERLAND
STUDENT HELPLINE
THE STUDENT GATEWAY
CHESTER ROAD
SUNDERLAND SR1 3SD
t: 0191 515 3000 f: 0191 515 3805
e: student.helpline@sunderland.ac.uk
// www.sunderland.ac.uk

QW38 BA English and Creative Writing
Duration: 3FT Hon
Entry Requirements: *GCE:* 260-360.

P390 BA Scriptwriting: Film, Television and Radio
Duration: 3FT Hon
Entry Requirements: *GCE:* 260-360. *IB:* 30.

S85 UNIVERSITY OF SURREY
STAG HILL
GUILDFORD
SURREY GU2 7XH
t: +44(0)1483 689305 f: +44(0)1483 689388
e: ugteam@surrey.ac.uk
// www.surrey.ac.uk

Q3W8 BA English Literature with Creative Writing (3 years)
Duration: 3FT Hon
Entry Requirements: *GCE:* 320.

Q3WV BA English Literature with Creative Writing (4 years)
Duration: 4SW Hon
Entry Requirements: *GCE:* 320.

W6W8 BA (Hons) Film Studies with Creative Writing (3 or 4 years)
Duration: 3FT/4SW Hon
Entry Requirements: *GCE:* ABB. *IB:* 34.

T20 TEESSIDE UNIVERSITY
MIDDLESBROUGH TS1 3BA
t: 01642 218121 f: 01642 384201
e: registry@tees.ac.uk
// www.tees.ac.uk

Q3W8 BA English Studies with Creative Writing
Duration: 3FT Hon
Entry Requirements: *GCE:* 280. *IB:* 25.

T80 UNIVERSITY OF WALES TRINITY SAINT DAVID
COLLEGE ROAD
CARMARTHEN SA31 3EP
t: 01267 676767 f: 01267 676766
e: registry@trinitysaintdavid.ac.uk
// www.tsd.ac.uk

W801 BA Creative Writing
Duration: 3FT Hon
Entry Requirements: GCE: 120-360. IB: 26. Interview required.

QW38 BA Creative Writing and English
Duration: 3FT Hon
Entry Requirements: GCE: 120-360. IB: 26. Interview required.

WV85 BA Creative Writing and Philosophy
Duration: 3FT Hon
Entry Requirements: Contact the institution for details.

U40 UNIVERSITY OF THE WEST OF SCOTLAND
PAISLEY
RENFREWSHIRE
SCOTLAND PA1 2BE
t: 0141 848 3727 f: 0141 848 3623
e: admissions@uws.ac.uk
// www.uws.ac.uk

WW68 BA Filmmaking and Screen Writing
Duration: 4FT Hon
Entry Requirements: GCE: BC-CC. SQAH: BBC. Interview required. Portfolio required.

W20 THE UNIVERSITY OF WARWICK
COVENTRY CV4 8UW
t: 024 7652 3723 f: 024 7652 4649
e: ugadmissions@warwick.ac.uk
// www.warwick.ac.uk

QW38 BA English Literature and Creative Writing
Duration: 3FT Hon
Entry Requirements: GCE: AAA. SQAAH: AA. IB: 38. Interview required.

W50 UNIVERSITY OF WESTMINSTER
2ND FLOOR, CAVENDISH HOUSE
101 NEW CAVENDISH STREET,
LONDON W1W 6XH
t: 020 7915 5511
e: course-enquiries@westminster.ac.uk
// www.westminster.ac.uk

QW38 BA English Language and Creative Writing
Duration: 3FT Hon
Entry Requirements: GCE: BBC. SQAH: BBCCC. SQAAH: BCC. IB: 30. Portfolio required.

QW3V BA English Literature and Creative Writing
Duration: 3FT Hon
Entry Requirements: GCE: BBC. SQAH: BBCCC. SQAAH: BCC. IB: 30. Portfolio required.

QW18 BA Linguistics and Creative Writing
Duration: 3FT Hon
Entry Requirements: GCE: BBC. SQAH: BBCCC. SQAAH: BCC. IB: 30. Portfolio required.

W75 UNIVERSITY OF WOLVERHAMPTON
ADMISSIONS UNIT
MX207, CAMP STREET
WOLVERHAMPTON
WEST MIDLANDS WV1 1AD
t: 01902 321000 f: 01902 321896
e: admissions@wlv.ac.uk
// www.wlv.ac.uk

WQ83 BA Creative & Professional Writing and English
Duration: 3FT Hon
Entry Requirements: GCE: 160-220.

QW38 BA English Language and Creative Professional Writing
Duration: 3FT Hon
Entry Requirements: GCE: 160-220.

VW58 BA Philosophy and Creative Professional Writing
Duration: 3FT Hon
Entry Requirements: GCE: 160-220.

W76 UNIVERSITY OF WINCHESTER
WINCHESTER
HANTS SO22 4NR
t: 01962 827234 f: 01962 827288
e: course.enquiries@winchester.ac.uk
// www.winchester.ac.uk

TWR8 BA American Studies and Creative Writing
Duration: 3FT Hon
Entry Requirements: Foundation: Distinction. GCE: 260-300. IB: 25. OCR ND: D OCR NED: M2

VWK8 BA Archaeology and Creative Writing
Duration: 3FT Hon
Entry Requirements: Foundation: Distinction. GCE: 260-300. IB: 24. OCR ND: D OCR NED: M2

NWC8 BA Business Management and Creative Writing
Duration: 3FT Hon
Entry Requirements: Foundation: Distinction. GCE: 260-300. IB: 25. OCR ND: D OCR NED: M2

LW5V BA Childhood Youth & Community Studies and Creative Writing
Duration: 3FT Hon
Entry Requirements: *GCE:* 260-300. *IB:* 24.

W800 BA Creative Writing
Duration: 3FT Hon
Entry Requirements: *Foundation:* Distinction. *GCE:* 260-300. *IB:* 26. *OCR ND:* D

WL8J BA Creative Writing and Criminology
Duration: 3FT Hon
Entry Requirements: *Foundation:* Distinction. *GCE:* 260-300. *IB:* 25. *OCR ND:* D *OCR NED:* M2

WX83 BA Creative Writing and Education Studies
Duration: 3FT Hon
Entry Requirements: *Foundation:* Distinction. *GCE:* 260-300. *IB:* 25. *OCR ND:* D *OCR NED:* M2

WXW3 BA Creative Writing and Education Studies (Early Years)
Duration: 3FT Hon
Entry Requirements: *Foundation:* Distinction. *GCE:* 260-300. *IB:* 25. *OCR ND:* D *OCR NED:* M2

WX8H BA Creative Writing and Education Studies (Modern Liberal Arts)
Duration: 3FT Hon
Entry Requirements: *Foundation:* Distinction. *GCE:* 260-300. *IB:* 25. *OCR ND:* D *OCR NED:* M2

QW38 BA Creative Writing and English
Duration: 3FT Hon
Entry Requirements: *Foundation:* Distinction. *GCE:* 260-300. *IB:* 25. *OCR ND:* D *OCR NED:* M2

WQ83 BA Creative Writing and English Language Studies
Duration: 3FT Hon
Entry Requirements: *Foundation:* Distinction. *GCE:* 260-300. *IB:* 25. *OCR ND:* D *OCR NED:* M2

WW86 BA Creative Writing and Film & Cinema Technologies
Duration: 3FT Hon
Entry Requirements: *Foundation:* Distinction. *GCE:* 260-300. *IB:* 25. *OCR ND:* D *OCR NED:* M2

VWC8 BA Creative Writing and History
Duration: 3FT Hon
Entry Requirements: *Foundation:* Distinction. *GCE:* 260-300. *IB:* 25. *OCR ND:* D *OCR NED:* M2

WW8X BA Creative Writing and Modern Liberal Arts
Duration: 3FT Hon
Entry Requirements: *Foundation:* Distinction. *GCE:* 260-300. *IB:* 25. *OCR ND:* D *OCR NED:* M2

WWL8 BA Creative Writing and Performing Arts (Contemporary Performance)
Duration: 3FT Hon
Entry Requirements: *Foundation:* Distinction. *GCE:* 260-300. *IB:* 25. *OCR ND:* D *OCR NED:* M2

WL82 BA Creative Writing and Politics & Global Studies
Duration: 3FT Hon
Entry Requirements: *Foundation:* Distinction. *GCE:* 260-300. *IB:* 25. *OCR ND:* D *OCR NED:* M2

WL83 BA Creative Writing and Sociology
Duration: 3FT Hon
Entry Requirements: *Foundation:* Distinction. *GCE:* 260-300. *IB:* 25. *OCR ND:* D *OCR NED:* M2

WNW8 BA Creative Writing and Sports Management
Duration: 3FT Hon
Entry Requirements: *GCE:* 260-300. *IB:* 24.

WC86 BA Creative Writing and Sports Studies
Duration: 3FT Hon
Entry Requirements: *Foundation:* Merit. *GCE:* 260-300. *IB:* 24.

VW68 BA Creative Writing and Theology & Religious Studies
Duration: 3FT Hon
Entry Requirements: *Foundation:* Distinction. *GCE:* 260-300. *IB:* 25. *OCR ND:* D *OCR NED:* M2

MW18 BA Law and Creative Writing
Duration: 3FT Hon
Entry Requirements: *Foundation:* Distinction. *GCE:* 260-300. *IB:* 25. *OCR ND:* D *OCR NED:* M2

W80 UNIVERSITY OF WORCESTER
HENWICK GROVE
WORCESTER WR2 6AJ
t: 01905 855111 f: 01905 855377
e: admissions@worc.ac.uk
// www.worcester.ac.uk

WW68 BA Animation and Screen Writing
Duration: 3FT Hon
Entry Requirements: *GCE:* 220-300. *IB:* 24. *OCR ND:* D Interview required. Portfolio required.

WQ82 BA Creative & Professional Writing and English Literary Studies
Duration: 3FT Hon
Entry Requirements: Contact the institution for details.

WW82 BA Creative & Professional Writing and Illustration
Duration: 3FT Hon
Entry Requirements: Contact the institution for details.

W990 BA Creative & Professional Writing and Screenwriting
Duration: 3FT Hon
Entry Requirements: Contact the institution for details.

WW6V BA Digital Film Production and Screen Writing
Duration: 3FT Hon
Entry Requirements: *GCE:* 220-300. *IB:* 24. *OCR ND:* D Interview required. Portfolio required.

QW3V BA English Language Studies and Screen Writing
Duration: 3FT Hon
Entry Requirements: *GCE:* 240-260. *IB:* 24. *OCR ND:* D *OCR NED:* M3

Y75 YORK ST JOHN UNIVERSITY
LORD MAYOR'S WALK
YORK YO31 7EX
t: 01904 876598 f: 01904 876940/876921
e: admissions@yorksj.ac.uk
// w3.yorksj.ac.uk

WQ83 BA Creative Writing and English Language
Duration: 3FT Hon
Entry Requirements: *GCE:* 220-260. *IB:* 24.

WQ8H BA Creative Writing and English Literature
Duration: 3FT Hon
Entry Requirements: *GCE:* 220-260. *IB:* 24.

Q3W8 BA English Literature with Creative Writing
Duration: 3FT Hon
Entry Requirements: *GCE:* 220-260. *IB:* 24.

PERFORMING ARTS

B22 UNIVERSITY OF BEDFORDSHIRE
PARK SQUARE
LUTON
BEDS LU1 3JU
t: 0844 8482234 f: 01582 489323
e: admissions@beds.ac.uk
// www.beds.ac.uk

W491 BA Theatre and Professional Practice
Duration: 3FT Hon
Entry Requirements: *GCE:* 160. Interview required.

B25 BIRMINGHAM CITY UNIVERSITY
PERRY BARR
BIRMINGHAM B42 2SU
t: 0121 331 5595 f: 0121 331 7994
// www.bcu.ac.uk

W490 BA Community and Applied Theatre
Duration: 3FT Hon   CRB Check: Required
Entry Requirements: *GCE:* 240. *IB:* 28. Interview required.

B38 BISHOP GROSSETESTE UNIVERSITY COLLEGE LINCOLN
BISHOP GROSSETESTE UNIVERSITY COLLEGE
LINCOLN LN1 3DY
t: 01522 583658 f: 01522 530243
e: admissions@bishopg.ac.uk
// www.bishopg.ac.uk/courses

CW84 BA Applied Drama with Psychology
Duration: 3FT Hon   CRB Check: Required
Entry Requirements: Contact the institution for details.

C8W4 BA Psychology and Applied Drama
Duration: 3FT Hon   CRB Check: Required
Entry Requirements: Contact the institution for details.

B50 BOURNEMOUTH UNIVERSITY
TALBOT CAMPUS
FERN BARROW
POOLE
DORSET BH12 5BB
t: 01202 524111
// www.bournemouth.ac.uk

W491 FdA Performing Arts: Contemporary Theatre
Duration: 2FT Fdg
Entry Requirements: *Foundation:* Distinction. *GCE:* 120. *IB:* 24. Interview required.

B92 BROOKSBY MELTON COLLEGE
MELTON CAMPUS
ASFORDBY ROAD
MELTON MOWBRAY
LEICESTERSHIRE LE13 0HJ
t: 01664 850850 f: 01664 855355
e: heenquiries@brooksbymelton.ac.uk
// www.brooksbymelton.ac.uk

094W HNC Community Theatre
Duration: 1FT HNC
Entry Requirements: Contact the institution for details.

C10 CANTERBURY CHRIST CHURCH UNIVERSITY
NORTH HOLMES ROAD
CANTERBURY
KENT CT1 1QU
t: 01227 782900 f: 01227 782888
e: admissions@canterbury.ac.uk
// www.canterbury.ac.uk

WQ43 BA Creative Arts
Duration: 3FT Hon
Entry Requirements: Interview required.

W490 BA Performing Arts
Duration: 3FT Hon
Entry Requirements: *GCE:* 240. *IB:* 24. Interview required.

C35 CENTRAL SCHOOL OF SPEECH AND DRAMA, UNIVERSITY OF LONDON
EMBASSY THEATRE
64 ETON AVENUE
LONDON NW3 3HY
t: 0207 722 8183 f: 0207 722 4132
e: enquiries@cssd.ac.uk
// www.cssd.ac.uk

W490 BA Drama, Applied Theatre and Education
Duration: 3FT Hon
Entry Requirements: *GCE:* BBB. Interview required.

W491 BA Theatre Practice: Stage Management
Duration: 3FT Hon
Entry Requirements: *GCE:* BBC. Interview required. Portfolio required.

W493 BA Theatre Practice: Technical and Production Management
Duration: 3FT Hon
Entry Requirements: *GCE:* BBC. Interview required. Portfolio required.

C64 CITY COLLEGE COVENTRY
SWANSWELL
50 SWANSWELL STREET
COVENTRY CV1 5DG
t: 0800 616 202 f: 024 7622 3390
e: courses@covcollege.ac.uk
// www.covcollege.ac.uk

194W HNC Performing Arts
Duration: 1FT HNC
Entry Requirements: Contact the institution for details.

C71 CLEVELAND COLLEGE OF ART AND DESIGN
CHURCH SQUARE
HARTLEPOOL
CHURCH SQUARE TS24 7EX
t: 01642 288888 f: 01642 288828
e: studentrecruitment@ccad.ac.uk
// www.ccad.ac.uk

W490 BA(Hons) Entertainment Design Crafts
Duration: 3FT Hon
Entry Requirements: *Foundation:* Pass. *GCE:* 120. Interview required. Portfolio required.

C99 UNIVERSITY OF CUMBRIA
FUSEHILL STREET
CARLISLE
CUMBRIA CA1 2HH
t: 01228 616234 f: 01228 616235
// www.cumbria.ac.uk

W493 BA Production Top-Up
Duration: 1FT Hon
Entry Requirements: Interview required. HND required.

D39 UNIVERSITY OF DERBY
KEDLESTON ROAD
DERBY DE22 1GB
t: 01332 591167 f: 01332 597724
e: askadmissions@derby.ac.uk
// www.derby.ac.uk

W490 BA Creative Expressive Therapies (Drama)
Duration: 3FT Hon   CRB Check: Required
Entry Requirements: *Foundation:* Distinction. *GCE:* 280. *IB:* 28. *BTEC Dip:* D*D*. *BTEC ExtDip:* DMM. *OCR NED:* M2 Interview required.

E42 EDGE HILL UNIVERSITY
ORMSKIRK
LANCASHIRE L39 4QP
t: 01695 657000 f: 01695 584355
e: study@edgehill.ac.uk
// www.edgehill.ac.uk

WB49 BA Performance and Health
Duration: 3FT Hon   CRB Check: Required
Entry Requirements: *GCE:* 280. *IB:* 26. *OCR ND:* D *OCR NED:* M2 Interview required.

E70 THE UNIVERSITY OF ESSEX
WIVENHOE PARK
COLCHESTER
ESSEX CO4 3SQ
t: 01206 873666 f: 01206 874477
e: admit@essex.ac.uk
// www.essex.ac.uk

W496 BA Acting and Community Theatre
Duration: 3FT Hon   CRB Check: Required
Entry Requirements: *GCE:* 160. *IB:* 24. Interview required.

W494 BA Physical Theatre
Duration: 3FT Hon
Entry Requirements: *GCE:* EE. *IB:* 24.

W495 BA World Performance
Duration: 3FT Hon
Entry Requirements: *GCE:* 260. *SQAH:* BBBCC. *SQAAH:* BBC. *IB:* 28. *OCR ND:* D Interview required.

H60 THE UNIVERSITY OF HUDDERSFIELD
QUEENSGATE
HUDDERSFIELD HD1 3DH
t: 01484 473969 f: 01484 472765
e: admissionsandrecords@hud.ac.uk
// www.hud.ac.uk

W490 BA Performance (Top-Up)
Duration: 1FT Hon
Entry Requirements: Interview required. HND required.

H73 HULL COLLEGE
QUEEN'S GARDENS
HULL HU1 3DG
t: 01482 329943 f: 01482 598733
e: info@hull-college.ac.uk
// www.hull-college.ac.uk/higher-education

WW14 FdA Visual Arts
Duration: 2FT Fdg
Entry Requirements: GCE: 80. Interview required. Portfolio
required.

K24 THE UNIVERSITY OF KENT
RECRUITMENT & ADMISSIONS OFFICE
REGISTRY
UNIVERSITY OF KENT
CANTERBURY, KENT CT2 7NZ
t: 01227 827272 f: 01227 827077
e: information@kent.ac.uk
// www.kent.ac.uk

**WQ43 BA Drama & Theatre Studies and
English Language & Linguistics**
Duration: 3FT Hon
Entry Requirements: GCE: ABB. SQAH: AAABB. SQAAH: ABB. IB:
33. OCR ND: D OCR NED: M1

L27 LEEDS METROPOLITAN UNIVERSITY
COURSE ENQUIRIES OFFICE
CITY CAMPUS
LEEDS LS1 3HE
t: 0113 81 23113 f: 0113 81 23129
// www.leedsmet.ac.uk

W492 BA Performance Arts
Duration: 1FT Hon
Entry Requirements: Interview required. HND required.

L48 THE LIVERPOOL INSTITUTE FOR
PERFORMING ARTS
MOUNT STREET
LIVERPOOL L1 9HF
t: 0151 330 3000 f: 0151 330 3131
e: admissions@lipa.ac.uk
// www.lipa.ac.uk

W491 BA Community Drama
Duration: 3FT Hon
Entry Requirements: GCE: 180. Interview required.

N30 NEW COLLEGE NOTTINGHAM
ADAMS BUILDING
STONEY STREET
THE LACE MARKET
NOTTINGHAM NG1 1NG
t: 0115 910 0100 f: 0115 953 4349
e: he.team@ncn.ac.uk
// www.ncn.ac.uk

W490 BA Theatre Arts (Top-up)
Duration: 1FT Hon
Entry Requirements: Interview required. HND required.

N37 UNIVERSITY OF WALES, NEWPORT
ADMISSIONS
LODGE ROAD
CAERLEON
NEWPORT NP18 3QT
t: 01633 432030 f: 01633 432850
e: admissions@newport.ac.uk
// www.newport.ac.uk

W490 BA Applied Drama
Duration: 3FT Hon
Entry Requirements: GCE: 260. IB: 24.

QW34 BA Applied Drama and English
Duration: 3FT Hon
Entry Requirements: GCE: 260. IB: 24. Interview required.

P60 PLYMOUTH UNIVERSITY
DRAKE CIRCUS
PLYMOUTH PL4 8AA
t: 01752 585858 f: 01752 588055
e: admissions@plymouth.ac.uk
// www.plymouth.ac.uk

WW46 BA Digital Performance Arts
Duration: 1FT Hon
Entry Requirements: HND required.

P80 UNIVERSITY OF PORTSMOUTH
ACADEMIC REGISTRY
UNIVERSITY HOUSE
WINSTON CHURCHILL AVENUE
PORTSMOUTH PO1 2UP
t: 023 9284 8484 f: 023 9284 3082
e: admissions@port.ac.uk
// www.port.ac.uk

W491 BA Drama and Performance
Duration: 3FT Hon
Entry Requirements: *GCE:* 240-300. *IB:* 25. *BTEC SubDip:* P.
BTEC Dip: DD. *BTEC ExtDip:* DMM. Interview required.

Q25 QUEEN MARGARET UNIVERSITY, EDINBURGH
QUEEN MARGARET UNIVERSITY DRIVE
EDINBURGH EH21 6UU
t: 0131474 0000 f: 0131 474 0001
e: admissions@qmu.ac.uk
// www.qmu.ac.uk

W490 BA Drama and Performance
Duration: 4FT Hon
Entry Requirements: *GCE:* 300. *IB:* 30.

S21 SHEFFIELD HALLAM UNIVERSITY
CITY CAMPUS
HOWARD STREET
SHEFFIELD S1 1WB
t: 0114 225 5555 f: 0114 225 2167
e: admissions@shu.ac.uk
// www.shu.ac.uk

W490 BA Performance and Professional Practice
Duration: 1FT Hon
Entry Requirements: HND required.

W491 BA Performance for Stage and Screen
Duration: 3FT Hon
Entry Requirements: *GCE:* 240.

N8W4 BSc Events Management with Arts & Entertainment (Top-up)
Duration: 1FT Hon
Entry Requirements: HND required.

S30 SOUTHAMPTON SOLENT UNIVERSITY
EAST PARK TERRACE
SOUTHAMPTON
HAMPSHIRE SO14 0RT
t: +44 (0) 23 8031 9039 f: + 44 (0)23 8022 2259
e: admissions@solent.ac.uk
// www.solent.ac.uk/

W490 BA Performance
Duration: 3FT Hon
Entry Requirements: *Foundation:* Distinction. *GCE:* 240. *SQAAH:*
AA-CCD. *IB:* 24. *BTEC ExtDip:* MMM. *OCR ND:* D *OCR NED:* M3
Interview required.

S32 SOUTH DEVON COLLEGE
LONG ROAD
PAIGNTON
DEVON TQ4 7EJ
t: 08000 213181 f: 01803 540541
e: university@southdevon.ac.uk
// www.southdevon.ac.uk/welcome-to-university-level

WN48 FdA Drama, Performance and Arts Management
Duration: 2FT Fdg
Entry Requirements: Contact the institution for details.

S72 STAFFORDSHIRE UNIVERSITY
COLLEGE ROAD
STOKE ON TRENT ST4 2DE
t: 01782 292753 f: 01782 292740
e: admissions@staffs.ac.uk
// www.staffs.ac.uk

W491 BA Entrepreneurship in Theatre Arts
Duration: 1FT Hon
Entry Requirements: Interview required. Portfolio required.

S74 STRATFORD UPON AVON COLLEGE
THE WILLOWS NORTH
ALCESTER ROAD
STRATFORD-UPON-AVON
WARWICKSHIRE CV37 9QR
t: 01789 266245 f: 01789 267524
e: college@stratford.ac.uk
// www.stratford.ac.uk

194W HND Performing Arts (Musical Theatre)
Duration: 2FT HND
Entry Requirements: *GCE:* 200. Interview required.

S84 UNIVERSITY OF SUNDERLAND
STUDENT HELPLINE
THE STUDENT GATEWAY
CHESTER ROAD
SUNDERLAND SR1 3SD
t: 0191 515 3000 f: 0191 515 3805
e: student.helpline@sunderland.ac.uk
// www.sunderland.ac.uk

W490 FdA Performing Arts
Duration: 2FT Fdg
Entry Requirements: *GCE:* 80-220. *SQAH:* CCCC. *IB:* 22.
Interview required.

T20 TEESSIDE UNIVERSITY
MIDDLESBROUGH TS1 3BA
t: 01642 218121 f: 01642 384201
e: registry@tees.ac.uk
// www.tees.ac.uk

W499 BA Performance and Events Production
Duration: 1FT Hon
Entry Requirements: Interview required.

W493 BA Performing Arts
Duration: 1FT Hon
Entry Requirements: Interview required.

W490 FdA Performance and Events Production
Duration: 2FT Fdg
Entry Requirements: *GCE:* 80-100. *IB:* 24. Interview required.

W492 FdA Performing Arts
Duration: 2FT Fdg
Entry Requirements: *GCE:* 120. *IB:* 24. Interview required.

U65 UNIVERSITY OF THE ARTS LONDON
272 HIGH HOLBORN
LONDON WC1V 7EY
t: 020 7514 6000x6197 f: 020 7514 6198
e: c.anderson@arts.ac.uk
// www.arts.ac.uk

W490 BA Theatre and Screen : Costume Design
Duration: 3FT Hon
Entry Requirements: *Foundation:* Pass. *GCE:* 80. *IB:* 28.
Foundation Course required. Interview required. Portfolio required.

W491 BA Theatre and Screen : Costume Interpretation
Duration: 3FT Hon
Entry Requirements: *Foundation:* Pass. *GCE:* 80. *IB:* 28.
Foundation Course required. Interview required. Portfolio required.

W492 BA Theatre and Screen: Technical Arts and Special Effects
Duration: 3FT Hon
Entry Requirements: *Foundation:* Pass. *GCE:* 80. *IB:* 28.
Foundation Course required. Interview required. Portfolio required.

W76 UNIVERSITY OF WINCHESTER
WINCHESTER
HANTS SO22 4NR
t: 01962 827234 f: 01962 827288
e: course.enquiries@winchester.ac.uk
// www.winchester.ac.uk

LW3K BA Criminology and Performing Arts (Contemporary Performance)
Duration: 3FT Hon
Entry Requirements: *Foundation:* Distinction. *GCE:* 260-300. *IB:* 24. *OCR ND:* D *OCR NED:* M2

QW3K BA English Language Studies and Performing Arts (Contemporary Performance)
Duration: 3FT Hon
Entry Requirements: *Foundation:* Distinction. *GCE:* 260-300. *IB:* 25. *OCR ND:* D *OCR NED:* M2

NW8K BA Event Management and Performing Arts (Contemporary Performance)
Duration: 3FT Hon
Entry Requirements: *Foundation:* Distinction. *GCE:* 260-300. *IB:* 24. *OCR ND:* D *OCR NED:* M2

WW64 BA Film & Cinema Technologies and Performing Arts (Contemporary Performance)
Duration: 3FT Hon
Entry Requirements: *Foundation:* Distinction. *GCE:* 260-300. *IB:* 24. *OCR ND:* D *OCR NED:* M2

MW1K BA Law and Performing Arts (Contemporary Performance)
Duration: 3FT Hon
Entry Requirements: *Foundation:* Distinction. *GCE:* 260-300. *IB:* 25. *OCR ND:* D *OCR NED:* M2

WW94 BA Modern Liberal Arts and Performing Arts (Contemporary Performance)
Duration: 3FT Hon
Entry Requirements: *Foundation:* Distinction. *GCE:* 260-300. *IB:* 25. *OCR ND:* D *OCR NED:* M2

LW2K BA Performing Arts (Contemporary Performance) and Politics & Global Studies
Duration: 3FT Hon
Entry Requirements: *Foundation:* Distinction. *GCE:* 260-300. *IB:* 24. *OCR ND:* D

WNKV BA Performing Arts (Contemporary Performance) and Sports Management
Duration: 3FT Hon
Entry Requirements: *Foundation:* Pass. *GCE:* 260-300. *IB:* 24. *OCR ND:* D

VW63 BA Performing Arts (Contemporary Performance) and Theology & Religious Studies
Duration: 3FT Hon
Entry Requirements: *Foundation:* Distinction. *GCE:* 260-300. *IB:* 25. *OCR ND:* D *OCR NED:* M2

**W81 WORCESTER COLLEGE OF
TECHNOLOGY**
DEANSWAY
WORCESTER WR1 2JF
t: 01905 725555 f: 01905 28906
// www.wortech.ac.uk

094W HND Theatrical Make-Up and Costume
Duration: 2FT HND
Entry Requirements: *GCE:* 80.

PS